RESEARCH HANDBOOK ON CORPORATE BOARD DECISION-MAKING

Research Handbook on Corporate Board Decision-Making

Edited by

Oliver Marnet

Associate Professor of Accounting, Southampton Business School, University of Southampton, UK

EE Edward **Elgar**
PUBLISHING

Cheltenham, UK • Northampton, MA, USA

Published by
Edward Elgar Publishing Limited
The Lypiatts
15 Lansdown Road
Cheltenham
Glos GL50 2JA
UK

Edward Elgar Publishing, Inc.
William Pratt House
9 Dewey Court
Northampton
Massachusetts 01060
USA

Paperback edition 2024

A catalogue record for this book
is available from the British Library

Library of Congress Control Number: 2022944630

This book is available electronically in the **Elgar**online
Business subject collection
http://dx.doi.org/10.4337/9781800377189

ISBN 978 1 80037 717 2 (cased)
ISBN 978 1 80037 718 9 (eBook)
ISBN 978 1 0353 4055 2 (paperback)

Printed and bound by CPI Group (UK) Ltd, Croydon, CR0 4YY

Contents

PART III   BOARD DECISION-MAKING IN PRACTICE

PART IV   BOARD DECISION-MAKING IN EXTREME SITUATIONS

Figures

Tables

Contributors

Geofry Areneke is a Senior Lecturer and Head of Research and Knowledge Exchange in the Accounting, Finance and Banking department at Manchester Metropolitan University Business School. His research transverses comparative corporate governance, corporate finance, developmental and microfinance. He possesses a multi-disciplinary perspective in accounting and finance research, infused with international business, leadership, law and sociology. His work has been published in top journals, including the *Journal of World Business*, *Journal of Business Research*, *International Journal of Finance and Economics* and *Managerial Auditing Journal*.

Ilias G. Basioudis is Senior Lecturer/Associate Professor of Financial Accounting & Auditing in the Accounting Department at Aston University in Birmingham, UK, and Chairman of the Auditing Group of the British Accounting & Finance Association. He is a Fellow of the Academy of Higher Education and Editor of the *International Journal of Auditing*, and has been an external examiner in various universities. Ilias has written two textbooks, the most recent one being *Financial Accounting: The Basics* (Routledge, 2019). He does research in auditing and accounting education.

Roy Edwards is a Lecturer in Accounting at Southampton Business School. By background he is a business historian researching the history of accounting and management information. More recently he has published on British government business relationships with special regard to the role of the Industrial Reorganisation Corporation in 1960s industrial policy. He was on the Executive of the Business Archives Council.

Moataz Elmassri, PhD, is Senior Lecturer of Management Accounting in the Centre for Sustainability and Responsible Management at the University of Roehampton. His research interests are in the areas of investment appraisal, strategic investment decisions, management control, accountability and performance management. His research has been published in internationally refereed high-quality academic journals (ranked A* by the Australian Business Deans Council); e.g., *British Accounting Review* and *Accounting, Auditing & Accountability Journal*. He has an interest in accounting and social theory, especially applying strong-structuration theory to his research.

Richard Fairchild, PhD, is Senior Lecturer in Behavioural Finance and Financial Economics in the School of Management, University of Bath. Prior to academe, he worked at Airbus (Bristol), and was involved in project reporting, investment appraisal, budgeting, forecasting and planning. Richard's research focuses on behavioural and emotional finance, behavioural game-theoretic approaches to venture capital/entrepreneur financial contracting, the behavioural economics approach to understanding social investing and social entrepreneurship, and the behavioural economics of corporate fraud. Richard has published widely in internationally renowned finance, economics and management journals, and has presented his research at many international conferences.

Elaine Harris is Emerita Professor at the University of Roehampton, where she headed up the Accounting and Management Control research group and ran the Business School doctoral programme. She edited the 2018 *Routledge Companion to Performance Management and Control*. Her latest research investigates the strategic investment decisions in universities, decisions made by sell-side analysts, sustainability in business acquisitions and project appraisal. Elaine is an Honorary Professor at Aston Business School, Chair of the Management Control Association and Associate Editor of *British Accounting Review*. She was awarded a lifetime achievement award (2020) by the British Accounting & Finance Association.

Bruce Hearn is a Professor of Accounting & Finance at the University of Bradford and a Professor (Visiting) at the University of Southampton. His research focuses on corporate finance and corporate governance in emerging economies and has been published in journals such as the *Journal of Corporate Finance*, *Journal of World Business* and *Journal of Business Venturing*.

Jaskaran Kaur is a Lecturer in Accounting & Finance at the University of Bradford. Her research focuses on corporate governance and audit. Her teaching interests are in corporate finance and governance.

Khairul Ayuni Mohd Kharuddin is an Associate Professor at the Faculty of Accountancy, Universiti Teknologi MARA (UiTM), Malaysia. She formerly taught at Loughborough University and Aston University, and worked as a Senior Auditor in Ernst & Young, Malaysia. She is an Executive Committee member for the Audit Group of the British Accounting & Finance Association. She is a Fellow member of the Association of Chartered Certified Accountants and the UK Higher Education Academy, as well as Associate Editor of the *Asian Journal of Accounting Research*.

Muhammad Khawar is a Lecturer in Accounting & Finance at the University of Bradford. His research and teaching interests focus on corporate governance, management and cost accounting. He has considerable professional experience in establishing and founding modules and courses at undergraduate, postgraduate and MBA levels.

Wafa Khlif is Professor in Management Accounting at Toulouse Business School, Barcelona. Her research interests focus on board director efficiency, and corporate board roles, duties and composition as well as issues in accounting and sustainability. Her research has been published in various internationally recognised journals such as the *International Small Business Journal*, *Journal of Small Business and Enterprise Development*, *Journal of African Business*, *Society and Business Review* and *Technovation*.

Danson Kimani is a Lecturer in Accounting at Essex Business School, University of Essex, United Kingdom. His research interests are in the areas of auditing and corporate governance, biodiversity/environmental accounting, taxation, and emerging technologies in accounting and finance. His research has been published various leading and international journals, such as *Corporate Governance: An International Review*, *Critical Perspectives on Accounting* and the *Journal of World Business*. Danson is also involved in collaborative engagements with several corporate governance professional and policy bodies based in Africa.

Jia Liu is a Professor in Finance at the University of Portsmouth. Her research focuses on accounting, finance, corporate governance and business economics, which she integrates with a wide range of business management disciplines, including law, business ethics, leadership, entrepreneurship, R&D, economic behaviour and organisation, strategic management, public administration and management, fintech, big data, the green economy and social inclusion/diversity. She publishes in the *Journal of Corporate Finance* and *British Journal of Management*, among others, and has written books on governance, sustainability and decision-making. Her research has featured in media including *The Conversation*.

Oliver Marnet is an Associate Professor in Accounting at Southampton Business School, and investigates behavioural and cognitive factors affecting the quality of judgement and decision-making of those charged with governance, and their monitors and gatekeepers. He has conducted research for the Institute of Chartered Accountants in England and Wales and the Leadership Foundation for Higher Education; provided evidence to the Department for Business, Energy & Industrial Strategy, Competition and Markets Authority, Institute of Chartered Secretaries and Administrators, Pensions & Investment Research Consultants, and the European Commission on audit and governance reform; acted as an academic adviser to the Financial Reporting Council's Guidance on Board Effectiveness, and presented evidence to the French audit regulator (Le Haut Conseil du commissariat aux comptes).

Steve Maslin is a chartered accountant whose commercial and charitable non-executive director roles include Nuffield Health, Carey Group and the Royal Collection Trust. Steve spent 28 years as a partner with Grant Thornton, where his leadership roles included Chair of the Partnership Board, Head of Assurance and Managing Partner London Satellite Offices. Steve chaired the Global Public Policy Committee, which represents the six largest global accounting networks with government, the Financial Stability Board, regulators and other policy makers.

Vinita Mithani is a Fellow Chartered Accountant with 20 years' experience at senior levels in accountancy practice and industry, and several years' experience as a module leader and lecturer at undergraduate level. She has published opinion articles on auditor independence in the online magazine of the Institute of Chartered Accountants in England and Wales. She has also given oral and written evidence and acted as adviser to the Business Parliamentary Select Committee on its Future of Audit inquiry.

Alexander Mohr is a Professor of International Business at the Vienna University of Economics and Business. His research focuses on international strategic management, international governance modes and non-market strategies. His work has been published in journals such as the *British Journal of Management*, *Journal of International Business Studies* and *Journal of World Business*.

Chiharu Narikiyo is a research student in the Centre for Sustainability and Responsible Management at the University of Roehampton. Her research explores how organisational decision-making balances financial and non-financial considerations to achieve sustainable development goals as well as financial goals. Her research is fully funded by a Business School Scholarship of the University of Roehampton. Her research interests include strategic investment decision-making, green/ethical investment and environmental accounting.

Donald Nordberg is Associate Professor at Bournemouth University Business School and author of *The Cadbury Code and Recurrent Crisis* (Palgrave, 2020) and *Corporate Governance: Principles & Issues* (SAGE, 2011). His research has been published in *Corporate Governance: An International Review*, *Business History*, *Leadership*, *Philosophy of Management*, the *European Management Journal* and other journals. He also serves as chair of a major social care provider and as non-executive director of a performing arts organisation. Earlier in his career, he was a management consultant specialising in information businesses, and an editorial executive at Reuters.

Teerooven Soobaroyen is a Professor in Accounting at Essex Business School. His research examines the interplay between accounting, accountability and governance, mainly in the context of emerging economies. His research has been published in various internationally recognised journals, such as *Critical Perspectives on Accounting*; *Accounting, Organizations and Society*; *Accounting Forum*; *Accounting, Auditing and Accountability Journal*; and *Corporate Governance: An International Review*.

Leslie Spiers is a visiting lecturer at several universities. His PhD was concerned with corporate governance in small companies and its contribution to risk and crisis management. Leslie has been a company director for over 38 years and has chaired more than 500 board meetings. His special interest is how small and medium-sized enterprises develop and implement strategy, and how that contributes to resilience.

Laura F. Spira is an Emeritus Professor of Corporate Governance. Her research interests encompass aspects of governance and accountability with a particular interest in using qualitative approaches to undertake research in corporate governance. She was a founder member of the British Accounting & Finance Association Corporate Governance Special Interest Group, and has been Research Relationships Adviser to the Institute of Chartered Accountants in England and Wales (ICAEW) and a member of the ICAEW Research Advisory Board. Laura acted as academic adviser to the Financial Reporting Council's Turnbull Review Group, and completed a study of the Cadbury Committee, published by Oxford University Press in 2013.

Krishanthi Vithana (Krish) is a Lecturer in Accounting with Southampton Business School. Her research focus is on accounting for human capital resources in organisational contexts. She has published her research in the *Journal of Business Ethics*, *Accounting Forum* and the *International Journal of Human Resource Management*. Krish has been the principal investigator for Economic and Social Research Council Impact Acceleration Account-funded research projects, including An Investment Case on Real Living Wage Accreditation. Krish has actively engaged with industry partners, including the Global Responsible Investment team of Aviva Investors, the Living Wage Foundation and Platform Living Wage Financials.

David Weir has been a dean/director of several business schools and a professor in several universities, including ancient universities, former colleges of advanced technology, municipal colleges, colleges of education, colleges of theology and French *grandes écoles*, and is a former company director. He served on research council committees and the (Finniston) Committee of Inquiry into British Engineering. He consults globally on organisational excellence and higher education. Author of many publications, he is a member of the Business Excellence Institute and Foundation Fellow of the Leadership Trust.

Geoffrey Wood is a Professor and DanCap Private Equity Chair, and Department Chair DAN Management, at Western University in London, Canada, and Visiting Professor at Trinity College, Dublin. Previously, he served as Dean and Professor of International Business at Essex Business School and before then as Professor of International Business at Warwick Business School, Coventry, UK. He is Editor in Chief of *Human Resource Management Journal* (ABS [Association of Business Schools] 4* Journal of Distinction) and Incoming Editor in Chief of *Academy of Management Perspectives* (ABS 4).

Rashid Zaman is a Lecturer in Accounting at Edith Cowan University, Western Australia. His areas of research include corporate social and environmental/sustainability accounting, corporate governance and corporate fraud/misconduct. Rashid has published 19 refereed articles in leading international journals, 14 ranked A*/A on the Australian Business Deans Council List. Rashid's research has featured in several media outlets (e.g., *Irish Times*, *The Conversation*, *ACCA Global Accounting and Business*). He has secured funding from multiple research-grant-awarding bodies in Australia, New Zealand and the United States.

Acknowledgements

As editor, I owe a debt of gratitude to many and can repay little. I thank all the authors for their excellent contributions to this *Handbook* and for their patience. In addition to the authors, I also thank the many colleagues who contributed to the discussion on corporate governance, board decision-making, fraud, bias and heuristics, and external audit. A special debt is owed to the late Professor David Gwilliam, for always encouraging the author to think outside the box and take the road less travelled. His insights are ever so missed. I also wish to thank the Edward Elgar team for their assistance in preparing this *Handbook*.

1. Introduction to the *Research Handbook on Corporate Board Decision-Making*

Oliver Marnet

There is no shortage of concerns on corporate governance, the role of companies large and small, their impact on society and the environment, how companies should meet their diverse obligations, what these are, and how corporate decisions are made, and for whom. For many decades, these and related issues have provided researchers, practitioners, policy makers and regulators with a broad arena for discussion and reform efforts, prompted updates to corporate governance codes and company laws, led to the introduction of stewardship codes, and yielded corporate commitments to a plethora of codes of conduct and best practice at national and global level.

Alas, these concerns do not seem to diminish over time, and prominent corporate scandals reoccur with frightening frequency and impact to remind the observer that many critical corporate issues are yet to be meaningfully addressed, let alone resolved. At times, it feels like "Groundhog Day",[1] where another year surprises observers, some at least, with another governance, accounting, environmental or political scandal involving high-profile companies, which is followed by stern calls for inquiries and reform, solemn proclamations and declarations, more rules and regulations, tighter monitoring, greater fines and penalties, and corporate leaders, monitors, gatekeepers, and institutions proclaiming to do better in the future, only for this pattern to repeat itself not long after.

Some empathy is perhaps due to those charged with corporate governance, and their monitors, who seem to frequently get caught in the middle when corporate events become news for all the wrong reasons. Company boards are accountable to many diverse stakeholders with at times diametrically opposed goals and expectations, often run by dominant CEOs and powerful chairs (where these two functions are separated), and typically faced with agendas where the pressing tends to crowd out the important. A cynical observer might think the placing of important decisions at the end of packed agendas to be a deliberate practice to push through projects with limited meaningful review by those tasked with governance. Overwhelming the non-executive directors (NEDs) with tasks and preventing them from providing proper but perhaps unwelcome scrutiny and due diligence, or providing insufficient time, or late, partial, and/or irrelevant information, while emphasising the critical need for unanimity, and impressing on these actors the urgency of 'once in a lifetime' opportunities can result in boards unanimously agreeing to significant institutional obligations and massive risks after no more than a superficial presentation by the CEO designed to awe the audience. Pity the NED.

Of course, the CEO/president and chair might have moved on to greener pastures, or be in the process of doing so, just in case, as and when the events unfold differently from those rose-coloured presentations. Therein lies the crux. Typically, executive managers have little to lose from a negative institutional impact of past decisions. At times this may even be the case in situations where managerial fraud was an underlying factor. Even with the best of intentions, unexpected events may come along, and massive expenditures and investments, endless takeovers, and risky business models, once touted with the promise of never-ending bounty, may quickly become unpalatable. Sometimes, NEDs might agree to such proposals in the hope that this time it will be different, with groupthink, selective perception, biased judgement, blind trust, dominant leadership and overoptimism combining to degrade meaningful risk assessments to tick-box exercises, where due diligence is neglected as an onerous regulatory exercise, another 'thing one must do' but does not see much use for otherwise in the heat of the moment.[2] This might be harsh, and some boards do an excellent job, at times. Certainly, all listed companies have good governance on paper and prominently list their ethical principles on corporate websites, as did Enron, whose 64-page Code of Ethics now resides at the Smithsonian's National Museum of American History.[3] History shows that there is ample potential for overoptimism, hubris, fraud and groupthink, on top of plain and simple mistake-making in the decisions made by executive managers, and their boards which approve and support these. While we tend to be smarter with hindsight, especially observers who were not part of the initial decisions, we need to critically reflect on the fact that we often make decisions under uncertainty, with limited information, in a hurry, labouring from prior beliefs and as members of a group, which can affect the quality of judgement and that of the resulting decisions, even when these decisions are made with the best of intentions.[4]

Regardless of the limitations of the human mind, individually and in the collective, it has become increasingly clear that while the continued development and reform of corporate governance best practice guidelines are necessary for good governance, they may not be sufficient on their own. Boards increasingly need to reflect deeply about the way they carry out their role and the behaviours that they display during judgement formation and decision-making, and are strongly encouraged to consider how the way in which decisions are taken might affect the quality of those decisions.[5] Hence, it is not only important to reflect on what boards decide upon, and for whom, but increasingly also on how they make these decisions.

Boards urgently also need to reflect on the very reason of their existence and that of the organisations they supervise. The COVID-19 pandemic; political disturbances; critical questions on environmental, social and governance (ESG) issues; and the Global Financial Crisis of 2008/2009 (GFC) provide sufficient proof that going back to 'business as usual' is not an option, and organisations need to reflect how they can contribute positively to these global issues if they wish their organisations to be truly sustainable and if they desire to be part of a solution rather than being an ever larger part of the problem. This is also relevant for the various monitors and gatekeepers in corporate governance, the regulators and supervisors.

There frequently is little anticipation. There is also a void of evidence on the existence of a consistent, systematic and deliberate use of processes and procedures to systematically mitigate cognitive bias during judgement formation and review past decisions, and the need to focus not only on the ultimate merits of a decision itself but also on the decision-making process leading up to it, and the lessons to be learnt from past mistakes and failures.

It is for these reasons that this *Handbook* aims to encourage thinking outside the box, reviews issues with a broad and novel perspective on and approaches to governance, and aims to provide critical interpretations on the meaning, value, contribution, quality and purpose of the decision-making by those charged with corporate governance, and of those looking over their shoulders. What boards decide, how they make these decisions, what they focus on in boardroom deliberations, how they balance diverse stakeholders' interests and how they even remotely hope to reassure themselves that their decisions are in the best interest of these stakeholders and the organisation as a whole are but some of the questions explored in this *Handbook*.

The *Handbook* presents a wide range of topics and contributions related to board decision-making and expands the discussion to a broad range of issues related to and affecting decision-making and their outcomes at board level. This includes reflections on the expected roles and duties of board directors vs observed behaviours; the impact of regulations/guidelines on the quality of board decision-making; independence, competence, ethics and diversity; the meaning of responsible decision-making; factors which impede meeting the expected duties of those in charge of corporate governance; factors which impede good decision-making; behavioural/cognitive factors in judgement formation and the quality of board decision-making; exploring whether directors/boards learn from past mistakes, or whether there are tendencies to go back to business as usual; whether there are solid procedures in place to encourage good decision-making; exploring what best practice is vs what perhaps it should be; exploring issues of adherence to the spirit vs the letter of the law/rules/regulations/guidelines; what issues should boards be looking at vs those that they primarily engage in; factors which encourage the spread of fraud within organisations; and board decision-making under extreme circumstances/in extreme environments (for example, the GFC, COVID-19 or global environmental threats). A broad range of authors, with very diverse backgrounds, research interests and professional perspectives, contributed to this *Handbook* to provide rich insights into some of these questions and frequently contrast fact with proclaimed intentions, providing suggestions on how to move forward.

Part I of the book discusses questions of who makes the decisions in the boardroom, who these are made for and to what end. Geoffrey Wood explores the relationship between institutions and firm-level decision-making and reviews the circumstances under which firm-level actors might be particularly prone to challenging existing institutional configurations, and how recent events have impacted on the relationship between embedded rules and firm level choices. Laura F. Spira considers the relationship between corporate board composition and decision-making, outlining the conventional wisdom on board composition with specific regard to independence and diversity. She identifies research in a range of disciplinary areas which challenges underpinning assumptions, and discusses further questions that could or should be explored in order to provide a more extensive evidence base to influence and support regulatory and policy development. Donald Nordberg expands on the liminality of NEDs, exploring their freedom from hierarchy and creative space – the service role of boards, which he sees progressively at odds with a board agenda weighted towards compliance – its control role. Through a series of thought experiments, fictional cases drawn from real-life experiences, he explores how the collective engagement of directors in decision practices can induce the development of commitment and psychological ownership that stewardship requires. Leslie Spiers, meanwhile, looks at the contributions from small non-listed companies, the particular challenges they face, responses that are typically unplanned and often chaotic should a crisis occur, and the consequences of unpreparedness, inevitably resulting in failure and personal losses for the entrepreneur. The author explores the role and nature of corporate governance in small companies, very different to that in publicly quoted entities and requiring a meaningful, appropriate and relevant approach if it is to contribute towards the resilience of the small company.

The chapters in Part II of the book explore aspects of governance best practice, what it is and what it might be. Vinita Mithani addresses two significant gaps in knowledge about the role and effectiveness of NEDs. One relates to the likely impact of their activities on firm performance. The other major gap in knowledge concerns the antecedents to NEDs' behaviour. The aim of her contribution is to provide a roadmap to advance knowledge on the generative mechanisms underlying NEDs' behaviour and consequently their effectiveness. Steve Maslin provides evidence of a positive correlation between good corporate governance behaviour and enhanced financial performance, drawing on recent empirical research carried out by the Grant Thornton Governance Institute, which demonstrated a strong link between effective corporate governance and value creation. His research identifies six areas of governance behaviour that provide reliable predictors of superior financial performance. The second part of the chapter provides a series of case studies in support of the theoretical conclusions. Roy Edwards explores a historical debate concerning the reporting of non-financial performance in the context of government investigation and proposed regulation of railway accounts and statistics in the first quarter of the 20th century. The chapter seeks to explore one element of how the relationships between owners, managers, customers and the legislature developed at a specific point in time, when the nature of governance and its relationship with management control was being contested, and all too often equated with compliance. Specifically, the chapter reveals the concerns expressed by railway management regarding the knowledge required to interpret the performance of complex operations, and explores contending scientific approaches to management derived from systems of train control that were not recognised by external stakeholders such as journalists, government and some investors acting through lobby groups. Lessons are outlined for today's scholars and practitioners from this historical experience. Krishanthi Vithana explores gaps in accounting and financial reporting in the recognition of human capital investment; disjoints between researchers' efforts on valuing, accounting for and financial reporting recognition of human capital investment; and practitioners' efforts in applying these concepts. In identifying practical and empirical gaps, her chapter critically evaluates the relevant academic and practitioner literature, with an emphasis on board decision-making and corporate governance practices, highlighting the practical significance of recent research projects published from a broad human capital accounting and disclosure perspective. The author provides guidance on the development of a human capital resource disclosure framework and encourages the integration of human capital resource information for firm decision-making at strategic and operational level.

Part III turns to board decision-making in practice, contrasting often lofty goals and proclamations with realities and observations on the ground. David Weir questions the basis of the general perception of universities that they, like most educational institutions, can be trusted, and counter-balances this with a brief case history which indicates that truth may perhaps be a contested terrain and that universities may be tempted to conceive of themselves as permitted to be generic arbiters of the truth as embodied in the knowledge they choose to impart and research, contrasting this with opportunities for conflict and outcomes which might show otherwise. Chiharu Narikiyo, Elaine Harris and Moataz Elmassri provide a structured review of literature on strategic investment decision-making. Drawing upon literature from corporate social responsibility (CSR) and finance on 'green' investment, they develop a conceptual framework to interrogate the financial and narrative information publicly available. The authors encourage future case-based research using primarily archival methods, supplemented by key stakeholder interviews, to investigate how 'ethical' or green corporate decision-making is (what they do) compared with strategies and public relations statements (what they say) in companies that are considered to be performing well as 'green investments', and recommend a critical approach to corporate decision-making research, based on the concepts of steward-ship, social contracts and stakeholder theory. Rashid Zaman and Jia Liu note that corporate social irresponsibility (CSiR) incidents, such as those involving Volkswagen (VW), British Petroleum (BP) and Wells Fargo, have not only highlighted the importance of CSR but have also made the effective implementation of CSR a global policy issue. In reflection on the revised New Zealand Stock Exchange (NZX) Corporate Governance Code 2017, which gives special attention to CSR issues with the objective of promoting ESG activities among NZX-listed firms, these authors identify, classify and prioritise CSR initiatives to propose a CSR model applicable to listed firms, to enhance the understanding and promotion of responsible business practices. Geofry Areneke, Wafa Khlif, Danson Kimani and Teerooven Soobaroyen provide a detailed review of published articles and existing codes in multiple African contexts, revealing that the efficacy of many codes remains very limited in terms of pragmatic outcomes while firms in countries that have adopted codes continue to face uneven performance and poor accountability. The authors urge for an understanding of the reasons underlying such results, and recommend an African-led re-think (re independence, ownership, board processes) of existing codes to make them more aligned with the governance needs of African firms and their complex sociocultural backgrounds, highlighting a need for further research to illuminate Africa's actual governance experiences and necessities.

Part IV turns its attention to board decision-making in extreme situations, investigates information asymmetries, looks at the effectiveness of governance agents during global crises, and explores cognitive behavioural factors underlying corporate fraud, how managers can succumb to fraud and how fraud might spread within the company to become a defining character of its operations. Bruce Hearn, Alex Mohr, Muhammad Khawar and Jaskaran Kaur explore information asymmetries in the financial sector and NEDs' ability to influence these. The authors investigate the relationship between NED personal ownership and firms' bid–ask spreads in listed firms from 179 companies listed on eight Caribbean offshore securities exchanges, and report that bid–ask spreads increase with NED ownership. However, this result is negatively moderated in the context of higher formal institutional quality and also if the territory has a fixed exchange rate regime, but positively moderated if the firm is located within an offshore jurisdiction. Overall, they note the effectiveness of NEDs to be highly contingent upon the specific institutional context, with higher formal institutional quality and the presence of strong macroeconomic ties between territory and Organisation for Economic Co-operation and Development country leading to a reduction in these costs, while offshore financial centres lead to their increase. Khairul Ayuni Mohd Kharuddin and Ilias G. Basioudis investigate the effectiveness of audit committees and the internal audit function in conjunction with the impact of the GFC on company decision-making. The authors find little evidence of audit committee involvement in company financial reporting decisions, as they have neither moderated companies' earnings management nor had any effect on the auditor's opinion issued during the GFC period. Instead, their results indicate that the internal audit function and joint industry audit specialists promoted higher earnings and audit quality. These suggest that the internal and external audit functions seemed to be more effective than the audit committee in contributing to improved quality in a company's financial reporting and audit, and hence were the more important pillars of board performance management and decision-making during the turbulent GFC time. In the conclusion of this part and the book, Richard Fairchild and Oliver Marnet reflect on the combined effects of economic, behavioural, psychological, emo-tional and psycho-analytical factors on the managerial propensity to commit corporate fraud.

They develop a behavioural game-theoretical and Freudian psycho-analytical framework of corporate fraud and consider the effect of a Freudian super-ego, acting as a moral compass, on managerial fraud. Furthermore, they analyse the contagious spread of fraud across an organisation from unethical to ethical managers. The behavioural insights gathered are applied to a case review into remuneration practices at Enron to demonstrate how these may have encouraged the spread of fraud within the company. The chapter concludes with an in-depth review of policy makers and practitioners as they are beginning to appreciate and incorporate the behavioural economics approach in developing better policies to address corporate fraud.

As the chapters in this *Handbook* demonstrate, much remains to be discussed and resolved in the area of governance and the role of boards therein, their overall purpose, the quality of their decision-making and the outcomes of the decisions made at board level. The debate continues to grapple not only with the who and the what for, but also on the how of boardroom processes and procedures, and how the governance paradigm can motivate, enable, enhance and support the quality of the work of those charged with corporate governance and that of their monitors and gatekeepers. One frequently emerging insight is that the tone at the top really matters. It affects, influences and often determines the ultimate outcome of the decisions made at board level, regardless of lofty vision and mission statements, and the impact of those decisions on institutional sustainability, its capital valuation, and its impact on society and the environment. It is hoped that the contributions in this *Handbook* provide the reader with valuable insights into the debate on corporate issues.

NOTES

1. "Groundhog Day" refers to the 1993 movie which shows the main character being trapped in a time loop where he repeats one particular day over and over until he finally escapes the cycle. The term "Groundhog Day" has since become part of the English language, meaning a monotonous, unpleasant, hopeless and endlessly repetitive situation. While the movie has been interpreted in numerous different ways, a central message common to many interpretations seems to be in the need to make a meaningful change in order to break a repetitive pattern. Einstein may or may not ever have said that "The definition of insanity is doing the same thing over and over again and expecting different results", but the gist of the message is the same.
2. The late 'Tiny' Rowlands has famously been accredited with dismissing NEDs as "baubles on a Christmas tree", reflecting how little chief executives respected these members of the board. Upon reflection on many interviews with auditors and board members on the value of external audit, auditors might be considered the tinsel. Nice to have, and of course part of regulatory requirements for listed companies, but adding what value if external audit is dismissed so readily by key stakeholders? The editor of this book does not necessarily share this view, and in some of his research explores the social role of auditors in promoting functioning capital markets and how this role may be enhanced.
3. The Code's foreword by former CEO Kenneth Lay contains this rather delightful line: "We want to be proud of Enron and to know that it enjoys a reputation for fairness and honesty and that it is respected." Ironically, the Code also suggested that no Enron employee should trade in Enron's stock while in the possession of material non-public information regarding the company. Apparently, this did not prevent Ken Lay from selling 1.8 million Enron shares between early 1999 and July 2001, for some $100 million, five months before Enron filed for bankruptcy (*New York Times*, January 13, 2002, and SEC, July 8, 2004), as a leading example to the many other senior Enron executives who successfully offloaded their Enron shares in the run-up to the company's demise, at a time when ordinary employees, holding Enron shares in their 401(k) retirement plans, were prevented from switching investments.

4. See Daniel Kahneman, Paul Slovic and Amos Tversky (eds) (1982), *Judgment under Uncertainty: Heuristics & Biases* (Cambridge, MA: Cambridge University Press); Financial Reporting Council (2018), *Guidance on Board Effectiveness*, available at www.frc.org.uk/images/uploaded/ documents/Guidance on board effectiveness FINAL6.pdf; and John C. Coffee Jr., Understanding Enron: "It's about Gatekeepers, Stupid", 57 *Bus. Law.* 1403 (2002), available at https://scholarship .law.columbia.edu/faculty_scholarship/2117, for explorations of the impact of mental shortcuts and cognitive biases on the quality of judgement.
5. Financial Reporting Council (2018), *Guidance on Board Effectiveness*.

PART I

BOARD DECISION-MAKING: BY WHOM, AND WHO FOR?

2. Institutions and corporate decision-making
Geoffrey Wood

INTRODUCTION

It is generally recognized that the decisions made by firms are to a lesser or greater extent bound up with contextual circumstances (Gupta et al., 2020; Wood et al., 2014). This explains long consistencies in organizational decision-making, an often alarming reticence to take account of events and a tendency towards greater experimentation in times of flux. However, what constitutes an institution is open to much debate, and again, the role of managers and owners as active agents impacting back on social structures is open a wide degree of debate and controversy. Schotter et al. (2021) divided institutional theory into organizational, economic and comparative. This chapter introduces different ways in which institutions and institutional change may be understood. Particular attention is accorded to those in wide usage in understanding how corporations are governed, and how this is moulded and remoulded by managerial decision-making; in other words, the strands of institutional thinking encompassed in the latter category. Hence, this chapter focuses on macro-institutional accounts, economic institutionalism and comparative institutionalism, although it is recognized that the more micro-orientated organizational institutionalism may be of considerable value in understanding everyday relations at horizontal and vertical levels within organizations.

ECONOMIC INSTITUTIONALISM

Economic institutionalism argues that institutions are providers of incentives and disincentives to rational economic agents (Goergen et al., 2009). In terms of a highly influential account by North (1990) and later work by La Porta and colleagues (2008), the most important institutional dimension was that pertaining to the protection of private property rights. It was held that strong private property rights provided the best incentives for economic agents to make the optimal decisions (Goergen et al., 2009). La Porta et al. (2008) argued that common law systems provided the best protection of private property rights, and held that in turn this would make for optimal decision-making across an economy, and hence superior growth. Although not one and the same as agency theory, in the finance and business and management literature there has been a long-standing tendency to combine the two (see La Porta et al., 2000). In part, this reflects a rather sketchy understanding of decision-making within the firm within the original articles by La Porta et al. (Armour et al., 2009); the firm is assumed to be a kind of transmission belt translating institutional effects into macro economic outcomes (Wood and Brewster, 2016).

Agency theory is, quite simply, a way of understanding contracting (Lambert, 2001). A major concern of applications of agency theory is that managers are agents of property owners; managers, however, will selfishly pursue their own ends of empire building and prestige unless they are firmly subordinated to the interests of owners, who, in turn, are really only concerned about maximizing returns (Jensen, 1994). Where economic institutionalism comes in is the assumption that in some systems – in other words, those with superior property rights – are agency problems most likely to be mitigated (La Porta et al., 2000). In such settings, managerial tenure, especially that of senior managers, will be tied to following shareholder interests, with carrots being provided in the form of rewards linked to increases in share price and the like (Datta et al., 2009).

There are a number of critiques of this argument. The first is that focusing on management as the main cite of perceived agency failure might obscure agency failings elsewhere in the system. For example, within developed common law systems, institutional investment funds are likely to be particularly powerful (Allen, 2001). In turn, this may mean that fund managers may pursue their own interests (maximizing their own incentives and prestige) at the expense of ordinary investors; whilst the former will have an interest in short-term returns, the latter may have an interest in promoting longer-term organizational strategies and, potentially, more stable and predictable income flows (Folkman et al., 2007). In other words, even if (or because) managers have their realm for autonomous action restricted, ordinary investors may similarly lose out and have their own concerns ignored.

The second is that the taxonomies for categorizing national systems may be overly simplistic. For example, the UK and Canada are not uniformly common law across their national territories, exceptions being Scotland and Quebec (Deakin and Pistor, 2012). Again, much of corporate law even in the US and the UK is not judge-made (the defining feature of common law); much of it is enacted via legislation, as is the case in civil law countries (ibid.). Here it has been argued that perhaps of greater impact is the electoral system, with the in-built right-wing bias in most first-past-the-post systems, owing to the greater possibilities of gerrymandering, and the disproportionate power accorded to small groups of swing voters with few ideological commitments that might easily be swayed by moneyed interests (Armour et al., 2009; Goergen et al., 2009; Pagano and Volpin, 2005). In other words, even if managers may have less autonomy and investors (or at least investment funds) more power in the major common law systems, this may be to do with other institutional features than the law (cf. Dibben et al., 2015). Of course, if institutions exert many different effects at different levels, then this is hard to reconcile with assumptions that the most important and over-riding effects of institutions centre around the relative protection of private property.

The third is, if one takes account of the process and outcomes of managerial decision-making, there seems to one some variation in how good managerial decision-making is in common law (and for that matter civil law) systems. For example, in recent years, common law countries have a generally poor track record in incrementally innovative manufacturing (Harcourt and Wood, 2007). On the one hand, it could be argued that this does not matter, and capital is better deployed elsewhere (Arslan-Ayaydin et al., 2014). On the other hand, if managers are seeking to preserve the capital of their investors, then perhaps a longer-term view (and, indeed, room to take a longer-term view), and associated patterns of decision-making, might be more appropriate (Jackson and Deeg, 2008).

Finally, there is the assumption of very pronounced path dependency (Zattoni et al., 2020). There are very few recent examples of countries successfully transforming their legal system. This would suggest that managers in civil law countries will be more prone to 'wrong' decision-making, when there is plenty of evidence to the contrary; it has been persistently possible for many firms to prosper and owners to do well without a root and branch reform of the legal system (Armour et al., 2009). La Porta et al. justify their arguments through citing economic evidence as to superior growth of common law systems, but this conclusion only held for a very specific time, their results also being helped through the inclusion of franco-phone West Africa (civil law) in their analysis (Wood and Brewster, 2016). A significant body of economic literature points to the increasing disarticulation between policy prescriptions and growth, which would further challenge the linkages between institutional protections of property rights, superior decision-making by firms and overall growth.

COMPARATIVE INSTITUTIONALISM

The broad comparative institutionalist literature (or literature on comparative capitalism) seeks, once more, to explain why patterns of firm-level decision-making replicate themselves within specific contexts (Crouch, 2020; Dibben et al., 2015). This body of literature draws on a number of distinct theoretical traditions. For example, the influential account by Hall and Soskice (2001) draws on the assumption of Coasian economics that actors will seek to mitigate transaction costs through imparting a certain predictability into exchange relations (cf. Hall and Soskice, 2003). Other work draws on the Parisian regulationist tradition that in turn seeks to explain how always spatially and temporarily confined institutional fixes can stabilize economic activity and help secure the basis of growth (Jessop, 2001). Still other accounts draw on the 'old' or historic institutionalist tradition to explain how formative historical events or disjunctures lead to periods of sustained institutional redesign; actors have an interest in hanging onto such institutional solutions owing to their increasingly tested nature, and the failure of past experiments (Thelen, 1999).

What all these accounts have in common is their view that embedded social ties matter (Jackson and Deeg, 2019). Exchange relationships are not simply about 'arm's length contracting', and hence actors do not frame their decisions simply in terms of immediate costs and gains (Hall and Soskice, 2003; Schmid and Kwon, 2020). In practical terms, this means that within and between firms, it is not just the economic but also the social that counts (Roberts and Kwon, 2017). In contrast, more traditional, orthodox economic approaches to institutions would suggest that social ties may be an impediment to rational decision-making (Jackowicz and Kozłowski, 2019).

Again, it is held that in some contexts, actors are bound together with denser or 'thicker' ties than in others (Jackson and Deeg, 2008). Hence, it is in such settings that 'arm's length' contracting is much less likely to represent the default in terms of both inter- and intra-organizational transactions (Jackson and Deeg, 2019). In terms of the former, this would encompass relations with customers and suppliers, and indeed, in terms of transactions involving, on a direct or indirect basis, the wider community. This would include longer-term relations with key suppliers and a focus on building customer loyalty, and a greater representation of stakeholder interests on corporate boards (Prevezer, 2017; Zattoni et al., 2020). An example of the latter would be the employment relationship embodied in greater job security and a tendency to invest more in organization-specific skills (Goergen et al., 2012). Rather than impediments to market efficiency, this literature holds that such types of longer termism can be highly functional, in helping to promote great commitment and sustain higher-value-added production paradigms (ibid.). Again, closer ties between firms enable the sharing of knowledge, conducive to incremental innovation (Mikler and Harrison, 2012; Schmid and Kwon, 2020). In such settings, there is more room for a professional manager with industry-relevant technical skills and knowledge whose skills lie in reconciling different stakeholder interests and who has a longer-term interest in a career with the organization and, indeed, sustaining the latter (Crouch et al., 2009). As employees and their representatives are likely to have more rights under the law, firms are more likely to make usage of formal structures for collective bargaining and engagement around the organization of work (ibid.; Hall and Soskice, 2001). Whilst greater stakeholder rights mean that executive decision-making may accordingly be somewhat circumscribed, this is compensated for by a higher security of tenure, and the intrinsic rewards associated with sustaining an organizational ecosystem. Such settings are commonly referred to as Coordinated Market Economies (CMEs, or stakeholder capitalism), and would encompass Scandinavia, the Rhineland nations and Japan (Hall and Soskice, 2001).

In contrast, other settings are characterized by a stronger emphasis on short-termism, characterized by more instrumental approaches to contracting, where the relative worth of each transaction in its own terms counts for much more than the ties between actors (Hall and Soskice, 2001). Such settings were referred to as Liberal Market Economies (LMEs, the developed Anglo-Saxon nations, otherwise known as shareholder capitalism) (ibid.). Jobs are much less likely to be secure, there are higher staff turnover rates and, indeed, the main focus of training is more likely to be on induction; skills needs will be filled through recourse to the external labour market (Allen, 2004; Hall and Soskice, 2001). Investors are more likely to be committed to a specific firm, and will be quick to exit should better rates of return present themselves elsewhere (Harrison et al., 2016). In turn, managers are more likely to be firmly subordinated to shareholders, and aligned to their interests through reward packages linked to share prices. In other words, each model both constrains managerial decision-making and incentivizes managers to make some decisions over others, but in different areas, making for quite distinct organizational outcomes.

This work was initially focused on the mature markets, and argued that each model had equal viability. This is quite different to the economic approaches to institutions, which assumed that shareholder primacy, enforced by strong property rights under the law, worked best. However, it was held that emerging markets would gradually develop towards one or other of these two mature models (Hall and Soskice, 2001; Wood et al., 2014).

Later work sought to extend this analysis to emerging markets, exploring the different patterns of relations and ties that tended to predominate there; for example, the operation of extended informal networks of support (Wood and Frynas, 2006). Again, it was not assumed that such models were necessarily of universally lower functionality; such models could work quite well for selected actors, even if progress might be quite uneven across firms and societies (Feldmann, 2019; Wood and Frynas, 2006). In practical terms, again, the choices of actors was again circumscribed by structures, and the associated type and density of social ties. In practical terms, managers would make decisions both in compensation for gaps in formal regulation, and to build on strengths in other parts of the system; for example, those that might be imparted through the operation of network ties (Witt and Redding, 2013). Again, if regulation and enforcement might be patchy, there may be sufficient in some areas – most notably in terms of governing the activities of large firms – to both circumscribe behaviour and encourage managerial decision-making to opt for decisions that might be beneficial for other economic agents and indeed the country at large (ibid.; Wood and Frynas, 2006).

DECISION-MAKING AND THE DECLINE OF CAPITALIST DIVERSITY?

The course of events in the late 1990s and early 2000s led to substantial revisions to this body of theory. The quite strong performance of the LMEs during this period, and a seeming lack of confidence in the CME model, led to predictions of a gradual unwinding of the latter, and an inevitable convergence with the LME one (Streeck, 2009). This did not necessarily mean that all economies would become alike, as, in turn, the LMEs appeared to be moving towards a 'purer' or more extreme model (ibid.; Streeck, 1997). Other work ascribed this to the dominance of market liberalism as an ideology, and the challenges in developing viable alternatives and/or updates to the CME model to make it relevant to a changing world (Bruff, 2010).

Still other accounts focused on the role of domestic managers and investors as insurgents or norm entrepreneurs, contributing to the erosion of the CME model from within (Carroll et al., 2019). This might also reflect the rising power of trans-national institutional investors, imposing their will and agendas on firms in CMEs (Boselie and Koene, 2010), and in turn shifting managerial decision-making to one prioritizing shareholder value. Particular attention was accorded to the possible role of foreign activist investors spreading their ways of doing things from abroad (Boselie and Koene, 2010). Moreover, it was argued that as firms were increasingly inserted in global production networks, this forced successive realms of cost-cutting; codetermination and taking account of the needs of different stakeholders was a luxury that was no longer affordable. Longer-term historically rooted perspectives might suggest that the kind of social compromises that underlie CMEs were forged after the crises of the 1930s and World War II; as memories of historical traumas fade, the need to compromise appears somehow less necessary (Lane and Wood, 2009; Mahoney, 2017). A variation of this argument is that actors will always seek to test restraints on their behaviour, and if ground is conceded, events will rapidly snowball (Hall and Soskice, 2003; Lane and Wood, 2009). In other words, work in this genre focused on how, whilst structural changes in the global economy may have provided opportunities or driven difficult choices, ultimately it was the choice of actors that drove changes.

THE RETURN OF DIVERSITY AND THE REMAKING OF CHOICE

The 2008 economic crisis and its aftermath challenged the assumption of the LME as the benchmark for successful capitalism and financial service deregulation as a positive good. Moreover, despite liberalization, the CMEs continued to retain their distinct identities. The rise of right-wing populist extremism in the two largest LMEs, the US and the UK, highlighted the limitations of these economies: overall growth masked rising inequality, falling living standards for many and, indeed, infrastructural decay (Cumming et al., 2020). In turn, this raised questions around choices of investors, managers and organizations, encompassing shifts towards precarious labour, and large-scale tax avoidance (Inanc, 2020); it seemed that the 'robber baron' model had returned, and as with the 1920s, it brought with it the threats of existential economic crisis and social disorder (Kotz, 2018).

If institutions are about agreed restraints on behaviour, with the purposes of alleviating transaction costs and/or developing social ties and relations with other actors, this raises the issue as to when and why owners, firms and/or managers might seek to abrogate their side of the social contract. The first explanation, and the simplest, is that there are historical conjunctures where opportunities present themselves for doing so. Such opportunities might include a period of sustained economic crisis suggesting that old recipes might no longer work, a crisis of confidence among elites as to the feasibility of the status quo (whether for real or imagined reasons) or simply that ad hoc opportunistic decision-making snowballs, with earlier choices creating space for ever more bold challenges to the systemic order (Kotz, 2018). However, the challenging of an existing order does not necessarily make for a new one; rather there may be a sustained period of transition or flux (ibid.). In such periods, more predatory actors may seize on the opportunity to expropriate more resources, to capture components of the state or otherwise further undermine the position of other stakeholders or the system at large (Foweraker, 2020; Richardson, 2020).

At the same time, whilst it may be possible, and indeed easy, to challenge the weaker aspects of a system, initiating or challenging existing institutional arrangements and firm practices represents a departure to an unknown destination. Whilst actors may be well aware of the immediate benefits and some of the risks of initiating systemic changes, the outcomes will always be unpredictable, and indeed may ultimately destroy their own position; even reactionary revolutions have something of a knack for devouring their own children. Those undermining an existing order often register short-term gains, but even in a period of flux it is often second movers who gain more, as the first become discredited by their excesses and/or because precipitate action is often matched by a lack of planning.

Changes in the composition of elites may be destabilizing. It has been argued that the divisions between different elite segments may become more permeable, allowing for, for example, a more rapid and larger-scale movement between the public and private sectors, contributing to the subordination of the former to the interests of the latter (Froud et al., 2017; Savage and Williams, 2008). Alternatively, it has been argued that if commercial interests assume paramountcy over other elite segments, such as technocrats and intellectuals, there is much less interest in forging or sustaining social compromises (Priestland, 2013).

A second explanation, by no means exclusive to the first, is that there are structural reasons why actors tend to work for systemic change at particular times. In other words, the scale and scope of the existing crisis means that prevailing firm and policy remedies no longer seem effective. If actors normally agree to maintain a system owing to its known benefits or for want of known alternatives, an extended crisis can challenge such assumptions (Hollingsworth, 1998). In turn, this would increase the incentives for coming out with firm-level remedies or, at least, coping mechanisms even if they erode or challenge the prevailing formal and informal regulatory order. This does not necessarily mean the breaking of the law, but rather the spirit underlying it and/or unwritten informal conventions. Again, not all crises lend themselves to firm- or property-owner-driven drivers for systemic reconfiguration (Jackson and Sorge, 2012; Lane, 2000). It is possible that both groupings may leave themselves so utterly discredited by the failure of a past order as to open up space for coalitions of other actors to play the dominant or at least major role in rule-writing (Jackson and Sorge, 2012; Lane, 2000); a recent example of this would be the Chilean elected constitutional convention, although more commonly cited ones are the continental European post-war settlements.

A third explanation is that actors accept compromises when impelled to do so by extraordinary historical events. However, compromises are always painful and a long period of stability can lead to memories fading as to the reasons for the compromise in the first place (Lane and Wood, 2009). In turn, this will lead to a period of sustained challenges (ibid.). However, the assumptions as to fixed institutional 'shelf lives' may be challenged, as there are many examples of some institutional arrangements sustaining themselves even after their original purposes are of little present relevance (Crouch et al., 2005; Lane and Wood, 2009). Indeed, it has been argued that often seemingly obsolete institutions may be deployed to new purposes, in other words, remaining a relevant and valuable tool for solving coordination problems as and when they arise (Crouch et al., 2005; Hancké, 2009; Lane and Wood, 2009).

Fourthly, long periods of institutional crisis, followed on by responses by actors that challenge existing ways of doing things have been tied to long energy transitions (Verbeke, 2021; Wood et al., 2020). The latter fundamentally challenge existing allocations of capital, and the relative competitive position of industries and nations. A growing body of work highlights that some types of institutional regimes are more conducive to particular energy sources than others (Doh et al., 2021; Wood et al., 2020). The LMEs coped much better with the move from coal to oil and gas in the first half of the twentieth century, reflecting more mobile investors and the natural resource endowments conferred by territorial expansionism or empire (Wood et al., 2020). In contrast, the CMEs have tended to make much better progress in the present switch to renewables, given the latter require more patient capital and incremental innovation, and because the oil and gas lobby wields significantly less political clout than is the case in the major LMEs (Wood et al., 2020). This represents a further illustration of how institutional configurations may support or allow space for specific patterns of decision-making.

A variation of this argument highlights the new challenges posed by the rupturing of humanity's relationship with the natural world, evidenced by runaway climate change and pandemics (Phan and Wood, 2020). Again, whilst this poses hard choices for firms around the world, in some contexts it is easier to make decisions to implement remedial actions (Doh et al., 2021); although earlier work might suggest that once again the advantage lies with CMEs, the growing interest of many LME investors in environmental issues might suggest that meaningful action in the latter contexts cannot be ruled out (Doh et al., 2021). At the risk of being excessively optimistic, this might suggest that even if patterns of firm decision-making remain profoundly different between LMEs and CMEs, there may be room in each model for meaningful action against climate change (ibid.). Against this must be considered the efficiency of the oil and gas industry's usage of non-market political strategies (Green et al., 2020), especially in first-past-the-post electoral systems, which, as noted above, are typically decided by a relatively small body of swing voters more easily swayed by campaign spending than the general electorate (Goergen et al., 2009; Wood and Brewster, 2016).

CONCLUSION

This chapter explores how and why institutions may sustain particular patterns of decision-making, and how, in turn, choices by actors within and beyond firms may sustain or challenge an existing institutional order. In any national contexts, there are common patterns of embedded behaviour within and beyond firms that sustain and are sustained by institutions (Hall and Soskice, 2001; Lane and Wood, 2009). Whether these institutions may primarily sustain private property rights, ease transaction costs or do much more may be debated. However, whatever one's views on the different main strands of institutional theorizing, it is evident that national diversity remains remarkably persistent, despite the world ecosystemic dominance of particular policy recipes (whether at governmental or firm level).

This is not to suggest that actors do not seek to change institutions, nor that they are, at times, remarkably successful in such endeavours (Boyer et al., 2018). However, institutional changes in one area may lead to unforeseen outcomes for firms and, indeed, for other institutional realms. Actors may respond to challenges by improvising new solutions, making for renewed, if altered, diversity, or seek to revitalize past remedies through planned adjustments, hybridization, or experimentation (ibid.).

This leads to the question as to why actors may be seemingly more emboldened to work for systemic change at particular times. There are many reasons as to why this may be the case, from the quotidian tendency of actors to opportunistically test the boundaries of the system, through to structural changes in the global economy (Hall and Soskice, 2003; Jessop, 2019). Recent work has highlighted the material dimensions of institutional change, encompassing the effects of long energy transitions and even the changing nature of humanity's relationship with the natural world (Phan and Wood, 2020; Wood et al., 2020). When faced with profound challenges, actors may be compelled to adopt completely different ways of doing things, and entire business models or even sectors may be rendered obsolete. However, institutions are quite resilient, and in such instances the range of choices and likely patterns of decision-making will reflect present institutional realities, even if the latter may face existential crisis and quite radical redesign. There is a very large literature on the relationship between decision-making and social structure that draws attention to the dynamic and dualistic nature of this process (Hvinden and Halvorsen, 2018). However, the increasing incidence of world-changing events in recent years, both within the world economy and in the physical ecosystem, both raises the stakes in organizational decision-making and challenges existing rules and remedies.

REFERENCES

Allen, F., 2001. Do financial institutions matter? *Journal of Finance*, *56*(4), pp. 1165–75.

Allen, M., 2004. The varieties of capitalism paradigm: not enough variety? *Socio-Economic Review*, *2*(1), pp. 87–108.

Armour, J., Deakin, S., Sarkar, P., Siems, M., and Singh, A., 2009. Shareholder protection and stock market development: an empirical test of the legal origins hypothesis. *Journal of Empirical Legal Studies*, *6*(2), pp. 343–80.

Arslan-Ayaydin, Ö., Florackis, C., and Ozkan, A., 2014. Financial flexibility, corporate investment and performance: evidence from financial crises. *Review of Quantitative Finance and Accounting*, *42*(2), pp. 211–50.

Boselie, P., and Koene, B., 2010. Private equity and human resource management: 'Barbarians at the gate!' HR's wake-up call? *Human Relations*, *63*(9), pp. 1297–319.

Boyer, R., Uemura, H., Yamada, T., and Song, L., 2018. *Evolving Diversity and Interdependence of Capitalisms*. Cham: Springer.

Bruff, I., 2010. European varieties of capitalism and the international. *European Journal of International Relations*, *16*(4), pp. 615–38.

Carroll, T., Gonzalez-Vicente, R., and Jarvis, D.S., 2019. Capital, conflict and convergence: a political understanding of neoliberalism and its relationship to capitalist transformation. *Globalizations*, *16*(6), pp. 778–803.

Crouch, C., 2020. The state and innovations in economic governance. In Budd, L., Charlesworth, J., and Paton, R. (eds), *Making Policy Happen*. Abingdon: Routledge, pp. 94–104.

Crouch, C., Schröder, M., and Voelzkow, H., 2009. Regional and sectoral varieties of capitalism. *Economy and Society*, *38*(4), pp. 654–78.

Crouch, C., Streeck, W., Boyer, R., Amable, B., Hall, P.A., and Jackson, G., 2005. Dialogue on 'Institutional complementarity and political economy'. *Socio-Economic Review*, *3*(2), pp. 359–82.

Cumming, D.J., Wood, G., and Zahra, S.A., 2020. Human resource management practices in the context of rising right-wing populism. *Human Resource Management Journal*, *30*(4), pp. 525–36.

Datta, D.K., Musteen, M., and Herrmann, P., 2009. Board characteristics, managerial incentives, and the choice between foreign acquisitions and international joint ventures. *Journal of Management*, *35*(4), pp. 928–53.

Deakin, S., and Pistor, K., 2012. *Legal Origin Theory*. Cheltenham, UK and Northampton, MA: Edward Elgar Publishing.

Dibben, P., Wood, G., and Williams, C.C., 2015. Pressures towards and against formalization: regulation and informal employment in Mozambique. *International Labour Review*, *154*(3), pp. 373–92.

Doh, J., Budhwar, P., and Wood, G., 2021. Long-term energy transitions and international business: concepts, theory, methods, and a research agenda. *Journal of International Business Studies*, *52*, pp. 951–70.

Feldmann, M., 2019. Global varieties of capitalism. *World Politics*, *71*(1), pp. 162–96.

Folkman, P., Froud, J., Johal, S., and Williams, K., 2007. Working for themselves? Capital market intermediaries and present day capitalism. *Business History*, *49*(4), pp. 552–72.

Foweraker, J., 2020. *Oligarchy in the Americas: Comparing Oligarchic Rule in Latin America and the United States*. Cham: Springer Nature.

Froud, J., Johal, S., Moran, M., and Williams, K., 2017. Outsourcing the state: new sources of elite power. *Theory, Culture & Society*, *34*(5–6), pp. 77–101.

Goergen, M., Brewster, C., and Wood, G., 2009. Corporate governance regimes and employment relations in Europe. *Relations industrielles/Industrial Relations*, *64*(4), pp. 620–640.

Goergen, M., Brewster, C., Wood, G., and Wilkinson, A., 2012. Varieties of capitalism and investments in human capital. *Industrial Relations: A Journal of Economy and Society*, *51*, pp. 501–27.

Green, J.F., Hadden, J., Hale, T., and Mahdavi, P., 2020. *Transition, Hedge, or Resist? Understanding Political and Economic Behavior toward Decarbonization in the Oil and Gas Industry* (September 17, 2020). Available at SSRN: https://ssrn.com/abstract=3694447 or http://dx.doi.org/10.2139/ssrn .3694447.

Gupta, K., Crilly, D., and Greckhamer, T., 2020. Stakeholder engagement strategies, national institutions, and firm performance: a configurational perspective. *Strategic Management Journal*, *41*(10), pp. 1869–900.

Hall, P.A., and Soskice, D., 2003. Varieties of capitalism and institutional change: A response to three critics. *Comparative European Politics*, *1*(2), pp. 241–50.

Hall, P.A., and Soskice, D. (eds), 2001. *Varieties of Capitalism: The Institutional Foundations of Comparative Advantage*. Oxford: Oxford University Press.

Hancké, B. (ed.), 2009. *Debating Varieties of Capitalism: A Reader*. Oxford: Oxford University Press.

Harcourt, M., and Wood, G., 2007. The importance of employment protection for skill development in coordinated market economies. *European Journal of Industrial Relations*, *13*(2), pp. 141–59.

Harrison, R.T., Botelho, T., and Mason, C.M., 2016. Patient capital in entrepreneurial finance: a reassessment of the role of business angel investors. *Socio-Economic Review*, *14*(4), pp. 669–89.

Hollingsworth, J.R., 1998. New perspectives on the spatial dimensions of economic coordination: tensions between globalization and social systems of production. *Review of International Political Economy*, *5*(3), pp. 482–507.

Hvinden, B., and Halvorsen, R., 2018. Mediating agency and structure in sociology: what role for conversion factors? *Critical Sociology*, *44*(6), pp. 865–81.

Inanc, H., 2020. Varieties of precarity: how insecure work manifests itself, affects well-being, and is shaped by social welfare institutions and labor market policies. *Work and Occupations*, *47*(4), pp. 504–11.

Jackowicz, K., and Kozłowski, Ł., 2019. Social ties between SME managers and bank employees: financial consequences vs. SME managers' perceptions. *Emerging Markets Review*, *40*, p. 100619.

Jackson, G., and Deeg, R., 2019. Comparing capitalisms and taking institutional context seriously. *Journal of International Business Studies*, *50*(1), pp. 4–19.

Jackson, G., and Deeg, R., 2008. Comparing capitalisms: understanding institutional diversity and its implications for international business. *Journal of International Business Studies*, *39*(4), pp. 540–61.

Jackson, G., and Sorge, A., 2012. The trajectory of institutional change in Germany, 1979–2009. *Journal of European Public Policy*, *19*(8), pp. 1146–67.

Jensen, M.C., 1994. Self-interest, altruism, incentives, and agency theory. *Journal of Applied Corporate Finance*, *7*(2), pp. 40–45.

Jessop, B., 2019. Authoritarian neoliberalism: periodization and critique. *South Atlantic Quarterly*, *118*(2), pp. 343–61.

Jessop, B., 2001. *Regulation Theory and the Crisis of Capitalism*. Cheltenham, UK and Northampton, MA: Edward Elgar Publishing.

Kotz, D.M., 2018. *The Rise and Fall of Neoliberal Capitalism*. Cambridge, MA: Harvard University Press.

La Porta, R., Lopez-de-Silanes, F., and Shleifer, A., 2008. The economic consequences of legal origins. *Journal of Economic Literature*, *46*(2), pp. 285–332.

La Porta, R., Lopez-de-Silanes, F., Shleifer, A., and Vishny, R.W., 2000. Agency problems and dividend policies around the world. *Journal of Finance*, *55*(1), pp. 1–33.

Lambert, R.A., 2001. Contracting theory and accounting. *Journal of Accounting and Economics*, *32*(1–3), pp. 3–87.

Lane, C., 2000. Globalization and the German model of capitalism: erosion or survival? *British Journal of Sociology*, *51*(2), pp. 207–34.

Lane, C., and Wood, G., 2009. Capitalist diversity and diversity within capitalism. *Economy and Society*, *38*(4), pp. 531–51.

Mahoney, J., 2017. Shift happens: the historical institutionalism of Kathleen Thelen. *PS: Political Science & Politics*, *50*(4), pp. 1115–19.

Mikler, J., and Harrison, N.E., 2012. Varieties of capitalism and technological innovation for climate change mitigation. *New Political Economy*, *17*(2), pp. 179–208.

North, D.C., 1990. *Institutions, Institutional Change and Economic Performance*. Cambridge: Cambridge University Press.

Pagano, M., and Volpin, P.F., 2005. The political economy of corporate governance. *American Economic Review*, *95*(4), pp. 1005–30.

Phan, P.H., and Wood, G., 2020. Doomsday scenarios (or the black swan excuse for unpreparedness). *Academy of Management Perspectives*, *34*(4), pp. 425–33.

Prevezer, M., 2017. *Varieties of Capitalism in History, Transition and Emergence: New Perspectives on Institutional Development*. London: Taylor & Francis.

Priestland, D., 2013. *Merchant, Soldier, Sage: A New History of Power*. Harmondsworth: Penguin.

Richardson, H.C., 2020. *How the South Won the Civil War: Oligarchy, Democracy, and the Continuing Fight for the Soul of America*. Oxford: Oxford University Press.

Roberts, A., and Kwon, R., 2017. Finance, inequality and the varieties of capitalism in post-industrial democracies. *Socio-Economic Review*, *15*(3), pp. 511–38.

Savage, M., and Williams, K., 2008. Elites: remembered in capitalism and forgotten by social sciences. *Sociological Review*, *56*(1_suppl), pp. 1–24.

Schmid, J., and Kwon, S., 2020. Collaboration in innovation: an empirical test of varieties of capitalism. *Technological Forecasting and Social Change*, *157*, p. 120099.

Schotter, A.P., Meyer, K., and Wood, G., 2021. Organizational and comparative institutionalism in international HRM: toward an integrative research agenda. *Human Resource Management*, *60*(1), pp. 205–27.

Streeck, W., 2009. *Re-forming Capitalism: Institutional Change in the German Political Economy*. Oxford: Oxford University Press on Demand.

Streeck, W., 1997. German capitalism: does it exist? Can it survive? *New Political Economy*, *2*(2), pp. 237–56.

Thelen, K., 1999. Historical institutionalism in comparative politics. *Annual Review of Political Science*, *2*(1), pp. 369–404.

Verbeke, A., 2021. The long-term energy transition and multinational enterprise complexity: a BJM–JIBS joint initiative. *Journal of International Business Studies*, *51*, pp. 803–6.

Witt, M.A., and Redding, G., 2013. Asian business systems: institutional comparison, clusters and implications for varieties of capitalism and business systems theory. *Socio-Economic Review*, *11*(2), pp. 265–300.

Wood, G., and Brewster, C., 2016. Corporate governance and human resource management. *Annals of Corporate Governance*, *1*(4), pp. 249–319.

Wood, G., Dibben, P., and Ogden, S., 2014. Comparative capitalism without capitalism, and production without workers: the limits and possibilities of contemporary institutional analysis. *International Journal of Management Reviews*, *16*(4), pp. 384–96.

Wood, G., Finnegan, J.J., Allen, M.L., Allen, M.M., Cumming, D., Johan, S., Nicklich, M., Endo, T., Lim, S., Tanaka, S., and Wood, G., 2020. The comparative institutional analysis of energy transitions. *Socio-Economic Review*, *18*(1), pp. 257–94.

Wood, G., and Frynas, J.G., 2006. The institutional basis of economic failure: anatomy of the segmented business system. *Socio-Economic Review*, *4*(2), pp. 239–77.

Zattoni, A., Dedoulis, E., Leventis, S., and Van Ees, H., 2020. Corporate governance and institutions: a review and research agenda. *Corporate Governance: An International Review*, *28*(6), pp. 465–87.

3. Board composition and decision-making: who makes the decisions?

Laura F. Spira

1. INTRODUCTION

An investigation of board decision-making may be framed by a series of questions.

What do boards decide? In the corporate governance literature, the areas of board decision-making have typically been divided into dual aspects: strategy/oversight, advisory/monitoring or performance/conformance. While these seem to be neat descriptors, in practice there are aspects of board work that may span both areas, such as defining and managing risk, and this binary approach may not capture the complexity of board activity.

How do boards decide? The literature on group and organisational decision-making is extensive and spans a range of academic disciplines. There is also a sizeable grey literature offering practical guidance to board members. While this may sometimes be written by academics (e.g., Useem, 2006) it is rarely informed by the findings of academic research.

Important influences on the processes around board decision-making include information channels, agenda setting and the roles of the company secretary and other internal and external advisors. Board structure, in particular the role of board sub-committees, is important in considering board processes. The accountability structures within which boards operate could also be relevant to decision-making. Board members have statutory responsibilities: does this make the board different from other organisational groups or teams? Do boards in public and third sector organisations operate differently?

When are decisions are made? For example, how much decision-making is delegated to board sub-committees and when do they meet in relation to the main board? In theory, decisions made by sub-committees have to be ratified by the full board, but how far is this a process of rubber-stamping?

Where are decisions made? Does all decision-making take place behind the boardroom door? How does the environment affect decision-making? Hassink (1996, 2011) provided an interesting visual examination of the boardroom locus. The increasing use of virtual board meetings is also an important area for investigation, particularly in the context of the Covid-19 pandemic.

A more fundamental question, which directs attention to underpinning assumptions about corporate structures and processes, could be: why do boards decide? Could companies be governed differently? US legal scholars have begun to explore some fundamental changes (Alces, 2011; Bainbridge and Henderson, 2018; Bainbridge, 2019; Gilson and Gordon, 2019; Henderson 2019).

While recognising that all these questions are important and interlinked, this chapter focuses more narrowly on the question of who makes the decisions, considering the importance of board composition and its influence on decision-making.

The relationship between board composition and board performance in general remains unclear, in spite of a significant stream of research seeking links, but it is reasonable to assume that the composition of a board will have some effect on how it arrives at decisions, and that this relationship is therefore worth investigating.

Regulatory and policy decisions with regard to board composition are frequently made without reference to academic research. Policy makers often regard academic research as too slow and too equivocal. Occasionally, specific academic research is commissioned to underpin policy prescriptions,[1] but more often the authors of reports rely on anecdotal information and surveys of varying design quality, or take a selective approach to available research in order to support pre-planned recommendations. Where consultation takes place on proposed regulations, the comments received are frequently published on the web sites of government and regulatory bodies, but little indication is provided as to how such feedback is taken into account in developing the eventual outcome.

This lack of congruence between policy and research is particularly notable in two areas of UK policy which centre on board composition: board independence and board diversity.

Discourse around both topics focuses on achieving levels of independence and diversity which are assumed to have positive effects on board activities, but the empirical evidence and underpinning assumptions are rarely explored.

2.   BOARD COMPOSITION: THE IMPORTANCE OF INDEPENDENCE

The ideal model of a board is probably that of a group of directors around a table, experienced and competent, knowledgeable about the company, provided with accurate and relevant information which they will approach with a critical eye in formulating decisions about the strategy and control of the company. The group may include both executive directors with management leadership roles and non-executive directors (NEDs) who are not involved in day-to-day management.

The assumption underpinning corporate governance structures and processes is that management cannot be entirely trusted to work on behalf of shareholders and that some form of independent oversight is needed. Historically, such oversight has centred on financial aspects, provided by independent external auditors appointed by the shareholders in annual general meetings. More recently, the focus has shifted to an expectation that independent NEDs should have a broader internal oversight role.

What does independence mean in the board context? Independence has been conceptualised as an unbiased approach which is difficult to assess for any individual, so in practice evidence of independence depends on a lack of connection between the people involved. This notion of independence is assumed to be compromised by close relationships and, even where these do not exist, continuing association is seen as a threat to the independence of long-serving NEDs. Thus, within corporate governance policy and regulation, independence of connection, which may be objectively determined, has come to stand as a proxy for independent thinking. However, neither form of independence is simple to establish, and the idea of independence remains theoretically and practically ambiguous.[2]

The Cadbury Committee, whose report and Code of Best Practice was published in 1992, enshrined the importance of the NED role in the UK corporate governance landscape but side-stepped a detailed definition of independence and left it to individual companies to determine:

> An essential quality which non-executive directors should bring to the board's deliberations is that of independence of judgement. We recommend that the majority of nonexecutives on a board should be independent of the company. This means that apart from their directors' fees and shareholdings, they should be independent of management and free from any business or other relationship which could materially interfere with the exercise of their independent judgement. It is for the board to decide in particular cases whether this definition is met. (Cadbury, 1992: 4.12)

This approach was very much in keeping with the spirit of the Code, which introduced the principle of "comply or explain". In drafting the Code, the Cadbury Committee hoped that explanations of non-compliance would prompt ongoing conversations between boards and investors, giving individual companies the flexibility to adopt corporate governance structures and processes which would be appropriate for their specific context, with due regard to best practice (Spira and Slinn, 2013: 199–206). Subsequent iterations of the UK Corporate Governance Code have prescribed more detail about criteria for establishing the independence of NEDs, but retain the provision that the board may determine that a director is independent even if such criteria are not met, as long as a "clear explanation" is given.[3] The type of engagement envisaged by the Cadbury Committee has not noticeably become general practice and the quality of explanations of non-compliance varies markedly, but this flexible approach to the definition may still serve a useful purpose, in avoiding potentially negative consequences of detailed prescription. For example, studies have demonstrated that, in some circumstances, social ties between NEDs and management, which would be considered as threats to independence, may in fact be beneficial (Westphal, 1999; Adams and Ferreira, 2007; Hoitash 2011).

Mandating the appointment of independent NEDs has provided a quick fix for policy makers and regulators:

> Independent directors are a plausible fix for any and all problems, and they can credibly be sold as such. Independent directors are viewed differently by various constituencies: investors view them as advocates for shareholder wealth maximization; employees view them as advocates for institutional stability; financial creditors view them as a voice of reason against excessive risk-taking; environmentalists view them as stewards of our environment; and still other interests view them as representatives of the public interest. Their appointment placates all interested constituencies, from shareholders to populists, and satisfies the demand for regulation. (Velikonja, 2014: 904)

The appointment of NEDs is relatively cheap, compared to requirements for structural changes to boards or increased disclosure demands. However, the effectiveness of the policy has been questioned in the academic literature for many years (Karmel, 1984; Baysinger and Butler, 1985; Bhagat and Black, 1999). Recent history shows that independent NEDs on boards do not prevent financial scandals. The question usually asked when these occur is: where were the auditors? Rarely is the failure of scrutiny by NEDs raised. It is indeed difficult to understand how they can be effective monitors in practice, given that they work part-time and the requirement of distance to maintain independence may act against their opportunities to develop sound knowledge of complex companies. Given these obvious limitations, why then have they become such an established feature of corporate governance policy?

3.   THE NON-EXECUTIVE DIRECTOR: A BRIEF HISTORY

The rise of the independent director has been well documented, particularly by legal scholars such as Boyle (1978), who was writing in the early days of their establishment in the UK; Parkinson (2000), who traced further developments in the UK; and Baum (2017), who provided a comprehensive overview of their rise in the US, the UK and continental Europe. The following brief summary highlights the assumptions which have driven this process.

In the UK in the nineteenth century, a series of financial scandals led to general distrust of companies and their directors. To reassure investors and creditors, company promoters sought out titled people to sit on their boards. Popular culture at the time suggests that this strategy may not have been very successful: for example, the Oxford English Dictionary definition of "guinea pig" includes the following citation from 1871:

> 'Guinea pigs,' the pleasant name for those gentlemen of more rank than means … who have a guinea and a copious lunch when they attend board meetings.

Increasingly, other directors who would be considered "non-executive" were also invited to become board members. Professional advisors such as solicitors and accountants could provide useful expertise. Appointments might be prompted by personal relationships, possibly as a means of accessing resources. Directors might also bring to the board the advantage of other business connections, representing suppliers or customers, or political links through which influence which might be exercised on the company's behalf. But the idea of independence in the context of such appointments did not exist. Companies legislation did not distinguish between executive and non-executive directors – and still does not. NEDs, if they did anything at all, performed an advisory role but appointments were frequently symbolic.

Little changed in the first half of the twentieth century. Writing of the 1930s, Sargent Florence observed:

> Where a large supply of capital must be drawn from the inexpert or 'sucker' public, a director may be appointed solely for his drawing power. Reputation for honour and honesty is for this purpose more important than actual efficiency, and in Britain the mere possession of a title or 'handle to one's name' may apparently take the place of experience or even competence to watch the interest of the investing 'sucker'. (Sargent Florence, 1961: 206)

Events involving unexpectedly poor financial results in the late 1960s/early 1970s, such as the GEC–AEI merger (Rutherford, 1996) and the collapse of Rolls-Royce (Bowden, 2002), revealed the extensive scope for judgement in financial reporting, particularly in the valuation of assets. Attention became focused on the role of directors and auditors, driven in part by the increasingly important influence of institutional investors who demanded improved monitoring (Hill, 1995).[4] The Watkinson Committee in 1973[5] proposed that NEDs should be appointed to company boards. A 1977 White Paper on the conduct of company directors[6] drew on practice in the US and recommended that boards should establish audit committees, composed wholly or mainly of NEDs, to deal with issues around financial reporting.

In 1978 the accountancy firm Deloitte Haskins & Sells commissioned a report on the role of the NED and the audit committee which noted a new emphasis on the importance of the NED monitoring role:

> The argument now being advanced is that there is another underlying reason for the interest in non-executives which is to provide, and be seen to provide, a counterweight to managerial power. Tricker (1978: 5.2)

Further impetus was provided by the launch in 1982 by the Bank of England of an agency, PRONED, to support the appointment of NEDs to corporate boards, although at least one commentator observed that the task of corporate governance reform was far more substantial than the improvements NEDs might provide, urging institutional investors to undertake a consensus-building exercise to identify the main issues and possible solutions (Knight, 1986).[7] This early suggestion that too much might be expected of NEDs was ignored as they came to be regarded as a panacea for corporate governance problems. The Cadbury Committee's Code of Best Practice firmly placed NEDs as central to effective corporate governance:

> The Committee believes that the calibre of the non-executive members of the board is of special importance in setting and maintaining standards of corporate governance. (Cadbury Committee, 1992: 22)

Although the approach of the Code was not without its critics (Corrin, 1993; Spira and Slinn, 2013), it embedded the monitoring aspect of the NED role even further by providing a structural framework within which it could be exercised, recommending the establishment of audit, remuneration and nomination sub-committees of the board, members to be drawn from NEDs. Expectations of NEDs continued to rise thereafter: they were described as "the custodians of the governance process" (Higgs, 2003: 11) and as "guardians of the corporate conscience" (ACCA, 2008: 3).

Deakin (2011: 541), analysing the role of corporate governance in the global financial crisis, highlighted an important consequence of the shift to monitoring boards – a diminishing emphasis on expertise and knowledge as criteria for NED appointments:

> the transformation in the structure and function of corporate boards that took place in the United States and Britain in the period of deregulation and financialization of the economy ... began in the 1980s. At the start of this period, corporate boards consisted largely of insiders with a deep knowledge of companies for which, in many cases, they had worked continuously throughout their careers. The task of the board was principally managerial, that is, to set and implement corporate strategy. At the end of this period, boards consisted mostly of outsiders who viewed their role as representatives of the shareholder interest and whose task was understood to be the monitoring of managers. Independence had replaced working knowledge of the company as the principal criterion for appointment to the board.

In contrast to the expectation enshrined in regulatory policy that NEDs on boards will provide effective monitoring, it is noteworthy that the UK corporate governance survey published annually by accountancy firm Grant Thornton[8] has for many years identified the Code requirement for independent NED appointment as the most significant area of non-compliance. Further, while delineating the historical context and the influences which increased the appointment of independent NEDs to boards, the literature which deals with their history pays little attention to the pervasive scorn with which NEDs have been regarded, reflected in popular culture in the UK from their earliest appearance.

Boards and the symbolic appointment of directors were satirised by Trollope, Gilbert and Sullivan and Agatha Christie, among others.[9] More recently, NEDs have been described using such unflattering epithets as "Christmas tree decorations",[10] "chairman's pet rocks",[11] "chairman's poodles",[12] "bidets",[13] and "knitted toilet roll covers".[14] At the time of writing, a conversation in the ICAEW (Institute of Chartered Accountants in England and Wales) Corporate Governance Community group on LinkedIn includes this comment: "INEDs only turn up to board meetings for tea and biscuits (joke!)"[15]

Thus we can identify two paradoxes which potentially complicate expectations of NEDs.

Firstly, they have been given a monitoring role, although under UK law all directors have equal responsibilities. Ezzamel and Watson (1997) argued that this tension would make it impossible for NEDs to fulfil their monitoring role effectively without major change to the unitary board framework, although a study commissioned in support of the Higgs Review suggested that in practice the situated role of the NED is far more complex than this simple opposition of roles indicates, and the way in which NEDs manage their roles in practice is very context dependent (Roberts et al., 2005: S17).

Secondly, in spite of the espoused expectations of those designing regulatory policy, NEDs are widely perceived as ineffective monitors. The next section explores the literature on NEDs to see how far research studies provide support for this popular view.

4.   WHAT DO WE KNOW ABOUT NEDS?

Literature produced by accountancy firms and professional bodies may be designed to assist NEDs in undertaking their role or may be commissioned as part of policy reviews. This literature rests in large part on implicit assumptions about the value of independence, usually undefined, and anecdotal assertions of "best practice", but rarely indicates a grounding in any rigorous academic research.

The academic literature approaches the NED role from varying perspectives. This section does not attempt to provide a full-scale literature review but highlights different streams of research where potential challenges to the assumptions underpinning proposals for corporate governance reform have been found.

Economics and Finance

Research relevant to NEDs often focuses on models of board structure and composition which are tested econometrically, using publicly available data. A widely cited challenge to the assumptions about the value of independent directors was presented by Bhagat and Black (1999), who surveyed evidence on the relationship between board composition and performance and concluded that a balance of inside and outside directors could be more effective than an all-outsider board. Recent contributions to this literature indicate that there is no robust evidence that board independence improves firm performance – indeed, in some circumstances, a lack of board independence may be value-enhancing. Adams used a comprehensive survey to explore directors' perceptions of their role, concluding that:

> Directors who consider their role to consist primarily in monitoring do not feel that they participate as much in discussions or that their input is as valued by the CEO as other directors. This raises doubts that increasing the monitoring strength of the board will necessarily lead directors to be more effective, as governance standards often implicitly assume. (2009: 28)

Faleye et al. (2011) demonstrated that firms with stronger monitoring boards may innovate less. Fahlenbrach et al. (2010) presented evidence that outside directors may damage firm performance by resigning when problems arise and their input may be most needed. Fahlenbach and Stulz (2011) found some evidence that banks with CEOs whose incentives were better aligned with the interests of shareholders – i.e., with more independent boards – actually performed worse in the global financial crisis, and no evidence that they performed better. Recent studies have paid more detailed attention to board sub-committees (Lee, 2020; Adams et al., 2021) highlighting the constraints on NED roles within board structures as mandated within US regulations.

This developing stream of research, while predominantly based on US data, suggests that the contribution of independent directors to corporate governance may depend on complex and company-specific factors which regulatory requirements relating to board composition may not recognise.

Law

Legal scholars have approached the NED role by considering it within the appropriate statutory and regulatory framework. Papers published in the US in the 1970s and 1980s suggest that a more critical assessment of the role was being aired there at around the time when NEDs were being strongly promoted in the UK (Solomon, 1978; Brudney, 1982).

Gilson and Kraakman (1991) called in a similar way to Knight (1986) for collective action by institutional investors, urging them to appoint to boards a new breed of professional outside director who would take on the monitoring role and be directly accountable to investors. In a more recent development of this idea, Gilson and Gordon (2019) analysed the history of the board from the original advisory model to the change to a monitoring focus and, identifying the ineffectiveness of the monitoring approach, proposed two potential solutions drawn from the way in which private equity boards work. Their vision involves either appointing directors with specific competences and experience empowered to monitor management through a strategy review committee, supported by a dedicated office – which they admit would be a costly process – or treating private equity as a "relational investor" to fulfil the longer-term monitoring approach that institutional investors have failed to do.

Langevoort (2000, 2002) drew on behavioural research to demonstrate the unintended consequences of a regulatory approach to board composition and director independence.

Clarke (2007) demonstrated the confusion around the definition of independent directors and argued that the lack of theorisation around their purpose leads to inconsistent regulations. Rodrigues (2008) argued that repeated attempts to narrow definitions of independence have been unproductive: she proposed that independence should be defined within the context of transactions where board members might have conflicts of interest. Sharpe (2012) argued that criteria of time, information and knowledge are as important as structural independence in considering optimal board composition. Le Mire and Gilligan (2013) analysed independence theoretically into four components: structural relationships, capacity, status and power. They suggested that paying greater attention to the relationships between these elements could improve the development of regulatory policy.

Fairfax (2010), setting out a case for more inside (executive) directors on US boards, observed that independent directors are viewed as an ideal substitute for external regulators because they have better inside knowledge of corporate behaviour and their independence makes then suitably objective. However, she noted many constraints on the beneficial exercise of independence and observed that:

> Because independent directors rarely face liability for their actions, the focus on independent directors means that the corporate-monitoring system depends upon the least accountable actors in the corporate regime. (2010: 174)

Rodrigues (2013) argued that increasing board independence had not improved monitoring effectiveness, and proposed a conflict primacy model which could refocus monitoring more narrowly and reduce unrealistic expectations of the NED role. Velikonja (2014) observed that both institutional investors and corporate management favour independence in spite of its deficiencies because it avoids the need for more costly regulatory reform. Avci et al. (2018) tested the effect of independent directors by analysing empirical evidence on insider trading, identifying further limitations on their monitoring role. Kress (2018) argued that membership of several boards undermines the potential for NEDs to monitor effectively, and suggested reforms to alleviate this overcommitment. Nili (2020) demonstrated the limitations of the assumption that independence of connection will guarantee functional independence and effective monitoring.

The general focus of this stream of US literature prescribes caution in adopting legislative solutions to strengthening the role of the independent NED. However, while addressing some general issues relating to independent directors, much of this debate is centred on the US regulatory environment where corporate governance issues are more likely to be dealt with by legislation than in the UK, where the Cadbury Committee established a more mixed tradition of voluntary code compliance within a less closely specified legal framework.

In the UK, Belcher explored responses to the consultation on the Higgs Review and, assessing these within the framework of both statutory provision and case law relating to directors' duties, argued that, despite strong support for the concept of the unitary board among the Higgs consultation respondents, the effect of the adoption of the recommendations with their increased focus on the monitoring role would mean that in practice the unitary board would "cross the line from fact into fiction" (2003: 148). Nolan (2006) presented a critique of the Higgs Review proposals and observed that the NED role remained "mixed and unfocused", arguing that independent NEDs should act as monitors only. Wheeler (2009) noted the important point that criteria for determining independence focus on an individual NED's relationship with one company and ignore broader network ties which might also be considered to compromise independence.

Following the increased emphasis on the NED role in policy prescriptions responding to the global financial crisis, Deakin observed that the UK banks which had to be bailed out had boards which complied with all current corporate governance requirements; he noted that NEDs on those boards were probably unable to avert the effects of the crisis, but commented, somewhat acerbically, on their success in protecting shareholder interests:

> The events surrounding the financial crisis suggest that there are limits to the effectiveness of independent directors as monitors that derive from the complexity of modern business organizations and the volatility of the markets in which they operate. Independent directors appear, on the other hand, to have been highly effective in articulating shareholder concerns and in ensuring that executives orientated their own conduct to maximizing shareholder wealth. In performing this part of their role with such effectiveness, boards may have exacerbated the pressures which led to the critical corporate failures of 2008. (2011)

Sociology, Political Economy

Some attention has been paid to the NED role by scholars in sociology and political economy. Hill's study, based on interviews with board members in the 1980s, highlights the prevailing view of NEDs at that time and notes the shift, driven by institutional investors, for the NED role to include monitoring of the board (Hill, 1995).

Network analysis was used by Davis and Robbins in an exploration of board centrality; i.e., boards' connections to other boards. Using a US sample between 1982 and 1994, they found that boards looked to appoint well-connected directors in situations where they needed to display status because their governance practices were under close scrutiny. They observed that:

> centrality evidently increases the corporation's esteem in the eyes of external constituencies while leaving operating performance unchanged … symbolic displays appear to be sufficient, even if detached from substantive reform. (2005: 307)

Froud et al. (2008) drew on the data from the Higgs Review and used network analysis to demonstrate that there is a well-established process of exchange of NEDs among boards of major companies. Analysis of a case study illustrates their argument that the impact of increased numbers of NEDs on boards has changed the way in which boards respond to take-over bids: the role of NEDs appears to have shifted from saving the company from predatory acquisition and asset stripping, to ensuring that the highest price possible is obtained. Their study is one of the few to consider NED motivation. Their approach, grounded in the shift to shareholder value preoccupations, resonates with that of Gordon (2007), who explained the increased focus on the importance of NEDs in the US between 1950 and 2005 in the context of the shift to shareholder wealth maximisation as a primary corporate aim and the greater informativeness of stock prices. His explanation is that NEDs solve three problems: they align managerial interests with shareholder objectives through a focus on stock prices; they improve the reliability of company information disclosure and thus the signalling effects of stock prices; and they contribute to the view that stock market prices are the most reliable firm performance measure.

Management and Organisational Behaviour

The perspective of organisational behaviour has generated an extensive literature on boards. Again, much of it focuses on the US context. Some studies suggest new theoretical approaches which might throw light on the NED role. Shropshire (2010) looked at board interlocks, considering the individual characteristics that might make interlocking directors successful in knowledge transfer. She did not look explicitly at the monitoring role, but she did raise the issue of board receptivity, a factor which is generally ignored in policy debates about NEDs, where the outcomes of constructive challenge are assumed to be beneficial.

Westphal and Graebner (2010) argued that external factors such as negative reports by analysts may prompt changes in board composition which, through a process of impression management, appear to enhance the capacity for monitoring and control but do not increase that capacity in practice. This resonates with Roberts et al., relating to the Higgs Review, who presented a far more nuanced picture of the NED role in the UK corporate environment and observed that:

> Since reform typically follows failure, the kneejerk reaction is often calls for a yet further strengthening of the independence and control exercised by the non-executives over the executives. More non-executive and more independent non-executives here are grasped as visible sources of confidence to distant investors (and governments concerned with reforming national systems of corporate governance). But the danger is that such visible reassurance is pursued at the expense of actual effectiveness. (2005: S21)

Capezio et al. argued that "the structural emphasis on board independence stands to draw attention away from board decisional processes and capabilities" (2011: 505). Boivie et al. (2016) provided a comprehensive review of the US literature, questioning the effectiveness of the NED monitoring role and positing information processing as an important factor. Veltrop et al. (2021) used a micro-level approach to investigate the limitations on the NED monitoring role, identifying the importance of the psychological safety of NEDs as a key factor.

This brief literature summary[16] highlights selected studies from a range of disciplines which challenge the assumption that the appointment of independent NEDs to boards represents an unalloyed benefit to corporate governance, but the paradoxes remain unexplained. The varying perspectives on the tension between monitoring and strategic roles are not resolved in the studies discussed: some suggestions are made about how it might be resolved, while other studies indicate that, in practice, it may not be a problem. The lack to date of clear theoretical or empirical explanations of the paradoxes suggests that the role of NEDs is far more complex than research or policy making has recognised, and that general prescriptions about board composition may do little to improve board effectiveness and may indeed impede it. This has not diminished the reliance of regulators and policy makers on pursuing such prescriptions, and attention has turned to promoting board gender diversity.

5.   BOARD DIVERSITY

Calls for greater board diversity are closely related to the demand for greater board independence but have also been influenced by broader social and political concerns.

A developing focus on the role of the company in society (see, for example, Mayer, 2013, 2018) has led to calls for boards to focus on environmental, social and governance (ESG) issues and to broaden their remit beyond a narrow shareholder focus. While board independence remains embedded in regulatory policy as an important factor in effective oversight of the management of finance and risk, the need to consider the interests of a wider range of stakeholders has prompted demands for greater board diversity. A new conventional wisdom assumes that homogeneity in board composition hampers board effectiveness by adversely affecting the processes of board decision-making. Can diversity of board membership achieve the broader approach to board decision-making that independent membership alone has not managed?[17]

What does diversity mean in the board context? Definitions of diversity carry similar problems to those noted earlier around independence. To date, much of the debate has focused on gender diversity, a characteristic assumed – as with independence of connection – to be easily definable and to stand as a proxy for diversity of thought.[18]

The Higgs Review noted the importance for boards of diversity of skills and experience, and this was also emphasised in the Tyson Report[19] which followed, with recommendations for increasing the available pool of NEDs. While Tyson noted the limited number of women on boards, the report approached diversity more generally. However, gender diversity became an increasing focus, partly driven by political concerns about the representation of women in senior positions within arenas of power across society. Moral, social and political arguments for increasing numbers of women in such contexts are rarely articulated in the discourse around board gender diversity (Choudhury, 2014, is a notable exception) and policy debates have generally centred on "the business case".[20] This attempts to demonstrate a causal link between female representation on boards and corporate performance. While correlations have been observed, causality is far more difficult to establish, as academic research acknowledges, but this fact is glossed over in many reports.[21] The weakness of the business case has in part been obscured by a policy approach which focuses on methods of increasing female representation on boards: the assumption that board gender diversity is a worthwhile objective is no longer questioned.

The Davies Report on women on boards was published in 2011,[22] setting out a voluntary target of 25 per cent women board members of FTSE 100 companies by 2015, a target that was achieved. This voluntary policy was taken over and extended by the Hampton Alexander review[23] in 2016, but the undoubted success in the progress of promoting board gender diversity has not to date been accompanied by rigorous examination of its impact.

As noted in the early history of NEDs, there may well be a symbolic element to the appointment of female directors, providing a useful way for companies to differentiate themselves. Tokenism may be mitigated by increasing numbers: one mantra associated with the board gender discourse is "One is a token, two is a presence, three is a voice" (Torchia et al., 2011). Although there is little evidence of the range of derogatory epithets applied to NEDs noted earlier, boards slow to embrace diversity are often described as "male, pale and stale", pithily drawing attention to gender, ethnicity and age characteristics.

Beecher-Monas (2007) examined the limitations of director independence as a means of improving monitoring, and argued that redefining independence to include diversity of thought and willingness to dissent would enable a culture which would improve board decision-making. She drew extensively on the literature on group dynamics in constructing her argument but did not identify boards as a particular type of group.[24] This is an important gap in our understanding. Research into the impact of diversity on organisational behaviour has a long history with varied conclusions about its effects. Seminal articles by Milliken and Martins (1996) and Williams and O'Reilly (1998) surveyed prior research and cautioned that potentially negative effects of diversity needed careful management. A more recent study by Harrison and Klein (2007) identified inconsistencies of approach to the definition of diversity, and proposed an analytical framework featuring separation, variety and disparity. While valuable insights into all aspects of diversity may be drawn from this literature, the specific context of the corporate board is not addressed. How might boards differ from other organisational groups and teams? Unlike groups within organisations, they sit within a different accountability structure, subject to external regulation: what impact, if any, does this have on their behaviour?

Literature on board gender diversity falls into similar disciplinary categories as those identified for independence. In the area of finance, seminal studies have been provided by Ferreira (2010) and Adams and Ferreira (2009). Legal scholarship includes work by Fairfax (2005,

2011) and Burch (2011), the latter extending the board diversity discussion to include race and worldview as well as gender. In organisational behaviour, a study by Triana et al. (2014) argued that board gender diversity could support or impede strategic change, depending on contextual factors. Additionally, scholars in the areas of business ethics and political science can provide significant insights into broader arguments for diversity (Torchia et al., 2011) and issues around female representation and quotas (Murray, 2014).

While the literature on board gender diversity is growing rapidly, the gap between research and policy in this area is, as with other aspects of corporate governance, considerable: Ferreira (2015) reflected on the importance of this gap. References to research in policy documents rarely distinguish between peer-reviewed studies and less rigorous anecdotal reports; research which does not support predetermined policy outcomes is often ignored. Just as research into aspects of corporate governance often seeks to identify links with firm performance, much of the literature on board gender diversity follows a similar pattern, using similar theoretical frameworks and methodological approaches, and providing similarly equivocal results.

6. AREAS FOR RESEARCH: INFORMATION AND CONSENSUS

Having outlined broad areas of existing research about board composition with regard to independence and diversity, we can return to consider the specific relationship of these factors to board decision-making and identify areas where research effort could usefully be directed.

Board decision-making depends crucially on two factors: information and consensus.

Information

To perform any useful role, NEDs need to gather and assess information. This presents a third paradox for their monitoring role, since, like external auditors, they are dependent on management – the people they are monitoring – for the information required. The issue of independent authentication of information has been discussed in the context of audit (Wolnizer, 1987) but little attention has been paid to the way in which independent directors can assure themselves that internal information is reliable.

Adams and Ferreira (2007) argued that management-friendly boards, as opposed to monitoring boards, may be optimal in some circumstances, where the value of information exchange in supporting strategic decisions outweighs the costs of monitoring. The growing literature on busy boards suggests that there is some advantage to the networking connections of busy directors which benefits their advisory role, although their monitoring role may be impaired (Field et al., 2013). Duchin et al. (2010) considered the impact of information cost on the effectiveness of monitoring. Boivie et al. (2016) used an information-processing approach to consider the monitoring role of the board, providing a comprehensive literature summary on monitoring and noting that "one-size-fits-all prescriptions" are unsatisfactory.

Given the importance of information to the oversight role (Sharpe, 2012), it is notable that information flows around the board have received little attention. Board and sub-committee structure are influential factors on information flows.

Free et al. (2021) used a qualitative approach interviewing audit committee chairs in Australian public companies to explore how audit committees process information. Adams and Ferreira (2007) observed that the effect of increasing board independence could have a negative impact on information sharing by management, depending on board structure. Adams et al. (2021: 47) examined the role of board sub-committees and concluded that

> As the formal authority of inside directors declines, they may strategically withhold information in an attempt to increase their real authority. Thus, even in equilibrium, boards may not be able to take steps to improve communication when formal authority is constrained by regulation.

Gai et al. (2021) studied the structure of board committees, noting potential silo effects between them and exploring the effects of directors sitting on multiple board committees.

In UK companies with a unitary structure but operating with a majority non-executive membership and a separate executive group, how do the two communicate? When NEDs no longer sit round the boardroom table with executive directors, they potentially lose an opportunity to interact with them informally. If the only executive board members are the chief executive and the chief financial officer, information is likely to be mediated through them, placing them in a powerful position that contrasts oddly with the notion that management needs to be constrained by independent oversight.

Beyond the structure of boards and their committees, there has been little investigation of the relationship of NEDs with two important corporate actors and sources of information: the internal auditor and the company secretary.

Assuming that NEDs can acquire relevant and reliable information, how do they use it? Do NEDs, working part-time and often with other board appointments, have time to get to grips with large complex organisations in order to interpret information in context?

There is thus considerable scope for research into how the information needs of boards are met and the impact of information flows on board decision-making.

Consensus

Our ideal board will arrive at its decisions through a process of reasoned debate based on the available information, with competent independent NEDs drawing on their experience to advise and monitor colleagues and management. But it is notable that metaphors of conflict are often used in reports of what happens behind the boardroom door.[25] Effective decision-making requires the achievement of consensus. Underpinning the drive to increase the independence and diversity of boards is the assumption that homogeneity of board composition provides the conditions leading to the phenomenon of "groupthink", considered to lead to poor decision-making. The work of Janis (1971) that originally provided evidence of the deleterious effects of groupthink is widely cited but rarely examined closely: Janis' analysis of structural and situational factors enabling groupthink addressed more than just homogeneity of group membership. Consensus does not necessarily imply groupthink: differing opinions may be expressed in arriving at consensus. Nor does apparent lack of groupthink guarantee good decision-making.

Similar concepts appear in the literature of social psychology and organisational management, identifying the constraints on decision-making of the operation of social norms – for example, the Abilene paradox (Harvey, 1988) and pluralistic ignorance (Westphal and Bednar, 2005). Morck (2008) drew on research in social psychology to argue that "reflexive subservience" is a continuing constraint on the exercise of constructive challenge within existing board structures.

The exercise of "productive disagreement" or "constructive challenge" expected from independent NEDs is seen as a means to combat groupthink. In practice, its effectiveness may be limited. At one end of the spectrum, it may be a symbolic performance; at the other it may lead to division and conflict, undermining consensus. A balance must be struck, and the role of the chair and internal dynamics of the board will undoubtedly play an important moderating role. Marchetti et al. (2017) is one of relatively few studies which examine dissent in the boardroom. Using data from Italy, they explored the impact of dissent on the market, observing that disclosure of the detail of decisions might mitigate this. From the perspective of dissenting directors, they suggested that incentives for dissent might be affected by risk of liability, and fear of this might lead to more negotiation outside the boardroom, a potentially "questionable" governance practice. They also stressed the importance of accurate and comprehensive minutes of board meetings.

A growing literature examines the impact of demographic fault lines on board activity and identifies this as a potential problem arising from increased board diversity (Veltrop et al., 2015; Van Peteghem et al., 2018).

Further research into how boards achieve consensus could test the assumption of the value of challenge and enhance policy prescriptions around both the monitoring and advisory roles of NEDs.

7.   CONCLUSION

Adams (2017: 292) observed:

> While conceptually appealing, the evidence that conventional measures of board independence matter is inconclusive … Even more worrisome, banks with more independent boards had worse outcomes during the financial crisis … Instead of being a panacea, independence may be a problem. While this is bad news for those who want easy answers, it is good news for academics interested in challenging research.

Academic papers in the corporate governance literature usually end with a call for further research but little concrete guidance on how this could be pursued. This chapter has raised a series of questions that could usefully be explored and has drawn on literature from a range of disciplines and research approaches, with the intention of offering signposts for future research.

A first challenge for such research would be situating a potential study within existing knowledge. A helpful starting point could be the very comprehensive survey of the literature on boards assembled by Adams (2017), covering many of the issues highlighted in this chapter. Klausner (2018) provided a helpful overview of US research on the value of independent boards, noting the methodological difficulties of identifying causation. Ferreira (2015) offered some important reflections on research into board diversity.

Much corporate governance research is undertaken within academic "silos". As well as disciplinary, these may be geographical (US studies do not always draw on relevant research in Europe, Asia or Africa), theoretical (agency theory tends to dominate) and methodological (qualitative approaches are relatively under-represented). Studies using mixed methods or drawing together different disciplines may present practical challenges to researchers but offer the potential for valuable insights to support policy developments.

It is particularly important to recognise the potential contribution from other academic disciplines in considering studies that claim to provide meta analyses or systematic literature reviews. For example, Nguyen et al. (2020) surveyed a long list of journals addressing issues around women on boards but did not include any law journals; the systematic literature review of corporate board committees by Alhossini et al. (2021) also ignored law journals. Yet, as this chapter has demonstrated, legal scholars have contributed significantly to debates about board independence and diversity.

A second challenge is access to data, which can be a particular issue for researchers using qualitative approaches to investigate boardroom dynamics. How can we get behind the board-room door? Leblanc and Schwartz (2007) provided a good starting point for addressing this, drawing on their own experience and suggesting some practical solutions. Research methods continue to evolve: Veltrop et al. (2021) developed a micro-level approach using videos of meetings to investigate the limitations on the NED monitoring role.

Research from a variety of disciplinary perspectives suggests that policy makers and regulators should exercise caution in regulating board composition, but the extent to which research directly influences the development of policy and regulation is unclear.[26] Corporate governance policy making has developed a pattern, often prompted by responses to critical events, whereby regulatory bodies establish a process of evidence collection and public consultation, led by an individual or group recognised as having the necessary experience to pronounce authoritatively on the findings. While the responses may be made public, the process by which these responses are collated, summarised and used remains opaque and the influence of academic research seems to be very limited.[27] Very few academics respond formally, and it is unclear whether policy makers are directed to appropriate research during their deliberations.[28]

Although NEDs may not be represented in quite such unflattering terms as in the past, the idea that they are weak monitors and should offer more challenge seems entrenched in recommendations for increasing board independence and diversity. The recent emphasis in the UK on increased shareholder engagement with boards as a route to improved corporate governance will also impinge on the role of NEDs: to what extent will the development of new relationships of boards with investors support or undermine the NED's capacity to offer "constructive challenge"? Demands for board-level risk committees will also have an impact, with possible blurring of responsibility: Li and Wearing (2010) argued that proposals that NEDs should form risk committees are unsound because risk and return are inherently linked and the management of risk must be an executive function.

Can mandating board composition ever improve the functioning of boards? How can nomination committees construct a board of NEDs with appropriate skills and experience which is also sufficiently diverse across a range of characteristics? The work of audit and remuneration committees has been studied in more detail than that of nomination committees, but their work is fundamental to any consideration of board composition.

Mandating board composition remains an attractive solution for policy makers and regulators seeking to address perceived problems with corporate governance. It can be relatively easily implemented and costs less than increased disclosure demands, but its effectiveness remains questionable. This chapter has identified some of the questions that need to be pursued.

As Sir John Kay observed in his interim review of UK equity markets and long-term decision-making:

Perhaps there is no set of rules that can define the composition of an effective board. (2012: 17)

NOTES

1. See Roberts et al. (2005) and McNulty et al. (2005) for discussion of the research undertaken for the 2003 Higgs Review of the role and effectiveness of non-executive directors.
2. Le Mire and Gilligan (2013) provided a useful theoretical analysis of independence, emphasising the contextual nature of its definition and interpretation. The use of the term remains ambiguous in practice. Page and Spira (2005) discussed the protective role of ambiguity in the context of auditor independence.
3. Crespí-Cladera and Pascaul-Fuster (2014) examined the implications of independence misclassification.
4. The accountancy profession responded to criticism by introducing a programme of accounting standard-setting, although this response was not without its critics (Baxter, 1981).
5. *The Responsibilities of the British Public Company*, CBI, 1973.
6. *The Conduct of Company Directors*, Command Papers 7037, HMSO, 1977.
7. Knight's comments presage the Walker Review recommendation: "Institutional investors and fund managers should actively seek opportunities for collective engagement where this has the potential to enhance their ownership influence in promoting sustainable improvement in the performance of their investee companies." (Recommendation 21, Walker 2009, p. 19).
8. Every year since 2001 the accountancy firm Grant Thornton has published a review of corporate governance disclosures of FTSE 350 companies, examining the level of compliance with the UK Corporate Governance Code.
9. Anthony Trollope, *The Way We Live Now*, 1875; Gilbert & Sullivan, *Utopia Ltd*, 1893; Agatha Christie, *The Seven Dials Mystery*, 1929.
10. Mace, M. (1971) *Directors: Myth and Reality*, Harvard University Press.
11. Attributed to Ross Perot.
12. Holmes, G., and Sugden, A. (1995), Useful Watchdog or Chairman's Poodle?, *Investors Chronicle*, 3 November, 21.
13. Michael Grade, *Have I Got News for You*, BBC 1, 18 May 2001.
14. Coggan, P. (2002), "Days of the Golf Buddy Are Passing", *Financial Times*, 27 April.
15. https://tinyurl.com/48r4zauf (accessed 4.6.21).
16. See Adams (2017) for a comprehensive literature survey on board membership.
17. Wheeler (2012) described this new focus as "independence plus", a hybrid which combines (and confuses) structural independence with demographic characteristics assumed to provide desirable cognitive skills.
18. Both literature and practice have yet to consider explicitly issues around gender definition.
19. Available at http://facultyresearch.london.edu/docs/TysonReport.pdf (accessed 18.6.21).
20. Possibly because this is seen by advocates as more objective and the most effective way to convince male directors.
21. See, for example, a report published by the International Finance Group of the World Bank at https://openknowledge.worldbank.org/bitstream/handle/10986/31057/Women-in-Business-Leadership-Public-Sector-Opinion-42-PUBLIC.pdf?sequence=1&isAllowed=y (accessed 21.6.21), which assembles a range of relevant literature including the meta analysis conducted by Post and Byron (2015) but fails to note that the authors are clear that their work posits an association but not causality; in contrast, a widely cited report by Credit Suisse (2012) drew on a range of academic research and emphasised that while correlations have been observed no claims for causality are made.
22. Available at https://assets.publishing.service.gov.uk/government/uploads/system/uploads/attachment_data/file/31480/11–745-women-on-boards.pdf (accessed 18.6.21).
23. https://ftsewomenleaders.com/about-us/ (accessed 18.6.21).

24. Boivie et al. (2016) addressed this difference in exploring the monitoring role of boards.
25. Some examples: "PIRC sides with activist investor in Exxon boardroom battle City AM", www
     .cityam.com/pric-sides-with-activist-investor-in-exxon-boardroom-battle/   (accessed   25.5.21);
     "Nominet boardroom battle may already be over as campaign to oust management hits critical
     milestone", www.theregister.com/2021/02/02/nominet_board_battle/ (accessed 25.5.21); "Yingde
     boardroom battle escalates ahead of shareholder meeting", www.reuters.com/article/yingde-gases
     -ma-idUSL3N1GK3BD (accessed 25.5.21).
26. Adams (2017: 348) made this point particularly strongly.
27. Roberts et al. (2005) reflected on the way in which their research was incorporated into the Higgs
     Report.
28. Walker (2009), Annex 4, drew on research in social psychology.

REFERENCES

ACCA (2008) Resigning From a Board: Guidance for Directors, www.accaglobal.com/ca/en/technical
     -activities/technical-resources-search/2008/december/resigning-from-a-board-guidance-for-directors
     .html (accessed 22.6.21).
Adams, R. (2009) *Asking Directors about Their Dual Roles*. Finance and Corporate Governance
     Conference 2010 Paper, available at SSRN: https://ssrn.com/abstract=1362339 or http://dx.doi.org/
     10.2139/ssrn.1362339.
Adams, R. (2017) Boards and the Directors Who Sit on Them. In Hermalin, B., and Weisbach, M. (eds),
     The Handbook of the Economics of Corporate Governance. Elsevier Science.
Adams, R., and Ferreira, D. (2007) A Theory of Friendly Boards. *Journal of Finance*, 62(1), 217–50.
Adams, R., and Ferreira, D. (2009) Women in the Boardroom and Their Impact on Governance and
     Performance. *Journal of Financial Economics*, 94(2), 291–309.
Adams, R., Ragunathan, V., and Tumarkin, R. (2021) Death by Committee? An Analysis of Corporate
     Board (Sub-) Committees. *Journal of Financial Economics*, doi: https://doi.org/10.1016/j.jfineco
     .2021.05.032 (in press, accessed online 23.6.21).
Alces, K.A. (2011) Beyond the Board of Directors, *Wake Forest Law Review*, 46, 783–836.
Alhossini, M., Collins G., Ntim, C., and Mansour Zalata, A. (2021) Corporate Board Committees and
     Corporate Outcomes: An International Systematic Literature Review and Agenda for Future Research.
     International Journal of Accounting, 56(1), doi: 10.1142/S1094406021500013.
Avci, S., Schipani, C., and Seyhun, H. (2018) The Elusive Monitoring Function of Independent
     Directors. *University of Pennsylvania Journal of Business Law*, 21(2), 235–87.
Bainbridge, S.M. (2019) Rethinking the Board of Directors: Getting Outside the Box. 74 The Business
     Lawyer 285 UCLA School of Law, Law-Econ Research Paper No. 18–15, available at SSRN: https://
     ssrn.com/abstract=3302927 or http://dx.doi.org/10.2139/ssrn.3302927.
Bainbridge, S.M., and Henderson, M.T. (2018) *Outsourcing the Board: How Board Service Providers
     Can Improve Corporate Governance*. Cambridge University Press.
Baum, H. (2017) The Rise of the Independent Director: A Historical and Comparative Perspective,
     available at SSRN: https://papers.ssrn.com/sol3/papers.cfm?abstract_id=2814978.
Baxter, W.T. (1981) Accounting Standards: Boon or Curse? *Accounting and Business Research*, Winter,
     3–10.
Baysinger, B.D., and Butler, H. (1985) Corporate Governance and the Board of Directors: Performance
     Effects of Changes in Board Composition. *Journal of Law, Economics and Organization*, 1, 101–24.
Beecher-Monas, E. (2007) Marrying Diversity and Independence in the Boardroom: Just How Far Have
     You Come, Baby? *Oregon Law Review*, 86, 373–412.
Belcher, A. (2003) The Unitary Board: Fact or Fiction? *Corporate Ownership and Control*, 1(1), 139–48.
Bhagat, S., and Black, B. (1999) The Uncertain Relationship Between Board Composition and Firm
     Performance. *Business Lawyer*, 54(3), 921–63.
Boivie, S., Bednar, M., Aguilera, R., and Andrus, J. (2016) Are Boards Designed to Fail? The
     Implausibility of Effective Board Monitoring. *Academy of Management Annals*, 10(1), doi:
     10.1080/19416520.2016.1120957.

Bowden, S. (2002) Ownership Responsibilities and Corporate Governance: The Crisis at Rolls-Royce, 1968–71. *Business History*, 44(3), 31–62.

Boyle, A.J. (1978) Company Law and the Non-Executive Director: The U.S.A. and Britain Compared. *International and Comparative Law Quarterly*, 27(3), 487–509.

Brudney, V. (1982) The Independent Director: Heavenly City or Potemkin Village? *Harvard Law Review*, 95, 597–600.

Burch, R. (2011) Worldview Diversity in the Boardroom: A Law and Social Equity Rationale. *Loyola University Chicago Law Journal*, 42, 585–628.

Cadbury Committee (1992) Report of the Committee on the Financial Aspects of Corporate Governance. Gee & Co.

Capezio, A., Shields, J., and O'Donnell, M. (2011) Too Good to be True: Board Structural Independence as a Moderator of CEO Pay-for-Firm-Performance. *Journal of Management Studies*, 48(3), 487–513.

Choudhury, B. (2014) New Rationales for Women on Boards. *Oxford Journal of Legal Studies*, 34, 511–42.

Clarke, D. (2007) Three Concepts of the Independent Director. *Delaware Journal of Corporate Law*, 32, 73–9.

Coggan, P. (2002) Days of the Golf Buddy Are Passing. *Financial Times*, April.

Corrin, J. (1993) A Blatant Slur on Executive Directors' Integrity. *Accountancy*, April, 81–2.

Credit Suisse Research Institute (2012) *Gender Diversity and Corporate Performance*, available at www.mmfoundation.org/sites/mmf/files/Em(pfehlung_csri_gender_diversity_and_corporate_performance.pdf (accessed 27.6.21).

Crespí-Cladera, R., and Pascual-Fuster, P. (2014) Does the Independence of Independent Directors Matter? *Journal of Corporate Finance*, 28, 116–34.

Davis, G., and Robbins, G. (2005) Nothing but Net? Networks and Status in Corporate Governance. In Knorr Cetina, K., and Preda, A (eds), *The Sociology of Financial Markets*. Oxford University Press.

Deakin, S. (2011) What Directors Do (and Fail to Do): Some Comparative Notes on Board Structure and Corporate Governance. *New York Law School Law Review*, 55, 525–41.

Duchin, R., Matsusaka, J., and Ozbas, O. (2010) When Are Outside Directors Effective? *Journal of Financial Economics*, 96, 195–214.

Ezzamel, M., and Watson, R. (1997) Wearing Two Hats: The Conflicting Control and Management Roles of Non-Executive Directors. In Keasey, K., Thompson, S., and Wright, M. (eds), *Corporate Governance: Economic, Management and Financial Issues*. Oxford University Press.

Fahlenbrach, R., Low, A., and Stulz, R. (2010) *The Dark Side of Outside Directors: Do They Quit When They Are Most Needed?* NBER Working Paper No w15917, available at SSRN: https://papers.ssrn.com/sol3/papers.cfm?abstract_id=1590746 (accessed 25.6.21).

Fahlenbrach, R., and Stulz, R. (2011) Bank CEO Incentives and the Credit Crisis. *Journal of Financial Economics*, 99(1), 11–26.

Fairfax, L. (2005) The Bottom Line on Board Diversity: A Cost-Benefit Analysis of the Business Rationales for Diversity on Corporate Boards. *Wisconsin Law Review*, 795.

Fairfax, L. (2011) Board Diversity Revisited: New Rationale, Same Old Story? *North Carolina Law Review*, 89, 855–85.

Fairfax, L.M. (2010) The Uneasy Case for the Inside Director. *Iowa Law Review*, 96, 127–93.

Faleye, O., Hoitash, R., and Hoitash, U. (2011) The Costs of Intense Board Monitoring. *Journal of Financial Economics*, 101(1), 160–81.

Ferreira, D. (2010) Board Diversity. In Anderson, R., and Baker, H. (eds), *Corporate Governance: A Synthesis of Theory, Research, and Practice*. John Wiley & Sons.

Ferreira, D. (2015) Board Diversity: Should We Trust Research to Inform Policy? *Corporate Governance: An International Review*, 23(2), 108–11.

Field, L., Lowry, L., and Mkrtchyan, A. (2013) Are Busy Boards Detrimental? *Journal of Financial Economics*, 109(1), 63–82.

Free, C., Trotman, A., and Trotman, K. (2021) How Audit Committee Chairs Address Information Processing Barriers. *Accounting Review*, 96(1), 147–69.

Froud, J., Leaver, A., Tampubolon, G., and Williams, K. (2008) Everything for Sale: How Non-executive Directors Make a Difference. *Sociological Review*, 56(Supplement 1), 162–86.

Gai, L., Cheng, Y.-J., and Wu, A. (2021) Board Design and Governance Failures at Peer Firms. *Strategic Management Journal* (in press, https://doi.org/10.1002/smj.3308, accessed 25.6.21).

Gilson, R., and Kraakman, R. (1991) Reinventing the Outside Director: An Agenda for Institutional Investors. *Stanford Law Review*, 43(4), 863–906.

Gilson, R.J., and Gordon, J.N. (2019) Board 3.0: An Introduction. *Business Lawyer*, 74, 351.

Gordon, J. (2007) The Rise of Independent Directors in the United States: Of Shareholder Value and Stock Market Prices. *Stanford Law Review*, 59, 1465–568.

Harrison, D., and Klein, K. (2007) What's the Difference? Diversity Constructs as Separation, Variety, or Disparity in Organizations. *Academy of Management Review*, 32(4), 1199–28.

Harvey, J. (1988) The Abilene Paradox: The Management of Agreement. *Organizational Dynamics*, Summer, 17–43.

Hassink, J. (1996) *The Table of Power*. Menno van de Koppel.

Hassink, J. (2011) *The Table of Power 2*. Hatje Cantz.

Henderson, M.T. (2019) Outsourcing the Board: A Rebuttal. *Business Lawyer*, 74(2), 373–85.

Higgs, D. (2003) *Review of the Role and Effectiveness of Non-Executive Directors*. DTI, available at https://ecgi.global/code/higgs-report-review-role-and-effectiveness-non-executive-directors (accessed 9.8.22).

Hill, S. (1995) The Social Organization of Boards of Directors. *British Journal of Sociology*, 46(2), 245–78.

Hoitash, U. (2011) Should Independent Board Members with Social Ties to Management Disqualify Themselves from Serving on the Board? *Journal of Business Ethics*, 99, 399–423.

Holmes, G., and Sugden, A. (1995) Useful Watchdog or Chairman's Poodle? *Investors Chronicle*, November, 21.

Janis, I. (1971) Groupthink. *Psychology Today*, 5(6), 43–6.

Karmel, R. (1984) The Independent Corporate Board: A Means to What End? *George Washington Law Review*, 52, 534–56.

Kay, J. (2012) The Kay Review of UK Equity Markets and Long-Term Decision-making: Interim Report, available at www.gov.uk/government/consultations/the-kay-review-of-uk-equity-markets-and-long-term-decision-making (accessed 29.6.21).

Klausner, M. (2018) Empirical Studies of Corporate Law and Governance: Some Steps Forward and Some Steps Not. In Gordon, J., and Ringe, W. (eds), *The Oxford Handbook of Corporate Law and Governance*. Oxford University Press.

Knight, A. (1986) The Politics of Management: The Corporate Governance Issue. *Government and Opposition*, 21(3), 286–99.

Kress, J.C. (2018) Board to Death: How Busy Directors Could Cause the Next Financial Crisis. *Boston College Law Review*, 59, 877.

Langevoort, D. (2000) The Human Nature of Corporate Boards: Law, Norms and the Unintended Consequences of Independence and Accountability. *Georgetown Law Journal*, 89(4), 797–832.

Langevoort, D. (2002) Monitoring: The Behavorial Economics of Corporate Compliance with Law. *Columbia Business Law Review*, 71, 77–120.

Leblanc, R., and Schwartz, M. (2007) The Black Box of Board Process: Gaining Access to a Difficult Subject. *Corporate Governance: An International Review*, 15(5), 843–51.

Lee, W.-M. (2020) The Determinants and Effects of Board Committees. *Journal of Corporate Finance*, 65, 101747.

Le Mire, S., and Gilligan, G. (2013) Independence and Independent Company Directors. *Journal of Corporate Law Studies*, 13(2), 443–75.

Li, C.A., and Wearing, R.T. (2012) Risk Management and Non-Executive Directors in UK Quoted Banks and Other Financial Institutions. *International Journal of Disclosure and Governance*, 9, 226–37.

Marchetti, P., Siciliano, G., and Ventoruzzo, M. (2017) Dissenting Directors. *European Business Organization Law Review*, 18, 659–700.

Mayer, C. (2013) *Firm Commitment: Why the Corporation Is Failing Us and How to Restore Trust in It*. Oxford University Press.

Mayer, C. (2018) *Prosperity: Better Business Makes the Greater Good*. Oxford University Press.

McNulty, T., Roberts, J., and Stiles, P. (2005) Undertaking Governance Reform and Research: Further Reflections on the Higgs Review. *British Journal of Management*, 16, S99–S107, doi: 10.1111/j.146 7–8551.2005.00451.x.

Milliken, F., and Martins, L. (1996) Searching for Common Threads: Understanding the Multiple Effects of Diversity in Organizational Groups. *Academy of Management Review*, 21(2), 402–33.

Morck, R. (2008) Behavioral Finance in Corporate Governance: Economics and Ethics of the Devil's Advocate. *Journal of Management and Governance*, 12, 179–200.

Murray, R. (2014) Quotas for Men: Reframing Gender Quotas as a Means of Improving Representation for All. *American Political Science Review*, 108(3), doi: 10.1017/S0003055414000239.

Nguyen, T., Ntim, C., and Malagila, J. (2020) Women on Corporate Boards and Corporate Financial and Non-Financial Performance: A Systematic Literature Review and Future Research Agenda. *International Review of Financial Analysis*, 71, 1–24 [101554].

Nili, Y. (2020) The Fallacy of Director Independence. *Wisconsin Law Review*, 491, 512.

Nolan, R. (2006) The Legal Control of Directors' Conflicts of Interest in the United Kingdom: Non-Executive Directors Following the Higgs Report. In Armour, J., and McCahery J. (eds), *After Enron*. Hart Publishing.

Page, M., and Spira, L.F. (2005) Ethical Codes, Independence and the Conservation of Ambiguity. *Business Ethics: A European Review*, 14(3), 301–16.

Parkinson, J. (2000) Evolution and Policy in Company Law: The Non-Executive Director. In Parkinson, J., Gamble, A., and Kelly, G. (eds), *The Political Economy of the Company*. Hart Publishing.

Post, C., and Byron, K. (2015) Women on Boards and Firm Financial Performance: A Meta-Analysis. *Academy of Management Journal*, 58(5), 1546–71.

Roberts, J., McNulty, T., and Stiles, P. (2005) Beyond Agency Conceptions of the Work of the Non-Executive Director: Creating Accountability in the Boardroom. *British Journal of Management*, 16, S5–S26.

Rodrigues, U. (2008) The Fetishization of Independence. *Journal of Corporation Law*, 33, 447–96.

Rodrigues, U. (2013) A Conflict Primacy Model of the Public Board. *University of Illinois Law Review*, 1052–55.

Rutherford, B.A. (1996) The AEI-GEC Gap Revisited. *Accounting, Business and Financial History*, 6(2), 141–61.

Sargent Florence, P. (1961) *The Logic of British and American Industry*. Routledge.

Sharpe, N. (2012) Questioning Authority: The Critical Link Between Board Power and Process. *Journal of Corporate Law*, 38(1), 1–51.

Shropshire, C. (2010) The Role of the Interlocking Director and Board Receptivity in the Diffusion of Practices. *Academy of Management Review*, 35(2), 246–64.

Solomon, L.D. (1978) Restructuring the Corporate Board of Directors: Fond Hope–Faint Promise? *Michigan Law Review*, 76, 581–610.

Spira, L.F., and Slinn, J. (2013) *The Cadbury Committee: A History*. Oxford University Press.

Torchia, M., Calabrò, A., and Huse, M. (2011) Women Directors on Corporate Boards: From Tokenism to Critical Mass. *Journal of Business Ethics*, 102(2), 299–317.

Triana, M., Miller, T., and Trzebiatowski, T. (2014) The Double-Edged Nature of Board Gender Diversity: Diversity, Firm Performance, and the Power of Women Directors as Predictors of Strategic Change. *Organization Science*, 25(2), 609–32.

Tricker, R.A. (1978) *The Independent Director: A Study of the Non-Executive Director and the Audit Committee*. Tolley.

Useem, M. (2006) How Well-Run Boards Make Decisions. *Harvard Business Review*, November, 130–38.

Van Peteghem, M., Bruynseels, L., and Gaeremynck, A. (2018) Beyond Diversity: A Tale of Faultlines and Frictions in the Board of Directors. *Accounting Review*, 93(2), 339–67.

Velikonja, U. (2014) The Political Economy of Board Independence. *North Carolina Law Review*, 92(3), 855–916.

Veltrop, D., Bezemer, P.-J., Nicholson, G., and Pugliese, A. (2021) Too Unsafe to Monitor? How Board–CEO Cognitive Conflict and Chair Leadership Shape Outside Director Monitoring. *Academy of Management Journal*, 64(1), https://doi.org/10.5465/amj.2017.1256.

Veltrop, D., Hermes, N., Postma, T., and de Haan, J. (2015) A Tale of Two Factions: Why and When Factional Demographic Faultlines Hurt Board Performance. *Corporate Governance: An International Review*, 23(2), 145–60.

Walker, D. (2009) *A Review of Corporate Governance in UK Banks and Other Financial Industry Entities*, available at http://webarchive.nationalarchives.gov.uk/+/http://www.hm-treasury.gov.uk/d/walker_review_261109.pdf (accessed 26.6.21).

Westphal, J.D. (1999) Collaboration in the Board Room: Behavioral and Performance Consequences on CEO Board Social Ties. *Academy of Management Journal*, 42(1), 7–24.

Westphal, J.D., and Bednar, M. (2005) Pluralistic Ignorance in Corporate Boards and Firms' Strategic Persistence in Response to Low Firm Performance. *Administrative Science Quarterly*, 50(2), 262–98.

Westphal, J.D., and Graebner, M. (2010) A Matter of Appearances: How Corporate Leaders Manage the Impressions of Financial Analysts about the Conduct of Their Boards. *Academy of Management Journal*, 53(1), 15–43.

Wheeler, S. (2009) Non-Executive Directors and Corporate Governance. *Northern Ireland Legal Quarterly*, 60(1), 51–62.

Wheeler, S. (2012) Independent Directors and Corporate Governance. *Australian Journal of Corporate Law*, 27, 168–87.

Williams, K., and O'Reilly, C. (1998) Demography and Diversity in Organizations: A Review of 40 Years of Research. *Research in Organizational Behavior*, 20, 77–140.

Wolnizer, P. (1987) *Auditing as Independent Authentication*. Sydney University Press.

4. Liminality, purpose, and psychological ownership: board decision practices as a route to stewardship

Donald Nordberg

INTRODUCTION

Boards sit at the apex of the organisation. Through their collective decision-making, directors take legal responsibility for the outcomes and the processes. And when things go seriously wrong, someone is sure to ask: "Where was the board?" (MacAvoy, 2003). But the individuals who sit on corporate boards sit outside the day-to-day flows of information required for evidence-based decision-making and separated from the insights to be gathered from the nuances of corporate culture. Moreover, many are only involved part-time with the business. That brings benefits, of course, but it also raises questions about their commitment to collective aims. In unitary boards, where executives sit alongside the outside, non-executives, those executives are asked in law and codes of conduct to set internal allegiances aside when working on board business. That is, directors – especially but not only the non-executives – are liminal actors in the workings of corporations, neither inside nor outside. They perch on the threshold between the organisation and the outside world of shareholders and stakeholders. When important issues require decisions, how do these outside-insiders or inside-outsiders decide, with what degree of commitment, and with what sense of purpose? Under these circumstances, in what ways is director stewardship likely to emerge?

This chapter explores those questions through examination of prior studies of board decisions, insights from corporate directors gathered informally over long periods in different settings and countries, and board experiences of the author. It draws on theoretical perspectives in anthropology, sociology, and social psychology, which provide different perspectives from those of economics-led writing on corporate governance. Doing so lets us glimpse a director's-eye view, in which "agency" refers to the latitude directors have and the discretion they exercise (Sewell, 1992), rather than to the "problem" posited in agency theory (Dalton, Hitt, Certo, and Dalton, 2007; Fama and Jensen, 1983). That can involve setting aside structures of control and mechanisms designed to enhance corporate governance to create opportunities in which director commitment can arise, and with them the possibility of stewardship.

We begin by examining ideas of corporate purpose and director stewardship, and what liminality and commitment entail. We will then examine how these concepts manifest in types of major decisions that organisations face: mergers and acquisitions, recruitment and remuneration of senior executives, financial decisions, and questions of how to govern during crises. These cases of concern different organisation types: private, for-profit businesses or those listed on public markets, and not-for-profits. The chapter develops a framework for analysing routes to stewardship and concludes by examining the research questions that arise. We will also speculate on why board decision-making often fails, sometimes with catastrophic consequences for the constituencies with which the board interacts, and for the directors themselves.

PURPOSE, STEWARDSHIP

In the middle of 2019, a decade after the worst financial crisis since the Great Depression of the 1930s and half a year before the Covid-19 pandemic turned the world of organisations upside down, an important US business lobbying organisation announced a seemingly sweeping change in direction. The Business Roundtable, a club of CEOs of listed companies, orchestrated a statement from its members. No longer would they set their goals by the principle of shareholder value or accept the primacy of shareholders in guiding their decisions (Business Roundtable, 2019). Its message echoed one delivered 18 months earlier by the chairman of the largest asset management firm in the world; that is, the world's largest shareholder (Fink, 2018). Instead, decisions would be guided towards creating value for a wide range of stakeholders. These statements crystallised a line of thought that had been building across large swathes of opinion, for some under the banner of "CSR", or corporate social responsibility; for others as "ESG" (environmental, social and governance) concerns; for others still as "sustainability". The Business Roundtable proclamation was billed as a call for a re-orientation of decision-making and the attitudes that directors bring to the task. It sought a fresh sort of answer to the question: what is a company – what is *this* company – for?

In conventional thinking, if shareholder primacy is the guiding principle – and if shareholders see "value" as the sum of capital gains and monies returned (Rappaport, 1986) – then board decisions should maximise return on investment, with the principal levers of growth and profitability above the cost of capital. Under modern portfolio theory (MPT), board decisions should accept any project that met those criteria and reject any that did not. With Business Roundtable's manifesto on corporate purpose, were directors to understand that MPT was officially eMPTy? If so, what other criteria should apply? Or was this statement little more than an attempt to deflect criticism? If directors have accountability to a range of stakeholders, they may play the needs of one point of accountability against the others. In doing so, they may exhibit accountability to none (Bebchuk, 2020).

Business Roundtable's acceptance of this change of purpose has not been universally accepted, even among academics who consider themselves advocates for social responsibility and adherents to stakeholder theory (e.g., Edmans, 2011, 2020). If shareholders tend to take a short-term view of returns, does that mean that corporations will respond with decisions that favour short-term gains at the expense of long-term value? There is evidence for such a conclusion, not least that the growing presence of "transient" investors is often followed by reductions in spending on research and development and a short-lived boost to share prices, followed by a subsequent decline (Cremers, Pareek, and Sautner, 2020). But there is also evidence that activism focusing on strategic change, including by hedge funds, can lead to sustained improvement in performance even if followed by the activists' exit soon after the decision to change is announced (Bebchuk, Brav, and Wei, 2015; Becht, Franks, Grant, and Wagner, 2015). Moreover, the dramatic growth in investment in ESG funds offered by mainstream asset management firms shows a growing appetite for something other than narrowly defined ideas about shareholder value. These observations suggest ways in which corporate purpose might align with a shareholder-centric notion of accountability. If so, then the remedies of agency theory, which include monitoring and control of executives as well as incentives to align with shareholder interest, might indeed have some merit.

If the purpose of the organisation is to create value – for whomever – and to continue to do so for the long term, then the organisation requires decisions to be made by people acting for the long-term good of the organisation; that is, to be stewards. Stewardship theory, however, suggests processes and practices that are the polar opposites of those in agency theory (Davis, Schoorman, and Donaldson, 1997). In agency theory, managers are assumed to be self-interested economic actors. Stewards are temperamentally other-regarding not self-regarding, self-actualising not self-aggrandising. They give priority to the collective. They thrive on trust and respond with service; they rebel against monitoring and control. Moreover, stewards demonstrate cognitive alignment and emotional attachment (Hernandez, 2012); these are the ingredients of psychological ownership (Pierce, Kostova, and Dirks, 2001) and of corporate purpose. Stewards take that stance even in the absence of legal ownership of corporate equity.

It can be argued, therefore, that individual stewards relegate personal reward for corporate purpose. Through their activities, they pursue intrinsic goods, the exercise of what Aristotle (1962) called the virtue of *phrónēsis*, often translated as the practical wisdom. But they are also guided by "generosity and self-control"; that is, moral virtues "formed by habit" (pp. 32, 33). Like Aristotle, the contemporary moral theorist Alasdair MacIntyre (2007) sees practical wisdom, exemplified by the artist, arising through repeated practice, though he is famously sceptical of whether practices associated with management can be virtues as they are based in the pursuit of extrinsic rewards. Sinnicks (2014, p. 236), however, argues that managerial disciplines, rather than overall management, do have that character, adding: "Employees may initially require supervision and direction before they are eventually able to understand the [internal] goods present in their roles" (see also Newton, 1992). Practice, in pursuit of excellence, makes virtuous.

These are manager- and employee-centric arguments. Translating such stewardship to the boardroom may seem obvious, but it is not so simple. Directors oversee the work of managers, some of whom are stewards, proud of the work they do, the company and its products and services. Moreover, success in business sometimes comes from being self-interested and having that self-interest aligned with the interests of owners. Such alignment is what we see in early-stage, entrepreneurial enterprises, when venture capital backs acceleration of development of the business (Filatotchev, Toms, and Wright, 2006). But the needs may change as businesses mature, list on stock exchanges, and alter their financial structures. Then imperatives for governance shift to a more hierarchical form of accountability to distant and more fragmented owners.

Boards, as the first line of governance, need to adapt to those changing circumstances. Moreover, numerous writers see the work of the board as involving two often conflicting roles: service and control (Åberg, Bankewitz, and Knockaert, 2019; Hillman and Dalziel, 2003; Zahra and Pearce, 1989). Moreover, some scholars argue that these roles are even more distinct, as they are driven by different theoretical mechanisms (Mooney, Brown, and Ward, 2021). Doing both at the same time requires stewards, at the risk of pursuing one over the other. However, as we shall see, many strategic decisions arise in contexts that play both roles at the same time and with the same action. Moreover, boards need to do so under conditions of incomplete information about the past and uncertainty about the future, which seems to point towards (a) a need for commitment to the organisation, engendered through cognitive and affective engagement with its overriding purpose, and (b) achieving that while maintaining the detachment associated with sitting perpetually on the threshold.

LIMINALITY, COMMITMENT, AND "OWNERSHIP"

With unitary boards modelled on British and American practice, non-executive directors sit with one foot inside and one foot outside.[1] Their roles grant them access to confidential internal information, while their external orientation provides different perspectives of the business environment. However, by standing outside for much of their time, they are also cut off from internal networks and can remain uninitiated in the nuances of how the business works. By contrast, executives on the board are insiders, deeply steeped in its internal workings and culture. But when acting as directors they are asked, often in law, to set aside internal allegiances and join the non-executives on that threshold.

In the dual-board systems common in continental European companies, or in single but entirely non-executive boards we often see in charities, the ultimate decision-makers may have no full-time role with the company and yet bear personal liability for their decisions. As outsiders, directors thus face a psychological impediment to developing the sense of commitment. In short, their work is liminal.

Moreover, the place of board work can signify liminality. In practical terms, boardrooms are often separated from the everyday experience of employees. Boardrooms have physical barriers that separate them from everyday experience. They are filled with special furniture as well, giving a symbolic meaning to both the occupants and the those not entitled to use them. As a consequence, boardrooms, both physically and psychologically, are often sacred spaces, controlled by remote, supposedly wise men and women who engage in rituals often alien to the ordinary affairs of the corporation. Is there something in the process, the ritual practices, and symbolic meaning of place that allows liminality to achieve a deeper sense of belonging?

The Liminal

The concept of liminality entered discussions of management from an unlikely source. A half-century ago, the anthropologist Victor Turner studied rites of passage for boys in tribal settings. Building on earlier findings of Van Gennep (1909/2013), he observed that in a variety of societies, boys were introduced to manhood through rituals that involved entering a sacred place. In these repeated practices, each boy encounters adult males, often in costume, who engage in ritualised play, creative indulgences that gradually introduce the adolescents to adult ways and recognition of social structures (Turner, 1977). Step by step, they learn the lessons needed to engage in the protection and governance of society. Crucial to the exercise is the child-like lack of hierarchy at the start of the process, which gradually fades as lessons are learned. At the end, the initiand takes an appropriate position in the social structure and develops commitment to place society's needs ahead of personal desires.

The concept of using such liminal spaces has been used in management studies (Söderlund and Borg, 2018) to describe induction of new employees (Guimarães-Costa and Pina e Cunha, 2013), those working on temporary contracts (Garsten, 1999), entrepreneurs trying to break into the corporate world (Gartner and Shane, 1995), foreign managers (Guimarães-Costa and Pina e Cunha, 2009), and the status of doctoral students on the threshold of academic careers (Gatfield, 2005). Management consultants and professionals (e.g., auditors and legal counsel) seem to engage in permanent, rather than transitional, liminality (Czarniawska and Mazza, 2003). Informality is also important, and so such activities often take place not in the controlled place of headquarters, where hierarchy reigns, but in some other, separate and freer space – a hotel or conference venue, a pub – where dress codes may be relaxed, and hierarchies can be set aside.

This discussion adopts the terminology of "space" and "place" as used by de Certeau (1984), in which "place" signifies a physical setting that is controlled by a larger force and thus controls the behaviour of those who occupy it. For Certeau, "space" is open, unconquered territory, where the rules are laws of nature, not socially constructed constraints. Hjorth (2004) develops this idea in connection with entrepreneurship and creativity, seeing entrepreneurs as those often cast out of the places occupied by corporations. These entrepreneurs then seek to carve out their own place from unoccupied space. "Place" and "space" thus have symbolic as well as physical significance. In contemporary practice, this vocabulary and these concepts apply now to abstractions, including now dematerialised marketplaces, like stock exchanges, and the more playful and open online "marketspaces" (Ozuem, Howell, and Lancaster, 2008).

Boards are, at least notionally, non-hierarchal. To be sure, the chair and committee chairs hold levers of power that other directors do not, and subject expertise of individual directors brings influence. But such equality creates the legal expectation that any such informal hierarchy can and should be set aside on important matters, and that board work can be and will become liminal when the directors themselves choose. That means non-executive directors have the option of staying permanently on the threshold, and executive directors have the right to discard hierarchical subservience in favour of liminality any time they choose. Consider: an operations director may identify professionally with the organisation (self-identity, as an engineer and producer of products) and personally with the CEO and top management (social identity, as a team). But when appointed to the main board, she can conspire with non-executives to fire her boss; she must in law if the actions of the CEO are harming the business. If directors are always on the threshold, how do they build the commitment to the organisation that director duties[2] require? How do they achieve the stewardship associated with taking a long-term perspective that policy seeks?

From Commitment to "Ownership"

Commitment to the organisation motivates work in different ways from identification with the organisation. According to Meyer and Allen (1991), work commitment has affective, continuance, and normative elements: a desire, a need, and an obligation. To be committed, one has to like the place of work, the people, the products and services, and the reputation of the organisation. But liking is not enough. One must also feel a need to continue to work there, which can override the appeal of other workplaces and impede the desire to explore alternatives. More than that, however, one needs a sense of duty to the others; this other-regarding element means that commitment is a social phenomenon, not just an individual one. Such commitment can be damaged or lost, of course, if another individual or the organisation fails to reciprocate. This may be especially damaging when someone who is temperamentally a steward feels untrusted. Yet the affective element of commitment – desire – can be reinforced by repeated reciprocity, which strengthens the normative element – obligation.

Table 4.1   *Sources and expectations of psychological ownership of directors, boards*

Sources of "ownership"	Forces supporting	Forces constraining
Control	Legally strong; effected collectively by boards	Constrained by local circumstances; individual directors' control depends on persuasiveness in boardroom
Knowing	Notionally directors have full rights to internal information; non-executives have ability to add external perspective	Organisational factors can restrict information available to liminal actors; nuances of organisational culture may be out of sight
Investment: time, effort, also finance	Investments in time and effort and individuals' commitment are mutually reinforcing, leaving the issue of how to start the process Some directors may hold shares; i.e., financial investment Employee share options create financial investment, reinforcing time and effort on path to psychological ownership	Governance codes generally discourage options and other equity-based rewards for board service, limiting ways to foster financial investment
Safety	Sanctity of physical and mental boardroom offers safety; board cohesion and trust reduce risk	Justice, trust, closeness dependent on local conditions
Expectations of "ownership"	*Forces supporting*	*Forces constraining*
Rights	Considerable latitude prescribed in law; board has discretion over scope of delegated authority	Implementation depends on local factors; e.g., wilful CEO can impede exercise of rights
Responsibilities	Personal liability for decisions, mitigated in part by directors' and officers' insurance; individuals may select specific duties	Director discretion can lead to shirking in absence of commitment (i.e., absence of desire, need, or sense of obligation)
Change	Depends on sources of individual's motivation beyond status and remuneration	Directors' lack of commitment may lead to apathy about change

Source: Author

While organisational commitment helps to explain why people continue to work at organisations and may even make sacrifices to remain, in the view of other psychology scholars there is another state of mind that goes further. Etzioni (1991, p. 466) argues that people often develop symbolically a sense of property about their association with objects and practices with which they engage; this dual creation is "part attitude, part object, part in the mind, part 'real'". Pierce et al. extend these ideas to develop a theory of psychological ownership, in which the possessed object is viewed as an extension of the self, part of "me". Psychological ownership is thus not just entitlement; it also satisfies three human motives: to have an effect, to extend self-identity, and to possess "territory or space"; that is, to carve out a "place", a home (2001, p. 300).

Pierce et al. (2001) see several routes to the development of psychological ownership. Employee control over, intimate knowledge of, and personal investment – in time and effort, in aspects of the organisation – increase the sense of ownership.[3] Having such a sense effect brings rights and responsibilities as well, as does the expectation that actions will create change; having change imposed, however, can diminish the sense of ownership.

In a meta-analysis of empirical studies, Zhang, Liu, Zhang, Xu, and Cheung (2021) identify another component – safety – which they describe as comprising organisational justice, trust, support, and emotional closeness. Moreover, they find that psychological ownership goes beyond both commitment to and identification with the organisation as a motivating force for employees. Moreover, psychological ownership may be reinforced through financial investment as well as time and effort (McCarthy and Palcic, 2012), though the effects may be constrained by institutional arrangements in different settings (Oehmichen, Wolff, and Zschoche, 2018). These forces encouraging development of a sense of ownership face obstacles as well, of course (see Table 4.1). While these perspectives focus on developing commitment and psychological ownership among employees, we need to consider whether and how this concept can be extended to boards.

BOARD PROCESSES, PRACTICE, AND "OWNERSHIP"

How do non-executive directors overcome liminality to develop the commitment and sense of ownership that permit stewardship? How do the executives who sit on the board develop the detachment from the inner workings of the organisation sufficiently to become a controlling force over other executives and their own, pecuniary self-interest? The answer to these questions may lie in board processes, and particularly those that lead to strategic decisions.

Forbes and Milliken (1999) developed a model of board work with processes at its centre. They argue that having knowledge and skills among the directors is important only if the board's processes engage them. Expectations of discipline and engagement – that is, "effort norms" – are needed. So too is constructive challenge involving episodes of "cognitive conflict". In dysfunctional boards, these processes are turned inside out. Expectations of sliding through – by not reading through the board papers, arriving late, or not showing up at board meetings – can become norms in themselves, with corrosive effect. Individual directors may fail to use the knowledge they have, but so too the processes themselves may inhibit directors from engaging constructively. Conflict that is not constructive may arise because it is rooted in negative affect, rather than cognition; or it may fail to appear because of positive affect: the board is too cohesive.

These elements – effort norms, use of skills, cognitive conflict – suggest an understanding of "process" quite distinct from that of standard procedures and fixed decision paths. They point towards what we might call the board's *ethos*, a word Aristotle used to describe habits derived from practice.[4] Cognitive conflict is a practice of control, in which directors assert the board's control over management. It also acts as a mechanism to assure just outcomes. Effort indicates investment of time and energy, the use of knowledge. That a board is cohesive makes it a safe group in which to operate. Board practices thus align with the sources of psychological ownership. They thus provide a route through which liminal actors can develop it, which goes beyond just commitment to the organisation and its goals. It extends to establishing those goals – that is, articulating corporate purpose – and then ensuring its delivery.

Commitment to the company that gives rise to psychological ownership generates an expectation of responsibility for it, and with that a sensation of being accountable. In a recent study, Elms and Nicholson (2020) show the wide variety of directors' commitment to and identification with the companies they serve, and the implications for their "felt accountability", an "intrinsic, subjective state and a matter of individual perception" (Fry, 1995, p. 183).[5] Elms and Nicholson's invocation of "felt accountability" suggests they see affect as well as cognition at work, pointing to the building blocks of stewardship.

So far, this discussion has dealt mainly with directors controlling management, often associated with challenging management, seeking explanations for actions and plans, and in doing so creating accountability. It is a role often associated with agency theory and using the board as a tool to align management interests with those of shareholders. As we have seen, however, board work also has another facet: service. This is, by contrast, a more creative activity, contributing insights and facilitating access to scarce resources that can help the business accelerate. This is collaborative work of executives and non-executives on unitary boards or between the supervisory and management bodies in dual-board systems. By spanning organisational boundaries, directors not part of management can help the firm overcome resource constraints and help to surface unconventional approaches to problem solving (Hillman and Dalziel, 2003; Hillman, Withers, and Collins, 2009).

This dichotomy tells only part of the story, however, in at least two regards. First is the stance that individuals take towards their work. The study by Elms and Nicholson (2020) suggests that having an identity as an *expert* – for example, as an accountant – leads directors to concentrate on narrow aspects of board work, while achieving a more dominant identity as *director* leads to concern for the overall performance of the company. The latter points to greater engagement with collective decision-making and a more balanced approach to service and control roles. Second, and often absent from the theoretical intent of academic literature, is the practical dimension of being on a board. Service often takes place intimately co-mingled with control activities. As we will see, some actions of directors may have a disciplinary function even as they support management to achieve its aims. The two roles become, as practiced, indistinguishable.

Yet, as concerns about problems in corporate governance have mounted, through recurrent cases of loss of control and waves of corporate collapses, a board's agenda can become overwhelmed with compliance activities (part of its *control* role) and in so doing squeeze out other more creative ideas and the playfulness associated with innovating business practices (*service*). A study of boards of hospitals in the UK National Health Service found agendas overloaded with routine and compliance matters. Strategic decisions were regularly placed at the end of long agendas and thus rarely got more than cursory attention. Big, important, and exciting decisions were cramped by agendas stifled with routine and compliance (ICSA, 2011). What directors attend to in practice becomes institutionalised, constraining attention given to other tasks (Ocasio, 2011).

For this reason, boards often leave the boardroom itself, a place increasingly associated with "control", to find alternative, informal ways of interacting for the more creative, "service" work. In the aftermath of the great financial crisis of 2007–09 and the long recession that followed, Concannon and Nordberg (2018) explored attitudes of directors of companies mainly in the heavily regulated financial service firms. Their formal agendas had become dominated by control activities of audit and compliance, leading directors to seek out informal settings to conduct their blue-sky thinking and product and process innovation. That is, the boardroom was no longer playful and non-hierarchical, but instead the site of struggles over control of the existing resource base. The boardroom has ceased to be a liminal space.

Figure 4.1 then shows how directors, bumping against a threshold that can inhibit direct development of psychological ownership, can find a path through board processes and practices to develop the knowledge, exercise control, and invest the time and energy that Pierce et al. (2001) see as sources of claiming the organisation as a part of self. Following the line of reasoning in Concannon and Nordberg (2018), the investment seems likely to appear in strategic decision-making, which engenders cognitive and affective engagement as well as responsibility alongside the rights that directorship entails.

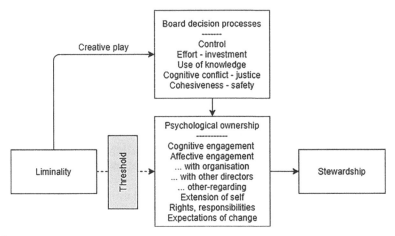

Figure 4.1   *Board decision processes as path to director stewardship*

For non-executives, this rationale is clearer than for executive directors, who already sit inside the organisation. Yet they too may face a hurdle to psychological ownership. From within the organisation, they may have commitment; that is, the desire and need to continue with the organisation and a sense of obligation to it and those who work there. But this theoretical discussion points to "ownership" as something different, the sense of property as extension of one's self. Coming into liminal space and engaging in the non-hierarchical and creative work of boards may be what they too need to make the ownership leap.

DECISIONS AND DECIDING

The important decisions that boards make are often said to fall into a handful of categories, four of which dominate: (1) strategic decisions, including mergers and acquisitions, and business entry and exit; (2) CEO and board succession, and executive pay; (3) financial matters, including dividends, leverage, and capital allocation; and (4) governance matters, concerning organisational structure, processes, and decision rules (McKinsey & Co., 2021). With the framework developed above in mind, let us consider four thought experiments in which boards need to make strategically important decisions concerning problems where expedience conflicts with longer-term aspirations and societal needs. These examples are cases are fictional but with analogues in real organisations. They have been developed in part from incidents in which board work was confidential. Some were important enough to attract public attention, or directors have voiced their opinions informally and not for attribution. Details of the processes may, therefore, be reconstructed from outcomes or the fragmented accounts of interested parties.

I make no claims of representativeness or completeness, only of validity. These cases are not products of research per se, but instead provocations for research. Each case asks two questions, neither about the outcome: how does the process affect directors' commitment and sense of ownership, and how does that represent the other-regarding yet self-actualising stance we associate with stewardship of corporate purpose?

Case 1: The Merger

Let us call it that, a merger not an acquisition. But we both know (*you and I*) that our side is the winner and theirs the loser. The label – whether *M* or *A* – is mainly a matter of saving taxes. When it is an acquisition, the other company's shareholders have to offload some of their shares in the new firm to pay capital gains tax, driving down their price and the value of the shares that *you and I* each hold. If it is a combination of equals, all that untidiness goes away. Agreed?

You are chief operating officer, only recently appointed to the main board. I am the lead non-executive, newly appointed to that role but with three years' service. The CEO has a good relationship to the chair, who has been with our company from the start a dozen years ago, when they patched together several unwanted initiatives of banks and insurance firms. They took those service ideas and turned them into a mobile phone app that that revolutionised payments. Users faced much lower costs than credit cards, though consumers in major Western economies like ours were slow to adopt them. The explosive growth came mainly in East Asia and the United States, though in the latter serious competition was just around the corner. Still, we listed on the stock exchange a half-dozen years ago, and last year won a spot in a major index, attracting new investors and pushing up the share price, and with it your wealth and mine, as well as theirs.

At today's board meeting, the chief financial officer (CFO) presented a proposition: a South Asian entrepreneur – operating in a large market we have not yet cracked – mimicked our initial business model, buying up a string of exciting but under-capitalised start-ups and incorporating a holding company for them in London. Each of the businesses has real customers, and their numbers are growing rapidly. Like us, they deduct a small fee from every transaction, as we did at the beginning. But the plan, as ours was from the outset, is to morph into a deposit-taking organisation. For that, they need a partner with the knowledge of how best to navigate banking regulation and manage the awkward transition from being a tool that banks use to being a competitor. The entrepreneur is looking for shares and cash, so the tax position is important. But he does not want a seat on the board. This is his exit, and he sees our shares as a good, long-term investment, with liquidity should he wish to complete the exit soon. Besides, he knows we will not offer an all-cash deal. The chair, smiling, wants both of us to join an ad hoc committee to evaluate the proposal. The seller understands these things take time. But he is pressing nonetheless for a quick-ish decision. How should we, the board, *you and I*, decide?

Case 2: The CEO

You chair the nominations committee. We meet to discuss the sense that I have, as a new non-executive, that something is not right with the CEO. He seems lethargic, dismissive, complacent, more concerned with his legacy than our future. It does not help that his share options are underwater. In the current climate, our investors will not tolerate a re-pricing of past remuneration decisions. What do we do?

Textbooks speak of our role as one of constructive challenge, but the CEO is playing rope-a-dope in meetings. The expression gained attention when in 1974 Muhammad Ali told officials to loosen the ropes of the boxing ring so the ropes, rather than Ali's torso, would absorb the force of body blows from his opponent, George Foreman. Our CEO is just lying against the ropes, deflecting our questions about gaps in the explanations of variances from budget. At the moment, the mainstays of the board all seem friendly – too friendly – with both the CEO and CFO. The worst example is the chair himself, who seems to be playing rope-a-dope himself, on the other side of ring, where no one is even throwing a punch.

Over time we have quiet discussions – at coffee before the board meeting, on the phone afterwards – and we share our concerns. Then, we organise a couple of dinners in high-sided booths of an old-fashioned Victorian chop house in the city centre, the sort of place where the movers and shakers in politics and commerce have long conspired. At these soirees, a few of the other directors confide that they, too, have felt uncomfortable. One is considering making her excuses and leaving the board as soon as her elected term is up. Another has been speaking of his concerns to a personal coach, coyly not naming names, but he is getting anxious that the smokescreen of anonymity is not very strong. Is this a consensus developing? Or have we, in initiating the discussions, merely offered our colleagues a chance to nod, much as they have nodded to the actions of the CEO and the inactions of the chair? It is time to decide. What is the next step?

Case 3: The Dividend

We, the board – like most sensible, intelligent people – have joined the consensus that climate change is the most important issue facing humanity, and the most intractable. Our product is a big part of the problem, and our company – let us call it Gigantic Petroleum – should be part of the solution. Outside the annual meeting, and on many days outside our headquarters, protestors decry not just the carbon emissions of our operations, but those of our customers. For years, one activist group of environmentalist investors has been demanding that we shift all future capital investment to renewables. Now it has captured the ear of several hedge funds and a large asset management firm working on behalf of pension funds. Together, they hold many more of our shares than the environmentalists, though still nothing like a majority.

But today, that investor coalition has notified us of a new demand: that we cease making dividend payments altogether until our operations are carbon-neutral and renewables make up at least half of the revenue of the firm. Led by specialist environmental-activist funds, the effort has attracted a wider following. At least one of the hedge funds that joined is reputed to engage regularly in short selling.

Our CFO scoffed at the demand. Had we not seen the argument advanced by none other than some of the world's top scholars in corporate finance, law and governance? They argue that Gigantic ought to increase its payout, not cut it, she says. That way all our investors would get more money to invest as they see fit, which would make more capital available for renewables, once the return looked attractive. She told us to look up their manifesto, their *démarche*: Edmans, Enriques, and Thomsen (2021). What next?

Case 4: Governing in a Crisis

We have just joined the board of a medium-sized charity, using premises donated by a corporation and surplus to its requirements, or by a municipal government for the sake of creating a community service. We operate a sports hall, auditorium and playing fields that can be rented out for events or used for other forms of local entertainment, outfitted over the years through donations, ticket sales, and an occasional boost from local government funds. The board has its regularly scheduled meeting to consider the next year's budget, but the day before a disaster has arisen. It might have been a flood or a fire, which would have had a similar effect. It was, however, a decision by central government to put the entire community into lockdown for the coronavirus SARS-CoV-2, known colloquially as Covid. The venue must close, and we – the charity, that is – have no debt but only minimal physical assets. Our working capital is sufficient to operate for a few weeks. When it is gone, we will be insolvent. In good years we operate at only a bit better than breakeven, so reserves are very modest, perhaps not even sufficient to pay statutory severance to the workforce on whose goodwill we have repeatedly drawn. There is emergency funding available backed by the state, but no prospect of revenue for the foreseeable future.

The board is made up entirely of volunteers, 12 of us, working without pay. More than half are in full-time employment elsewhere. In this case, unlike in a fire or flood, the various organisations that employ us are all panicking too. Eight of the directors have strong emotional ties to the type of community service we deliver, either from having worked in that type of service or from family members who have at one time relied on this type of service. Four do not; they joined principally to gain experience of boards in the hopes of gaining a promotion. After very careful, iterative reforecasting, using varying assumptions, we decide to bid for a central government grant, but only after projecting three (of five) scenarios in which the organisation can survive. Moreover, the chair has decided – *no*, he corrected himself, *recommended* – to appoint an emergency board, made up of five of the 12 of us, with power to act for the board as a whole. You have been invited to join. I have not.

PRACTICES AND "OWNERSHIP"

These four cases suggest practices that can lead to – or away from – imbuing stewardship in board. They show varying degrees of control and circumstances that make it possible. In *Merger* the directors (*you and I*) may have the ability to control the situation, but we choose to go with the comfortable flow; our effort is weak, because we see it adding little to the outcome. While we have the skills to intervene, to challenge, we choose not to bother. In this cohesive board we see no need to act, but is the decision safe, or have we overlooked the possibility that the CFO has different and undeclared intentions?

In *CEO*, by contrast, we seem not to be in control. Over time, through effort and by using informal communication channels, we understand that our control is greater than we initially thought. Our scope for cognitive conflict grows as we use our intellect, collaboratively, in seeking a just outcome, taking the interests of the directors justly into account. In *Dividend*, the board has to decide; the decision lies outside the legal competence of the executive. For directors the question is one of effort: of developing a better understanding of the logic of what appears to be a self-regarding approach as we educated ourselves about the counterin-

Table 4.2   *Decision process elements by case*

	Merger	2. CEO	3. Dividend	4. Crisis
Control	Strong, though ceded by the directors in the case	Impaired by controlling CEO, chair	Strong	Weak: insuperable external forces; managing as *coping*, rather than *controlling*
Effort, investment	Weak, deemed unnecessary	Strong among allies	Strong: decision requires rethinking theory, practice	Strong
Use of knowledge	Passive	Strong among allies	Strong	Strong
Cognitive conflict, justice	Weak	Strong among allies	Strong, challenge forces re-think of basis of justice	Strong, in particular in need for justice
Cohesiveness, safety	Presumed strong; may overlook divided objectives of other directors	Strong among allies, but may divide board, risking dysfunction	Strong: CFO's *démarche* calls for collective effort	Strong, though safety sought is that of beneficiaries, not self

Source: Author

tuitive, other-regarding proposition whose irony may be missed by those voices reaching the board that take a more ideological form of conflict. Does dividing the board open the door to dysfunction?

In *Crisis*, the board faces insuperable forces; while it may control the executive, it cannot possibly do more than cope with the pandemic. It invests effort and uses the knowledge and skills at its disposal to generate what is hopefully a less unjust outcome. Cognition is in evidence, but not conflict, until in a heavy-handed way the chair tells you how much he values your input and infers how little he values mine. Cohesion is placed in jeopardy, which now relies on my identification with and commitment to corporate purpose, unsupported by affective ties to the board itself. The results of this analysis are summarised in Table 4.2.

Psychological ownership, with its cognitive and affective dimensions, is possible in each case, though affect is less evident in the largely self-interested directors (*you and I*) in *Merger*. The directors there seem to disregard responsibilities while asserting personal rights; the sense of self is supported but not extended, and the directors look petty as a result. In joining the ad hoc committee to examine the deal, they have the opportunity to build commitment through engagement. Together they have detailed inside understanding (the operations director) and outside perspective (non-executive), if they could get outside the confines of the physical boardroom. But more important is to get outside the hierarchy of the chair, who is already agitating for a quick decision. There will not be time for creativity and play, or an opportunity to explore options about the purpose of this deal, or the merger.

In *Crisis*, by contrast, affective engagement may even pre-date appointment to the board, as charity directors seem often to have a strong appreciation of the cause before finding the organisation in which to pursue it (Nordberg, 2021), alignment therefore with purpose before it is incorporated in the organisation. For them, board practice may well be the pursuit of internal goods and intrinsic value not just of the charity but also of board work itself. But some of the board members clearly have external goods in mind and extrinsic motivations. Engaging repeatedly through the pandemic in board work may guide them to see the internal goods, much as Sinnicks (2014) suggests can happen as employees commit to and identify with the organisation in which they work. But there is a risk: you may have been ordained (by the chair) to act as saviour. By contrast, I have been ejected from the liminal space, excluded from creative if very serious play, into the cold. Yet I remain, legally, liable for the mistakes you may make.

In *CEO*, we see strong and growing engagement on both cognitive and affective levels, a strong sense of responsibility and a modest but an indeterminant ability to exercise the right to effect change. The directors' acquiescence to the current state of decline is a board-level example of what Fragale, Sumanth, Tiedens, and Northcraft (2012, p. 373) call "lateral deference", a communication strategy in which deferring to peers is used to protect their "hierarchical positions". In boards, directors are formally equal, whatever the informal position might be. Directors may thus defer to peers without accepting the position and then find that doing so solidifies their position and builds support for action later. Directors are not only entitled to object to the actions of their peers; they have an imperative as stewards to act. In this case, acting as a *control* is at once a creative process and a *service*. Engaging in such practices, without hierarchy (and without the chair) shows the rudiments of a practice that grows with each encounter, building affective and cognitive social ties between the dissidents and disgruntled. The question then is whether to act immediately or later, as evidence of injustice or threats to safety mount.[6]

In *Dividend*, we see a position of a dominantly other-regarding stance, though given the puzzle posed by the counterintuitive, politically incorrect yet appealing analysis, board members face a call to look at themselves in an academic mirror. This form of self-regard is a questioning one, however, asking: where do you or I stand? It engages us cognitively, but quite possibly separately. Solving puzzles together might increase affective engagement with each other and with corporate purpose, and the exercise itself seems likely to stretch the muscles of our identity, self- and social. (For a summary of the analysis of "ownership", see Table 4.3.)

Moreover, some of the questions these cases raise lead us to recognise how difficult it is to separate control from service, and thus how difficult it is to separate the agency problem from the problem of the lack of stewardship. While *Merger* might be the agency problem incarnate, affective engagement with corporate purpose is evident, as articulated in its strategy. These directors (*you and I*) have to decide whether to act on it. Yet we know, or at least sense, that the others will even go ahead without us. What is missing among the ingredients for stewardship is the cognitive engagement associated with responsibility, which might be triggered by processes of strong cognitive conflict. We failed to ask the question: why is this proposal coming from the CFO and not the CEO or top management as a team? Failing to ask the question is not just a missing opportunity to control; it is a disservice to the board, perhaps to senior management, and quite possibly to shareholders, customers, and others, when the merger imperils corporate stability.

In *Crisis*, by contrast, the scope for personal gain was close to zero and the threat to corporate purpose was extreme. Here we asked questions that we could not possibly answer, but in asking them, we alert each other – board and senior management – to possible future states and the risk and opportunities they entail. Such attention accustoms us to thinking of alternatives, mental exercises that can increase our fitness to decide, when decisions become imperative. In setting aside procedures, we allow ideas to surface that might not arise in more open processes. But then an act of misguided direction by the chair – deciding, not being open to options, and imposing hierarchy on what had been a free-wheeling discussion – puts the consensus of the board at risk.

Table 4.3   *Facets of psychological ownership by case*

	1. Merger	2. CEO	3. Dividend	4. Crisis
Self- or other-regarding	Dominantly self: focus on personal share ownership, corporate tax considerations	Dominantly other: concern for business, shareholder interest	Dominantly other: self-regard comes from satisfaction derived from solving puzzle	Dominantly other
Cognitive engagement	Strong, but potentially misdirected: they overlook self-regarding intent of CFO, other executives	Strong	Strong	Strong
Affective engagement	Strong, given the statement of corporate purpose	Strong in some relationships	Unclear: exercise has potential to build ties	Strong; affective engagement may precede board membership
Extension of self	Self-identity supported, not challenged	Social identity expanded	Exercise stretches self- and social identity	Self- and social identity both expanded
Rights	Strong: focus on shareholder rights and directors as shareholders	Strong, but ability to exercise them seems limited by current practice	Strong	Strong legal rights have little scope to deal with environmental challenge
Responsibilities	Weak	Strong	Strong, but consensus on object conflicted	Strong
Expectation of change	Strong	Strong	Strong	Strong, even though objective may be to retain prior status in face of potential catastrophe

Source: Author

In all these cases, the directors (*you and I*) need to play with ideas, so we opt for avenues of communication separate from the formalities, and to meet in places where hierarchy matters less than it seems to in the boardroom. That freedom to play lets us imagine alternatives, free (for a time) from the need to act and from the standard procedures designed to maximise the control associated with accountability and compliance. That freedom to play is the fun of being a director.

PRACTICES, NOT DECISIONS

Let us recall the task we set at the beginning: identifying ways that boards of directors can foster stewardship through the decisions they take. One of the first things we notice is that all these decisions involve complex processes. None fits neatly into any one of the four categories we outlined. Separating strategy, human resources, finance, and governance arrangements from each other is impossible. Strategy and governance questions spill across many categories of business issues. What looks like a matter of performance management in an ordinary employee becomes a strategic risk in the boardroom. What looks like a simple question of affordability becomes a statement of strategic intent and an act of defiance to many investors and the public at large. The activities of the directors within each case involve service *and* control in the same breath, not the distinct and opposite things we learn in theory.

What the Cases Suggest

Getting from liminality to stewardship is also not a straightforward process. In *Crisis*, it should be. Affective engagement is there at the outset. Without it, the directors would probably not bother. But even there the path has obstacles. We work pro bono for the sake of corporate purpose but also simultaneously because the work is fun. We like the cause, but we also like the process of engaging in the debate, especially in this time of crisis, when the mental exercise is exhilarating. In *Merger*, we disengage from affect and feel a need – short of an imperative – to withdraw from cognitive engagement. Does a steward leave quietly? On the other hand, we could look the others in the eye and see ourselves. Other-regarding in the boardroom is an exercise of self-regard, we feel (that is, not think). We fail to ask the penetrating and uncomfortable question. Stewardship does not arise.

In *Dividend*, we see a cognitive puzzle that increases our enjoyment of the activities of being a director. That enjoyment is of short duration, however, and without the power to motivate a long-term attachment that allows identification with purpose to become commitment to its pursuit. In *CEO*, we see division, not cohesion, and cognitive effort that does not immediately become evident in constructive challenge. Here, however, seeds of engagement are growing roots. In this case, our sense of self expands as our concern for the other(s) grows.

Implications

From the four cases, several tentative ideas emerge about the progress from liminality to stewardship. What seems easy to appreciate is the way that using one's knowledge and skills, and engaging in the effort of board work, are likely to build a sense of ownership irrespective of whether directors have made a financial investment as well. Doing the work collectively creates affective links among the directors as well, and the formation of a group through interaction will extend social identity and could contribute to build a strong self-identity as they gain esteem for their current knowledge and discover new facets of self. These point towards the development of psychological ownership that leads to stewardship (Figure 4.1). Beyond that lie some other insights from these cases, but given the plausible but fictional case details, it would be rash to make strong claims. Yet we might (*you and I*) raise these ideas as questions.

How important to stewardship is the ability to control? Controlling is an important process in corporate governance, yet in these scenarios the ability did not matter very much in *Merger* or *Crisis*. Stewardship seemed unlikely to arise in the former, whatever the decision was, and quite likely in the latter. In legal ownership of property, control is a right. Being unable to control must affect our engagement with the processes. The case of *Crisis*, however, suggests that engagement may depend less on having control than in not having to cede control to another actor.

How does justice in process relate to the sense of safety? The theorising in Forbes and Milliken (1999) suggests an uneasy interaction of cognitive conflict and the cohesiveness of boards. They posit an inverted-U relationship with outcomes, in which conflict stimulates until it retards progress, and cohesion helps until it spills into cosiness. Conflict in the pursuit of justice can feel dangerous, as it does in *CEO*, in which both just processes and just outcomes are at stake. But it also creates purpose and energises engagement. In so doing, it reinforces the other-regarding, responsibilities-led elements of ownership, though at the risk of cohesion. In *CEO*, however, cohesion between the CEO and chair has already tipped towards the counter-productive side of the inverted U.

What roles do different forms of affect have on development of stewardship? The model in Figure 4.1 identifies affective engagement with both the board and the organisation. In most situations those might seem like the same thing. Yet in *CEO* we have seen affective ties between the chair and CEO that threaten ties to other board members, and then affect developing among the reticent but dissident directors, who defer to the chair and CEO *for the moment*. Emotional ties to the organisation, its products and services, and its employees might well in this case be accompanied by loathing for other individual directors. The contributions of self- and other-regarding seem in this case difficult to separate, and their impact on stewardship seems to depend upon which "other" one regards.

What roles does corporate purpose play in fostering director stewardship? Corporate purpose is an important in policy (Tomorrow's Company, 2016) and in public discussion of corporate governance (e.g., Business Roundtable, 2019; Fink, 2018), though in this form it has not quite worked itself into academic theorising and empirical examination of stewardship. Some have invoked investor stewardship into the debate (e.g., Edmans, 2020; Mayer, 2020), often in the context of rejection of shareholder value as the driving force of corporate decision-making and investor stewardship as a potential countervailing force. The management literature often equates stewardship with long-term orientation and thus the willingness to forgo short-term gains for the sake of investments with a longer time horizon. The cases postulated in the chapter also treat purpose only tangentially. *Crisis* deals with a volunteer board and an organisation with beneficiaries who are not easily seen as owners, investors, or customers. *Dividend* raises the question of purpose, in a sense, through the back door. In *Crisis*, the organisation's purpose is clear to directors before they join the board; it motivates the decision to become a director, perhaps much more than the modest benefit of being allowed to call oneself a director. In *Dividend*, however, we have to consider whether the CFO's suggested sense of purpose might disguise ulterior motives hidden behind a smokescreen of academic credibility. Does she see the purpose of Gigantic Petroleum to be a producer of cash flow and dividends, to be allocated efficiently by the magic of markets? Or is its purpose to use the intellectual, commercial, logistic, and financial resources to identify new and innovative ways of providing energy to its customers; that is, basically, everyone? In either case, in what ways – through what practices – does director stewardship shift the balance in decision-making? And through what mechanisms does purpose affect the sense of psychological ownership that stewardship seems to require?

Is there a danger that psychological ownership can spill over into a feeling of entitlement? The sense of emotional attachment that workers may feel for an employer may be reinforced by participating in share option programmes or profit-sharing remuneration. But among directors, psychological ownership combined with power over decision-making might reinforce a sense, as we see in *Merger*, that the organisation owes something to the director, rather than the other way around.

HOW THIS MATTERS

These questions help us to see the implications of this field of inquiry for organisations, their directors, and academic inquiry in corporate boards and the psycho-social aspects of their decision-making. They and the cases we have considered illustrate the need for a liminal agent (director) to attach to the organisation. They do so through participation in processes and practices that bring familiarity with the organisation *and* aspects of the business environment to which it might not have seemed connected before. Familiarity with the organisation is a larger obstacle for non-executive directors, but they bring experiences from outside the organisation that help executive directors to identify connections, including personal connections with other directors. In board work, liminality brings the critical distance needed for monitoring and control, yet it is also a barrier to commitment. Building attachment may work better in informal, liminal settings where hierarchy is less important, and the work takes on a more playful character.

For organisations seeking stewards as directors, and for directors seeking to act as stewards, this line of thinking suggests that the necessary formality associated with legal compliance and reinforcing protocols might benefit from a more open approach, at least as a supplement. Openness in process seems more likely to encourage activities that generate cognitive engagement, while offering routes to affective attachment and extension of both self- and social identity. That might involve experimenting with creative work and forward-looking inquiry in open mental and perhaps less formal physical spaces (in the sense that de Certeau, 1984, uses the term "space"), while suspending critical questioning for another time and (appropriated and controlled) place. Doing so could open the path to discussion of the dimensions of corporate purpose.

Research into this field will of course face the obstacles of access to private and often commercially sensitive discussions that have long impeded work on corporate governance. Studies that have managed to do so suggest benefits of behavioural, and not just demographic, diversity (Klarner, Probst, and Useem, 2020). We have also seen nuanced uses board chairs make of their power as they reduce and increase the scope for engagement by other directors (Bezemer, Nicholson, and Pugliese, 2018). Researchers with such access might extend their efforts to examine decision events to understand what practices, ritualised or improvised, foster the engagement of directors and build commitment to the organisation and psychological ownership of it, and thus the role that process plays.

CONCLUSIONS

The argument of this chapter is not a manifesto to do away with structures and mechanisms of corporate governance. Nor does it consider how affective engagement with creative practices might provide *service* but jeopardise *control*. Instead, it seeks to heighten attention to the paradoxes of being a director and the puzzle they create for directors when they make major decisions. Piecing together theoretical approaches and empirical evidence, it presents a tentative model of a path from liminality to psychological ownership that seems an antecedent of director stewardship.

Sitting on the threshold has advantages. It permits directors to distance themselves from the implementation of policies and thus to exercise control over them. Asking inside, executive directors to join non-executives on the limen should help them to overcome internal allegiances that impede the cognitive conflict that is central to strong governance. Inviting outside, non-executive directors to engage liminally allows them to gain channels to information that will make their control of the company better informed. But liminality has a drawback. Executive directors may fail to see an incentive to set aside self-interest and develop the other-regarding character of a steward. Non-executives may fail to develop the commitment necessary to develop the affective element of commitment to the company.

This chapter has argued that the barrier that liminality presents to psychological ownership and thus stewardship may be overcome by paying attention to the other side of board work – its service role – through less structured, even deliberately non-hierarchical methods. Such work – such as awaydays, collective learning exercises, or meeting in informal settings – can prevent compliance from crowding strategy off the agenda of formal board meetings. Through its thought experiments, it has shown how engagement creates in directors a sense of obligation to each other. It also fosters desire for the success of the business, thus contributing to stewardship. It can thus provide opportunities to rebalance service and control.

The thought experiments also illustrate downsides that can arise from the failure to develop stewardship on corporate boards, how self-interest or excessive deference can lead to poor board decisions. Such problems arise in both processes and outcomes. Those problems occur when the liminal space remains hide-bound in hierarchy, and the path to imagination is squeezed out of board work, or never allowed to develop.

That path involves circumventing the obstacle of the limen, the threshold, using liminality to the full through ritualised openness and uncritical playfulness for at least parts of the process of board work. Structure and control are set temporarily aside, while commitment grows and identification, with the organisation, the board, and perhaps corporate purpose, builds. When the board returns to the structure of its agendas and to its control tasks of compliance, it may retain some of the freedom to think and act.

NOTES

1. NB With adoption of its code of corporate governance in 2016, Japan has joined the jurisdictions where such unitary boards, including non-executive (or outside) directors alongside executives (Hiura and Ishikawa, 2016), a retreat from the all-executive boards that had been commonplace.
2. As a matter of law, director duties will vary by jurisdiction, but with considerable similarity. In UK Company Law, directors are required to "promote the success of the company for the benefit of members as a whole", where "members" means shareholders or the equivalent in other forms of incorporation. Even a director nominated by a large shareholder must set aside specific interests of the shareholder they represent. Executive directors should be directors first and executives only after the board adjourns.
3. The "investment" factor here is not financial. But using the term points towards benefits for work motivation that can arise from employee equity ownership, which combine legal and psychological ownership. Studies of psychological ownership often focus on employee stock ownership plans (Avey, Avolio, Crossley, and Luthans, 2009; Pierce and Rodgers, 2004).
4. It may help to keep the definition of practice of MacIntyre (2007, p. 187) in mind: "any coherent and complex form of socially established co-operative human activity through which goods internal to that activity are realized". He goes on to say that these activities are conducted in the pursuit of standards of excellence appropriate to that activity, and that the activity thus extends both human powers to achieve excellence and our conceptions of the ends and the goods involved. He thus sets

a high bar for what constitutes practices that leads to virtue. Bad habits are not virtuous. The *ethos* of some boards may thus be both dysfunctional and vicious.

5.   NB Fry (1995) writes of "felt responsibility"; Elms and Nicholson (2020) translate that to "felt accountability". Fry says felt responsibility helps individuals to be accountable to themselves and others, which resonates with the observations on horizontal and vertical accountability by Roberts (1991, 2001).

6.   I am indebted to Professor Terry McNulty for originally alerting me to this idea. An as yet unpublished conference paper (Stiles, McNulty, and Roberts, 2017) develops this theme further.

REFERENCES

Åberg, C., Bankewitz, M., and Knockaert, M. (2019). Service tasks of board of directors: A literature review and research agenda in an era of new governance practices. *European Management Journal*, *37*(5), 648–63. doi:10.1016/j.emj.2019.04.006.

Aristotle (1962). *Nicomachean Ethics* (M. Ostwald, Trans.). Indianapolis, IN: Library of Liberal Arts.

Avey, J.B., Avolio, B.J., Crossley, C.D., and Luthans, F. (2009). Psychological ownership: theoretical extensions, measurement and relation to work outcomes. *Journal of Organizational Behavior*, *30*(2), 173–91. doi:10.1002/job.583.

Bebchuk, L.A. (2020, April). The illusory promise of stakeholder governance. *Forthcoming in Cornell Law Review*. Retrieved from https://ssrn.com/abstract=3544978.

Bebchuk, L.A., Brav, A., and Wei, J. (2015). The long-term effects of hedge fund activism. *Columbia Law Review*, *115*(5), 1085–1155.

Becht, M., Franks, J., Grant, J., and Wagner, H.F. (2015, March). The returns to hedge fund activism: an international study. *European Corporate Governance Institute (ECGI) – Finance Working Paper No. 402/2014*. Retrieved from http://dx.doi.org/10.2139/ssrn.2376271.

Bezemer, P.-J., Nicholson, G., and Pugliese, A. (2018). The influence of board chairs on director engagement: a case-based exploration of boardroom decision-making. *Corporate Governace: An International Review*, *26*(3), 219–34. doi:10.1111/corg.12234.

Business Roundtable (2019, August). *Statement on the Purpose of a Corporation*. Retrieved from https://opportunity.businessroundtable.org/wp-content/uploads/2019/08/Business-Roundtable-Statement-on-the-Purpose-of-a-Corporation-with-Signatures.pdf.

Concannon, M., and Nordberg, D. (2018). Boards strategizing in liminal spaces: process and practice, formal and informal. *European Management Journal*, *36*(1), 71–82. doi:10.1016/j.emj.2017.03.008.

Cremers, M., Pareek, A., and Sautner, Z. (2020). Short-term investors, long-term investments, and firm value: evidence from Russell 2000 Index inclusions. *Management Science*, *66*(10), 4535–51. doi: https://doi.org/10.1287/mnsc.2019.3361.

Czarniawska, B., and Mazza, C. (2003). Consulting as a liminal space. *Human Relations*, *56*(3), 267–90. doi:10.1177/0018726703056003612.

Dalton, D.R., Hitt, M.A., Certo, S.T., and Dalton, C.M. (2007). The fundamental agency problem and its mitigation: independence, equity, and the market for corporate control. *Academy of Management Annals*, *1*, 1–64. doi:10.5465/078559806.

Davis, J.H., Schoorman, F.D., and Donaldson, L. (1997). Toward a stewardship theory of management. *Academy of Management Review*, *22*(1), 20–47. doi:10.5465/amr.1997.9707180258.

De Certeau, M. (1984). *The Practice of Everyday Life* (S. Rendall, Trans.). Berkeley, CA: University of California Press.

Edmans, A. (2011). Short-term termination without deterring long-term investment: a theory of debt and buyouts. *Journal of Financial Economics*, *102*(1), 81–101. doi:10.1016/j.jfineco.2010.11.005.

Edmans, A. (2020). Company purpose and profit need not be in conflict if we "grow the pie". *Economic Affairs*, *40*(2), 287–94. doi:https://doi.org/10.1111/ecaf.12395.

Edmans, A., Enriques, L., Fried, J.M., Roe, M., and Thomsen, S. (2021, April). Call for reflection on sustainable corporate governance. *Policy Statement by Members of the European Corporate Governance Institute*. Retrieved from https://ecgi.global/content/call-reflection-sustainable-corporate-governance.

Elms, N., and Nicholson, G. (2020). How director identification shapes accountability and scope of contribution. *Accounting, Auditing & Accountability Journal*, *33*(8), 1815–34. doi:10.1108/aaaj -12–2019–4358.

Etzioni, A. (1991). The socio-economics of property. *Journal of Social Behavior and Personality*, *6*(6), 465–468. Retrieved from www.gwu.edu/~ccps/etzioni/A208.pdf.

Fama, E.F., and Jensen, M.C. (1983). Agency problems and residual claims. *Journal of Law and Economics*, *26*(2), 327–49. doi:10.1086/467038.

Filatotchev, I., Toms, S., and Wright, M. (2006). The firm's strategic dynamics and corporate governance life-cycle. *International Journal of Managerial Finance*, *2*(4), 256–79. doi:10.1108/ 17439130610705481.

Fink, L. (2018, January 17). A sense of purpose. *Post on the Harvard Law School Forum on Corporate Governance*. Retrieved from https://corpgov.law.harvard.edu/2018/01/17/a-sense-of-purpose/.

Forbes, D.P., and Milliken, F.J. (1999). Cognition and corporate governance: Understanding boards of directors as strategic decision-making groups. *Academy of Management Review*, *24*(3), 489–505. doi: 10.5465/AMR.1999.2202133.

Fragale, A.R., Sumanth, J.J., Tiedens, L.Z., and Northcraft, G.B. (2012). Appeasing equals: lateral deference in organizational communication. *Administrative Science Quarterly*, *57*(3), 373–406. doi: 10.1177/0001839212461439.

Fry, R.E. (1995). Accountability in organizational life: problem or opportunity for nonprofits? *Nonprofit Management and Leadership*, *6*(2), 181–95. doi:10.1002/nml.4130060207.

Garsten, C. (1999). Betwixt and between: temporary employees as liminal subjects in flexible organiza-tions. *Organization Studies*, *20*(4), 601–17. doi:10.1177/0170840699204004.

Gartner, W.B., and Shane, S.A. (1995). Measuring entrepreneurship over time. *Journal of Business Venturing*, *10*(4), 283–301. doi:10.1016/0883–9026(94)00037-U.

Gatfield, T. (2005). An investigation into PhD supervisory management styles: development of a dynamic conceptual model and its managerial implications. *Journal of Higher Education Policy & Management*, *27*(3), 311–25. doi:10.1080/13600800500283585.

Guimarães-Costa, N., and Pina e Cunha, M. (2009). Foreign locals: a liminal perspective of international managers. *Organizational Dynamics*, *38*(2), 158–66. doi:10.1016/j.orgdyn.2009.02.002.

Guimarães-Costa, N., and Pina e Cunha, M. (2013). The inevitability of liminality in organising. *International Journal of Management Concepts and Philosophy*, *7*(1), 47–63. doi:10.1504/IJMCP .2013.052831.

Hernandez, M. (2012). Toward an understanding of the psychology of stewardship. *Academy of Management Review*, *37*(2), 172–93. doi:10.5465/amr.2010.0363.

Hillman, A.J., and Dalziel, T. (2003). Boards of directors and firm performance: integrating agency and resource dependence perspectives. *Academy of Management Review*, *28*(3), 383–96. doi:10.5465/amr .2003.10196729.

Hillman, A.J., Withers, M.C., and Collins, B.J. (2009). Resource dependence theory: a review. *Journal of Management*, *35*(6), 1404–27. doi:10.1177/0149206309343469.

Hiura, T., and Ishikawa, J. (2016, February). Corporate governance in Japan: board membership and beyond. *Report for Bain & Co*. Retrieved from www.bain.com/insights/corporate-governance-in -japan-board-membership-and-beyond/#.

Hjorth, D. (2004). Creating space for play/invention: concepts of space and organizational entrepreneur-ship. *Entrepreneurship & Regional Development*, *16*(5), 413–32. doi:10.1080/0898562042000197144.

ICSA (2011, July). Mapping the gap: highlighting the disconnect between governance best practice and reality in the NHS. *Institute of Chartered Secretaries and Administrators*. Retrieved from www.icsa .org.uk/assets/files/pdfs/NHS/ICSA%20mapping%20the%20gap%20report.pdf.

Klarner, P., Probst, G., and Useem, M. (2020). Opening the black box: unpacking board involvement in innovation. *Strategic Organization*, *18*(4), 487–519. doi:10.1177/1476127019839321.

MacAvoy, P. (2003). "Where Was the Board?" Share Price Collapse and the Governance Crisis of 2000–2002. In P. MacAvoy and I. Millstein (Eds), *The Recurrent Crisis In Corporate Governance* (pp. 66–94). Basingstoke: Palgrave Macmillan.

MacIntyre, A. (2007). *After Virtue: A Study in Moral Theory* (3rd ed.). Notre Dame, IN: University of Notre Dame Press.

Mayer, C. (2020). The future of the corporation and the economics of ourpose. *Journal of Management Studies*, online first. https://doi.org/10.1111/joms.12660.

McCarthy, D., and Palcic, D. (2012). The impact of large-scale employee share ownership plans on labour productivity: the case of Eircom. *International Journal of Human Resource Management*, *23*(17), 3710–24. doi:10.1080/09585192.2012.655762.

McKinsey & Co. (2021, April). Boards and decision-making. *Inside the Strategy Room: A Report of Strategy & Corporate Finance Practice*. Retrieved from www.mckinsey.com/business-functions/strategy-and-corporate-finance/our-insights/boards-and-decision-making.

Meyer, J.P., and Allen, N.J. (1991). A three-component conceptualization of organizational commitment. *Human Resource Management Review*, *1*(1), 61–89. doi:10.1016/1053-4822(91)90011-Z.

Mooney, A., Brown, J., and Ward, A. (2021). The effects of director tenure on monitoring and advising: new insights from behavioral governance and learning theories. *Corporate Governance: An International Review*, online first. doi:https://doi.org/10.1111/corg.12373.

Newton, L. (1992). Virtue and role: reflections on the social nature of morality. *Business Ethics Quarterly*, *2*(3), 357–65. doi:10.2307/3857538.

Nordberg, D. (2021). Who's in charge, in whose interest? The experience of ownership and accountability in the charity sector. *Management Research Review*, *44*(3), 460–76. doi:10.1108/MRR-04-2020-0190.

Ocasio, W. (2011). Attention to attention. *Organization Science*, *22*(5), 1286–96. doi:10.1287/orsc.1100.0602.

Oehmichen, J., Wolff, M., and Zschoche, U. (2018). Employee participation in employee stock ownership plans: cross-level interaction effects of institutions and workgroup behavior. *Human Resource Management*, *57*(5), 1023–37. doi:10.1002/hrm.21885.

Ozuem, W., Howell, K.E., and Lancaster, G. (2008). Communicating in the new interactive marketspace. *European Journal of Marketing*, *42*(9/10), 1059–83. doi:10.1108/03090560810891145.

Pierce, J.L., Kostova, T., and Dirks, K.T. (2001). Toward a theory of psychological ownership in organizations. *Academy of Management Review*, *26*(2), 298–310. doi:10.5465/amr.2001.4378028.

Pierce, J.L., and Rodgers, L. (2004). The psychology of ownership and worker-owner productivity. *Group & Organization Management*, *29*(5), 588–613. doi:10.1177/1059601103254270.

Rappaport, A. (1986). *Creating Shareholder Value: The New Standard for Business Performance*. New York, NY: Free Press.

Roberts, J. (1991). The possibilities of accountability. *Accounting, Organizations and Society*, *16*(4), 355–68. doi:10.1016/0361-3682(91)90027-C.

Roberts, J. (2001). Trust and control in Anglo-American systems of corporate governance: the individualizing and socializing effects of processes of accountability. *Human Relations*, *54*(12), 1547–72. doi:10.1177/00187267015412001.

Sewell, W.H., Jr. (1992). A theory of structure: duality, agency, and transformation. *American Journal of Sociology*, *98*(1), 1–29. doi:10.1086/229967.

Sinnicks, M. (2014). Practices, governance, and politics: applying MacIntyre's ethics to business. *Business Ethics Quarterly*, *24*(2), 229–49.

Söderlund, J., and Borg, E. (2018). Liminality in management and organization studies: process, position and place. *International Journal of Management Reviews*, *20*(4), 880–902. doi:10.1111/ijmr.12168.

Stiles, P.G., McNulty, T., and Roberts, J. (2017). Lateral deference in the boardroom. *Academy of Management Annual Meeting Proceedings, 2017*. doi:10.5465/AMBPP.2017.14192abstract.

Tomorrow's Company (2016, July). *Governing Culture, Risk & Opportunity: A Guide to Board Leadership in Purpose, Values & Culture. Tomorrow's Company Contribution to the FRC Consultation on Board Culture*. Retrieved from http://tomorrowscompany.com/wp-content/uploads/2016/07/Governing-Culture-Risk-and-Opportunity-FINAL-lv.pdf.

Turner, V.W. (1977). *The Ritual Process: Structure and Anti-Structure*. Ithaca, NY: Cornell University Press.

Van Gennep, A. (1909/2013). *The Rites of Passage*. London: Routledge.

Zahra, S.A., and Pearce, J.A., II (1989). Boards of directors and corporate financial performance: a review and integrative model. *Journal of Management*, *15*(2), 291–334. doi:10.1177/014920638901500208.

Zhang, Y., Liu, G., Zhang, L., Xu, S., and Cheung, M.W.-L. (2021). Psychological ownership: a meta-analysis and comparison of multiple forms of attachment in the workplace. *Journal of Management*, *47*(3), 745–70. doi:10.1177/0149206320917195.

5. Beyond the listed company: meaningful, appropriate and relevant governance in SMEs

Leslie Spiers

INTRODUCTION

This chapter considers the nature of governance in small companies where, in many instances, formal decision-making processes are secondary to the wishes and diktats of the owner-manager who may be the sole shareholder or own the majority of the shares, and where the board may comprise just one individual – the owner-manager.

The first section explores the nature and dynamics of small companies and the idiosyncratic application of what may be considered to be "corporate governance", a term that is, however, rarely mentioned within the walls of small businesses.

Section 2 examines corporate governance, its context and purpose, and then moves on to expand on how it applies to small companies. The section highlights the differences between small businesses and their larger counterparts through the lenses of codification; matters such as structure, power and the gallimaufry of additional controls with which listed entities must comply or "explain" their non-conformities.

The third section uses the International Finance Corporation's (IFC's) *SME Governance Guidebook* (2019) as a template for what the writers of the guide consider to be appropriate guidelines for decision-making at the various growth stages of a small company as it moves from pupa to fully fledged and "oven-ready". This section also uses Carey's Better Governance Construct (2020) to place decision-making as one of three major contributors to boardroom excellence.

Finally, the chapter concludes with some remarks drawn from research conducted by the author in his capacity as a person who has chaired over 500 board meetings in small companies across a range of sectors. Such experience offers a rare insight into the "black box" that is the boardroom and shines a light on a space that is inherently difficult for researchers to access.

1.   THE NATURE AND DYNAMICS OF SMALL COMPANIES

UK-based small companies are, in common with much of the rest of the world, a significant element within the national economy (Hiebl 2012, Hong et al. 2012, Yiannaki 2012, Verbano and Venturini 2013, Vrečko and Širec 2013, Farooq et al. 2014). Summarising their significance, Tilley states,

> it is possible to conclude that small firms can no longer be viewed, individually or collectively, as an insignificant component of the economy or the environment. (2000, p. 33)

The extant literature reveals that within the overall typology of small to medium-sized enterprises (SMEs), into which micro and small companies are bracketed together as a sub-sector, there is a pronounced heterogeneity where, for example, management style, resources, planning capabilities and skills differ widely between companies that vary in size from a sole trader to a business deploying significant tangible and intangible assets (Ang 1991, Brunninge et al. 2007, Uhlaner et al. 2007, Kohler and Deimel 2012, Blackburn et al. 2013, Karoui et al. 2014). Blackburn et al. (2013) state that those differences are evident even between those "small companies" segregated as a sub-set within the overall SME sector. The differences occur largely as a consequence of the aspirations and gender of the founder, antecedent attributes, prior experience, education levels, industry sector and location (Blackburn et al. 2013). As such, it could be argued that there is a need to recognise that definitions and characteristics that are frequently based upon employee numbers, as is the case in the UK, offer a one-dimensional perspective and a somewhat crude basis for analysis.

Lobonţiu and Lobonţiu (2013) concur with this view and aver that a small business has a series of fundamental features that differentiate it from a medium-sized or large company. The first of these is an absence of functional managers where, in many cases, control of a small business is vested in one person. Lobonţiu and Lobonţiu (2013) go on to add that there are also thresholds and discontinuities in a small business that limit growth and capacity due in part to both restricted working capital and market incoherence. Finally, Lobonţiu and Lobonţiu (2013) see the owners' socio-emotional identification with the business and his or her associated beliefs, attitudes, behaviours and values as a key differentiator between small companies themselves, and between small companies and their larger counterparts.

Bannock, however, defines small companies in terms of characteristics that comprise: a small market share, managed in a personalised way and independence in the exercise of management responsibility. This leads him to conclude that "each small business is unique" (2005, p. 7).

Despite these differences of approach, the literature does identify a homogeneous trait pertaining to all small companies as being one of fragility and a limited capacity to withstand unwanted business interruptions (Spillan and Hough 2003, Betts et al. 2012, Clancy et al. 2013). Herbane (2015) and others, for example, point out that vulnerability is inversely proportional to size; hence, as organisational size decreases so susceptibility to adversity and perturbation increases (Corey and Deitch 2011, Asgary et al. 2012). Despite the inherent flexibility of small companies, their widespread use of relatively simple technology, limited resource requirements and high levels of social capital, the impact of acute business interruptions can be severe and constitute an existential threat (Irvine and Anderson 2004, Lampel et al. 2014, Kurschus et al. 2015).

A potential threat that subsequently morphs into to a business interruption in a small company differs fundamentally from a similar disruptive event occurring in a large business (Budge et al. 2008). In the case of a small company, the impact of the disruption goes beyond what might be called the business sphere and has the potential to impinge directly upon the income, lifestyle and personal assets of the owner-manager (Drummond and Chell 1994, Bodmer and Vaughan 2009, Hiebl 2012). Whilst small companies tend to be agile and able to adapt to changing and unforeseen circumstances (Doern 2016), they nevertheless have little slack and are generally resource-limited (Verbano and Venturini 2013). This has been graphically demonstrated with the Covid-19 lockdown resulting in great numbers of small businesses floundering in jurisdictions throughout the world. Doern (2016) concludes that in view of the high mortality rate of businesses within the small company sector, improving resilience, competence and capability in such companies is both a macroeconomic imperative as well as a social benefit to the communities in which those businesses are located.

Definition of Small Companies

Definitions vary as to what is, and is not, included within the largely meaningless umbrella term "small to medium-sized enterprise" or within the "small company" sector (Clarke and Klettner 2009, Berisha and Pula 2015). Scholars and practitioners use criteria emanating from international institutions, national legislation or industry-derived metrics, or a melange of measures that include such items as revenue or asset value (Ayyagari et al. 2007, Berisha and Pula 2015). This multi-dimensional approach contrasts greatly with the Bolton Report (1971) on small businesses that uses only employee numbers as its definitional base (Berisha and Pula 2015) and which continues to be the critical measure prevalent in 2018 despite its inherent flaws.

Reflecting the lack of consensus concerning the definition of an SME, Karoui et al. (2014) contend that, even within the SME sub-sector of "Small", there are wide disparities, and whilst a measure of employee numbers within specified ranges is a convenient approach to labelling, it could be argued that a more rigorous categorisation is required based upon criteria such as industry sector, finance, attitudes and governance structure. Brooksbank (1991) supports this widening of criteria and proposes a mix of quantitative (employees and revenue) and qualitative (scope and products) benchmarks. Gibson and Van der Vaart, however, conclude that "we are far from an international consensus on what constitutes SMEs" (2008, p. 8), thereby echoing the view of Berisha and Pula (2015) and Tommaso and Dubbini (2000), who concur that the typology is not a scientific division based on macroeconomic indicators, but rather a statistical arbitrariness designed to facilitate comparable performance and a common classification.

In spite of the claim that the typology is arbitrary and the author's view that the term "SME" is meaningless, at the end of 2017 the UK Government's Department for Business Innovation and Skills determined that small companies (including micro businesses) comprising 0–49 employees accounted for 99.3 per cent of all private sector businesses in the UK, 48 per cent of private sector employment and 37 per cent of private sector turnover (UK Government 2017).

However, it could be claimed that this seemingly discrete and precise categorisation can lead to confusion. An enterprise, for example, towards the upper decile of the definition of "small" is likely to have a relatively developed infrastructure and internal management systems. It may own premises as well as significant fixed and current assets (Pal 2013). Such a business (for one of which the author is chairman of the board) may also have external directors, shareholders and investors, and hence, according to Karoui et al. (2014), the assumption of homogeneity within the sub-sector is misplaced. Herbane (2010), however, notes the particular importance of the micro and small company sectors in the UK but does not distinguish between the "Micro" and "Small" classification in his definition and by conflating the two groups may, as Karoui et al. (2014) argue, be failing to recognise a self-evident truth, that the internal dynamics of a sole trader working in a garden shed or from the back of a van have little in common with a business employing 49 staff.

Gibson and Van der Vaart (2008, p. 16) disagree with Karoui et al. (2014) and adopt a collectivist view, believing that it is time to move from a de facto merger of "small and medium"

Table 5.1   UK definition of company size using employee numbers

Micro firm: 0–9 employees	Small firm: 10–49 employees
Medium-sized firm: 50–249 employees	Large firm: over 249 employees

Source: UK Government (2014); contains public sector information licensed under the Open Government Licence v3.0

Table 5.2   EU classification of company size

Descriptor	Employees	Turnover € millions	Balance sheet € millions
Micro	<10	<2 m or	<2 m
Small	<50	<10 m or	<10 m
Medium	<250	<50 m	<43 m

Source: User Guide to SME Definition 2015 (European Union 2015, p. 11)

to a *de jure* recognition of SME as a single-size group, or developmental asset class. Gibson and Van der Vaart (2008) underscore their argument when they point out that at a global level the broad umbrella SME classification, using employee numbers, varies from an upper limit of 500 in the USA to a ceiling of 99 in Tanzania (OECD 2005).

Given the assortment of approaches, the UK Government generally defines the size of a business by the number of employees, but does choose, in specific circumstances, to use revenue as an alternative measure. The Companies Act 2006 s. 382 and 465, as amended, defines a small company as one that meets two of three conditions: a turnover of below £10.2 million, a balance sheet total of less than £5.1 million and fewer than 50 employees. (A medium-sized company must meet two of three conditions: a turnover of less than £36 million, a balance sheet total of less than £18 million and fewer than 250 employees.)

For statistical purposes, however, the Department of Trade and Industry (DTI), now known as the Department of Business, Energy and Industrial Strategy (BEIS), tends to use the definitions below (UK Government 2006b). Table 5.1 defines small companies in terms of employees and therefore it is this definition that, despite its vagaries, is used throughout this study. Whilst the European Union (EU) states that the definition of company size is a non-binding recommendation, it classifies companies in the terms set out in Table 5.2.

Characteristics of Small Companies

Although small companies account for a significant proportion of business activity in the UK and across the globe (Hiebl 2012, OECD 2015, UK Government 2015) (see Table 5.3), research relating to small firms is relatively scarce when compared to that pertaining to quoted companies (Tommaso and Dubbini 2000, Lynall et al. 2003, Bennett and Robson 2004, Torres and Julien 2005, Carney et al. 2013).

Accordingly, there is a rich stratum to be mined in order to explore, and thereby develop, our understanding of the dynamics of this critical and growing sector.

Acs et al. (1996) cite a speech given in 1939 by Winston Churchill when they choose to liken small companies to "a riddle wrapped in a mystery inside an enigma" and in so doing reflect and amplify the complex and diverse nature that pertains to small companies (Culkin and Smith 2000, Haugh and McKee 2004, Kotey and Slade 2005). This so-called "riddle" encapsulates the personality-driven, reactive and loosely structured nature of small companies

Table 5.3   *Estimated number of businesses in the UK private sector, associated employment and turnover (by size of business, December 2019)*

	Number of businesses	Employment	Turnover (£ millions)
All businesses	5,867,770	27,498,000	4,149,973
All SMEs (0–249 employees)	5,860,085	16,630,000	2,168,005
Small and micro businesses (0–49 employees)	5,824,500	13,157,000	1,528,684
0 employees	4,457,820	4,835,000	304,508
1–9 employees	1,155,385	4,206,000	595,013
10–49 employees	211,295	4,116,000	629,163
50–249 employees	35,585	3,473,000	639,321
250+ employees	7,685	10,868,000	1,981,968

Source: UK Government, Department of Business, Innovation and Skills (BIS): *Business Population Estimates for the UK and Regions*, December 2019; contains public sector information licensed under the Open Government Licence v3.0

and whilst much of the literature views small companies through the formal lenses of structure, process and strategic orientation, researchers frequently assert that it is the influence, attitudes, idiosyncrasies and behaviours of the founding owner-manager that decide upon the character and culture of a small company (Deakins and Freel 2006, Uhlaner et al. 2007, Lobonţiu and Lobonţiu 2013).

Yet whilst management structures in small companies are frequently ad hoc and reactive (Coulson-Thomas 2007), the vagaries of unitary control in a personality-dominated structure seem to offer contemporaneous contrasts of opportunity and risk, simplicity and complexity, and dynamism and stagnation (Hmieleski and Baron 2009). Hence Gibb and Davies (1992) note that the personal goals, beliefs and attributes of the founding owner-manager of a small company are instrumental in determining the culture of the company, its orientation and its vision. However, Gibb and Davies resist over-emphasising a characteristics model and propose a contingency approach "that concentrates not upon the characteristics of the entrepreneur-social, psychological, or economic – but his/her behaviours" (1992, p. 8). In so doing they acknowledge that different types of behaviour, traits, skills and decision-making competencies are required due to the degrees of uncertainty and intricacies in the marketplace.

Gibb and Davies (1992) add that knowledge and skills are underdeveloped in small companies and that as money invested in the business is, in some measure, derived from personal resources rather than from distant and impersonal investors this results in a parsimonious attitude towards expenditure that is not perceived as a direct profit-related expense. Training and development may be one such example where the returns on expenditure are viewed as uncertain and distant when compared with purchases of raw materials.

It is possible to conclude that Acs et al. (1996) choose to liken small companies to an enigmatic conundrum as a consequence of a key characteristic of such enterprises: namely that of opaqueness and its resemblance to a black, impenetrable box. Small companies are not subject to external audit nor detailed reporting and disclosure in the wider public arena. Changes in reporting requirements with effect from January 2016 requires that most small companies in the UK need only submit abbreviated financial information to Companies House in the form of a signed balance sheet, although more detailed information must be provided for Her Majesty's Revenue and Customs and the shareholders, who are in many cases the directors

Table 5.4   Key characteristics of small enterprises

Key characteristics of small enterprises	86% registered for VAT	71% limited company 61% family owned
Key characteristics of their owners and leaders	9% work from home	33% have two owners 61% with a women owner
Recent turnover and employment growth	86% level or growing in past year; 90% forecast to grow	79% were profitable in current year
Capabilities (ability to innovate, export, train)	83% had innovated new product or process in past year	26% had exported in past year; 80% had training
Accessing finance	69% had not sought finance in the past year; 72% had a good relationship with the bank	21% were unable to access finance in the past year
Use of business support	59% aware of Local Enterprise Partnership (LEP) as a support vehicle; 13% used mentors	51% sought business advice regarding growth

Source: Department for Business, Innovation and Skills (2015), *Small Business Survey 2014: SME Employers*; contains public sector information licensed under the Open Government Licence v3.0

Table 5.5   Storey's characteristics approach

The entrepreneur	The firm	Strategy
Motivation	Age	External equity
Education	Legal form	Market positioning
Managerial experience	Location	New product introduction
Teams	Size	Management recruitment

Source: Author, based upon Storey (2011)

themselves (UK Government 2016). Consequently, in part due to restricted publicly available documents, empirical research into the inner workings and dynamics of small companies is limited, and accordingly a pre-requisite to empirical research into these enterprises is the open-handed participation of the owner-manager.

Research published in the *Small Business Survey 2014: SME Employers* (BIS, 2015), suggests that small companies display structural characteristics that are unique to the sector (see Table 5.4). BIS surveyed 1,714 small enterprises, all of whom employed fewer than 50 people, from which a snapshot emerged regarding ownership, legal structure, resource management and financial performance. However, rather than a focus upon merely a list of procedural factors, of benefit would have been an insight into the importance of the behaviours of the owner-manager and assertation that these are a fundamental determinant of the culture and ethos of the business (Carter and Jones-Evans 2006, Deakins and Freel 2006, Uhlaner et al. 2007).

In contrast with the mainly quantitative data in the *Small Business Survey 2014* (BIS, 2015), Deakins and Freel (2006, p. 167) cite Storey (2011), who adopts an interpretivist perspective and posits that small firms are driven by three interrelated components: the entrepreneur, the firm itself and strategy (see Table 5.5). The characteristics approach advocated by Storey (2011) deals with the formal, objective and visible aspects of the company, but does not see the axiological perspectives of the owner-manager as a significant influence in contrast with others who would assert the primacy of her values and beliefs as the dominant paradigm (Haugh and McKee 2004). Accordingly, decision-making, whether there is a functioning board or not, is the preserve of the shareholder-manager.

Owner-managers, whose personalities, ambitions and values are embedded within each and every element of a small firm, can rarely be detached from the role of key decision-maker (Haugh and McKee 2004, Kotey and Slade 2005, Carter and Jones-Evans 2006). Therefore, to explore decision-making within the operational, tactical and strategic functioning inside a small firm, where the influence of the owner-manager within a compressed hierarchy is ubiquitous must be understood. Given that it is the owner-manager who ultimately decides upon such matters as the legal form and location of the business as well as funding and product-related issues, it is axiomatic therefore that the lynchpin around which everything revolves is the owner-manager themselves, and as Culkin and Smith state, "the heart of the small business decision-making unit is essentially the owner/manager" (2000, p. 148). Culkin and Smith (2000) do however acknowledge that as the enterprise grows, decision-making and leadership will become decentralised and distributed as other directors and senior managers are appointed, but nevertheless note that for the owner-manager and principal risk-taker, the business and personal spheres remain interlinked. Those overlaps between private life and business activity fluctuate according to circumstances and pressures. Decisions are inevitably made within the context of competing force fields.

Overlapping of the twin spheres of "business" and "personal" is exemplified by the close coincidence of ownership and management interests residing in the hands of the owner-manager (Long et al. 2005), or the cadre of owner-managers, which, in practice, limits the likelihood of behaviours associated with the widely-accepted notion of agency theory (Bennett and Robson 2004, Karoui et al. 2014). Hence, in view of the foregoing it may be argued that there is little need for outside directors to exercise the control function of the board. Nonetheless, Bartholemeusz and Tanewski (2006) point out that there is, however, an agency issue within small companies that adopts a different guise to the traditional model proposed by Jensen and Meckling (1976). What may be called "the issue of internal agency" occurs when salaried directors are appointed in addition to shareholder directors, and notwithstanding their equal status in law, a de facto dyadic relationship is created where the two conjoined parties may assume differing attitudes on matters such as remuneration, expense allowances, pension provision, transport, socio-economic wealth, commercial objectives and matters of asymmetry of information. In particular, the question of deciding upon dividend distribution is a sensitive matter due to the intimate working relationships existing between shareholding directors and non-shareholding directors.

A further issue of overlap concerns the dual roles of ownership and control performed as both shareholder and director where limited liability status does little to protect the owner-manager who will, in either the role of shareholder or director in many cases, have given personal guarantees as loan collateral, thereby increasing exposure to risk (Ang 1991), unlike his fellow salaried directors.

An additional and ever-present characteristic of small companies relates to the issue of specialisation. Unlike large enterprises, where specialists are to be found in areas such as human resource management, IT, marketing and purchasing, small companies tend to be resource-limited and accordingly owner-managers are intimately engaged, often as an enthusiastic and well-intentioned amateur, in a wide range of activities from the mundane and workaday to matters of compliance and strategy (Culkin and Smith 2000, Carter and Jones-Evans 2006, p. 419). This "Swiss Army knife" approach is the norm in many small companies, as Kotey and Slade note: in small companies, owner-managers undertake "most business activities themselves or directly supervise the performance of these activities" (2005, p. 19).

Wright and Ashill (1998) identify a further characteristic of small companies – that of identity, whereby owner-managers exhibit a widely held perception of uniqueness that in turn can lead to a fortress-like mentality where reversion to personal experiences is used to resolve threats and challenges.

Researchers recognise a further characteristic of small companies; that of the widespread use of support and information exchange networks in both a real and virtual sense (Karoui et al. 2014, Kitching 2015). Advice and information is sought from a variety of sources that include friends and family, staff, customers, suppliers, peers, professionals (Kuhn et al. 2016) and bodies such as the Chamber of Commerce (London Chamber of Commerce and Industry 2016) and the Federation of Small Business (2016). Virtual networks may include special interest groups on LinkedIn and Facebook or more specialist advice from such as the PwC Governance Insights Center website (PwC 2015) and professional bodies such as the Institute of Chartered Secretaries (ICSA The Governance Institute 2016). Given that sole directors in small companies are, *ipso facto*, constrained in seeking internal advice, it would appear that the value of formal, virtual and "pop-up" networks offers a potentially inexpensive and supportive bulwark to the, at times, beleaguered entrepreneur (Burn-Callander 2016).

Fragility and Vulnerability of Small Companies

Whilst the overall tenor of the *Small Business Survey 2014* (BIS, 2015) is positive and reflects the natural optimism of the entrepreneur (Hmieleski and Baron 2009, Storey 2011), small companies along the spectrum of size have significant weakness in infrastructure, systems and processes (Sullivan-Taylor and Branicki 2011, Gao et al. 2013) and are, according to Drummond and Chell, fragile and lacking in resilience. They state that "Of all organizations at risk, small businesses are the most vulnerable" (1994, p. 37). Atherton (2003), also commenting on the fragile nature of small companies, makes specific reference to owner-managers, whom, he claims, perceive a high level of impotence with particular regard to events driven by the external environment and the consequential impact created by unforeseen hazards.

The literature furthermore suggests that, born from the inherent fragility of small companies, there is a widespread and recurring concern at the temporality and survival rate of such enterprises (Ricketts-Gaskill et al. 1993, Perry 2001, Spillan and Hough 2003, Runyan 2006, Vargo 2011, Kraus et al. 2013, Lampel et al. 2014, Herbane 2015, Kurschus et al. 2015). From start-up to demise is, for many, no longer than five years (Jones 2009, Storey 2011, Smit and Watkins 2012). Herbane, reflecting upon the business interruptions on the limited lifespan of SMEs and the associated social consequences for particular sections of society, writes,

> The impact of acute business interruptions on SMEs is beyond doubt – not least given the continuing importance of SMEs in terms of economic growth, employment, innovation and opportunities for economic migrants and black and minority ethnic groups. (2015, p. 585)

Relatively few small and fragile businesses trading in an environment of complexity (Santana 1997, Perrow 1999) grow and develop to become medium-sized companies, either through, in some cases, lifestyle choices made by owner-managers, or due to other factors such as investment and working capital limitations (Ayyagari et al. 2007, Storey 2011), external hazard events or matters such as weak governance, strategy, skills and managerial incompetence (Mitroff and Anagnos 2000, Smith 2007). Highlighting what he refers to as a "one way bet" related to the high chance of business failure, Storey (2011, p. 307) cites Coad et al. (2011) whose research into UK start-up companies and survival rates, based upon bank data, shows the temporal nature of many small companies, with closure rates varying between 13.2 per cent and 25.1 per cent.

Bodmer and Vaughan (2009) further underline the fragility of the small company and note how the business sphere and the private sphere are intrinsically intertwined, thereby adding another layer to an already complex issue when they write that, with regard to family-controlled companies, where crisis management planning is not a routine activity,

> Close relations between the entrepreneurial and the private sphere of the entrepreneur's life are usual and can be an additional source for crisis emergence (e.g. the threat of a divorce). (Bodmer and Vaughan 2009, p. 41)

Expanding upon the link between the business and private spheres in small companies, Carter and Jones-Evans state that the penalties of failure in such enterprises vary with the degree of personal commitment, the availability of other income streams or employment opportunities, and the nature of social provision. They stress that risk is a distinctive feature of a small company and that failure "usually involve[s] high personal cost" (2006, p. 35).

Jones, referring to SMEs (which includes small companies) in the USA states,

> The history of SMEs is one where many have gone but few have succeeded. The average lifecycle of many SMEs is in the region of five years or less. (2009, p. 3)

In a similar view of small businesses in the UK, the RSA Insurance report *Growing Pains* reflects the situation described in the USA by Jones and states that in the UK around 55 per cent of new businesses do not survive beyond five years (RSA Insurance 2014). Likewise, Gray, Saunders and Goregaokar state that after five years, fewer than 45 per cent of businesses will have survived. They add that "small firms are more likely to die than larger firms" (2013, p. 1).

Alluding to survival rates, a Higher Education Funding Council for England (HCFCE) report concerning small companies situated in Dorset, a rural county in the UK, states that between 2011 and 2014 there were 1,988 start-ups, with 57 per cent (2 per cent greater than the UK norm) remaining in business after three years had passed (Bonner et al. 2015). A total of 5.8 per cent of companies within the same time period reached a turnover in excess of £1 million, thereby suggesting that there are significant barriers relating to achieving growth within the small company sector (Lee 2011).

Other researchers aver that such rates of attrition are not only destructive at a personal level (Drummond and Chell 1994, Bodmer and Vaughan 2009) or at the level of the enterprise itself, but agglomerated have far-reaching implications for employment, wealth creation, supply chain fragility (Sterling 2011) and wider society (Spillan and Hough 2003, Kurschus et al. 2015). Emphasising this point, a UK Government briefing document reflects concern regarding the resilience of small companies, half of whom have no plan for managing a crisis or for recovery post-crisis event (UK Government 2006c). Spillan and Hough (2003) state that 90 per cent of businesses without a plan for recovery will fail within two years of a crisis event. Undated evidence from the website of Cross-Sector Safety and Security Communications (CSSSC), a national charity, asserts that commercial fire losses are on the rise and that 85 per cent of SMEs suffering a serious fire never recover or cease trading within eight months

(Cross-Sector Safety and Security Communications 2014). Such details point towards the physical and psychological aspects relating to recovery and the hill that has to be climbed in order to recommence trading.

The 80 per cent figure is referenced by Penrose (2000), citing Brown's article in the edition dated 1 October 1993 of *Management Today* which posits that around eight from 10 businesses will fail within two years after encountering a crisis. There is, however, little agreement in the literature, the relevant professional institutions and the trade bodies as to the veracity of this claim.

Summarising the status of small companies and their tendency towards fragility, the literature concludes that managers default to a reactionary posture (Budge et al. 2008), resources tend to be scarce (Aleksić et al. 2013), planning is weak (Corey and Deitch 2011), and that business skills (Minichilli and Hansen 2007) and governance are lacking (Ricketts-Gaskill et al. 1993, Herbane 2010, Faghfouri et al. 2015). Finally, with regard to the possibility of a crisis event, denial and disavowal trump any attempt to embrace reality and to acknowledge the consequences of a crisis (Mitroff et al. 1989, Mitroff and Anagnos 2000).

2.   SMALL COMPANIES AND CORPORATE GOVERNANCE

Having reviewed the nature of fragile small companies, the focus of this chapter moves on to consider the definition of corporate governance and the issues related to both its theory and practice in its widest context, and then examines how and in what forms this may apply, or not, to small companies.

"Corporate governance", the derivation of which is the Latin verb "*gubernare*", meaning "to steer", is the broad term that describes the processes, customs, policies, laws and regulations that direct the boards of companies and organisations with regard to the means by which they administer and control their business. It is the mechanism by which boards of directors seek to achieve the aims and objectives of the organisation and manage often complex relationships with a wide range of internal and external stakeholders.

Whilst the foregoing paragraph summarises a plethora of definitions, amongst researchers, scholars and practitioners there is a divergence of opinion as to the nature and scope of corporate governance. Some definitions focus upon the legal aspects (Johnston 2004), others emphasise the relationships of the entity with a wider stake-holding and corporate social responsibility (Mason and O'Mahony 2008), whilst a third stream of thinking on corporate governance references the internal processes as a schema within which the board is encouraged, or required, to operate (Seidl 2006, Wymeersch 2006).

Pieper distinguishes between "goal-orientated" definitions, which strive to determine the aim and outcomes of corporate governance, whilst "task-orientated" definitions focus upon the tasks that must be undertaken in order to meet the ultimate goal. Pieper adds that within the nature of the tasks to be undertaken there is a dimensional aspect relating to scope that he identifies as being either "narrow" or "broad" (2003, p. 3), the former of which is allied to a shareholder model whilst the latter is aligned to a stakeholder model.

The absence of a clear and common definition of corporate governance is in part due to the differing national systems across a range of jurisdictions where corporate law affords specific and unique rights and obligations (OECD 2015). Additionally, the weight of research into corporate governance rests upon the separation of ownership and control in a distributed shareholding with principals and agents as the central actors. However, La Porta et al. (1998) claim that this model is a rare phenomenon and that it is concentrated ownership within and beyond families that is the dominant structure. Hence, there are structural limitations relating to definitions of corporate governance that assume a model largely based upon the thinking of Berle and Means (1932). Such restricted cognition has failed to appreciate the subsequent and developing diversity of business ownership structures, management, direction and governance. It is not difficult to conclude that until the second decade of the current millennium the entire dialogue concerning corporate governance and the work of boards is one in which the directors of small companies have been marginalised to the extent that they have not even been in the room whilst the conversation has been taking place!

According to Mason and O'Mahony (2008) the term "corporate governance" is first mentioned in 1981, although Sicoli (2013) states that it is used to indicate the structure and functioning of company policy. Irrespective of its antecedent, Becht et al. argue that,

> the term corporate governance derives from an analogy between the government of cities, nations or states and the governance of corporations. (2007, p. 834)

Whilst the early literature in this field views such "representative government" (Mead 1928, p. 31) as an important advantage of the corporation when compared with partnerships, there appears to be little agreement on the purpose of corporate governance and the question of whose interest it serves in practice.

Despite the debate concerning its purpose, "corporate governance" has nevertheless become a commonplace term in the discourse of business (Keasey et al. 2005), and following the financial scandals involving companies such as Enron, WorldCom, Maxwell Communications, BHS (and more recently Carillion) and others engaged in abuses of corporate power, interest in corporate governance has grown significantly (Becht et al. 2007, Webster 2007, Monks and Minnow 2011, Nordberg 2011, Tricker 2011). The financial crash of 2008 drew further attention to matters related to corporate governance and triggered, according to the Financial Reporting Council (FRC),

> widespread reappraisal, locally and internationally, of the governance systems which may have alleviated it. (2012, p. 2)

The UK Corporate Governance Code (UKCGC), published in 2014 (previously known as "the Combined Code"), emphasises the key features of corporate governance as being those of temporality, innovation and risk management together with its orientation towards goals and positive outcomes when it states that,

> The purpose of corporate governance is to facilitate effective, entrepreneurial and prudent management that can deliver the long-term success of the company. (Financial Reporting Council 2014, p. 1)

A shift in focus can be seen from the current version of the code when set alongside the task-oriented view of its antecedent, *The Report of the Committee on the Financial Aspects of Corporate Governance*, published in 1992 by the so-called Cadbury Committee, that defines corporate governance in more prosaic and direct terms as, the system by which companies are directed and controlled. Boards of directors are responsible for the governance of their companies. (Cadbury 1992, p. 12)

Irrespective of its terse tone and length of service, much of the literature continues to use this "classic" definition offered by Cadbury (Financial Reporting Council 2014, p. 1), although the Institute of Directors (IOD) points out that governance priorities today bear little resemblance to those under consideration at the time of the deliberations of Sir Adrian Cadbury and his committee (Institute of Directors 2016). A reader of this comment may well conclude that, notwithstanding the oblique and genteel language of the IOD, the underlying message clearly asserts that this definition has long passed its "sell-by date".

In contrast to the UKCGC, the definition of corporate governance proposed by the Organisation for Economic Co-operation and Development (OECD) has at its focus relationships and structural matters as the means of achieving and scrutinising performance objectives, stating that,

> Corporate Governance involves a set of relationships between a company's management, its board, its shareholders and other stakeholders. Corporate governance also provides the structure through which the objectives of the company are set, and how the means of attaining those objectives and monitoring performance are determined. (Johnston 2004, p. 11)

The OECD does, however, concede that "There is no single model of good corporate governance" (Johnston 2004, p. 13).

Differing from the OECD, the World Bank posits that a twin approach to corporate governance is needed with the first category highlighting the lived behaviour of companies, their performance, use of resources, innovation, financial structure, and relationships with shareholders and the wider stakeholders. The second category relates to the normative framework – the rules under which companies operate. Those rules derive from the legal system, professional and institutional practices, market directives, and local regulations (World Bank 2005). Referring to the World Bank's view of corporate governance, McNutt describes corporate governance as

> more of a process and less of an obligation on individuals to perform in an ethical way, that is, to be held responsible for their actions by fulfilling their duties. (2010, p. 742)

With this view, McNutt (2010) places the onus not upon the company, thought of by some as a legal fiction (Schane 1986), but upon individuals within the company, and as a consequence, the governance regimen is defined by a code of ethics and ingrained values, and not by an ethos of accountability and compliance.

Millstein (2014) is cited by the Global Governance Forum in *Toolkit 2: Developing Corporate Governance Codes of Best Practice* and in a comprehensive and lofty definition of corporate governance states that

> Corporate governance refers to that blend of law, regulation and appropriate voluntary private sector practices which enables the corporation to attract financial and human capital, perform efficiently and thereby perpetuate itself by generating long-term economic value for its shareholders, while respecting the interests of stakeholders and society as a whole. (Quoted in Gregory 2003)

The IOD, reflecting, in part, the Cadbury Report, differs from Millstein (2014) and chooses to emphasise a prescription of managerial oversight, skills and ethical considerations that go beyond concern for shareholders alone and acknowledge that effective governance, whilst being multi-dimensional, does have, at its core, a compliance component:

> 'Governance' means rigorous supervision of the management of a company; it means ensuring that business is done competently, with integrity and with due regard for the interests of all stakeholders. Good governance is, therefore, a mixture of regulation, structure, best practice and board competency. (Institute of Directors 2004, p. 5)

Given that the majority of IOD members were and continue to be directors of SMEs, this definition leans heavily towards the large corporation and appears to have little in common with the needs of its membership. The *Financial Times* offers yet another definition of corporate governance that incorporates a range of specific elements, some of which reflect the thrust of the Companies Act 2006 and in particular pay heed to the requirements of sections 171–7 of the act with regard to director duties. It defines corporate governance in terms of

> How a company is managed, in terms of the institutional systems and protocols meant to ensure accountability and sound ethics. The concept encompasses a variety of issues, including disclosure of information to shareholders and board members, remuneration of senior executives, potential conflicts of interest among managers and directors, supervisory structures. (*Financial Times* 2014)

Nordberg summaries corporate governance "in the narrow sense" as

> the mechanisms put in place inside companies to guide their actions and monitor their performance. (2011, p. 5)

However, Nordberg (2011) adds a series of specific elements upon which scholars tend to focus when considering the nature of corporate governance – matters such as the role of the board, creating strategy, appointing managers, accountability and performance. Nordberg (2011) then goes on to assert that a central tenet of corporate governance is the relationship between shareholders, who have invested in the company, and the board of directors who are charged with a duty of care related to the efficient utilisation of the capital supplied by shareholders. This definition, however, once again bears little relevance to most small companies.

Durst and Henschel (2014) agree with Nordberg (2011) in that seeking a concise definition of corporate governance is difficult. They conclude that as corporate governance is a concept without clarity, it is preferable to use context-based variables to assess the optimum configuration. Where a degree of homogeneity of corporate governance standards exists, such as in public markets, they contend that an appropriate, industry-driven code offers a practical solution to the question of definition. However, where no such homogeneity prevails, as is the case in the small company sector, a less rigid definition of corporate governance is required that is contingent and fit for purpose. Durst and Henschel therefore propose a sector-specific definition in respect of small private companies and, as such, acknowledge that corporate governance is not simply a means of control but also acts as a mechanism for the future health of the business, stating,

> the corporate governance system involves the structures, processes and relationships with relevant stakeholders that help owner-managed firms not only to control the firm but also to facilitate strategic change. (2014, p. 18)

This view is analogous to Nordberg's notion of corporate governance involving a triumvirate of the "steering wheel, the brake and the accelerator" (2011, p. 7) and the IOD's contention that corporate governance fulfils the role of both "watchman and pilot" (Barker 2008, p. 3).

In summary, the UKCGC is the (non-statutory) instrument that sets the governance parameters to which companies with a premium listing of equity shares, regardless of whether they are incorporated in the UK or not, must adhere. Aguilera et al. point out that the text of the code itself also makes a clear statement that corporate governance is not about "box ticking compliance" (2008, p. 488). Listing rules require that companies must either comply with the terms of the code or explain their non-compliance. The FRC, custodian of the UKCGC, summarises a definition of corporate governance in terms of a value-driven approach and makes clear the difference between governance and operational management, an issue that is particularly germane to unlisted, smaller companies (Abor and Adjasi 2007):

> Corporate governance is therefore about what the board of a company does and how it sets the values of the company. It is to be distinguished from the day to day operational management of the company by full-time executives. (Financial Reporting Council 2014, p. 1)

Corporate Governance: A Historical Perspective and the Dominance of Agency Theory

Defining and scoping corporate governance by the FRC and others has almost developed into a mini-industry alongside the development of codes of governance at a national, regional and international level. Such endeavours are relatively recent, yet the driving force behind much of the thinking on what is at the heart of corporate governance emanates from the long-standing agency issue. The tension pertaining to relationships between owners and managers was identified by Berle and Means (1932) when they declared in their book *The Modern Corporation and Private Property* that within the largest American corporations, a new condition had developed in that there were no dominant owners and that control was, to a large degree, separated from ownership, thus creating dissonance as a consequence of contradictory aims.

This view dominated thinking about corporate governance (Hawley and Williams 2000) during the 20th century and into the 21st century as the default paradigm (Cheffins and Bank 2009). Nevertheless, this commonly held perception has been challenged (Hannah 2007, Holderness 2009) with claims that far from a diversified ownership, those same American corporations had a concentrated ownership with fewer shareholders owing greater percentages of the equity. The work of, among others, Veblen (1997), in his book *Absentee Ownership*, first published in 1923, pre-dates Berle and Means' seminal publication, and reflects wide concern relating to issues of governance in the early years of the twentieth century. Veblen (1997) refers to the separation of ownership and control and to the disparate interests between managers and shareholders (Lewis 2010), and is a link in the chain of thought that culminates half a century later with the work of Jensen and Meckling (1976) and the enduring concept of agency theory.

The shareholder, Berle and Means (1932) claim, has limited interest in genuine and active ownership, and postulate that the shareholder's prime concern is the capital growth of their investment and the dividends receivable. They argue that with reduced engagement by shareholders, a culture of "managerialism" (Armour and Gordon 2009) would result in executives developing policies that would be inimical to shareholders' interests and would allow both egocentricity and pressure groups to unduly influence the management of the business.

Whilst rapacious managers reward themselves handsomely, the shareholders, whose investments tend to be growing, choose to relegate corporate governance to the backseat (Rappaport 2006) and in so doing, it may be argued, they give tacit approval to abuses of power whilst capital growth and dividends are flowing their way in what could be viewed as an act of complicity and an unwise adventure of common purpose.

Agency Theory

Berle and Means (1932) point towards the uneasy relationship that existed, and continues to exist, between owners (the principals) and the managers (who may, in some cases, have the title of "director") (the agents) appointed to control and manage the company, and underline the differences that can occur between parties with differing and competing interests and goals.

The work of Berle and Means (1932) is developed by others who later call the issue raised by them the "agency problem" (Jensen and Meckling 1976, Fama 1980, Fama and Jensen 1983). "Agency theory", as it is widely known, is described in simple terms by Eisenhardt as

> the ubiquitous agency relationship, in which one party (the principal) delegates work to another (the agent), who performs that work. (Eisenhardt 1989, p. 58)

Figure 5.1 illustrates the essence of this seemingly uncomplicated agency relationship as described by Eisenhardt (1989). In Figure 5.1, the agents are exemplified as "directors". Such "directors" are synonymous with the "managers" as referred to by Jensen and Meckling (1976). However, the neat lines and straightforward relationships belie a gallimaufry of dysfunctionality reflecting in large part the complex, self-serving and acquisitive nature of the human condition (Fama 1980, Clarysse et al. 2007, Smith 2007, Letza et al. 2008, Wellage 2011, Schneider and Scherer 2013).

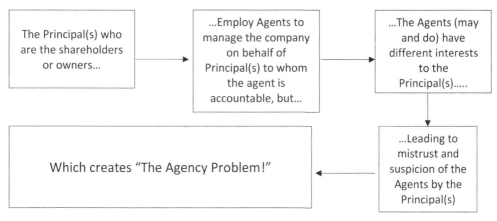

Source: Author

Figure 5.1   Overlapping spheres in small companies

Mallin, citing Blair, reflects both the *de jure* and de facto roles of the agents, but in recognising the frequently contentious nature of the relationship emphasises the need for monitoring and control based on an a priori assumption that an abuse of power is likely to occur. She writes that managers (for which also read directors) are "supposed" to act as agents of the shareholders (who own a bundle of rights related to the company), but recognises that such managers must be monitored and proper arrangements must provide "checks and balances to make sure they do not abuse their power" (2004, p. 11).

Mallin's use of the word "supposed" could be interpreted as a pejorative term reflecting the default position of the agent as being that of a proclivity towards self-interest, excess and covetousness, conditions therefore that require policing.

Over 150 years before scholars in the twentieth century were ruminating on the issue of principal and agent, and with what may be considered remarkable prescience, Adam Smith, in 1776, wrote that

> The directors of such [joint-stock] companies, however, being the managers rather of other people's money than of their own, it cannot well be expected, that they should watch over it with the same anxious vigilance with which the partners in a private copartnery frequently watch over their own. Like the stewards of a rich man, they are apt to consider attention to small matters as not for their master's honour, and very easily give themselves a dispensation from having it. Negligence and profusion, therefore, must always prevail, more or less, in the management of the affairs of such a company. (Smith 2008, Book 5, Part 3, Article 1)

Scholars such as Mallin (2004) and Zahra (2009) are united in their view that agency theory is the most commonly cited phenomenon within the context of corporate governance. Mallin, however, adds that within an agency relationship there is an additional risk. She refers to a risk beyond the abuse of power, to a risk of the agent adopting an attitude of cautiousness and in so doing failing to exploit commercial opportunities. She writes that beside the risk of abuse of power there is also a risk that "the agent is not sufficiently adventurous" (2004, p. 11).

Mallin (2004) also articulates a further problem related to the relationship between agent and principal as being that of information asymmetry, whereby the agent has access to more detailed information than the principal, and furthermore, the agent can decide on what information to give to, or withhold from, the principal.

This asymmetry thereby creates an unbalanced dyadic relationship of dependency on the part of the principal. The agent is thus in a position, as controller and arbiter, to determine the information provided to principals upon which they depend in order to make decisions (Nordberg 2011).

However, such concerns have minimal and tangential relevance to owner-managed small businesses where, in many instances, the owner-manager is the sole shareholder and the sole manager, and is frequently the sole director acting as the thinking and controlling mind of the entity (Abu-Bulgu 2007).

In contrast, it can be argued that whilst agency theory, in its generally accepted sense, is not prevalent in small companies, the control role of the board in companies with concentrated ownership and associated high levels of hegemony can nevertheless result in internal agency issues relating to minority owners, dormant owners and non-shareholder directors.

Equally, at such a time when additional, non-shareholding directors are appointed there is a risk of an agency situation arising where goals and objectives may diverge and information asymmetry occurs (Huse 2007).

This issue is compounded as the Companies Act 2006 deems that risk and liability can be apportioned to all directors equally, whilst, in practice, executive directors, who are both shareholders and non-shareholders, have more information and knowledge than non-executive directors (NEDs) who seek to add value through their independence. Accordingly, the NED faces risks as a result of information asymmetry with such information being mediated and determined by others.

If, however, NEDs have the same information as executive directors that very independence for which they are appointed is, *ipso facto*, weakened and the likelihood of "going native" increases.

Eisenhardt (1989) summaries the features of agency theory, and like Mallin (2004) she appears to use conditionality whilst expressing the main idea that the principal–agent relationship "should" rather than "does" reflect efficacy. She states the key idea as being one of a principal–agent relationship that reflects efficient organisation of information and risk-bearing costs that exists within a contract between those two parties. Her unit of analysis, the contract between the principal and the agent, is similar to Jensen and Meckling's (1976) description of this relationship using the metaphor of a contract.

Eisenhardt (1989) concludes that such a contract has inbuilt moral hazard, and points out that there are differing goals and attitudes towards risk between principal and agent. A final point of note is made with regard to the asymmetry of information whereby the balance of power resides with the agent who is in a position to modify, nuance or adapt such information in its transmission to the principal if he or she so chooses.

3.   CORPORATE GOVERNANCE IN SMALL COMPANIES – AS ONE SIZE DOES NOT FIT ALL!

Levrau and Du Bus challenge the normative view of corporate governance as a valuable resource and pose the question as to why corporate governance, if it has intrinsic value, is largely viewed with negativity within small companies, and suggest that it is often linked to

> establishing order where there is none; integrating discipline where there seems to be confusion; infusing fairness where there is egregious greed; and protecting shareholder interests where there is abuse. (2014, p. 1)

They argue that for companies that view themselves as well-managed, ethical and vanilla in their purpose, corporate governance appears to be associated with bureaucracy, inefficiency and waste, and as such, codes which are fundamentally designed for listed companies, and which appear to have failed in curtailing executive excess, offer an uninviting prospect.

In spite of referring to negative attitudes by owner-managers of small companies, Levrau and Du Bus present the view that there is, nonetheless, an inherent relationship between good governance and the long-term success of small companies. They claim that the purpose of appropriate governance models is

> not to disarm the capable entrepreneur of his/her ability to take good decisions, but rather to strengthen those elements. (2014, p. 1)

Levrau and Du Bus see the value and contribution of corporate governance in a small enter-prise as that of a stepping stone to business development and growth and preparation for the day when the capacity of the owner-manager will be such that a single-handed approach will not be sustainable and to continue as such could be a precursor of failure. They suggest that the output of the resource that is corporate governance will be "increased discipline, professionalism and long term survival" (2014, p. 1). This statement may appear to some to be an axiomatic, self-evident truth, yet in spite of the advantages claimed by proponents of corporate governance, amongst owner-managers of small companies there nevertheless remains a stubborn resistance towards the adoption of corporate governance principles at any level (Miller et al. 2013). In an article published by the IOD entitled "Why good governance is a must for SMEs" in its February 2017 edition of *The Director*, Estelle Clark of the Chartered Quality Institute counters the resistance that prevails in small companies concerning corporate governance and says that "it is as relevant for a company of five people as it is for 5,000" (Herman 2017, p. 17). Clark adds that she would like to see governance in small companies to be on "the agenda for every company, not just those listed on the Stock Exchange" (Herman 2017, p. 17).

Whilst most of the corporate governance literature is concerned with public companies, the vast bulk of UK businesses, both incorporated and unincorporated, are private companies (UK Government 2015), the majority of which are small companies and sole traders. They operate in a variety of guises and are registered, in many cases, at Companies House as Limited or Limited by Guarantee, Partnerships, Limited Liability Partnerships, Community Interest Companies, Industrial and Provident Societies or as unregistered, unincorporated Sole Traders.

Both the UKCGC and the abridged, less demanding, Alternative Investment Market (AIM) Code are, however, primarily designed for, and apply to, listed public companies. These codes are an integral part of listing rules. Accordingly, Lane et al. (2006) and Saxena and Jagota (2015) believe that adoption of such codes by a small company would be inappropriate and would likely incur a burdensome and bureaucratic overhead. Relating to small companies in the USA, Lane et al. pose a rhetorical question and ask,

> What is the significance of these governance reforms, de jure and de facto, for the publicly held corporation's distant, smaller but economically robust brethren – namely the closely-held, family-owned business? Should these family-owned entities be held to the same governance guidelines and standards that apply to those firms making up the ranks of the Fortune 500 for example? (2006, p. 147)

Gibson et al. (2013) and Torres and Julien (2005) likewise note that there are consequences of ignoring the differences between small business and publicly quoted firms when considering matters of corporate governance due to the contextual differences and the economic inefficiencies generated. Clarke and Klettner (2009), referring to codes designed for quoted companies, support this view and argue that there is an inequitable financial burden through transaction costs related to corporate governance activities foisted upon smaller companies that creates economic inefficiencies, and that widely differing contexts do not warrant such an imposition.

Beyond the uncertain world of early-stage growth when (or if) a company, having survived the pains of birth and infancy, moves through the cycle from "micro" to "small", more formal corporate governance arrangements are, however, likely to feature as a matter of increasing interest to the board as a means of managing and mitigating risk (Ansong 2013). The adoption and implementation of an appropriate set of corporate governance principles "*in toto*", or amended if need be, can be a critical tool in creating and enhancing resilience, developing resources and contributing to competencies (Abor and Adjasi 2007). The 2012 Chartered Management Institute survey into business continuity management (BCM) concludes,

Corporate governance remains the biggest external driver of BCM, with 42 per cent of managers highlighting it as a catalyst for their organisation implementing or changing BCM. (Pearson and Woodman 2012, p. 4)

Despite the number and disparity of small companies and their productive contribution to the economy, there is comparatively little research into corporate governance in this sector (Lane et al. 2006, Uhlaner et al. 2007, Siebels and zu Knyphausen-Aufseß 2012, Saxena and Jagota 2015).

Furthermore, Lane et al. (2006) claim that not only is there a general lack of research into small companies but that, in particular, there is also a paucity of research relating to the usage and application of corporate governance codes within small companies.

The Paradigm of Elasticity in Small Companies

Despite the claims of limited research into the functioning of codes, researchers have nevertheless seen small companies as being somewhat homogeneous in their operating mode (Brooksbank 1991), intuitive in their approach and dominated by the owner-manager (Torres and Julien 2005), thereby implying a universal yet informal modus operandi as to governance and strategy. However, Curran and Blackburn state unequivocally that this is not the case, and tacitly support the paradigm of the elasticity of small companies and their concomitant fuzzy characteristics. They write,

> Small enterprises have an extreme range of forms. They operate in every sector of the economy, from computer software to candle-making and from insurance broking to instrument manufacturing. Entrepreneurs and owner-managers come from different genders and/or a wide range of ethnic, cultural and educational backgrounds and from every age group. (2001, p. 6)

Thus, corporate governance for this array of small companies represents something quite different in both meaning and application compared to the onerous and costly compliance requirements and standardised obligations of large organisations and the associated implications of agency theory (Pieper 2003, Gibson et al. 2013). Contingency theory proponents such as Aguilera et al. (2008) and Uhlaner et al. (2007) argue, however, that the governance regime for any given entity needs to be appropriate and relevant to both its circumstances and context. Uhlaner et al. (2007) also point out that there are few formal contracts in small companies and that social control behaviour amongst directors and managers is prevalent. Hence they propose that governance procedures are based around stewardship assumptions rather than exercised through an alternative, prescriptive model (Uhlaner et al. 2007).

Relationships and Socio-Economic Wealth

Vandekerkhof et al. (2011) lend weight to the argument proffered by Uhlaner et al. (2007) when they state that small businesses, and especially family firms, display normative isomorphism as a consequence of intimate relationships and, as such, the relevance of formal corporate governance such as that propounded across codes is diminished. Vandekerkhof et al. (2011) point out, however, that as the business grows and outside managers are recruited, so the significance of personal relationships and socio-economic wealth diminishes as professionalism takes on the mantle of moderator and hence a new and more structured corporate governance paradigm emerges. Yet, preferring relevance and relationships to rigidity, Durst and Henschel (2014) argue for a definition of corporate governance that is fit for purpose with regard to small companies and call attention to the danger of using concepts of corporate governance related to large corporations. Durst and Henschel then go on to define corporate governance in small companies as a system that

> involves the structures, processes and relationships with relevant stakeholders that help owner-managed firms not only to control the firm but also to facilitate strategic change. (2014, p. 18)

Stressing the need for a pro-active engagement in corporate governance practices in small companies, Saxena and Jagota believe that "governance is critical for smaller firms" (2015, p. 55). However, other researchers challenge this view and claim that empirical evidence has failed to confirm that, in family-controlled small businesses in particular, there is a positive impact on performance as a consequence of good corporate governance (Seidl 2006). Researchers point to the distinctive characteristics of small, family-controlled companies that differ from those of managerial-controlled small companies (Gómez-Mejía et al. 2007, Chrisman et al. 2013) where, in the former, the importance of socio-economic wealth establishes legitimacy and can override the goal of economic gain.

Contingent or Universal Application of Corporate Governance?

Contrary to the widely held view that corporate governance must be contingent, Maassen (2004) proposes that certain elements of corporate governance principles are universal and can be as relevant to small companies as they are to their larger counterparts. In his work on corporate governance in Macedonian small businesses, he states that practices such as transparency, openness and corporate social responsibility are important manifestations of mature approaches to corporate governance and are, accordingly, germane in attracting finance. Such a position is consistent with both stakeholder theory and the view of practitioners as stated in the preamble contained within the IOD's *Corporate Governance Guidance and Principles for Unlisted Companies in the UK*, which states that

> Good governance can also play a crucial role in gaining the respect of key external stakeholders – even unlisted companies have to devote attention to their stakeholder responsibilities. (Institute of Directors 2010, p. 6)

However, directors of small companies tend to view corporate governance as being of limited importance or relevance compared with the imperatives related to survival (Uhlaner et al. 2007, Clarke and Klettner 2009). Yet Crossan et al. point out that a lack of governance in small companies is a contributory factor in business failure, stating,

> Many of these failures can be mitigated by the introduction of robust governance structures that would potential[ly] provide better planning and management structures. (2015, p. 3)

Steier et al. state that

> Governance is widely recognised as a key determinant in the success and failure of all organizing activity. (2015, p. 266)

The literature in this respect points towards a lapse on the part of owner-managers to recognise, appreciate and act upon the issue of causality that links failures of corporate governance to business decline and mortality. Seeking to unwrap this fundamental contra-intuitive paradigm that appears to be the antithesis of rationality represents a challenge to owner-mangers concerning the nature, scope and adoption of corporate governance in small companies.

In spite of limited awareness and widespread antipathy by directors of small businesses towards corporate governance (Lane et al. 2006), the IOD is nevertheless promoting and encouraging the boards of small companies to adopt *appropriate* forms of governance procedures that go beyond a mechanistic, box-ticking approach that assumes the agency problem.

Barker, in an IOD Briefing Paper, notes a fundamental issue:

> However, the governance of SMEs is not subject to the same sort of dialogue with institutional investors as is the case with larger companies. (2008, p. 7)

The IOD goes on to observe that, referring to the Combined Code, "An alternative approach would be to develop an alternative code of best practice for smaller companies" (Barker 2008, p. 8). The IOD then concludes that smaller companies would gain benefit from a bespoke corporate governance code in preference to the Combined Code (Barker 2008).

Adding to Barker's words, Clarke and Klettner (2009) refer to the pervasive governance model which for many smaller operators is an unwanted imposition, whilst Uhlaner et al. use contingency theory to propose that "the appropriate governance design for a particular firm likely depends on the context" (2007, p. 227).

In the foreword to *Corporate Governance Guidance and Principles for Unlisted Companies in the UK* (2010), the director general of the IOD states that

> The IOD is convinced that appropriate corporate governance practices can contribute to the success of UK companies of all types and sizes, including those that are unlisted or privately held. (Institute of Directors 2010, p. 5)

Prior to November 2010, the launch date of the IOD's *Corporate Governance Guidance and Principles for Unlisted Companies in the UK*, the UKCGC and its antecedents, together with the Quoted Companies Alliance (QCA) AIM code (first published in 2005), were the only UK reference sources for companies wishing to adopt a recognised national governance code. (Other codes, such as the Belgian Code Buysse [Committee on Corporate Governance for Non-Listed Enterprises 2009], had, however, been published outside the UK.) *Corporate Governance Guidance and Principles for Unlisted Companies in the UK* does not have at its heart a "comply or explain" requirement but seeks to promote appropriateness based on practices and processes that add value and ensure resilience, profitability and sustainability. This notion is expanded upon by the IOD, referring to corporate governance codes serving the twin role of "watchman and the pilot", and in the case of the SME, the dominant role being that of the "pilot" (Barker 2008, p. 3).

Despite a fanfare launch of the IOD Principles, little is known as to the up-take of codes of governance of any kind within small companies either prior to or since the launch of *Corporate Governance Guidance and Principles for Unlisted Companies in the UK* in 2010 (Barker 2014). Additionally, according to Ponomareva and Ahlberg (2016) and Seidl (2006), there is a paucity of research that supports the normative assumptions that underpin codes of corporate governance, raising thereby an opportunity for further investigation.

Reflecting a murmuring of interest in corporate governance amongst small firms and the need for relevant and appropriate processes, the British Standards Institution (BSI) publishes a code of practice, BS 13500:2013 for delivering effective governance of organisations, stating,

> In a small organisation, there may be only a sole trader who owns, governs and manages their business. Complex, formal arrangements are not necessary, but applying the principles of good governance is still important for sustainable success. (British Standards Institution 2013, p. 2)

The notion of good governance as expressed by the BSI would appear to reflect a growing ideology that seeks to maximise shareholder value *and* promote stakeholder engagement, which, according to Ponomareva and Ahlberg (2016), has increased attention in, and subsequent adoption of, what might be called good corporate governance. Drawing on institutional theory, this paradigm shift, Pieper (2003) claims, has led to the growth of a dominant institutional logic that exhorts small companies, and especially family businesses, to adopt corporate governance codes and its associated processes and practices.

The literature therefore would appear to conclude that corporate governance codes of an appropriate, relevant and meaningful nature can contribute to the performance and resilience of small companies and that an overarching "one size fits all" is not a practicable approach to guide and enable directors of smaller companies to conduct effective governance (Sullivan-Taylor and Branicki 2011).

The IFC Decision-Making Model for Small Companies

Whilst the earlier sections of this chapter take a theoretical and conceptual perspective, the third section moves away from "knowing about" to "knowing how" and offers a practical model of decision-making in boards of small companies, using the work of the IFC, part of the World Bank. The IFC has, at the heart of its mission, a desire to improve the resilience of the millions of small companies across the globe. In the introduction to its *SME Governance Guidebook* Mary Porter Peschka, IFC Director, Environmental, Social and Governance Department, states,

> When asked about corporate governance, owners of small and medium enterprises (SMEs) often are sceptical of its value add. They either believe that the business is too small or that it is too early in its development to benefit from building out corporate governance systems and processes. For those interested small business owners, most corporate governance principles and standards are not fit for their business. Implementing policies and procedures designed for larger companies can represent an overly complex and resource-intensive effort for the typical resource-strapped SME. (IFC 2019, p. v)

The introduction to the *Guidebook* goes on to refer to decision-making as the first of a raft of key challenges for SME owner-managers:

> In practice, the most common SME governance challenges involve decision-making, strategic oversight, recruitment and retention of qualified management staff, succession, and establishing standardized internal control mechanisms and policies. These challenges stem from the very nature of SMEs, many of them family businesses, which typically experience organic growth, and more often than not, the systems, policies, and processes required for the proper governance of the business lag behind. (IFC 2019, p. vii)

The word "decision" is highlighted above as the first in a litany of challenges and is mentioned 151 times in the *Guidebook*. Furthermore, an entire chapter is devoted to the subject of decision-making, thus reflecting the importance that the IFC attaches to this element of governance as a key to SME success and growth. To achieve the holy grail of successful growth, the IFC recommendations, with regard to a best practice governance model for SMEs, are grouped around five governance topics. These are:

1. Culture and Commitment to Good Governance
2. Decision-making and Strategic Oversight
3. Risk Governance and Internal Controls
4. Disclosure and Transparency
5. Ownership

Through the four stages of growth from start-up to what the IFC refers to as the "Business Expansion" phase, the question of decision-making is a central theme.

The processual model suggests that from early days, decision-making is centralised and the owner-manager is firmly embedded in an autocratic and dictatorial mode where it's "my way or the highway". This, the IFC suggests, is the principal modus operandi until the company moves beyond the UK definition of a "small company" to the lower limit of the "medium-sized company". The IFC concludes that there is a discrete dividing line, this process of moving from an autocratic to a distributed decision-making structure is gradual, as the founder recognises that he or she cannot simultaneously play the roles of goalkeeper, centre half, striker and referee!

As the company grows, decision-making becomes less centralised, more collaborative and more widely distributed, but nevertheless there remains little doubt amongst managers and directors where the basis of power resides. Such executives, and in particular directors, may face the "mortgage conundrum" where in any given instance they firmly oppose the decision of the owner-manager they are then faced with a choice of acquiescence or resignation. As the Companies Act 2006 requires directors to be independent, there is a clear risk of falling foul of the law where a director may ignore what is the right thing to do in favour of the continuation of his or her creature comforts, the expense account and the company car. Such a decision may in turn lead to disqualification or prosecution of the director where ignorance (and self-interest) is no defence.

It is often the case that around this metamorphic stage of growth the company may decide to appoint an NED, or "outside director" as they are sometimes known. NEDs are a common feature in large companies, with the benefits of such appointments, whilst expensive, being appreciated by owner-managers of SMEs. An advantage of such an appointment to the decision-making team is that the "mortgage conundrum" is irrelevant and enables a truly independent voice to challenge fearlessly and offer a non-partisan opinion, often based on many years of leadership in other organisations. The NED is especially valuable in handling sensitive discussions such as balancing internal capital requirements and determining the level of dividend the owner-manager (or their spouse) is seeking. In many cases, such a discussion around an issue such as this would be difficult for salaried directors to negotiate. In more enlightened companies it may not be an issue at all.

The way in which decision-making is integrated within an overarching governance model has been developed by Guernsey-based commentator Perrin Carey (2020). Carey's wholistic approach shows three nodes linking directly with Decision-Making – these are Information

Quality, Information Flow and the Quality of Decision Maker. The decision-making element of the model complements Implementation and Culture as a triad of factors that in turn contribute to "Better Governance". Replication of the IFC model in terms of adding "Strategic Oversight" to "Decision-Making" could, however, improve what is nevertheless a well-developed construct.

Carey has written extensively with regard to the importance of culture as a core element of effective governance and places great emphasis on the ethical stance of the board over and above the strictures of process that he appears to suggest have dominated the conversation with ever more prescriptive requirements from regulators. This notion of values-based governance is gaining traction despite the present emphasis on process and procedures.

4.   PERSONAL EXPERIENCES, REFLECTIONS AND OBSERVATIONS: SHEDDING LIGHT ON DECISIONS FROM INSIDE THE BLACK BOX

The final section of this chapter contains reflections and observations based upon my 36 years of service as a director on the boards of large, medium and small companies across a range of sectors. Over this time period, I have chaired over 500 board meetings in addition to conducting board evaluations, strategy and planning meetings, and task-related working groups. The following paragraphs are based upon my life experience as a director in small companies and reflect my personal perceptions as to what happens inside the so-called black box that is the boardroom, and indeed beyond its marbled walls and well-stocked drinks cabinets, both of which are utterly misplaced notions, I hasten to add!

Having sat as both an executive and non-executive director in addition to my role as a board consultant, I have been in the rare and privileged position of witnessing at first hand, and from an insider perspective, the day-to-day functioning of boards in small companies. From my observations and insight into the workings of such boards, there is a distribution profile whereby the high-performing board is the exception, with the remainder being high on enthusiasm but weak in both corporate governance and leadership skills. Strategy development, and implementation in particular, tends to be flaky at best and non-existent in many cases, largely due to the pressure of the immediate – a force field that simply will not abate nor vanish.

I acknowledge, however, that those companies in which I have acted as an NED may not be representative of the small company sector overall in that the appointment of an NED suggests a modicum of interest in corporate governance and its associated disciplines, as well as a desire to add to its social network, improve its socio-economic wealth, create resilience and seek excellence. Not all small companies by any means would list those goals as being of great importance, however. As such, I could stand accused of offering a biased view and may be found guilty of dissecting the sector and presenting a view that over-states the buy-in to high governance standards.

In order to establish criteria against which to assess the performance of boards in small companies and the decisions that they make, I have established a baseline from the BSI publication BS 13500:2013, entitled *Code of Practice for Delivering Effective Governance of Organizations*:

The reasons for this choice relate to the code's focus away from the conceptual and its emphasis upon practical application and the abundance of examples, checklists and templates contained within the guide. These 'ready to use tools' address a question asked by directors of small companies that is related to 'Know How' rather than necessarily 'Know About'. This code tacitly acknowledges that there are barriers that hinder the acquisition of knowledge and understanding that impact upon the implementation of innovative corporate governance processes. By implication, it further recognises that corporate governance and directors of small companies are not comfortable bedfellows. (Spiers 2017, p. 219)

In its style and structure the BSI code is non-academic and is more akin to a guidebook. It avoids "academic speak" and language that may limit the practitioner's engagement and inclusivity. Harvard academics Abraham and Allio (2006) would appear to agree with this view, stating that

> research is not designed with managers' needs in mind, nor is it communicated in the journals they read … For the most part it has become a self-referential closed system [irrelevant to] corporate performance. (2006, p. 8)

It is apparent that whilst procedure and process matters are crucial in establishing a workable corporate governance regime, it is the attitudes, values, beliefs and decisions of owner-managers and directors that are the foundation stones of effective corporate governance.

> It is the ability and desire of those key actors to move away (invariably for a short period) from a pre-occupation with the immediate and the urgent to develop a regime that has strategy, risk, accountability and policy formulation as its foundation stones. This may not be the 'super-tanker' corporate business model with its five-year horizon and sensitivity analyses, but the model should nevertheless, have regard to a timeframe that is strategic in nature, yet remains flexible and responsive to emergent events. (Spiers 2017, p. 120)

In considering the ingredients for successful corporate governance in an SME (I prefer to call it Boardroom Brilliance) I have isolated eight recurrent themes that are evident irrespective of the sector, the scope and the structure of the entity.

High-Level and Strategic Matters

Firstly, corporate governance as it relates to decision-making, risk, strategy and policy-making is a matter of peripheral concern to directors of small companies, and I doubt if it occupies a great deal of the day-to-day thinking of most directors in SMEs. When asked, however, directors will aver that corporate governance is of importance, but it is not viewed as a high-priority matter upon which valuable time and resources should be spent.

> Corporate governance attracts immediate and identifiable additional costs where the associated benefits accruing are unclear or, at best, will only to be realised at some time in the future. Corporate governance, beyond that prescribed by the law, is not perceived as being a pressing need but a process that adds another layer to an already burdensome bureaucracy. In summary, corporate governance is seen as an 'ok to have' but not 'a must have'. (Spiers 2017, p. 121)

Size and Legitimacy Matter

The second theme that is evident is that corporate governance is a function of size and assumes greater importance as the company grows and increases its capital through wider shareholding beyond the founders. Allied to this, and the responsibilities associated with debt finance, an associated driver towards engagement in corporate governance emanates from customers seeking legitimacy in their supply chain through assurances on matters of corporate governance alongside other quality-standard verifiers.

Corporate Governance as "Turning a Sow's Ear into a Silk Purse"

Theme number three is that corporate governance has cosmetic value and can be a valuable tool for public relations purposes. An independent NED in the role of chair of the board can add credibility in the eyes of internal and external stakeholders. Corporate governance nevertheless can be presented by the venal and unscrupulous as a smokescreen for dark and avaricious behaviours, thus giving superficial credence to the world at large, evidence of which has been seen in recent times in some of the well-publicised failures.

The Non-Executive as an Agent of Change

Theme number four: although NEDs in small companies are an expensive item, the appointment of an NED can tilt a board of directors away from an agenda that is largely operational towards the adoption of a strategic posture that inculcates decisions that relate to a longer-term vision concerning the future of the business. The decision to appoint an NED suggests directors and shareholders are, however, positively disposed towards the adoption of a corporate governance model of one form or another.

   In spite of a contract that specifies the duties and time commitment of an NED, owner-managers tend to have an unrealistic expectation as to what an NED can achieve in one day or so per month. In small, bordering micro, companies the realisation that the cost of one day's work by an NED often equates to greater than a week's wages for an operative tends to lead to a significant reduction in interest in the appointment of an NED.

Moving from Process to Profit

The fifth theme that emerges is that directors often perceive corporate governance as a matter for the company secretary or external accountants, and do not see it in the context of decision-making and strategic oversight. Directors frequently perceive corporate governance as being mostly concerned with administrative processes related to the board, such as the compilation and distribution of agendas, reports, minutes and other matters related to internal and external compliance.

Putting Risk as a Core Topic on the Board Agenda

The sixth theme addresses director attitudes towards decisions concerning risk in the context of sound corporate governance practices. Directors tend to view risk through a narrow prism in terms of health and safety operations, sales and finance. There is an unfounded belief that risk transfer through insurance cover provides adequate protection.

Providing the Reality Check

Theme number seven emerges when a crisis arises that may be both internally or externally driven. I suggest that the prevalent attitude of directors is one of crisis denial – "Crises happen to other companies – not to us." Boards overestimate and overstate their coping mechanisms, believing that if a crisis occurred it could be easily managed and contained. It is also clear that within small companies there is limited internal capacity or knowledge to resource, create, monitor and test a crisis management plan.

Embedding Values within the Corporate DNA

The final theme relates to the owners' values. The beliefs, attitudes, decisions and values of the owner-manager are the key factor in the perception and adoption of an appropriate corporate governance model. In so embracing, the owner-manager is ceding a measure of control and influence and, by extension, is acknowledging a dilution of personal power. For most owner-managers this step across the Rubicon requires a fundamental shift of thinking.

What Next?

In terms of governance, what then might the immediate future hold for the millions of small companies in the UK and beyond? The coronavirus has disproportionally affected the very existence of small businesses over a period of longer than a year, the result of which is that many have vanished never to re-emerge. Whatever the new normal, SMEs will rise from the ashes and continue to be a forceful sector in the UK and elsewhere and the decisions that boards make will be instrumental in creating a more resilient sector. Risk and crisis management will be items on the menu in the eternal search for successful formulae beyond a narrow focus on financial performance. Decisions will be tempered by consideration of sustainability and environmental issues that will appear on a triple bottom line as the co-partners and adjutants of finance. Just as the term "servant leader" has emerged, so too will the notion of the servant board, and a wider form of distributed leadership will emerge with the board being no longer a "controlling mind" but a force for creativity, innovation and wider participation.

REFERENCES

Abor, J., and Adjasi, C., 2007. Corporate governance and the small and medium enterprises sector: Theory and implications. *Corporate Governance*, 7 (2), 111–22.

Abraham, S., and Allio, R.J., 2006. The troubled strategic advice industry: Why it's failing decision makers. *Strategy & Leadership*, 34 (3), 4–13.

Abu-Bulgu, M., 2007. *Corporate Crisis and Risk Management: Modelling Strategies and SME Application*. London: Elsevier.

Acs, Z., Carlsson, B., and Thurik, R., 1996. *Small Business in the Modern Economy*. Oxford: Blackwell.

Aguilera, R.V., Filatotchev, I., Gospel, H., and Jackson, G., 2008. An organizational approach to comparative corporate governance: Costs, contingencies, and complementarities. *Organization Science*, 19 (3), 475–92.

Aleksic, A., et al., 2013. An assessment of organizational resilience potential in SMEs of the process industry: A fuzzy approach. *Journal of Loss Prevention in the Process Industries*, 26 (6), 1238–45.

Ang, S., 1991. Small business uniqueness and the theory of financial management. *Journal of Entrepreneurial Finance*, 1 (1), 1–14.

Ansong, A., 2013. Risk management as a conduit of effective corporate governance and financial performance of small and medium scale enterprises. *Developing Country Studies*, 3 (8), 159–63.

Armour, J., and Gordon, J., 2009. *The Berle–Means Corporation in the 21st Century*. Cambridge: University of Cambridge.

Asgary, A., Anjum, M., and Azimi, N., 2012. Disaster recovery and business continuity after the 2010 flood in Pakistan: Case of small businesses. *International Journal of Disaster Risk Reduction*, 2, 46–56.

Atherton, A., 2003. The uncertainty of knowing: An analysis of the nature of knowledge in a small business context. *Human Relations*, 56 (11), 1379–98.

Ayyagari, M., Beck, T., and Demirguc-Kunt, A., 2007. Small and medium enterprises across the globe. *Small Business Economics*, 29 (4), 415–34.

Bannock, G., 2005. *The Economics and Management of Small Business: An International Perspective*. Abingdon: Routledge.

Barker, R., 2008. *The UK Model of Corporate Governance: An Assessment from the Midst of a Financial Crisis* [online]. Institute of Directors. Available from: www.iod.com/intershoproot/eCS/Store/en/pdfs/policy publication_The_UK_Model_of_Corporate_Governance.pdf [accessed 25 February 2015].

Barker, R., 2014. Informal conversation with author.

Bartholomeusz, S., and Tanewski, G.A., 2006. The relationship between family firms and corporate governance. *Journal of Small Business Management*, 44 (2), 245–67.

Becht, M., Bolton, P., and Röell, A., 2007. Corporate Law and Governance. In: Polinsky, A., and Shavell, S., eds., *Handbook of Law and Economics, Volume 2*. Amsterdam: Elsevier BV.

Bennett, R., and Robson, P., 2004. The role of boards of directors in small and medium-sized firms. *Journal of Small Business and Enterprise Development*, 11 (1), 95–113.

Berisha, G., and Pula, J., 2015. Defining SMEs: A critical review. *Academic Journal of Business, Administration, Law and Social Sciences*, 1 (1), 17–28.

Berle, A., and Means, G., 1932. *The Modern Corporation and Private Property*. New York, NY: Macmillan.

Betts, S.C., Huzey, D., and Vicari, V., 2012. Crisis management for small business: Advice for before, during and after a crisis. *Journal of International Management Studies*, 12 (4), 27.

Blackburn, R.A., Hart, M., and Wainwright, T., 2013. Small business performance: Business, strategy and owner-manager characteristics. *Journal of Small Business and Enterprise Development*, 20 (1), 8–27.

Bodmer, U., and Vaughan, D., 2009. Approaches to preventing crises in family controlled small enterprises. *Journal of Neuroscience, Psychology and Economics*, 2 (1), 41–58.

Bolton, J.E. (1971) *Report of the Committee of Enquiry into Small Firms*. Cmnd 4811. London: HMSO.

Bonner, K., et al., 2015. *Collaboration between SMEs and Universities: Local Population, Growth and Innovation Metrics*. Bristol: HEFCE Enterprise Research Centre.

British Standards Institution, 2013. *Code of Practice for Delivering Effective Governance of Organizations*. London: BSI Standards.

Brooksbank, R., 1991. Defining the small business: A new classification of company size. *Entrepreneurship and Regional Development*, 3 (1), 17–31.

Brunninge, O., Nordqvist, M., and Wiklund, J., 2007. Corporate governance and strategic change in SMEs: The effects of ownership, board composition and top management teams. *Small Business Economics*, 29 (3), 295–308.

Budge, A., Irvine, W., and Smith, R., 2008. Crisis plan? What crisis plan! How microentrepreneurs manage in a crisis. *International Journal of Entrepreneurship & Small Business*, 6 (3), 337–54.

Burn-Callander, R., 2016. *Mumpreneurs and Networking* [online]. *Daily Telegraph*. Available from: www.telegraph.co.uk/connect/small-business/business-networks/mumpreneurs-networking-prove-they-know-best/ [accessed 9 December 2016].

Cadbury, A., 1992. *Report of the Committee on the Financial Aspects of Corporate Governance*. London: Gee.

Carey, P. 2020. *Better Governance Construct*. Unpublished working paper.

Carney, M., et al., 2013. What do we know about private family firms? A meta-analytical review. *Entrepreneurship Theory and Practice*, 39 (3), 513–44.

Carter, S., and Jones-Evans, D., 2006. *Enterprise and Small Business: Principles, Practice and Policy*. Harlow: Pearson Education.

Cheffins, B., and Bank, S., 2009. Is Berle and Means really a myth? *Business History Review*, 83 (3), 443–74.

Chrisman, J., et al., 2013. The influence of family goals, governance, and resources on firm outcomes. *Entrepreneurship: Theory & Practice*, 37 (6), 1249–61.

Clancy, K., Hanover, A., and Masini, A., 2013. Complacency not an option. *Financial Executive*, 29 (3), 24–7.

Clarke, T., and Klettner, A., 2009. Governance issues for SMEs. *Journal of Business Systems, Governance and Ethics*, 4 (4), 23–40.

Clarysse, B., Knockaert, M., and Lockett, A., 2007. Outside board members in high tech start-ups. *Small Business Economics*, 29 (3), 243–59.

Coad, A., Frankish J., Roberts, R.G., and Storey, D.J., 2011. Growth paths and survival chances, *SPRU Working Paper Series*, 195 (SPRU – Science Policy Research Unit, University of Sussex Business School).

Committee on Corporate Governance for Non-Listed Enterprises, 2009. *Code Buysse II*. N.p.: Author.

Corey, C.M., and Deitch, E.A., 2011. Factors affecting business recovery immediately after Hurricane Katrina. *Journal of Contingencies and Crisis Management*, 19 (3), 169–81.

Coulson-Thomas, C., 2007. SME directors and boards: The contribution of directors and boards to the growth and development of small and medium-sized enterprises (SMEs). *International Journal of Business Governance and Ethics*, 3 (3), 250–61.

Cross-Sector Safety and Security Communications, 2014. The business case for sprinkler systems [online]. London: Available from: www.vocal.co.uk/cssc/the-business-case-for-sprinkler-systems/ [accessed 23 June 2015].

Crossan, K., Pershina, E., and Henschel, T., 2015. A model analysis of internal governance for SMEs. *Interdisciplinary Journal of Economics and Business Law*, 4 (4), 1–26.

Culkin, N., and Smith, D., 2000. An emotional business: a guide to understanding the motivations of small business decision takers. *Qualitative Market Research: An International Journal*, 3 (3), 145–57.

Curran, J., and Blackburn, R., 2001. *Researching the Small Enterprise: The Need for Small Business Research* [online]. London: SAGE. Available from: http://methods.sagepub.com/book/researching -the-small-enterprise/n1.xml [accessed 20 May 2017]

Deakins, D., and Freel, M., 2006. *Entrepreneurship and Small Firms*. Maidenhead: McGraw-Hill Education.

Department for Business, Innovation and Skills (BIS), 2015. *Small Business Survey 2014: Employers*. BIS Research Paper 214, Department for Business, Innovation and Skills. Crown copyright 2015. Publication is licensed under the terms of the Open Government Licence v3.0. Available from: www .gov.uk/government/publications/small-business-survey-2014-businesses-with-employees [accessed 11 March 2022]

Doern, R., 2016. Entrepreneurship and crisis management: The experiences of small businesses during the London 2011 riots. *International Small Business Journal*, 34 (3), 276–302.

Drummond, H., and Chell, E., 1994. Crisis management in a small business. *Management Decision*, 32 (1), 37–40.

Durst, S., and Henschel, T., 2014. Governance in small firms: A country comparison of current practices. *International Journal of Entrepreneurship and Small Business*, 21 (1), 16–32.

Eisenhardt, K., 1989. Agency theory: An assessment and review. *Academy of Management Review*, 14 (1), 57–74.

European Union, 2015. *User Guide to SME Definition*. Luxembourg: EU. Available from: https://ec .europa.eu/regional_policy/sources/conferences/state-aid/sme/smedefinitionguide_en.pdf [accessed 10 August 2022].

Faghfouri, J., et al., 2015. Ready for a crisis: How supervisory boards affect the formalized crisis procedures of small and medium-sized family firms in Germany. *Review of Management Science*, 9 (2), 317–38.

Fama, E., 1980. Agency problems and the theory of the firm. *Journal of Political Economy*, 88 (2), 288–307.

Fama, E., and Jensen, M., 1983. Separation of ownership and control. *Journal of Law and Economics*, 26 (2), 301–25.

Farooq, W., et al., 2014. SMEs' preparedness to face economic crisis: A proposed framework from Malaysian SMEs. *World Applied Sciences Journal*, 30 (30), 1–7.

Federation of Small Business, 2016. Home page. Available from: www.fsb.org.uk/ [accessed 25 August 2016].

Financial Reporting Council, 2012. *UK Corporate Governance Code Draft Revisions*. London: FRC.

Financial Reporting Council, 2014. *The UK Corporate Governance Code*. London: FRC.

Financial Times, 2014. *Defintion of Corporate Governance* [online]. Available from: http://lexicon.ft .com/Term?term=corporate-governance [accessed 17 October 2016].

Gao, S.S., Sung, M.C., and Zhang, J., 2013. Risk management capability building in SMEs: A social capital perspective. *International Small Business Journal*, 31 (6), 677–701.

Gibb, A., and Davies, L., 1992. Methodological problems in the development of a growth model of business enterprise. *Journal of Entrepreneurship*, 1 (1), 3–36.

Gibson, B., Vozikis, G., and Weaver, M., 2013. Exploring governance issues in family firms. *Small Enterprise Research*, 20 (2), 87–97.

Gibson, T., and Van der Vaart, H., 2008. Defining SMEs: A less imperfect way of defining small and medium enterprises in developing countries. Brookings Institution. Available from: www.brookings .edu/research/defining-smes-a-less-imperfect-way-of-defining-small-and-medium-enterprises-in -developing-countries/ [accessed 10 August 2022].

Gómez-Mejía, L., et al., 2007. Socio-emotional wealth and business risks in family-controlled firms: Evidence from Spanish olive oil mills. *Administrative Science Quarterly*, 52 (1), 106–37.

Gray, D. Saunders, M. and Goregaokar, H., 2013. *Success in Challenging Times: Key Lessons for UK SMEs*. Annual International Conference on Innovation and Entrepreneurship. Guildford: University of Surrey.

Gregory, H., 2003. *International Comparison of Corporate Governance Guidelines and Codes of Best Practice*. New York: Weil, Gotshal and Manges LLP.

Hannah, L., 2007. The "divorce" of ownership from control from 1900 onwards: Recalibrating imagined global trends. *Business History*, 49 (4), 404–38.

Haugh, H., and McKee, L., 2004. The cultural paradigm of the smaller firm. *Journal of Small Business Management*, 42 (4), 377–94.

Hawley, J., and Williams, A., 2000. The emergence of universal owners: Some implications of institu-tional equity ownership. *Challenge*, 43 (4), 43–61.

Herbane, B., 2010. Small business research: Time for a crisis-based view. *International Small Business Journal*, 28 (1), 43–64.

Herbane, B., 2015. Threat orientation in small and medium-sized enterprises. *Disaster Prevention and Management*, 24 (5), 583–95.

Herman, R., 2017. Why good governance is a must for SMEs. *The Director*, February, 17–19.

Hiebl, M.R.W., 2012. Risk aversion in family firms: What do we really know? *Journal of Risk Finance*, 14 (1), 49–70.

Hmieleski, K., and Baron, A., 2009. Entrepreneurs' optimism and new venture performance: A social cognitive perspective. *Academy of Management Journal*, 52 (3), 473–88.

Holderness, C.G., 2009. The myth of diffuse ownership in the United States. *Review of Financial Studies*, 22 (4), 1377.

Hong, P., Huang, C., and Li, B., 2012. Crisis management for SMEs: Insights from a multiple-case study. *International Journal of Business Excellence*, 5 (5), 535–53.

Huse, M., 2007. *Boards, Governance and Value Creation: The Human Side of Corporate Governance*. Cambridge: Cambridge University Press.

ICSA The Governance Institute, 2016. Home page. Available from: www.icsa.org.uk/ [accessed 25 August 2016].

Institute of Directors, 2004. *Corporate Governance*. London: IOD.

Institute of Directors, 2010. *Corporate Governance Guidance and Principles for Unlisted Companies in the UK*. London: ECODA.

Institute of Directors, 2016. *The 2016 Good Governance Report*. London: IOD.

International Finance Corporation, 2019. *SME Governance Guidebook*. Washington, DC: IFC.

Irvine, W., and Anderson, A., 2004. Small tourist firms in rural areas: Agility, vulnerability and survival in the face of crisis. *International Journal of Entrepreneurial Behavior & Research*, 10 (4), 229–46.

Jensen, M.C., and Meckling, W.H., 1976. Theory of the firm: Managerial behavior, agency costs and ownership structure. *Journal of Financial Economics*, 3 (4), 305–60.

Johnston, D., 2004. *OECD Principles of Corporate Governance*. Paris: OECD.

Jones, N., 2009. SME's life cycle: Steps to failure or success. *AU-GSB e-Journal*, 2, 3–14.

Karoui, L., Khlif, W., and Ingley, C., 2014. Board directors in private SMEs beyond one form fits all. *European Conference on Management, Leadership and Governance*. Reading: Academic Conferences and Publishing International.

Keasey, K., Thompson, S., and Wright, M., 2005. *Corporate Governance and Accountability: Enterprise and International Comparisons*. Chichester: John Wiley & Sons.

Kitching, J., 2015. Between vulnerable compliance and confident ignorance: Small employers, regulatory discovery practices and external support networks. *International Small Business Journal*, 34 (5), 601–17.

Kohler, J., and Deimel, M., 2012. Corporate and good governance in German SMEs. Tefen Management Consulting. Available from: www.tefen.com/insights/services/operation_Organization/corporate_and_good_governance_in_german_smes [accessed 10 August 2022].

Kotey, B., and Slade, P., 2005. Formal human resource management practices in small growing firms. *Journal of Small Business Management*, 43 (1), 16–40.

Kraus, S., et al., 2013. Crisis and turnaround management in SMES: A qualitative investigation of 30 companies. *International Journal of Entrepreneurial Venturing*, 5 (4): 406.

Kuhn, K., et al., 2016. Near, far, and online: Small business owners' advice-seeking from peers. *Journal of Small Business and Enterprise Development*, 23 (1), 189–206.

Kurschus, R.-J., Sarapovas, T., and Cvilikas, A., 2015. The criteria to identify company's crisis in SME sector. *Engineering Economics*, 26 (2), 152–58.

La Porta, R. et al., 1998. *Agency Problems and Dividend Policies around the World*. Cambridge, MA: Harvard Institute of Economic Research, Harvard University.

Lampel, J., Bhalla, A., and Jha, P., 2014. Does governance confer organisational resilience? Evidence from UK employee owned businesses. *European Management Journal*, 32 (1), 66–72.

Lane, S., et al., 2006. Guidelines for family business boards of directors. *Family Business Review*, 19 (2), 147–67.

Lee, N., 2011. *Barriers to Growth*. London: Work Foundation.

Lewis, M.K., 2010. Did Berle and Means get it wrong? Reflections on Thorstein Veblen, Paul Samuelson, and "Corporate Strategy Financialized." *Accounting Forum*, 34, 222–7.

Letza, S., Kirkbride, J., Sun, X., and Smallman, C., 2008. Corporate governance theorising: Limits, critics and alternatives. *International Journal of Law and Management*, 50 (1), 17–32.

Levrau, A., and Du Bus, S., 2014. Governance in small and medium-sized entreprises: Setting the course for success. *Business Compliance*, 3 (5), 5–17.

Lobonțiu, G., and Lobonțiu, M., 2013. The owner-manager and the functional management of a small firm. *Procedia – Social and Behavioral Sciences*, 124, 552–61.

London Chamber of Commerce and Industry, 2016. Home page. Available from: www.londonchamber.co.uk.

Long, T., Dulewicz, V., and Gay, K., 2005. The role of the non-executive director: Findings of an empirical investigation into the differences between listed and unlisted UK boards. *Corporate Governance: An International Review*, 13 (5), 667–79.

Lynall, M., Golden, B., and Hillman, A., 2003. Board composition from adolescence to maturity: A multitheoretic view. *Academy of Management Review*, 28 (3), 416–31.

Maassen, G., 2004. *Corporate Governance and Small and Medium-Sized Enterprises: How SMEs Can Benefit from Corporate Governance Principles and CSR*. Washington, DC: United States Agency for International Development.

Mallin, C., 2004. *Corporate Governance*. Oxford: Oxford University Press.

Mason, M., and O'Mahony, J., 2008. Post-traditional corporate governance. *Journal of Corporate Citizenship*, 31 (Autumn), 1–14.

McNutt, P., 2010. Edited ethics: Corporate governance and Kant's philosophy. *International Journal of Social Economics*, 37 (10), 741–54.

Mead, E., 1928. *Corporation Finance*, 6th Edition. New York, NY: D. Appleton and Company.

Miller, D., Le Breton-Miller, I., and Lester, R., 2013. Family firm governance, strategic conformity, and performance: Institutional vs. strategic perspectives. *Organization Science*, 24 (1), 189–209.

Millstein, I., 2014. *International Comparison of Selected Corporate Governance Guidelines and Codes of Best Practice*. New York, NY: Weil, Gotshal & Manges LLP.

Minichilli, A., and Hansen, C., 2007. The board advisory tasks in small firms and the event of crises. *Journal of Management & Governance*, 11 (1), 5–22.

Mitroff, I., and Anagnos, G., 2000. *Managing Crises Before They Happen*. New York, NY: Amacom.

Mitroff, I., Pauchant, T., Finney, M., and Pearson, C., 1989. Do (some) organisations cause their own crises? *Industrial Crisis Quarterly*, 3 (4), 269–83.

Monks, R., and Minnow, N., 2011. *Corporate Governance*, 5th Edition. Chichester: John Wiley & Sons.

Nordberg, D., 2011. *Corporate Governance Principles and Issues*. London: SAGE.

OECD, 2005. *SME and Entrepreneurship Outlook*. Paris: OECD. Available from: https://stats.oecd.org/glossary/detail.asp?ID =3123.

OECD, 2015. *Taxation of SMEs in OECD and G20 Countries Tax Policy Studies No 23*. Paris: OECD.

Pal, R., 2013. *Organizational Resilience through Crisis Strategic Planning*. Doctoral thesis, Tampere University of Technology.

Pearson, G., and Woodman, P., 2012. *Planning for the Worst: The 2012 Business Continuity Management Survey*. London: Chartered Management Institute.

Penrose, J.M., 2000. The role of perception in crisis planning. *Public Relations Review*, 26 (2), 155–71.

Perrow, C., 1999. Organizing to reduce the vulnerabilities of complexity. *Journal of Contingencies and Crisis Management*, 7 (3), 150–155.

Perry, 2001. Relationship between business plans and the failure of small businesses. *Journal of Small Business Management*, 39 (3), 201–8.

Pieper, T., 2003. Corporate governance in family firms: A literature review. *Insead Working Paper series*, 97 (IIF), 1–27.

Ponomareva, Y., and Ahlberg, J., 2016. Bad governance of family firms: The adoption of good governance on the boards of directors in family firms. *Ephemera Theory and Politics in Organisations*, 16 (1), 53–77.

Price Waterhouse Coopers (PwC), 2015. Governance Insights Center [online]. Available from: www.pwc.com/us/en/governance-insights-center.html [accessed 23 August 2015].

Rappaport, A., 2006. Ten ways to create shareholder value [online]. *Harvard Busines Review*. Available from: https://hbr.org/2006/09/ten-ways-to-create-shareholder-value [accessed 20 October 2016].

Ricketts-Gaskill, L., Van Auken, H., and Manning, R., 1993. A factor analytical study of the perceived causes of small business failure. *Journal of Small Business Management*, 31 (4), 1–7.

RSA Insurance, 2014. *Growing Pains: How the UK Became a Nation of "Micropreneurs"*. London: RSA Group.

Runyan, R.C. 2006. Small business in the face of crisis: Identifying barriers to recovery from a natural disaster. *Journal of Contingencies and Crisis Management*, 14 (1), 12–26.

Santana, G., 1997. *Crisis Management: Towards a Model for the Hotel Industry*. PhD thesis, Bournemouth University.

Saxena, A., and Jagota, R., 2015. Should the MSMEs be governed the corporate governance way? *Indian Journal of Corporate Governance*, 8 (1), 54–67.

Schane, S., 1986. The corporation is a person: The language of a legal fiction. *Tulane Law Review*, 61 (3).

Schneider, A., and Scherer, A.G., 2013. Corporate governance in a risk society. *Journal of Business Ethics*, 126 (2), 309–23.

Seidl, D., 2006. *Regulating Organizations through Codes of Governance*. Cambridge: ESRC Centre for Business Research.

Sicoli, G., 2013. Role of corporate governance in the family business. *Global Conference on Business and Finance* (Vol. 8). San Jose, Costa Rica: IBFR.

Siebels, J.-F., and zu Knyphausen-Aufseß, D., 2012. A review of theory in family business research: The implications for corporate governance. *International Journal of Management Reviews*, 14 (3), 280–304.

Smit, Y., and Watkins, J., 2012. A literature review of small and medium enterprises (SME) risk management practices in South Africa. *African Journal of Business Management*, 6 (21), 6324–30.

Smith, A., 2008. *An Enquiry into the Nature and Causes of the Wealth of Nations*. Oxford: Oxford University Press.

Smith, C.W., Jr., 2007. On governance and agency issues in small firms. *Journal of Small Business Management*, 45 (1), 176–8.

Spiers, L., 2017. Corporate governance, risk and crises in small companies: Shedding light from inside the boardroom black box. *Economics and Business Review*, 3 (17), 112–26.

Spillan, J., and Hough, M., 2003. Crisis planning in small businesses: Importance, impetus and indifference. *European Management Journal*, 21, (3), 398–407.

Steier, L.P., Chrisman, J.J., and Chua, J.H., 2015. Governance challenges in family businesses and business families. *Entrepreneurship: Theory & Practice*, 39 (6), 1265–80.

Sterling, S., 2011. Encouraging resilience within SMEs. *Journal of Business Continuity and Emergency Planning*, 5 (2), 128–39.

Storey, D.J., 2011. Optimism and chance: The elephants in the entrepreneurship room. *International Small Business Journal*, 29 (4), 303.

Sullivan-Taylor, B., and Branicki, L., 2011. Creating resilient SMEs: Why one size might not fit all. *International Journal of Production Research*, 49 (18), 5565–79.

Tilley, F., 2000. Small firm environmental ethics: How deep do they go? *Business Ethics: A European Review*, 9 (1), 31–41.

Tommaso, M., and Dubbini, S., 2000. *Towards a Theory of the Small Firm Theoretical Aspects and Some Policy Implications*. Santiago: United Nations Restructuring and Competitiveness Network Division of Production, Productivity and Management.

Torres, O., and Julien, P., 2005. Specificity and denaturing of small business. *International Small Business Journal*, 23 (4), 355–77.

Tricker, B., 2011. Re-inventing the limited liability company. *Corporate Governance: An International Review*, 19 (4), 384–93.

Uhlaner, L., Floren, R., and Geerlings, J., 2007. Owner commitment and relational governance in the privately-held firm: An empirical study. *Small Business Economics*, 29, (3), 275–93.

UK Government, 2006a. *Companies Act*. London: HMSO.

UK Government, 2006b. *Small and Medium Enterprise (SME) – Definitions*. London: HMSO.

UK Government, 2006c. *How Resilient Is Your Business to Disaster*. Available from: https://www.gov.uk/government/publications/how-resilient-is-your-business-to-disaster.

UK Government, 2014. *Business Population Estimates for the UK and Regions*. Available from: https://www.gov.uk/government/statistics/business-population-estimates-2014.

UK Government, 2015. *Business Population Estimates for the UK and Regions 2015*. London: HMSO.

UK Government, 2016. Prepare annual accounts for a private limited company. HMRC. Available from: https://www.gov.uk/annual-accounts.

UK Government, 2017. *Business Population Estimates for the UK and Regions 2017*. London: HMSO.

Vandekerkhof, P., et al., 2011. Professionalization of TMT in private family firms: The danger of institutionalism. *Proceedings of the European Conference on Management, Leadership & Governance*, 419–26.

Vargo, J. 2011. Crisis planning for SMEs: Finding the silver lining. *International Journal of Production Research*, 49 (18), 5619–35.

Veblen, T., 1997. *Absentee Ownership*. Abingdon: Transaction Publishers. (Originally published in 1923.)

Verbano, C., and Venturini, K., 2013. Managing risks in SMEs: A literature review and research agenda. *Journal of Technology Management and Innovation*, 8 (3), 186–97.

Vrečko, I., and Širec, K., 2013. Managing crisis of SMEs with restructuring projects. *Business Management Dynamics*, 2 (8), 54–62.

Webster, M. (Ed.) 2007. *The Director's Handbook*, 2nd Edition. London: IOD in association with Pinsent Masons.

Wellage, N., 2011. Agency costs ownership and corporate goverance mechanisms: A case study in New Zealand unlisted small companies. *Journal of Business Systems, Governance and Ethics*, 6 (6), 53–66.

World Bank, 2005. *The World Bank Annual Report 2005: Year in Review, Volume 1*. Washington, DC: World Bank.

Wright, M., and Ashill, N., 1998. A contingency of marketing information. *European Journal of Marketing*, 32 (1/2), 125–44.

Wymeersch, E., 2006. Corporate Governance Codes and their Implementation. In: *Private and Commercial Law in European and Global Context, Festschrift für Norbert Horn*. Berlin: Walter de Gruyter.

Yiannaki, S., 2012. A systematic risk management for SMEs under financial crisis. *International Journal of Organizational Analysis*, 20 (4), 406–42.

Zahra, S.A., Gedajlovic, E., Neubaum, D.O., Shulmand, J.M., 2009. A typology of social entrepreneurs: Motives, search processes and ethical challenges. *Journal of Business Venturing*, 24 (5), 519–532.

PART II

GOVERNANCE BEST PRACTICE

6. Non-executive directors' behaviour and activities, and firm performance

Vinita Mithani

1. INTRODUCTION

The development of capital markets, especially in the highly capitalist countries like the United States of America (US) and the United Kingdom (UK), has meant that the largest companies have their shares traded on a public market (Armour et al., 2009). Those who own these entities – i.e., shareholders – are therefore not the ones running them; i.e., corporate management (Petrovic, 2008). In other words, ownership has become fully separated from control for companies with shares listed on the stock market. This has brought to the fore the agency problem discussed by Jensen and Meckling (1976), whereby managers (the agent) cannot be trusted to always make decisions in the best interests of shareholders (the principal). Yet, the large number of dispersed shareholders are not able to collaborate in monitoring management's activities (Petrovic, 2008). To address this issue, boards were expected to appoint independent non-executive directors (NEDs) as monitors of executive directors (EDs), alongside their other roles. However, the corporate scandals at the turn of the 21st century led to NEDs' characteristics and monitoring duties being defined more specifically and legislated through the Sarbanes–Oxley Act in the US in 2002; these were also incorporated in the Corporate Governance Code in the UK in 2003 (Roberts et al., 2005). Monitoring duties were to be performed through designated board committees, including audit, remuneration, and nomination committees (Akbar et al., 2016).

It was expected that NEDs who were seen to be independent of management would possess the necessary objectivity required to appraise EDs effectively (Westphal and Bednar, 2005). Also, their limited involvement in the day-to-day running of the business would make for less biased assessments of the firm's performance and strategies (Westphal and Bednar, 2005; Pugliese et al., 2009). In other words, NEDs' detachment from management and detailed business operations meant that they would be highly suited to address the agency problem between shareholders and management. However, numerous high-profile corporate failures resulting from poor monitoring of corporate management have raised serious doubts over NEDs' ability to deliver on such expectations.

An alternative view challenges the existence of an agency problem between management and shareholders. Stewardship theory proposes that managers' and shareholders' interests are naturally aligned as the firm's performance impacts the manager's reputation and shareholders' wealth simultaneously (Daily et al., 2003). In this context, NEDs' role is more one of supporting rather than monitoring EDs (Pugliese et al., 2009). Indeed, resource dependence theory suggests that firms require access to external resources for their survival and success (Pfeffer and Salancik, [1978] 2003). NEDs with their external outlook are considered well positioned to enable such access (Pugliese et al., 2009). Resources would range from strategic advice to connections with providers of finance, government bodies, and potential suppliers and customers (Hillman and Dalziel, 2003; Nicholson and Kiel, 2007; Pugliese et al., 2009). Regulators, however, have been more concerned about the need to control EDs' behaviour driven by their self-interests.

Certainly, there has been a large amount of empirical research testing agency theory; i.e., testing for the effectiveness of NEDs' monitoring role (Jermias and Gani, 2014; Boivie et al., 2016; Adams, 2017). This testing has involved attempting to find a correlation between NEDs' independence from management (based on observable characteristics) and firm performance (Brennan, 2006). However, these studies have produced inconclusive results (Brennan, 2006; Hillman et al., 2008; Boivie et al., 2016). More recent studies that address endogeneity issues do not, however, find a significant statistical association between measures of NEDs' independence and firm performance, not even in the longer term. For example, Akbar et al. (2016) used the reported independence of NEDs on the monitoring committees of UK listed companies as an indicator of good governance. They designed their study to address risks of reverse causality between firm performance and good governance, arising from multiple sources. They observed firm performance over three consecutive years and did not find any relationship with the governance indicator, and suggested that any prior studies that may have found a positive relationship most probably had not controlled for reverse causality. An earlier UK study by McKnight and Weir (2009) found a negative relationship for both the existence of a nomination committee and the independence of NEDs on the nominating committee. Such findings have raised doubt over the benefit of NEDs' monitoring role and called into question the purpose of extensive regulations in this regard (Boivie et al., 2016). However, many have suggested that it is the underlying assumptions in these empirical studies that are flawed; i.e., that NEDs, who appear independent of management, will deliver on their monitoring duties and that monitoring positively impacts firm performance (Brennan, 2006; Hillman et al., 2008; Boivie et al., 2016).

Much less research activity has been devoted to testing resource dependence theory (Adams, 2017). The testing here has focused on finding a relationship between NEDs' 'capital' and firm performance, 'capital' being conceived in terms of NEDs' skills, knowledge, expertise, and reputation (Hillman et al., 2008). Jermias and Gani (2014) indeed found a positive and significant correlation in the US context. They proxied NEDs' capital by considering the other positions they held outside the focal firm, namely serving as an ED or NED in other listed companies, or being a university professor or a government officer. However, not only are quantitative archival studies relying on proxies of NEDs' abilities, many argue that it is also unclear even if NEDs possessed such capital whether they were indeed able to use it to make a difference to the firm's performance (Adams, 2017). In other words, we are still in the dark when it comes to the mechanism involved. A few decades ago, Pfeffer and Salancik ([1978] 2003) pointed to the lack of true empirical engagement with resource dependence theory. While there has been some progress here, their criticism of the lack of further development of the theory still stands.

Given the nature of research in respect of both the monitoring and resource provision roles of NEDs, several questions remain unanswered. Brennan (2006) called for research to explain how NEDs decide which role they focus on, what duties they indeed carry out, how effectively they perform them, how they contribute, and what the effects are of social interactions on the board. She argued that this would help us get closer to closing the 'expectations gap' on NEDs' contributions, an area of research that has been neglected. Petrovic (2008) also highlighted knowledge gaps in terms of what roles NEDs play in practice and what makes them effective in those roles. Although we have a long list of questions that still need answering, there has been little systematic guidance on exactly how these voids are to be filled comprehensively. In the meantime, the tradition of quantitative studies attempting to link NEDs' observable characteristics to firm performance continues (Petrovic, 2008). This in turn prevents the necessary advances in knowledge (Daily et al., 2003) that could have had greater currency in driving policy in this area (Roberts et al., 2005). This chapter aims to address these weaknesses specifically by providing a clear, structured, and extensive road map for future research.

The first step, as presented in Section 2, is an analysis of the intermediate stages in the posited connections between the observable characteristics of NEDs and firm financial performance, what the determinants of those intermediate stages are and what their impact is. In doing so, it considers both the monitoring and resource provision roles of NEDs. A visual representation of the (assumed) links (Figure 6.1) helps to disentangle the different problem areas. It also enables a clearer grasp of the reasons underlying the inconclusiveness of empirical research in the field. The analysis goes beyond simply pointing out the major 'inferential leaps' (Pettigrew, 1992, p. 171). It discusses the precise ways in which these connections may or may not operate; it does so by incorporating empirical evidence from the different lines of research within corporate governance. This is intended to guide future research in terms of the matters that need to be considered to ensure the production of credible and meaningful knowledge. The two main problem connections that are addressed are (1) the assumption that NEDs' observable characteristics directly predict their behaviour, and (2) the assumption that their behaviour in turn predicts the firm's financial performance. Section 2.2 of this chapter discusses the former assumption and the current state of knowledge on the determinants of NEDs' behaviour. Section 2.3 addresses the latter assumption by considering the possible mechanisms through which NEDs' activities may impact firm financial performance. Section 3 leads on from Section 2.2 and presents an extensive framework to guide future research in respect of the determinants of NEDs' behaviour. It does so to enable the development of a complex substantive theory that would pave the way for a move away from the blind pursuit of testing grand theories in an area little understood (Huse, 2007).

2.   THE MISSING CONNECTIONS

2.1   Introduction

As discussed above, empirical studies seeking to find a statistical correlation between NEDs' observable characteristics and firm performance have assumed the association without empirical knowledge of the intermediate connections (Pettigrew, 1992). Figure 6.1 attempts a visualisation of the (broken) links between NEDs' discernible attributes and organisational performance; i.e., the A$\tilde{q}$D relationship which is the one predominantly observed and measured. NEDs' activities/behaviours (B) tend to be assumed based on their traits, as manifest from archival sources (A); i.e., the A$\tilde{q}$B relationship is assumed (Petrovic, 2008; Adams, 2017). However, a whole field of behavioural psychology would argue that there are many other factors (Z) impacting human actors' behaviour (Z$\tilde{q}$B). A few studies – e.g., Finkelstein and Mooney (2003), Ingley and Van der Walt (2005), and Roberts et al. (2005) – have used surveys and interviews to throw light on NEDs' activities/behaviours, as discussed in detail in Section 2.2 below. Some studies have also attempted to study the impact on NEDs' behaviour of factors other than their observable characteristics, as analysed in Section 3. However, we are far from developing a comprehensive behavioural framework for NEDs, one that will better guide policy (Adams, 2017). Another segment of research, discussed in detail in Section 2.3 below, has studied the links between NEDs' attributes and the expected direct outcomes (A$\tilde{q}$C) of their assumed activities (B). These avoid making any inferential leaps from those expected direct outcomes of NEDs' activities to firm performance; i.e., they do not proceed to claim the (C$\tilde{q}$D) relationship. However, they do not observe the activities/behaviours themselves (B) let alone consider the other factors likely impacting NEDs' behaviour (Z$\tilde{q}$B). As a result of the above, we are left with a considerable void, firstly in terms of what is truly driving NEDs' behaviour and how; i.e., little is known regarding the (Z$\tilde{q}$B) mechanism. Secondly, we remain in the dark about the extent to which the direct outcomes of NEDs' activities impact firm performance; i.e., the (C$\tilde{q}$D) relationship has been given little attention.

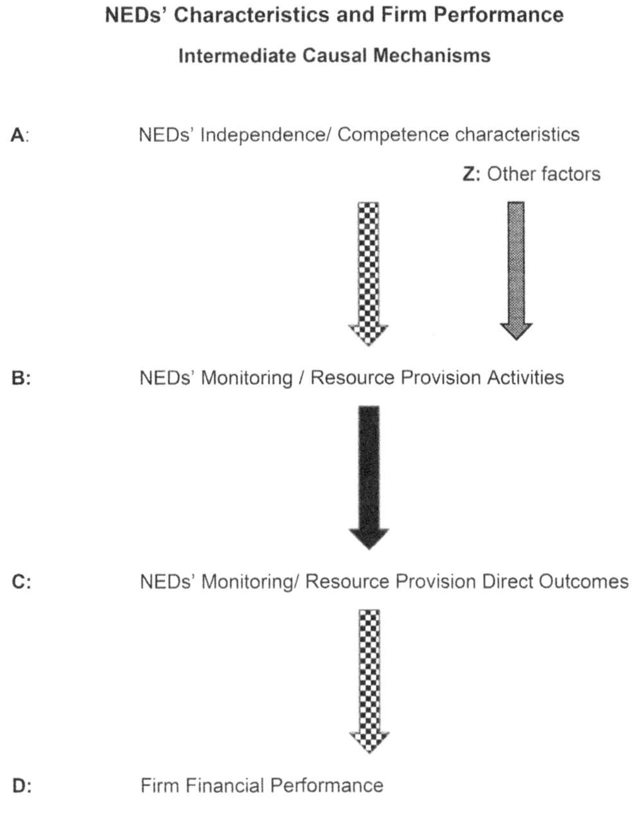

NEDs' Characteristics and Firm Performance

Intermediate Causal Mechanisms

A: NEDs' Independence/ Competence characteristics

                                                   Z: Other factors

B: NEDs' Monitoring / Resource Provision Activities

C: NEDs' Monitoring/ Resource Provision Direct Outcomes

D: Firm Financial Performance

Figure 6.1   *NEDs' characteristics and firm performance intermediate causal mechanisms*

2.2   Determinants of NEDs' Behaviour/Activities (Z$\tilde{q}$B)

Many scholars have called for much more research that directly studies NEDs' behaviour (B), rather than assumes it based on their observable attributes relating to independence and competence in terms of knowledge and skills (Petrovic, 2008; Adams, 2017); i.e., to refrain from assuming the (A⫶B) relationship. There is indeed little doubt that it is NEDs' actual conduct in terms of willingness to challenge and contribute that determines their effectiveness (Pye and Pettigrew, 2005; Roberts et al., 2005; Petrovic, 2008); i.e., it is the (B⫶C) link that is truly effective. As such, many have attempted to understand board work processes; e.g., Finkelstein and Mooney (2003), Ingley and Van der Walt (2005), and Roberts et al. (2005). However, while these studies have given some insight into what NEDs do (B), or at least claim they do, they fail to explain why NEDs focus on what they do. In other words, they do not provide any insight on the (Z⫶B) relationship. For example, Finkelstein and Mooney (2003) used structured interviews with chief executive officers (CEOs) and NEDs to gain their perspective on what makes boards work; i.e., the different behaviours that make for a successful board, such as finding the confidence to challenge, insisting on full and timely information, etc. This specifically concerns the (B⫶C) relationship. However, what remains unclear is why boards fail to engage in such idyllic behaviours, what those structures are, and how much agency NEDs have within those structures. Roberts et al. (2005) used transcripts of interviews carried out as part of a UK regulatory review to study NEDs' behaviour relative to EDs. However, besides the validity issues arising from their vested interests when responding to a regulatory review, the evidence did not shed light on the drivers of their behaviour. Similarly, Ingley and Van der Walt (2005) surveyed directors to gauge their perception of their contributions and found that directors felt their contribution to be limited. However, the study did not address the factors inhibiting their full influence.

It is not to say that the study of structures impacting NEDs' behaviour has not received any attention; i.e., the (Z⫶B) relationship. Indeed, there have been separate investigations of some individual factors; for example, the power of the CEO vis-à-vis NEDs, and financial incentives for NEDs, amongst others. However, these have often used proxies for NEDs' behaviour. Also, many of the likely causal forces have not been studied from a behavioural perspective; i.e., how social structures impact attitudes and actions, which then determine outcomes. Individual factors have also not been woven together into a comprehensive behavioural framework. Boivie et al. (2016) certainly discussed the findings of studies on several factors likely impeding NEDs' monitoring role. However, the constraints they discussed regarding NEDs' monitoring role are likely only part of the elements that would feed into NEDs' decision-making about the focus of their roles. The effects of regulatory, legal, and reputational influences on NEDs' perception of accountability would likely also bear heavily on their actions, not to mention the impact of NEDs' personal motivations and incentives. Langevoort (2001) argued the need to study how NEDs make sense of the 'institutional and legal constraints' on their behaviour (p. 831). This proposal takes that on board and goes much further. Brennan (2006) indeed discussed multiple factors likely creating an 'expectations gap' in relation to NEDs' monitoring activities. She proposed that groupthink in the boardroom, EDs' control of business information, EDs' appointment of NEDs, the latter's general lack of detailed knowledge of business operations, and their limited time commitment to the role possibly limit their ability to monitor in the way that stakeholders expect. However, there was limited discussion of empirical evidence on each of the factors. Section 3 of this chapter uses a behavioural theory lens and available evidence on several factors to build and propose a comprehensive analytic framework for the study of NEDs' behaviour. The methodology that would be appropriate for such research is also discussed. It is hoped that this will provide the necessary guidance for future research in this area, which has been neglected but which could significantly advance knowledge in the field.

In other words, what is proposed in Section 3 goes significantly beyond the type of knowledge that others have called for; e.g., greater understanding of how NEDs choose to behave, what they achieve, and what they should do to be effective (Petrovic, 2008). Instead, it puts forward a schema that would enable an examination of the underlying forces that explain those behaviours. Such knowledge is essential to ensure effective policy formulations; it will at the very least set the right expectations of what certain regulations can achieve. To reduce the variability arising from different regulatory environments, it is proposed that such behavioural studies are situated in a specific context. In this chapter, the discussion about the implications of the regulatory environment is based on the UK context as an illustration; it should still be able to guide studies relating to other jurisdictions.

2.3   Expected Direct Outcomes of NEDs' Activities and Firm Performance (C$\tilde{a}$D)

As discussed, a large body of research has sought to find the (A$\tilde{a}$D) relationship between corporate governance attributes/activities and the company's financial performance, the latter being used as a proxy for NEDs' effectiveness (Nicholson and Kiel, 2007). A separate corpus of empirical studies has instead focused on the relationship between NEDs' attributes and their expected direct outcomes (A$\tilde{a}$C). However, the implication of the latter body of research for the former has not been considered. In other words, there has been little study of the relationship between the expected direct outcomes of NEDs' activities and firm financial performance (C$\tilde{a}$D). Yet this may elucidate on the seemingly inconclusive results emanating from the search for a link with organisational performance. Boivie et al. (2016) did indeed raise the question of whether NEDs' monitoring role can be expected to improve a firm's performance, but they did not elaborate further on this. Brennan (2006) also considered this issue and suggested the possibility that monitoring dampened management's efforts to add value, although she did not discuss the likely effects of the different and specific monitoring activities. This section of the chapter analyses the implications of the findings of empirical studies on the direct outcomes of the various distinct monitoring activities of NEDs in the context of their likely impact on financial performance. It then does the same for resource provision activities.

Monitoring activities
Research on NEDs' specific monitoring activities has been split along the lines of the three main board committees prescribed by corporate governance regulations, namely audit, remuneration, and nomination committees (FRC, 2018b). The findings from each are therefore considered in turn in the discussion below. A risk committee, separate from the audit committee, is required for some sectors, and recommended generally (FRC, 2018a, 2018b). However, research on risk committees has been very limited. Nonetheless, the available research findings for risk committees and risk management activities generally are also discussed below.

Audit committee
This is the one area of NEDs' monitoring activity that has received the most attention in terms of academic research (J.R. Cohen et al., 2008). The expected direct outcomes of the monitoring activities of audit committees also provide the clearest and strongest evidence against a link between such activities and firm financial performance measures. The monitoring role of

audit committees relates to the quality of a firm's financial reporting (FRC, 2018b). Research has therefore focused on finding evidence of the audit committee's effectiveness at reducing the likelihood of reported financials being manipulated by the management team. Financial statements are a means of providing the necessary signal to investors about the competence of management in ensuring the sound financial performance and position of the company they have been entrusted to run. As a result, management tends to have a strong motivation for manipulating reported figures (Dechow et al., 1996), hence the significance of the monitoring role of audit committees (Xie et al., 2003). The principle of accruals accounting (as compared to cash accounting) creates opportunities for such manipulation (Xie et al., 2003). A highly effectual audit committee would be expected to prevent such misrepresentations (Bédard et al., 2004) through their oversight of the choice of accounting policies and of judgements used in calculating estimated/forecast figures (Basu and Liang, 2019). Another significant way in which audit committee NEDs impact the reliability of financial statements is through their role in ensuring the independence of external auditors from management (Carcello and Neal, 2003).

Indeed, most empirical studies of the association between independent and competent audit committee members and earnings manipulations have found an expected negative relationship; e.g., Klein (2002), Xie et al. (2003), Bédard et al. (2004), and Peasnell et al. (2005). Abbott et al. (2004) also found that audit committee independence and meeting frequency were negatively associated with the restatement of financial statements. Beekes et al. (2004) and Ahmed and Duellman (2007) found such attributes related to accounting conservatism; i.e., persistent prevention of overstatements of earnings over multiple consecutive periods. Of course, there are endogeneity issues with most of these studies; in any case, their relational nature means that causality is neglected (Xie et al., 2003). Also, the studies do not observe audit committees' monitoring activities directly; instead, they assume that such activity would follow from the observable independence and competence characteristics and meeting frequency of NEDs (Beekes et al., 2004). In other words, they also assume the (A$\overset{a}{\rightarrow}$B) relationship. Nonetheless, they are in line with the outcomes one would expect of an audit committee of NEDs actively and rigorously discharging its monitoring duties.

The implications, therefore, are that the more effectively NEDs perform their monitoring duties within audit committees, the more conservative the reported financials are. In other words, highly active NEDs meeting the expectations of the investing public and regulators would prevent inflated financials from being reported. Notably, therefore, the opportunity to manipulate reported financial performance implies that it may not always reflect true financial performance. Studies attempting to find a positive association between NEDs' characteristics and firm financial performance may therefore be wrongly concluding ineffectiveness on the part of NEDs if they do not consider the effects of monitoring for earnings manipulation. Indeed, such studies rarely control for it.

In any case, it is difficult to identify a mechanism by which effectual active audit committees would directly contribute to the underlying economic performance of the firm, especially in the short term and in the way that is measured by most quantitative studies. Instead, in monitoring the reliability of financial information presented to investors, they would contribute to the efficient running of capital markets generally. Their work does certainly also ensure that the board itself has reliable information to make the appropriate strategic interventions, which would ensure the much-longer-term success of the firm, and would possibly avert a corporate collapse, as in the high-profile cases of this generation. Reorienting research to capture the longer-term effects of true guardianship by NEDs may therefore be more fruitful. Case study designs might be particularly suitable for such investigation as the richness of individual cases would allow the unfolding of mechanisms over time to be observed more firmly (Blatter and Blume, 2008).

Remuneration committee

Remuneration committees are meant to play a prime role in ensuring that executives' pay structure and levels are effective in motivating them to maximise shareholder value (Anderson and Bizjak, 2003). Ensuring the alignment of EDs' financial incentives with those of share-holders and thereby reducing the agency cost (Jensen and Meckling, 1976) is therefore a key aspect of NEDs' role as part of the compensation committee (Sapp, 2008). Indeed, the UK Corporate Governance Code prescribes the long-term holding of equity by EDs as a means of ensuring such alignment (FRC, 2018b). The level at which remuneration is set is also meant to adequately reflect the input of the executive to ensure they do not extract excessive compensation, and thereby to protect shareholder wealth (Bebchuk et al., 2002).

Empirical studies attempting to find an association between directors with observable independence characteristics and executives' pay structure and/or level have reported mixed results. For example, Sapp (2008) found evidence of weaker boards increasing excess executive pay; i.e., pay not supported by firm performance. Similarly, Larcker et al. (2005) found more socially connected boards linked to higher levels of excess executive pay. Additionally, the findings of Van Essen et al. (2015) showed that more powerful boards can control total executive compensation levels and ensure a greater proportion of share-based executive remuneration. On the other hand, Anderson and Bizjak (2003) found no evidence of more independent remuneration committees preventing excessive pay or poorly structured packages in terms of the alignment of incentives. Gregory-Smith (2012) and Guthrie et al. (2012) also detected no relation.

The above studies of course do not observe actual board activity/processes, which may partly explain the inconclusive results overall. However, executive pay levels and structures are also likely to be heavily determined by market forces (Gregory-Smith, 2012). NEDs' monitoring role within remuneration committees may therefore be limited to ensuring that EDs' pay is at par with the market. Ultimately, they need to ensure that the pay level and structure can secure the talent required by the firm (Anderson and Bizjak, 2003) while also not being excessive. The UK Corporate Governance Code also sets out the expectations of remuneration committees in terms of EDs' pay levels and structure; e.g., the revised Code requires executive compensation to be set in the context of other workers' pay, and that incentives have a long-term focus (FRC, 2018b). In other words, the flexibility available to NEDs in influencing executive pay may indeed be quite restricted. As a result, their monitoring activities in relation to executive remuneration policies may not have any significant influence on firm performance.

Besides, although a more equity-based compensation package was intended to align management and shareholder interests (Dobbin and Jung, 2010), such packages also incentivise management to manipulate reported financial performance. This is particularly the case with stock options as executives can influence share prices to their advantage by managing reported earnings (D.A. Cohen et al., 2008). This is exacerbated if the vesting of stock options is conditional on meeting certain performance targets, as evidenced also by UK studies; e.g., Conyon et al. (2000) and Kuang (2008). In other words, management pay packages which contain a substantial equity element may not necessarily be in shareholders' interest, and although they may be correlated with reported financial performance, this may not reflect the firm's true performance. Therefore, to the extent that NEDs can ensure EDs' compensation packages have a greater variable performance-based component, they may be deemed to be discharging their duties effectively even though such activity may have negative consequences for investors.

There are clearly strong reasons to believe that the relationship between NEDs' monitoring activities within the remuneration committee and firm financial performance is somewhat vexed.

Nomination committee

NEDs within the nomination committee are responsible for appointing, appraising, and dismissing other company directors (Faleye et al., 2011; Guo and Masulis, 2015). They therefore play a crucial role in determining the quality of the board (Withers et al., 2012; Guo and Masulis, 2015), which in turn has potentially the most impact on the future value of the firm. Although there has been very limited research on nomination committees, especially compared to the other two main committees (Kaczmarek et al., 2012), there are some studies on the outcomes of their activities. Guo and Masulis (2015), for example, found that the more independent the NEDs on the nomination committee the greater the chance of the CEO being dismissed following weak firm performance. Faleye et al. (2011) also observed this phenomenon when the same NEDs were on at least two or more monitoring committees. To proceed with a decision to dismiss the CEO requires adequate timely appraisal and the willingness to act despite the uncertainty linked to a new CEO, which would be a strong indicator of NEDs' true independence from management (Guo and Masulis, 2015). NEDs would have been acting in shareholders' interests by attempting to quickly reverse a low performance trend and ensuring the continued success of the firm. However, it is unlikely that a suitable new CEO could be recruited quickly and even less likely that they would be able to impact firm performance in the short term. Therefore, while NEDs would be delivering on their duties to shareholders, this is not likely to be easily captured in short-term financial data. Indeed, regulatory guidance for boards specifically refers to the need to make appointment decisions in view of the company's long-term success (FRC, 2018a).

In relation to the recruitment of other NEDs by the nomination committee, Eminet and Guedri (2010) discovered that boards with nominating committees were more likely to recruit other NEDs with strong monitoring reputations. Through this act, NEDs on nominating committees increase the overall monitoring effectiveness of the board and better protect shareholder interests (Eminet and Guedri, 2010). However, if the various monitoring activities discussed above cannot be easily linked to short-term financial performance, then the nomination committee's role in recruiting better monitors will not necessarily translate into improved firm performance in the short to medium term.

Risk committee

The risk committee, either separate to or a sub-set of the audit committee, is charged with identifying, managing, and reporting on the key risks to the business (FRC, 2014). As mentioned above, empirical research relating to risk committees and firm-level risk management has been extremely limited (Hoyt and Leibenberg, 2011; Elamer and Benyazid, 2018; Malik et al., 2020). The studies that have been conducted have generally been quantitative based on archival data, attempting to find an effect on firm financial performance/value. Even these have failed to present conclusive evidence of such a relation (Gordon et al., 2009; Elamer and Benyazid, 2018; Malik et al., 2020). For example, a UK study spanning the period 2003 to 2008 by Elamer and Benyazid (2018) found that the existence, independence, and activity of risk committees all had a negative impact on accounting measures of firm performance. On the other hand, a more recent UK study covering the period 2012 to 2015 by Malik et al. (2020) found that the composite indices for both risk committee capability and risk management activity were positively related to firm value. They argued that the effect on accounting measures would likely take time while the share price would be able to reflect the expected impact on future performance. However, market expectations may not equate to actual future performance. It is also unknown how well the market perceives the capacity of risk committees and the quality of risk management to be able to price these in appropriately. The study also does not control for other factors that would be more salient to the market, namely dividend pay-out policy and history, free cash flow, growth rate, etc. However, an earlier US study by Hoyt and Leibenberg (2011) also found a positive effect of risk management on market value, even after controlling for dividend payments, sales growth, and profitability. Yet, Gordon et al. (2009) found that risk management only impacted one-year excess stock returns when it was aligned with the business environment in terms of uncertainty, competition, and operational complexity, and this only for high-performing companies.

The lack of conclusive findings suggests that empirical research on risk management would benefit from focusing on the direct outcomes of risk management activities. Certainly, such research is extremely limited. Lam (2014), however, does discuss the direct benefits through a series of case studies. He explains that in the 1970s and 1980s, the focus of risk management was on minimising the possibility of losses, and therefore key activities related to credit control, liquidity, and insurance. Evidently, while such activities would prevent exceptional/non-recurrent losses from being incurred, they are unlikely to translate into a sustained increase in earnings. In the 1990s, risk management began to also encompass the minimisation of earnings volatility arising from fluctuations in foreign exchange rates, interest rates, inflation rates, etc. (Lam, 2014). As a result, risk-transfer products such as financial derivatives became popular; as investors valued earnings stability, they priced the shares of such companies accordingly (Lam, 2014). Again, however, these activities would result in smoother earnings rather than consistently higher profits. Pagach and Warr (2010), however, argue that both loss and volatility minimisation would improve companies' credit rating and reduce the cost of capital. Nocco and Slutz (2006) also refer to such an effect from the mere reporting of risk management activities. Easier and cheaper access to capital could certainly translate into more profitable projects being invested in, although the effects on profits are not likely to be observed over a short period, but rather as long-term projects begin to pay off. Most recently, risk management has taken a less defensive turn, aiming in the main to have better understanding of the risk profiles of different investments and activities, and therefore making better risk-return based decisions in the choice of projects (Lam, 2014). This would likely translate into higher returns (Nocco and Slutz, 2006; Hoyt and Leibenberg, 2011). However, once again, these are likely to be over an extended time period. Certainly, the US study by Pagach and Warr (2010) comparing earnings for the two years before the implementation of risk management practices to earnings for the two years after only found evidence of reduced volatility. They did not find any improvement in profitability or firm value. They also did not find changes in other variables likely to present more direct evidence of improved investments, namely borrowings, surplus cash, other reserves, asset types, research, and development, amongst others. They suggested that the effects of risk management may indeed only materialise over a much longer period.

There is clearly a need for considerable empirical research that traces the entire chain of effects of risk management activities, through direct outcomes to possible financial performance. This would help ensure that quantitative studies attempting to find an effect on firm performance are better designed to not only study the intermediate effects but also to consider the appropriate time horizon.

Monitoring in relation to strategy

NEDs' monitoring role in relation to strategy is likely to be one of the most impactful in ensuring shareholder resources are being deployed on the most productive ventures, and that the approved ventures are being well implemented (Stiles, 2001). Faleye et al. (2011), however, found that firms where boards monitored more intensely displayed less innovation. The mechanism they posit is that EDs would view such a board as less supportive for the approval of higher risk projects, and so these would not be put forward. They also identified that when firms are in high need of advisory input from NEDs, they suffer loss in value if their boards are overly focused on monitoring, at the expense of providing support. In relation to strategy, therefore, monitoring could have a direct negative impact on firm performance.

Monitoring activities, collectively considered

Clearly, there are multiple reasons why one should not expect to see a strong positive correlation between monitoring activity and firm financial performance, especially short-term performance. Consequently, conclusions from such quantitative archival studies about the effectiveness and usefulness of monitoring also need to be reconsidered. For example, Shaukat and Trojanowski (2018) build a composite governance index incorporating the UK Corporate Governance Code's prescriptions relating to the independence of the board and the three main monitoring committees (remuneration, audit, and nomination). They find a significant association between this measure and subsequent period financial performance for UK listed companies. However, subsequent period performance appears to be closely correlated with financial performance in the index measurement year but is not controlled for in this element of the study. Indeed, others, such as Akbar et al. (2016), found considerable evidence of endogeneity between financial performance and a similar corporate governance index for UK listed companies. Shaukat and Trojanowski (2018) attempt to address endogeneity concerns by also analysing the relationship between drops in the index and financial performance in the subsequent period. They find a significant association and conclude that this provides evidence of managerial opportunism rather than efficiency motives, and that it also proves that monitoring capacity translates into monitoring activity which then disciplines management into delivering better financial performance. However, the implications of managerial opportunism require further consideration. The only plausible form of managerial opportunism in this case would be that management had knowledge of a likely forthcoming deterioration in financials and wanted to purposefully reduce the monitoring capacity of the board and its committees to reduce the accountability pressure. This certainly does not suggest that management would have wanted to lower monitoring activity knowing this would directly lead to reduced financial performance on which their many incentives depend. In sum, much more empirical research is needed to elucidate these mechanisms.

Resource provision

The relationship between resource provision activities and firm performance may be easier to rationalise. Indeed, Hillman and Dalziel (2003) proposed such a link, and Jermias and Gani (2014) found a positive and significant association between board capital and firm performance in terms of market value relative to book value. However, the time it would take from the performing of resource provision activities (by a board with capital) to its effects manifesting in reported financial performance/share price would be considerable, as the following discussion demonstrates by analysing each of the different aspects of resource provision in turn. Future research will therefore need to recognise this lag to give greater credence to its findings.

Pfeffer and Salancik ([1978] 2003) conceptualised firms as being dependent on their environments for their success. NEDs, with their external exposure and networks, are considered vital in enabling firms to connect with the outside world on which they rely (Hillman and Dalziel, 2003). They would, therefore, be instrumental in matters such as securing private and/ or government finance, identifying acquisition targets, and sealing important business deals, amongst others (Hillman and Dalziel, 2003). Such activities ensure the firm continues to thrive into the future; their announcements may also trigger share price rises based on expectations of future firm performance. However, the actual realisation of the benefits of such access would take place over a long period of time as they are put to good use in the business.

NEDs also tend to be from diverse backgrounds, from the legal profession to academia; many also continue to serve as executives in other businesses or have knowledge of government workings from their previous posts (Hillman and Dalziel, 2003). They are, therefore, very well placed to advise and support management in developing as well as implementing strategy (Pfeffer and Salancik, [1978] 2003; Jermias and Gani, 2014; Boivie et al., 2016). Pugliese et al. (2009) indeed discuss some evidence of such activities from other studies. NEDs' advisory and support activities are expected to ensure higher-quality decisions and greater operational effectiveness by management, which would feed into enhanced firm performance (Jermias and Gani, 2014). However, this is likely to be a gradual effect over a long period of time, as it takes time for decisions to be implemented and for their rewards to be reaped.

An even more indirect and unclear effect on firm performance would emanate from NEDs' involvement in bridging the communication gap with external stakeholders, a role considered significant by many; e.g., Pfeffer and Salancik ([1978] 2003) and Boivie et al. (2016). This has certainly come into focus with the revised UK Corporate Governance Code emphasising the need to consider the interests of all stakeholders (FRC, 2018b). Additionally, the UK's revised Stewardship Code requires greater engagement of investment managers with corporate directors on such matters as well as those impacting shareholders more directly (FRC, 2019). Better communication may improve transparency with investors and others and help raise the firm's reputation (Boivie et al., 2016). This may indeed positively impact the share price and perhaps also ensure easier access to funds subsequently. While this may in turn ensure the future survival and ongoing success of the firm, it is less clear whether the benefits would materialise into enhanced distributable profits in the shorter term.

In summary, research will need to take a more careful and considered approach, acknowledging the complex mechanisms linking monitoring and resource provision activities to observable firm performance, if it is to credibly advance the state of knowledge in this field.

3.   A BEHAVIOURAL ANALYTIC FRAMEWORK

3.1   Introduction

Jon Elster (2000) modified Max Weber's theory of rationality using advances in the domain of cognitive psychology to develop a more comprehensive behavioural theory. Within this framework, an individual's decision/action/behaviour is never objectively rational, but subjectively so; i.e., it is perceived to be optimal by the individual. The decision/action/behaviour itself is determined by a complex interplay of one's desires and beliefs, themselves conditioned by the information one obtains/receives. The behavioural analytic framework proposed for the study of NEDs' actions is an adaptation and an application of the modified theory presented by Jon Elster (2000). The term 'desires' is substituted by the term 'aims' and the concept of 'beliefs' is replaced by 'perceptions' as they fit better within the context of corporate governance.

Figure 6.2 summarises the key constructs that are considered and discussed below within each of these main determinants of NEDs' behaviour. 'Aims' capture NEDs' possible motivations for taking on these roles; these are expected to significantly impact their focus. Perceptions have two main elements: NEDs' perceptions of their accountability (to whom and for what) and their perceptions of constraints in their role. Information from the environment feeds back into both aims and perceptions. Regulatory prescriptions about the role of NEDs are expected to influence both the aims and the accountability perceptions of NEDs. As highlighted earlier, the regulatory environment discussion relates to the UK but can be adapted for studies in other countries.

Within the behavioural framework, it is also possible that NEDs adjust/set their aims subject to who they perceive to be accountable to and what they perceive to be achievable in the role. The resulting behaviour encompasses both the monitoring and resource provision roles and the degrees of intensity with which the respective roles may be performed. The framework attempts to capture the key factors that can be expected to shape NEDs' behaviour. The framework guided by Elster (2000), and as summarised in Figure 6.2, therefore provides an organising structure for the study of the interplay of factors that have typically been studied independently. This addresses calls by Fairchild et al. (2019) and Marnet (2007) for the development of a more comprehensive framework for the study of corporate governance actors, one that incorporates the 'social and psychological factors' impacting NEDs' behaviour. It responds to the need to look beyond the effects of rules, regulations, and legal repercussions to access other possibly more salient factors motivating behaviour, which would better inform policy formulations (Marnet, 2007). Accordingly, the framework includes factors possibly constraining NEDs' behaviour, such as social ties with EDs, dependence on EDs for remuneration but also information, the need to conform, and the effect of dominant personalities; i.e., key factors highlighted by Fairchild et al. (2019) and Marnet (2007). The UK regulatory guidance for directors on how to ensure board effectiveness specifically refers to the likely impact of several of these socio-psychological factors, namely conflicts of interest, emotional attachments, inadequate knowledge, information and time, and groupthink, amongst others (FRC, 2018a). The proposed framework, as summarised in Figure 6.2 and discussed further below, includes these factors alongside the regulatory structures.

However, a study of how each of these factors individually and together impacts NEDs' behaviour requires an appreciation of the bounded rationality of humans; i.e., the limitations of human processing capabilities (Simon, 1972; Simon et al., 2000). For example, NEDs may not

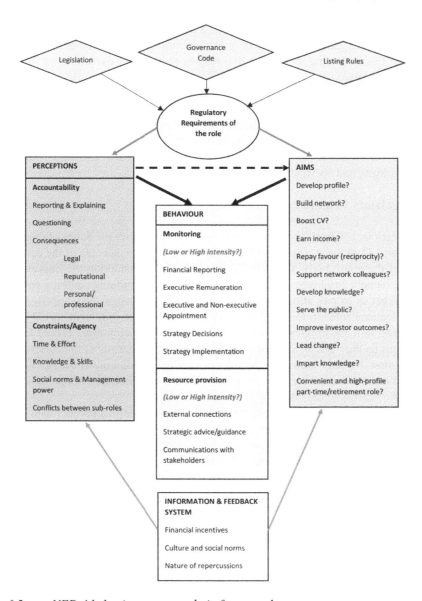

Figure 6.2   NEDs' behaviour – an analytic framework

have clear understanding of their aims; and even if they do, they may not behave consistently with their aims (Marnet, 2007). They are also unlikely to have comprehensively considered all the factors in the framework when deciding on their position, especially as the factors represent conflicting forces (Kahneman, 2003; Marnet, 2007). They may also not have correctly interpreted the impact of behavioural and cognitive factors (Kahneman, 2003; Marnet, 2007); e.g., they may simply not have an appropriate awareness of the risk of legal repercussions. Tversky and Kahneman (1974) and Kahneman (2003) discuss the implications of the ease with which such factors and their characteristics can be evoked. Lau and Coiera (2007) discuss the exposure effect. Certainly, therefore, a lack of exposure to information about legal repercussions could mean that this factor is not appropriately weighted or even considered. Alternatively, despite having the facts, NEDs may be particularly overconfident or optimistic in their interpretation of the likelihood of certain outcomes (Langevoort, 1998; Fairchild et al., 2019). Humans tend to over-discount future uncertain events (Kahneman and Tversky, 1979; Langevoort, 1998; Kahneman, 2003). Also, NEDs may simply not have conscious awareness of their biases created by the complex interplay of the factors (Bazerman et al., 2002; Fairchild et al., 2019). Understanding how this imperfect reasoning takes place in the context of multiple forces and how this then sets up NEDs' behaviour is key to be able to assess the relative effects of regulatory, legal, and social structures (Marnet, 2007).

3.2   Regulatory Requirements of the Role

In the UK, Sections 170 to 177 of the Companies Act 2006 specify the duties of directors (CA, 2006). Section 172 of the Act refers to the 'Duty to promote the success of the company' for the benefit of the entire body of shareholders, while also considering the interests of other stakeholders, namely employees, suppliers, customers, the community, and the environment. It requires directors to pay attention to the longer-term success of the company. The other noteworthy sections refer to the need to 'exercise independent judgment' (s173), 'exercise reasonable care, skill and diligence' (s174) and 'avoid conflicts of interest' (s175). Essentially, there is a focus on the need to act with integrity, putting the interests of the company and the shareholders first. Notably, however, the Act (as in other jurisdictions) does not differentiate between EDs and NEDs, and certainly does not delineate the roles of EDs from those of NEDs in ensuring the success of the company (Aguilera, 2005).

The UK Corporate Governance Code, on the other hand, is aimed predominantly at NEDs and emphasises their role as monitors of management's performance (FRC, 2018b). It sets out the specific expectations of directors' responsibilities as members of the main monitoring committees, namely audit, nomination, and remuneration. It makes explicit the need to consider the long-term success of the company. While compliance with the Code is not obligatory, the UK's Listing Rules do require disclosure of how the principles of the Code have been applied, and to provide explanations if any have not (MacNeil and Li, 2006; FRC, 2018b).

The UK Corporate Governance Code certainly refers to the need for the unitary board to focus on identifying opportunities and risks and on devising appropriate strategy for long-term success (FRC, 2018b). However, its specific guidance on NEDs' role relates to the monitoring committees. NEDs could therefore perceive that they would be most accountable for their role as monitors of management, rather than as providers of resources, namely advice, connections, etc. (Boivie et al., 2016). The particular emphasis on the functioning of the audit, nomination, and remuneration committees within the Code also appears to leave out other possibly more significant monitoring activities. For example, Stiles (2001) discusses the board's monitoring role with respect to strategy as assessing management's strategy proposals and their subsequent implementation. Clearly, the effect of the Act and the Code in NEDs' formulation of their aims and focus deserves attention from an empirical perspective.

3.3   Perceptions of Accountability

As discussed above, Section 172 of the Companies Act 2006 refers to directors needing to work in the interests of shareholders collectively. Certainly, the UK regulatory framework sets out mechanisms to ensure NEDs are accountable to shareholders through the requirements for reporting, explaining/justifying, being questioned, and bearing the consequences of poor conduct (Keay and Loughrey, 2015).

Reporting and explaining
In terms of reporting and explaining, the Companies Act 2006 requires directors to publish (as part of the annual report) the company's audited financial statements, a directors' report, reports of the work of the audit committee, and a strategic report to explain how they have met their statutory obligations under s172 to ensure the long-term success of the company for shareholders (CA, 2006, Keay and Loughrey, 2015). The recently revised UK Corporate Governance Code, which came into effect at the beginning of 2019, now also requires greater reporting on engagement with the workforce, building the appropriate culture for the long-term success of the company, the skills mix of directors, board evaluation, succession planning, and executive remuneration needing to consider workforce remuneration (FRC, 2018b).

The Business, Energy, and Industrial Strategy (BEIS) department of the UK government has also published proposals for detailed reporting on some additional areas, namely the effectiveness of internal controls; the impact of proposed dividends on distributable reserves and solvency; measures to address the short-, medium-, and long-term risks facing the business, including climate change; the wider scope of their audit and assurance policy; and supplier payment practices (BEIS, 2021). The reporting and explaining requirements are the first layer of ensuring directors feel accountable to shareholders (Keay and Loughrey, 2015), many of whom also make decisions based on companies' regard for the environment and society generally (FRC, 2019). However, the extent to which reporting and explaining requirements mould NEDs' perceptions of who they are accountable to and for what is an unknown.

There is, however, evidence that the 'comply or explain' principle underlying the UK Corporate Governance Code may not be achieving its aims. For example, MacNeil and Li (2006) report that the compliance assessment by PIRC (Pensions Investment Research Consultants) in 2004 showed that, in their reports, companies were greatly over-stating their degree of compliance. The recent review of the application of the revised UK Corporate Governance Code by the regulator, the Financial Reporting Council (FRC), also highlighted companies' persistence at claiming full compliance when in fact they were not compliant (FRC, 2020). The FRC's report also found that, generally, explanations were poor and there was a 'tick-boxing' attitude to compliance. Shaukat and Trojanowski (2018) also found that actions to reduce the independence of the key monitoring committees preceded deterioration in financial performance; i.e., management can opportunistically reduce monitoring capacity because of the flexibility provided by the 'comply or explain' principle of the Code. The lack of commitment to adhering to the Code's principles and to providing adequate explanations suggests that perhaps UK corporate boards may not perceive themselves as being accountable to shareholders, let alone wider stakeholders.

Questioning

As regards the next layer of accountability – i.e., being subject to questioning by shareholders – MacNeil and Li (2006) discuss the likely difficulty of investors in assessing directors' reports on compliance. They also refer to evidence showing a positive association between non-compliance and financial performance, suggesting that investors may be forgiving any possible non-compliance where companies were performing well financially. Certainly, Coffee (2006) discussed this behaviour in relation to Enron and the stock market bubble. The generally documented lack of engagement by institutional investors also adds to weaknesses in this layer of accountability mechanism (BEIS, 2019, p. 19). It is unclear, however, whether the new UK Stewardship Code 2020 which requires reporting by investment managers on how they have discharged their duties (FRC, 2019), will make investment managers more proactive in addressing issues with corporations. There are certainly fears that it would lead to another layer of 'boiler-plate' reporting, this time from the representatives of investors (Webster in Irvine, 2019). Such behaviour on the part of investors likely feeds back into directors' perceptions of accountability.

Consequences

Shareholder action ex ante

UK law confers considerable powers to shareholders to prevent boards making significant decisions that are not in shareholders' interests (Armour et al., 2009). However, for most major decisions, only a simple majority shareholder approval is required (CA, 2006). Also, in many instances where shareholder dissent fails to reach the 51 per cent mark, the board is under no legal obligation to consider the view of the dissenting shareholders. Additionally, for some matters, the shareholder vote only has advisory status; i.e., it is not binding on the board, as in the case of the Directors' Remuneration Report (DRR) Regulations introduced in 2002 requiring an annual shareholder vote on directors' remuneration (Conyon and Sadler, 2010). Nonetheless, one would expect NEDs acting on the remuneration committee to take seriously shareholder dissent relating to executive compensation. Certainly, the UK Code requires the board to understand the reasons for significant shareholder disagreement and to report on its actions in relation to the matter (FRC, 2018b). However, over 30 UK listed companies were on the Investment Association's register of investor revolts (shareholder dissent of 20 per cent or over) for two consecutive years for the same issue, mainly regarding directors' remuneration and re-election (Irvine, 2018). Other high-profile cases of shareholder rebellions against excess executive pay and stubbornly unresponsive remuneration committees have led the UK Parliamentary Work and Pensions Committee to intervene and write to the remuneration committee, as in the case of the Lloyds Banking Group (McCance, 2019). The evidence therefore appears to suggest that despite the structures in place for investors to voice their opinions, they may not be the body NEDs feel singularly accountable to.

Legal enforcement as an ex-post mechanism

The perception of the possibility of legal action and the ensuing financial and reputational repercussions would be expected to impact NEDs' behaviour and thereby the outcomes for the firm (Basu and Liang, 2019). However, Armour et al. (2009) find that the UK 'has strong substantive corporate law but almost no formal private enforcement of that law against directors of publicly traded companies' (p. 721). They explain that UK directors' duties are primarily to the company, albeit for the benefit of shareholders, hence the near absence of direct legal enforcement by shareholders. Any litigation would have to be by the company itself, and the board would generally not turn against one of its NEDs (Armour et al., 2009). In addition to the lack of evidence of private enforcement, they also find minimal cases of public enforcement by the Financial Conduct Authority, the securities regulator. Disqualification of directors of insolvent public limited companies (PLCs) by the BEIS department is also rare as it is uncommon for PLCs to enter insolvency proceedings (Armour et al., 2009). Disqualification, if not for a substantial period, may also have little deterrence effect. For example, there was widespread criticism of the relatively short periods of three to six years for which the directors of MG Rover Group were disqualified to act as directors of other UK companies (I&L, 2011). Some argued they should have been made to repay the very large sums they had drawn from the company, which ultimately became insolvent (I&L, 2011). Disqualification proceedings have also begun against the directors of Carillion, which collapsed in 2018, although there is concern about the generally low likelihood of success with such proceedings (Lex, 2021).

Additionally, based on evidence from the US, one would expect that where private or public legal enforcement against directors did take place, it would be the executives rather than the non-executives who would be the main targets (Armour et al., 2009; Brochet and Srinivasan, 2014). However, US evidence also shows that NEDs who serve as members of the audit committee and are therefore responsible for financial reporting and controls are more likely to be named in securities lawsuits; these are also more likely to be settled, and for higher amounts (Brochet and Srinivasan, 2014). In other words, while the likelihood of enforcement is low, and particularly so for NEDs, they are somewhat more exposed for their monitoring roles, especially in respect of financial aspects of governance. It is unclear, however, whether this may be leading to a bias in their focus. In any case, Director and Officer (D&O) insurance generally covers any legal settlement costs that may arise for NEDs, unless the case relates to fraud (Black, Cheffins, and Kausner, 2006, in Brochet and Srinivasan, 2014).

While objectively there appears to be a low legal risk for NEDs and even more so in the UK, it is possible that they may be perceiving the risk to be higher than it truly is, with lawyers and the press likely exaggerating the risk (Langevoort, 2001). On the other hand, NEDs, as with EDs, may possess attributes of over-confidence, leading them to discount any possible legal threat (Langevoort, 2001). The distant and uncertain nature of such repercussions may also mean they are given even less consideration and weight than economic rationality would suggest (Langevoort, 1998). Although it is indeed the perceived rather than the actual threat that would drive NEDs' behaviour, this is an area that has received little empirical research (Langevoort, 2001).

Nonetheless, the numerous high-profile cases of failures in corporate governance and a less than threatening legal environment have led the BEIS department to consider proposals for greater public enforcement by the proposed new regulator, ARGA (Audit, Reporting and Governance Authority), due to replace the FRC (BEIS, 2021). These powers are intended to include clawbacks of directors' remuneration for wrongdoing (BEIS, 2021). The effectiveness of these powers will certainly depend on successful enforcement. However, some, like Jensen (1993) and Langevoort (2001), have argued that legal and regulatory controls create an environment where boards are more concerned with 'covering their backs' than driving long-term success for the company. Others, on the other hand, like Basu and Liang (2019), appear to support greater director liability as they provide evidence of a link in the US between reductions in director liability and the expected outcomes of reduced monitoring of financial reporting. The behavioural mechanism, however, in terms of how changes in regulatory repercussions impact risk perception by directors and how that affects their focus, has not been directly studied. Kleck et al. (2005) empirically studied this issue in relation to crime generally using a large-scale telephone survey. They found that higher actual levels of punishment did not translate into a perception of more severe legal repercussions, most likely because of limited exposure to information about such risks. They argue therefore that greater deterrence measures do not have the desired effects and that measures that address core motives would likely be more productive.

Reputational consequences
Fama and Jensen (1983) argued that the need to maintain a good reputation as effective monitors would be sufficient motivation for NEDs. The question then is to what extent are monitoring failures punished by the market for NEDs, and how much weighting do NEDs place on this effect. To this end, Fich and Shivdasani (2007) found that NEDs of US companies sued for financial fraud lost a considerable number of seats at other boards, and this effect was greater for NEDs who served on the audit committee. Institutional Shareholder Services (ISS) play a key role in this process through their recommendations to shareholders on director voting decisions (Cai et al., 2009). ISS's policy is to recommend a vote against directors involved in misconduct on other boards, or for major corporate governance failures (ISS, 2020). Cai et al. (2009) found that such a recommendation from ISS led to a 19 per cent drop in vote share in their US study, although it did not generally lead to the director being removed. However, they found that improvements in governance practices did follow shareholder dissent. To the extent that these US studies also reflect the UK environment, there would appear to be reputational repercussions of poor monitoring in the UK too. One would therefore expect UK NEDs to be aware of these, and to consequently maintain high monitoring intensity.

Companies' poor financial performance also appears to have reputational effects for NEDs in terms of offers to join other boards, as per the US archival study by Ferris et al. (2003). This clearly reflects investors' expectations of NEDs' contributions. However, to what extent NEDs believe they indeed influence a company's financial performance is another matter. If indeed NEDs perceive that resource provision – i.e., the provision of advice, support, and connections – has the most significant impact on firm financial performance, then one would expect them to focus their efforts on this role. Monitoring, on the other hand, may have the opposite effect on their reputation, especially when aimed at preventing the reporting of inflated financials. Lower monitoring may allow financials to reflect a rosier picture, thereby boosting their reputation in the market.

Indeed, Westphal and Stern (2007) found that greater advisory work and lower monitoring activity were associated with a larger number of new seats on other boards for US NEDs both before and after the Sarbanes–Oxley Act came into effect. However, the reputational effects they found were related to NEDs' image in the eyes of the executives rather than investors, as validated by their pre- and post-survey interviews with NEDs. Through interviews and a survey, Westphal and Khanna (2003) also found that US NEDs experienced 'social distancing' on other boards if they had been involved with implementing stricter governance practices on a board. NEDs reported being left out of decision-making or having their views and advice ignored. As a result, they would subsequently avoid engaging in the set-up of greater executive monitoring systems. Campbell-Meiklejohn and Frith (2012) indeed discuss how one's social behaviour is subconsciously guided by what one perceives gives us a reputation for cooperation. Certainly, in relation to NEDs' behaviour, there is a need to study the effect of such perverse reputational effects, alongside their perceptions of other incentives and deterrents within a specific regulatory context.

Personal, professional, and social consequences
Clearly, despite the legal position whereby NEDs are meant to be accountable to shareholders, who they truly feel accountable to may be quite different. Aguilera (2005) highlights the significance of NEDs' nomination process in terms of who they might perceive allegiance towards. She points to the relative impotence of the legal right of shareholders to approve NEDs' appointments to the board vis-à-vis executives' roles in identifying suitable NEDs and putting them forward for nomination.

Indeed, considerable research effort has been devoted to studying social ties between executives and non-executives and their impact on monitoring outcomes. Bruynseels and Cardinaels (2014), for example, found that such social connections existed in about 40 per cent of cases, years after the passage of the Sarbanes–Oxley Act. They also found that such links were associated with lower financial reporting quality and less disclosure of internal control weaknesses, suggesting possibly lower monitoring effort by NEDs. Larcker et al. (2005) found that the closer NEDs' network links with executives through other boards, the higher the CEO's pay, and they highlighted the fact that such complex links through a network of boards are not caught by corporate governance rules on independence. Stern and Westphal (2010), through a survey and interviews, found that NEDs and EDs of large US firms had fellow directors on other boards who were able to propose their appointment to those other boards. They also found that the more directors engaged in 'ingratiatory' behaviour towards their colleagues, the greater their chances of being put forward for appointments on other boards. Fracassi and Tate (2012) also found evidence of CEOs continuing to select NEDs from their network, which was then associated with flawed business acquisition decisions. However, as they rightly point out, there remains a gap in empirical knowledge about why such connected NEDs may be exerting less monitoring effort: is it to sustain valuable relationships or because they naturally support the CEO's agenda, coming from the same background? Indeed, UK governance guidance emphasises the need for diversity in the boardroom in terms of skills and background (FRC, 2018a). However, it is unclear how strong the incentives are for directors to ensure true diversity and encourage real challenge. As Langevoort (2001) explained, regulations have little sway on how boards are constituted; instead, the general rule of ensuring a good working relationship dominates director selection.

Although, according to Fama and Jensen (1983), one would expect EDs to choose their NEDs based on how they could contribute to the business, they certainly did not anticipate that such choice would create monitoring weaknesses. In fact, notwithstanding the existence of social ties, the sheer dependence on the CEO for their appointment could sway NEDs' accountability to management rather than shareholders. Boivie et al. (2016) discuss NEDs' possible feelings of obligation towards a CEO if the latter had been instrumental in their appointment; they may then perceive that their role should primarily be to 'rubber-stamp' the CEO's activities. Indeed, Coffee (2006) highlighted this issue as explaining the passivity of NEDs in the Enron case, and Langevoort (2001) pointed to the strong reciprocity culture in boardrooms. Fairchild et al. (2019) also identify this as a key ingredient in explaining the cases of corporate failure they study. However, there is certainly a need for more research in this area which accesses direct empirical evidence of these behavioural mechanisms, and in the broader population of boardrooms. Generally, other than some case studies of serious corporate failures, the focus has been on demonstrating a statistical association between indicators of CEOs' involvement in board selection and the likely outcomes of less than effective monitoring; e.g., financial statement restatements by Carcello et al. (2011).

UK policy makers are clearly becoming increasingly concerned with the issue of management effectively selecting its own monitors, and the implications for accountability. This is evident from the latest proposals from the UK's BEIS department requiring more direct supervision of audit committee activities by the regulator (BEIS, 2021). However, an assessment of the likely impact of such regulation requires substantial empirical research on how NEDs balance these personal, professional, and social consequences against other regulatory forces and how this leads them to adjust their monitoring/resource provision activities.

3.4   Perceptions of constraints vs agency

Notwithstanding social ties and consequences, there may be factors constraining well-intentioned NEDs in their ability not only to discharge their monitoring duties but also to deliver on resource provision.

Time and effort
The time available to NEDs as compared to the time and effort that would be required for them to perform both roles effectively is considered a possible significant constraint on them (Brennan, 2006; Boivie et al., 2016). Multiple directorships are believed to exacerbate this problem; e.g., Sharma and Iselin (2012) found that where audit committee members served on multiple boards, there was a greater likelihood of financial misstatements, suggesting they 'may be stretched too thinly to effectively perform their monitoring responsibilities' (p. 149). However, Ferris et al. (2003) found that multiple directorships did not reduce NEDs' activity level in terms of number of meetings attended. They also found no relation between multiple directorships and litigation. The issue certainly needs to be studied directly from the perspective of NEDs' lived experiences. It may be that an awareness of these constraints leads NEDs to choose to perform a passive role.

Knowledge and skills
Boivie et al. (2016) discuss the salience of the knowledge barrier. They contend that the monitoring role, especially in relation to strategy, would require NEDs to have a thorough grasp of the business and the environment within which it operated, and yet most NEDs would not have such extensive knowledge, especially for large and complex organisations. They argue that the effort that would be required for NEDs to gain the necessary knowledge and understanding would be prohibitive. As a result, NEDs may simply not be able to deliver on their monitoring duties and may therefore focus on resource provision activities as these would make less demand on their time and cognitive effort (Boivie et al., 2016).

Not having the necessary skills or training may also be an impediment to monitoring. Coffee (2006) certainly highlighted NEDs' reliance on external advisors for their monitoring duties; he referred to the 'gatekeepers' being the auditors, the lawyers, and the analysts. Indeed, through interviews, Beasley et al. (2009) found that audit committee members were not confident in their ability to detect fraud or the misstatement of reported financials; they relied instead on external auditors. Reliance on management for the information NEDs need to monitor them also presents a significant challenge (Jensen, 1993; Aguilera, 2005). Turley and Zaman (2007) concluded the same based on a case study of audit committee processes. They noted that the audit committee's activities were limited by the extent to which internal auditors, external auditors, and management provided them with the necessary information and on time. Fairchild et al. (2019) also refer to these issues in their study of four high-profile cases of corporate governance failure. Similar findings also emerged from a unique ethnographic case study of governance by Collier (2005) where he was a board member for a quasi-public sector entity over a period of three years. He found that governance was constrained by the selectivity of information and narrative presented by management, and by NEDs' own limited financial competence.

Additionally, through interviews, Hendry et al. (2010) found considerable evidence of NEDs' and EDs' perception that NEDs did not have the necessary in-depth knowledge of the business to be able to make a significant contribution to strategy. In other words, NEDs' lack of knowledge and skills may be constraining their ability to meet the high expectations of them in multiple areas.

Social norms and management power

Behaviour is believed to also be determined by the need to belong to a social group; this creates a tendency towards conformity; i.e., matching one's views and actions with the expectations of others around us to be accepted into the group (Campbell-Meiklejohn and Frith, 2012). Boivie et al. (2016) refer to 'norms of deference to the CEO' that may exist on corporate boards and that would dictate NEDs' behaviour. Marnet (2007) discusses the effect of social pressures to conform. Indeed, Jensen (1993) discussed how CEOs' own insecurities would lead them to create an environment that discourages monitoring effort, and that regulations would remain ineffectual in the face of such culture.

Bebchuk et al. (2002) analysed a large body of work to conclude that the prevalence of sub-optimal executive remuneration packages implied management was heavily involved in the decision process, and that competent and independent NEDs did not appear to be able to change the course of events. From an analysis of interviews with US NEDs as audit committee members, Beasley et al. (2009) also concluded that NEDs' ability to play a 'substantive role' was limited by management's determination to control processes and outcomes. In the same vein, interviews with US external auditors by Cohen et al. (2010) revealed that management continued to steer decisions on the hiring and dismissing of auditors. The interviews also highlighted that half of audit committee members did not have a significant input even in the resolution of disputes between auditors and management. Fiolleau et al. (2013) also found the same in a Canadian case study, as well as Dhaliwal et al. (2015) using archival US data. Similarly, with involvement in strategy, many NEDs felt heavily constrained by management even when they had the necessary knowledge to contribute (Hendry et al., 2010). NEDs and CEOs interviewed by Finkelstein and Mooney (2003) for their US study both highlighted CEOs' disapproval of disputes in the boardroom. This dissuaded the necessary challenge that NEDs are generally expected to bring to the table. Langevoort (2001) and Hambrick et al. (2008) also referred to the general tendency towards agreement rather than challenge in boardrooms.

However, despite some inroads, as discussed above, generally the issue of behavioural constraints created by such socio-psychological dynamics has received little attention in terms of empirical academic research (Marnet, 2007; Hambrick et al., 2008; Fairchild et al., 2019).

Certainly, NEDs' inability to impose a different culture and mode of operation is likely linked to their perception of accountability to management. Alternatively, it may indeed be a case of 'pluralistic ignorance' such that each NED perceives that they may be the only one feeling uneasy and that they are unlikely to have the support of other NEDs in pushing a different agenda (Westphal and Bednar, 2005).

John Roberts argues that excessive focus on the 'formal, hierarchical system of accountability' – i.e., with NEDs tasked to control EDs – can have negative consequences, and that 'socialising forms of accountability' based on informal relationships and interactions and a sense of reciprocity can provide a better forum for open discussions (Roberts, 1991, 2001). However, his argument is on the basis that power is distributed equally amongst the parties in the informal realm. This may indeed not be the case, as discussed above, with management effectively controlling NEDs' appointment, and having far superior knowledge of the business.

Conflicts between sub-roles
The agency of NEDs also needs to be considered in the context of the likely behavioural implications of managing their seemingly conflicting roles of monitoring versus supporting (Hillman et al., 2008; Pugliese et al., 2009). Ethiraj and Levinthal (2009) explored the cognitive challenge involved in working across incompatible goals within a business environment, even when there are no issues relating to inherent commitment to the respective goals. Unsworth et al. (2014) studied a large body of work on behaviour when faced with multiple divergent goals and derived some general principles that in such situations one proceeds to resolve the conflict primarily through some means of prioritisation. It could be that the goal/role that better enables one's higher personal aims to be achieved is prioritised, or the goal/role that brings us the most intrinsic satisfaction or that requires the least effort to achieve (Unsworth et al., 2014). However, empirical research on this dilemma within the corporate governance context is all but lacking. One could conjecture, based on the foregoing discussions, that NEDs would perceive the monitoring role to be less pleasant given that it may put them in a confrontational position vis-à-vis management. This may also cost them in terms of possible seats at other boards. Monitoring would also require considerable collaboration from management in terms of the provision of information needed to carry out the monitoring. As a result, NEDs may prioritise resource provision at the expense of monitoring. Stiles (2001) indeed found evidence from interviews with directors that they were focusing more on contributing to strategy than on monitoring activities. However, NEDs' role in relation to strategy was found to be more of a monitoring nature, whereby they would simply carry out some questioning on management's proposals, which itself led to limited changes to strategy.

An alternative view that has been put forward is that NEDs successfully navigate the supposedly contradictory requirements of their role. Sundaramurthy and Lewis (2003) suggested that by collaborating with and supporting management, NEDs help develop management's trust. This in turn makes management more forthcoming with information that NEDs would need to better monitor them; they would also then be more open to constructive feedback. Adams and Ferreira (2007) put forward a similar theory. Langevoort (2001) also supported the view that excessive challenge reduces trust, which then impedes communication and leads management to engage in more 'image management', all of which makes monitoring more difficult. Evidence from interviews carried out as part of a regulatory review in the UK suggests NEDs indeed engage in this complex act of assistance/encouragement/support alongside questioning/debate/challenge (Roberts et al., 2005). However, given the circumstances of the interviews, it is possible that NEDs may have presented a picture of proficiency at all their sub-roles for fear of more draconian regulatory measures.

Further goal conflict is likely arising from the increasing regulatory emphasis on meeting the needs of a wider set of stakeholders as the financial success of the company is required to be considered alongside the interests of workers, business partners, the environment, and society at large (Nicholson and Kiel, 2007; FRC, 2018b). As mentioned earlier, the revised UK Corporate Governance Code now requires more emphasis on such matters when directors report on how they have discharged their duties under s172 of the Companies Act 2006 (FRC, 2018b). The pressure on directors could be expected to have increased further following the issuance of the revised Stewardship Code. The new Code requires investment managers as representatives of investors to report on their activities in holding directors to account on these matters (FRC, 2019). This added layer of complexity in NEDs' prioritisation activities further supports the need for more comprehensive empirical research on how NEDs perceive and manage these goals and why.

3.5   Aims

Personal aims

Ultimately one's actions are determined by both one's perceptions ('beliefs'), themselves constructed from the information we gather/receive, and one's aims ('desires') (Elster, 2000). The reasons, therefore, why NEDs take on these roles would have a significant impact on understanding the choices they make in terms of their focus, and yet our knowledge of this area is minimal (Hambrick et al., 2008; Fracassi and Tate, 2012; Withers et al., 2012). This issue becomes even more salient given the numerous likely constraints on their ability to deliver on their roles, which NEDs would have already perceived. In other words, the question is why would NEDs take on duties they knew they would struggle to discharge? Indeed, their perceptions (of their accountability and constraints) may themselves influence their motivations/aims.

Hambrick et al. (2008) contemplate several possible aims that NEDs may entertain, namely increasing their income sources, gaining knowledge of other boards and businesses, raising their profile, and/or reciprocating on their obligation to other directors. Fracassi and Tate (2012) question if NEDs take on these roles to support the plans of CEOs whom they may have ties with. Adams (2017) also suggests the need to consider the possibly specific psychological attributes of directors which would condition their aims. Undoubtedly, regulators and investors would hope that directors' aims would relate to serving the investing public, protecting stakeholders' interests, imparting knowledge, leading positive change, and enforcing high ethical standards. However, direct access to NEDs' motivations and how these interact with their perceptions of accountability and constraints to impact their behaviour has been limited. Yet, the resulting knowledge would be vital to ensure policy formulations have the desired effects.

Incentives

While personal aims refer more to intrinsic motivations, incentives represent an extrinsic motivational factor to influence behaviour that may not already be aligned with the desired outcomes. Fama and Jensen (1983) posited that NEDs' incentives to monitor relate to their need to maintain a reputation for monitoring. They believed that this would be strong enough to deter NEDs conspiring with EDs in acting against shareholder interests. However, as the foregoing discussion on reputational consequences has shown, the more relevant reputation may be vis-à-vis management itself. With multiple forces pulling NEDs towards allying with EDs, and a weak system of legal and reputational repercussions, there is potentially a case for strong monetary incentives to tilt the balance for NEDs towards protecting shareholders (Bebchuk et al., 2002). To this end, Jensen (1993) and Elson (1996) argued for NEDs to have a substantial shareholding in the company as a means of aligning their economic incentives with those of the remaining body of shareholders. Yet, the UK Corporate Governance Code on the independence of NEDs requires that they do not have any major shareholding in the company (FRC, 2018b). Certainly, the liquidity of shareholdings in listed companies presents challenges of its own as it can encourage short-term opportunistic behaviour (Zeff, 2003; D.A. Cohen et al., 2008).

In terms of empirical research in this area, a meta-analysis by Dalton et al. (2003) found that NEDs' equity holdings have a very low impact on firm financial performance. However, as discussed at length in Section 2 of this chapter, this outcome is plausible even in the context of high monitoring activity by NEDs. A study by Bhagat and Black (2002) which was not included in the meta-analysis by Dalton et al. (2003) did indeed show a positive association with long-term financial performance. More importantly, those studying the impact of equity holdings on direct outcomes of monitoring tend to find a stronger link. For example, Carcello and Neal (2003) found that the larger the equity holdings of audit committee members, the less likely they were to dismiss external auditors for issuing an audit report qualified for going concern. Ahmed and Duellman (2007) also found a positive link with greater accounting conservatism, while Sapp (2008) found greater NED shareholdings associated with lower CEO remuneration. These studies, however, do not confirm causality and certainly do not capture the full behavioural mechanism in terms of how the financial incentives may overcome or exacerbate the other forces at play for NEDs, and it would be difficult to recommend changes to the Code without such clarity.

Nonetheless, what is evident is that the need to incentivise NEDs reflects an agency problem between shareholders as principals and NEDs as agents, something that has not been given due attention. Notably, Jensen and Meckling (1976) expected that the agency problem would not arise solely between shareholders and management, and that it would be prevalent in many other relationships. They also believed that the exploration of other agency situations would advance organisational theory. Indeed, gaining clarity on the effect of accountability structures and incentives on NEDs' attitude towards discharging their responsibilities to investors would significantly improve policy decisions. However, the constraints to their agency would also need to be considered concurrently.

3.6   Résumé

The foregoing discussion in sections 3.1 to 3.5 relates to the academic evidence on the multitude of factors which are expected to impact NEDs' behaviour. These factors are listed and categorised in Figure 6.2. In sum, what aspect of their role NEDs focus on and with what intensity depends on the influence of many different elements. One is their perception of accountability (to whom and for what), and this in turn is partly determined by regulatory prescriptions and mechanisms including legal repercussions. Accountability is also shaped by other perceived consequences relating to their reputation/career opportunities and personal relationships. NEDs' perception of accountability, however, does not exclusively determine their behaviour. This is also impacted by the constraints they perceive in their role. These include the time available to them versus the demands of the role, their relatively limited knowledge and understanding of the entity's business environment, and their restricted skills set. Constraints also relate to their dependence on EDs for information, the social norms of behaviour, and the balance of power in the boardroom. The challenge of reconciling their monitoring and advisory/support roles also presents an impediment to the effective discharge of their duties. The added requirement to consider the needs of a wider stakeholder group may also generate a cognitive challenge. Finally, NEDs' motivations for taking on the role would weigh heavily on their chosen focus within their role.

However, as demonstrated in the discussion above, direct empirical evidence of the impact of these factors on NEDs' behaviour is sparse. Not only are the causal mechanisms unclear for individual determinants, but there is also limited understanding of how NEDs' focus comes to be shaped in the presence of conflicting influences. Unravelling the relative significance of the different elements as experienced by NEDs should enable more targeted and effective policies to be designed to ensure NEDs truly deliver on their roles within the corporate governance framework.

Undeniably, the proposed analytic framework is extensive, requiring the study of multiple inputs into NEDs' behaviour. It is hoped, however, that the complexity will not deter the determined researcher, as it is only through the examination of the impact of this comprehensive set of factors that theory can be fully developed. This in turn should pave the way for more evidence-based policy formulations. Section 3.7 next provides guidance on what would constitute an appropriate methodology for a study of this kind.

3.7   Methodology

Critical realism

A critical realist philosophy would be best suited for the investigation detailed above, for multiple reasons. Firstly, to be able to guide policy, behavioural research in this field crucially needs to reveal the underlying structures and the mechanisms by which they are enabling or constricting NEDs' agency, a central theme in critical realism (Fleetwood, 2005; Bisman, 2010; Smith and Elger, 2014). It also recognises that access to such knowledge can only be gained through the minds of the field actors (Fleetwood, 2005; Bisman, 2010). Indeed, the analytic framework proposed focuses on how actors' perceptions of repercussions and social dynamics affect their decisions and behaviours (Bisman, 2010). However, with a critical realist philosophy, the search is for broader generative mechanisms that transcend actors' different experiences and behaviours (Bisman, 2010; Bygstad et al., 2016). Such an approach is necessary to be able to support policy initiatives which will impact all actors across the board. Calls for regulatory changes will also not be convincing without a clear understanding of how the interaction of the different factors generate those mechanisms. Research guided by a critical realist philosophy would be able to deliver such knowledge (Bygstad et al., 2016). The well-developed framework would also help researchers discuss with actors the possible impact of factors they may not have been conscious of, a key strength of a critical realist methodology (Smith and Elger, 2014).

Qualitative interviews

As discussed, the proposed study would aim to understand how various factors are considered and weighed up by NEDs (consciously or subconsciously) in determining what aspect(s) of their role they focus on and with what intensity. This decision-making process is also likely to be impacted by actors' bounded rationality, adding another layer of complexity to the study. The study will therefore require direct access to NEDs and a qualitative approach. Indeed, many have called for qualitative interview-based studies given our limited knowledge in this area and the need to understand it from within; e.g., Daily et al. (2003), Hermalin and Weisbach (2003), and Eminet and Guedri (2010).

However, the formidable challenge of accessing such data has also been quoted widely; e.g., by Daily et al. (2003) and Eminet and Guedri (2010). Also, studies where such access has been obtained have pointed to the possible issues with the validity of accounts provided by currently serving NEDs; e.g., Roberts et al. (2005). Certainly, due attention needs to be given to the purposive nature of human actors and in particular NEDs' acute awareness that the findings of research may feed into new regulations affecting them. Participant-observer research into board processes as carried out by Collier (2005) and Marnet (2011) is one way of gaining direct access to governance mechanisms. However, it requires long periods of engagement and can only study a small number of cases. Another way in which both access and validity issues may be addressed while also capturing broader tendencies is to seek out as participants a fair number of NEDs who have left the corporate sphere either because they have retired fully or because they have changed career direction completely. Although they are still likely to have a strong social network linked to the corporate world, they are likely to have fewer direct vested interests and should therefore be able to discuss matters candidly. A relatively large sample would enable the necessary cross-validation of the general underlying structures and mechanisms. Many individuals now make information on their prior and current roles available publicly through web-based professional networks. Therefore, the problem of identifying and contacting such individuals may not be as insurmountable as it used to be. This in addition to snowballing (where participants identify further suitable participants from their contacts) should be able to yield an appropriate sample of former NEDs willing and able to share faithful accounts of their prior experiences and decision-making processes.

As regards the interview mode itself, a semi-structured approach is warranted, guided by the analytic framework while still allowing sufficient flexibility to accommodate the different contexts within which the interviewees would have performed their NED role. A brief interview guide is presented in the Appendix, building on the analytic framework in Figure 6.2 such that a set of sub-themes/questions are suggested for the discussion around each factor. These aim to address the knowledge gaps discussed above. The intention is to firstly ascertain the focus of their activities as NEDs before moving the discussion onto each likely antecedent in turn. In this respect, the objective is to understand their awareness and perception of these factors and the underlying reasons for their relative salience to NEDs. This will also develop knowledge about the mental processes involved; it should reveal the way in which their bounded rationality leads them to consider and weigh risks and rewards. What the principal drivers are and why, when it comes to NEDs' behaviour, can thereby be revealed. Consequently, a clearer appreciation should emerge of the reasons why regulations may be limited in their ability to affect NEDs' behaviours, and where solutions may be found.

Analysis of the qualitative data would need to focus on identifying common patterns of behavioural mechanisms across interviews rather than accounting for the myriad of different and specific experiences, interpretations, and actions. This would help derive conclusions on the most likely impact of factors on NEDs' behaviours generally, in line with the critical realist philosophy. Indeed, this is necessary to ensure that arguments for any policy changes are convincing.

Despite the complexity and challenge of the study being proposed, the knowledge that such research will generate will allow us to move away from blindly expecting NEDs with certain observable attributes to behave in certain ways, and to see their reality for what it is. In other words, the study should enable the development of a substantive middle-range theory of corporate governance (Huse, 2007). This may in turn reveal the true relevance and positioning of the grand theories of agency, resource dependency, and stewardship within the corporate governance realm (Huse, 2007). Of course, whether researchers take on this challenge would depend on their own aims and perceptions.

4.   CONCLUSION

The chapter aimed to address two significant gaps in knowledge in respect of NEDs' role and effectiveness within corporate governance. Empirical research has been focused on testing broad theories, namely agency, stewardship, and resource dependence. Such testing has involved attempting to find a link between NEDs' observable attributes (independence from management, and competence/capital) and organisational performance. It is generally assumed that NEDs with those visible characteristics would deliver effectively on their role, and that such activities (monitoring and/or resource provision) would lead to improved firm performance. Yet, findings from this line of research remain inconclusive, especially with respect to monitoring activities.

There has also been considerable research that focuses on the direct outcomes of NEDs' monitoring and resource provision activities. These have been more conclusive than studies attempting to find improvement in firm financial performance. However, the two lines of research have not been reconciled; i.e., the possible mechanisms by which the direct results of NEDs' activities and behaviours might impact the organisation's success have not been fully analysed. Section 2 presents evidence from this line of research to discuss these channels and their plausibility. It considers the consequences of the main monitoring activities; i.e., in relation to financial reporting, risk management, executive remuneration, director appraisal, appointment, and dismissal, and finally strategy. The analysis also covers the different aspects of NEDs' resource provision role, namely advising and supporting executives, enabling connections to the external world, and improving communications with it. The analysis suggests that NEDs' specific activities, even when diligently performed, may not impact reported firm financial performance, especially not in the short term. It therefore makes a case for more comprehensive research which attempts to empirically observe and uncover the mechanisms by which the direct outcomes of NEDs' activities impact firm performance. Clear evidence and therefore better understanding of the operation of these channels might allow research to move beyond inconclusive testing of theories.

The other major area of assumption has been what drives NEDs' behaviour. Studies have presupposed NEDs' activities based on their manifest characteristics. The true antecedents to NEDs' behaviour have received very little empirical attention. More importantly, they have not been studied as part of a holistic behavioural framework. Section 3 presents a road map to enable this gap to be filled. It first considers available evidence on the multiple posited determinants of NEDs' behaviour to propose an extensive analytic schema using behavioural theory. The framework is grounded in the need to study NEDs' behaviour in the context of their aims and perceptions. Perceptions relate to accountability as well as constraints within their role. Perceptions of accountability are proposed to be conditioned by regulatory prescriptions and the perceived regulatory, legal, reputational, and personal/social repercussions of their behaviour. Constraints relate to the time, effort, knowledge, and skills required to deliver on their roles, as well as social norms within the board and difficulties in reconciling their possibly conflicting roles of monitoring and supporting management. These perceptions would interact with NEDs' personal aims and incentives to determine what they conceive to be the most optimal behaviour for them. A suitable methodology for studying NEDs' behaviour through this lens is also proposed. The ensuing empirical research would support the development of a comprehensive theory of NEDs' behaviour. In other words, it would not simply present findings of what NEDs do but explain the forces behind such behaviours. This should help to fill some of the major gaps in knowledge and to develop substantive theory in this area which could provide the necessary foundation for recommendations on appropriate policy action.

In conclusion, investors, other stakeholders, and regulators place great reliance on corporate governance and the role of NEDs within it. However, major strides in academic research are needed for the development of truly consequential knowledge, to better serve these interest groups. This chapter hopes to provide some insights and direction to guide such research.

REFERENCES

Abbott, L.J., Parker, S., and Peters, G.F. (2004) 'Audit Committee Characteristics and Restatements', *Auditing: A Journal of Practice & Theory*, 23(1), pp. 69–87.

Adams, R.B. (2017) 'Boards, and the Directors Who Sit on Them', in Hermalin, B.E., and Weisbach, M.S. (eds) *The Handbook of the Economics of Corporate Governance*. Amsterdam: North-Holland, pp. 291–382.

Adams, R.B., and Ferreira, D. (2007) 'A Theory of Friendly Boards', *Journal of Finance*, 62(1), pp. 217–50.

Aguilera, R.V. (2005) 'Corporate Governance and Director Accountability: An Institutional Comparative Perspective', *British Journal of Management*, 16, pp. S39–S53.

Ahmed, A.S., and Duellman, S. (2007) 'Accounting Conservatism and Board of Director Characteristics: An Empirical Analysis', *Journal of Accounting and Economics*, 43(2), pp. 411–37.

Akbar, S., Poletti-Hughes, J., El-Faitouri, R., and Shah, S.Z.A. (2016) 'More on the Relationship between Corporate Governance and Firm Performance in the UK: Evidence from the Application of Generalized Method of Moments Estimation', *Research in International Business and Finance*, 38, pp. 417–29.

Anderson, R.C., and Bizjak, J.M. (2003) 'An Empirical Examination of the Role of the CEO and the Compensation Committee in Structuring Executive Pay', *Journal of Banking and Finance*, 27(7), pp. 1323–48.

Armour, J., Black, B., Cheffins, B., and Nolan, R. (2009) 'Private Enforcement of Corporate Law: An Empirical Comparison of the United Kingdom and the United States', *Journal of Empirical Legal Studies*, 6(4), pp. 687–722.

Basu, S., and Liang, Y. (2019) 'Director–Liability–Reduction Laws and Conditional Conservatism', *Journal of Accounting Research*, 57(4), pp. 889–917.

Bazerman, M.H., Loewenstein, G., and Moore, D.A. (2002) 'Why Good Accountants Do Bad Audits', *Harvard Business Review*, 80(11), pp. 87–102.

Beasley, M.S., Carcello, J.V., Hermanson, D.R., and Neil, T.L. (2009) 'The Audit Committee Oversight Process', *Contemporary Accounting Research*, 26(1), pp. 65–122.

Bebchuk, L.A., Fried, J.M., and Walker, D.I. (2002) 'Managerial Power and Rent Extraction in the Design of Executive Compensation', *University of Chicago Law Review*, 69(3), pp. 751–846.

Bédard, J., Chtourou, S.M., and Courteau, L. (2004) 'The Effect of Audit Committee Expertise, Independence, and Activity on Aggressive Earnings Management', *Auditing: A Journal of Practice & Theory*, 23(2), pp. 13–35.

Beekes, W., Pope, P., and Young, S. (2004) 'The Link Between Earnings Timeliness, Earnings Conservatism and Board Composition: Evidence from the UK', *Corporate Governance: An International Review*, 12(1), pp. 47–59.

BEIS (2019) *The Future of Audit: Nineteenth Report of Session 2017–19, HC 1718*. London: Business, Energy, and Industrial Strategy Parliamentary Select Committee. Available at https://publications.parliament.uk/pa/cm201719/cmselect/cmbeis/1718/1718.pdf (accessed 16 April 2021).

BEIS (2021) *Restoring Trust in Audit and Corporate Governance: Consultation on the Government's Proposals*. London: Department for Business, Energy & Industrial Strategy. Available at https://assets.publishing.service.gov.uk/government/uploads/system/uploads/attachment_data/file/970676/restoring-trust-in-audit-and-corporate-governance-command-paper.pdf (accessed 16 April 2021).

Bhagat, S., and Black, B. (2002) 'The Non-Correlation Between Board Indpendence and Long-Term Firm Performance', *Journal of Corporation Law*, 27(2), pp. 231–73.

Bisman, J. (2010) 'Postpositivism and Accounting Research: A (Personal) Primer on Critical Realism', *Australasian Accounting Business & Finance Journal*, 4(4), pp. 3–25.

Blatter, J., and Blume, T. (2008) 'In Search of Co-Variance, Causal Mechanisms or Congruence? Towards a Plural Understanding of Case Studies', *Swiss Political Science Review*, 14(2), pp. 315–56.

Boivie, S., Andrus, J.L., Bednar, M.K., and Aguilera, R.V. (2016) 'Are Boards Designed to Fail? The Implausibility of Effective Board Monitoring', *Academy of Management Annals*, 10(1), pp. 319–407.

Brennan, N. (2006) 'Boards of Directors and Firm Performance: Is There an Expectations Gap?', *Corporate Governance: An International Review*, 14(6), pp. 577–93.

Brochet, F., and Srinivasan, S. (2014) 'Accountability of Independent Directors: Evidence from Firms Subject to Securities Litigation', *Journal of Financial Economics*, 111(2), pp. 430–49.

Bruynseels, L., and Cardinaels, E. (2014) 'The Audit Committee: Management Watchdog or Personal Friend of the CEO?', *Accounting Review*, 89(1), pp. 113–45.

Bygstad, B., Munkvold, B.E., and Volkoff, O. (2016) 'Identifying Generative Mechanisms through Affordances: A Framework for Critical Realist Data Analysis', *Journal of Information Technology*, 31(1), pp. 83–96.

CA (2006) *The Companies Act 2006, c.46*. Available at www.legislation.gov.uk/ukpga/2006/46/contents (accessed 12 June 2021).

Cai, J.I.E., Garner, J.L., and Walkling, R.A. (2009) 'Electing Directors', *Journal of Finance*, 64(5), pp. 2389–421.

Campbell-Meiklejohn, D., and Frith, C.D. (2012) 'Social Factors and Preference Change', in Dolan, R.J., and Sharot, T. (eds) *Neuroscience of Preference and Choice: Cognitive and Neural Mechanisms*. San Diego, CA: Elsevier Academic Press, pp. 177–206.

Carcello, J.V., and Neal, T.L. (2003) 'Audit Committee Characteristics and Auditor Dismissals following "New" Going-Concern Reports', *Accounting Review*, 78(1), pp. 95–117.

Carcello, J.V., Neal, T.L., Palmrose, Z.-V., and Scholz, S. (2011) 'CEO Involvement in Selecting Board Members, Audit Committee Effectiveness, and Restatements', *Contemporary Accounting Research*, 28(2), pp. 396–430.

Coffee, J.C., Jr. (2006) *Gatekeepers: The Role of the Professions in Corporate Governance*. Oxford: Oxford University Press.

Cohen, D.A., Dey, A., and Lys, T.Z. (2008) 'Real and Accrual-Based Earnings Management in the Pre- and Post-Sarbanes-Oxley Periods', *Accounting Review*, 83(3), pp. 757–87.

Cohen, J., Krishnamoorthy, G., and Wright, A. (2010) 'Corporate Governance in the Post-Sarbanes-Oxley Era: Auditors' Experiences', *Contemporary Accounting Research*, 27(3), pp. 751–86.

Cohen, J.R., Krishnamoorthy, G., and Wright, A.M. (2008) 'Form versus Substance: The Implications for Auditing Practice and Research of Alternative Perspectives on Corporate Governance', *Auditing: A Journal of Practice & Theory*, 27(2), pp. 181–98.

Collier, P.M. (2005) 'Governance and the Quasi-Public Organization: A Case Study of Social Housing', *Critical Perspectives on Accounting*, 16(7), pp. 929–49.

Conyon, M., and Sadler, G. (2010) 'Shareholder Voting and Directors' Remuneration Report Legislation: Say on Pay in the UK', *Corporate Governance: An International Review*, 18(4), pp. 296–312.

Conyon, M.J., Peck, S.I., Read, L.E., and Sadler, G.V. (2000) 'The Structure of Executive Compensation Contracts: UK Evidence', *Long Range Planning*, 33(4), pp. 478–503.

Daily, C.M., Dalton, D.R., and Cannella Jr, A.A. (2003) 'Corporate Governance: Decades of Dialogue and Data', *Academy of Management Review*, 28(3), pp. 371–82.

Dalton, D.R., Daily, C.M., Certo, S.T., and Roengpitya, R. (2003) 'Meta-Analyses of Financial Performance and Equity: Fusion or Confusion', *Academy of Management Journal*, 46(1), pp. 13–26.

Dechow, P.M., Sloan, R.G., and Sweeney, A.P. (1996) 'Causes and Consequences of Earnings Manipulation: An Analysis of Firms Subject to Enforcement Actions by the SEC', *Contemporary Accounting Research*, 13(1), pp. 1–36.

Dhaliwal, D.S., Lamoreaux, P.T., Lennox, C.S., and Mauler, L.M. (2015) 'Management Influence on Auditor Selection and Subsequent Impairments of Auditor Independence during the Post-SOX Period', *Contemporary Accounting Research*, 32(2), pp. 575–607.

Dobbin, F., and Jung, J. (2010) 'The Misapplication of Mr. Michael Jensen: How Agency Theory Brought Down the Economy and Why It Might Again', in Lounsbury, M., and Hirsch, P.M. (eds) *Markets on Trial: The Economic Sociology of the U.S. Financial Crisis: Part B (Research in the Sociology of Organizations, Vol. 30 Part B)*. Bingley: Emerald Group, pp. 29–64.

Elamer, A.A., and Benyazid, I. (2018) 'The Impact of Risk Committee on Financial Performance of UK Financial Institutions', *International Journal of Accounting and Finance*, 8(2), pp. 161–80.

Elson, C.M. (1996) 'Director Compensation and the Management-Captured Board: The History of a Symptom and a Cure', *SMU Law Review*, 50(1), pp. 127–74.

Elster, J. (2000) 'Rationality, Economy, and Society', in Turner, S. (ed.) *The Cambridge Companion to Weber*. Cambridge: Cambridge University Press, pp. 19–41.

Eminet, A., and Guedri, Z. (2010) 'The Role of Nominating Committees and Director Reputation in Shaping the Labor Market for Directors: An Empirical Assessment', *Corporate Governance: An International Review*, 18(6), pp. 557–74.

Ethiraj, S., K., and Levinthal, D. (2009) 'Hoping for A to Z While Rewarding Only A: Complex Organizations and Multiple Goals', *Organization Science*, 20(1), pp. 4–21.

Fairchild, R., Gwilliam, D., and Marnet, O. (2019) 'Audit Within the Corporate Governance Paradigm: A Cornerstone Built on Shifting Sand?', *British Journal of Management*, 30(1), pp. 90–105.

Faleye, O., Hoitash, U., and Hoitash, R. (2011) 'The Costs of Intense Board Monitoring', *Journal of Financial Economics*, 101(1), pp. 160–81.

Fama, E.F., and Jensen, M.C. (1983) 'Separation of Ownership and Control', *Journal of Law and Economics*, 26(2), pp. 301–25.

Ferris, S.P., Jagannathan, M., and Pritchard, A.C. (2003) 'Too Busy to Mind the Business? Monitoring by Directors with Multiple Board Appointments', *Journal of Finance*, 58(3), pp. 1087–111.

Fich, E.M., and Shivdasani, A. (2007) 'Financial Fraud, Director Reputation, and Shareholder Wealth', *Journal of Financial Economics*, 86(2), pp. 306–36.

Finkelstein, S., and Mooney, A.C. (2003) 'Not the Usual Suspects: How to Use Board Process to Make Boards Better', *Academy of Management Executive*, 17(2), pp. 101–13.

Fiolleau, K., Hoang, K., Jamal, K., and Sunder, S. (2013) 'How Do Regulatory Reforms to Enhance Auditor Independence Work in Practice?', *Contemporary Accounting Research*, 30(3), pp. 864–90.

Fleetwood, S. (2005) 'Ontology in Organization and Management Studies: A Critical Realist Perspective', *Organization*, 12(2), pp. 197–222.

Fracassi, C., and Tate, G. (2012) 'External Networking and Internal Firm Governance', *Journal of Finance*, 67(1), pp. 153–94.

FRC (2014) *Guidance on Risk Management, Internal Control and Related Financial and Business Reporting*. London: Financial Reporting Council. Available at www.frc.org.uk/getattachment/ d672c107-b1fb-4051–84b0-f5b83a1b93f6/Guidance-on-Risk-Management-Internal-Control-and -Related-Reporting.pdf (accessed 8 August 2021).

FRC (2018a) *Guidance on Board Effectiveness*. London: Financial Reporting Council. Available at www.frc.org.uk/getattachment/61232f60-a338–471b-ba5a-bfed25219147/2018-guidance-on-board -effectiveness-final.pdf (accessed 8 August 2021).

FRC (2018b) *The UK Corporate Governance Code*. London: Financial Reporting Council. Available at www.frc.org.uk/getattachment/88bd8c45–50ea-4841–95b0-d2f4f48069a2/2018-UK-Corporate -Governance-Code-FINAL.pdf (accessed 15 April 2021).

FRC (2019) *The UK Stewardship Code 2020*. London: Financial Reporting Council. Available at www .frc.org.uk/getattachment/5aae591d-d9d3–4cf4–814a-d14e156a1d87/Stewardship-Code_Dec-19 -Final-Corrected.pdf (accessed 15 April 2021).

FRC (2020) *Review of Corporate Governance Reporting*. London: Financial Reporting Council. Available at www.frc.org.uk/getattachment/c22f7296–0839–420e-ae03-bdce3e157702/Governance -Report-2020–2611.pdf (accessed 16 April 2021).

Gordon, L.A., Loeb, M.P., and Tseng, C.-Y. (2009) 'Enterprise Risk Management and Firm Performance: A Contingency Perspective', *Journal of Accounting and Public Policy*, 28(4), pp. 301–27.

Gregory-Smith, I. (2012) 'Chief Executive Pay and Remuneration Committee Independence', *Oxford Bulletin of Economics & Statistics*, 74(4), pp. 510–31.

Guo, L., and Masulis, R.W. (2015) 'Board Structure and Monitoring: New Evidence from CEO Turnovers', *Review of Financial Studies*, 28(10), pp. 2770–811.

Guthrie, K., Sokolowsky, J.A.N., and Wan, K.-M. (2012) 'CEO Compensation and Board Structure Revisited', *Journal of Finance*, 67(3), pp. 1149–68.

Hambrick, D., C., Werder, A., and Zajac, E., J. (2008) 'New Directions in Corporate Governance Research', *Organization Science*, 19(3), pp. 381–85.

Hendry, K.P., Kiel, G.C., and Nicholson, G. (2010) 'How Boards Strategise: A Strategy as Practice View', *Long Range Planning*, 43(1), pp. 33–56.

Hermalin, B.E., and Weisbach, M.S. (2003) 'Boards of Directors As an Endogenously Determined Institution: A Survey of the Economic Literature', *Federal Reserve Bank of New York Economic Policy Review*, 9(1), pp. 7–26.

Hillman, A.J., and Dalziel, T. (2003) 'Boards of Directors and Firm Performance: Integrating Agency and Resource Dependence Perspectives', *Academy of Management Review*, 28(3), pp. 383–96.

Hillman, A.J., Nicholson, G., and Shropshire, C. (2008) 'Directors' Multiple Identities, Identification, and Board Monitoring and Resource Provision', *Organization Science*, 19(3), pp. 441–56.

Hoyt, R.E., and Liebenberg, A.P. (2011) 'The Value of Enterprise Risk Management', *Journal of Risk & Insurance*, 78(4), pp. 795–822.

Huse, M. (2007) *Boards, Governance and Value Creation: The Human Side of Corporate Governance*. Cambridge: Cambridge University Press.

I&L (2011) *'Why Didn't Insolvency Service Prosecute MG Rover's Phoenix Four?'* London: Insolvency & Law. Available at https://insolvencyandlaw.co.uk/why-didnt-insolvency-service-prosecute-mg -rovers-phoenix-four/# (accessed 8 August 2021).

Ingley, C., and Van der Walt, N. (2005) 'Do Board Processes Influence Director and Board Performance? Statutory and Performance Implications', *Corporate Governance: An International Review*, 13(5), pp. 632–53.

Irvine, J. (2018) 'FTSE Companies Named and Shamed by Investors', Economia. London: Institute of Chartered Accountants in England and Wales, 5 December. Available at https://wayback.archive -it.org/13284/20191231132313/https://economia.icaew.com/news/december-2018/ftse-companies -named-and-shamed-by-investors (accessed 16 April 2021).

Irvine, J. (2019) 'FRC Sets Bar High with Its Revised Stewardship Code', Economia. London: Institute of Chartered Accountants in England and Wales, 25 October. Available at https://wayback.archive-it .org/13284/20191231121120/https://economia.icaew.com/news/october-2019/frc-sets-bar-high-with -its-revised-stewardship-code (accessed 16 April 2021).

ISS (2020) *United Kingdom and Ireland Proxy Voting Guidelines, Benchmark Policy Recommendations*. London: Institutional Shareholder Services. Available at www.issgovernance.com/file/policy/active/ emea/UK-and-Ireland-Voting-Guidelines.pdf (accessed 16 April 2021).

Jensen, M.C. (1993) 'The Modern Industrial Revolution, Exit, and the Failure of Internal Control Systems', *Journal of Finance*, 48(3), pp. 831–80.

Jensen, M.C., and Meckling, W.H. (1976) 'Theory of the Firm: Managerial Behavior, Agency Costs and Ownership Structure', *Journal of Financial Economics*, 3(4), pp. 305–60.

Jermias, J., and Gani, L. (2014) 'The Impact of Board Capital and Board Characteristics on Firm Performance', *British Accounting Review*, 46(2), pp. 135–53.

Kaczmarek, S., Kimino, S., and Pye, A. (2012) 'Antecedents of Board Composition: The Role of Nomination Committees', *Corporate Governance: An International Review*, 20(5), pp. 474–89.

Kahneman, D. (2003) 'A Perspective on Judgment and Choice: Mapping Bounded Rationality', *American Psychologist*, 58(9), pp. 697–720.

Kahneman, D., and Tversky, A. (1979) 'Prospect Theory: An Analysis of Decision under Risk', *Econometrica*, 47(2), pp. 263–91.

Keay, A., and Loughrey, J. (2015) 'The Framework for Board Accountability in Corporate Governance', *Legal Studies*, 35(2), pp. 252–79.

Kleck, G., Sever, B., Li, S., and Gertz, M. (2005) 'The Missing Link in General Deterrence Research', *Criminology*, 43(3), pp. 623–60.

Klein, A. (2002) 'Audit Committee, Board of Director Characteristics, and Earnings Management', *Journal of Accounting and Economics*, 33(3), pp. 375–400.

Kuang, Y.F. (2008) 'Performance-Vested Stock Options and Earnings Management', *Journal of Business Finance & Accounting*, 35(9/10), pp. 1049–78.

Lam, J. (2014) *Enterprise Risk Management: From Incentives to Controls*. Hoboken, NJ: John Wiley & Sons.

Langevoort, D.C. (1998) 'Behavioral Theories of Judgment and Decision Making in Legal Scholarship: A Literature Review', *Vanderbilt Law Review*, 51(6), p. 1499.

Langevoort, D.C. (2001) 'The Human Nature of Corporate Boards: Law, Norms, and the Unintended Consequences of Independence and Accountability', *Georgetown Law Journal*, 89(4), pp. 797–832.

Larcker, D.F., Richardson, S.A., Seary, A.J., and Tuna, A.I. (2005) 'Back Door Links Between Directors and Executive Compensation'. University of Pennsylvania. Available at http://citeseerx.ist.psu.edu/viewdoc/download?doi=10.1.1.207.4262&rep=rep1&type=pdf (accessed 15 April 2021).

Lau, A.Y.S., and Coiera, E.W. (2007) 'Do People Experience Cognitive Biases while Searching for Information?', *Journal of the American Medical Informatics Association*, 14(5), pp. 599–608.

Lex (2021) 'Carillion/Directors: Dysfunctional Disqualifications', *Financial Times*, 16 Jan. Available at www.ft.com/content/b9ea3a30–8d27–4b51-b326–1091644308bb (accessed 8 August 2021).

MacNeil, I., and Li, X. (2006) '"Comply or Explain": Market Discipline and Non-Compliance with the Combined Code', *Corporate Governance: An International Review*, 14(5), pp. 486–96.

Malik, M.F., Zaman, M., and Buckby, S. (2020) 'Enterprise Risk Management and Firm Performance: Role of the Risk Committee', *Journal of Contemporary Accounting & Economics*, 16(1).

Marnet, O. (2007) 'History Repeats Itself: The Failure of Rational Choice Models in Corporate Governance', *Critical Perspectives on Accounting*, 18(2), pp. 191–210.

Marnet, O. (2011) 'Bias in the Boardroom', *International Journal of Behavioural Accounting and Finance*, (3/4), p. 238.

McCance, D. (2019) 'Lloyds' Executive Pensions Show "Boundless Greed", Say MPs', Economia. London: Institute of Chartered Accountants in England and Wales, 16 May. Available at https://wayback.archive-it.org/13284/20191231124730/https://economia.icaew.com/news/may-2019/lloyds-executive-pensions-show-boundless-greed-says-mps (accessed 16 April 2021).

McKnight, P.J., and Weir, C. (2009) 'Agency Costs, Corporate Governance Mechanisms and Ownership Structure in Large UK Publicly Quoted Companies: A Panel Data Analysis', *Quarterly Review of Economics and Finance*, 49(2), pp. 139–58.

Nicholson, G.J., and Kiel, G.C. (2007) 'Can Directors Impact Performance? A Case-Based Test of Three Theories of Corporate Governance', *Corporate Governance: An International Review*, 15(4), pp. 585–608.

Nocco, B.W., and Stulz, R.M. (2006) 'Enterprise Risk Management: Theory and Practice', *Journal of Applied Corporate Finance*, 18(4), pp. 8–20.

Pagach, D.P., and Warr, R.S. (2010) *The Effects of Enterprise Risk Management on Firm Performance*. Available at SSRN: https://ssrn.com/abstract=1155218 (accessed 8 August 2021).

Peasnell, K.V., Pope, P.F., and Young, S. (2005) 'Board Monitoring and Earnings Management: Do Outside Directors Influence Abnormal Accruals?', *Journal of Business Finance & Accounting*, 32(7/8), pp. 1311–46.

Petrovic, J. (2008) 'Unlocking the Role of a Board Director: A Review of the Literature', *Management Decision*, 46(9), pp. 1373–92.

Pettigrew, A.M. (1992) 'On Studying Managerial Elites', *Strategic Management Journal*, 13, pp. 163–82.

Pfeffer, J., and Salancik, G.R. ([1978] 2003) *The External Control of Organizations: A Resource Dependence Perspective*. Stanford, CA: Stanford University Press.

Pugliese, A., Bezemer, P.-J., Zattoni, A., Huse, M., Van Den Bosch, F.A.J., and Volberda, H.W. (2009) 'Boards of Directors' Contribution to Strategy: A Literature Review and Research Agenda', *Corporate Governance: An International Review*, 17(3), pp. 292–306.

Pye, A., and Pettigrew, A. (2005) 'Studying Board Context, Process and Dynamics: Some Challenges for the Future', *British Journal of Management*, 16, pp. S27–S38.

Roberts, J. (1991) 'The Possibilities of Accountability', *Accounting, Organizations and Society*, 16(4), pp. 355–68.

Roberts, J. (2001) 'Trust and Control in Anglo-American Systems of Corporate Governance: The Individualizing and Socializing Effects of Processes of Accountability', *Human Relations*, 54(12), pp. 1547–71.

Roberts, J., Stiles, P., and McNulty, T. (2005) 'Beyond Agency Conceptions of the Work of the Non-Executive Director: Creating Accountability in the Boardroom', *British Journal of Management*, 16, pp. S5–S26.

Sapp, S.G. (2008) 'The Impact of Corporate Governance on Executive Compensation', *European Financial Management*, 14(4), pp. 710–746.

Sharma, V.D., and Iselin, E.R. (2012) 'The Association between Audit Committee Multiple-Directorships, Tenure, and Financial Misstatements', *Auditing: A Journal of Practice & Theory*, 31(3), pp. 149–75.

Shaukat, A., and Trojanowski, G. (2018) 'Board Governance and Corporate Performance', *Journal of Business Finance & Accounting*, 45(1/2), pp. 184–208.

Simon, H.A. (1972) 'Theories of Bounded Rationality', in McGuire, C.B., and Radner, R. (eds) *Decision and Organization*. Amsterdam: North-Holland, pp. 161–76.

Simon, M., Houghton, S.M., and Aquino, K. (2000) 'Cognitive Biases, Risk Perception, and Venture Formation: How Individuals Decide to Start Companies', *Journal of Business Venturing*, 15(2), pp. 113–34.

Smith, C., and Elger, T. (2014) 'Critical Realism and Interviewing Subjects', in Edwards, P.K., O'Mahoney, J., and Vincent, S. (eds) *Studying Organizations Using Critical Realism*. Oxford: Oxford University Press, pp. 109–31.

Stern, I., and Westphal, J.D. (2010) 'Stealthy Footsteps to the Boardroom: Executives' Backgrounds, Sophisticated Interpersonal Influence Behavior, and Board Appointments', *Administrative Science Quarterly*, 55(2), pp. 278–319.

Stiles, P. (2001) 'The Impact of the Board on Strategy: An Empirical Examination', *Journal of Management Studies*, 38(5), pp. 627–50.

Sundaramurthy, C., and Lewis, M. (2003) 'Control and Collaboration: Paradoxes of Governance', *Academy of Management Review*, 28(3), pp. 397–415.

Turley, S., and Zaman, M. (2007) 'Audit Committee Effectiveness: Informal Processes and Behavioural Effects', *Accounting, Auditing & Accountability Journal*, 20(5), pp. 765–88.

Tversky, A., and Kahneman, D. (1974) 'Judgment under Uncertainty: Heuristics and Biases', *Science*, 185(4157), pp. 1124–31.

Unsworth, K., Yeo, G., and Beck, J. (2014) 'Multiple Goals: A Review and Derivation of General Principles', *Journal of Organizational Behavior*, 35(8), pp. 1064–78.

Van Essen, M., Otten, J., and Carberry, E.J. (2015) 'Assessing Managerial Power Theory: A Meta-Analytic Approach to Understanding the Determinants of CEO Compensation', *Journal of Management*, 41(1), pp. 164–202.

Westphal, J.D., and Bednar, M.K. (2005) 'Pluralistic Ignorance in Corporate Boards and Firms' Strategic Persistence in Response to Low Firm Performance', *Administrative Science Quarterly*, 50(2), pp. 262–98.

Westphal, J.D.., and Khanna, P. (2003) 'Keeping Directors in Line: Social Distancing as a Control Mechanism in the Corporate Elite', *Administrative Science Quarterly*, 48(3), pp. 361–98.

Westphal, J.D., and Stern, I. (2007) 'Flattery Will Get You Everywhere (Especially if You Are a Male Caucasian): How Ingratiation, Boardroom Behavior, and Demographic Minority Status Affect Additional Board Appointments at U.S. Companies', *Academy of Management Journal*, 50(2), pp. 267–88.

Withers, M.C., Hillman, A.J., and Cannella, A.A. (2012) 'A Multidisciplinary Review of the Director Selection Literature', *Journal of Management*, 38(1), pp. 243–77.

Xie, B., Davidson, W.N., and DaDalt, P.J. (2003) 'Earnings Management and Corporate Governance: The Role of the Board and the Audit Committee', *Journal of Corporate Finance*, 9(3), pp. 295–316.

Zeff, S.A. (2003) 'How the U.S. Accounting Profession Got Where It Is Today: Part II', *Accounting Horizons*, 17(4), pp. 267–86.

APPENDIX

Former NEDs: Behavioural Effects of Multiple Factors – Interview Guide

Experience as NED: period, nature of entities (industry, size, etc.), experience of monitoring committees

Role
Perception of requirements of role
Own focus within NED role(s)
How role is interpreted in context of UK Corporate Governance Code

Accountability
Who feel accountable to?

Code
Response to 'reporting and explaining' requirements of Code. Compliance-mindset? Why?

Shareholder involvement
Engagement by shareholders (inc. institutional investors $\tilde{\alpha}$ Impact on accountability
Experience of shareholder votes, nature of outcomes, nature of board responses

Legal consequences
Awareness of legal repercussions for failings in role: private enforcement, public enforcement, disqualification
Extent of consideration of such repercussions
Effects of awareness, uncertainty, and distant nature of such risks
EDs' responsibilities and accountability vs NEDs'
Effect of directors' insurance

Financial consequences
View of likely impact of remuneration clawbacks if implemented as proposed?

Reputational consequences
Experience of shareholder revolt against director nomination – basis for revolt and actions taken by board
How NED roles obtained
Salience of reputation within director community
Qualities sought by director community
Characteristics disliked by director community
Impact on focus within role

Regulator monitoring of the monitors?!
Likely impact of regulatory monitoring of NEDs' activities and decisions?

Constraints

Time and effort
Time available vs time and effort needed to deliver $\tilde{\alpha}$ impact on focus
Effect of multiple directorships

Knowledge and skills
Industry knowledge and experience
Business operations knowledge (linked to time constraint?)
Dependence on EDs for information
Competence; e.g., financial expertise

- Impact of above constraints on monitoring and advisory role
- Reliance on external experts due to above constraints?

Social norms and management power
Norms of behaviour in boardroom re challenge/support/advice
Relative power of EDs vs NEDs

- Antecedents to that power
- EDs' resulting behaviour
- Effects on NEDs' behaviour of the power structures

Monitoring vs advisory roles
Perception of the requirements of the two roles: complementary or conflicting
Basis of perception as complementary
If conflicting, how resolved. Which prioritised, and why

Shareholders vs wider stakeholders
How the needs of all are considered and reconciled. Challenges $\tilde{\alpha}$ impact on focus

Aims and incentives
Motivation(s) for taking on NED role $\tilde{\alpha}$ Impact on focus within role
Impact of accountability structures and role constraints on overall personal goals
Views on likely effect of alternative structures of financial incentives

7. Driving higher enterprise value through good governance
Steve Maslin

1. INTRODUCTION

In this chapter, I advance the case that research demonstrates a positive correlation between good corporate governance behaviour and enhanced financial performance. This enhanced financial performance can be measured in better returns to shareholders as well as lower leverage and greater liquidity, which means that the companies with the best governance behaviour should require premium interest from both investors and other capital providers, such as lenders.

I then present some case studies which support this case, based upon my experience as a non-executive director on various boards. I also describe how using an effective corporate governance framework has helped those companies navigate the crisis brought on by Covid.

Finally, I highlight what I see as some of the key themes that will drive governance behaviour over the next few years, based on drivers from both the capital markets and regulators.

While most commentators agree that well-run companies are more likely to succeed than poorly-run ones, opinion is often divided when it comes to the role played by corporate governance. While some argue that effective governance is an integral tool in optimising an entity's financial performance and enterprise value, others argue that it is a regulatory burden that brings inflated cost for little real value. This is in part because the evolution of governance codes derives from market regulators rather than capital markets or academic research.

The first formal corporate governance code for companies came in the UK and followed the *Cadbury Report* in 1992.[1] The Cadbury Committee was formed by the London Stock Exchange and Financial Reporting Council (FRC) following concerns raised on the standard of financial reporting and accountability. The original Cadbury Code has been revised several times and now exists as the UK Governance Code issued by the FRC.[2] It is the parent of similar codes, and its recommendations have been used to varying degrees to establish other codes such as those of the Organisation for Economic Co-operation and Development, the European Union, the US and the World Bank. The FRC in the UK issued the Wates Principles[3] in 2019, and these principles are intended to be a corporate governance code for large private companies. These codes are valuable but viewing them solely through a regulatory lens is a missed opportunity.

Fortunately, we now have authoritative research that provides empirical evidence linking good governance with superior financial return. In 2019, the Grant Thornton Governance Institute (GT Governance Institute) published a White Paper entitled *Corporate Governance and Company Performance: A Proven Link between Effective Corporate Governance and Value Creation*.[4] This research is based upon a study of the UK FTSE (i.e., the 350 largest companies by market value listed on the main UK Stock Exchange) between 2007 and 2017 and supported by academic studies globally between 1996 and 2012.

The findings are stark. The FTSE companies with the best governance behaviour create greater value than their peers: double the total shareholder return and over three times the operational cashflow. They also show more effective value retention than their peers, being 15 per cent less leveraged and 25 per cent more liquid than peers. These findings mean that the best-governed companies should attract premium interest from both investors and other funders, such as banks.

The model that underpins the GT Governance Institute research has been compiled over 18 years and comprises both quantitative and qualitative data points to provide an evaluation of the degree to which FTSE 350 companies truly embrace the spirit of the UK Governance Code, rather than merely "tick the boxes" to provide a veneer of compliance. Those companies that are assessed as truly embracing the UK Governance Code consistently show superior performance from those that simply tick the boxes or who show limited appetite to comply.

The GT Governance Institute research goes on to suggest that there are six areas of governance behaviour that, based on its findings, are the most reliable predictors of superior financial performance. These are: (i) business model clarity and connectivity, (ii) culture and value integration, (iii) risk management, (iv) internal controls, (v) board effectiveness and (vi) succession planning.

These research findings can be supported by real-life examples of how companies have embraced, and invested in, effective corporate governance while at the same time demonstrating superior financial performance. In this chapter I outline two case studies, of boards on which I served as a non-executive director, which support the research findings that effective corporate governance drives superior financial performance. The first is Nuffield Health, where a new CEO and Executive Team applied a rigorous approach to defining its business model and connectivity, based on culture and values, to carve out a unique place in its crowded markets; this led to both superior financial performance and a significantly improved social return regarding Nuffield Health's charitable purpose. The second is Grant Thornton, where a new CEO and chair embraced a brand new governance code specific to its sector (the Audit Firm Governance Code) to ensure there was greater challenge and diversity with the board, including being the first large audit firm to appoint independent non-executives to its board, and to drive significantly enhanced engagement with external stakeholders, such as institutional investors and clients; again, this led to a period of superior financial returns, growth in market share and positive recognition.

The Covid crisis that began in 2020 provided a dramatic real-life stress-test for UK businesses on the effectiveness or otherwise of the governance behaviour that they had embedded throughout their organisations. I provide some practical examples of the types of governance framework used by some boards, again where I served as a non-executive director, and risk and audit committees to help the company take decisive and swift actions to balance competing needs such as protecting the workforce in the short term with ensuring financial resilience once Covid is more controlled. In both cases, Carey Group and Nuffield Health, the businesses faced virtually a 100 per cent loss of revenues overnight, in the case of Nuffield at the cost of hundreds of millions of pounds in lost income. However, by adopting a clear decision-making framework to guide the multiple decisions that were necessary to ensure survival and resilience during the lockdown imposed as a result of Covid, often on a daily or hourly basis, both businesses have emerged from lockdown with more resilient business models and enhanced reputations with stakeholders.

These case studies support the contention that effective corporate governance helps to drive superior financial performance and enterprise value during both a normal economic cycle and also during periods of crisis.

Towards the end of this chapter, I provide a personal view of the themes that I believe will dominate governance developments over the next decade. Three of these – sustainability and the use of scare resources, social governance and further requirements on internal controls environments – have been the subject of much writing elsewhere. So, the issue that I choose to highlight as my final tip on a governance area that will help drive financial performance and enterprise value in coming years is diversity. There are now multiple sources of soft and hard regulation that attempt to drive greater diversity in boards. Enlightened boards see the drive towards greater diversity as a means to improve board decision-making, increasing appeal to new markets and enhancing the organisation's access to talent.

However, my main message is that companies who embrace effective corporate governance and see good governance as a vital tool to achieve success, rather than as a regulatory burden, offer themselves the best chances to drive superior financial performance and enterprise value.

2.   CORPORATE GOVERNANCE AND COMPANY PERFORMANCE: A PROVEN LINK BETWEEN EFFECTIVE CORPORATE GOVERNANCE AND VALUE CREATION

Much of the first part of this chapter is drawn from research by the GT Governance Institute. The Institute was first established in the early 2000s by my former colleague Simon Lowe, and is now led by another former colleague, Sarah Bell; both are partners in Grant Thornton. The work of the GT Governance Institute has frequently been referenced by the FRC in the UK, and its senior members have been consulted from time to time by government and the FRC to advance UK corporate governance codes; for example, I was consulted by the FRC when it was advancing the case of investor needs ("effective stewardship") when drafting the 2012 UK Corporate Governance Code.[5]

The GT Governance Institute started tracking the way UK FTSE companies adopted the (then Cadbury) Code in 2002, since when it has published an annual review of corporate governance behaviour and trends within the UK FTSE 350, and now has a unique dataset built over 18 years. This data underpins the aforementioned 2019 White Paper on corporate governance and company performance.

The methodology used in Grant Thornton's Annual Governance Review creates an annual score that measures corporate governance behaviour ("the CG Index") of every company within the UK FTSE 350, excluding all investment trusts, as these are advised to adopt their own sector-specific code, as recommended by the FRC. The CG Index is derived from both quantitative and qualitative data. For example, when assessing the governance processes over internal control, a company might be awarded points for an explicit statement to confirm the company has complied with the Code requirements to assess the effectiveness of internal controls; however, additional points can be awarded where the company provides greater colour in its disclosures, say, by providing some insight into how that assessment has been made and how weaknesses have been addressed. In this way the CG Index goes beyond a mere survey of what a company board states it has done and evaluates the degree to which the company appears genuinely to address the spirit and intention of the Code.

The GT Governance Institute does not publish its precise methodology for awarding points for qualitative factors or for weighting quantitative versus qualitative scores. However, its latest annual research findings of FTSE 350 governance[6] provides some insights into the qualitative factors that are included in the CG Index, and a summary is included here in the Appendix.

The 2019 research critically analyses this data in the 10-year period from 2007 to 2017, creating upper- and lower-quartile governance performance scores, which are then further analysed into the 10 industry sectors recognised by the UK Listing Authority and also size of entity.

The term financial performance is measured through three separate lenses: the company's perspective, shareholders' perspective and lenders' perspective.

The 2019 research also distils 183,000 academic research pieces on corporate governance between 1996 and 2012, focussing on those studies reflecting the G7, G20, BRICS (Brazil, Russia, India, China and South Africa) and APEC (Asia-Pacific Economic Cooperation) countries.

3.   GT GOVERNANCE INSTITUTE RESEARCH FINDINGS: COMPANY PERSPECTIVE, STRONGER RESULTS

The 2019 research identified four key financial performance measures that are relevant from a company perspective: operating margin, contribution, return on capital employed and operating cashflow.

The top quartile of best-governed companies, as measured by the CG Index, outperformed the bottom quartile for each of these four financial measures.

With regard to operating margin, the best-governed companies produced an operating margin that was over 40 per cent greater than their worst-performing peers over 10 years. The improved operating margin in best-governed companies was observed every year from 2007 to 2017 and was consistent across all 10 industry sectors. The correlation of good governance and higher operating margin was significant, with a correlation coefficient of 0.179. The outperformance probability measured was 100 per cent; i.e., every company in the top quartile outperformed the bottom quartile.

The trend for operating cashflow was consistent with operating margin. The improved operating cash flow in the best-governed companies was more than twice as good as the worst-governed ones. Again, this outperformance was observed in all 10 years of the research and consistent across all 10 industry sectors. The correlation coefficient was high at 0.337 and, just as for operating margin, the outperformance probability was 100 per cent; i.e., once again every company in the top quartile outperformed those in the bottom quartile.

Average return on capital employed over 10 years for the best-governed companies was 45 per cent compared with 35 per cent for the worst, and as with operating margin and cashflow the finding was consistent across all 10 industry sectors. The outperformance probability was 80 per cent; i.e., four in five companies within the top quartile of governance outperformed their worst-performing peers on this measure.

Finally, the best-governed companies produced a contribution margin more than double that of their worst-performing peers. This finding was pronounced in five of the 10 industry sectors (healthcare, industrial, oil and gas, technology and utilities) with no discernible difference in five others, but again there was a high outperformance probability factor of 70 per cent.

4.   GT GOVERNANCE INSTITUTE RESEARCH FINDINGS: SHAREHOLDERS' PERSPECTIVE, HIGHER RETURNS

To measure investor return, the 2019 research identified four key financial performance measures: free cashflow, cashflow per share, dividend per share and total shareholder return.

Once again, there was a statistically significant finding that the best-governed companies outperformed the worst-governed across all four financial measures.

The top quartile returned nearly 3.4 times greater free cashflow over 10 years and produced higher free cashflow in every one of the 10 years of the research. This finding was consistent across all 10 industry sectors and good governance was a 100 per cent predictor of outperformance.

The best-governed companies produced 50 per cent greater cashflow per share than the worst across all industry sectors and 60 per cent greater dividends per share, the latter finding being across five industry sectors (healthcare, technology, industrials, oil and gas, and utilities).

Most notably, on the key measure of total shareholder return, the best-governed companies produced a 20 per cent better performance than their worst-performing peers.

5.   GT GOVERNANCE INSTITUTE RESEARCH FINDINGS – LENDERS' PERSPECTIVE, STRONGER COVENANTS

Finally, the 2019 research examined financial performance from a lender's perspective, analysing the financial prudence of companies based upon: current ratio, quick ratio, financial leverage and free cashflow.

Once again, the best-governed companies outperformed the worst-governed by statistically significant amounts.

The current ratio is a measure of the company assets that it can swiftly convert into cash to meet its short-term liabilities. The top quartile had an average current ratio of 1.7 compared with 1.5 for the worst, with seven sectors conforming to trend (basic materials, consumer goods, financial services, industrials, telecoms, technology, and oil and gas). This measure is a 50 per cent effective measure of outperformance.

The quick ratio is a measure of the company's assets that it can very swiftly convert into cash to meet its day-to-day liabilities. The top quartile had an average quick ratio of 1.0, 25 per cent higher than the bottom quartile, which had an average quick ratio of 0.8. A quick ratio of less than 1.0 leaves the company vulnerable to short-term liquidity pinch points. The seven industry sectors conforming to this trend were consistent with the findings for current ratio. This measure was a 90 per cent effective predictor of good financial performance.

The best-governed companies had an average leverage of 1.1 compared with the worst at 1.3, and eight industry sectors conformed with trend (with utilities being added to the seven sectors identified in the current ratio measure above). Good governance was a 70 per cent effective predictor of lower leverage.

And, as seen above, good governance was a strong predictor of good financial performance measured by free cashflow, with the best-governed companies producing more than 2.3 times greater free cashflow than their worst peers, a finding consistent across all 10 sectors.

6.   THE SIX GOVERNANCE BEHAVIOURS THAT MOST RELIABLY PREDICT STRONGER FINANCIAL PERFORMANCE AND RETURNS ON CAPITAL

The GT Governance Institute has analysed the UK FTSE over the 10 years from 2007 to 2017 and identified six key areas that appear to mark out the best-governed companies and which have a significant impact on driving stronger financial performance and enterprise value. These are:

- Business model clarity and connectivity;
- Culture and value integration;
- Risk management;
- Internal controls;
- Board effectiveness; and
- Succession planning.

These areas of governance and their linkage to strong financial performance and enterprise value can be observed in practice and the following sections of this chapter are based upon my experiences as an audit partner and non-executive director.

6.1   Business Model Clarity and Connectivity

Business model clarity starts with considering what the entity's purpose is. A good way to test purpose is to ask the question that one CEO I once worked with would ask: "If my company did not exist, would society find a reason to invent it?" If the answer to that question is yes, the board can start to build the business model with that clear purpose of its contribution to society and the markets in mind. If the answer is no, the board should question whether it has a sustainable and profitable business model as its goods or services might easily be easily provided by others.

Another of the most successful and strategically minded CEOs I ever worked with once said to me that if your business, or its component parts, cannot easily be seen to be in the top two competitors in its market or markets, then you have to question whether it is going to be successful in the medium term. Market leadership could be defined in various ways, not just size, but the definition needed to be credible through the eyes of the external market. It was a question he addressed rigorously on a regular basis, and he was prepared to make bold changes to the business's direction as soon as its leadership positioning was threatened.

Of course, visionary entrepreneurs such as Elon Musk might argue that the success of Tesla refutes the case that purpose comes from whether society would invent your business if it did not exist; in his words "We don't know what we don't know." However, I believe that the answer to Tesla's success is that once society knew what new products and services could exist (commercially viable electric cars, affordable and safe space travel) it realised it would have invented them if only it had the vision.

Connectivity is another key question for boards to address in arriving at a successful business model. Do all the parts of the business fit? Too often, I witness boards whose instinct is to work bottom-up when formulating the business model; "Here is what we do now and here is how we do it, let us work that into something that sounds like a connected business model." A better platform for building the business model is to view what the business should do and how it should aim to do it is through the eye of external stakeholders. A rigorous top-down approach to building the business model allows legacy business components that can no longer be said to be market-leading to be sold or disinvested before they suck valuable capital and resources from those business components that have a clearer route map to market leadership. The top-down approach paves the way for the board to be able to continually challenge itself on the sustainability of the business model.

6.2   Culture and Value Integration

For me culture and value integration are often a significant, and costly, blind spot of many boards. There are positive and negative reasons for boards to nurture an authentic, success-oriented culture and to work to embed that culture firmly throughout the organisation.

The negative reason for embedding an effective culture is the avoidance of harm. While many of the spectacular corporate collapses of the early 2000s saw accounting impropriety and failure being at the centre of a suddenly collapsed entity (Enron, Parmalat, WorldCom, AIG et al.), more and more examples of collapsed enterprise value in the late 2000s and 2010s are linked to a poor culture.

It seemed, apparently, okay for a tier of the management team of VW (and some others in the automotive industry) to falsify carbon emissions test results for short-term gain, but the uncovering of that deception led to immediate collapse in the company's market value, and it will now be involved in litigation for years with exposure to hundreds of millions of Euros. WeWork is a fast-growing US real estate business that had to suspend its flotation after the CEO was forced to resign after claims of widespread bullying of staff. Boeing, Nissan and Uber are all companies that have seen market value massively affected by claims of poor culture and ethics leading to the exit of a CEO. Whether justified or not, the absence of clear evidence of a strong culture and ethical framework creates a vulnerability when such allegations surface.

Indeed, even the accounting and banking scandals of earlier decades could all be argued to have had their roots in poor culture: overly aggressive CEOs who pursued profit and personal gain above any sense of doing the right thing by the workforce, shareholders and wider society.

However, there are also positive reasons for boards to pay greater attention to building a strong culture and to foster strong ethical values. Health psychologist Dr Brian Marien of Positive Group is just one of those who has published compelling research to show that good culture, such as showing kindness to colleagues, has a demonstrable and positive impact on corporate success.

Dr Marien has summarised over 20 pieces of research to support this contention in an article published for Positive Group entitled "Lessons in Kindness".[7] For individuals, these lessons include increased psychological wellbeing and enhanced longevity; for groups, reduced anxiety, fewer punitive actions against others, reduced employee turnover and improved perception of leadership and trust. In fact, Dr Marien observes, just witnessing kindness encourages people to act for the common good. "Research carried out here at Positive supports this: we have found that staff who feel their line managers care about their wellbeing score significantly higher across all wellbeing and performance metrics."[8]

At Nuffield Health, where I serve as audit committee chair, we are embracing this philosophy, and kindness will be the primary quality looked for in recruitment, evaluation and promotion of our leaders. SAP is a good example of a fast-growth technology company that replaced its entire suite of reporting metrics, which became focussed on the wellbeing and happiness of its workforce; SAP recognised that its primary driver of financial performance and enterprise value was the innovation and ingenuity of its workforce, and that it needed lead indicators to ensure that it was recruiting, retaining and motivating that workforce to deliver its ambitious financial targets.

It is interesting when consulting a business's current or potential workforce to hear how many of them have a detailed knowledge of the business's social policies, and insider accounts of how well, or otherwise, those policies play out in practice.

People who feel that they are able to bring their authentic selves to work make for a more effective workforce than those who feel they are always looking over their shoulders.

Many of the companies I refer to above that suffered sudden and catastrophic loss of entity value would have had values and culture statements that had a veneer of plausibility. So how can one obtain an insight into what is the real culture within an organisation?

I have yet to find a model that can evaluate culture reliably. However, there is one test that I apply when assessing culture that I have found helpful in assessing whether an entity's stated values are authentic and consistent with those that play out in practice throughout the organisation as a whole. I find it revealing to test how curious a board is about the lived experiences of its workforce and other stakeholders and whether those lived experiences align with the board's vision of culture.

Culture is not something that can be defined or created via a memo or a slide on a website. Rather it is the social behaviour and norms that permeate the entity and play out every day in the way the entire workforce interacts with one another and external stakeholders. In my experience, the most authentic value statements (and therefore the ones most to be trusted when assessing governance effectiveness) are those which are driven from the bottom up; i.e., statements which are built up from an extensive enquiry of all stakeholder groups as to how they view the entity's culture. The reverse is true; those values statements which emanate from a "white board" session of solely board members or senior executives are almost always a wish-list and not based on how the entity actually behaves or is seen from outside the board.

Many boards, I fear, pay lip service to gaining external validation of their culture and explain away potentially negative evidence from sources such as workforce engagement surveys, gender pay reports and ethnic representation data. The stated values of such boards should be treated with suspicion. However, increasingly, more enlightened boards are passionate about monitoring source data points with regard to the culture as represented through actual lived experiences. Inevitably such boards will continually test reasons for negative evidence (e.g., low workforce engagement, wide gender pay gaps, low levels of ethnic representation), will create safe spaces for workforce and other stakeholders to express concerns where the lived experience differs from the stated values statement, and will act swiftly and boldly where there are indications that the current culture is not what the board aspires to.

This issue, of the curiosity of the board about its actual culture as viewed through the lens of the workforce and other stakeholders, is included in the CG Index inputs. Two of the questions addressed by the GT Governance Institute are: what methods does the board use to monitor culture? What sources of information do companies use to assess culture? They are questions that should be asked of the company when trying to obtain a genuine picture of the culture.

6.3　Risk Management

Risk management is another area that is often seen as a regulatory or defensive management tool, and clearly there are important reasons for identifying and mitigating against those risks that can cause catastrophic failure. However, the best-governed boards, who drive strong financial performance, use risk management as a positive factor in creating value.

Identifying catastrophic risks (say, premises burning down) and mitigating actions (fire safety measures and insurance) are generally relatively easy to include in the risk register. However, the most successful boards go further to consider what might harm their chances to achieve success in the longer term. Changes in market buying patterns (say, office vs home working), a supply chain (say, threat of conflict in an overseas territory), a workforce (failure of, say, the sector to train people in sufficient quantities to allow future market need to be met) or technology (say, changes in market demand for digital technologies) can be more subtle risks that are harder to identify and overcome; but those companies that navigate such longer-term challenges and plan well in advance will normally be those that financially out-perform peers over time.

6.4　Internal Controls

In the aftermath of accounting scandals at Enron, WorldCom, Global Crossing et al., the US authorities introduced the Sarbanes–Oxley Act;[9] Section 404 of that Act imposes a duty upon management to certify that the entity's internal control framework has been evaluated for robustness and found to be working effectively. Section 404 is widely considered in the US to have been one of the pieces of regulation or legislation that had the most beneficial impact on strengthening reporting practice and, as a consequence, the US capital markets.

While governance regulations such as the UK Governance Code and Auditing Standards make reference to internal controls of public companies, the rigour they impose is far less stringent than that required by Sarbanes–Oxley. While annual reports often assert that the internal control framework has been reviewed, frequently boards give little colour as to how that evaluation has been conducted, the depth of the review or what weaknesses were identified.

At the time of writing, the UK awaits government responses to two significant reports on corporate governance and the audit market (Kingman and Brydon).[10,11] It is my expectation that a more robust requirement on companies and auditors to report to the market on their respective evaluation and conclusions on internal controls will be a prime recommendation to be implemented by BEIS (the UK's Department for Business, Energy & Industrial Strategy) and AGRA (Audit, Reporting and Governance Authority). Regardless, the research by the GT Governance Institute points to a rigorous evaluation of internal controls as a key driver of stronger financial performance and enterprise value, and any new regulatory requirements should be seen as a value driver and not just a regulatory burden.

6.5　　Board Effectiveness

It has taken some UK boards a good deal of time truly to embrace a disciplined approach to board effectiveness reviews, but most UK FTSE companies now have mature effectiveness reviews.

Virtually all human communities will have pockets of frustration, latent ideas and rivalries, and boards are no different. A good board effectiveness review should provide a safe space for all board members, and those closely connected to them, to provide an honest voice about what is working well at the board and committees and what needs to be changed. A crucial element of the effectiveness review is culture within the boardroom and an assessment of whether the chair truly draws views from all directors or whether one or two views dominate discussion and decision-making.

6.6.　　Succession Planning

The sixth key governance behaviour that will determine whether the company can be predicted to outperform the market in financial performance and enterprise value measures is succession planning, which needs to be linked to the other areas discussed in this section, such as risk and business model.

In 2017 over 90 per cent of the UK FTSE identified IT and cyber as a key risk; but fewer than 50 per cent reported that they had a leader with deep IT and cyber experience on the main board or senior leadership team. Again, many companies referred to fast-moving demands for new digital ways of delivering goods or services, but few had the age demographic on the board who are most likely to understand that changing demand and which of emerging technologies are gaining traction with a younger generation.

Effective succession planning needs to drill down to talent supply at several tiers of leadership, well below board level. How can a board director properly devote his or her energies to the strategic opportunities and challenges that the board must face while having one eye on whether their deputies are executing the business model well?

6.7　　Conclusion

The research published by the GT Governance Institute paints a compelling picture that companies who adopt and embed the most effective governance frameworks have a very high probability of outperforming their peers in terms of financial performance and value creation.

Those companies that avoid box-ticking and voluminous compliance reporting but think deeply about the business model, culture, risk management, internal controls, board effectiveness and leadership succession are the ones most likely to provide a compelling picture of their effective corporate governance and to enjoy the financial success that is likely to ensue.

7.　　CASE STUDIES: A LINK BETWEEN EFFECTIVE CORPORATE GOVERNANCE AND VALUE CREATION

Having set out the case above that there is a provable link between good corporate governance and stronger financial performance and enterprise value, and identified the six most important governance areas that predict good financial performance, I have included in this section two case studies based on my time as a board member. First is Nuffield Health and second is Grant Thornton. Both case studies show how significant investment in establishing effective corporate governance linked neatly with periods of strong financial performance and growth.

7.1 Nuffield Health

Nuffield Health is a leading UK healthcare provider. It operates 31 private hospitals throughout the UK and 111 wellbeing centres, which are primarily private gyms that provide clinical services such as doctors, physiotherapy and mental wellbeing support in addition to traditional gym facilities and fitness classes. In recent years its revenues have been around £1 billion and EBITDA (earnings before interest, taxes, depreciation and amortisation) £100 million.

Nuffield Health operates in two highly competitive markets (private hospitals and gyms), both of which have seen a number of corporate failures and declines in the last two decades. Unlike its direct private sector competitors, Nuffield Health is a charity and does not have share capital or pay dividends. It is the UK's largest healthcare charity.

In 2015, the board recruited a new CEO, Steve Gray, with a view to developing its business model and governance practices. In particular, the board wished to build the business model and purpose around Nuffield Health's unique place in its markets as a charity. Hitherto its annual surpluses were fully reinvested in delivering health and fitness services, as there was no dividend to pay. However, the old business model and governance practices made no further specific reference to the company's charity status, and its key internal and external performance metrics and investment criteria were traditional financial ones. The board embarked on a journey to establish a clear charitable purpose for Nuffield Health and to place that charitable purpose at the heart of its strategy, business model and governance.

The board began by formulating its purpose and mission, which is "To help build a healthier nation". Its service offering was then defined by three stage-of-life categories under the banners "Healthy Start", "Healthy Living" and "Healthy Aging", and the services that Nuffield Health delivers are rigorously reviewed against how well they match these categories.

Five key measurable strategic goals were developed to allow the board to measure success and progress against achieving the company's desired strategic outcomes. The board recognised that it needed to be financially strong, both in terms of earnings (for example, so that as much cash generated as possible was redirected to providing front line services) and viability (since over £100 million is invested in maintaining, repairing and replacing the estate annually). However, unlike the previous key performance indicators (KPIs), financial measures were seen as an enabler, and set alongside other measures, rather than being the primary focus of performance.

The five strategic pillars were:

- Reach – i.e., the number of people who receive a health outcome from Nuffield Health;
- Quality and Safety – as reported by the CQC, the industry regulator;
- Market Share – the proportion of consumers who use Nuffield Health in its two sectors;
- Awareness – the proportion of the population at large that recognise and trust the Nuffield Health brand, both prompted and unprompted; and
- Earnings – traditional finance measures based on EBITDA and operational cash generation.

Moreover, whereas previously the two main divisions (Hospitals and Wellbeing Centres) had separate leadership and targets, and indeed there was a good deal of autonomy in each of the organisation's 31 hospitals, following the new strategy the business plans and investment allocations for the whole group became connected.

The board measures progress against these strategic measures every quarter. The board reviews the business model twice a year, not to keep changing strategy but to ensure it remains relevant to emerging market needs.

Going hand in hand with development of a clear purpose and business model has been a suite of programmes to embed an appropriate culture within the organisation. For example, the organisation is very risk averse with regard to clinical outcomes, and among the programmes rolled out is "Speaking Up". The Speaking Up programme makes every person who has a touchpoint with a patient or wellbeing consumer feel responsible for the health and welfare of the people they are looking after, from hospital porter to senior consultant surgeon.

The risk register evaluation has been revamped from being a backwards-facing process dominated by checks on outstanding internal audit recommendations to a dynamic, forward-looking process. At every meeting of the risk and audit committee, the CEO and senior executive team are invited to reflect on current and emerging trends, time is devoted to the key challenges the organisation faces to execute its strategy and what opportunities and threats lie over the horizon, and the board and Executive consider how best they can work constructively to overcome those challenges.

The board effectiveness review has helped the board to change the balance of its agenda to spend less time on assessing functional reports and more time on a rich discussion of strategic challenges and opportunities, with a rigorous focus on how Nuffield Health is delivering on its charitable purpose.

The succession planning process has helped the board to challenge itself on its diversity. For example, a significant proportion of its wellbeing consumers are from a younger demographic, and the board has challenged itself on how well that demographic is represented on the board and Executive. The succession planning process has also allowed the organisation over time to refresh and strengthen leadership teams in the levels below the Executive with an eye to having a candidate capable of stepping up to replace each senior Executive role should an emergency need arise.

What has been the outcome from these governance developments and a focus on defining and achieving Nuffield Health's charitable purpose rather than viewing success predominantly through a financial lens?

Excellent progress has been made in achieving Nuffield Health's charitable purpose, for which there are now three KPIs:

- Reach – the number of people who receive a health or wellbeing outcome;
- Social return on investment – the measurable financial return to the individuals who receive a health outcome (e.g., their ability to regain employment) and the savings to society (e.g., from reducing the call on NHS [National Health Service] services by those individuals); and
- Inclusion – the proportion of patients who receive a health or wellbeing service who come from less well-resourced backgrounds and who would not normally be able to access private healthcare or wellbeing services.

Since the implementation of the new strategy in 2016 the total reach has increased each year and has grown from 0.9 million in 2015 to 1.6 million in 2020. In the first year it was measured, the social return on investment was £30 million and the organisation is well on track to achieve its strategic target of achieving a social return on investment of over £120 million by 2023. In 2020, 85,000 people from less well-resourced backgrounds were able to access health or wellbeing services, and the organisation is on track to meet its target of increasing this number to 200,000 by 2025.

While the organisation remains ever vigilant, Nuffield Health has achieved excellent health and safety outcomes on the key measures identified by the industry regulator, the CQC. Twenty-nine of its 31 hospitals were rated good or outstanding by the most recent CQC inspections, a result which outperforms the NHS and all other private healthcare providers. The two hospitals that did not achieve that rating on the most recent independent inspections have addressed all issues raised. They have not been re-inspected by the regulator on the basis they are seen as low-risk.

At the same time as achieving these improved social measures and the charitable purpose, Nuffield Health has outperformed most of its competitors in terms of financial performance. This period has seen significant challenges to actors in both the healthcare and wellbeing (gyms) markets, and a number of entities have failed or required bail-outs, but until the outbreak of the pandemic (when its entire income flows from traditional sources ceased) Nuffield Health continued to grow revenues and operational cash flows and outperform sector norms.

7.2   Grant Thornton

Another first-hand illustration of the linkage of effective corporate governance and outstanding financial performance came from my time as Chair of the Grant Thornton Partnership Oversight Board from 2009 to 2016.

At the beginning of that period Grant Thornton was the fifth largest UK audit firm, and the UK (and global) audit profession was under close scrutiny from governments, regulators and investors after a series of shock corporate collapses. The UK regulator, the FRC, published a new Corporate Governance Code for the largest UK audit firms,[12] based on the Murray Report,[13] in January 2010.

This Audit Firm Governance Code encouraged large audit firms to implement enhanced governance in six areas:

- Leadership;
- Values;
- Independent non-executives;
- Operations;
- Reporting; and
- Dialogue with institutional investors.

The board and I agreed that it was important reputationally for Grant Thornton to be seen to be in the forefront of good governance, a message we were conveying to our own clients, and that instead of a piecemeal adoption of the Code, the firm would seek to be first (and rigorous) adopters.

In common with many other large audit firms, Grant Thornton already had governance processes in place under many of these headings that at least met the Code. However, the Code requirement for audit firms to appoint independent non-executives (INEs) was, at the time, hugely controversial. The board at Grant Thornton concluded that it would embrace the new Audit Firm Governance Code; while many firms responded by creating a new "public interest oversight body" and allowed newly appointed INEs access to only restricted information, Grant Thornton felt it should appoint its new INEs to its main board, where they would have unfettered access to information on all aspects of the firm, and became the first audit firm to do so.

While the Code required a minimum of two INEs, the firm appointed three. The firm looked for a balanced INE team. One INE had a background as CEO of an institutional investor, as it was felt that this experience would help the firm to address the challenge it saw in institutional preference for the Big Four audit firms. A second INE had experience as both executive and non-executive of large public companies, as this was seen as a key growth area for the firm. The third INE had extensive leadership experience in a large legal practice, as it was felt that this knowledge of professional practices would balance the perspectives of the other two INEs, who came from a corporate background.

Grant Thornton also embraced the Code requirement to establish regular dialogue with the institutional investor community. It formed a working group that brought together members of the board with representatives of the investor community and met at least annually. This group allowed the firm to explain its business model, ambitions, challenges and governance to the investors, and allowed the investors to set out the issues of current interest where they wanted audit firms to challenge the companies they audited. Again, Grant Thornton became the first firm to allow the institutional investors to meet privately with its INEs, without the presence of the partner members of the board, to facilitate a free exchange of views.

The other key response was for the firm to look more clinically at its leadership framework. The firm had traditionally delegated significant powers to a CEO, who appointed their own senior leadership team, while the board had historically overseen the activities of the CEO. However, there was frequently a lack of clarity over the respective roles and authorities of the senior leadership team and the board.

As Chair, I worked closely with the CEO to ensure the leadership accountability was articulated much more clearly. This created clarity on which powers were reserved for the board, which were delegated to the CEO (reporting back to the board) and which were delegated to the CEO but required consultation with the board before decisions were taken. This made for much swifter and more confident decision-making by the CEO and senior leadership team and led to more focussed challenge of the CEO by the board.

In the first five-year period of the new strategy and governance procedures, the firm's revenues grew from £350 million to £500 million, average profit per partner doubled from £200,000 to £400,000, and the firm's prompted and unprompted awareness doubled.

I believe that the Nuffield Health and Grant Thornton case studies are good illustrations of how investing in embedding high corporate governance standards can be linked to strong financial performance.

Those who regard corporate governance as a regulatory burden fail to see the enormous advantages that flow from exemplary governance. For example:

• Rigorous analysis of purpose and clarity of business model is an essential element in determining where the entity has the best chance of securing competitive advantage and that it continually challenges its purpose and business model to remain as a leader in its chosen markets;

- Attention to embedding the appropriate culture and ethical values ultimately allows the entity to gain access to the largest pool of talent and to allow that talent to give of their best and thrive;
- Turning risk management from a historical, defensive tool into a forward-looking and dynamic one allows the entity continually to navigate evolving opportunities and threats and to develop the most effective route maps to pursuing opportunities and mitigating threats;
- Seeking assurance on the strength of the internal control framework is an essential element of ensuring that the Board understands how the control framework is operating in practice, as opposed to how it is supposed to work in a manual, and that weaknesses are highlighted and rectified quickly;
- Reviewing board effectiveness, especially if conducted by an external agency, is the most reliable way of ensuring that board is fit for purpose to meet the opportunities and challenges of today and tomorrow, and not just a legacy of yesterday's issues; and
- Leadership succession allows the entity to ensure that it is constantly replenishing and nurturing talent throughout so that potential gaps are filled before those gaps damage performance.

This conclusion – i.e., that strong corporate governance and outstanding financial performance go hand in hand – is consistent with some of the findings of the International Integrated Reporting Council (IIRC).[14] The IIRC was spawned by the work of the Prince of Wales Accounting for Sustainability programme.

The IIRC has developed a framework for corporate reporting which starts with the premise that to assess entity value it is necessary to consider the sustainability of the business model rather than traditional but narrower, and often short-term, financial measures. While the IIRC framework is focussed on responsible corporate reporting, rather than wider governance behaviour, effective reporting goes hand in hand with effective governance; one cannot assess entity value and be assured of effective governance without a reliable reporting measure.

The IIRC faced the same challenges as presented to the early corporate governance codes; i.e., was this something that is a "nice to have" or even "another regulatory burden"? Or, was it a framework that, by focussing attention on what really drives entity value, would enable entities to pull new levers and so enhance that entity value? There was much early scepticism, but the results from the early adopters of the IIRC framework have been encouraging, and increasingly the IIRC framework is being supported by institutional investors and stock exchanges around the world.

The IIRC provides a framework that encourages reporting entities to prepare the annual reports in a holistic fashion to shine a light on the sustainability of the business model. The IIRC framework deploys six "capitals", being:

- Financial;
- Manufactured;
- Intellectual;
- Human;
- Social and relationship;
- Natural.

The point of the IIRC framework is that to be successful on a sustained basis, an entity has to invest in and measure all six capitals rather than just focus on short-term financial performance. A weakness in investment in any of the capitals will inevitably create a threat to the business model at some point and could present a catastrophic challenge to that model and entity value.

The IIRC reporting framework has now been adopted by over 250 of the world's largest companies, such as Anglo American (Europe), AXA (UK), BP (Europe), Coca-Cola (US), SAP (Europe), Tata (Asia), Transnet (Africa) and Canadian Real Estate Investment Trust (North America).

One of the most interesting findings from the early days of the IIRC came from its CEO Committee, which comprised some of the CEOs of the global corporations who were the early implementers of the IIRC framework. Many of those CEOs said that they had adopted the IIRC framework from a reputational perspective; i.e., they thought that it was an important statement to their shareholders and markets that they were taking sustainability of the business model seriously. However, many of them reported that the discipline imposed by this framework based on six capitals (rather than a predominantly financial one) had brought a greater focus in their leadership teams in vigorously defining purpose, culture, leadership and the entity's relationship with its workforce, external stakeholders and the environment. This in turn was bearing fruit in improved financial performance. In other words, good governance and outstanding financial performance are not competitors but go hand in hand.

8.   EXAMPLES OF HOW A STRONG GOVERNANCE FRAMEWORK ENABLES A COMPANY TO DEAL EFFECTIVELY WITH AN UNEXPECTED EMERGENCY

In the earlier sections of this chapter I looked at the evidence that good corporate governance behaviour drives enhanced financial performance and enterprise value. I also provided some case studies that illustrate the point.

In this section, I look at two case studies that show how a good corporate governance framework can protect financial performance and enterprise value when a crisis arises, in this case the Covid emergency.

The rapid emergence of the Covid pandemic at the beginning of 2020 provided companies with an unprecedented set of challenges. ("Unprecedented" is an overused term but in this case it is correct.) Not since wartime has the state imposed such onerous restrictions on the free movement of its people and the forced closure, redeployment or requisitioning of private business as was witnessed in many countries, notably in Europe and North America.

Covid posed a series of challenges to boards. First, the nature of the business interruption was not something previously experienced and the length of that interruption could not be forecast with any precision. Second, the scale for many businesses was potentially catastrophic, and companies had to learn quickly what support from government and other agencies would be put in place and how that support could be accessed.

In my experience, there were two over-riding and immediate issues to address. First, an enhanced governance framework was needed to help the company to navigate its way through multiple layers of complexity and uncertainty which created decision-making that balanced competing priorities; for example, how to balance the need for the company to play its part in containing the spread of Covid with the need to keep the company afloat. Second, a new governance relationship between the board and the Executive was required; certainly, at the start of the government lockdown restrictions, companies were faced with a wave of major decisions on a daily, sometimes hourly, basis and the traditional model of executive decisions waiting for monthly or quarterly board or committee approval would be too slow.

At such a time of stress, those businesses that went into the crisis brought on by the pandemic with a foundation of strong corporate governance had a clear advantage. For example, a well-articulated risk appetite helped agile decision-making in the early days of lockdown; the day your board discovers that all sources of revenue have stopped overnight is not the time to start drafting a business continuity plan.

However, the boards that I saw deal most effectively and sensitively with the Covid crisis quickly embedded a principled framework specifically to guide decision-making through the pandemic.

8.1   Carey Group

Carey Group is a family-owned civil engineering and construction group with revenues of £500 million and an employed workforce of 1,000 and which complements its own workforce with a series of sub-contractors. In March 2020 there was considerable political and media pressure to close the construction sector because of fears around the large number of construction workers who were using very crowded public transport networks at peak rush hours and the close working proximities of thousands of construction workers on sites. However, given the scale of many key construction projects, closure of sites could quickly wipe millions of pounds from entity balance sheets.

The board at Carey's quickly adopted a four-point governance framework to deal with the specific challenges of Covid and the Executive's deployment of the business continuity process. I am indebted to my friends at EY who suggested the framework, which was built around four principles:

- Keeping our people safe;
- Acting responsibly and doing the right thing by society;
- Communicating swiftly and frequently with all key stakeholders; and
- Securing the financial strength of the group.

Clearly there were often extreme tensions between these principles for many of the decisions required in the early days, but these principles provided an essential framework against which we could judge each key decision, and they forced the board to justify why we might appear to be contravening any one principle. Without such a framework, the board and Executive would quickly have become swamped by a series of one-off decisions with little cohesion in how decisions were arrived at.

One of the first decisions the board made was to close, on a voluntary basis, every site (other than where ongoing maintenance was essential to maintain safety), acknowledging that this would cause a cessation of all revenue streams, other than a small amount of rental income. While health and safety are paramount at all Carey's sites, the actions necessary to keep people safe in a Covid environment were simply untried or unknown at that time and government guidance was moving daily. Moreover, we could not convince ourselves it was responsible to society to ask our workforce to travel on crowded public transport, causing heightened risk of infection to them and fellow passengers.

As events transpired, a little time later government closed all construction sites. However, before that time, the board had judged that its responsibilities to our people and to society outweighed the financial cost of closure. We also concluded that waiting until being coerced into closing sites would do severe damage to our reputation.

The next action was to bring into operation the emergency communications strategy. The Covid Response Team met daily. We needed to reassure our people that we were looking after their safety but also give what reassurance we could about their longer-term job security. We also decided to speak on a daily basis at that time with clients to explain why we were exiting sites and to agree key needs such as how to continue essential safety maintenance. We needed to reassure clients about our financial resilience and also seek reassurance from them that they would honour debts due for the work we had done. Similarly, we spoke on a daily basis with all key suppliers to reassure them of our ability to pay the debts that were due to them and satisfy ourselves as to which suppliers would be able to continue to supply materials once sites were re-opened.

The period of mandatory lockdown gave the Executive team time to develop a back-to-work strategy for when government allowed construction sites to re-open. A key concern was the mental wellbeing of our people, who themselves were coping with tension between health and financial pressures. Once government gave the green light for construction sites to re-open, every member of our workforce was required to have a one-to-one meeting before returning to work to assess their physical and emotional readiness to return to work; for example, people worried about their health could be a danger to themselves and others on a construction site. We responded to public concerns about construction workers causing crowding on public transport by providing private means of transport for every site worker so that they did not need to use public transport (and they were not allowed to do so).

A detailed risk assessment was carried out on every site, and no site was allowed to open unless it had been certified as Covid-secure, assurances about payment had been received from clients and the supply chain was secured.

Communication with clients and suppliers continued to be key and we maintained the frequent, often daily, conversation with key partners to build mutual trust that both sides would use best endeavours to allow projects to continue and to commit to pay for services and work supplied.

Cash management clearly became a priority; three-week rolling cash forecasts were updated daily by the Executive and monitored weekly by the board so that there was a coordinated plan of action where short-term pressure points were foreseen.

Carey's frequent and transparent communications extended to the banks and HMRC (Her Majesty's Revenue and Customs). In our case, Allied Irish Bank waived its covenant requirements and provided emergency Covid funding within 24 hours of our request. Similarly, HMRC was very accessible and agreed a combination of Value Added Tax and Pay As You Earn tax payment deferrals and paid cash to the group for provisional R&D tax credit claims, within days of the group making the requests. While the large banks and HMRC do not often come in for widespread praise, in my experience both the banking system and HMRC performed superbly in the Covid crisis, not only putting in place massive emergency support packages but also short-cutting many of their normal review and approval processes.

During the height of the crisis, after a consultation process, the group asked its workforce to participate in a voluntary salary reduction. This was tiered so that those on lower incomes did not suffer a reduction while reductions of up to 30 per cent were sought from the highest pay grades, including members of the board and Executive. As a result of the frequent and transparent communications the group had had with its people, all bar less than a dozen of its 1,000 people agreed to that salary-sacrifice request. Happily, the group has now repaid all of the amount that our people voluntarily agreed to give up.

While neither Carey Group nor the construction sector as a whole is complacent about the lingering impact of Covid, in the case of Carey Group we have arrived at a place where our business is considerably stronger than it was immediately before the pandemic hit.

First, while areas of uncertainty continue within the workforce, our people engagement has been strong, and the management are holding monthly "town hall" meetings at which all 1,000 people can hear the latest news on the group from the CEO and Executive and post their questions and comments.

Second, our relationships with key clients and suppliers are stronger than they have been for years, giving both parties greater confidence in the delivery of existing contracts and the successful outcomes of future ones.

Third, our relationship with the bank is stronger and we have been able to agree a long-term financing package to enable the group to prepare for post-Covid growth with confidence.

Fourth, our decision to close sites on a voluntary basis at the height of the first Covid wave has helped our profile and reputation with local communities and fostered a relationship built on trust.

Finally, the group's forecasting ability is at a record high and its finances and cash position are stronger than they have been at any time in recent years.

Carey Group's success in navigating the crisis brought about by the first year of Covid is a testament to its leadership, people and external stakeholders. But I doubt that the board and Executive would have steered such a steady path and maintained and built enterprise value and improved financial performance without a solid governance framework with which to determine the many critical decisions, which involved conflicting pressures, often on a daily basis.

8.2   Nuffield Health

The impact of Covid on Nuffield Health was equally dramatic. Within days, the NHS requested us to cease treatment in all our private patient activity and devote all 31 hospitals to emergency NHS Covid and oncology cases. At the same time, with minimal warning, all 111 gyms and wellbeing centres were forced to close.

The governance framework adopted by Nuffield Health was similar to Carey's and involved three pillars:

- Protecting our people;
- Doing the right thing by society; and
- Building sustained financial resilience.

It was immediately clear that the group would need to adapt its normal governance structures as so many crucial decisions were having to be made daily. The board agreed high-level principles by which additional authority was devolved to the Executive and much of the board's work was delegated to standing and ad hoc committees that allowed smaller groups of the Executive and board members to work collaboratively in agile fashion.

Our first priority was our 15,000 people. Some of the people challenges were relatively easy; for example, ensuring they had access to adequate personal protective equipment. This was dealt with by agreeing very strict contractual terms with local health trusts. However, other people challenges have been much harder. For example, our teams usually do not routinely become involved in acute surgery, and while deaths occur, they are unusual. However, now most of our hospital teams were dealing every day with multiple fatalities, and we believe, as a result, that many will need mental health support for years to come. And it is our responsibility to identify and meet those needs.

A second challenge was how to do the right thing by our clients and society – clearly it was right to agree to the request from government to make our hospitals available to the NHS for Covid intensive care treatment and emergency cancer cases. The cost of losing our income from gyms and giving up our income from hospitals was enormous; however, the board and Executive felt that morally we had no option but to do the best we could for society and provide the NHS with our hospital capacity.

However, a conflict arose once the first Covid surge died down. The NHS understandably wanted to retain the additional hospital capacity for an extended time; its focus was on being able to deal with the risks of a second and third spike in infections later on. But utilisation of beds and surgeries at some of our hospitals was less than 20 per cent. The company had a long list of private patients, many with serious surgical needs whom we had not been able to help, and some of whom were at risk of harm as an indirect consequence of Covid. We wanted to get back to providing those clients with the healthcare they needed and to start to rebuild the company's financial resilience.

So we had to balance those competing needs and embark on complex negotiations with the NHS and local health trusts to try to identify innovative and agile working methods that allowed the NHS capacity in all hospitals as Covid cases increased but allowed some provision of care to our private patients.

Third was the financial challenge. We were about to start a £400 million re-financing with banks before Covid struck. We had so many vulnerabilities in forecasts that scenario planning, while vital, was extremely hard. While we recovered the cost of some of the hospital services, we had lost all revenue from traditional sources. We had no sight as to when we could return our hospital capacity for our own patients. We had no visibility on when we could open our gyms. And even when we were able to open, we had no foresight on customer behaviours – would there be pent up demand with customers flooding back to gyms our would they be hesitant to return to group settings?

So we worked up a plan with our banks to roll over our facilities for a further 12 months, and they provided us with a small Covid contingency fund. But we deferred the long-term re-financing until we all had a better idea of the shape of the business going forward. And we have worked closely with them on a monthly basis so there are no surprises about our results or any concerns they might have about continuing to lend.

Since Nuffield Health has been able to re-open its hospitals to its own patients, this side of the operation has been operating at record levels. The company has emerged with a strong balance sheet and its lenders have sufficient confidence in the company's financial resilience that they are planning to agree a new five-year financial package shortly.

The company has emerged from lockdown with a strongly enhanced reputation, a committed workforce and financial resilience.

While Carey Group and Nuffield Health operate in very different sectors and their outcomes were varied, both showed immense resilience in overcoming the loss of their entire revenue streams almost overnight, took care of their workforces, acted responsibly towards society, and emerged with strong growth potential and strong balance sheets.

The point of these case studies is to underline the vital role that establishing a strong governance framework, to deal with the specific challenges of Covid, played in ensuring that a company takes coherent decisions in a time of crisis. I find it difficult to imagine that such coherence would have been as readily achieved among companies that did not adopt such a governance framework or which focussed solely on short-term financial goals. Having a robust governance framework to deal with an emergency gives the company the best chance to emerge both financially strong and with a sustainable business model intact that allows it to take advantage of the inevitable opportunities that will flow in the aftermath of that emergency. In other words, effective corporate governance protects financial performance and enterprise value when an unexpected emergency arises.

9.   EMERGING GOVERNANCE AREAS THAT WILL LIKELY DRIVE ENTERPRISE VALUE IN FUTURE

In Section 6 of this chapter, I set out the six key governance behaviours highlighted by the GT Governance Institute research that most reliably predict stronger financial performance. I close this chapter by suggesting the governance areas that I believe will be similarly crucial for boards to address in coming years.

As mentioned above, three of these – sustainability and the use of scare resources, social governance and further requirements on internal controls environments – have been the subject of much writing elsewhere. So, the issue that I choose to highlight as my final tip on a governance area that will help drive financial performance and enterprise value in coming years is diversity.

9.1   Diversity

Gender diversity within a UK corporate environment was first raised in a governance context by the report of Lord Davies in 2011.[15] Lord Davies recommended that the UK FTSE 100 should aim for a minimum 25 per cent female representation on boards by 2015. This was supported by the 30% Club, established by Helena Morrissey, and which established an aspirational target of 30 per cent women on boards by 2015.

The gender diversity mantle was taken on by the Hampton–Alexander Review of 2016[16] which promoted a target of 33 per cent female representation on FTSE 350 boards by the end of 2020. Business Secretary Alok Sharma raised his concern earlier in 2021 that over 40 per cent of companies had failed to meet that target. Some institutional investors are now expressing publicly that they will be prepared to vote down director appointments where boards pay insufficient attention to gender diversity.

One of the outcomes of the tragic death of George Floyd in the US has been a spotlight on the severe shortage of ethnic diversity on boards and, to me, it is an inescapable conclusion that ethnic diversity will be brought into the ambit of regulatory governance codes in the near future.

I welcome these initiatives to drive greater diversity throughout organisations, but especially at board and Executive level. However, companies that see the promotion of diversity as a regulatory cost are missing an opportunity. Just as with risk management as discussed earlier, there are compelling business (as well as moral) reasons for promoting diversity in many aspects; these are both negative reasons (avoiding harm; e.g., improving the company's ability to identify and mitigate key risks) and positive ones (identifying growth opportunities) for boards to regard promotion of diversity as a crucial tool in driving stronger financial performance and enterprise value.

There is a range of research that points to diversity leading to stronger companies. However, I believe this conclusion is best illustrated non-empirically by Matthew Syed in his inspirational book *Rebel Ideas*,[17] which provides excellent case studies of how a lack of diversity in leadership structures has led to catastrophic failure while broad diversity has been an enabler of exceptional growth.

With regard to the former (failure to avoid catastrophe), Syed cites the failure of the CIA to identify the seriousness of the threat posed by Osama bin Laden and al-Qaeda despite having many warning signs in the years leading up to 9/11. He links this failure to a recruitment process that focussed on "the best of the best" from an Ivy League, and therefore, predominantly white, background and argues that this narrow perspective within the CIA meant that the severity of the emerging al-Qaeda threat could not be comprehended by a non-diverse class which could not understand the power of the symbolism that was being portrayed, and who dismissed bin Laden as an isolated oddball stuck in a cave. Whereas, Syed argues, had the CIA's recruitment driven greater diversity (including people more in tune with Islamic thinking) within its tiers, the threat would have been only too obvious well before the loss of nearly 3,000 lives.

Syed also discusses lack of diversity of thinking in hierarchical structures. He cites the example of the failure of an attempt on the Everest summit, with consequent loss of lives, by a team of experienced climbers and links the failure to a hierarchical leadership structure that did not tolerate leadership challenge. He argues that the hierarchical structure arose because the leaders believed that there was no time for debate and discussion when there was such a limited time window for a successful ascent. That structure worked well while things were going to plan; however, when an unexpected crisis arose, too much responsibility fell upon the leader, who was so overwhelmed he was too slow to recognise that the plan had to be changed if the team was to survive. Even though the experienced support leaders could see the problems, the power of the hierarchical culture meant that they failed to challenge and support the leader, with fatal consequences. There was insufficient diversity of thinking to change the plan in time to save lives.

Syed contrasts these catastrophic failures with the explosive growth enjoyed by many giant technology companies where diversity of thinking and perspective tend to be promoted and facilitated by flatter leadership structures and collaborative working practices.

The Race at Work Charter[18] sponsored by Business in the Community has prompted a range of interesting tools to emerge to help boards. Innovative ideas are now being deployed to promote diversity by some successful boardrooms who see achieving more diverse environments as a driver of stronger financial performance and enterprise value as well as a moral imperative. Ideas include:

- Allyship;
- Incentives;
- Curiosity;
- Networks;
- Data; and
- Reverse and two-way mentoring.

9.2   Allyship

It is common for newly appointed board members and commentators to express concern about how challenge can be delivered, and received, constructively. How does one learn to speak up, go against the grain, ruffle some feathers, break groupthink, etc., without being booted off the board, and get a board to learn to appreciate and actively seek this? How does one convince the chair and CEO that diversity in thought, constructive criticism and devil's advocate thinking can drive positive outcomes, even if only by validating original propositions?

The concept of allyship can be helpful in this regard; i.e., being willing to argue someone else's case. For example, in the case where the chief information officer is arguing the case for greater technology investment, say to improve business connectivity or increase cyber resilience, it is likely to be more compelling if the point is argued or supported from outside the IT Department.

The concept of allyship takes on particular importance in breaking down lack of diversity based on characteristics, encouraging those in the majority to be alert to situations where people might be suffering from negative bias. It is commonly argued that you cannot be neutral on sexism, racism, etc.; one either speaks out against such biases or one is part of the problem ("Silence is not an option"). I have witnessed, even on boards where I rate culture and values highly, an almost imperceptible rolling of the eyes when a person of colour or a woman attempts to point out a lack of ethnic or gender diversity; it is much harder for such scepticism to take hold when I make the point (as a white man).

9.3   Incentives

It is common, in my experience, for boards to view a lack of diversity through the wrong end of the telescope; to receive another depressing set of reports on a lack of diversity, to have a collective sucking of teeth, and to shake heads and say the board has done all it can, that the lack of diversity is the problem of those "outside groups". To create truly diverse thinking and culture, a board that sees there is a lack of diversity (i.e., at present, sadly, most boards) must take ownership and see this as a problem for the organisation, not for those who are under-represented.

By and large, managers are good problem-solvers; this is what allowed them to be promoted in the first instance. By making a lack of diversity a problem for the organisation to solve, and incentivising managers to reach solutions, the dynamic changes; creating a more diverse culture becomes a management opportunity (e.g., for financial gain or approval) rather than someone else's problem.

9.4   Curiosity

I expressed the view above, in the section on culture, that curiosity is a key determinant of effective board behaviour and good governance. This is especially the case when it comes to creation of diverse and inclusive cultures. Boards should not explain away lack of diversity (e.g., low representation or negative pay gaps) with cursory arguments. Boards need constantly to be vigilant in seeking evidence as to whether the real lived experiences of their workforce and external stakeholders align with the desired and stated culture and, in the frequent cases where they do not fully align, be rigorous in seeking ways to address the problems.

The most powerful tool I have seen over the past 12 months to exhibit this curiosity, and to ensure the board has a much deeper understanding of the barriers to diversity and inclusivity, is the concept of facilitated conversations that create a safe space for all people within the workforce to speak about their lived experiences and the barriers they have faced. This can be done in small groups, but equally I have seen this concept deployed very effectively via virtual global conversations.

Participating (by listening) in these conversations has opened my eyes to the barriers that are frequently faced by people based on gender, ethnic, religious, age and sexual orientation prejudices, and the debilitating cumulative impact that micro-aggressions, which might seem trivial in isolation, have when repeated systemically. For example, a woman who is told repeatedly that she is being "bossy" when a male colleague might be viewed as being "a leader" for behaving in an identical way; a person of colour who is constantly told they are being "chippy" when a white colleague might be viewed as "standing up for themselves"; a gay man on a building site who is subjected to a taunt daily (hourly) that is justified as "just a bit of banter"; or a young person who is told that they "do not understand how things are done around here" when a more experienced colleague would be lauded as being "innovative" for making the same point.

I was talking recently to the CEO of a global professional practice (both the organisation and the CEO are exemplars of a business and leader who believe passionately in building diverse and inclusive cultures, and indeed have had measurable success in doing so) and I recognised his new awareness from these conversations that often the micro-aggressions that hold back people from under-represented groups occur outside the workplace, but have a debilitating cumulative impact that the individual takes into the workplace. That enlightened leader, and his global organisation, are now vocal about taking ownership of these "out of workplace" micro-aggressions and recognising that, even though the source of exclusive behaviour is outside the business, it is the responsibility of the business and its leaders to help those people overcome the obstacles and to feel safe in bringing their authentic selves to work.

While I describe this facilitated conversation to be a powerful tool, that description only applies where the conversations and proposals that arise from them are at the heart of the board's agenda. Another common failure of boards to drive diversity effectively is to regard the matter as a project to be led outside the board, say by the HR function. Hearing the obstacles faced by under-represented groups, and how their real lived experiences in the workplace differ from the desired culture, can make for uncomfortable hearing in the boardroom, but it is only by hearing, and acting upon, these uncomfortable conversations that a board can fully commit to doing all that it can to improve diversity and inclusion.

9.5   Networks

Creating networks of under-represented groups can be impactful in improve the inclusiveness of a culture, but only if the networks are genuinely sponsored by board leadership and their views and recommendations acted upon. For example, seemingly small steps such as recognising non-Western religious or festival days can have an immediate and widespread impact throughout the organisation. Whereas, if the network is simply left to get on without authentic board sponsorship and a voice to facilitate change, the network risks reinforcing exclusivity.

9.6   Data

It is a well-used phrase in business that what gets measured gets done. Reliable and objective data – for example, workforce engagement, pay gap and representation reports – are essential tools for boards to determine the success or otherwise of their programmes to create diverse and inclusive cultures and the measures they are taking to overcome areas of poor culture.

9.7   Reverse and Two-Way Mentoring

As I approach one of the later stages of my professional career, I have found reverse or two-way mentoring to be an incredibly rich source of learning and engagement, both for me and my reverse mentors. This concept pairs an established board colleague with a less experienced person from a very different background. In my case, my reverse mentors are younger people from a different ethnic background.

When I joined the two-way mentoring programme of a particular organisation, this concept was sold to me as being an opportunity for me to help my reverse mentors by helping them to form strategies to develop their career paths more effectively and for my reverse mentors to give me a better insight into their lived experiences, and the micro-aggressions they experience, inside and outside the workplace. Indeed, this programme has delivered both those objectives and has been rewarding for all participants as a result. However, I have found that I have gained so much more by being challenged with a totally fresh perspective, and this has helped me grow both in my professional career and indeed my personal life.

None of these tools should be seen as a silver bullet. However, there is no doubt that those boards and leaders who deploy a selection of them can achieve measurable success in driving ever more diverse and inclusive cultures.

9.8   Conclusion on Diversity and Inclusion

Increasingly the case for diversity goes beyond better decision-making in organisations. New, younger customer bases tend to be much more attuned to an entity's culture, values and practices, and a company that fails to promote itself as diverse puts at risk a significant element of its potential customer base. Despite the march of technology, many sectors continue to have access to talent as a key risk, and a company that fails to exude a culture which welcomes talent from all genders, ethnic backgrounds, faiths, ages and sexual orientations is immediately constructing an obstacle to mitigating that risk.

Alongside the environment and use of scare resources, I see diversity and representation as the key social issue of the 2020s, and I would urge all boards to place the creation of a diverse and inclusive culture at the heart of their agendas.

10.   CONCLUSIONS

The UK has had a formal corporate governance code for listed and public interest entities for around 30 years, since the publication of the Cadbury Report in 1992. However, while most commentators agree that well-run companies are more likely to succeed than poorly-run ones, opinion has often been divided when it comes to the role played by corporate governance in driving financial performance. Some argue that effective governance is an integral part of optimising an entity's financial performance and enterprise value; others argue that it is a regulatory burden that brings inflated cost for little real value.

Fortunately, we now have authoritative research that provides empirical evidence linking good governance with superior financial return. Research published by the GT Governance Institute based on observable data from FTSE 350 companies over 10 years shows that there is a demonstrable link between good corporate governance behaviours and stronger financial performance and enterprise value.

Moreover, this positive correlation is based on financial performance based on each of the company perspective (e.g., operating margin), shareholder perspective (e.g., total shareholder return) and lenders' perspective (e.g., leverage).

The GT Governance Institute has identified six governance behaviours that are good predictors of strong financial performance. These are: (i) business model clarity and connectivity, (ii) culture and value integration, (iii) risk management, (iv) internal controls, (v) board effectiveness and (vi) succession planning.

This link can be observed in companies who embrace effective corporate governance to build financial performance and enterprise value in a normal cycle and also to protect enterprise value in times of crisis.

The areas of (i) sustainability and the use of scare resources, (ii) social governance, (iii) further requirements on internal controls environments and (iv) diversity are ripe for new regulatory requirements. However, of these, I believe that diversity offers rich opportunities for improving financial performance in the short term.

My main conclusion from many years of studying this space is that companies who embrace effective corporate governance and see good governance as a vital tool to achieve success, rather than as a regulatory burden, offer themselves the best chances to drive stronger financial performance and enterprise value.

NOTES

1.   Cadbury Report on Corporate Governance, issued by the Committee on the Financial Aspects of Corporate Governance, May 1992.
2.   The UK Corporate Governance Code, issued by the Financial Reporting Council, July 2018.
3.   The Wates Corporate Governance Principles for Large Private Companies, issued by the Financial Reporting Council, December 2018.

4. https://www.grantthornton.co.uk/globalassets/1.-member-firms/united-kingdom/pdf/documents/corporate-governance-and-company-performance.pdf, issued by the Grant Thornton Governance Institute, December 2019.
5. The UK Corporate Governance Code, issued by the Financial Reporting Council, October 2012.
6. *Corporate Governance Review 2020*, published by Grant Thornton Governance Institute.
7. "Lessons in Kindness", article published by the Positive Group, May 2020. https://www.positivegroup.org/loop/articles/lessons-in-kindness.
8. Ibid.
9. The Sarbanes–Oxley Act, enacted July 2002.
10. The Independent Review of the Financial Reporting Council, led by Sir John Kingman, issued December 2018.
11. The Report of the Independent Review into the Quality and Effectiveness of Audit, led by Sir Donald Brydon CBE, December 2019.
12. The Audit Firm Governance Code Revised by the Financial Reporting Council, July 2016.
13. The Audit Firm Governance Code, a Project for the Financial Reporting Council, issued January 2010.
14. The Consultation Draft of the International Integrated Reporting Framework, released April 2013.
15. Independent Review into Women on Boards, led by Lord Davies, published February 2011.
16. Improving Gender Balance in FTSE Leadership, issued by the Hampton–Alexander Review, published in November 2016.
17. *Rebel Ideas: The Power of Diverse Thinking*, by Matthew Syed, published April 2020.
18. https://www.bitc.org.uk/race/.

APPENDIX

Summary of Qualitative Assessments Included in the 2020 Corporate Governance Review 2020 Published by the Grant Thornton Research Institute (permission for reproduction of this summary granted by authors Sarah Bell and Simon Lowe)

Purpose, value creation and protection
Do companies define their purpose?
Does the annual report explain the board's activities in relation to assessing if the company's policies, practices and behaviours are aligned with the company's purpose and values?
To what extent do companies describe their business model?
What is the quality of descriptions of principal risks and uncertainties?
To what extent do companies provide a balanced and comprehensive analysis of their business?
To what extent do companies describe KPIs that measure the performance of the business?
What is the average number of financial KPIs disclosed?
To what extent do companies describe the likely future development of the business?
How many companies disclose technology/cyber security as a principal risk?

Culture
To what extent does the annual report address culture and values?
Does the chair discuss the culture and values of the company, and where?
Does the CEO discuss the culture and values of the company?
What methods does the board use to monitor culture?
What sources of information do companies use to assess culture?

Stakeholder engagement
Does the board explain in the annual report how their stakeholders' interests and the matters set out in section 172 influenced decision-making?
How does the board gather the views of the workforce?
To what degree does the board demonstrate the steps taken to understand the views of major shareholders?
Does the chair meet with shareholders, and do they discuss governance and performance against the strategy?
Who attends meetings with major shareholders?

ESG [Environmental, social and governance]
To what extent does the company explain environmental matters?
To what extent does the company explain social, community and human rights activities?
To what extent does the company explain employee matters?

Board composition, responsibilities and effectiveness
How many board members with experience in the specified areas?
Why are non-executive directors not considered independent?
How much explanation is there of how the board, committees and individual directors are annually formally evaluated for their performance?
To what extent are the outputs and actions arising from the board evaluation disclosed?

What development areas have been identified from the evaluation conducted during the year?

Nomination Committee

To what extent do companies describe board succession planning?

To what extent does the board describe the company's succession planning for senior management and development of a diverse pipeline?

How much explanation is there of the company's policy on gender diversity in the boardroom?

How much explanation is there of the company's policy on other aspects of diversity in the boardroom?

What other kinds of diversity are mentioned?

Audit Committee

How well is the viability statement summarised?

How many years are assessed in the company viability statement?

How much information is there about the company's internal control systems?

How much information is provided on the process the board have applied in reviewing the effectiveness of the internal control system?

How much information does the audit committee report provide on how it reached its recommendation to the board on the appointment, reappointment or removal of the external auditors?

If the auditor provides non-audit services, is there a statement as to how the auditor's objectivity and independence is safeguarded?

Remuneration Committee

How clearly are companies describing their remuneration policies?

What metrics are used in executive annual bonuses?

What metrics are used in executive long-term performance-based remuneration?

What is the retention (additional holding) period of awards after vesting?

What is the minimum shareholding requirement for the CEO?

Is there a clawback provision?

Are executive pensions aligned to workforce pensions?

Does the description of the work of the remuneration committee include the details of what engagement has taken place to explain how executive remuneration aligns with the wider workforce?

Does the description of the work of the remuneration committee include the details on what engagement has taken place with shareholders and the impact this has had on remuneration policy and outcomes?

Annual report and quality of reporting

How much information does the board provide as to why it considers the annual report fair, balanced and understandable?

How detailed is the personal commentary from the chair?

8. Knowledge, experience and measurement for stakeholder decision-making: a historical case study

Roy Edwards

INTRODUCTION

The history of management in Britain has developed significantly in the last 30 years. The survey by John Wilson and Andrew Thompson published in 2006 provides a comprehensive text summarising a range of disciplines, professions and practices that constitute management practice within a historical context. Their analysis concluded that insofar as British management was professionalised, there was more "reflectivity" from management, in an economy that had transitioned from manufacturing and services (Wilson and Thompson, 2006, p. 273). To this might have been added the gradual expansion of business techniques into areas of the economy such as education, health and general public administration that created new opportunities for consulting, outsourcing of goods and services that required business language to frame contracts and monitor performance. The past 120 years seemed to be a period where a systematic approach to management was extending and developing throughout the economy. From the factory floor to the office and boardroom, information was being collected, collated and analysed using a variety of techniques, from mathematics to accounting and even engineering. Alongside management for internal control and decision-making, accounting and business historians explored the development of company law and associated transformation of financial reporting (see Harris, 2000, for further details). Similarly, J.R. Edwards covered the development of financial reporting through the 19th and 20th centuries (Edwards, 2019). This chapter seeks to explore one element of how the relationship between owners, managers, customers and the legislature – stakeholders – developed at a specific point in time, when the nature of governance and its relationship with management control was being contested. All too often governance is equated with compliance and the necessity to report information to overcome the asymmetries associated with the principal–agent relationship. More cynically, it may the case that attention is focused on whatever issue has attracted scrutiny from an indignant media, prompting an eventual legislative response that demonstrates the latter's concern that such egregious behaviour should be allowed.

This chapter explores a debate surrounding the performance measurement and disclosure at the turn of the 20th century in a period when government intervention and shareholder pressure was slowly becoming a legitimate means of overcoming perceived – if not actual – poor management and operating performance. A comprehensive analysis of railway returns reported that "average returns of railway ordinary and preference shares were the poorest amongst domestic sectors" before concluding "railways could have been better managed and the average social rate of return could have been higher" (Mitchell, Chambers and Crafts, 2009, pp. 17 and p. 24). This chapter accepts this conclusion but with an important caveat, that some railway companies were investing in new management techniques, but that they did not fit within what might be called a financial model of the firm. The wider rationale for this analysis is that it explores the debate on railway management and information disclosure when sector-specific knowledge and experience was critical in understanding the reality of what reported statistics meant. In terms of the history of accounting, this idea resonates with the critique of management accounting during the 1980s where Western business performance and management control of complex industries required non-financial operating information to supplement financial information. Johnson and Kaplan's (1987) critique of management accounting examined the information needed for internal control, including enhanced non-financial metrics to supplement cost accounting, compared to financial reporting. This chapter shows that this was not confined to the 1980s, nor just manufacturing. The effectiveness of individual management control was being challenged by new approaches to management control that sought the de-personalisation of management and the idiosyncratic experience that went with it. Senior railway management rejected this view as an assault on their methods of management, viewing disclosure as problematic, because knowledge and experience was critical to effectively interpreting measures of management control, and the relevance of reporting to performance.

There are two reasons to be interested in the historical context of performance measurement, management control and reporting in the context of board decision-making and wider interaction with shareholders and managers. Firstly, it reveals more detail on the contested nature of the development of new management methods, from existing management. Secondly historical case evidence improves understanding of how techniques emerge and offers alternatives to be considered, and through this more effective reflection on the existing approach to management decision-making. More recent emphasis on the importance of stakeholder involvement comes from, for example, Spitzeck and Hansen (2010), who have stressed the importance of stakeholders in the survival of the organisation. For this, it is important that there is effective reporting of key management information to said stakeholders. This chapter will explore government investigation – by the Board of Trade – of railway accounts and statistics where a particular measurement was being pushed as an example of what might be called, then, modern scientific management. The evidence from this case will be used to tease out the conflicting views on reporting and the conflation of measurement for reporting and management control within this investigation. This will be contrasted with a more effective real-time method of management, train control, that was rejected by the critiques of railway management because they did not understand how it was able to supplement and systematise their *bête noire* of personal supervision.

HISTORICAL BACKGROUND AND CONTEXT

The chapter explores the debate surrounding the collection and use of accounting and statistical information in the British railway sector, at a time when concerns were being raised by some shareholders and government at the performance of railway companies and their failure to introduce new measures of performance developed primarily in the United States. As the railway companies had merged over the course of the 19th century, more complex organisational structures had developed, and this was coupled with a belief that the performance of individual companies was not what it should be. The emphasis here will follow the contemporary debate on the performance of rail freight operations, cast in terms of the ton-mile (see below) and derivative statistics. The analysis is framed by exploring how reported information needed to be interpreted by individuals with knowledge and experience, in addition to accounting and performance measurement. Previous authors exploring the history of management information and railway performance have criticised the railways for not adopting a more "scientific" approach to management. Derek Aldcroft, for example, admonished the railways for not paying "sufficient attention" to improving techniques. He argued that they had "little conception of the economic science of transportation", concluding that as regards ton-mileage, "If the railways were to be run scientifically and economically it was essential that it was possible for such data [to] be collected" (Aldcroft, 1968, pp. 160 and 172). This is not the case.

The debate has affected the way in which railway management has been subsequently portrayed. The debate has always been framed in terms of the criticisms made by critics of railway management from the financial and trade press, given formal voice through representations as members of government investigations and under cross-examination. A departmental committee of the Board of Trade was established in response to collected evidence on accounting and statistical information between 1907 and 1910. This investigation led in turn to the Railway Companies (Accounts and Returns) Act of 1911 (Kirkus, 1927). This chapter revisits the written evidence to explore in more detail some of the evidence presented by witnesses and comments made by the committee during the process of cross-examination. This chapter will conclude that the debate over reporting managerial performance was not as straightforward as historians have surmised, and that this has implications for how we understand the nature of reporting and the value of information in the governance and decision-making process – in both historical and contemporary contexts.

This matters because the history of management information in general has often been cast as the triumph of scientific method over outdated, rule-of-thumb and ad hoc management techniques. Yet at the time, this was not always recognised as being the case. Senior railway managers thought that outsiders did not understand the complexity of day-to-day railway operations, if they understood the industry at all. This belief questioned the ability of outsiders to make realistic judgements on performance. The debate assumed increasing importance given the increasing interest in regulation by the state during the first quarter of the 20th century. Government needed to understand cause and effect in aspects of railway management in order to intervene in internal railway operating and commercial routines. This meant that measures such as the ton-mile were seen as the foundation for intervention because they measured the net result of operating processes. The ton-mile was a physical measure of output quantifying how much weight was carried a given distance: for example, 1 ton carried 10 miles and 10 tons carried 1 mile would equate to 10 ton-miles. It did not reflect the cubic capacity of a load, so 10 tons of hay would take up more space, and hence require more wagons, than 10 tons of coal. However, the debate on the ton-mile statistic as a unit of performance measurement was also confused with concerns over the lack of a cost-based basis for price-setting in charging for freight haulage. Investors being discouraged by diminishing returns led to calls for greater intervention by government, and accountability from those in charge of the companies through the structure of railway pricing – called rates. This was reflected in further investigations by government. From 1906 to 1910 the Board of Trade investigated railway accounts and statistics, followed in 1911 by another departmental committee, on railway agreements and amalgamations. A select committee of Parliament on transportation in general reported in 1918, having been curtailed by the intervention of the First World War. The war itself led to centralised government control by a Railway Executive of the network from 1914 until 1921. This was a solution to the wartime pressures on the network, but by definition did not replicate peacetime conditions, nor the rapidly changing commercial environment that would be faced in the post-war period. While nationalisation was considered to improve the efficiency of railway working, this was rejected in favour of forced mergers, and greater government control on day-to-day commercial decision-making. A new Ministry of Transport was established in 1919, and the 1921 Railway Act ended government control of the railways and forced the merger of the 120-plus railways into four regional railway monopolies. These lasted until more government control in the Second World War and then nationalisation in 1947.

What was not appreciated by many external stakeholders in the period from 1900 to 1914 was the degree to which road transport and a variety of new methods of haulage – compression ignition, internal combustion, steam and even electric – road vehicles would destroy the monopoly position of railways. Railway managers were well aware of this threat. Despite attempts to pursue integrated railway/road strategies, government and other interest groups prevented the suggested solutions. Ironically, the members of the new Ministry of Transport were supportive of the railways but were unable to convince Parliament and the government of their case (Edwards, 2015). The regulatory settlement reached in 1921 would be compromised by competition, and the financial base of the new merged companies eroded. The regulation of the railways in the 1921 Act was based upon each company achieving a given standard net revenue, determined after a series of public hearings and wider consultation with stakeholders. This revenue base was never achieved by any of the companies. This was a failure of regulation to take into consideration changing technology and market conditions. The basis of price-setting for freight haulage was a commodity classification based on factors such as the value of goods in their final market, together with the cost of haulage, calculated through proxies rather than direct knowledge of costs because of the complexity surrounding traffic costing. The Rates Classification used had an explicit cross-subsidy to allow low-value traffic to be cross-subsidised by high-value. A ton of coal or iron was thus subsidised by the higher-value ton of furniture. These rates were subject to statutory agreement through a Railway Rates Tribunal. All rates were to be published so that customers, and competitors, could see the prices being charged on each contract. Such disclosure was catastrophic for the railways because road hauliers would examine these prices and adjust so they were just below them to win the traffic. This resulted in the cross-subsidy diminishing as the road carriers were able to "skim the cream" of the traffic that was the source of the profit. This background is important, because the discussion of the ton-mile and derivative statistics informed the nature of this regulation. It created a climate in which both Parliament and civil servants in Whitehall believed that the railways were not being run effectively, while ignoring the impact of economic change exogenous to the railways. It also ignored the engineering and operational aspects of railway management.

This historical example will be used as a means of exploring issues surrounding the development of external reporting and its relationship to management control and attempts by external users to shape the direction of business though government intervention. This suggests the value of a historical approach in shaping reporting of information and governance, and therefore contributes to the wider literature on the history of corporate governance, albeit from the perspective of the knowledge and experience required to interpret measurements used to report performance.

The rationale for using the railway sector at this time as an exemplar of changing attitudes to reporting and governance is that it represented a point in time when a debate on operational control and a scientific/systematic approach to management was taking place, combined with the possibility of more direct government intervention in the sector. Issues were arising that combined internal performance and reporting for the purpose of external control of internal routines. While financial reporting was the context within which the debate took place, it went beyond the accounting profession and developed within transport as an emerging profession. The mainline network was complete, and railways had a monopoly of inland transport, although there was competition from sea lanes, with tramp shipping still able to impact inland rates. Managers giving evidence before government investigations felt that they had enough data and experience of railway working to interpret such information as was available without the difficulty of using and interpreting an average like the ton-mile. The regulations the railways were placed under by Parliament were many: they could not refuse freight since they were considered common carriers, and prices were fixed, as were charges for facilities.

The debate on measurement and performance was brought into focus by a collection of articles, reprinted by Sir George Paish, from the journal *The Statist*. The foreword was written by the North Eastern Railway (NER) General Manager Sir George Gibb and reflected criticisms of the management methods as practised by British railway managers. Historians have tended to view Gibb uncritically as a major management innovator, especially after Irving's study of the North Eastern. The latter argued that the introduction of statistical measures "meant that what Paish liked to call 'scientific management' had replaced 'rule-of-thumb' on the North Eastern Railway" (Irving, 1976, p. 219). By this he meant that statistical measures were in place as part of the organisations management control systems. These measures of ton-mileage, wagon loading, average receipts per ton-mile, etc., were therefore being used to plan and monitor operations. The NER was viewed as an example of model management practice then, and is now, because it collected ton-mile statistics. Irving includes details of this debate on management reform (1976, pp. 250–266). However, too much emphasis has been placed on the NER both in terms of best practice and the conclusions to be drawn as regards techniques of management control and the implementation of statistical measurement.

The central critique by Paish was that compared to US performance, British trains and wagons were poorly loaded. This problem was compounded by the failure to account sufficiently for their operating and commercial activities. That is, most railways did not collect ton-mile statistics. The ton-mile was seen both by historians and contemporaries alike as a measure of "scientific management." This view has influenced historians to conclude that railways were not being run well. Yet few have considered what was meant by "scientific" in the context of this debate, nor what the ton-mile was and was not capable of.

We need to consider the debate over the ton-mile in a little more depth as it was representing a consensus in the business community of what passed for scientific management in the context of transportation. The question we have to ask is whether the debate reflected fairly on the railway companies. Was this ton-mile the only measure of management success or were there other more valid claims?

THE TON-MILE AND THE BOARD OF TRADE INVESTIGATION

The Departmental Committee on Railways Accounts (hereinafter the Departmental Committee) was established in 1907 and reported in 1910 to the Board of Trade. These were general instruments of administration that drew together expert witnesses that could be cross-examined as to the voracity of the evidence. In general, a committee was established with expertise from across the board, often covering all aspects of views under consideration, and including in this case industry expertise. The evidence was published as part of the so-called blue books, more formally known as Parliamentary Papers, with the committee publishing a report. Sometimes there were dissenting reports drawing different conclusions or questioning some aspect of the evidence and its interpretation. As historical documents the resulting verbatim evidence is valuable, but it results in a significant amount of material. While it is tempting to use an index to seek evidence on specific topics, it is only through reading the entire document that the sense of these committees emerges. In this case, an in-depth reading of all 424 pages reveals that the concept of the ton-mile was not accepted as a legitimate measure of supervision and control by most managers and directors, aside from those associated with the NER. Those supporting the use of this data struggled to find clear evidence that it was effective for internal control, never mind external reporting.

The resulting report recommended new statutory forms of returns and accounts but fell short of compulsory collection and publication of the ton-mile statistic. This prompted two reservations to the report, rather than minority reports. However, insofar as the report is remembered for having these, it is the dissent of the ton-mile enthusiast that is remembered, rather than that of the railway managers and accountants. The evidence presented to the committee was in general against (at least the compulsory) collection of the ton-mile but reservations were also expressed as to the measure's usefulness. The evidence suggested that yardmasters and superintendents were expected to check train running and observe yard activity in person, not rely on disembodied statistics collected by others as a data collection exercise. This was a more effective means of control and should not be conflated with what would now be termed disclosure.

The evidence presented was a mix of home and overseas railways, including those from the British Empire. The NER was the only one of the former in favour of the ton-mile as part of a system of statistical analysis, but this is not surprising given that George Gibb was General Manager of the North Eastern and an enthusiastic endorsement of Paish's journalism. Philip Burtt, the Goods Manager of the NER, supported the adoption of ton-miles as well as more detailed statistics: "[Railways] cannot be administered efficiently without efficient information with which to administer and with which to govern, and amongst that efficient information I should put knowledge of tons and miles amongst the very first" (Departmental Committee Q5806, 1910; all further references are to the question number, rather than the page number of the printed evidence). In his memorandum of evidence, Burtt indicated that the ton-mile was a useful indicator of work done, with ton-miles per engine hour giving the overall measure of operating efficiency for haulage. The train load as a ratio of the ton-mile and the train mile was used by district superintendents as a measure of weight carried, and that of wagon to train miles for the load in terms of wagons. They also used the wagon load at the starting point as indicative of the efficiency of wagon loading at each terminal point. Data collected was said by Burtt to enable the future to be forecast by producing a profile of the past (Departmental Committee, Q5108, 1910).

Burtt's evidence also strayed further from just performance measurement and into more ten-dentious areas with little evidence. It was perhaps indicative of his, and the NER's, enthusiasm for modernisation of management. He attempted to link the gains made by introducing large capacity wagons, in which the NER was a pioneer, to the use of improved statistical method. The issue here was that coal wagons were small relative to those in the United States. Clearly if larger loads were carried, running would be more economical. But this ignored the market for coal transport, dominated by small collieries with their own private sidings and handling infra-structure. Domestic coal haulage was also small-scale in nature, requiring smaller loads being sent more often than large-scale, concentrated haulage. Much like the ton-mile, this was to be a source of constant criticism until much later nationalisation changed the market for both rail haulage in general and coal in particular. This connection between wagon size and ton-mile as a source of inherent inefficiency seems tenuous at best and there was no evidence of causation in Burtt's evidence. Similarly, he also suggested that in some way the collecting of statistics could help determine rates, something that even many of the supporters of ton-miles would not claim (Departmental Committee, Q5081, Q5141 and Q5739, 1910).

The lack of detail in evidence was not confined to Burtt either. In his evidence, Gibb found difficulty in giving any specific examples of ton-miles improving performance. All he could do was "point to the whole of my experience. Supervision has been totally different, more searching, more intelligent, and more fruitful in result than it ever was before" (Departmental Committee, Q9723, 1910). When questioned further, Gibb referred simply to "the daily and monthly business" before finally giving engine movement as an example where ton-miles could be of use (Departmental Committee, Q9724 and Q9727, 1910). The management reforms, including statistical collection, introduced at the turn of the century on the NER made its officers important witnesses for the committee, but they were not unbiased. Dissenting voices were plentiful in the witness statements and under cross-examination.

The London and North Western Railway (LNWR) certainly expressed doubts on the value of the proposed statistics, but not in the collection and use of information. In a memorandum of evidence, its staff stated their objections to the collection of the ton-mile as being that it was too slow in its preparation (about two months), that different units were combined and that the result was misleading at best. Furthermore, the task they were supposed to fulfil, monitoring operations, could be achieved with the statistics that they already had, so they were not reject-ing statistical analysis outright, but rather questioning the specific value of certain measures (Departmental Committee, 1910a, p. 111). The memorandum reported that more useful data was the "hourly, daily and weekly statistics of the loading of every train and wagon", rather than an average, with information from the guard's journal copied into so-called train books for the use of the district superintendent in supervision (Departmental Committee, 1910b, p. 112). This detail is important because it demonstrates the type of information being col-lected and how it informed management control. This was processed every morning for the preceding day's traffic in his office and divided into several categories: mineral and "less important" traffic was the first category with the express and regular transhipment trains. Any light loading was reported to the district office and thence to headquarters. The average train load was sampled "spasmodically" from the guard's journal in number of vehicles rather than actual tonnage, either gross or net. The wagon load was taken from each individual wagon return. Light loading was also checked by the so-called loading books kept at each stop where loads were exchanged, and these could be regularly inspected by the district superintendent's travelling inspectors. These forms and ledgers contained the information used to supplement the personal supervision of managers throughout the organisation.

Once collected, the results were compared "man with man, section with section, station with station, District with District" (Departmental Committee, 1910b, p. 114). Large stations furnished daily returns and the smaller stations monthly and half yearly. The loading of wagons was reported weekly and monthly to the district goods manager, who also received notice of light loading once a week. The performance of engines was monitored in daily or weekly returns depending on the size of station, large or small respectively. A daily statement from the goods agent to a district officer contained details of how many wagons were dealt with and how quickly they were dealt with, thus providing an indicator of shunting performance. Larger stations gave returns on how foremen, inspectors and other officials spent their time, and on the "power" expended in yard operations. More general reports were also submitted to headquarters by the district goods managers and district superintendents (Departmental Committee, 1910a, p. 115).

The committee heard that "experts attached to the District Offices and Headquarters are sent from place to place, wherever ... it is considered the best is not being done" (Departmental Committee, 1910a, p. 114). To conclude their memorandum, the LNWR staff stated that they dealt "day by day in detail by means of useful statistics" (Departmental Committee, 1910a, p. 116). The use of an average negated the value, so they thought, and this was a common criticism throughout the proceedings. An average disguised underlying operating and commercial conditions and rendered comparison between routes, loads and services problematic. Even the same service over the same route might face different conditions. Far from enhancing management control, such averages might make matters worse. For the LNWR, the emphasis was on understanding the operating conditions (Departmental Committee, 1910a, p. 10).

This view was supported by evidence from the Great Western Railway (GWR). Its memorandum of evidence drew attention to the myriad operating conditions – different traffics over different sections of line, pointing out that there was no consideration of the terminal cost. On the GWR similar use was made of the guard's journal but with a monthly return instead collated in the district superintendent's office and then sent to the superintendent of the line. These showed average loading and the average number of minutes late. Poor loading was then discussed in a monthly meeting between the divisional superintendent and the goods manager. The chief manager's office also monitored wagon loading on a quarterly basis via a sample of wagon loading for each station, and inspectors could also, as on the LNWR, make surprise visits to the stations. The board of directors was also informed of poor loading by the presentation of such data either directly or within minutes presented to the board and its constituent committees.

As with the LNWR, there was a comprehensive information gathering mechanisms. For example, the average train load was not taken as a useful figure, but the load of each individual wagon was known at each point. The measure of sophistication suggested by the GWR evidence was that of earnings per train mile, as they included terminal costs. Under cross-examination, the GWR witness was Mr T.H. Rendell, the Chief Goods Manager, and former Assistant General Manager of the GWR. He noted in a reply to George Paish, "I think the difference between us is that you are contending for averages, and I say we know the load, because we take it between every point" (Departmental Committee, Q4469, 1910).

Further evidence of the deficiencies of the ton-mile came from the Great Central Railway (GCR), represented by its General Manager Mr Sam Fay. His evidence reveals some of the problems in discussing the application of statistics. Like the GWR there seems to have been much "hands on" supervision of operations with inspectors from the goods manager's office (Departmental Committee, 1910b, p. 281). The wagon load was recorded and sent to the district goods manager, where an average was compiled before going on to the chief goods manager. Monthly meetings between the goods and traffic offices ensured that poor loading could be checked. Returns were similarly received from the train – i.e., the guard's journal – and sent to the district superintendent's office for daily analysis. A weekly report was submitted to the superintendent of the line, and the general manager had a monthly return of train loading sheets which he would take to a meeting of the goods and traffic offices. Comparative statements of expenditure incurred were made every fortnight, and were scrutinised by the finance committee.

The point of the variety of detail from different companies is to underline that there existed a considerable amount of information collection, collation and analysis that related directly to operating and commercial analysis without being subjected to averaging and hence distancing from actual activities that drove performance. Given the time taken to produce the data, it is difficult to see how the ton-mile could be used to monitor performance in a control sense, since the conditions could vary considerably. The ton-mile statistic and its derivatives would develop into what can be seen as an "official" system producing "information too late and at too aggregate a level to be helpful for operational control" (Johnson and Kaplan, 1987, p. 194).

The investigation by the committee seems to have conflated two separate issues: firstly, the use of ton-miles as instruments of management control, and secondly the desirability of reporting such information to other stakeholders through a public, regulated process. Furthermore, it was not clear what the relationship should be between the financial and non-financial measures, yet this was implied by the critique of outsiders like Paish. It seemed that the committee was side-tracked – "captured" is too strong a word – by the ton-mile as a management idea that should be used for management control. Judging from the evidence, the proxy used by the committee for efficient management seems to have been whether ton-mile statistics were collected or not. Hence, both the members of the committee and the witnesses were sometimes talking at cross purposes, and this led to the minority reservations being expressed on both sides of this ideological divide. Those supporting the ton-mile saw a spectrum of uses to which these measures could be applied, from internal management control and financial reporting within an annual report to their use by the Board of Trade or intervention mechanisms such as the Railway & Canal Commission that regulated prices. The thrust of the reformers' argument was that the railway industry had been mismanaged and hence needed measures which government, shareholders and directors could use to intervene. To the likes of Paish and Gibb, it did not matter that the information was too late to be of use to managers as they were not the audience at which it was aimed. But at the same time, they were promoting the use of the ton-mile as a key measure of internal control. The final report recognised the distinction between the analyses of statistics, which, as noted above, was not always clear from the evidence presented. For the practical use of statistics

> to those actually responsible for the working of a railway, it is necessary to draw a distinction between the working returns taken out at short intervals, merely embodying detached information for the use of subordinate officers in the daily conduct of the business, and the more generalised figure prepared for the use of higher officials and directors. (Departmental Committee, 1910a, paragraph 53).

However, this distinction was not always made clearly by those calling for ton-miles. For example, in evidence the representative of a lobbying group, the Railway Shareholders' Committee, stated, "It is a lamentable fact, widely recognised, that for many years this country has lagged behind others in scientific organisation" (Departmental Committee, 1910a, p. 327). This clearly represented outsiders taking a view on inside management processes, rather than just reporting performance. Of course, this was what the information was designed to do, but at what cost? Sir Sam Fay of the GCR was well aware of the possible costs in a comment under questioning as to the value of the ton-mile: "I think you have got to deal with all sorts of peculiar people in this country. You have got to deal with Committees of Parliament, and I should be afraid of anything a Committee of Parliament did, from my experience of some of them" (Departmental Committee, Q7960, 1910).

It is perhaps not surprising that the report was not unanimous. The main body of the report was endorsed by all members, but three were reserved in their comments. Sir Charles Owen and two others rejected the endorsement of such statistics. Citing the terms of reference of the committee, these three did not believe that a departmental committee of the Board of Trade was competent enough to deal with such questions. William Acworth, H. Fountains and George Paish offered further reservations, this time backing the compulsory collection of statistics. So, while all signed the main report there were two supplemental "reservations" added. One group thought the report should have gone further to support the ton-mile. William Acworth was a lawyer who had been involved in the setting up of the Railway Department at the London School of Economics and was well known as what we might now call a policy analyst. He was therefore interested in getting more information which he could use in his teaching and publishing. George Paish was a journalist and as editor of *The Statist* and *The British Railway Position* had built a career on proselytising statistics for management control. George Peel seems to have been a writer on politics and economics and would later, briefly, become a Member of Parliament (MP). Those against more disclosure of this type, and the use of the ton-mile for internal control were Charles Owens, General Manager of the London & South Western Railway; Walter Bailey, Chief Accountant of the Midland Railway; and G.J. Whitelaw, Chief Accountant of the GWR. All professional railwaymen with a clear understanding of how the industry operated, and regarding the latter two, the difficulties associated with the collection, collation and analysis of the ton-mile. While it might be argued that they had a vested interest in keeping disclosure to a minimum, this has also to be set against the very real problems that they were identifying. It is this latter group's report that is of value here because it summarises the belief that aside from cost, there was an issue with interpretation at a distance.

These dissenting comments concerned the remit of the committee and referred to the question of mechanisms of control versus measures of output and performance. Concerning the main report, they believed that the committee had "travelled" beyond its terms of reference because it was discussing "matters affecting the internal working of railways". They cited the terms of reference: "to consider and report what changes, if any, are desirable in the form and scope of the Accounts and Statistical Returns (Capital, Traffic, Receipts and Expenditure) rendered by Railway Companies under the Railway Regulation Acts". This meant that the committee "has not been entrusted with the duty of expressing an opinion upon the value to those actually responsible for the working of British Railways of certain statistics". Furthermore, they noted that this was in spite of their making representations to this effect during the proceedings (Departmental Committee, 1910a, p. 24).

This critique went further, into the cost and effectiveness of collecting the information. For ton-miles alone they estimated a cost of at least £35,000 per annum (Departmental Committee, 1910a, p. 27). Both Bailey and Whitelaw would be in a position to know, given their role as chief accountants, but even if this is accepted as an overstatement, the additional information would be expensive. They went further, charging that the committee itself had stated that it could not find a single case where a "definite increase of earnings or decrease of expenditure" had been achieved as a result of the ton-mile. Indeed, they recognised that even then, existing management control as outlined in evidence could achieve the same outcome. "Every witness who supported the Ton Mile Statistic was challenged to produce such concrete cases, and not one could do so" (Departmental Committee, 1910a, p. 25).

Finally, the validity of an average was contested in the specific context of monitoring the cost per ton per mile of working, "on the absurdity of a common average covering the cost of working a ton of furniture and a ton of coal … not one witness has attempted to define any method by which a satisfactory division of expenses between the various classes of traffic could be made" (Departmental Committee, 1910a, p. 26). Not even Sir George Gibb thought that such figures should be published, even were it possible to provide a meaningful calculation. Later experience showed that this was indeed the case when attempts at traffic costing were investigated in the mid-1930s (Edwards, 2015).

The debate engendered by this investigation would provide a foundation for later discussion on the nature of management control and reporting in the railway sector. However, this was not the whole story. At the same time as the committee was taking evidence and preparing its report, other management ideas were being applied that could have informed more effective reporting and certainly improved operating performance. It is also instructive in terms of understanding the importance of distance from decision-making, and associated understanding of operating and commercial realities, to appreciate what these were, and how they compared with the ton-mile approach.

OPERATIONAL MANAGEMENT USING TRAIN CONTROL

Within the responses of the witnesses giving evidence in support of more statistics, there was sometimes a dismissive tone, some doubt that railway managers could personally supervise railway activities. Certainly, the growing complexity of operations in a comprehensive network would require additional information to reflect the span of control required to co-ordinate traffic and assets. A system was being developed on the Midland Railway that would soon spread across various companies and become the foundation for computerised control systems in the 1960s. The key component of this was the telephone and, to a lesser extent, the telegraph. Not only did this control system facilitate internal control, but it was an alternate approach to management that might have improved the basis for reporting – had the critics of management such as Paish understood its full implications. It is ironic that one of the key texts in train control written in the 1920s would be written by Philip Burtt of the NER, who gave evidence in supporter of the ton-mile (Burtt, 1926).

Train control was tried on the lines of several companies, including the LNWR, Lancashire & Yorkshire, NER and GWR. But it was on the Midland (and, post-1923, the London, Midland and Scottish) that centralised control first emerged – at the time of the investigation into railway accounts and statistics. By using the telegraph and telephone in a system of management control the process of conveyance could be monitored and information extracted for use by management, and could have informed reporting performance as well, although the problem of interpretation and experience would remain. The evidence presented here comes from the internal company documents, together with commentary from the technical press and textbooks. The latter were written by railway insiders as sources for education and training; the former was often based upon content provided by insiders and published as commentary. That said, opinion pieces and independent analysis were also carried in the pages of these publications.

Reporting the ongoing development of train control in 1921, the *Railway Gazette* commented that "The train control system is undoubtedly the most ambitious scheme conceived with the object of determining the utilisation of track capacity and plant, and of securing a more efficient and economic user" (Anon., 1921). By this time the value of this type of control had been proved. The origins of the system emerged from specific concerns over the performance of the Midland's coal trains into London around 1907.

The movement of coal from collieries in the Midlands and beyond was arranged using 10- and 12-ton wagons. These were relatively small to allow for rapid loading and movement, in what was often a retail market for coal. Asset specificity precluded the creation of large wagons for dedicated movement of trainload coal, although this was a common occurrence to ports for export and power stations. So, a key element to the movement of this traffic was the use of many small wagons that needed monitoring and allocating to traffic. In addition, many of these wagons were not owned by the railway companies but the collieries, although they were built to a Railway Clearing House industry standard. Train control initially stemmed from the need to relieve congestion and improve the relief of guards, firemen and drivers. The Midland had a so-called small engine policy that supposedly allowed for flexibility of motive power by using smaller locomotives, but also doubled the crew required for heavy train loads because it required the use of two engines. Reflecting on the introduction of control, a Midland report written in 1914 observed that there was a general need to improve overall working without increasing the capital expenditure relative to revenue (RAIL/491/815, 1914). Building additional running lines was ineffective, being limited by lack of space in the urban areas often created by rail transport. Wagons from private sidings – collieries, factories, wharfs, etc. – would spill into the surrounding railway-owned depots and storage facilities, and sometimes block running lines. During some periods of congestion, a crew might start a shift on a locomotive and only move a couple of hundred yards down the line. The impact of this was recorded as: 24,760 cases of firemen and drivers working more than 15 hours a day, resulting in increased fatigue and payments for longer shifts (RAIL/491/815, 1914, p. 2). The introduction of an eight-hour working day also provided an incentive for more effective management of crew if costs were going to be minimised.

The initial installation of train control on the Midland was on a 10-mile section of line beginning in 1907, with the aim of managing coal train working in the Masboro (now Masbrough) area of Yorkshire. This was a limited test, using telephones as the basis for reporting movement and events across the rail network, alongside that of an expanded centralised set of documents recording information generated by reports and conversations. This system of train control supervised local working of traffic with the issue of operating principle, "discussed and controlled" by the superintendent of freight trains, who was in turn a representative of the general superintendent responsible for traffic movement at headquarters at Derby. A series of district controllers reported to the superintendent of freight trains and in addition they discussed the previous 24 hours' working (RAIL/491/815, 1914, p. 9). The basis for control, and how it differed from anything that had gone before, was the collection of information linked to discussions in distinctive offices using the telegraph and telephone. Information concerning operating conditions, traffic and the movement of wagons was telephoned into the control office via reporting points throughout the network by so-called train reporters. As trains entered and left sections, the engine number, class of train (slow, fast, freight, passenger, etc.), train identification (time or named train), actual time of passing and time cleared were phoned through (RAIL/491/815, 1914, p. 12).

This process of control began with a census of both locomotive and crew availability communicated to the control office, which merged this with knowledge of areas where traffic was collecting. This information was recorded on "traffic cards" and enabled the controllers to manage locomotive and wagon assets effectively (RAIL/491/815, 1914, p. 22). The ability of crews to meet their allotted train on time and at the right place was ensured, and any non-attendance or failures of crew allocation could be monitored. Management was able to plug gaps in operating more effectively and provide information to all levels of the organisation to examine why such failures occurred.

Given this process of allotting assets to create trains, it was possible to integrate the timetabling and planning functions into control. Many trains – especially passenger – run to a planned timetable where it is crucial that they run to time. But for freight haulage, trains were created to reflect the needs of traffic, so managers needed to be able to plan the route they would take subject to the already published timetable. There was also the need to manage the progress of these trains within the paths required for passenger services (Anon., 1921). Squared paper was used to represent the route and time (24 hours), with the important stations, sidings, yards and other facilities such as private sidings and terminal equipment. A distinction was made between slow and goods lines, colour-coded red and green. The steeper the diagonal lines connecting locations on the squared paper, the faster the train, with horizontal lines indicating where and for how long stops were scheduled. At no point should any of the lines meet, as this would indicate two trains on the same track at the same time. This process, known as "diagramming", helped to facilitate the co-ordination of freight train movements across fixed track capacity and maximised the workable running capacity of the line. Once the diagrams had been agreed by staff in the superintendent's office they were written up as the "Midland Railway Freight Train Working Time Book". These train diagrams were used to improve the performance of heavy coal trains to London by retiming them. The success of this was revealed by a survey of 428 trains that revealed 258 arriving on time, 148 less than 10 minutes late (RAIL/491/815, 1914).

The movement of trains was monitored by a "train card" which contained the names of the crew, the time they started duty, the number of wagons, the destination and an identifying locomotive number. This card was placed on a "train board" and the card moved according to its location based on reports on its movement at each point on its journey – from locomotive allocation to yard and other reporting points throughout its journey. Similarly, traffic awaiting collection was recorded by a "traffic card", also displayed on the train board. Reports were expected every two hours from "sidings, Inspectors, Foremen, Siding Porters etc who are stationed at the point where traffic originates". They provided the information that allowed controllers to organise the movement of trains and position of wagons and locomotives and their crews (RAIL/491/815, 1914, p. 21).

The above was enough to create a picture for managers of what was happening on the network. The real value added was created by the ability to communicate to outlying terminals, yards and sidings what was happening if traffic was building up to a level where running lines and sidings might be blocked. A "Stopped Traffic" card was used if there was a build-up of traffic "owing to an abnormal run of traffic, or other cause, [and] a consignee is unable to receive his traffic it becomes necessary to stop or restrict its despatch from the starting point" (RAIL/491/815, 1914, p. 23). Any yard or terminal could request authority from the district control office to modify movement across the network. As long as the station/yard card was held at source, it acted as the authority to restrict the traffic. The position was reviewed every two hours with details recorded on a "traffic sheet", followed by a review the following morning at 8 o'clock. This enabled those responsible to check on the availability of assets and where cover might be needed to move wagons, crew and locomotives to clear traffic.

In a review of the initial performance of the control system, the Midland Railway noted that the "Train Control System has produced an inseparable link between the Central Control Offices and the District Controllers, the daily conferences establishing an equitable distribution of working difficulties and harmony which is most healthy to work amongst" (RAIL/491/815, 1914, p. 62). The impact on congestion was immediate, and this had an ongoing impact on resources. In 1907 on the Midland, there were 5,936 drivers and firemen, falling to 5,780 in 1910. More significantly, there were 2,830 goods guards and brakemen, costing £240,368. These were the crew responsible for the management of the train as they operated the brakes in conjunction with the driver of the locomotive. By 1910 it was £176,124 with 2,200 men. Overall, the wage bill for the Midland fell from £783,237 to £698,971, and senior management attributed this to the introduction of train control (RAIL/491/815, 1914, p. 71).

Before control was introduced, the process of train movement and terminal operations was a matter of purely local management that would take several hours to determine by in-person supervision. Note that a distinction is being drawn here between this and personal supervision discussed by the Departmental Committee. Control augmented in-person management because it extended the reach of managers, with visits by travelling controllers and inspectors. This represented a real-time mechanism for monitoring and control that was designed to supplement, rather than replace, personal supervision. It certainly countered the claims within the Departmental Committee evidence that it was not possible to monitor such large networks as the Midland Railway. This formed the foundation for the creation of a more developed capability to then monitor the development of asset use more widely and monitor what we would now call the real-time status of the railway, its assets and traffic. The system only fully disappeared in the 1960s with the development of centralised computer control. Information provided by this system enabled individual supervision to be better informed about the status of the entire network in a timelier manner than averages. The evidence presented to the Departmental Committee did not discuss the introduction of train control – probably because it was still in its early stages when the committee was sitting and taking evidence. However, the ongoing debate on management control and the use of the ton-mile remained an issue. Following the publicity given to the Midland's system, *The Statist* carried a correspondence that illustrates the tension between the two perspectives.

The Statist was still claiming in 1914 that the performance of the railways was problematic and that "scientific material about British railways is neither compiled nor permitted to be compiled, except by the North Eastern Railway" (Paish, 1914a, p. 363). The letters page contained thereafter a series of responses by anonymous correspondents. This was not unusual and may have been official responses from railway companies disguised, but is also likely to be employees wanting anonymity. "A Traffic Manager" provided a response over several weeks, pointing out that there was more to a scientific approach to railway management than the ton-mile. He cited the advantages of train control, noting that it was "infinitely more useful as a guiding or saving factor than any amount of ton-mile statistics can possibly be to the operating officer" (A Traffic Manager, 1914a, p. 421). In another letter the following week he observed that the variety of traffic and conditions involved in rail transport meant that "meaningless averages" were unscientific (A Traffic Manager, 1914b, p. 486). The response of the editorial opinion, still led by Paish, failed to engage with the wider issue of train control and doubled-down with not a little hostility. This sort of criticism proved that managers were not following "scientific management" (Paish, 1914b, p. 486). A further anonymous letter appeared, this time apparently from a director, "A Railway Director" supporting the stance of Paish. Once again, the practicality of personal supervision was rejected: "The truth is that your correspondent is not and cannot be in close touch from day to day and from hour to hour with the working of his railway" (A Railway Director, 1914, p. 486). This apparent director did not appear to be aware of how train control functioned. It is especially ironic because at about the same time, the NER was itself introducing train control, albeit more piecemeal than the Midland in its extent. This issue was once again conflated with issues of disclosure and performance. A letter from William Burdett-Coutts, an MP representing the Railway Shareholders Committee, who noted that shareholders had "no means of gauging the competence of those who control and manage the enterprise other than by the dividend paid" (Burdett-Coutts, 1914, p. 326). Burdett-Coutts had presented evidence to the Departmental Committee and spoke in Parliament when the 1911 Act was being debated. He noted in the first reading debate in the House of Commons that the bill was about the nation and "the scientific organisation of its industries" (Burdett-Coutts, 1910, 1407). Here again we see this conflation of ton-mile statistics and scientific methods. By any measure, the system of train control was far more effective than the ton-mile at this function. It was more scientific, it could capture data rapidly, it was not an average and it would illustrate the key drivers for the cost of operations and revenue generation – and the relationship between the two. What the correspondence in *The Statist* demonstrates is that the ton-mile was, in a sense, a fashionable management technique, possibly even a fad, with which to attack railway management. This is supported by referencing the wider debate on what constituted scientific management at the time.

There was then a wider agreement as to what constituted a scientific approach to management. The wider "scientific management" literature viewed a scientific approach to management as more than a measure of output. For example, in a text collecting papers on scientific management methods, summarising what might be called best practice across a number of sectors and authors of differing experience, it was noted that information needed to be "systematically collected" so as to be "instantly available" (Cardullo, 1922, p. 62). The function of scientific management was "to bring together, analyse and prove the vast amount of knowledge making up the trade" and "this must be classified, tabulated, and made available ... to all men, whereas formerly it was scattered" (Hathaway, 1922, p. 369). This later correspondence reveals something of the mindset of the reform movement associated with Paish and others. Control was clearly a scientific method of management according to the widespread meaning of the time, but it seems not to have found favour with the likes of Paish and others. There was an agenda to seek information, and individuals found common cause according to their interest: Acworth for his teaching and publications, Burdett-Coutts for shareholders, and

Paish as part of what might be called a crusading journalism. Control and ton-miles might be complementary, of course. Information from train control would provide investors and other stakeholders with details of operating performance, but there were two problems. Firstly, it was too good, and therefore commercially sensitive. This was not because other railway companies might somehow use the information to obtain a comparative advantage, but the existing coastal shipping and emerging road haulage companies might be able to derive some knowledge of traffic flows and local performance. Secondly, the use of control might have revealed better performance and therefore be useful in management rebuttal of criticisms of performance. The minority report noted that the Departmental Committee's conclusions had strayed into performance measurement rather than the reporting of performance. Had the Midland chose to, it could have reported in some detail on the development of train control to rebut the accusations of unreflective learning. That it did not probably reflects the early stages of its implementation, although the archive is silent on this.

The future of train control reveals more on the dynamics behind management innovation, and the dangers of capabilities becoming rigidities and the consequences for the lessening of usable experience and local knowledge. Under the Midland Railway the Control Office was staffed by those who had experience of signalling and working in specific locations. However, under the London, Midland and Scottish Railway through to British Railways in the 1950s it seems that the role became salaried – that is, managerial – with less of an emphasis on knowledge of local conditions.

DISCUSSION

The historical debate on the use of management information has been an important sub-set of the wider history of management and history of accounting. The work of JoAnne Yates (1987) and Ted Porter (1995) established a foundation for examining the development of management ideas and techniques in practice. Through a mix of organisations, from Du Pont and the Illinois Central Railroad to the Corps of Engineers in the United States, these authors emphasised the development of information and its use within the context of a development of systematic approaches to management, and how these might be applied within an organisational context. The recent exploration of routines in a historical context expands the position of information in the organisation across a variety of management practices, industries and time periods, although most from within the United States. The edited volume by Philip Scranton and Daniel Raff (2017) offers a perspective of how this approach might inform the history of management and decision-making. From a historical perspective we can map, with sufficient archival evidence, where routines might have resided in an organisation. The historical emergence of management techniques represents the creation of such routines and the gradual systemisation of personal and ad hoc decision-making. The management process itself also requires that what was tacit becomes codified. This process is at the heart of the historical development of knowledge in general, and management in particular. The work of Joel Mokyr has put the development and application of knowledge at the forefront of industrialisation in an analysis of knowledge applied and based upon technical practice, rather than scientific theory (Mokyr, 2002, 2009). This analysis is focused on the emergence of an "industrial enlightenment" through understanding how knowledge informed Britain's industrial revolution. Such an approach recognises the importance of experience and tacit knowledge in the context surrounding the historical emergence of ideas and techniques in practice. This chapter suggests that a similar approach to the development of management ideas and practices as knowledge would illuminate the historical processes behind their adoption. The emphasis on experience and the codification of tacit knowledge derived from operations and their management fits with the historical evidence presented above. Indeed, much of what constitutes an archive will represent the remains of a codification process – the reports and records of meetings, drawings, operating instructions, etc. Of course, this does not negate ad hoc responses to events as being important to a business, and these will also have to be monitored by management. Indeed, routines might emerge from ad hoc practice. But in the context of this framework, and indeed the historical emergence of routines of monitoring and control, it is the routinisation aspect that is important. The emergence of train control was an example of a mix of routinised and ad hoc responses to events that improved supervision and potentially provided information for management control.

This chapter engages with a similar approach, seeking to examine the different conceptualisations of what constituted scientific management at this time. The historical evidence contained within the written evidence of the Departmental Committee illustrates the tensions between different ideas of what constituted management knowledge. It is as if the two sides of the debate were talking across each other, and this confusion was revealed in the dissenting comments made by both supporters and detractors of the ton-mile noted above.

This historical debate is interesting because it appears just before the experience of the First World War boosted the careers of consultants in fields of accounting and engineering who later engaged in conversations with government and business over "wasteful" competition and the importance of planning and centralised administration, rather than the market. The experience of wartime administration had seen transport heavily involved across all theatres of war under government control. The railway companies themselves were developing a series of training schemes and expanding the engineering apprenticeship model to that of commercial and operating traffic schemes from the 1890s onwards. The London School of Economics had a successful suite of railway courses led by William Acworth, who, it will be remembered, was a member of the Departmental Committee on Accounts and Statistical Returns. A Railway Department was established at LSE offering full- and part-time degree-level study taught by a mix of experienced railway managers and academics throughout the interwar period. A Chartered Institute of Transport was founded in 1919 to professionalise transport with professional exams and meetings designed to disseminate knowledge and encourage reflection on all aspects of the transport business. In short, there was no shortage of interest in management ideas within managers of the railways in the first half of the 20th century. The argument against the ton-mile was less against management and more about the use and interpretation of information by those without the means to interpret the data.

The ton-mile debate demonstrated that there was no agreement on how management and reporting related to each other. The question was, and remains, how best to measure the activities of an organisation within a coherent framework that facilitates decision-making. One way of looking at this is to extend the notion of internal organisational learning to that of wider stakeholder learning, where information crosses the barrier of the firm to shareholders, financial institutions and government. This wider information ecology results in a shift away from the locus of performance, beyond even that of management control, and sets up a conflict between the internal performers and the managers and outsiders who shape the future of the enterprise. This is especially problematic if the outsiders impact not just the resources and strategic direction of the firm, but the performance of critical operating and commercial routines. These latter are vital for successful competition in the marketplace, where it is possible that even well-intentioned intervention can cause harm to the enterprise. It is very difficult, if not impossible, to locate cause and effect between decisions that are made or indeed not made. Both outsiders and management might make decisions that are detrimental to the execution of strategy and implementation of the business model, reversing gains made and preventing innovation through a perception that a given action, event or set of techniques are desirable. There are many reasons why this might be the case depending on the management attention and incentives existing at the time. Certainly, new management fads might boost the status of a manager or policy maker, and provide income for the consultant, but do they really create value that can be captured? Will the business be sustainable in the longer term because of these techniques? Or will they dull innovation, make the product less effective and ruin the firm's ability to compete? Certainly, it is possible that the effectiveness of product delivery might be compromised with intervention from those least placed to understand the consequences of their actions.

The development of train control was more representative of a scientific approach to management than the ton-mile. The importance of experience in control recognised the role of tacit knowledge, that which is difficult and/or expensive to communicate effectively, and how it might be codified for dissemination and discussion within the organisation. This perspective values the experience of doing something – loading and unloading of wagons, operating signalling equipment, running trains, etc. Information for management control was not always the same as actually doing the task; it was another "barrier" to effective understanding of what might be happening at the point of service delivery. This was at the heart of disputes in the evidence presented concerning the problems of the ton-mile and interpretation of averages.

The importance of personal experience and its application in management control, and hence the effective running of the business, lay in the articulation of information and observations of performance in meetings – in person or later in telephone conversations and conferences (Zollo and Winter, 2002). The points being raised by railway officials in evidence to the Departmental Committee were that these meetings were the venues for articulation where those with the tacit knowledge crystallised through discussion and communication responses to events and the eventual evaluation of performance. In this case the introduction of telephone-based train control expanded the ability of controllers to augment personal supervision by enabling telephone conversations – shifting discussions that were face to face to remote locations in control offices.

The process of codification through train control required an additional investment organisational time and attention where the results of control conferences might then be used to inform new operating instructions and working practices (Zollo and Winter, 2002, p. 342). This was the output of the various internal committees where railway managers developed the operating instructions for working that arose out of performance measurement and monitoring of operating and commercial activity. This process of codification left a trail of documents that acted as communications system and organisational memory. Codification in this sense was deliberate and the end product of a clearly thought through process. But there would also be what might be called "small c" codification where experiences are written down to be discussed – articulated – later, and performance reviews under articulation would also generate written material. Another example would be the various cards and forms generated by train control that captured aspects of railway operation to inform reflection on operations and route planning, timetables, etc. In a sense the gradual introduction of train control was enhancing the personal management style criticised by some of the witnesses.

This sense of personal, almost intimate knowledge of how the railways operated expressed itself through the experience of work and its supervision. To appreciate the significance of events, the response of the railway and use of assets to deliver traffic required a knowledge of transport. This might be acquired by a period of working within a railway company before becoming a journalist or investor, or through textbooks or even a degree program in transport such as operated at the LSE. But there is a difference between theory and practice. The introduction of statistics on top of existing financial information shifted attention away from the actual delivery of the product. Board-level decision-making and the communication of information outside of the firm operated at a distance from the delivery of service. The points that the critics of the ton-mile were making drew on the problems of interpretation at a distance without any of the experience of managers. Communicating statistics that were averages required an understanding of variance under actual conditions if they were to be used effectively. What were the conditions on a given section of line that might diminish performance of a given district? Just what were shareholders and government going to do with these figures?

The contrasting approaches to management represented by ton-mile and train control represented the different needs of stakeholders with different experiences and hence knowledge. The witnesses before the Departmental Committee and the minority comments against the ton-mile are evidence that management realised this. They were genuinely concerned about reporting because they knew it might be used for regulation. Of course, it might also be in their interest to have a quiet life, but surely the ton-mile was not the solution. It was more likely to lay within the systems offered by train control. The point here is that investors and government officials would not have the knowledge to hold companies to account using the ton-mile. This required a more in-depth understanding of operations – engineering, operations, commercial, etc. – that was difficult to obtain. The formal professionalisation of transport in the period after 1918 was providing a foundation of knowledge that would enable different parts of the organisation to work together more effectively. Further research might reveal that government officials also took professional transport examinations so that they would have that similar knowledge base where they could at least have a conversation with railway management with an understanding of railway operation.

A similar critique can be levelled at those involved in the implementation of government intervention in Britain. The first Chairman of the British Transport Commission was Cyril Hurcomb, a life-long civil servant with experience of the General Post Office, and then the Ministry of Transport (becoming permanent secretary from 1927 to 1937), then Shipping and War Transport before assuming his role at the pinnacle of the nationalised transport industry. But he had no experience of operations, sales and wider commercial product sensing roles. The Industrial Re-Organisation Corporation, a government merchant bank designed to create "national champions" correcting so-called market failures, supported mergers by rejecting knowledge of operations and engineering strategy (Gandy and Edwards, 2019). The knowledge base that it drew on was predominantly accounting and what might be called general business, rather than a background in engineering and the associated product markets.

CONCLUSION

Are there lessons for today's scholars and practitioners from this historical experience? Perhaps the most important one is humility in the face of real-world complexity. While the railway network rapidly diminished in extent from the 1960s onwards, the practice of logistics remains a complex business. Chemical and materials science companies, financial institutions, electronics and computers all involve enormous complexity and yet performance is reviewed through financial reporting, investor presentations and analysts who may or may not have science or engineering qualifications, never mind experience of working in the industries they analyse.

This chapter suggests that in a world of complexity, contact with the delivery of any product, be it transport, steel or even university education, needs a combination of knowledge and experience that relates to practice. Without the latter, the former remains disembodied out of context and errors can be made. This is the point that the railway managers were making about the ton-mile statistics, and it was certainly part of the rationale behind train control to augment close supervision and expand the circle of those with experience and knowledge of railway operations. This chapter suggests that historians of both management and transport have been too accepting that the introduction of management techniques and governance structures has had a positive impact or more importantly is evidence of efficient working.

BIBLIOGRAPHY

A Railway Director (1914) *The Statist*, March 4.
A Traffic Manager (1914a) *The Statist*, February 28.
A Traffic Manager (1914b) *The Statist*, March 7.
Aldcroft, D. (1968) "The Efficiency and Enterprise of British Railways", *Explorations in Economic History*, 5(2), pp. 158–74.
Anon. (1921) "The Train Control System of the Midland Railway", *Railway Gazette*, July 8.
Anon. (1929) "Traffic Control on the LMS", *Railway Gazette*, February 22.
Burdett-Coutts, W. (1910) *Hansard House of Commons Debates*, 15 June 1910, Vol. 17.
Burdett-Coutts, W. (1914) *The Statist*, March 7.
Burtt, P. (1926) *Railway Rates, Principles and Problems*, London: Pitmans.
Cardullo, F.E. (1922) "Industrial Administration and Scientific Management" in C.B. Thompson (ed.) *Scientific Management*, London: Harvard University Press.
Departmental Committee on Railway Accounts and Statistical Returns (1910a) Final Report, *Parliamentary Papers*, Vol. LVI.
Departmental Committee on Railway Accounts and Statistical Returns (1910b) Minutes of Evidence, *Parliamentary Papers*, Vol. LVI.
Edwards, J.R. (2019) (2nd ed.) *A History of Corporate Financial Reporting in Britain*, Abingdon: Routledge.
Edwards, R. (2015) "Shaping British Freight Transport in the Interwar Period: Failure of Foresight or Administration?" in R. Roth and C. Divall (eds) *From Rail to Road and Back Again*, Farnham: Ashgate.
Gandy, A., and Edwards, R. (2019) "Enterprise vs Product Logic: The Industrial Reorganisation Corporation and the Rationalisation of the British Electrical/Electronics Industry", *Business History*, 61(7), 1236–57. https://doi.org/10.1080/00076791.2018.1462796.
Harris, R. (2000) *Industrializing English Law: Entrepreneurship and Business Organization, 1720–1844*, Cambridge: Cambridge University Press.
Hathaway, H.K. (1922) "The Planning Department, Its Organisation and Function" in C.B. Thompson (ed.) *Scientific Management*, London: Harvard University Press.

Irving, R.J. (1976) *The North Eastern Railway*, Leicester: Leicester University Press.

Johnson, H., and Kaplan, R. (1987) *Relevance Lost: The Rise and Decline of Management Accounting*, Boston: Harvard Business Review Press.

Kirkus, A.E. (1927) *Railway Statistics: Their Compilation and Use*, London: Sir Isaac Pitman and Sons.

Lewis, M.L., Lloyd-Jones, R., Maltby, J., and Matthews, M. (2011) *Personal Capitalism and Corporate Governance: British Manufacturing in the First Half of the Twentieth Century*, Farnham: Ashgate.

Mokyr, J. (2002) *The Gifts of Athena: Historical Origins of the Knowledge Economy*, Princeton: Princeton University Press.

Mokyr, J. (2009) *The Enlightened Economy: Britain and the Industrial Revolution, 1700–1850*, New Haven: Yale University Press.

Mitchell, B., Chambers, D., and Crafts, N. (2009) "How Good Was the Profitability of British Railways, 1870–1912?" *Warwick Economic Research Papers*.

Paish, G. (1914a) *The Statist*, February 21.

Paish, G. (1914b) *The Statist*, March 7.

Porter, T. (1995) *Trust in Numbers: The Pursuit of Objectivity in Science and Public Life*, Princeton, Princeton University Press.

RAIL 491/815 (1914) No Author, Midland Railway Train Control, Control Office, Derby.

Scranton, P., and Raff, D. (eds) (2017) *The Emergence of Routines: Entrepreneurship, Organisation and Business History*, Oxford, Oxford University Press.

Spitzeck, H., and Hansen, E.G. (2010) "Stakeholder Governance: How Stakeholders Influence Corporate Decision-making", *Corporate Governance*, 10(4), 378–91. https://doi.org/10.1108/14720701011069623.

Wilson, J.F., and Thomson, A.W. (2006) *The Making of Modern Management: British Management in Historical Perspective*, Oxford: Oxford University Press.

Yates, J. (1987) *Control through Communication: The Rise of System in American Management*, Baltimore: Johns Hopkins University Press.

Zollo, M., and Winter S (2002) Deliberate Learning and the Evolution of Dynamic Capabilities, *Organization Science*, 13(3), pp. 339–51.

9. Human capital resources accounting and firm value creation: a governance and board decision-making perspective

Krishanthi Vithana

1. INTRODUCTION

According to the findings of a recent survey of public company directors commissioned by the EY UK Centre for Board Matters, "79% of directors say their board spends more time discussing talent strategy than it did just five years ago". This is despite many boards "not monitoring key talent metrics" and the fact that "nearly 85% of directors support investment in employee training and reskilling to secure long term value benefits even if they may not deliver short term returns" (Corporate Board Member, 2020, p. 1). Additionally, institutional investors increasingly tend to inquire how businesses are integrating human capital resources into the overarching strategy to create value in the longer term. Influential investors have also made human capital resources a priority in their engagement with directors and senior management. This indicates that the board of directors in general can no longer be blinded to: (1) the human capital resources strategy, (2) how the investment in human capital resources helps businesses create value in the longer term, and (3) how information on human capital resources investment and its value creation can be communicated to the relevant stakeholders through accounting and financial reporting, even if investment in human capital resources may not necessarily lead to short-term accounting profits.

The concept of human capital, debated by scholars over the past several decades (Becker, 1962; Brummet, Flamholtz, and Pyle, 1968; Lev and Schwartz, 1971), has become a diversified research interest of many academicians and researchers (Abeysekera, 2008; McCracken, McIvor, Treacy, and Wall, 2018; Vithana, Jayasekera, Choudhry, and Baruch, 2018; Vithana, Soobaroyen, and Ntim, 2021). Many of them, relying on Marx's labour theory of "surplus value" and the value creation by the employees, have criticised the accounting treatment of human capital investment, which typically writes this off when calculating the economic profit under the neo-classical approach (Bryer, 1994; Dooley, 2005; Vithana et al., 2021). In spite of many previous measurement attempts (Brummet et al., 1968; Flamholtz, 1972; Lev and Schwartz, 1971), agreement on the recognition of human capital investment in accounting and financial statements – through critical arguments on measuring firm-level human capital resources investment using different valuation techniques and development of frameworks for reporting and disclosure – has yet to materialise (Roslender and Dyson, 1992). Although human capital resources are for the most part not captured as a financial indicator by firms, either as investments or capital components, they have been included under voluntary information disclosure as a decision-useful element (Abeysekera, 2008; Abeysekera and Guthrie, 2004; Lajili and Zéghal, 2006; McCracken et al., 2018; Vithana et al., 2021). Additionally, many initiatives introduced by influential groups such as the Global

Reporting Initiative (GRI), Embarkment Project for Inclusive Capitalism (EPIC), International Integrated Reporting Framework (IIRF) initiatives by the Sustainable Accounting Standards Board (SASB), Workforce Disclosure Initiative (WDI), and Business Roundtable (BRT), among others, identified human capital as a key driver in firm value creation, thus bringing it to the spotlight in practices including investment decision-making, investor engagement with directors and senior managers, and stakeholder management, and in designing financial reporting regulatory frameworks. Thus, there is increasing demand for information on human capital value creation by external stakeholders, requiring agreed principles and frameworks to capture this via accounting and financial reporting practices. Against this backdrop, this chapter focuses on: the significance of firm-level human capital resources investment for firm value creation in the longer term; a critical review of practitioner and academic contributions to human capital resources accounting and financial reporting; the decision-usefulness of firm-level human capital resources information and stakeholders' response to this information in the short, medium, and longer term; and guidelines on the development of human capital accounting and reporting frameworks with special emphasis on the role of the board of directors in incorporating firm-level human capital resources information in strategic decision-making, governance processes, and financial reporting practices.

2.   HUMAN CAPITAL

The arguments on human capital were initiated in the fields of economics (Becker, 1962) and accounting (Brummet et al., 1968; Flamholtz, 1972; Lev and Schwartz, 1971), taking into account the value creation for firms through people. Human capital is understood as the potential of employees themselves to generate more future wealth for firms (Vithana, 2014), which becomes the surplus value over returns on the other physical and financial assets of firms. This may be included in the balance sheet as a part of accounted intellectual asset components, or might exist unaccounted for as a part of the unrecognised/unaccounted intangible/intellectual assets of the firms. Human capital, according to several definitions, can be explained as existing in different levels, such as individual-level human capital, group- or organisational-unit-level human capital resources, and organisational-level strategic human capital resources (Ployhart, Nyberg, Reilly, and Maltarich, 2014; Wright, Coff, and Moliterno, 2014). Human capital at the individual person level is the value-creation potential of individuals as a result of the knowledge, skills, attitudes, and other characteristics that individuals possess (Becker, 1962; Lev and Schwartz, 1971), which is essential to make things happen in an organisation. Human capital at the individual level therefore is transferable from one firm to the other, unless there are exemption clauses, as firms do not necessarily own their employees. The human capital resources or the strategic human capital resources at the organisational unit level or the firm level define the value-creation potential of the organisational-unit-level or firm-level human capital resources that are captured by the firm through human capital management practices and organisational culture via emergence and complementarity (Crocker and Eckardt, 2014). This, however, is typically not transferable, and thus provides a competitive advantage for the firm. There could also be instances where employees with trade secrets may not be allowed to mobilise their human capital unless as a result of human-capital-driven corporate acquisition (Chen, Gao, and Ma, 2021). Leveraging individual-level human capital to organisational-unit- or firm-level human capital resources thus drives the value creation via human capital resources investment. This potential for value creation is recognised as a longer-term investment in human capital resources by both firms and external stakeholders (Vithana et al., 2021).

Due to the unique potential of employees, researchers have argued that spending on employees which results in increasing the productivity and capacity of employees should not just be treated as an expense in the year it is incurred, particularly since some employee expenditures may generate returns over a longer period of time (Brummet et al., 1968; Flamholtz, 1972; Vithana et al., 2018). This argument is subject to criticism for several reasons, such as: firms not being able to own the individual-level human capital, the inability to capture the investment component of the total spending on the employees, and the sensitivity of the value-creation potential of firm-level human capital resources to organisational and cultural changes. According to current accounting practice, only in strategic alliance situations such as mergers and acquisitions will this value-creation potential of the firm-level human capital resources be recognised as a portion of goodwill of firms. Thus, a considerable proportion of intellectual capital remains unrecognised or unaccounted for. Academics and practitioners continue to question how this proportion is to be recognised, particularly for the use of external stakeholders. Therefore, while it is evident that a general understanding of the concept of human capital resources in accounting contexts exists, a universally accepted and widely applicable definition for this and a framework to account for the firm-level human capital resources still does not, leading to several subjective interpretations at the level of both internal and most importantly external decision-making.

3.   HUMAN CAPITAL RESOURCES AND FIRM VALUE CREATION

Firms continue to write off the total spending on their employees as an expense irrespective of some components of this being associated with the firm's future earnings potential linked to employees. Due to the problems associated with this, development of an alternative measure to recognise human capital resources has been on the agenda for several decades now. Researchers have relied on many theoretical foundations, such as human capital theory (Flamholtz, 1972; Grove, Mock, and Ehrenreich, 1977; Lev and Schwartz, 1971), transaction cost theory (Coase, 1937; Foss, 2011; Lepak and Snell, 2002), and resource-based theory (Lepak and Snell, 2002), among several others, in developing these alternative measures, though with less success in terms of convincing practitioners. We have continuously witnessed the human capital resources budget being the most susceptible to downsizing, redundancies, temporary staff reductions, etc., in many adverse economic circumstances such as organisational crisis, financial crisis, and pandemic situations. These actions have continued despite their longer-term repercussions on firm performance and macroeconomic development. This is in part due to the inadequacy of human capital resources measures and an accounting and financial reporting framework to support information communication.

Human capital theory takes into account the concept of "service potential of employees of firm for the future" (Brummet et al., 1968; Lev and Schwartz, 1971). According to Lepak and Snell (1999), capitalising on human resources based on human capital and resource-based theories depends on two factors: speciality in skills and non-transferability. Therefore, only the skills development of employees, which are specific to the firm and cannot be utilised away from the firm, create a unique potential to generate wealth for the firm in future, which can be capitalised upon. However, in a highly sophisticated, competitive, and open business system, categorising human capital based on the speciality in skills and the non-transferability is understandably challenging. According to Grove et al. (1977), many attempts at human capital valuation are based on identifying the properties, attributes, or qualities of a concept and establishing empirical rules of correspondence between empirical object and the measurements. However, since these measures explain the empirical object but do not accurately measure the specific phenomenon, they are called surrogate measures. The surrogate-type human capital measurement indicators have basically been categorised into two groups based on input- or output-related measurements associated with the human value attribute for firms. The input-based indicators include the acquisition cost (Brummet et al., 1968), replacement cost, and discounted wage flows (Lev and Schwartz, 1971), while the output-based measurement systems include opportunity cost, market value, discounted earnings level, economic value, and group value model (Grove et al., 1977). According to transaction cost theory, firms choose to employ personnel in the most efficient way taking into account transaction costs for hiring and bureaucratic costs for training and development (Coase, 1937). Asset specificity and uncertainty have been identified as the key constructs in determining the alternatives between transaction vs bureaucratic costs (Lepak and Snell, 1999). The surrogate measures linked to human capital resources expenditures, however, would not usually be perceived by the external stakeholders as an investment which creates value for the firm, but rather as an outlay portraying value destruction. These measurement limitations tend to raise questions on the decision-usefulness of the human capital resources measures proposed and the measurement approach itself.

As a consequence, human capital resources expenditure disclosed in the income statement of annual financial reports tends to be the only and most widely used financial indicator used by the investors and external stakeholders for decision-making in relation to firm-level human capital investment (Higgins and Atwater, 2012). However, the economic short-termism in decision-making could lead investors to react myopically to human capital resources expenditure as an increase in such spending would depress short-term profit-based financial performance indicators. In one of our studies, this myopic reaction to the human capital expenditure approach was empirically tested by taking a market-based approach (Vithana et al., 2018; Vithana et al., 2021). Our results revealed that on the one hand, markets react myopically towards human capital resources expenditure. On the other hand, the reaction was reported non-myopic when firms' human capital resources investment was measured taking into account value creation by employee where the human capita resource was measured via the firm value added allocated to the employees as a proportion of the total value added (Vithana et al., 2018; Vithana et al., 2021). Our results also imply that the employee contribution in firm value added reported via the value-added statement in fact helps communicate information on firm value creation by employees. Besides disappearing from annual reports since the 1980s, value-added statements appear to continue to reflect social reality. Reinstatement of the value-added statement in the annual reports therefore could be one right step forward in terms of a human capital resources accounting point of view, since it effectively communicates information on the employee contribution to firm value creation, especially to external stakeholders.

In efforts to address the difficulty in conceptualising and measuring firm-level human capital resources and reflecting on risks associated with accounting for the direct measure of human capital resources of firms (such as claiming the ownership of the employees opposed to the other assets and the risk for manipulation), researchers have attempted to measure human capital as an efficiency indicator (Chan, 2009a, 2009b; Higgins and Atwater, 2012; Nazari and Herremans, 2007; Seetharaman, Sooria, and Saravanan, 2002) which may well be used in the decision-making process as well. Owing to the challenges in measurement as well as the lack of relevance and utility for decision makers due to the inconsistency in measurement approaches, the research trajectory since then has moved away from valuation to the financial reporting and disclosure of firm value creation via human capital through a variety of reporting frameworks developed by disclosure initiatives (Coalition for Inclusive Capitalism, 2018; Global Reporting Initiative, 2012; Woods, 2003) and academic research (Abeysekera and Guthrie, 2004; McCracken et al., 2018; Vithana et al., 2021). The more the measurement approaches are being questioned, the more the practice, profession, and academia have moved towards human capital resources disclosure through financial reporting. There have been several attempts to improve the disclosure practices via human capital resources disclosure initiatives, as discussed in the following section.

4. HUMAN CAPITAL RESOURCES ACCOUNTING AND DISCLOSURE INITIATIVES

There have been numerous initiatives by several influence groups to encourage the capturing of firm-level human capital resources in the stakeholder decision-making process. These include those by the GRI, EPIC, IIRF, SASB, WDI, BRT, Chartered Institute of Personnel and Development (CIPD), and several others. Stakeholder contributions in these projects include accounting and financial reporting regulators, businesses who are passionate about human capital resources investment and value creation, asset owners, asset managers, non-governmental organisations, and responsible investment charities, indicating the timely relevance of the recognition of human capital resources value creation through external financial reporting and disclosure, and their decision-usefulness.

The BRT, an initiative of influential CEOs of large corporations, focuses on delivering longer-term business value to a wide variety of stakeholders in addition to the shareholders, including employees, customers, suppliers, and the community. The early view – specially in 1980s – of the BRT statement of purpose of a corporation reflected the need for companies to invest in employees, communities, and other stakeholders. However, in 1997 the BRT reflected the importance of the shareholder emphasis – generation of economic return to its owners – as the principal objective of business enterprise. Recently, however, this view has been questioned, re-emphasising the importance of investing in employees and communities as this is believed to be the way to success in the longer term in a multiple-stakeholder perspective (Wustemann, 2021). The emphasis has been on sharing the benefit of capitalism more broadly, even though the evidence on the application of such sharing is yet to be seen in real-world practices.

The GRI is a long-term, multi-stakeholder international initiative that attempts to harmonise disclosure internationally by encouraging businesses to report relevant and credible corporate economic, environmental, and social performance information (Global Reporting Initiative, 2012; Woods, 2003). According to the GRI guidelines, disclosure of human capital resources information is included under the social dimension of the three dimensions: economic, environmental, and social. Human capital resources disclosure indicators covered under the GRI framework include but are not limited to the number of employees and the breakdown by gender and region in relation to employees and workers that are not employees, annual total compensation ratio and percentage increase in total compensation ratios, policy commitments to due diligence and human rights, stakeholder engagement practices, and occupational health and safety. Except for highlighting the information disclosure, limited attention is paid to capturing the value-creation potential of human capital resources in the longer term under the GRI framework. However, while providing a framework for more structured reporting, GRI guidelines also called for value-added indicators from a distributional fairness perspective. These consider how the value added by a firm is distributed among the key stakeholders, including employees.

The Integrated Reporting Council (IRC) framework, proposed by the International Integrated Reporting Council (IIRC) – formed in 2010 as a global coalition of regulators, investors, companies, standard-setters, the accounting profession, academia, and non-governmental organisations – also considers communication on value creation, preservation, and erosion as the next step in corporate reporting agendas. According to an IIRC (2013) report, the IRC particularly considers the return to six types of capital components: financial, manufactured, natural, intellectual, social and relationship, and human. Human capital resources disclosure under the IRC framework includes people's competences, capabilities, and experience, and their motivation to innovate, which in turn contribute to the value-creation potential of the employees. Under these elements, the IRC framework also expects firms to disclose employees' (1) alignment with and support for the organisation's governance framework, risk management approach, and ethical values; (2) ability to understand, develop, and implement an organisational strategy; and (3) loyalties and motivations for improving processes, goods, and services, including their ability to lead, manage, and collaborate (International Integrated Reporting Council, 2013). Thus the IRC framework supports integrated thinking, decision-making, and actions that focus on value creation over the short, medium, and longer term. Adopting a principle-based approach, the IRC framework discussed above tends to strike a balance between flexibility and prescription, allowing businesses to consider unique aspects that suggest organisational context, culture, etc., while also providing some basis for comparison, making the reporting framework more appealing for businesses (Dumay, Bernardi, Guthrie, and Demartini, 2016).

Recognising the importance of businesses to succeed in both the short term and the longer term, particularly for society and economies to thrive, the EPIC – an attempt to capture the business value that is increasingly not captured via the business balance sheet over a period – focused on the value drivers that are increasingly important to business today (Coalition for Inclusive Capitalism, 2018). Launched in 2017, the EPIC was an attempt to "identify and create new matrices to measure and demonstrate long term value to financial market" (Coalition for Inclusive Capitalism, 2018, p. 4). Out of the four key areas focused on in the EPIC report, the value-creation potential of human capital resources is reported as "Talent", under which aspects related to human capital development, organisational culture, and employee health and safety are discussed in detail based on a long-term value framework. Stakeholders that were consulted in development of the framework include companies, asset owners, and asset managers (Coalition for Inclusive Capitalism, 2018). The initiative, being led by investors and public listed companies, indicates the decision-usefulness of human capital resources value creation to both businesses and external stakeholders, particularly investors and financial analysists.

Among the five sustainability topics associated with SASB standards, the human capital dimension covers three general issue categories: employee health and safety; labour practice; and employee diversity, inclusion, and engagement. According to the SASB standards, human capital comes second only to climate risk as a thematic issue and has been widely discussed in a variety of platforms and through reporting initiatives (Sustainability Accounting Standards Board, 2020a, 2020b). The SASB's preliminary conclusion on accounting for human capital takes into account macroeconomic value drivers – the way in which businesses interact with the workforce and how this interaction drives long-term value creation – and business impact; i.e., how the macroeconomic value drivers affect the way businesses interact with their workforces. There are several other recent human-capital-resources-related disclosure initiatives, supported and endorsed by professional bodies and the investment community. These include the WDI, and the Corporate Human Rights Benchmark (CHRB), among others, which focus on overall human capital resources disclosure or individual aspects such as human rights, though such reporting would not necessarily focus on human capital value creation.

The adage "too many cooks spoil the broth" appears to be at work given the number and complexity of disclosure frameworks attempting to capture firm-level human capital resources value creation of listed firms over time. Empirical studies suggest a significant variability among the disclosure matrices used in practice and stakeholder responses and the decision-usefulness of the matrices used. Empirical analysis on firm-level human capital accounting and disclosure across the globe appears to provide a mixed and ambiguous picture because of the problems mentioned above (Abeysekera, 2008; Abeysekera and Guthrie, 2004; Abhayawansa and Abeysekera, 2008; Lajili and Zéghal, 2006; McCracken et al., 2018; Vithana et al., 2021), and efforts to provide more meaningful empirical insights have been less focused and subject to multiple interpretations as outlined in the section below.

5.   HUMAN CAPITAL DISCLOSURE: EMPIRICAL ANALYSIS

"Shifting away from the narrow economic-accounting perspective of the past to a broader social scientific perspective", attempts at putting people in the balance sheet have been diverted to generating softer accounting information (Roslender and Dyson, 1992, p. 311), with other researchers emphasising that external reporting of HR accounting information would impact the decisions of financial statement users, including managers, investors, financial and responsible investment analysts, and other stakeholders (Lajili and Zéghal, 2006; McCracken et al., 2018; Vithana et al., 2021). Given that firms' practice of human capital resources accounting is mostly limited to qualitative descriptions in the annual reports, researchers have also diverted their attention towards qualitative disclosures. Therefore, much research evidence is found on financial reporting recognition of human capital investment via voluntary disclosure in annual reports, despite the absence of a sound human-capital-reporting framework (Abeysekera, 2008; Abeysekera and Guthrie, 2004; Abhayawansa and Abeysekera, 2008; Lajili and Zéghal, 2006; McCracken et al., 2018; Vithana et al., 2021).

Human capital disclosure in annual reports on a voluntary basis has been identified as a means of reducing the information asymmetry and minimising the tension between firms and their constituents, especially in the interest of further capital accumulation (Abeysekera,

2008). Similar to the voluntary disclosure in general, human capital resources disclosure by firms as well has always been shaped and explained by theories such as agency, legitimacy, resource dependency, and stakeholder theory (Lajili and Zéghal, 2005, 2006; McCracken et al., 2018; Tinker, 1980; Vithana, 2014; Vithana et al., 2021). Going along the path of information disclosure, researchers have found that firms' reporting on human capital information in their annual reports has increased over time both in terms of amount of the depth and breadth of information disclosed as well as the meaningfulness of disclosure (Abeysekera, 2008; Abeysekera and Guthrie, 2004; McCracken et al., 2018; Vithana et al., 2021). However, research evidence also reveals that there is no consistency between the human capital management and reporting practices and the reporting practice across different contexts (Boedker, Guthrie, and Cuganesan, 2004; Subbarao and Zéghal, 1997). This perhaps may be attributable to the issues related to the aligning of human capital resources management practices with the human capital resources measurement and reporting frameworks, and the difficulty in diffusing measurement approaches and disclosure frameworks proposed by academia, professional bodies, and disclosure initiatives to real-world practice. This has led researchers to look at the old problem in a new light, proposing a paradigm shift (Abhayawansa and Abeysekera, 2008; Roslender and Dyson, 1992). Additionally, this inadequacy in softer accounting information about human capital resources might lead accounting and financial reporting practitioners to think about a balanced approach reflecting the value creation by employees, in terms of both quantitative and qualitative attributes, taking a principle-based approach to address the uniqueness of the practice and the contextual variations.

Human capital disclosure studies have focused on various aspects, such as motivations behind and the consequences of human capital resources disclosure (Abeysekera, 2008), the change in practice across geographical regions (Subbarao and Zéghal, 1997), theorising and the theoretical development of the human capital resources disclosure practice (Abhayawansa and Abeysekera, 2008; Vithana et al., 2021), and the historical development of the practice and the challenges in terms of the decision-usefulness of information disclosed (Lajili and Zéghal, 2005, 2006; McCracken et al., 2018). Geographical variance is revealed through empirical analysis, noting that European firms disclose more on human resources than Asian and North American firms. There is also a clear difference between the financial services sector and the manufacturing service sector (Subbarao and Zéghal, 1997). Results also imply a substantial variation in firms' practices due to firm-specific factors and employee relation ideologies of firms (Vithana et al., 2021), and other socio-economic factors which require further examination (Ax and Marton, 2008). Demonstrating that many different factors might affect human capital disclosure practices, Abeysekera and Guthrie (2004) also note a deviation from the studies carried out in developed countries in terms of the attributes mostly reported by firms. Even though the same content-analysis technique was adopted, no consensus was evidenced on human capital attributes included in disclosure indexes in the Australian context compared to the Sri Lankan context. Comparison with Australian studies revealed that the differences in the frequency and extent of disclosure are attributable to the socio-cultural values of the countries. As an example, entrepreneurial spirit has been highly valued by developed countries such as Australia but less so in developing countries such as Sri Lanka. Whereas more disclosure on results-driven attributes like, for example, value added is evidenced in the Sri Lankan context, process-driven attributes such as work-related knowledge were most reported by Australian firms (Abeysekera, 2008). These results clearly indicate that while there must be a basis for the analysis, any approach to account for and report on human capital resources requires a great deal of flexibility to capture the value in the context, be it geographical, indus-trial, or any other factor, justifying a principle-based approach in the development of human capital resources accounting and reporting frameworks.

Despite all the developments in the field and continuous attempts via disclosure initiatives, it is evident that many of the attempts regarding accounting and financial reporting recognition of human capital investment in general remain limited to descriptive disclosures. Furthermore, many of the regulatory bodies have limited their efforts on developing regulatory frameworks to merely capture qualitative human capital disclosure indicators, rather than quantification of human capital investment to include in the traditional financial statements in such a way that the value-creation potential of employees is communicated to the key stakeholders. Particularly, studies so far suggest that the practical gap in moving ahead with human capital resources accounting and disclosure arises because of the minimal involvement of the regula-tory and governance bodies and legislation. Even current studies on accounting and financial reporting recognition of human capital investment reveal some prejudices at the outset, being biased against investigating formal mechanisms to put the value-creation potential of human capital resources in financial statements. To address these issues, the accounting regulations, state control and the legislations should develop best practice guidelines for firms to mean-ingfully account for and disclose investment in people (Stittle, 2004; Vithana et al., 2018; Vithana et al., 2021). The next section discusses the factors to be considered in developing such a framework, taking into account the decision-usefulness of human capital resources information in the hands of the key stakeholders.

6.   BOARD DECISION-MAKING AND CONSIDERATIONS IN ACCOUNTING FOR HUMAN CAPITAL VALUE CREATION

Some of the social issues, such as rising economic inequality within countries, low public trust in businesses, increasing changes to the business models and the impact of them on the value drivers and longer-term value creation, and pressures for short-term financial performance by some investors, are inevitably linked to firms' human capital management and longer-term value-creation strategies. While some shareholders prefer short-term profit, others, such as pension funds, sovereign wealth funds, and institutional investors, will have to continually focus on the longer-term value creation. It is impossible for businesses to communicate the longer-term value if they continue to ignore the value-creation potential of human capital resources investment. Additionally, since employees are a key category of stakeholders, firms must develop trust that they recognise their employees for their value-creation potential. This is besides the current accounting treatment communicating the opposite – value destruction. Pressures for sustainable human capital management and the requirement for accounting for human capital resources are intensifying as more and more stakeholders are interested in these aspects. It is imperative that boards of directors are attuned to these issues, the relevance of them for firm-level human capital management or talent management strategies, and the importance of communicating information to relevant stakeholders. Given the challenges busi-nesses face in measuring human capital resources' value-creation potential, and in the absence of a standardised methodology, a principle-based approach considering both a quantitative as well as a qualitative analysis is called for.

Human capital as a thematic issue currently sits within the "social" component of the environmental, social, and governance (ESG) agenda of institutional investors. Investors, particularly institutional investors, are increasingly engaging with the firms they have invested in to pursue sustainable human capital management practices (Kotsantonis and Serafeim, 2020). From the business point of view, even though we use the terms "human capital" and "human asset", spending on employees is still a cost to the business. HR expenditure is one of the most sensitive budget titles, and tends to get curtailed in any adverse business or economic scenario. We have seen this time and time again during the economic crisis, financial crisis and COVID-19 pandemic. The redundancies and layoff decisions in such scenarios evidently have led to many repercussions, especially since the expected economic growth and development in a recovery phase can hardly be achieved in a low-wage economy. Moreover, businesses will not be able to cope with labour supply challenges in a recovery phase, should employees leave the industry and find their means of living elsewhere; as is reportedly the case for the post-pandemic hospitality industry.

In this context, boards have a responsibility regarding both businesses' human capital management practices as well as encouraging businesses to communicate firm-level human capital resources value creation via accounting and financial reporting practices to attract and retain the talent base. Stakeholders' extensive reliance on just the human capital resources expenditure can be avoided through alternative measures reflecting the human capital value creation. Employee contribution in firm value added appears to be one such general measure, implying the importance of the reinstatement of the value-added statement back with the conventional financial statements (Vithana et al., 2021). Industry-, sector-, or firm-specific alternative measures that can be disclosed in annual reports can also play a vital role in delivering information on human capital value creation. In this regard, academia, professional bodies, and disclosure initiatives can contribute to design the process requirement in developing the relevant measures as opposed to a common set of indicators, given the uniqueness in firm-level human capital resources value creation, taking a principle-based approach. The key questions to be asked include: (1) to what extent do businesses value and invest in people; (2) to what extent do businesses' accounting and financial reporting practices capture their investment in people and their value-creation potential, and finally, (3) how decision-useful is the information which businesses communicate to their stakeholders?

The extent to which firms value their human capital is reflected via their human capital/ talent management practices and the organisational culture. Therefore the accounting and financial reporting system should capture the human capital investment and human capital value creation though both quantitative and qualitative indicators. Breakdowns on firms' human resource expenditure, human capital value added as a portion of the total value added, investment in training and development per employee cost, or revenue-related indicators are used widely as quantitative financial indicators, whereas a variety of qualitative indicators can cover the qualitative aspect of the human capital resources value creation. Additionally, human capital disclosure frameworks to communicate human capital value creation should take into account the process of leveraging the individual-level human capital into the organisational-unit- or firm-level human capital resources. Therefore, the disclosure framework should capture the input indicators at the individual level, and process indicators at the organisational unit or firm level, with the output and outcome indicators measuring the value-creation process and outcome.

Knowledge, skills, attitudes, and other attributes of the employees account for the input indicators at the individual level. The process-level indicators meanwhile can take into account the human capital resources value-creation process through organisational culture and human capital management practices, considering induction, training and development, reskilling, coaching, mentoring, employee wellbeing and health, and contingency planning among several other industry- or firm-specific process-level indicators. The outcome-level indicators can highlight the value created because of the process through productivity, efficiency, satisfaction, engagement, and value added, among several other industry- or firm-specific outcome indicators. While it is possible for the disclosure initiatives or the financial regulators to come up with general indicators, it is essential to have flexibility over the industry- or firm-specific indicators to accurately capture and communicate the human capital resources value creation. Given the principle-based nature of the practice, boards of directors' role in strategy oversight, advising, monitoring, and governance oversight will be instrumental in the overall human capital management, accounting, and disclosure process.

7.   CONCLUSIONS

Over time, we have seen developments in the field of human capital resources management and accounting as well with regard to financial reporting recognition of value creation through firm-level human capital resources investment. Additionally, there is an extensive demand for the information on firm-level investment in human capital resources from asset owners, asset managers, financial analysts, ESG analysts, responsible investment charities, some non-governmental organisations, and regulatory bodies. From the supply end, however, standards, metrics, and regulations in terms of human capital management outcomes, accounting, and financial reporting recognition of firm-level human capital resources value creation appear to be still evolving. This is despite the significant contribution from the professional bodies such as the CIPD, SASB, Financial Reporting Council, IIRC, etc., as well as the contribution from practitioners and academics working in the field.

Against this backdrop, business leaders, executives, and boards of directors together shoulder a substantial responsibility in addition to the human capital management strategies towards understanding and measuring the outcomes of the human capital value-creation process, recognition of firm-level human capital investment and firm value creation, and most importantly the communication of this information to the relevant internal and external stakeholders. A principle-based approach appears to be the way forward in this regard in the absence of an advanced human capital management, accounting, and reporting framework, given the uniqueness in the practice of leveraging individual-level human capital through to firm-level human capital resources through organisational human capital management and value-creation practices and organisational culture. The exclusive responsibility of the board in this regard lies in providing the strategic direction in terms of human capital value creation and aligning human capital resources value with the key performance indicators and shaping the governance mechanism so that firms capitalise on the value-creation potential of their human capital resources. The failure in recognising human capital resources' value-creation potential could result in the undervaluation of the most crucial and strategically important asset of the firm, and exclusion of that in the firm's decision-making. This could be reflected via the firm's value in the longer term as well.

We require further research on commissioning a principle-based approach in recognising and communicating human capital value creation in corporate financial reporting. Additionally, further market-based and stakeholder-oriented approaches can be adopted to enhance understanding of the decision-usefulness of human capital resources investment information in the longer term. In addition to the general indications, a grounded approach providing the basis for the development of firm-specific value creation is also called for as a part of voluntary disclosure.

REFERENCES

Abeysekera, I. (2008). *Motivations behind Human Capital Disclosure in Annual Reports*. Paper presented at the Accounting Forum.

Abeysekera, I., and Guthrie, J. (2004). Human capital reporting in a developing nation. *British Accounting Review*, 36(3), 251–68.

Abhayawansa, S., and Abeysekera, I. (2008). An explanation of human capital disclosure from the resource-based perspective. *Journal of Human Resource Costing & Accounting*, 12(1), 51–64.

Ax, C., and Marton, J. (2008). Human capital disclosures and management practices. *Journal of Intellectual Capital*, 9(3), 433–55.

Becker, G.S. (1962). Investment in human capital: a theoretical analysis. *Journal of Political Economy*, 70(5, Part 2), 9–49.

Boedker, C., Guthrie, J., and Cuganesan, S. (2004). The strategic significance of human capital information in annual reporting. *Journal of Human Resource Costing & Accounting*, 8(2), 7–22.

Brummet, R.L., Flamholtz, E.G., and Pyle, W.C. (1968). Human resource measurement: a challenge for accountants. *Accounting Review*, 43(2), 217–24.

Bryer, R.A. (1994). Why Marx's labour theory is superior to the marginalist theory of value: the case from modern financial reporting. *Critical Perspectives on Accounting*, 5(4), 313–40.

Chan, K.H. (2009a). Impact of intellectual capital on organisational performance: an empirical study of companies in the Hang Seng Index (Part 1). *Learning Organization*, 16(1), 4–21.

Chan, K.H. (2009b). Impact of intellectual capital on organisational performance: an empirical study of companies in the Hang Seng Index (Part 2). *Learning Organization*, 16(1), 22–39.

Chen, D., Gao, H., and Ma, Y. (2021). Human capital-driven acquisition: evidence from the inevitable disclosure doctrine. *Management Science*, 67(8), 4643–64.

Coalition for Inclusive Capitalism (2018). *Embarkment Project for Inclusive Capitalism*. Retrieved from www.coalitionforinclusivecapitalism.com/wp-content/uploads/2021/01/coalition-epic-report.pdf.

Coase, R.H. (1937). The nature of the firm. *Economica*, 4(16), 386–405.

Corporate Board Member (2020). How the governance of human capital and talent is shifting. Retrieved from www.ey.com/en_us/board-matters/how-the-governance-of-human-capital-and-talent-is-shifting.

Crocker, A., and Eckardt, R. (2014). A multilevel investigation of individual- and unit-level human capital complementarities. *Journal of Management*, 40(2), 509–30.

Dooley, P.C. (2005). *The Labour Theory of Value*. Routledge.

Dumay, J., Bernardi, C., Guthrie, J., and Demartini, P. (2016). *Integrated Reporting: A Structured Literature Review*. Paper presented at the Accounting Forum.

Flamholtz, E. (1972). Toward a theory of human resource value in formal organizations. *Accounting Review*, 47(4), 666–78.

Foss, N.J. (2011). Human capital and transaction cost economics. *The Oxford Handbook of Human Capital*. Oxford University Press.

Global Reporting Initiative (2012). Home page. Online at: www.globalreporting.org/Pages/default.aspx.

Grove, H.D., Mock, T.J., and Ehrenreich, K.B. (1977). A review of human resource accounting measurement systems from a measurement theory perspective. *Accounting, Organizations and Society*, 2(3), 219–36.

Higgins, J., and Atwater, D. (2012). Linking human capital to business performance. *HCMI White Paper*.

International Integrated Reporting Council (IIRC) (2013). *The International IR Framework*. IIR Council.

Kotsantonis, S., and Serafeim, G. (2020). Human capital and the future of work: implications for investors and ESG integration. *Journal of Financial Transformation*, *51*, 115–30.

Lajili, K., and Zéghal, D. (2005). Labor cost voluntary disclosures and firm equity values: is human capital information value-relevant? *Journal of International Accounting, Auditing and Taxation*, *14*(2), 121–38.

Lajili, K., and Zéghal, D. (2006). Market performance impacts of human capital disclosures. *Journal of Accounting and Public Policy*, *25*(2), 171–94.

Lepak, D.P., and Snell, S.A. (1999). The human resource architecture: toward a theory of human capital allocation and development. *Academy of Management Review*, *24*(1), 31–48.

Lepak, D.P., and Snell, S.A. (2002). Examining the human resource architecture: the relationships among human capital, employment, and human resource configurations. *Journal of Management*, *28*(4), 517–43.

Lev, B., and Schwartz, A. (1971). On the use of the economic concept of human capital in financial statements. *Accounting Review*, *46*(1), 103–12.

McCracken, M., McIvor, R., Treacy, R., and Wall, T. (2018). *A Study of Human Capital Reporting in the United Kingdom*. Paper presented at the Accounting Forum.

Nazari, J.A., and Herremans, I.M. (2007). Extended VAIC model: measuring intellectual capital components. *Journal of Intellectual Capital*, *8*(4), 595–609.

Ployhart, R.E., Nyberg, A.J., Reilly, G., and Maltarich, M.A. (2014). Human capital is dead; long live human capital resources! *Journal of Management*, *40*(2), 371–98.

Roslender, R., and Dyson, J. (1992). Accounting for the worth of employees: a new look at an old problem. *British Accounting Review*, *24*(4), 311–29.

Seetharaman, A., Sooria, H.H.B.Z., and Saravanan, A. (2002). Intellectual capital accounting and reporting in the knowledge economy. *Journal of Intellectual Capital*, *3*(2), 128–48.

Stittle, J. (2004). UK corporate reporting of human capital: a regulatory failure to evolve. *Business and Society Review*, *109*(3), 311–37.

Subbarao, A., and Zéghal, D. (1997). Human resources information disclosure in annual reports: an international comparison. *Journal of Human Resource Costing & Accounting*, *2*(2), 53–73.

Sustainability Accounting Standards Board (December 2020a). *Human Capital: Preliminary Framework – Executive Summary*. Retrieved from www.sasb.org/wp-content/uploads/2020/12/Human-Capital_Executive-Summary_2020-December_FINAL.pdf.

Sustainability Accounting Standards Board (December 2020b). *Preliminary Framework on Human Capital and the SASB Standards*. Retrieved from www.sasb.org/wp-content/uploads/2020/12/Human-Capital_Preliminary-Framework_2020-December_FINAL.pdf.

Tinker, A.M. (1980). Towards a political economy of accounting: an empirical illustration of the Cambridge controversies. *Accounting, Organizations and Society*, *5*(1), 147–60.

Vithana, K., Jayasekera, R., Choudhry, T., and Baruch, Y. (2018). *HR as Cost or Investment: The Distinction between Short- vs. Long-Term Focus of Firm Valuation*. Paper presented at the Academy of Management Proceedings.

Vithana, K., Jayasekera, R., Choudhry, T., and Baruch, Y. (2021). Human capital resource as cost or investment: a market-based analysis. *International Journal of Human Resource Management*. https://doi.org/10.1080/09585192.2021.1986106.

Vithana, K., Soobaroyen, T., and Ntim, C.G. (2021). Human resource disclosures in UK corporate annual reports: to what extent do these reflect organisational priorities towards labour? *Journal of Business Ethics*, *169*(3), 475–97.

Vithana, V.K.G. (2014). *Accounting and Financial Reporting Recognition of Firms' Human Capital Investment: An Empirical Investigation of Firms in the FTSE 100 Listing of the London Stock Exchange*. Durham University.

Woods, M. (2003). The Global Reporting Initiative. *CPA Journal*, *73*(6), 60.

Wright, P.M., Coff, R., and Moliterno, T.P. (2014). Strategic human capital: crossing the great divide. *Journal of Management*, *40*(2), 353–70.

Wustemann, L. (2021). Human capital. *Professional Safety*, *66*(8), 18–19.

PART III

BOARD DECISION-MAKING IN PRACTICE

10. A device to attract the money? Or an invitation to partnership?[1]

David Weir

TRUSTED ORGANISATIONS

Some organisations are apparently regarded as worthy of being trusted more than others. Highly trusted institutions include hospitals and care homes, and, of course, churches and religious institutions are near the top end, police and prisons perhaps somewhere in the middle. The family itself may nowadays be less wholeheartedly acclaimed as a worthy social institution than in previous epochs, sometimes being strongly indicted as the source of troubles for many individuals (Laing, 1971). The conduct of business in the tradition of Adam Smith has been held to rest on ethical foundations (Smith, 2002; Werhane and Freeman, 1999). Trusts themselves, even family trusts (Hammar, Jagers and Nordblom, 2009), may in the light of current possibilities for evading tax and contributions to collective benefit appear more suspect if they appear to be merely vehicles for protecting economic advantage (Gosling, 2017).

It is not entirely clear where universities stand in this rubric. On the one hand the university must "take seriously and rigorously its role ... as interrogator of more and more complex ethical problems" (Morrison, 2002, p. 7), but in general, they are usually held to be worthy institutions, powers for good in society and worthy of support by both states and individuals. So for most, the intrinsic nature of a university entails virtue, and where ethical issues intrude it is usually the universities who are seen as the victim of damage from outside.

In the twenty-first century the public appears to be more sceptical of higher education than in the past (Immerwahr and Johnson, 2007). The concerns often relate to perceived conflicts of values that become visible when universities appear to be pressured into behaving like businesses. These sources of contagion have arrived from outside, and left to themselves these institutions would still be doing the right things because their core values are deeply rooted and intrinsically beneficial for the wider society. The imposition of commercial values has thus led to rising costs necessitating frequent appeals for increased funding in increasingly competitive though historically unfamiliar markets, unequal access and differential career prospects for their graduates (Bok, 2004). These are essentially consumer anxieties.

Probably this analysis needs to be more nuanced. On the one hand universities have been happy enough to be entrusted with the education of future members of the ruling elites. On the other hand, throughout their long history universities have been held somewhat responsible for the bad behaviour of their students, and plagiarism, cheating and hooliganism are often cited. In the new century, though, sometimes serendipitous virtue may be espied even in these excesses (Conlin, 2007) when cheating can be reframed as postmodern learning. This rebadging may be worthy of incorporation into Stephen Potter's legendary Academy of One-Upmanship (Potter, 1962).

There are fundamental issues around what universities really are and what their societal role ought to be. MacIntyre (1973, p. 7) comments that

> How we write the history of any particular educational institution will depend upon our judgments as to its continuity and identity; and these in turn will involve judgments as to generalizations about and norms governing educational practice. Normative debate is ineliminable from the question of how the concept of education is to be applied. The concept [...] turns out to be essentially contestable.

The normative claims of the university represent its social capital (Coleman, 1987) as at its core it is an institution that has strong normative objectives as its *raison d'être*. Etzioni (1961) identifies three types of organisational power – coercive, utilitarian and normative – and relates these to the three types of involvement available to participants as the alienative, calculative and moral. Universities have a range of available versions of normative/moral frames. They may claim to have special responsibilities for civic values (Ehrlich, 2000) and for democratic society more widely (Gutmann, 1987), and perhaps more especially for social cohesion (Moiseyenko, 2005). The normative nature of a university is clearly a different issue to that of the normative dimensions of commitment of individuals to an institution which is itself in these respects multidimensional (Penley and Gould, 1988). If a university is charged with cronyism that is no more nor less damaging than such an accusation against other types of institution.

But some dilemmas are inherent in times of social change (Bok, 2004) and become more visible in these periods involving scrutiny of wider societal values as a "fertile ground for ethical dilemmas to flourish ... [where] the two main categories of unethical practices identified by participants were academic dishonesty and inappropriate behaviour towards staff and students" (Ehrich, Cranston, Kimber and Starr, 2012, p. 99). Arguably such considerations are important in considering the moral careers of all pedagogical institutions (Gore, 1995).

The argument that the analysis of right or wrong in terms of conduct only apply to individuals and not to institutions has been ground well-fought over in relation to whether there can be a criminal offence of corporate manslaughter (Almond, 2013), and in principle answered in the affirmative, though the ensuing outcome in the UK is not without its critics (Gobert, 2008). However, the values identified as relevant to the trustworthiness of universities cannot be by any scalable metric mapped onto those individuals who at any specific time can claim membership of the institution. Academics as individuals are no more or no less moral than others.

The existence of a body within the structure of an institution that can effectively regulate institutional rectitude is no guarantee of good moral performance, for "ethical lapses by university governing boards are, unfortunately, all too common, even in countries with long-established boards" (Eckel, 2019).

Three helpful perspectives on the ethical issues confronting universities are those of professional ethics, an ethic of care and institutional ethics. These implicate the role of leadership, as "the ethical challenge facing leaders is multifaceted: it requires leading with integrity while respecting diverse, sometimes conflicting interests; it calls for leaders to be conscious about their own values and moral standards" (Maak and Pless, 2006, p. 36). Universities have specific responsibilities in respect of students, some originally designated under the rubric of "*in loco parentis*", and also in their role as employers and as rate- and tax-payers.

Questions of trust arise because a trustee holds assets or valuables as a proxy for their owners and can be expected to act in their interests even without necessarily having a fiduciary responsibility for applying the assets of others to the best advantage of the beneficial owners. Universities act often as stewards of the assets and opportunities of others in society, including students, teachers and partners. A fortiori, a breach of trust implies a conflict of interest exercised to the advantage of one of these parties against the interest of another.

But their central justification remains that they embody the rational values of reason itself: they are houses of reason. This justification is in one sense as old as society itself. The oldest university that I have ever visited is the 3,000-year-old Temple of Knowledge in Hanoi. In physical terms, possibly the first recorded site of a centre for universal learning based on the compilation of knowledge from other cultures and ideational sources in the Western traditions is probably the Baytal-Hikma, the House of Wisdom in the Baghdad of Harun al Rashid (Al-Khalili, 2011, p. 53; Gutas, 1998, pp. 53–60).

This line of justification is memorably put by Pirsig, who says,

> The real University … has no specific location. It owns no property, pays no salaries and receives no material dues. The real University is a state of mind. It is that great heritage of rational thought that has been brought down to us through the centuries and which does not exist at any specific location. It's a state of mind which is regenerated throughout the centuries by a body of people who tradition-ally carry the title of professor, but even that title is not part of the real University. The real University is nothing less than the continuing body of reason itself. (1974, p. 142)

We argue that universities are prime trustees for the wider society of the assets of knowledge (Geiger and Sá, 2008). But only some of these obligations are solidified in legally enforceable contracts, and some are merely desirable and aspirational (Hook, 1969). However, there is a penumbra of obligation about which there can be legitimate argument and thus sequences of events and actions that fall within the arena of ethical judgement, and it is the realm of these latter with which this chapter is concerned. It is a question of how to ensure that knowledge is based on truth. As MacIntyre (1973) warns, this is a contestable terrain.

Au fond, what is claimed is that the asset that is the special and unique object of the care of a university as the trustee for the wider society is that of *truth* and the search and proclamation of truths as far as they can be ascertained, and many universities issue statements of their aspiration embodying this claim. Thus, one university states on its website, "The University of Kent places value on critical thinking, the advancement of knowledge and the pursuit of truth" (University of Kent, 2021). Universities are expected to teach the truth and proclaim the results of research that are deemed to be true. They are also expected to act truthfully and, in their actions, to enact truth as fair dealing with the expectations of others with whom they enter willingly into contracts.

A BRIEF NOTE ON METHODOLOGY

First, a brief note on methodology. This section describes in some detail a series of events in which I was involved as a participant in a process that raised issues of practice, performance and identity at the time, but also, and partly with the advantage of hindsight, these experiences continue to raise issues of ethics appropriate to university life more generally.

To comply with the positioning of such a narrative it is necessary to relate some events which form part of the relevant historical context. They occurred a long time ago, in the 1970s to be exact, and it may well be relevant to ask why these recollections have taken so long to be put into the public domain. Specifically, why am I relating this history after such a lapse of time? One reason is summed up by Ehrich et al., who note: "One of the worrying aspects of this study's findings is the sense of powerlessness that many academics apparently feel when matters of ethics arise and confront them in their practice" (2012, p. 111). In fact these worries have engaged me all of my subsequent life and have never been satisfactorily dealt with by me.

Another author of a celebrated political memoir summed up his contribution in a title, *Old Men Forget* (Cooper, 1953), that deals with the life of a politician, statesman and participant in the political crises enveloping Europe in the late 1930s – but that is not the trouble here, which instead is that old men remember and often regret. The title is borrowed from Shakespeare's stirring speech by King Henry V before Agincourt:

> Old men forget: yet all shall be forgot,
> But he'll remember with advantages
> What feats he did that day. (Shakespeare, 1623, Act IV, Scene III)

The continuation of this speech contains another implication of senile recollection: that it may favour a version of events that over-praises its author's contribution to favourable outcomes. So, for the record this chapter records no claim to have been successful in any past "feats", but rather the contrary; this is written for the record with a sense of a participant's regret at outcomes and an unwillingness to see similar mistakes made again.

So, the incidents reported here are based on events that the writer was involved in and a party to. There are of course serious methodological grounds for criticism of auto-ethnographic writing based on data drawn from the memory of participants: Delamont (2007), for example, concludes that auto-ethnography is essentially harmful and that scholarly energy is best "put to work" doing other kinds of research, and I have tried to deal with these arguments elsewhere (Clarke and Weir, 2018).

However, these recollections may be valuable sources of knowledge. As Mills states, "to say that you can have experience, means, for one thing, that your past plays into and affects your present, and that it defines your capacity for future experience" (1959, p. 196). This chapter is thus in part an exercise in auto-ethnography penned by one who was a participant-observer with a non-trivial expertise in ethnographic method and subject to all of the methodological and ethical issues relative to such publications. Maybe also there is a more personal, intuitive sense that "when it comes, that is, when a man's autumn comes. He remembers forgotten things. Small sadnesses, brief pleasures and with the remembering comes the desire to make alterations, corrections. A futile desire" (Mangnall, 1988, p. 107).

Eliot warns that

> Time present and time past
> Are both perhaps present in time future,
> And time future contained in time past.
> If all time is eternally present
> All time is unredeemable. (Eliot, 1936)

However, ours is not Eliot's claim that all time is *unredeemable* but that such exercises are by no means futile if the review of past events can assist in a more precise or useful understanding of what really did happen in the past in order to understand how the past constrains the future if its lessons are misapplied in the present.

This is a "how" question, not a "why" question. Emotion, whether driven by guilt or satisfaction, is irrelevant. Redemption is unnecessary, even an obstruction. We did what we did. So did the other participants. There is no suggestion of deliberate malfeasance. But after the natural effluxion of time it may be valuable to reconsider.

These memoirs, stories and other species of narrative are thus not merely substitutes for further and better particulars or something to hang on to as second best until the real science is discovered. Nor are they inevitably inadequate speculations available when documentation and text are not, but they are also logically and psychologically prior because they are first-hand. Per contra the non-existence of text is not always accidental and sometimes hints at a need to account for the apparent non-existence of the evidential support for alternative narratives. The minutes of boardroom discussions often come as a surprise when they are subsequently read by those who were present at the meeting. Organisational crimes may be concealed by inadequate and incomplete reporting. Major crimes often require deliberate omission or collective amnesia ("Christmas party? What Christmas party?"). However, those listed as present can be asked for their version, and their testimonies have a right to be heard and at least be accounted as honest reportage and stand until they can be disproved, to stand or fall on their own merits as accounts.

After all the methodological arguments have been heard, there is still room for Motley's commonplace claim that "I have only to add that this work is the result of conscientious research, and of an earnest desire to arrive at the truth" (1873, p. vii). That has not quite the vigour of the Duke of Wellington's "publish and be damned", but it works for me.

THE STORY OF UK BUSINESS EDUCATION

In the early 1970s business education was seen as a desirable object both of public policy and of educational investment, as a credible addition to higher education in the UK, with the broader objective of increasing national economic performance and comparative competitiveness. By the end of the 1950s there had grown up a widespread understanding that the British economy had not reaped the expected benefits of being on the winning side in World War II, and that in particular the manufacturing sector had not merely fallen behind that of the United States but that areas such as marketing and design were labouring too.

One of the aspects of the US approach believed to contribute to the continuing American economic advantage was business education. This had been established in the United States when the Wharton School was founded at the University of Pennsylvania in 1881. The first business school in Europe, however, was the Ecole Speciale de commerce et d'industrie (now ESCP Europe) in Paris, established in 1819. It was later my privilege to create and launch the *European Management Journal* in partnership with the EAP (Ecole des Affaires de Paris) and still later to become a Professeur Permanent at CERAM (now SKEMA), a Grande Ecole de Gestion.

In April 1963 the National Economic Development Council (NEDC) recommended the establishment of a high-level business school or institute run on the lines of the Harvard Business School, the Wharton School or the School of Industrial Management at the Massachusetts Institute of Technology.

A committee was established under Lord Normanbrook, the former Cabinet Secretary, to consider the costs and practicalities of establishing two business schools. The committee recommended that the expenditure should be shared between the government, through the University Grants Commission (UGC), and business. As a result, the government agreed to bear half the capital and running costs of the two schools. The Foundation for Management Education, the Federation of British Industries, and the British Institute of Management sponsored an appeal for £3 million from the business world. The Franks Report (1963) recommended the establishment of two high-quality schools as part of existing universities (London and Manchester) but enjoying considerable autonomy. The schools would offer courses for about 200 postgraduates and 70–100 post-experience students.

At this point, therefore, several reports – including the Robbins Report (1963), the Normanbrook Report (1963) and the Franks Report (1963) – had identified the need for one or more business schools on the American pattern, located within universities and funded by both the state, through the funding body the UGC, and the private sector as the appropriate vehicles for these developments. It was assumed at the political level that these new schools would enjoy "considerable autonomy" within the systems of higher education. It was planned that the contribution of the public purse would be matched by equivalent amounts contributed from industry, for which the Council of Industry for Management Education as the fundraising institution and the Foundation for Management Education for distribution of the results of the appeal were nominated.

In terms of the assumptive values of these new institutions, the contemporary discourse provides several clues. These values were expected to derive principally from business and industry, and to be supported by the appointment of staff with such backgrounds and experience. For instance, the notion that most, if not all, members of the teaching staff would be expected to hold a PhD was never suggested in these discussions. There was a thread of partnership infusing all these statements of intent but no hint that the universities were to be regarded as the senior partners.

The initial recipients of the funding programme were to be the London Business School and the Manchester Business School (MBS) (Allen, 1979; Barnes, 1989) and it was subsequently accepted and noted in Parliamentary statements (Hansard, 1964) that the next beneficiary should be a Scottish business school. The same debate heard cross-party agreement on the central proposition and also support for other points, including that "full-time staff should have considerable latitude to supplement their academic income with outside fees and that a substantial part of the teaching should be carried on via a part-time basis by persons holding positions in industry and commerce, and that the trade unions should be involved".

The expectation was also expressed that "the teaching of languages in these schools which will be of help in our export drive" would be a central concern of these new institutions. The financing of these ventures was anticipated when one MP asked, "Would the Government be willing to enter into partnership on a [pound-for-pound] basis with industry in supporting management education courses and the like at our universities, including those in Scotland?" The answer was affirmative. The tenor of these debates was evidently that of pound for pound, equal investment for a presumed general social benefit.

In the "other place" (the House of Lords) the Noble Lord the Earl of Essborough explained, "The Working Party envisage that this financial burden should be shared equally between business and the universities. They also suggest how governing bodies should be constituted to carry out the principle of partnership" (Hansard, 1964). Again the leitmotif of these discussions was one of left hand and right hand working in harmony, business and industry on the right, education on the left.

The plan was to raise £3 million, but in the event this objective was comfortably surpassed, industry putting its hands in its pocket to the tune of £5 million. This was to be matched pound for pound by the state, through the UGC. The first two new institutions at London and Manchester were set up on slightly different bases, London as a fully independent institution associated with London University, and Manchester as a new faculty within Manchester University, situated, after a brief period in a former carpet warehouse in the downtown area, near Piccadilly, in brand new premises at Upper Brook Street, near the former Owens College site, but distinct from the existing management school in the University of Manchester Institute for Science and Technology.

In Scotland, after vain attempts by one university to scoop the whole pool, and a consequent somewhat bitter inter-institutional struggle, the foundation of a Scottish business school was agreed with a structural scheme to involve three of the universities in the central belt of Scotland, two ancient and one the inheritor of a college of advanced technology. Two of these universities (let us identify them as A and B) could claim some experience in business and management education, one as the home of the oldest undergraduate degree in business, the other as the home of a serious centre for postgraduate and post-experience programmes in these subjects. The third university (C), an ancient, medieval foundation, had several strong professional schools – in engineering (claimed to be the first in the world), law, medicine, architecture and veterinary science, for example – and a highly-esteemed tradition in social and economic research. However, it was not generally regarded as having any special interest or claim for standing in the fields of business and management and its appearance as a suitor for the new business school appeared to local observers to be somewhat surprising.

The ensuing three-way share of the increased grant money was used by each beneficiary in slightly different ways. University C seemed to take its time in making its first appointments, firstly announcing a plan to create three new professorships, in management, organisational behaviour and business policy respectively. Encouraged in the belief that the university was moving on acceptable lines, a private benefactor announced that University C would benefit from his generosity in endowing a fund in his name to create at least one additional professorial post. Unfortunately, doubtlessly on the advice of professional experts, this endowment was not to be in cash or tradable assets, but in the equity of his company, a private bank that quite soon after went bust.

An appointment to a professorial chair in management was made and a candidate from University A (though he was not in the Business Department there) was installed. He had a doctorate from a prestigious US university that had a world-rated school of management. His account of the circumstances leading to his appointment may be interesting; he would explain that he had crossed the central belt to give a scholarly seminar on his research into share price movements, involving interesting technical innovations of econometrics. After his presentation one of the participants had discussed whether he could be interested in being considered for a professorship in management, to which he had demurred, explaining that this was not his discipline. He had been surprised by the response from his interlocutor that this absence of that expertise could be just what they were looking for. He was duly appointed. On arrival he got to work and after some time introduced a new postgraduate degree, a Master of Administration, and established a claim for University C to create a doctoral programme under the auspices of the Scottish Business School. The Master of Administration programme, however, initially made little impact on the market.

Two years later the university advertised the other two foundational chairs, in organisational behaviour and in business policy, and an appointment was made to the former post. The author of this chapter was the appointee. I was at the time a Senior Lecturer at MBS and had discussed my application with my boss, the Director of MBS and a senior player in the UK business school scene. He had supported my application, and had surprised me by advising that if I were to get the post (which he doubted, because he feared it had come "too soon") it would be fortunate for my plans because "they have not yet spent their money". He explained that because of the industry money matched by the UGC, a large sum of money would be available to create a strong business/management school at University C because the money had been ring-fenced and protected in the grant allocation.

The interviews for the post took place in the morning, and following my interview I was asked if I would stay for lunch and make myself available for a meeting at 2 pm. At this meeting with the principal of the university I was offered the post, which I accepted. My great-grandfather had studied here and if it was good enough for him, that was good enough for me. The principal advised me in this one-on-one conversation that he expected things to happen as a result of my appointment, and mentioned that the university was coming under pressure from business people for a growing understanding that its progress had been rather slow and that they felt some ownership of the business school project as, after all, many of them had put their hands into their pockets to support the fundraising for it. After this I went to a meeting with the professor of management, the head of the Department of Management Studies, who was very amiable and showed me a piece of paper on which were handwritten a schematic set of planned appointments, of which between four and a dozen could be in my field, and we discussed these.

This was in mid-summer, and for several reasons I was not able to take up the position until the next February. Being slightly later than planned, I was naturally keen to get on and play my part in building an institution. We needed a credible programme and had had practically no takers for the only recently introduced Master of Administration, though no one seemed unduly concerned about that. But my time at MBS had taught me that business schools "on the North American pattern" invariably taught the MBA, and that industry expected this as criterial for their acceptance. Moreover a recent Social Science Research Council report had noted that this "American" degree had been the most widely accepted innovation in academic qualifications since the German-inspired PhD of the late nineteenth century.

It took a few weeks and several planning, hard-grafting and team-bonding meetings in the department to get a proposal before the Senatus Academicus. I was a new kid on the block, a new face across the Senate room, and nobody knew much about me. But some people had seen me coming. As I picked up my teacup in the pre-Senate meeting hall, I was approached by a venerable, distinguished, smooth-talking professor of mercantile law. The ensuing dialogue was straight out of Hollywood. "Ah, Professor Weir, is it not? The Clerk of Senate has asked me to pass on to you something which it is thought may prove to be a grave impediment against the proposal in your name to be laid before the Senatus this day."

Tremulously I enquired how this impediment had manifested itself. He proceeded very seriously to explain that it was a question of the colour of the hoods for the graduates of our new Master's degree; these were regulated by a definitive list of the colours of the wild flowers known to be growing on the mainland of Scotland; that is, excluding the Islands, even the big ones. He re-stressed the magic term "*definitive*", and noting my cue I enquired if that meant the list of colours appropriate for Masters' hoods was closed. "Indeed", answered the Great

Man, who moved to slide effortlessly towards the Senate room. As he departed, I announced boldly that this had indeed been considered by *my* committee and was not at all an impediment as I would, during my presentation of the rubric of the MBA, announce that as it had no applicants at present, the Master of Administration degree was to be suppressed immediately and the new degree would thus have hoods of an eligible colouration available for the graduates who would helpfully not be requiring them for at least 18 months.

In order to further sweeten the blow I pointed out that as a professor in a business school in a great university I would always be conscious of the pressing needs of trade in the city and its wider region, and that this decision would enable the crafters of hoods to continue to respect the university for recognising their need for certainty and reliability in production. This was not at all entirely fictitious, for I had previously discovered from family research that one of my ancestors, the grandfather of my great-grandfather, had been a man whose métier was that of a silk manufacturer in Paisley.

This same professor subsequently emerged as a sincere and reliable supporter of the aspirations and strategies of the business school. However, we never again referred to the singular circumstances of our first encounter. The only question raised during my introduction of the MBA to the Senatus Academicus was directed at my mis-spelling of the word "quantitative" as "quantative". I respectfully acknowledged serious error in this respect.

We had prepared draft regulations for both a full-time MBA route and a part-time version. After taking soundings within the university and more importantly in the industrial and commercial undertakings in the region, it became clear that there was an immediate and urgent need to re-qualify and re-skill the existing middle levels of management. I had in fact been spending most of my time in visiting companies and listening to their managers. This had been illuminating, as when I was once accused by a senior manager of having been mistaken about my institutional affiliation and suggested that it must have been my mistake because I must surely have been working at the other place, the "tech", because my interlocutor knew that the "uni" would never have any truck with a business school.

So we opened with the part-time MBA and printed rather well-designed glossy brochures with snazzy pictures of the university with its great tower, which also formed the template of the new business cards that were to be used by all members of our teaching faculty ("Business cards for lecturers?! Who sanctioned this unusual expenditure, Professor?").

As soon as our plans became publicly known outside the institution a great political fracas ensued. One of our partners in the three-legged partnership structure announced that they too had plans for a part-time MBA and that they expected our university to withdraw immediately from the field and give them a free run at a market that was much more suited to their expertise and skill base. This was of course a perfectly reasonable judgement, and one could not blame them for making this call. But we had got our blow in first.

I visited my principal and explained that as this course was all we had to offer we would not withdraw, adding that if he as principal instructed me to withdraw the MBA, I would of course have to do that but then would have to leave the university as I would know that we were not serious about our mission. He asked me to repeat what I had said and to repeat my reasoning, which I duly did, knowing that this was at least clearing my own mind about it all, and wondering if my house in Manchester was still unsold. Then he said cheerily, "You are the architect of this thing and we appointed you to know about these things so yours is the advice I must take. That is how the university runs. We appoint good people and we trust them." His eyes twinkled as he called his PA in and asked her to get the principal of University B on the phone. "Hello," he started, "you know we have a stramash just now about our new MBA degree?" There was a mutter from the receiver that rumbled on a bit. "Of course, you will not be surprised to know that we are going ahead. If you get your plans in order timeously there may be space enough for both of us!"

There were several memorable aspects to this brief telephonic encounter. One was my surprise at the style of my boss, who throughout clearly enjoyed the stylistic appurtenances of a playground stand-off between old sparring partners. The second was the clear intimation that this was a rough old world and it was up to the players to play dirty when appropriate. The other was to hear the somewhat archaic usage of the old Scots adverb "timeously" and the recall of the stress on the first syllable, and note that also for future reference.

The university's planning group asked what our projections for recruitment were. We had calculated that we could break even at 20, so I conservatively estimated 25. A senior colleague advised that this would be optimistic as there probably no more than around 50 qualified and interested potential customers in the region. In that first year we closed the book at 65 and never went below that for years after. We were the first university business school in the UK to offer such a programme.

In launching our new part-time MBA there ensued a telling telephone discussion with AMBA, the Association of MBAs, who advised that our course could not possibly expect to be recognised as preparing suitable candidates fitted to become members of their estimable association until these graduates had "proved their worth by experience". I pointed out that this proof by experience was precisely what our graduates had to have demonstrated before we would accept them on to our programme. We heard no more of this humbug.

By now we had another new professor. The excellent person who had been offered the Chair of Business Policy decided to accept another chair at an even more ancient foundation and we remained good friends. On re-advertisement we had several strong applications from good economists and social scientists whose claims were usually backed by supportive expressions from within our university. But none had the business experience or the street smarts that were being increasingly demanded by our new students aged between 30 and 50, most of whom were established and successful managers already.

Nonetheless, within the house, when it came to discussions of curricula, prerequisites, examination rubrics and the like we found we had to face imperceptible clouds of imprecision and latent scorn underlying such apparently innocuous questions as whether a Master's course in management or business could be regarded as worthy of a Master's qualification if it was not a "true postgraduate programme" but merely a (putatively inferior) postgraduating one when the university did not offer a Bachelor's programme in the same subjects. In due course, a decade later we did indeed yield to the hierarchy's lust for income by offering an undergraduate programme that instantly became exceedingly popular.

So I persuaded a former colleague at MBS to put his hat in the ring, and on the day he was interviewed he was duly offered the post. I knew his qualities as a colleague. He was a superb trainer and academic entrepreneur with a First Class degree in Marine Engineering; he had an inquiring, innovative and entrepreneurial mind allied to very strong industry experience, great presentation skills and vitally exciting ideas. At the time he had few journal articles published but those he had were read by managers. It was a good day when he joined us and we combined to form a good team.

We were growing by now on several fronts; but on one issue we were still not making progress. Of the two dozen or thereabouts new appointments we had expected and indeed believed we had been promised, we had been able to make fewer than half a dozen. We kept pushing at the doors of those senior colleagues who seemed to be publicly supportive of the university's plans for business education, but never received a clear explanation. It was a stalemate. On a research trip to London I called unexpectedly at the office of the FME, the Foundation for Management Education, to share our disappointment and to glean some relevant information from their records. They indeed had relevant paperwork and estimates of the value of the funds they had collected for the Scottish project, and knew how much this was worth per university when doubled to represent the UGC contribution and then divided by three to fairly reward the three claimants! One day a senior colleague enquired faux-naively about this mounting pressure from "outside the university", and his manner implied that I was evidently under suspicion as the source of this interest. I therefore started again to watch my back for fear of suspicion of fifth-column activity.

The FME also had comparative expenditure figures from the other two universities and knew at what rate they were continuing to grow, and started to ask our university some serious questions. One day I had a call from my new friend at FME to advise that he had discovered that the additional funds had indeed been duly added to the university's block grant at the agreed date, which was by now some five years earlier, and subsequently in later instalments. But it had not been "earmarked", merely "indicated". This constituted a significant distinction because had it been *earmarked* it could not be validly used for any other purpose; but if it was simply *indicated*, this only meant that it *should* be used for those purposes for which it had been claimed. The increase had gone into general funds. The force was moral, not contractual. Our treasure ship had already been unloaded and its contents warehoused somewhere untraceable.

But why would any university accept money for one purpose and then apply the funds for the benefit of other objectives? If you ask your parents for additional pocket money promising to use it for school books, they may be understandably miffed if they discover that it has been used for drugs, loose girlfriends and bacon sandwiches. But those who had given their share of the money through the Council of Industry for Management Education (CIME) Appeal had assumed that universities could be trusted to keep their promises.

By now we understood the history of these events quite well and were living and breathing the smell of the chase. In a conversation with a professor of engineering who had proved to be solidly sympathetic to our crusade, the term "Scottish business school" came up. "Peugh!" he snorted, "that was merely a device to attract the money!" This came to seem an apt title for the new business school.

There then entered a phase of computation and calculation of values, based on the appropriate formulae. In partnership with the FME this could be done quite accurately, and of course colleagues in universities A and B were helpful in sharing their assessments. A sum was determined and a bill presented to our principal. It came to more than half a million pounds. After some deliberation the answer came back that this sum appeared to be inflated and in any event the money did not exist anywhere. Of course it did not. It had been spent already.

But when we challenged the university's calculations on the grounds of unreasonable assumptions they were met with the gnomic response from a senior administrator that "for reasons that you will understand, the university does not give reasons". This seemed at the time to represent an odd line of argument, but this also has continued to be a useful guide to the meaning of silence in later experiences. The same senior administrator was a good source of gnomic utterances and meticulous in his expression, and one admired his mastery of the talk. Once, later, I was faced with what I deemed to be a state of emergency, crystallised by a confrontational decision of one of our tripartite partners that appeared to spell serious trouble for us, and took my problem to him. He mused quietly over the issue then averred quietly that it could be possible that the problem could solve itself with the aid of "the natural effluxion of time". I left the room snarling at the cautious attitude and was still grumbling in front of my secretary, who retorted sharply that "he could just be right, you know". I let it lie and she was right of course; both of them were.

Another recollection of this period came when I applied for and obtained the tenancy of a large family home in the Professors' Square, twelve (as when they were built there had been twelve professors) large Victorian houses in the heart of the university. In discussion with the outgoing tenants, on hearing of the title of my chair, my kindly new colleague observed that we were "bringing trade into the Square". It was presumably a light-hearted sally, a joke, possibly of the same genre as some of the Duke of Edinburgh's bons mots of the "slitty Chinese eyes" variety. My, how we laughed.

But such micro-exchanges underscored the reality of entering a new cultural world and exposure to new micro-cultural referencing. Another example came after I had been subjected to a boorish encounter in a public place with someone with whom I had presumed to be on collegial terms. When I noted this to a faculty colleague, he explained that this man did frequently behave in this threatening manner, but "after all, he was the dux [top pupil] at Allan Glen's", leaving me to ponder to which of my possible questions that could have been an appropriate answer. A good deal of tacit knowledge had therefore to be re-processed or assumed by a newcomer.

It is well understood that there is nothing automatic about the emergence and location of acceptable discourses in an institution, even one that can be authentically characterised as a Total Institution, for "These cultural identities do not automatically produce solidarity, but they can activate affinities amongst participants that allow access to a stock of collective culture that can ease belonging in the moment" (Scarborough, 2015, p. 3). These affinities build implicitly and often unremarkably into tacit knowledge, the ignorance of the subtlety of which may be damaging to the intruder into a new culture, as Rumsfeld (2011) famously noted as the unknown unknown.

My colleague and I occasionally recollect the subtlety of our shared experiences in University C, as when we were trying to put some of "the money" to appropriate advantage for a would-be business school, as a contribution to an adequate MBA suite for our managers, which we did, while digesting the inwardness of the implied rebuke that we were seeking to "embellish" the patently-not-fit-for-purpose physical teaching facilities. The "embellishment" that so threatened the sublime austerity of the nineteenth-century structure consisted of one tretford cord floor covering (available for one week only at a 40 per cent discount, if memory serves) and a coffee machine suitable for offering middle-level executives at least a warm drink between their days' working duties and their MBA evening classes.

As the new decade began, our embryonic business school burgeoned, not merely avoiding the savage cuts that damaged much of higher education but pioneering in the newer forms of university–industry partnership with the first non-science or engineering-based teaching company, the first of several teaching company partnerships with small and regionally significant partners, in creating a clutch of SME (small and medium-sized enterprise) support programmes and launching a new journal, the *European Management Journal*.

One day 10 years later I took a phone call from head-hunters enquiring about my availability to be interested in the directorship of an older, larger, long-established, internationally rated business school, which I laughed off, knowing there was much work still to do where I was. Soon afterwards, the invitation was repeated by a senior professor from that university, with the same message. I soon received a direct call from the vice chancellor of that university, asking me to at least "come down and see us, and see what you think". Before giving any definite answer, I sought an interview with our newly arrived principal, seeking at least a verbal assurance that he might consider ways to redeem the promises made to me fifteen years earlier and in particular whether there could be some movement towards provision of a purpose-built home for our business school as envisaged in discussions of more than a decade before. He advised that doubtless I would be well content with a move to the city in which I had been at school. One can take a hint.

Half a century later, University C now has a "business school"; that is to say it has a department of the university as part of a faculty of social studies, though not yet a "business school" of the sort the original money was collected to create. The MBA continues, though not apparently in its part-time executive-friendly mode, and recently celebrated the jubilee of its foundation with an event crafted around a preposterous mythic history embodied in a fanciful document produced for the occasion, apparently based on recovered memories of a fictional past relating an even flow of events instituted by the all-seeing and implausibly altruistic founding fathers.

But the truth is not in it. This is not what happened. The money had been won by promising an outcome that had not in reality been whole-heartedly attempted. The funds had been jointly raised for a business school embodying the values and practices of both the worlds of industry and academe and had after all produced another university department.

There need be no surprise in this outcome for values derive from the deep structures of ideation formed in early years and they are reinforced in early experience by supportive discourse and persuasive reinforcement. These combine to produce what in French is known as "*formation*" and incorporates the concepts of training and the wider infra-structures of autopoietic reproduction and the products of exaptative re-generation. Long-established institutions such as ancient universities find it hard to escape their own learned patterns of sense-making. To insiders nothing has happened here, no crime has been committed, nothing to see. Pass on, pass Go and collect the £200 as usual.

MAGDALEN LAUNDRIES AND INSTITUTIONAL OBLIGATIONS

Though it deals with more serious matters of life and death, the case of the Magdalen Laundries offers some parallels to the story recounted above (Killian, 2015). This history has become a cause célèbre not only in Ireland but throughout Christendom (McCarthy, 2010). The narrative has become one of apparently utterly worthy institutions designed to improve the life chances of women who had "fallen" from grace by conceiving and delivering illegitimate babies, but which had over time degenerated into highly-disciplined uncaring and vicious instruments of anti-female terror and lifelong punishment covering up a systematic exploitation of baby-sales for the enrichment of the institution (Hogan 2019).

The structuring of this narrative can be characterised as a representation of the degradation of compassion as "a complex social process embedded within power relations that can be disciplinary in nature and create ambivalent rather than wholly positive outcomes" (Simpson, Clegg, Lopes, e Cunha, Rego and Pitsis, 2014). It has also been a narrative of the perversion of institutional values and of the ideational imprisonment of "both the oppressors and the oppressed in such an institutional structure" (O'Rourke, 2011).

There is conflicted discourse in the explanations of survivors of the Magdalen Laundries who "felt both hatred and remorse, and seemed to be able to speak about their painful experience only by silencing others' liability, while making self-reproach and sympathy go hand in hand in their construal of both their past and themselves" (Hidalgo-Tenorio and Benitez-Castro, 2021, p. 315).

Control of the narrative is achieved by controlling long-term access to data or records that might tell a different story to the accepted, acceptable narrative (O'Mahoney, 2018, p. 456). But these "tales of brutality threatened to undermine the ethical foundations of the religious life" (Cullingford, 2007), and these stories were in some ways even more implicated in the classic organisational memes of money, exploitation, bribery, interlocking corruptions of public as well as private finance, condescension and defilement of the social under-classes (Raftery, 2011).

Students of aviation disasters know that behind each incident another may well be coming and many more have probably passed earlier. *Un train peut en cacher un autre* (one train passing through may hide another coming closely behind). So behind and contemporaneous with the exploitation of young women in the Magdalen Laundries was the exploitation of young men in industrial workshops uncovered by the Ryan Report (Keenan, 2012). What was known then had to be rediscovered later, and in the case of the Magdalen Laundries there are missing elements in the accepted discoursal strategies of the institutions which operated "a wilful obscuring of accountability and an excision of formality between these two bodies" (Killian, 2015, p. 17).

Arguably similar features occur in the careful amnesia regarding the logic of the acceptance and subsequent absorption of the additional monies that had accrued from the results of the CIME Appeal and the matching funds from the UGC. In this case the narrative of accountability omitted to consider these events in terms of contractual obligation. Thus, it appeared an acceptable in-group shorthand to speak of a commitment to establish a new kind of institution as a "device to attract the money", as an inadvertent peccadillo rather than an ostentatious breach of contract. But the decisions of other bodies and individuals had been contingent on an understanding that such a contractual basis existed in fact and could be presumed to have been understood by all parties as they in their turn made their dispositions.

Institutional control of the narrative can lead to presuming to write as judge in one's own cause and then to working up a readable narrative for the evening edition. This of course works pretty well in situations where only the judgement of peers is accepted as legitimate.

A story of the famous Scottish hanging judge Robert McQueen, Lord Braxfield, tells of his having to sentence to death a lifelong friend, Matthew Hay, with whom he had regularly played chess of a convivial evening. As his friend was brought before him for judgement the great man said, "I ken weel, Matthew that ye ken the rules of chess! Well, this is checkmate!" Witty indeed but possibly outdone by his jest on another similar occasion when the convicted person was a teenaged butcher's boy. "Do ye ken how to make meat good, Johnny?" To which the lad replied, "Sir, it is by hanging it well." "Aye, it is indeed Johnny, so by this method we hope to make you good" (see, for example, Roughead, 1914). My how the recipients of these fine jests must have chortled! The wit of the powerful is always worthy of critique, as are their claims of compassion, and the sordid history of the Magdalen Laundries implies also that the spokespeople and advocates of institutions that claim virtue are not infrequently smooth talkers. There is a comfortable common-room inwardness about the notion of "a device to attract the money".

The ethical basis of the Magdalen Laundries is in many respects contested terrain with no easy answers; but one other dimension of importance is that of discipline. It is defined "as readiness or ability to respect authority and observe conventional or established laws of society or of any other organisation" (Ajeyi and Adeniji, 2009). In a university culture it is conventional to accept the tacit assumptions of fair dealing by a hierarchy acknowledged as being wise; but this hierarchy ultimately decides what is to count as wisdom, and this can also be construed by the laity as marking one's own homework.

UNIVERSITIES AS TOTAL INSTITUTIONS

The concept of the "Total Institution" is usually associated with the great ethnographer Erving Goffman (1961) and still has wide currency (Serpa, 2018). Such institutions can be characterised by values that while they originate in cultures of imposition can "engender a kind of counter-vision of the world" (Goffman, 1999, p. 121). This strain of explanation of micro-events in such institutions has been revitalised by students of the writings of Foucault (1977). Total Institutions implicitly claim control over the discourse as well as the practices that reinforce the values of a docile membership of closed social systems that require permission to enter and also to leave, re-socialising participants into changed or new identities and roles.

Clegg (2006) rightly excoriates scholars for failure to understand the potential contribution these concepts can offer to the analysis of contemporary social issues, so, wishing to escape such censure we suggest that universities only narrowly evade depiction of themselves as Total Institutions and that the fact that many scholars evidently prefer their servitude is not justification enough for their having got away so lightly.

Institutions like the Magdalen Laundries and ancient universities as Total Institutions exercise long-term social control over participants in that they aim to control the discourse as well as the practices, enforcing compliance to those ways of looking at the world that impute special value to their own view of themselves. This can doubtless create opportunities for displaying exceptional virtue. But it also runs the risk of certifying over-claiming. If "a thing is what it is and no other thing" then the discoursal power lies also in the self-referential claim that the institution does indeed know and can legislate for the abolition and dismissal of competing claims.

This remains the master ground for justification in a university because it stands to reason that the university itself should legitimately offer to be judge in its own cause, for the university is by definition the master of reason. That is what it is instituted to do, and the unchallengeable assumption is that this is what it is still doing.

The cultures of Total Institutions promote conformity and acceptance of their own special values, and these assumptions work especially well when there exists a comfortable acceptance of its own history as illustrating some Ur-Spencerian notion of natural selection. A university that has stood for over five hundred years, high and proud on its towered hill at the apex of its educational hierarchical structures safeguarding its students, over 70 per cent of whom came from homes within a radius of 40 miles and whose ruling cadre was dominated by men whose whole educational experience has been moulded within these same regional parameters, may not have had much chance to develop grounds for self-critique or of the difference between its values and those of others outside its own milieu.

Such institutions operate a "capillary power", as Foucault termed it, that reaches deep down into the societal micro-structures, activating the micro-structures of organisational commitment and assent flowing through unquestioning channels of discourse that support the reproduction of institutional structure (Foucault, 1993). The reproduction of these social forms occurs through auto-poietic formulations (Varela, Maturana and Uribe, 1974) that may nonetheless repel the understanding of outsiders through their apparent opacity while remaining perfectly comprehensible to insiders. Hospitals and prisons and police organisations share some of these characteristics (Weir, Marsh and Greenwood, 2009).

There is a French proverb that asserts *"L'Habit ne fait pas le moine"* (the dress does not make the monk) and a traditional Jewish tale that implies a similar truth. An indolent son is chastised by his parents for his lack of a rewarding career. In an attempt to prove his parents wrong he buys a sea captain's cap from a second-hand shop and on returning home claims to have become a ship's master. His mother is delighted and wastes no time in advising her neighbours of the son's standing as "my son, the ship's captain". His father is less impressed and instead of berating his son for his insolence asks quietly, "To your mother, you're a captain. To the village you're a captain … To a ship's captain, are you a captain?"

This question has implications for universities that go beyond their institutional and personal experience in their claim for the ownership of reason and the definitions of knowledge. To other universities they are captains; to the state authorities with regulatory power over them, they may survive casual inspection; but to the business people who raised funds for their values to be respected because they have put their money into a deal voluntarily entered into on both sides, can they qualify as captains in a realm where obligation is sealed contractually? To a business school that does meet the expectations of the Franks or Normanbrook reports, is what we have in many of the UK university departments of Business and Management Studies a "business school"?

The relations between universities, industry and government form a triple helix of obligation and are occupied by partners presenting with disparate value-sets that require continual mediation (Etzkowitz and Leydesdorff, 2000). The logic of situations is understood differently in these distinctly different cultures, leading to "complex and complicated conflicts of interest" and "while general moral and social values are shared by industrial and university partners alike, individual researchers who bridge both kinds of organizations often nonetheless feel that they cannot solve value conflicts in a way that does justice to them both" (Hillerbrand and Werker, 2019, p. 1634). The values of theory are not necessarily well aligned with the values derived from practice. The notion of the "entrepreneurial university" seems threatening to many scholars and its behaviours are difficult to learn.

Likewise, while learning to fly in an airplane simulator is cost-effective, the experience is not the same as flying aircraft in real time, confronting difficult weather or unforeseen human–machine interactions (Weir, 1996). The crash in 2014 of a Richard Branson-led space vehicle was described by Christopher Hart, the chairman of the US National Transportation Safety Board investigating commission, as caused by a "failure to consider and protect against the possibility that a single human error could result in a catastrophic hazard to the SpaceShipTwo vehicle" (Malik, 2015). This judgement was based on predispositions to ignore the importance of learning under battle conditions and of a lack of understanding of the maxim gleaned from many examples that where complex socio-technical systems break down catastrophically it is usually due to human error rather than hardware failure (Weir, 1996, 2000, 2002). Moreover "the mistake is often a symptom of a flawed system" (Malik, 2015).

In taking advantage of a distinction between "indicated" and "earmarked" to permit their implicitly perceived comfort it would seem that University C had broken an implicit contract of fair dealing. They had not done what they were supposed to do and they did not care to take the time to enquire to be informed about what was implicitly promised in such a contract, promising to co-create new knowledge together with partners with other values sustaining diverse interests. As Killian notes of the Magdalen Laundries, "the informality was not accidental ... the problem was not accidental opacity but deliberate silence" (2015, p. 30).

However, it may be fair to reflect that the university staff were not used to this kind of relation with industry because they had not come into such a situation before. They had engaged in teaching and research in areas of knowledge in which they were expected to teach what they knew. They knew about political economy so could feel justified at re-mapping management as a subset of that. But after the Franks and Normanbrook formula had been endorsed by political agreement, they were being invited to co-create a new future in which they would have to accept both the knowledge of the other parties to such a contract but also their own relative ignorance. Universities do not in general like to admit to ignorance. They are supposed to know things and they come to believe that their knowledge in some areas compensates for their ignorance in others because they tend also to see themselves as impartial arbiters of what is useful knowledge, what it is important to know. But in this respect, they fall into the Rumsfeld trap of being ignorant of what they do not know or do not intend to find out about.

It is unnecessary to make any assumptions about individual motivation nor to blame individuals or even to invoke a capacity for "moral disengagement" (Johnson, 2014) to understand why this is suspect behaviour, even if the disengagement may be supplemented by the techniques of neutralisation described by Sykes and Matza (1957). In fact, what was meant by morality in respect of new knowledge was implicitly understood differently on the three sides of the bargain. Moral wrongdoing in organisations may be the outcome of "a process in which initial moral dissonance gives way to acceptance through a process of moral neutralization" (Kvalnes, 2019, p. 117). The blind eye sees no ships and all appears well.

The nuns in the Magdalen Laundries doubtless believed honestly that they were doing God's work. But their behaviour turns out to have been "a strange mixture of caring and corruption" (Coldrey, 2000). But this defence only appears strange to those for whom corruption does not require the claim of caring as its implicit justification. Of course they cared: they were nuns. Of course, great universities will not act unreasonably in preferring their own criteria of relevant knowledge to that of the practitioners in the apposite field of application. *They* are the arbiters of knowledge.

These debates have added resonance in our present situation where universities have "gone global" and are seen as "central to a knowledge society based on the belief that everyone can, through higher education, access universal truths and apply them in the name of progress" (Frank and Meyer, 2020, cover). A tacit assumption of this approach is that if one is discussing knowledge transfer, for instance, it is the university which is the originator of the knowledge and the industry partner merely provides the site of the application of that knowledge (De Wit-de Vries, Dolfsma, Van der Windt et al., 2019), though it may be that both parties can learn from the process (Cyert and Goodman, 1997). But it is more helpful to see these parties as mutually involved in an evolving process of co-creation.

Bandura (2004, p. 5) notes that "People do not ordinarily engage in reprehensible conduct until they have justified to themselves the rightness of their actions." He argued that this process of ethical justification is initiated by a stage of moral disengagement (Bandura, Barbaranelli, Caprara and Pastorelli, 1996). There is no need for an account of a university that defines its inhabitants as universally knowledgeable and to believe that its members act as "moral saints" (Wolf, 1982). But neither is it normally fair to judge that universities knowingly decide to act criminally either (Heath, 2008).

Institutions are neither "good" nor "bad" in and of themselves (Bhaumik and Dinova, 2004); they are discursively constructed artefacts of wide-ranging historically situated experience. In discussing Enron, Arthur Andersen or the London Metropolitan Police the notion of institutional corruption seems to be readily understood by academics (Armstrong, 2015). However, institutional corruption exists at three different but complementary levels: collective, cultural and individual.

Studies of Enron emphasise the interlocking nature of these mutually reinforcing levels creating a systemic cycle in which questionable objectives emphasising "income generation above all, regardless of means or sustainability, as long as it could be booked", are driving "a promotion and remuneration system which nurtured and rewarded unethical behaviour" and enforcing the compulsory exit of "low performers every six months, resulting in a culture where the unethical drove out the ethical, as only the former prospered. This quickly established behaviour patterns which yielded organization-wide corruption as the norm" (Fairchild and Marnet, 2018).

Several research studies illuminate the individual dimension and others concentrate on the risks to the (presumably virtuous) intrinsic educational values from the infective corruption of the (presumably questionable) ethical practices of commercialism (Bok, 2004; Washburn, 2008). However, there seem to be fewer studies of the two former levels, the collective and the cultural. Partly as far as universities are concerned this comes about because the role of the university (as that of a religious body, which of course historically is central to their history and evolution) is presumed to be a dimension of the stabilising and conservative elements of society.

But businesses can also be conservative and universities can be radical in any of these respects. One study that does attempt to identify some of the parameters is a study of universities in countries in Central Asia, which notes that "Universities may contribute to a nation's social cohesion through both direct and indirect means." And in an updated version of the injunction "physician, heal thyself" it concludes that "the single most important arena wherein universities can influence social cohesion in these countries is the manner by which they address education corruption" (Heynemann, 2007, p. 305).

The behaviour of institutional decision-makers is generally held to be pretty reasonable by the members of the institution in question who are of course already acculturated in its own special ways. This requires three stages, involving processes of encounters with other types of moral reasoning causing an experience of moral dissonance, in formal recognition of the need for moral neutralisation and the subsequent normalisation of questionable behaviour (Kvalnes, 2019).

In reviewing the moral careers of business institutions Donaldson argues that "bad practices can become institutionalized, and initial queasiness gives way to industry-wide acceptance"

(2012, p. 6). But there is no occasion for queasiness if all takes place under a moral umbrella that is similarly conformed in all its apparent manifestations. University C stands or stood at this time at the apex of a hierarchy of institutional deference. In this region nearly three-quarters of its students had historically been recruited from within a radius of 40 miles from its city centre. It had never been *one* of the universities of the city: it was *the* university: standing proud on its (self-created) history that represented the culmination of many a scholarly career that had commenced here and would finish here (for where would there be to go that could constitute a promotion?). It stood proud and visible for many miles around. It was *the* "house of reason" because it defined reason. So what it did was ipso facto reasonable.

Reason itself comes in many formats The Greek philosopher Archilocus is credited with the judgement πόλλ' οἶδ' ἀλώπηξ, ἀλλ' ἐχῖνος ἓν μέγα (in English, "A fox knows many things, but a hedgehog knows one big thing"). The now famous distinction became aphoristic after Isaiah Berlin's book *The Hedgehog and the Fox: An Essay on Tolstoy's View of History* that sought to interpret Leo Tolstoy's philosophy of history (Berlin, 1953).

Universities in most epochs lean more to the hedgehog style in their emphasis on monolithic disciplines and especially at present the constraining frameworks of best practice, rankings and formulaic, ritualised outputs of limited focus ("No more than 6,000 words for a four-star journal, Roger … and books don't count"). Industry meanwhile/in contrast increasingly seeks to innovate through privileging the behaviours of the fox as the epitome of entrepreneurship.

Business schools are not infrequently accused of hubris (Sadler-Smith and Cojuharenco, 2021), and accused of only teaching capitalist economics and of ignoring other than capitalistic types of management, encouraging short-term greed, damaging the "real" economy and, still more heinous, of damaging the idea of the university itself (Parker, 2018). But maybe that rot lies deeper in the intellectual fabric of some systems of higher education more generally and is based in the assumption that universities can be trusted to wish to find out what they do not know. But this implicit obligation may be ignored in case this curiosity subverts their general claim to knowledge on which their societal status depends.

Universities were invited by the state to *participate* but they have subtly and often by subterfuge apparently succeeded to *dominate* the form of these developments by a process of intellectual colonialism. So, for decision-makers in great universities confronted with the world of others there apparently existed a master justification because "the university does not give reasons (for reasons that you will understand)". One good reason for not asking these kinds of questions is because one *knows* that one already knows the answers.

Ajayi and Adesina argue that the external discipline required of organisational membership should be based on familial virtues of good home training to impart "self-control, restraint, respect for self and respect for others (Adesina, 1980). In addition, discipline calls for sacrifice, perseverance, tolerance and recognition of human dignity (Ogunsaju, 1989)" (Ajayi and Adeniji, 2009).

But these processes segue imperceptibly into an acceptance of unchallenged and unchanging ethical conformity embodied in a supportive culture if there is no opportunity to be regularly in diurnal practice confronted by alternatives. This segues in turn into a comfortable acceptance of what from other stances can seem uncomfortably close to corruption (Ashforth and Vikas, 2003) when senior decision-makers imperceptibly become judges in their own cause self-justifying with the precedents of 600 years. Adam Smith wrote for his own times and scarcely needs the comforting condescension of latter-day disciples.

Ethical conformity around historically accepted stereotypes is the bedrock of assent in institutions that have survived several generations of informal governance embodied in unchallenged practices. But contractual obligation needs more than this. Using a Bourdiesian framework (1990) Killian concludes that

> this underlines the importance of carefully building an architecture of accountability in the widest and most inclusive sense into all state relationships, particularly where services are delegated or outsourced, and doubly so when the services are targeted at groups who lack a clear voice. A system based on curated informality has a dangerous potential to alter the identities of those (un)accounted for, and these altered identities shift power. The state as instigator of this informality is rewarded with a convenient distance from these negative outcomes, and the people who enter the system without power find no means to progress, no familiar structure to navigate. (2015, p. 31)

A culture supports the behaviours of its members by rewarding their adherence to the values it claims despite the clear evidence that in its practice it often fails to exemplify those values by changes in its practice. But this becomes a circular process like the perpetual motion machines of the early part of the Scientific Revolution, doomed to failure because of their contradiction of the First Law, so energy always has to be added to keep the machine apparently reproducing it timelessly.

Universities are perceived deferentially by most members of a society in which such institutions are perceived as the ultimate custodians of the truth. But when they also define what truths are to be counted as truth and self-referentially choose the descriptors of truth that already fit them, and maybe them only ... *quis custodiet ipsos custodes?* (Who will guard the guards?)

Instead of a developing partnership between higher education and business and industry to improve the long-term needs of the economy to the leading edge of international practice that could have been led by new institutions with considerable operational independence, the business schools have been captured by the self-aggrandisement of institutions of the higher mediocrity and bureaucratic banality. But most of all they have succumbed to the creeping hegemonic dominance of a value system that has claimed to be judge in its own courts of where the virtues of reason should originate, instead of by relying on the values of respect for contracts and the evolving understanding of co-creation. What Killian depicts as "curated informality" becomes a device to cover up and provide incorrect narratives that contrive to deceive and blur institutional accountability (2015, p. 30).

The universities were generously funded by a partnership between the public purse and the private sector to serve five- or 10-course dinners of reputable fine dining cooked to the highest *trade* standards, and in return have cooked up a mess of pottage, a true "farce", a finely chopped meat and breadcrumb dish often used as a stuffing (though in my familial cuisine it regularly appears as a separate dish, a "savoury pudding" often prepared for the festive table; recipe upon application, send a stamped, addressed envelope for further particulars, cash is always acceptable).

The legacy asset base of the British university remains a powerful societal force because it rests upon an assumptive foundation of fair dealing that remains largely unquestioned because its intentions are not usually suspected. Sometimes this occurs because of its incorporation in larger entities and more evidently beneficial discoursal framings, such as "education" (who could criticise that?).

University business schools are seen by many in higher education as a great success story. They have certainly proven to be good business for the sector, with delivery costs at the lower end and pricing status at the premium end and contribution rates to its host institutions sometimes as high as 60 per cent. Vice chancellors agree: what is not to like about the cash-cow business school as a feeder into the *real* scholarly disciplines? But this has come at a fierce hidden cost to the business and industry sectors of the wider society that might have been better supported through a partnership model.

By the contemporary lights of the higher education sector, Business departments have done well. They are seriously profitable and attractive to wider markets than were ever envisaged. Good for Chinese industry but not what Robbins, Franks and Normanbrook envisaged and the CIME/FME contributed their share of the bargain to. The current UK Prime Minister was reliably reported to have ejaculated "F**k business!" (*National*, 2018) in response to being advised of the finding that much UK business and industry was exceedingly anxious about the possibility of a hard Brexit impacting negatively on their markets in the UK and globally. It turns out that over the longer haul there has been more than one way of doing just that, and that universities have also played their part.

The British Academy of Management (BAM) has grown to a powerful professional body, satisfying strong scholarly criteria (at least as far as its senior cadres are concerned), with a cadre of Fellows selected by their peers, supporting institutional ratings and rankings that drive academic careers and innumerable journals achieving high peer-rating acceptability. When the notion of introducing Fellows was raised at the Council of BAM, one member of the committee objected unless some at least, and preferably 50 per cent, of the Fellows came from business and industry. Off the cuff he proposed the names of three such possible candidates, one an FRS, FRSE, FR Society of Metallurgy, and former chairman of a major industrial corporation; one who had First Class Honours from University C, had been *Guardian* Young Chairman of the Year, and was a visiting professor also at University C and was CEO of a major supermarket group; and a third who had a PhD in marketing from a UK Business School and was at the time CEO of one of the world's most profitable food manufacturers. The chair of the meeting explained in a kindly way that clearly one member of the Council had not understood the inwardness of the definition of "Fellow" currently under discussion. But he had, he had. As George Bernard Shaw noted, "professions are conspiracies against the laity" (1911, Act 1) but some conspiracies are more profitable than others.

There are many interpretations of the story of business and management education in the UK, but in respect of the aspirations of the founding impulses represented in the reports of the Robbins, Normanbrook and Franks committees, they may be less comfortably judged to have failed miserably. In a period over which business education in UK universities has grown strongly, the relative standing of the UK economy has just as steadily declined. If there had been contracts tied to performance their obligations would not have been met.

To the other captains the UK business school higher education sector may be no longer entitled to its captain's cap. Perhaps it is not unreasonable to continue to question whether the university is "a bad public good" (Shaw, 2010). In a rigorous review of the ethical issues surrounding information systems it is claimed that "efficacy must be subordinate to ethicality – the system must not contravene the authentic values of those who use and are affected by the system" (Mingers and Walsham, 2010, p. 22). No one party to the ethical bargain can simply presume that its own reading of the values that might apply to a contractual engagement should hold undisputed hegemony.

Yet another story might seem appropriate to this perplexing narrative. It is that of the John Knox-like preacher who warns his errant flock of the possibility of their comeuppance on Judgement Day. It ends with the flock, faced with the imminence of their despatch to the underworld of Satan as the reward for their sinful behaviour, protesting that "Oh, Lord, we didnae ken, we didnae ken …"

But the preacher comforts them by reminding the congregation of the Guid Lord's generosity and forgiveness by intoning, "Then the Lord will look down on ye and in his infinite mercy and compassion he will say … Ah, weel, ye ken noo!"

NOTE

1. This chapter is based on true accounts of events that happened some time ago. There is no intention to imply wrongdoing or malicious intent on the part of any individual, but only to help in the understanding of how the culture of essentially virtuous institutions can operate to frustrate the equally good intentions of other participants in the democratic processes.

REFERENCES

Adesina, S. (1980) *Some Aspects of School Management*. Ibadan: Educational Industries.
Ajayi, K., and Adeniji, A. (2009) Pursuing discipline and ethical issues in tertiary institutions in Nigeria. *African Research Review*, 3(1).
Al-Khalili, J. (2011) *The House of Wisdom: How Arabic Science Saved Ancient Knowledge and Gave Us the Renaissance*. London: Penguin.
Allen, B. (1979) "Manchester Business School", *Education + Training*, 21(9), 265–66. https://doi.org/10.1108/eb002038.
Almond, P. (2013) *Corporate Manslaughter and Regulatory Reform*. London: Springer.
Armstrong, P. (2015) The discourse of Michel Foucault: A sociological encounter. *Critical Perspectives on Accounting*, 2, 29–42.
Ashforth, B., and Vikas, A. (2003) The normalization of corruption in organizations. *Research in Organizational Behavior*, 25, 1–52. https://doi.org/10.1016/s0191–3085(03)25001–2.
Bandura, A. (2004) Selective exercise of moral agency. In T.A. Thorkildsen and H.J. Walberg (Eds), *Nurturing Morality*. New York, NY: Kluwer.
Bandura, A., Barbaranelli, C., Caprara, G.V., and Pastorelli, C. (1996) Mechanisms of moral disengagement in the exercise of moral agency. *Journal of Personality and Social Psychology*, 71(2), 364.
Barnes, W. (1989) *Managerial Catalyst: The Story of the London Business School, 1964–1989*. London: Paul Chapman for London Business School.
Berlin, I. (1953) *The Hedgehog and the Fox: An Essay on Tolstoy's View of History*. London: Weidenfeld and Nicolson.
Bhaumik, S.K., and Dimova, R. (2014) Good and bad institutions: Is the debate over? Cross-country firm-level evidence from the textile industry. *Cambridge Journal of Economics*, 38(1), 109–26. https://doi.org/10.1093/cje/bes089.
Bok, D. (2004) *Universities in the Marketplace*. Princeton, NJ: Princeton University Press.
Clarke, D., and Weir, D. (2017) What makes the auto-ethnographic analysis authentic. In T. Vine, J. Stone, D. Weir and S. Richards (Eds), *Ethnographic Research and Analysis: Anxiety, Identity and Self*. London: Palgrave Macmillan.
Clegg, S.R. (2006) Why is organization theory so ignorant? The neglect of total institutions. *Journal of Management Inquiry*, 15(4), 426–30. https://doi.org/10.1177/1056492606294640.
Coldrey, B.M. (2000) A mixture of caring and corruption: Church orphanages and industrial schools. *Studies: An Irish Quarterly Review*, 89(353), 7–18.

Coleman, J.S. (1987) Norms as social capital. In G. Radmitzky and P. Bernholz (Eds), *Economic Imperialism*. New York, NY: Paragon Press.

Conlin, M. (2007, May 14) Cheating – or postmodern learning? Duke's b-school scandal points up the fuzzy ethics of a collaborative world. *Business Week*, 42.

Cooper, D. (1953) *Old Men Forget*. London: Rupert Hart-David.

Cullingford, E.B. (2007) "Our nuns are not a nation": Politicizing the convent in Irish literature and film. In W. Balzano, A. Mulhall and M. Sullivan (Eds), *Irish Postmodernisms and Popular Culture*. London: Palgrave Macmillan. https://doi.org/10.1057/9780230800588_5.

Cyert, R.M., and Goodman, P.S. (1997) Creating effective university–industry alliances: An organizational learning perspective. *Organizational Dynamics*, 25(4), 45–57.

Delamont, S. (2007) *Arguments against Auto-Ethnography*. Paper presented at the British Educational Research Association Annual Conference, Institute of Education, University of London, September 5–8, 2007.

De Wit-de Vries, E., Dolfsma, W.A., and Van der Windt, H.J., et al. (2019) Knowledge transfer in university–industry research partnerships: A review. *Journal of Technology Transfer*, 44, 1236–55. https://doi.org/10.1007/s10961–018–9660-x.

Donaldson, T. (2012) Three ethical roots of the economic crisis. *Journal of Business Ethics*, 106(1), 5–8.

Eckel, P.D. (2019) Towards ethical universities via ethical governing boards. *University World News*. Accessed at www.universityworldnews.com/post.php?story=20190326131223755 on December 29, 2021.

Ehrlich, T. (2000) *Civic Responsibility and Higher Education*. Washington, DC: ACE/Oryx.

Ehrich, L.C., Cranston, N., Kimber, M., and Starr, K. (2012) (Un)ethical practices and ethical dilemmas in universities: Academic leaders' perceptions. *International Studies in Educational Administration*, 40(2), 99–114.

Eliot, T.S. (1936) Burnt Norton. In *Four Quartets*. London: Faber & Faber.

Etzioni, A. (1961) *A Comparative Analysis of Complex Organizations*. Glencoe, IL: Free Press.

Etzkowitz, H., and Leydesdorff, L. (2000) The dynamics of innovation: From national systems and "Mode 2" to a triple helix of university–industry–government relations. *Research Policy*, 29, 109–23.

Fairchild, R.J., and Marnet, O. (2018) *Fraud-Perception, Superegos, and Cultural Spread of Unethical Behaviour: Theory and Evidence from Enron*. Available at SSRN: https://ssrn.com/abstract=3283883 or http://dx.doi.org/10.2139/ssrn.3283883.

Foucault, M. (1977) *Discipline and Punish: The Birth of the Prison*. New York, NY: Random House.

Foucault, M. (1993) The discourse on language (trans. R. Swyer). In *The Archaeology of Knowledge*. New York, NY: Barnes & Noble.

Frank, D.J., and Meyer, J.W. (2020) *The University and the Global Knowledge Society*. Princeton, NJ: Princeton University Press. https://doi.org/10.1515/9780691202075.

Franks Report (1963) *Report of the Franks Committee into Business and Management Education*. London: Foundation for Management Education.

Geiger, R.L., and Sá, C.-M. (2008) *Tapping the Riches of Science: Universities and the Promise of Economic Growth*. Cambridge, MA: Harvard University Press.

Gobert, J. (2008) The Corporate Manslaughter and Corporate Homicide Act 2007: Thirteen Years in the Making But Was It Worth the Wait? *Modern Law Review*, 71(3), 413–33.

Goffman, E. (1961) *Asylums: Essays on the Social Situation of Mental Patients and Other Inmates*. New York, NY: Anchor Books.

Goffman, E. (1999) *Os momentos e os seus homens* [The moments and their men]. Lisbon: Relógio d'Água.

Gore, J.M. (1995) On the continuity of power relations in pedagogy. *International Studies in Sociology of Education*, 5(2), 165–88. https://doi.org/10.1080/0962021950050203.

Gosling, T. (2017) Tory MP Jacob Rees Mogg's wife's ancestral home benefits from £7.6 million state rescue. *The Land Is Ours*. Accessed at https://tlio.org.uk/rees-mogg-wifes-ancestral-home-benefits -from-7–6m-state-rescue/ on December 3, 2021.

Gutas, D. (1998) *Greek Thought, Arabic Culture: The Graeco-Arabic Translation Movement in Baghdad and Early 'Abbāsid Society (2nd–4th/8th–10th Centuries)*. London: Routledge.

Gutmann, A. (1987) *Democratic Education*. Princeton, NJ: Princeton University Press.

Hammar, H., Jagers, S.C., and Nordblom, K. (2009) Perceived tax evasion and the importance of trust. *Journal of Socio-Economics*, *38*(2), 238–45.

Hansard (1964) *House of Commons Hansard Report of May 11 1964*. Accessed at https://api.parliament .uk/historic-hansard/commons/1964/may/11/business-schools-manchester-and-london and https:// hansard.parliament.uk/Lords/1964–05–11/debates/7498d9bf-5680–4fce-9da2–8e99547c8656/ BusinessSchoolsAtUniversities on December 11, 2021.

Heath, J. (2008) Business ethics and moral motivation: A criminological perspective. *Journal of Business Ethics*, 83(4), 595–614.

Heyneman, S.P. (2007) Three universities in Georgia, Kazakhstan and Kyrgyzstan: The struggle against corruption and for social cohesion. *Prospects*, *37*, 305–18.

Hidalgo-Tenorio, E., and Benitez-Castro, M.-E. (2021) The language of evaluation in the narratives by the Magdalen Laundries survivors: The discourse of female victimhood. *Applied Linguistics*, *42*(2), 315–41. https://doi.org/10.1093/applin/amaa029.

Hillerbrand, R., and Werker, C. (2019) Values in university–industry collaborations: The case of academics working at universities of technology. *Sci Eng Ethics*, *25*, 1633–56. https://doi.org/10.1007/ s11948–019–00144-w.

Hogan, C. (2019) *Republic of Shame: Stories from Ireland's Institutions for "Fallen Women"*. London: Penguin.

Hook, S. (1969) Barbarism, virtue, and the university. *Public Interest*, *15*(Spring), 23.

Immerwahr, J., and Johnson, J. (2007) *Squeeze Play: How Parents and the Public Look at Higher Education Today*. National Center Report #07–4. San Jose, CA: National Center for Public Policy and Higher Education.

Johnson, C.E. (2014) Why "good" followers go "bad": The power of moral disengagement. *Journal of Leadership* Special Issue, *13*(4), 36–50.

Keenan, M. (2012) *Child Sexual Abuse and the Catholic Church: Gender, Power and Organizational Culture*. Oxford: Oxford University Press.

Killian, S. (2015) For lack of accountability: The logic of the price in Ireland's Magdalen Laundries. *Accounting Organizations and Society*, *43*, 17–32. https://doi.org/10.1016/j.aos.2015.03.006.

Kvalnes, Ø. (2019) Moral neutralization. In: *Moral Reasoning at Work*. Cham: Palgrave Pivot. https:// doi.org/10.1007/978-3-030–15191–1_13.

Laing, R.D. (1971) *The Politics of the Family and Other Essays*. London: Tavistock Publications.

Maak, T., and Pless, N.M. (2006) Responsible leadership: A relational approach. In T. Maak and N.M. Press (Eds), *Responsible Leadership*. London: Routledge.

MacIntyre, A. (1973) The essential contestability of some social concepts. *Ethics*, *84*, 1–9.

Malik, T. (2015) Deadly SpaceShipTwo crash caused by co-pilot error: NTSB. *Space*. Accessed at www .space.com/30073-virgin-galactic-spaceshiptwo-crash-pilot-error.html on 15 December, 2021.

Mangnall, J. (1988) Vigil. Originally in *Ambit*, 107 (1987), reprinted in G. Gordon and D. Hughes (Eds), *The Minerva Book of Short Stories*. London: Heinemann.

McCarthy, R.L. (2010) *Origins of the Magdalen Laundries*. Jefferson, NC: McFarland.

Mills, C.W. (1959) *The Sociological Imagination*. New York, NY: Oxford University Press.

Mingers, J., and Walsham, G. (2010) Towards ethical information systems: The contribution of discourse ethics. *MIS Quarterly*, *34*(4), 833–54.

Moiseyenko, O. (2005) Higher education and social cohesion. *Peabody Journal of Education*, *80*(4), 89–104.

Morrison, T. (2002) How can values be taught in the university? *Peer Review*, *4*, 4–7.

Motley, J.L. (1873) *The Rise of the Dutch Republic*. London: George Routledge and Sons.

National (2018) EU diplomats reveal Boris Johnson said "f**k business" over Brexit fears. Accessed at www.thenational.scot/news/16310206.eu-diplomats-reveal-boris-johnson-said-f-k-business-brexit -fears/ on 30 December, 2021.

Normanbrook Report (1963) *Report of the Normanbrook Committee into Business and Management Education*. London: Council of Industry for Management Education.

Ogunsaju, S. (1989) *School Management without Crises*. Ibadan: Lavile Publications.

O'Mahoney, J. (2018) Advocacy and the Magdalen Laundries: Towards a psychology of social change. *Qualitative Research in Psychology*, *15*(4), 456–71. https://doi.org/10.1080/14780887.2017.1416803.

O'Rourke, M. (2011) Ireland's Magdalen Laundries and the state's duty to protect. 10 *Hibernian L.J.* 200.

Parker, M. (2018) *Shut Down the Business School: What's Wrong with Management Education.* London: Pluto Press.

Penley, L.E., and Gould, S. (1988) Etzioni's model of organizational involvement: A perspective for understanding commitment to organizations. *Journal of Organizational Behaviour*, 9(1), 43–59.

Pirsig, R.M. (1974) *Zen and the Art of Motorcycle Maintenance: An Inquiry into Values.* New York, NY: William Morrow.

Potter, S. (1962) *One-Upmanship: Being Some Account of the Activities And Teaching of the Lifemanship Correspondence College of One-Upness And Gameslifemastery.* Harmondsworth: Penguin.

Raftery, M. (2011) Ireland's Magdalen Laundries scandal must be laid to rest. *The Guardian*, June 8. Accessed at http://marilynsworld.com/docs/Irelands%20Magdalen%20laundries%20scandal%20must%20be%20laid%20to%20rest%20Mary%20Raftery%20The%20Guardian.pdf on December 8, 2021.

Robbins Report (1963) *Higher Education: Cmd 2154 – Report of the Committee Appointed by the Prime Minister under the Chairmanship of Lord Robbins.* London: Her Majesty's Stationery Office.

Roughead, W. (1914) Real Braxfield. Jurid. Rev., 26, 165.

Rumsfeld, D. (2011) *Known and Unknown: A Memoir.* New York, NY: Penguin.

Sadler-Smith, E., and Cojuharenco, I. (2021) Business schools and hubris: Cause or cure? *Academy of Management Learning and Education*, 20, 270–89. https://doi.org/10.5465/amle.2019.0289.

Scarborough, R.C. (2015) *Moments and Their Men: Cultural Architectures and Interactional Ecologies of Belonging and Inequality.* PhD dissertation, University of Virginia.

Serpa, S. (2018) On the concept of total institution. *International Journal of Social Science Studies*, 6(9). https://doi.org/10.11114/ijsss.v6i9.3467.

Shakespeare, W. (1623) Henry V. First Folio.

Shaw, G.B. (1911) *The Doctor's Dilemma.* Harmondsworth: Penguin Classics.

Shaw, J.S. (2010) Education: A bad public good? *Independent Review*, 15(2), 241–56. http://www.jstor.org/stable/24562365.

Simpson, A.V., Clegg, S.R., Lopes, M.P., e Cunha, M.P., Rego, A., and Pitsis, T. (2014) Doing compassion or doing discipline? Power relations and the Magdalen Laundries. *Journal of Political Power*, 7(2), 253–74. https://doi.org/10.1080/2158379X.2014.927684.

Smith, A. ([1759] 2002) *The Theory of Moral Sentiments.* Cambridge: Cambridge University Press.

Sykes, G.M., and Matza, D. (1957) Techniques of neutralization: A theory of delinquency. *American Sociological Review*, 22(6), 664–70.

University of Kent (2021) Responsibilities of the university and its students. Accessed at www.kent.ac.uk/welcome/responsibilities-of-the-university-and-its-students on December 3, 2021.

Varela, F.G., Maturana, H.R., and Uribe, H. (1974) Autopoiesis: The organization of living systems, its characterization and a model. *Biosystems*, 5(4), 187–96.

Washburn, J. (2008) *University, Inc.: The Corporate Corruption of Higher Education.* New York, NY: Basic Books.

Weir, D., Marsh, C., and Greenwood, W. (2009) How organisational DNA works. In L.A. Costanzo and R.B. Mackay (Eds), *Handbook of Research on Strategy and Foresight.* Cheltenham, UK and Northampton, MA: Edward Elgar Publishing.

Weir, D.T.H. (1996) The role of communication breakdown in plane crashes and business failure. In C. Hood and D. Jones (Eds), *Accident and Design.* London: UCL Press.

Weir, D.T.H. (2000) Communication failure in a socio-technical system. In B. Green (Ed.), *Risk Behaviour and Risk Management in Business Life.* Dordrecht: Springer.

Weir, D.T.H. (2002) When will they ever learn? Conditions for failure in publicly-funded high technology projects. *Disaster Prevention and Management*, 11(4), 299–307.

Werhane, P., and Freeman, R. (1999) Business ethics: The state of the art. *International Journal of Management Reviews*, 1(1), 1–16.

Wolf, S. (1982) Moral saints. *Journal of Philosophy*, 79(8), 419–39.

World Bank (2000) *Higher Education in Developing Countries: Peril and Promise.* Washington DC: World Bank.

11. How green is strategic decision-making in a 'green company'?

Chiharu Narikiyo, Elaine Harris and Moataz Elmassri

1. INTRODUCTION TO SUSTAINABLE (GREEN) DECISION-MAKING

Despite the significance of international Sustainable Development Goals (SDGs) in the policy world (United Nations, 2015), accounting researchers have been slow to participate in SDG-motivated research (Bebbington and Unerman, 2018). Research on sustainability in accounting has tended to focus on environmental and integrated reporting (past performance), rather than on strategic project appraisal (future performance). The gap we identified in the literature is whether and how organisational decision-making balances financial and non-financial considerations to achieve the SDGs as well as financial goals.

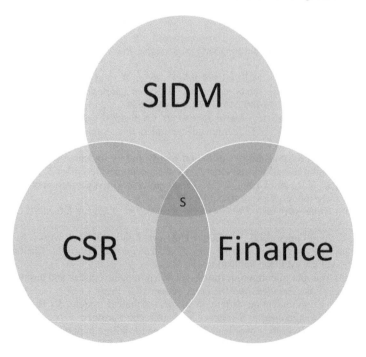

Figure 11.1   Fields of literature

In sections 2 to 4 we review the literature related to sustainability from three interconnected fields, as shown in Figure 11.1, taking strategic investment decision-making (SIDM) first, followed by corporate social responsibility (CSR) and finally ethical investment from the finance literature. First, we review key findings, then the predominant or prospective theories, followed by the methodologies used in relevant research.

2.   STRUCTURED LITERATURE REVIEW

A structured literature review (SLR) is defined by Massaro et al. (2016, p. 767) as 'a method for studying a corpus of scholarly literature, to develop insights, critical reflections, future research paths and research questions'. To fulfil this, a literature search using Business Source Premier, which covers all business disciplines with full text from over 2,100 journals (EBSCO, 2022) was conducted with two different keywords in all text for all work with full-text access published over the 10 years between 2011 and 2020. To assure credibility, the search was limited to peer-reviewed journals only. The first search, using the term 'strategic investment', found 21 publications, identified below. The top 10 articles were selected by sorting by relevance. In the same way, the second search, with the term 'capital expenditure', found 71 articles, which were narrowed down to 10 articles by relevance. This process was followed for the three fields identified in Figure 11.1.

   The key theories and methodologies applied and developed in this literature are identified and explained in sections 3 and 4, before we identify and illustrate how the literature gap may be explored through case analysis in Section 5. This leads us to consider future research avenues that might be fruitful to move research on in this crucial area in Section 6.

2.1   Strategic Investment Decision-Making and Sustainability Issues

Strategic investment decision-making is defined as the entire decision-making process, from the identification of a prospective project through design of a business case, and financial and non-financial analysis, to board approval, project execution and evaluation (Harris et al., 2018). SIDM plays a significant role in an organisation, functioning as the introduction of advanced manufacturing and business technologies, and substantial shifts in production capability. Typical examples of SIDM include company acquisitions and mergers, the introduction of major new product lines and the installation of new manufacturing processes (Alkaraan and Northcott, 2006). Traditionally, the motive of SIDM mainly arises from an economic and financial origin that can maximise the value of shareholders' financial capital, based on the consideration of the costs and benefits over a long period (Emmanuel, Harris and Komakech, 2010).

   When we look at papers from the accounting discipline, much current SIDM knowledge is based upon a quantitative perspective. Phulpagar et al. (2018), for instance, attempted to understand the factors that influence strategic investment decisions, with a focus on the power sector in India. They proposed a conceptual model of five factors that may influence the decision: organisation culture, internal resources and tools, industry, economic and technological environment, and socio-political environment factors. The model was tested with data relating to decision-makers in the Indian power sector. Their analysis tells us all five factors have a positive effect on the efficacy of strategic investment decisions at a 90 per cent confidence level (Phulpagar et al., 2018). This finding, however, opens a further question about whether and how organisational investment decision-making balances those multi-dimensional factors to implement the strategy. Furthermore, the authors suggested that strategic investment decisions are usually taken in line with the vision and objectives of the organisation.

Attig et al. (2014) investigated the impact of CSR on investment sensitivity to cash flows with a regression model. By using data from major US companies across sectors, their analysis concluded that increased CSR is related to a diminution in investment–cash flow sensitivity. One possible motive they give for this is that investing in relationships with a firm's major stakeholders would create competitive advantage, and may in turn enhance organisations' sustainability by improving their competitive position as well as their financial performance (Attig et al., 2014). However, their statistical method, focusing on major industries across the US, cannot show the detail behind the phenomena, due to the nature of quantitative methods. For this, methods such as the single-case-study approach are needed (Caldarelli et al., 2016) with rich contextual data as well as interviews data (Passetti and Rinaldi, 2020).

While the findings from the SLR indicate that SIDM is an active area of research, mainstream research tends to analyse the economic consequences by focusing foremost on the interests of shareholders or their agents. Critical research as well as sociologically based and qualitative research are relatively rare. Palea (2017) suggests that standardised approaches and monocentric concepts limit knowledge production and prevent the addressing of issues that are specific to different sociological contexts. This suggests that critical interpretations and flexibility in neutralising consensus would be encouraged (Palea, 2017). Such a proposal may aid a shift of emphasis in researcher traits: from an incremental gap-spotting research trait to a novel 'reflexive and path (up) setting scholar' (Alvesson and Sandberg, 2013).

Raising concern over sustainability issues in accounting has driven the motive of SIDM to a nuanced consequence of the decision-making, which indicates an implicit rather than explicit balance between competing elements and priorities (Gray et al., 2014). There are few theoretical frameworks to understand modern SIDM; therefore, cumulative knowledge-building and theorisation need further development (Harris et al., 2016). One of the few examples of the theorisation is presented by Bebbington et al. (2007), who developed the Sustainability Assessment Model (SAM) in British Petroleum (BP) plc. This is a thorough approach involving social and environmental issues that enables life-cycle evaluation and related life-cycle costing, contributing to capital investment appraisal (Bebbington et al., 2007). Building upon this notion, Vesty et al. (2015) demonstrate a multi-capital approach to capital investment appraisal in practice in Australia. Their case study research involving five organisations highlighted the growing multi-capital thinking that managers commit to, with sustainability measures embedded in management control systems. This has so far not been observed in the UK beyond the single case study at BP (Bebbington et al., 2007).

A recent SIDM study built upon the multi-capital approach (Harris et al., 2016) is presented by Narayanan et al. (2021). Their study sheds light on the extent to which investment decision-makers are willing to trade-off financial factors for environmental ones and vice versa. Positioned on the financialisation hypothesis, their finding suggests that decision-makers prioritise economic returns over carbon emissions. In order to understand SIDM with sustainability issues, the authors suggest examining different aspects of environmental impact other than carbon emissions or specific types of stakeholder pressure, which could provide useful insights into the managerial decision-making using non-financial decision attributes (Narayanan et al., 2021).

Global sustainability challenges beyond carbon emissions include air pollution, biodiversity loss, climate change, energy and food security, disease spread, species invasion, and water shortages and pollution (Liu et al., 2015). Raworth (2018) suggested the dimensions that modern organisations are facing to realise the 17 SDGs (United Nations, 2015), presented as a 'Doughnut of Social and Planetary Boundaries'. The Doughnut visualises safe and just space for humanity to realise regenerative and distributive prosperity that lies between 'a social foundation of well-being that no one should fall below and an ecological ceiling of planetary pressure that we should not go beyond' (Raworth, 2018:11). Taking one of those concepts as a guide, it could enable researchers to explore the extent to which organisations support or impinge upon them, either directly or indirectly (Bebbington, 2021). For instance, Walkiewicz et al. (2021) investigated a methodology to establish and combine sustainability control systems (SCS) with management control systems (MCSs). This case study focusing on the German-based food sector applied Raworth's (2018) Doughnut of Social and Planetary Boundaries framework to the design of the workshops to collect data (Walkiewicz et al., 2021).

One of the latest examples of SIDM in practice was introduced by Siemens Corporation (FT Climate Capital Council, 2021). It introduced a risk due diligence tool, an environmental, social and governance (ESG) radar, based on the material risk fields. This tool aims to help the company identify and assess likely ESG risks (Siemens Corporation, 2020). The company explained that the radar was designed by partnering with external and human rights experts, functioning as a checklist covering over 60 different risk indicators for individual business activities. While this would help the company mitigate existing risks associated with ESG, making a decision based on such an audit checklist would be disadvantageous if this is poorly used. For instance, checklists can be restrictive if used as the decision-makers' main support mechanism. Furthermore, generic checklists, which do not reflect the specific business case, may not add any value, and may interfere with decision-making. How the company can deal with the disadvantages and whether and how it can make a balanced decision between environmental and social sustainability and profitability remain unanswered.

In summary, these SIDM research projects show how integrated reporting (IR) has led to multi-capital-based thinking (Adams et al., 2016; Harris et al., 2018) and suggest the need for further research to explore how multi-capital-based thinking can lead to integrated decision-making. Furthermore, Narayanan et al. (2021) call for further considerations beyond carbon impact to understand modern SIDM. Together, the emerging framework of the Doughnut of Social and Planetary Boundaries suggests exploring as far as possible if and how all SDGs reflected in the Doughnut;s impact on SIDM (see Section 6).

2.2   Corporate Social Responsibility

The interaction of expectations from society and the ways that an organisation reacts to these pressures brought a transition in the definition of CSR. To avoid confusion, this chapter uses the definition of CSR as 'context-specific organisational actions and policies that take into account stakeholders' expectations and the triple bottom line of economic, social, and environmental performance' (Aguinis and Glavas, 2012: 933) as that was used in more recent CSR literature, including Tate and Bals (2018). Climate change and new carbon institutions inevitably influence corporate practices. In response, companies are expected to mitigate greenhouse gas emissions and are increasingly adopting a carbon accounting scheme (Wang et al., 2021). This interaction between carbon institutions, firms and their stakeholders has drawn considerable interest from scholars (He et al., 2021). There is an emergent professional field of carbon accounting, in a multi-actor arena (Gibassier et al., 2020).

Russell et al.'s (2017) literature review provoked researchers to reconsider their perceptions of 'accounts' and 'nature'. They reviewed knowledge from accounting, geography, sociology, political ecology, nature writing and social activism and offered a critique of key ideas relating to environmental accounting over four decades. They call for an expansion of interdisciplinary capability to contribute to ecological sustainability and social justice (Russell et al., 2017). He et al.'s (2021) review of accounting journals on carbon accounting illustrated the development and gaps in knowledge on carbon accounting. They identified carbon accounting as emerging as a distinct discipline, ramifying and creating four main streams of carbon accounting: carbon disclosure, management, performance and assurance (He et al., 2021).

Our search for research articles which include the terms 'carbon' and 'accounting' and 'document' published between 2011 to 2020 identified 17 articles. To expand the number of results, another search using the terms 'carbon' or 'accounting' or 'document' with the same condition of the first search returned 110,969 articles. Each list of the articles was sorted by relevance, and only empirical research papers were reviewed to understand the recent development of carbon accounting and understand the current knowledge gap. In this way, the top five articles of both, 10 articles in total, were identified and analysed in depth.

Overall, carbon accounting has been studied from a transdisciplinary perspective among the business research community. The most popular venue for the publication is accounting, followed by both management and cleaner production, six papers and two papers in the order given. Similarly, theories applied to the research vary, ranging from philosophical theories (Martineau and Lafontaine, 2020), institutional sociology theories (Gibassier et al., 2020; Mateo-Márquez et al., 2019) and legitimacy theories (Pitrakkos and Maroun, 2019). Applying multiple theories is also prevalent. For instance, Lemma et al. (2020) combined agency theory and information asymmetry theories to develop their theoretical framework.

In terms of research methods, qualitative methods slightly outnumber quantitative methods, taken by six papers and four papers, respectively. While current quantitative literature on carbon accounting mainly focuses on economic and regulatory influences (Wang et al., 2021), many qualitative research papers on this area take an exploratory approach to understand the new phenomena (Rietbergen et al., 2015). For instance, Le Breton and Aggeri (2018) aim to explore how carbon accounting practices could be performative; that is, able to deeply transform companies' practices and strategies. Their case study comprised 15 semi-structured interviews with the case company in France, and highlights that there are many different calculation acts, whose performativity is determined by their repetition over time, regarding a low-carbon strategy (Le Breton and Aggeri, 2018).

When it comes to data, this SLR shows a presence of the Carbon Disclosure Project (CDP) as a data source of a company's carbon credentials. The CDP offers self-disclosed environmental information for investors and academics (Gray et al., 2014). According to the CDP, the data have been utilised in 70 peer-reviewed papers in 2005–2015, being the leading source of environmental data for scholarly research (Griffin et al., 2017). For instance, Mateo-Márquez et al. (2019) attempted to unveil the relationship between nations' regulatory context and voluntary carbon disclosures from the new institutional sociology perspective in the global context. They used the Tobit regression model and analysed data from 2,183 companies in 12 countries that were invited to respond to the CDP questionnaire in 2015. Their results highlighted that countries' specific regulations regarding climate change influence both the involvement of the firms in the CDP and their quality, as quantified by the CDP disclosure score. Considering this was a deductively reasoned study, the sample size, restricted to 12 countries' regulatory environments, may be too small. Therefore, prudence should be exercised when it comes to generalising the results to other institutional backgrounds.

The most cited article, based on Google (on 6 July 2021), is Cho et al.'s (2015) paper focusing on sustainability disclosure. This research sheds light on the prevalence of the gap between corporate sustainability talk and actions. Taking a case study approach focusing on two large oil and gas companies, they analysed qualitative information from annual reports, websites and investor relations publications from the companies. Built upon two theoretical frameworks, organised hypocrisy and organisational façades, content analysis is critically conducted. Their findings conclude that both frameworks contribute to understanding sustainability disclosure, as they can help researchers understand how the economic system and confronting multi-stakeholders' demands constrict the practice of individual companies.

However, this research may have weaknesses in the data analysis methods. Even though achieving absolute validity and reliability would obviously be a difficult goal for any research effort, the content analysis they adopted is known to have several issues, mainly over comparability and credibility of the coding process. Vourvachis and Woodward (2015) analysed the use of content analysis in social and environmental reporting (SER) research. Their review comprised a quasi-systematic review of literature employing content analysis and an interpretive meta-analysis. Their findings underline some notable issues, pertaining to both validity and reliability. They argue that content analysts need to approach these goals by carefully balancing the various factors increasing credibility within the context of their particular research problems.

Acknowledgement of ecological and human rights obligations contributed to building the concept of the triple bottom line (TBL), which relates to people, planet and profit, as part of CSR. The beginning of the journey towards the establishment of TBL can be traced back to the 1960s. A pivotal contribution to trigger this was *Silent Spring*, which warns of the non-reversible effect of human activity on the natural environment (Carson, 1963). This influential book contends the complementarity in the three basic objectives of protecting human health, preserving non-human life and fostering human flourishing. The notion fostered public interest and resulted in the modern environmental movement beyond conservation (Cafaro, 2013). Regulation was also passed to deal with organisational environmental problems. The Brundtland Report (1987), commissioned by the United Nations (UN), stated a long-term concern and introduced the guiding principles for sustainable development. This defined sustainable development as 'a development that meets the needs of the present without compromising the ability of future generations to meet their own needs' (Brundtland, 1987). These developments encouraged managers to account for tracking and disclosing value added or destroyed based on TBL (Adams et al., 2016). There may be some researchers who view TBL as a theory and others who view it as a conceptual framework for corporate reporting practice. Most researchers would see TBL as falling within stewardship theory, explained in Section 3.

2.3   Finance and Ethical Investment

Utilising investment instruments to pursue social and environmental goals, ethical investment has considerably grown. Money invested in ethical funds soared from about USD 300 billion in 2011 to almost USD 900 billion in 2019, based on International Monetary Fund data (*Financial Times*, 2020). Defining ethical investment is not easy. Sparkes (2001) says that ethical investment has been based on the avoidance of unacceptable activities and/or a company with a notable failure in areas of ethical concern (Sparkes, 2001). Opposed to this negative screening, positive screening refers to when the investor picks out companies that meet certain ethical criteria to seek higher-risk-adjusted economic returns. The criteria have been conceptualised as ESG; therefore, this investment practice taking into consideration those ethical criteria is sometimes called 'ESG investing' (Eccles and Klimenko, 2019). To reduce misunderstanding in this chapter, the term 'ethical investment' will normally be used as a descriptive term to reach the broad idea of ethical and socially responsible investment behaviours.

As the evaluation of social, environmental capital has influenced investors' decision-making, TBL-based communication platforms have been introduced to integrate corporate accounting, stakeholder engagement and strategy. This led to the argument to establish new reporting standards, such as IR (Rinaldi et al., 2018). ESG-performance-rating businesses have also emerged to provide an inclusive listing of the 'best' companies based on a company's ethical performance, including Dow Jones Sustainability Indexes (DJSI) (Adams et al., 2016). However, the principle of ethical investment is not legally defined (Du Rietz, 2018). This unstandardised business practice has led to the mixed quality of ESG information; regarding sustainability, for example, ESG rankings do not always identify sustainable companies (Dhalla and Arndt, 2021). Conversely, the CDP has increased its presence as a source of a company's green credentials. This leads to our second research question.

It is likely that more sustainability factors may have been brought to bear in SIDM in 'green' companies than in companies not bearing this label, so examples of good practice might emerge. This may help other organisations by providing practical recommendations for effective decision-making that incorporates sustainability issues.

3.   RELEVANT THEORIES

In this section we start by setting out two relatively well-known theories, namely stewardship and stakeholder theories, that have been used in the literature reviewed above, in sections 3.1 and 3.2. We also include social contract theory in Section 3.3 as having the potential for use in research in the intersection of these fields, and follow this through in our recommendations for future research in Section 6. All three theories have their roots in social theory and are underpinned by the concepts of agency (Jack, 2017), which acknowledge the issues arising from the separation of ownership and management in organisations, such as the potential for goal incongruence if managers use their agent position to act in self-interest rather than in the interests of the principal or owner(s). We could have selected other theories, but argue that these are the three with the greatest potential to contribute to knowledge at the intersection of the fields shown in Figure 11.1.

3.1   Stewardship Theory

Along with the impetus for change brought about through the UN's SDGs factors, stewardship theory provides a basis for predictions as to why companies might engage in social investment (Adams et al., 2016). Motivations behind CSR including ethical investment can be explained by stewardship theories (it is a right thing to do) from a business ethics perspective (Adams et al., 2016). Stewardship in an organisational context is defined as 'the actions of managers in the discharge of their responsibilities to preserve the value of investors' capital investment and to earn a commensurate return on that investment' (Anderson et al., 2015: 100). Under this theory, managers follow a collective-serving model motivated by intrinsic values and a desire to do what is best, as a manager, for the corporate good (Donaldson and Davis, 1991). Where human activities intervene in the natural environment, however, stewardship may re-emerge and be re-theorised by arguments around organisational accountability for social and environmental factors (Bebbington et al., 2019).

To correctly assess stewardship, stakeholders must receive information that is adequately relevant and adequately specific for the task, and extricate management's impact on organisational performance from factors outside of conventional management control, such as environmental factors (Anderson et al., 2015). Stakeholders increasingly monitor the stewardship of organisations and initiate programmes to assure stewardship. For instance, the Church of England Pensions Board, a self-financing institutional asset manager, has established a new global standard to enhance stewardship by partnering with the UN and the Swedish National Pension Fund's Council on Ethics (*Church Times*, 2021). Analysing perceptions of those stakeholders towards an entity based on stewardship, therefore, could offer critical insights on the entity. With rising concerns around climate change (increasingly referred to as the 'climate crisis'), a new concept is emerging, that of 'biosphere stewardship' (Bebbington, 2021; Folke et al., 2019), which broadens the definition of stewardship to include a responsibility to the global environment and life on Earth.

3.2   Stakeholder Theory

Stakeholder theory suggests that the fundamental nature of business principally lies in developing relationships and generating value for all stakeholders, including employees, customers, communities, suppliers and financiers (Freeman and Dmytriyev, 2017). Authors such as Friedman (1970) traditionally advocated that a company's responsibility was all about increasing profits and how the results of operations impact its shareholders. Subsequently, he articulated that using shareholders' money for other purposes should be denied (Friedman, 1970). A rise in concerns regarding social and environmental issues, however, increased coverage of CSR topics in annual reports and suggested an awareness of multiple stakeholders (Tate and Bals, 2018). This suggests that shareholders are not the only ones who bear the fate of a company.

Unlike the narrow definitions of CSR, which take into account expectations of society at an abstracted level (Aguinis and Glavas, 2012), stakeholder theory attempts to understand what business in its entirety is about and tries to specify its range of responsibilities (Freeman and Dmytriyev, 2017). Based on the stakeholder theory, Carroll (1991) suggests that CSR is a pyramid that consists of four types of responsibilities: economic, legal, ethical and philanthropic. The concept has evolved from this, suggesting that modern CSR overlaps with concepts from business ethics, stakeholder theory and sustainability (Carroll and Shabana, 2010). Building upon this, Baden (2016) attempts to reconstruct Carroll's CSR pyramid by mirroring the social change in the 21st century. He points out that CSR differs greatly from Carroll's original shape, with a revised pyramid ranked as follows: ethical, legal, economic and philanthropic, based on the result of his global survey that contained 400 respondents' views from both business and the non-business community (Baden, 2016). This implies that the responsibility of corporations towards all the stakeholders may change.

3.3   Social Contract Theory

In ethics research in a business context, theory can be traced back to ancient ethical theory. Aristotle's moral virtues were founded on 'finding a mean between an excess and a deficiency' (Hadreas, 2002: 361). This virtue provides the foundation of social contract theory, defined as an 'implicit contract between the society and business that allows businesses the right to exist in return for the society partaking in the benefits of such an involvement' (Svensson and Wood, 2008). On the other hand, Blau (1986) conceptualised social exchange theory, building upon Aristotle's moral virtues. He defined social exchange as 'the voluntary actions of individuals that are motivated by the returns they are expected to bring and typically do in fact bring from others' (Blau, 1986: 94). The essence of it is the reciprocal financial and non-financial relationship between parties that accounts for loyalty, which has also applied to a company and its stakeholders. For instance, Frederick and Wasieleski (2002) describe how it carries both benefits and costs for the two sides and will be undertaken when each party believes the benefits to be gained outweigh the costs incurred (Frederick and Wasieleski, 2002).

In the field of accounting research, Tucker, Parker, and Merchant (2016) applied social exchange theory to their study, providing foundational insights into the co-authorship of accounting journal articles. Based on interviews with 76 academics from 67 universities located in the UK, US, Australia and European mainland, the authors found a broad classification of co-authorship styles with regard to the tendency to nurture more satisfactory working relationships and effectiveness of research outputs.

This could be applied to strategic alliances in business organisations and decisions concerning mergers and acquisitions, where the rationales go beyond the goal of maximising shareholder value. However, the factors that underpinned the social contract in the past have changed considerably, resulting in unprecedented challenges, including breaching the ecological ceiling and persistent deprivation (Raworth, 2018). This provokes a reconsideration of the social contract basis for determining CSR and encourages researchers to advance theories towards the potential of a capability approach (Bebbington and Unerman, 2018; Nussbaum, 2011).

4.   METHODOLOGIES

In this section, we present the methodologies used in accounting research on SDGs, using the SLR framework presented by Massaro et al., (2016). It is usually based on what has been published over a particular period in a selection of top journals (Speklé and Kruis, 2014). However, as this review aims to outline the methodological development in contemporary accounting research of our topic area, we do not have space to examine all papers published before 2016 or in other journals. O'Dwyer and Unerman (2016) identified the most prominent papers in the field of accounting for social sustainability as Tinker et al. (1991; see Tinker, 1980), Gray et al. (1997), Bebbington and Gray (2001) and Neu et al. (2001). Addressing these papers would thus provide us with a more thorough understanding of the field; therefore, they are covered in the literature review in addition to those published after 2016.

To identify the journals for our research topic, the guide provided by the Chartered Association of Business Schools is utilised. The accounting and management journals rated as 3 and above, which cover 'original and well-executed research papers and are highly regarded'

(Chartered Association of Business Schools, 2018), have been selected. These journals have then been filtered by the relevance to our methodological positions and qualitative research, and seven are listed as the top journals relevant to our research:

- *Accounting, Organizations and Society* (AOS)
- *Contemporary Accounting Research* (CAR)
- *Accounting, Auditing & Accountability Journal* (AAAJ)
- *Critical Perspectives on Accounting* (CPA)
- *Accounting Horizons* (AH)
- *British Accounting Review* (BAR)
- *Management Accounting Research* (MAR)

The research papers published in these journals were searched with the keyword 'sustainable development' and filtered by the year of publication from 2016 (the year after the UN published the SDGs) to 2020. All journals except AH showed articles with the search protocol; the outputs are sorted by relevance and the top five articles are reviewed in depth. As this review aims to find out how prior studies have been researched, non-empirical research papers are excluded from the review. Consequently, 24 articles were analysed, with the methodological approaches of the articles summarised in Table 11.1. Methodological categories have been abbreviated and are shown in a key under the table.

Table 11.1 shows that most of the recent accounting research on SDGs published in influential journals used qualitative methods (12 out of 17). Multi-method (qualitative) is the most prevalent methodological choice (seven), with five using a mono method (qualitative). When it comes to the research design, the single case study is the most frequently employed (eight), as this allows the researcher to explore issues in greater depth. In terms of the research strategy, documentary analysis and interviews are equally the most used (nine). When we look at the time frame of the research, longitudinal studies outnumbered the cross-sectional research (12 and five, respectively). Longitudinal studies are often employed with documentary analysis, also known as archival research (six) to examine changes in practice over time. In terms of the type of approach to theory development, the qualitative research papers analysed in this review mainly adopt inductive reasoning (nine). Abduction is only claimed by three papers, all in 2020, which may suggest it is gaining popularity. From this review, it can be concluded that case study research with a non-deductive approach is the research design most commonly used in our research area as it is most appropriate to explore a developing practice. It also best serves our aims in investigating green decision-making.

5.   ILLUSTRATIVE CASE ANALYSIS

In this section we present a brief empirical analysis of two strategic decisions, both business acquisitions, in a case company. Our case company, Unilever plc, has been crowned the most consistently influential sustainability leader globally (GlobeScan, 2020). Unilever is a major fast-moving consumer goods (FMCG) company operating in more than 190 countries, with a diversified product line ranging from personal care products, food and refreshment products to home care products (Unilever plc, 2020).

The company launched a bold sustainability initiative, the Unilever Sustainable Living Plan (USLP), that targets to double sales and halve the environmental impact of its products over

Table 11.1   *Analysis of the methodological approach in empirical accounting literature on SDGs: 2016–2020 (n=17 including * three published in 2021 available in early cite by 2020)*

Journal	Authors and year of publication	Theme	Methodological category	Type
AOS	Clune and O'Dwyer (2020)	CSR reporting	MOQL-SCAS-INT-LON	IND
	Grisard et al. (2020)	Organisational change	MUQL-SCAS-OBS-INT-LON	IND
	Tanima et al. (2020)	Women's empowerment	MUQL-SCAS-DOC-INT-CRO	ABD
	Green and Cheng (2019)	Non-financial performance measures	MOQA-STA-CRO	DED
CAR	Chen et al. (2021)*	Carbon reporting	MOQA-STA-LON	DED
	Wei (2021)*	Target setting	MOQA-STA-LON	DED
AAAJ	Sobkowiak et al. (2020)	Accountability of biodiversity	MUQL-SCAS-INT-DOC-LON	IND
	Charnock and Hoskin (2020)	Climate governance	MOQL-DOC-LON	ABD
	O'Dochartaigh (2019)	Storytelling in sustainable reporting	MOQL-DOC-CRO	IND
BAR	Cerbone and Maroun (2020)	Integrated reporting	MOQL-INT-CRO	IND
	Chi et al. (2020)	Voluntary CSR disclosure	MOQA-STA-LON	DED
	Passetti and Rinaldi (2020)	Moral legitimacy	MUQL-SCAS-INT-DOC-CRO	IND
	La Torre et al. (2019)	Integrated reporting	MOQL-DOC-LON	IND
	Brown et al. (2020)	Automation in management accounting	MUQL-SCAS-INT-OBS-DOC-LON	ABD
CPA	Pupovac and Moerman (2020)	Shadow accounts	MUQL-SCAS-DOC-LON	IND
	Eliwa et al. (2021)*	ESG practice and financial cost	MOQA-STA-LON	DED
MAR	Caldarelli et al. (2016)	Enterprise Risk Management	MUQL-SCAS-INT-DOC-LON	IND

Notes: MOQL: mono method qualitative (5), MUQL: multi-method qualitative (7), MOQA: mono method quantitative (5), SCAS: single case study, INT: interviews, DOC: documentary analysis, STA: statistics, OBS: observations, IND: inductive (9), ABD: abductive (3), DED: deductive (5), CRO: cross-sectional, LON: longitudinal

the next 10 years (*Guardian*, 2010). The following empirical analysis is based on archival evidence collected from the company's annual reports together with press releases and more independent news reports. We have selected two examples from a database of business acquisitions that is being developed for a longitudinal case study relating to two of the company's main business segments during the period 2017–2019 (see Table 11.2).

Table 11.2   Segmental analysis summary 2017–2019 (% contribution to revenue)

Business segment (product categories)	2019	2018	2017
Beauty and personal care (hair care, skin care and cleansing, deodorants)	38%	37%	35%
Food and refreshments (ice cream, savoury, tea, dressings and spreads)	35%	38%	41%
Home care (fabrics)	15%	15%	15%
Other	12%	10%	9%
Total	100%	100%	100%

Source: Authors, analysis based on data from Unilever Annual Report 2019 (sectors highlighted for illustrative takeovers)

5.1   Takeover of Tatcha

In 2019, Unilever acquired 95% of Tatcha, a premium skincare business in the US (Unilever plc, 2020). While the deal price was undisclosed, it was estimated to be around $500 million (Collins, 2019). Tatcha is an American premium skincare products brand founded by a Taiwanese American family in 2009, offering a unique skincare method inspired by traditional Japanese beauty rituals (Tatcha, 2021).

This acquisition project illustrates Unilever's attempt to increase its presence in the personal care segment. The transition in its strategic priorities is apparent as the turnover share of its Foods and Refreshment division fell from 49 per cent in 2011 to 37 per cent in 2019. Conversely, the share of its Personal Care division grew from 33 per cent to 42 per cent over the period given (Unilever plc, 2012, 2020). The premium skincare segment is a key driver of growth in this competitive market. Unilever says, 'Prestige brands continued to deliver double digit growth, with strong performances from brands such as Dermalogica, Hourglass and Living Proof' (Unilever plc, 2020). Adding Tatcha to its prestige brand portfolio, therefore, aligns with its strategic plan.

The presence of Tatcha in the North American market in 2019 was notable. According to Mintel (2019), 58 per cent of consumers supported the skincare approach offered by Tatcha and agreed on the link between confidence and skin health. Tatcha has established brand loyalty, not only the consumer–product relationship, by building the unique approach, acting on well-being (Mintel, 2019). Acquiring this distinguished brand, therefore, could enhance Unilever's competitive position for the following reasons. First, this acquisition enables Unilever to access critical mass and unique market positioning. Buying this brand could also be quicker than internal growth. Utilising its global sales channel and supply chain, Unilever could also expand the Tatcha brand outside North America efficiently (Mintel, 2019).

Assuming these were the rationales for Unilever's decision, they appear to arise mainly from a financial motive to maximise shareholders' financial capital, though it can still be positively aligned with the 'health and well-being' element of the UN's SDGs as it adds a 'natural' type of product. This case may illustrate that while not all strategic investment decisions are motivated to contribute to sustainable developments, they may be congruent with the SDGs.

5.2   Takeover of Betty Ice

In 2018, Unilever acquired Betty Ice, a Romanian ice cream producer, for an undisclosed sum (Unilever plc, 2019). Betty Ice is a major ice cream brand in Romania with a turnover of RON

126 million (around $30 million) in 2016, comprising 16.5 per cent of the ice cream market in Romania (*Romania Journal*, 2018).

This acquisition project illustrates Unilever's attempt to broaden its presence in the ice cream market. Table 11.2 shows the relevant contribution of this product category to the revenue. From this table, the strategic priority in the ice cream category is apparent. This category accounted for 13 per cent of the revenue from 2017 to 2019 continuously, which was the second-largest contribution. Unilever commented on this acquisition: 'Acquired Betty Ice, a leading ice cream business in Romania. The acquisition enriches Unilever's product range through local offerings and price tiers' (Unilever plc, 2020: 135). Acquiring Betty Ice, therefore, enables Unilever to access the established market positioning. Buying this brand would also be quicker than internal growth. Utilising its global sales channel and supply chain, Unilever can also expand the Betty Ice brand outside Romania efficiently. Those rationales primarily arise from a financial origin that leads to maximising shareholders' financial capital, based on the assumption of a cost and benefit over a long period (Emmanuel et al., 2010).

However, sugary food has been a serious health issue in society. Intake of excessive sugar in a person's diet can contribute to them being overweight and to obesity, which increases people's risk of illness, such as Type 2 diabetes, heart disease and some cancers (National Health Service, 2020). In 2016, a health campaigner criticised an ice cream producer over the sugar levels in its product (*Guardian*, 2016). In the same year, a UK government body also recognised that obesity was the largest public health crisis facing the UK. To deal with this obesity epidemic, Public Health England launched a programme to ask the relevant industry, including ice cream producers, to reduce sugar in their product (Public Health England, 2016). Those movements had happened two years before the Betty Ice acquisition.

So, while Unilever has divested other food products that have been associated with health risks – for example, its 'spreads' business (margarine sales moving from 6 per cent in 2017 to zero in 2019; Table 11.2) – this acquisition may illustrate the capital still being invested in products recognised as 'harmful' for people, even after the company had committed to improve the health and well-being of billions of people in its Sustainable Living Plan. This could be viewed negatively in terms of the green credentials of the company, even though it is still rated highly in the green stakes overall.

Further strategic decisions may be analysed and contrasted in this way in further research, summarised in the next and final section.

6.   RECOMMENDATIONS FOR FUTURE RESEARCH

We suggest useful future research might aim to provide a critique of specific companies with top 'green' credentials (according to sustainability performance measures) in terms of the how their strategic decisions relate to the SDGs (or not) using concepts from stewardship, social contract and stakeholder theories. This research may reveal that even in a so-called 'green' company, not all strategic decisions may have a positive impact on the environment, or align with SDGs or be ethically motivated, so this research should aim to apply a more stringent level of scrutiny than press coverage or their own internal processes alone might suggest.

Future research projects and associated theories are suggested in Table 11.3. In the first project, we seek to unpack sustainability credentials and performance through the stewardship theory lens, using data from the CDP.

Table 11.3   Future research projects and theories suggested

Suggested projects/ research questions	Theory	Method	Data
1. How has the 'green' company accounted for carbon impacts and activities protecting the environment?	Stewardship theory	Archival research	Secondary data (questionnaire from the CDP)
2. How has the 'green' company changed the narrative to describe its business acquisitions as socially responsible?	Social contract theory	Archival research	Press releases, news and annual reports
3. How do the 'green' company's stakeholders view the green aspects of its major business acquisition decisions?	Stakeholder theory	Semi-structured Interviews	Stakeholder interviews

Project two builds on the approach taken in Section 5 above and sheds further light on the last pillar of TBL, the social aspect. The narrative of its annual reports and press coverage are analysed based on social contract theory (positive or negative impacts in terms of the SDGs). In this research, the UN's SDGs are treated as forming a kind of social contract between society and the organisations (that have been labelled 'green') taking the SDGs on board.

Finally, project 3 aims to understand how multiple stakeholders view the green credentials of the company's major business acquisitions, based on the stakeholder theory. The results produced in projects 1 and 2 will inform the interview questions and prompts in the interview protocol. We recommend the use of a multi-method qualitative research design that uses a mix of archival and stakeholder interview evidence in longitudinal case studies to inform both a practice-based theory of SIDM and the practice of green decision-making. Through these projects we seek to develop knowledge in the sustainability intersection of the three fields of SIDM, CSR and green finance.

7.   CONCLUSIONS

This chapter methodically reviewed the literature on SIDM in relation to SDGs to understand current knowledge and identified a research agenda where future developments are strongly needed. We discovered a notable absence of knowledge about how organisational investment decision-making might balance financial goals and SDGs, despite the increase in the influence of SDGs in international policy. To approach this critical agenda, this chapter analysed the methodological development of the relevant research areas. We illustrated a case-based research design to explore the SIDM of a modern organisation that is recognised as a 'green company'. Drawing upon CSR, finance and 'green' investment literature, this chapter also discussed relevant theoretical lenses to interrogate financial and narrative information around a case company's decision-making. As illustrated in our case analysis, this in-depth case study approach can enable us to critically analyse how 'green' corporate decision-making is compared with strategies and public relations statements made by the company.

This research would provide a critique of leading companies with top 'green' credentials by adding those critical aspects to our knowledge of contemporary SIDM. These projects will contribute to the development of multi-capital decision-making theory, showing how the concepts from stewardship, social contract and stakeholder theories apply. One potential impact of the research suggested may be to draw up a blueprint for the green company of the future.

REFERENCES

Adams, C.A., Potter, B., Singh, P.J., and York, J. (2016) Exploring the implications of integrated reporting for social investment (disclosures). *British Accounting Review*, 48(3), 283–96. doi: 10.1016/j.bar.2016.05.002.

Aguinis, H., and Glavas, A. (2012) What we know and don't know about corporate social responsibility: A review and research agenda. *Journal of Management*, 38(4), 932–68. doi:10.1177/0149206311436079.

Alkaraan, F., and Northcott, D. (2006) Strategic capital investment decision-making: A role for emergent analysis tools? A study of practice in large UK manufacturing companies. *British Accounting Review*, 38(2), 149–73. doi:10.1016/j.bar.2005.10.003.

Alvesson, M., and Sandberg, J. (2013) Has management studies lost its way? Ideas for more imaginative and innovative research. *Journal of Management Studies*, 50(1), 128–52. doi:10.1111/j.1467–6486.2012.01070.x.

Anderson, S.B., Brown, J.L., Hodder, L., and Hopkins, P.E. (2015) The effect of alternative accounting measurement bases on investors' assessments of managers' stewardship. *Accounting, Organizations and Society*, 46, 100–114. doi:10.1016/j.aos.2015.03.007.

Attig, N., Cleary, S.W., El Ghoul, S., and Guedhami, O. (2014) Corporate legitimacy and investment–cash flow sensitivity. *Journal of Business Ethics*, 121(2), 297–314. doi:10.1007/s10551–013–1693–3.

Baden, D. (2016) A reconstruction of Carroll's pyramid of corporate social responsibility for the 21st century. *International Journal of Corporate Social Responsibility*, 1(1), 1–15. doi:10.1186/s40991–016–0008–2.

Bebbington, J. (2021) The foundations of environmental accounting. In Bebbington, J., Larrinaga, C., O'Dwyer, B., and Thomson, I. (eds) *The Routledge Handbook on Environmental Accounting*. London: Routledge. doi:10.4324/9780367152369.

Bebbington, J., Brown, J., and Frame, B. (2007) Accounting technologies and sustainability assessment models. *Ecological Economics*, 61(2), 224–36. doi:10.1016/j.ecolecon.2006.10.021.

Bebbington, J., and Gray, R. (2001) An account of sustainability: Failure, success and a reconceptualization. *Critical Perspectives on Accounting*, 12, 557–87.

Bebbington, J., Österblom, H., Crona, B., Jouffray, J.-B., Larrinaga, C., Russell, S., and Scholtens, B. (2019) Accounting and accountability in the Anthropocene. *Accounting, Auditing & Accountability Journal*, 33(1), 152–77. doi:10.1108/AAAJ-11–2018–3745.

Bebbington, J., and Unerman, J. (2018) Achieving the United Nations Sustainable Development Goals: An enabling role for accounting research. *Accounting, Auditing & Accountability Journal*, 31(1), 2–24. doi:10.1108/AAAJ-05–2017–2929.

Blau, P.M. (1986) *Exchange and Power in Social Life*, 2nd edn. Abingdon: Taylor & Francis.

Brown, P., Ly, T., Pham, H., and Sivabalan, P. (2020) Automation and management control in dynamic environments: Managing organisational flexibility and energy efficiency in service sectors. *British Accounting Review*, 52(2), 100840. doi:10.1016/j.bar.2019.100840.

Brundtland, G.H. (1987) The Brundtland Report: 'Our Common Future.' In *Report of the World Commission on Environment and Development*. New York: United Nations. doi:10.1080/07488008808408783.

Cafaro, P. (2013) Rachel Carson's environmental ethics. In Rozzi, R., Pickett, S.T.A., Palmer, C., Armesto, J.J., and Callicott, J.B. (eds) *Linking Ecology and Ethics for a Changing World: Values, Philosophy, and Action*. Dordrecht: Springer. doi.org/10.1007/978–94–007–7470–4_13.

Caldarelli, A., Fiondella, C., Maffei, M., and Zagaria, C. (2016) Managing risk in credit cooperative banks: Lessons from a case study. *Management Accounting Research*, 32, 1–15. doi: 10.1016/j.mar.2015.10.002.

Carroll, A.B. (1991) The pyramid of corporate social responsibility: Toward the moral management of organizational stakeholders. *Business Horizons*, 34(4), 39–48. doi:10.1016/0007–6813(91)90005-G.

Carroll, A.B., and Shabana, K.M. (2010) The business case for corporate social responsibility: A review of concepts, research and practice. *International Journal of Management Reviews*, 12(1), 85–105. doi: 10.1111/j.1468–2370.2009.00275.x.

Carson, R. (1963) *Silent Spring*. London: Hamish Hamilton.

Cerbone, D., and Maroun, W. (2020) Materiality in an integrated reporting setting: Insights using an institutional logics framework. *British Accounting Review*, 52(3), 100876. doi:https://doi.org/10 .1016/j.bar.2019.100876.

Charnock, R., and Hoskin, K. (2020) SDG 13 and the entwining of climate and sustainability metagovernance: An archaeological–genealogical analysis of goals-based climate governance. *Accounting, Auditing & Accountability Journal*, 33(7), 1731–59. doi: 10.1108/AAAJ-12–2018–3790.

Chartered Association of Business Schools (2018) The purpose of the Academic Journal Guide. Available at: https://charteredabs.org/academic-journal-guide-2018/ (accessed: 1 May 2021).

Chen, H., Letmathe, P., and Soderstrom, N. (2021) Reporting bias and monitoring in clean development mechanism projects. *Contemporary Accounting Research*, 38(1), 7–31. doi:10.1111/1911–3846 .12609.

Chi, W., Wu, S.-J., and Zheng, Z. (2020) Determinants and consequences of voluntary corporate social responsibility disclosure: Evidence from private firms. *British Accounting Review*, 52(6), 100939. doi: 10.1016/j.bar.2020.100939.

Cho, C.H., Laine, M., Roberts, R.W., and Rodrigue, M. (2015) Organized hypocrisy, organizational façades, and sustainability reporting. *Accounting, Organizations and Society*, 40, 78–94. doi: 10.1016/j.aos.2014.12.003.

Church Times (2021) Pensions board's first annual stewardship report highlights mining safety and climate change. Available at: www.churchtimes.co.uk/articles/2021/26-march/news/uk/pensions -board-s-first-annual-stewardship-report-highlights-mining-safety-and-climate-change (accessed: 20 July 2021).

Clune, C., and O'Dwyer, B. (2020) Organizing dissonance through institutional work: The embedding of social and environmental accountability in an investment field. *Accounting, Organizations and Society*, 85, 101130. doi:10.1016/j.aos.2020.101130.

Collins, A. (2019) Unilever acquires Tatcha in deal said approaching $500M. *WWD*. Available at: https:// wwd.com/beauty-industry-news/skin-care/unilever-acquires-tatcha-in-deal-said-approaching-500m -1203163718/ (accessed: 26 October 2021).

Dhalla, R., and Arndt, F. (2021) Sustainability rankings don' t always identify sustainable companies. *The Conversation*. Available at: https://theconversation-com.cdn.ampproject.org/c/s/theconversation .com/amp/sustainability-rankings-dont-always-identify-sustainable-companies-157023 (accessed: 1 May 2021).

Donaldson, L., and Davis, J.H. (1991) Stewardship theory or agency theory: CEO governance and shareholder returns. *Australian Journal of Management*, 16(1), 49–64. doi: 10.1177/031289629101600103.

Du Rietz, S. (2018) Information vs knowledge. *Accounting, Auditing & Accountability Journal*, 31(2), 586–607. doi:10.1108/AAAJ-01–2013–1198.

EBSCO (2022) Business Source Premier. available at: www.ebsco.com/products/research-databases/ business-source-premier (accessed: August 2022).

Eccles, R.G., and Klimenko, S. (2019) The investor revolution. *Harvard Business Review*, 2019(May– June), 106–16.

Eliwa, Y., Aboud, A., and Saleh, A. (2021) ESG practices and the cost of debt: Evidence from EU countries. *Critical Perspectives on Accounting*, 79, 102097. doi:10.1016/j.cpa.2019.102097.

Emmanuel, C., Harris, E., and Komakech, S. (2010) Towards a better understanding of capital investment decisions. *Journal of Accounting & Organizational Change*, 6(4), 477–504. doi: 10.1108/18325911011091837.

Financial Times (2020) Ethical funds are booming but there are obstacles to momentum. Available at: www.ft.com/content/97d005d4–07f3–4883–9d34–8c30b54f1853 (accessed: 1 May 2021).

Folke, C., Österblom, H., Jouffray, J.-B., Lambin, E.F., Adger, W.N., Scheffer, M., Crona, B.I., Nyström, M., Levin, S.A., Carpenter, S.R., Anderies, J.M., Chapin, S., Crépin, A.-S., Dauriach, A., Galaz, V., Gordon, L.J., Kautsky, N., Walker, B.H., Watson, J.R., … de Zeeuw, A. (2019) Transnational corporations and the challenge of biosphere stewardship. *Nature Ecology and Evolution*, 3(10), 1396–403. doi:10.1038/s41559–019–0978-z.

Frederick, W.C., and Wasieleski, D.M. (2002) Evolutionary social contracts. *Business and Society Review*, 107(3), 283–308.

Freeman, R.E., and Dmytriyev, S. (2017) Corporate social responsibility and stakeholder theory: Learning from each other. *Emerging Issues in Management*, 1, 7–15. doi:10.4468/2017.1.02freeman .dmytriyev.

Friedman, M. (1970) The social responsibility of business is to increase its profits. *New York Times*. Available at: https://graphics8.nytimes.com/packages/pdf/business/miltonfriedman1970.pdf (accessed: 1 May 2021).

FT Climate Capital Council (2021) FT Forums: How Businesses Can Balance Profitability and Sustainability. 17 June 2021.

Gibassier, D., El Omari, S., and Naccache, P. (2020) Institutional work in the birth of a carbon account- ing profession. *Accounting, Auditing & Accountability Journal*, 33(6), 1447–76. doi:10.1108/AAAJ -12–2014–1912.

GlobeScan (2020) The 2020 SustainAbility leaders. Available at: https://globescan.com/2020/08/12/ unilever-patagonia-ikea-interface-top-sustainability-leaders-2020/ (accessed: 1 May 2021).

Gray, R., Adams, C.A., and Owen, D. (2014) *Accountability, Social Responsibility, and Sustainability: Accounting for Society and the Environment*. Boston: Pearson Education.

Gray, R., Dey, C., Owen, D., Evans, R., and Zadek, S. (1997) Struggling with the praxis of social account- ing: Stakeholders, accountability, audits and procedures. *Accounting, Auditing & Accountability Journal*, 10(3), 325–64.

Green, W.J., and Cheng, M.M. (2019) Materiality judgments in an integrated reporting setting: The effect of strategic relevance and strategy map. *Accounting, Organizations and Society*, 73, 1–14. doi: 10.1016/j.aos.2018.07.001.

Griffin, P.A., Lont, D.H., and Sun, E.Y. (2017) The relevance to investors of greenhouse gas emission disclosures. *Contemporary Accounting Research*, 34(2), 1265–97.

Grisard, C., Annisette, M., and Graham, C. (2020) Performative agency and incremental change in a CSR context. *Accounting, Organizations and Society*, 82, 101092. doi: 10.1016/j.aos.2019.101092.

Guardian (2010) Unilever unveils ambitious long term sustainability programme. Available at: www.theguardian.com/business/2010/nov/15/unilever-sustainable-living-plan (accessed: 26 October 2021).

Guardian (2016) Prince Charles and Waitrose criticised over sugar levels in ice cream. Available at: www.theguardian.com/society/2016/oct/26/prince-charles-warned-about-sugar-levels-in-duchy -organic-ice-cream (accessed: 26 October 2021).

Hadreas, P. (2002) Aristotle on the vices and virtue of wealth. *Journal of Business Ethics*, 39(4), 361–76.

Harris, E., Northcott, D., Elmassri, M., and Huikku, J. (2016) Theorising strategic investment decision-making using strong structuration theory. *Accounting, Auditing & Accountability Journal*, 29(7), 1177–203. doi:10.1108/AAAJ-03–2015–2005.

Harris, E., Northcott, D., Elmassri, M., Huikku, J., and Silva de Souza, R. (2018) *Balanced Investment Decisions*. London: ICAEW.

He, R., Luo, L., Shamsuddin, A., and Tang, Q. (2021) Corporate carbon accounting: A literature review of carbon accounting research from the Kyoto Protocol to the Paris Agreement. *Accounting & Finance*, 62(1), 261–98. doi:10.1111/acfi.12789.

Jack, L. (2017) *Accounting and Social Theory: An Introduction*. London: Routledge.

La Torre, M., Dumay, J., Rea, M.A., and Abhayawansa, S. (2020) A journey towards a safe harbour: The rhetorical process of the International Integrated Reporting Council. *British Accounting Review*, 52(2), 100836. doi:10.1016/j.bar.2019.100836 (early cite: 2019).

Le Breton, M., and Aggeri, F. (2018) Counting before acting? The performativity of carbon accounting called into question – Calculation acts and dispositifs in a big French construction company. *M@n@ gement*, 21(2), 834–55. doi:10.0.15.77/mana.212.0834.

Lemma, T.T., Azmi Shabestari, M., Freedman, M., Lulseged, A., and Mlilo, M. (2020) Corporate carbon risk, voluntary disclosure and debt maturity. *International Journal of Accounting & Information Management*, 28(4), 667–83. doi:10.1108/IJAIM-06–2019–0064.

Liu, J., Mooney, H., Hull, V., Davis, S.J., Gaskell, J., Hertel, T., Lubchenco, J., Seto, K.C., Gleick, P., Kremen, C., and Li, S. (2015) Systems integration for global sustainability. *Science*, 347(6225), 1258832. doi:10.1126/science.1258832.

Martineau, R., and Lafontaine, J.-P. (2020) When carbon accounting systems make us forget nature: From commodification to reification. *Sustainability Accounting, Management and Policy Journal*, 11(3), 487–504. doi:10.1108/SAMPJ-07–2018–0178.

Massaro, M., Dumay, J., and Guthrie, J. (2016) On the shoulders of giants: Undertaking a structured literature review in accounting. *Accounting, Auditing & Accountability Journal*, 29(5), 767–801. doi: 10.1108/AAAJ-01–2015–1939.

Mateo-Márquez, A.J., González-González, J.M., and Zamora-Ramírez, C. (2019) Countries' regulatory context and voluntary carbon disclosures. *Sustainability Accounting, Management and Policy Journal*, 11(2), 383–408. doi:10.1108/SAMPJ-11–2018–0302.

Mintel (2019) Facial skincare and anti-aging: US – April 2019. Available at: https://reports-mintel -com.roe.idm.oclc.org/display/952630/?fromSearch=%3Ffreetext%3DTatcha (accessed: 26 October 2021).

Narayanan, V., Baird, K., and Tay, R. (2021) Investment decisions: The trade-off between economic and environmental objectives. *British Accounting Review*, 53(3), 100969. doi: 10.1016/j.bar.2020.100969.

National Health Service (2020) Sugar: The facts – Eat well. Available at: www.nhs.uk/live-well/eat -well/how-does-sugar-in-our-diet-affect-our-health/ (accessed: 26 October 2021).

Neu, D., Cooper, D.J., and Everett, J. (2001) Critical accounting interventions. *Critical Perspectives on Accounting*, 12(6), 735–62. doi:10.1006/cpac.2001.0479.

Nussbaum, M. C. (2011) *Creating Capabilities: The Human Development Approach*. Cumberland: Harvard University Press.

O'Dochartaigh, A. (2019) No more fairytales: A quest for alternative narratives of sustainable business. *Accounting, Auditing & Accountability Journal*, 32(5), 1384–413. doi:10.1108/AAAJ-11–2016–2796.

O'Dwyer, B., and Unerman, J. (2016) Fostering rigour in accounting for social sustainability. *Accounting, Organizations and Society*, 49, 32–40. doi:10.1016/j.aos.2015.11.003.

Palea, V. (2017) Whither accounting research? A European view. *Critical Perspectives on Accounting*, 42, 59–73. doi:10.1016/j.cpa.2016.03.002.

Passetti, E., and Rinaldi, L. (2020) Micro-processes of justification and critique in a water sustainability controversy: Examining the establishment of moral legitimacy through accounting. *British Accounting Review*, 52(3), 100907. doi:10.1016/j.bar.2020.100907.

Phulpagar, S., Maddulety, K., Jagannathan, S., and Kalia, S. (2018) Strategic investment decisions: An empirical study of power sector in India. *Journal of Accounting, Business and Management*, 25(2), 22–49. doi:10.31966/jabminternational.v25i2.354.

Pitrakkos, P., and Maroun, W. (2019) Evaluating the quality of carbon disclosures. *Sustainability Accounting, Management and Policy Journal*, 11(3), 553–89. doi:10.1108/SAMPJ-03–2018–0081.

Public Health England (2016) Industry attends PHE briefing on reduction and reformulation. Available at: www.gov.uk/government/news/industry-attends-phe-briefing-on-reduction-and-reformulation (accessed: 26 October 2021).

Pupovac, S., and Moerman, L. (2020) Bringing Shell and Friends of the Earth on stage: A one-act spectacle of oil spills in the Niger Delta. *Critical Perspectives on Accounting*, 102264. doi: 10.1016/j. cpa.2020.102264.

Raworth, K. (2018) *Doughnut Economics: Seven Ways to Think Like a 21st-Century Economist*. London: Random House Business Books.

Rietbergen, M.G., Van Rheede, A., and Blok, K. (2015) The target-setting process in the CO_2 Performance Ladder: Does it lead to ambitious goals for carbon dioxide emission reduction? *Journal of Cleaner Production*, 103, 549–61. doi: 10.1016/j.jclepro.2014.09.046.

Rinaldi, L., Unerman, J., and de Villiers, C. (2018) Evaluating the integrated reporting journey: Insights, gaps and agendas for future research. *Accounting, Auditing & Accountability Journal*, 31(5), 1294–318. doi:10.1108/AAAJ-04–2018–3446.

Romania Journal (2018) Unilever concludes Betty Ice acquisition. *Romania Journal*. Available at: www .romaniajournal.ro/business/unilever-concludes-betty-ice-acquisition/ (accessed: 26 October 2021).

Russell, S., Milne, M.J., and Dey, C. (2017) Accounts of nature and the nature of accounts. *Accounting, Auditing & Accountability Journal*, 30(7), 1426–58. doi:10.1108/AAAJ-07–2017–3010.

Siemens Corporation (2020) *Siemens Sustainability Information*. Available at: https://assets.new .siemens.com/siemens/assets/api/uuid:13f56263–0d96–421c-a6a4–9c10bb9b9d28/sustainability2020 -en.pdf (accessed: 20 July 2021).

Sobkowiak, M., Cuckston, T., and Thomson, I. (2020) Framing sustainable development challenges: Accounting for SDG-15 in the UK. *Accounting, Auditing & Accountability Journal*, 33(7), 1671–703. doi:10.1108/AAAJ-01–2019–3810.

Sparkes, R. (2001) Ethical investment: Whose ethics, which investment? *Business Ethics: A European Review*, 10(3), 194–205. doi:10.1111/1467–8608.00233.

Speklé, R., and Kruis, A.-M. (2014) Management control research: A review of current developments. In D. Otley and K. Soin (eds), *Management Control and Uncertainty*. Basingstoke: Palgrave Macmillan. doi:10.1057/9781137392121_3.

Svensson, G., and Wood, G. (2008) A model of business ethics. *Journal of Business Ethics*, 77(3), 303–22. doi:10.1007/s10551–007–9351–2.

Tanima, F.A., Brown, J., and Dillard, J. (2020) Surfacing the political: Women's empowerment, micro-finance, critical dialogic accounting and accountability. *Accounting, Organizations and Society*, 85, 101141. doi:10.1016/j.aos.2020.101141.

Tatcha (2021) Our story. Available at: www.tatcha.com/our-story.html (accessed: 26 October 2021).

Tate, W.L., and Bals, L. (2018) Achieving shared triple bottom line (TBL) value creation: Toward a social resource-based view (SRBV) of the firm. *Journal of Business Ethics*, 152(3), 803–26. doi:10.1007/s10551–016–3344-y.

Tinker, A. M. (1980) Towards a political economy of accounting: An empirical illustration of the Cambridge controversies. *Accounting, Organizations and Society*, 5(1), 147–60.

Tucker, B.P., Parker, L.D., and Merchant, K.A. (2016) With a little help from our friends: An empirical investigation of co-authoring in accounting research. *British Accounting Review*, 48(2), 185–205. doi:10.1016/j.bar.2015.10.001.

Unilever plc (2020) *The Unilever Annual Report and Accounts 2019*. Available at: www.unilever.com/Images/unilever-annual-report-and-accounts-2019_tcm244–547893_en.pdf (accessed: 26 October 2021).

United Nations, Department of Economic and Social Affairs (2015) Sustainable Development Goals. Available at: https://sdgs.un.org/goals (accessed: 1 November 2021).

Vesty, G., Brooks, A., and Oliver, J. (2015) *Contemporary Capital Investment Appraisal from a Management Accounting and Integrated Thinking Perspective: Case Study Evidence*. Melbourne: CPA Australia.

Vourvachis, P., and Woodward, T. (2015) Content analysis in social and environmental reporting research: Trends and challenges. *Journal of Applied Accounting Research*, 16(2), 166–95. doi:10.1108/JAAR-04–2013–0027.

Walkiewicz, J., Lay-Kumar, J., and Herzig, C. (2021) The integration of sustainability and externalities into the 'corporate DNA': A practice-oriented approach. *Corporate Governance*, 21(3), 479–96. doi:10.1108/CG-06–2020–0244.

Wang, H., Guo, T., and Tang, Q. (2021) The effect of national culture on corporate green proactivity. *Journal of Business Research*, 131, 140–150. doi:10.1016/j.jbusres.2021.03.023.

Wei, C. (2021). State ownership and target setting: Evidence from publicly listed companies in China. *Contemporary Accounting Research*, 38(3), 1925–60. doi: 10.1111/1911–3846.12665.

12. Corporate social responsibility and how the corporate sector should behave: a case study of New Zealand

Rashid Zaman and Jia Liu

INTRODUCTION

The recent surge in corporate social irresponsibility (CSiR) incidents, such as Enron, WorldCom, Volkswagen (VW), British Petroleum (BP) and Wells Fargo, have highlighted the importance of corporate social responsibility (CSR) (Voegtlin and Pless, 2014) – so much so that many now consider it a necessity for an organisation to both define its role in society and adhere to social, ethical, legal and responsible standards (Schembera, 2018). With the increasingly serious growth of CSiR issues in recent years, the effective implementation of CSR measures has also become a global policy issue (Farooq et al., 2021a; Farooq and De Villiers, 2019; Jain and Zaman, 2020; Pisani et al., 2017; Zaman et al., 2022). For example, legal authorities have mandated or introduced stakeholders' interests in the managerial decision-making process (Adams and Zutshi, 2004); the New Zealand Stock Exchange (NZX), for example, recently revised its Corporate Governance (CG) Code (2017) to encourage CSR practices among NZX-listed firms. Likewise, the Australian Securities Exchange (ASX) (2014) and Singapore Exchange Limited (SGX) (2016) CG principles on sustainability reporting; Bombay Stock Exchange's (BSE) mandatory environmental, social and governance (ESG) disclosure requirement; and the USA Dodd–Frank Wall Street Reform and Consumer Protection Act, 2010 – all have created a new set of practices and requirements to manage business risks.[1]

Such voluntary and mandatory developments have intensified the CSR implementation process globally. The majority of the Global 500 companies spent an average of US\$20 billion per year on CSR activities over the period of 2011 to 2013 (Dattani et al., 2015). Along similar lines, a KPMG (2013a) survey indicates that the number of firms implementing CSR activities dramatically increased from 52 per cent in 2005 to 93 per cent in 2013. However, despite the increasing trends in adopting CSR practices, irresponsible incidents (for example, Apple's planned obsolescence, VW's deception about vehicle emissions, Wells Fargo's cross-selling and Air New Zealand's price-fixing cartel case) have continued to rise.

CSR literature has identified two major factors behind the rise of CSiR: (i) management perceptions and (ii) a lack of understanding about CSR implementation (Farooq et al., 2021a; Farooq and De Villiers, 2019; Karaman and Akman, 2018; Lyon and Montgomery, 2015; Wickert and De Bakker, 2015). Firstly, management presumably portrays CSR as being of symbolic importance rather than a strategic framework for acting responsibly while also generating a profit (Farooq et al., 2021b; Wang et al., 2016; Zaman et al., 2021). For instance, management may embellish CSR initiatives to mislead consumers and build a good reputation and trust to increase profitability, rather than actually contributing to society and the environment (Farooq et al., 2021b; Lyon and Montgomery, 2015). These initiatives are possible because of a wide diversity of CSR implementation practices. Secondly, there is a notable lack of understanding of CSR design and implementation. Much of the existing literature focuses only on why companies should adopt CSR, with very little attention paid to how this might be achieved (Baumann-Pauly et al., 2013; Boesso et al., 2013; Farooq et al., 2021a; Lindgreen et al., 2009; Schembera, 2018; Yuan et al., 2011); there is a pressing need to adopt a more focused approach to CSR programme design and implementation.

Similarly, corporate sentiment towards CSR is primarily shaped by institutional logic, organisational structure, management preferences, organisational culture and the ideology of the majority of employees (Gupta et al., 2017), along with a long-term financial strategy and commitment to enhance competitive advantage (Boesso et al., 2013; Porter and Kramer, 2002) or to gain corporate reputation. Therefore, organisations often follow varied CSR schemes that can be aimed at influencing specific stakeholders; i.e., shareholders, employees, customers, the community or the environment (Dobbs and Van Staden, 2016). However, the effectiveness of each CSR scheme is debated in the literature. For instance, some scholars favour customer-focused CSR (Luo and Bhattacharya, 2006) for organisational profitability, while others are of the view that combined CSR schemes generate better results (Boesso et al., 2013; Martínez-Ferrero et al., 2015) and a number of CSR studies have focused on environmental or selected characteristics of the issue (Pisani et al., 2017). Hence, disentangling the determinants of CSR activities with the aim of proposing a CSR model could be a valuable contribution to the CSR literature in general, and especially in the New Zealand socio-economic context, where firms lack a formalised CSR system (Dobbs and Van Staden, 2016).

In addition, there is an apparent need to design effective CSR programmes in the NZX-listed firms' context due to the fact that recently the NZX initiated[2] a CSR disclosure requirement for New Zealand listed firms. Therefore, aiming for an appropriate CSR evaluation model for NZX-listed firms is timely. More specifically, this study focuses on two objectives: (i) identifying and classifying the CSR initiatives in NZX-listed firms using interviews with senior managers of those firms, and (ii) exploring the extent of identified CSR initiatives using the multi-criteria decision-making (MCDM) analysis, such as the analytical hierarchy process (AHP) and grey-AHP.

The results of this study have implications for literature as well as practice. First, the study's findings have the potential to serve as an effective tool for academics, practitioners and stakeholders (i.e., investors and shareholders) in assessing and benchmarking the existing CSR implementation of NZX-listed firms. Second, despite progression in empirical as well as theoretical literature on CSR, to date not much academic effort has been made to unmask the organisational CSR initiatives using managerial live experiences (Pisani et al., 2017). In this manner, some recent reviews' findings also confirm that the majority of CSR literature has predominantly focused on the antecedents and consequences of adopting such practices (Pisani et al., 2017, Zaman et al., 2022). Therefore, the proposed CSR model based on consideration of multiple CSR initiatives contributes to CSR literature and provides important policy implications by disentangling the priorities and identifying key factors for CSR resources allocation.

The remainder of this chapter is structured as follows: the second section reviews the literature and establishes the contextual setting, while the third provides the methodological justification of the study. The AHP and grey-AHP applications in the NZX-listed companies' context is presented in the fourth section, followed by findings and discussion in the fifth. The sixth section summarises and discusses future research suggestions.

LITERATURE REVIEW AND CONTEXTUAL SETTING

CSR is an evolving concept that lacks a single definition. Thus, scholars have developed different dimensions of CSR (Bhimani and Soonawalla, 2005; Carroll, 1991; Conner and Prahalad, 1996). For example, some scholars have classified CSR initiatives into four groups: political, ethical, instrumental and integrative (Garriga and Melé, 2004). Others view CSR as firm CSR initiatives in terms of environmental, community relations, diversity, employee relations and human rights (Hawn and Ioannou, 2016; Hou and Reber, 2011). Generally, there is a broad consensus among scholars that CSR initiatives can be divided into two categories: implicit and explicit CSR practices (Matten and Moon, 2008). Implicit CSR initiatives include organisational policies, procedures, codes and practices deemed useful for the welfare of internal stakeholders who operate within the narrow boundaries of organisations, such as employees (Brammer et al., 2007; Shen and Jiuhua Zhu, 2011; Turker, 2009). In contrast, explicit CSR initiatives are typically associated with volunteerism and philanthropy towards the environment and society, which help to strengthen a firm's legitimacy and reputation among external stakeholders (Brammer et al., 2007; Cornelius et al., 2008). External stakeholders typically lie outside organisational boundaries and may include society at large, governments, customers, suppliers, creditors and shareholders (Hawn and Ioannou, 2016).

CSR initiatives vary across institutional contexts contingent upon the prevalence of institutional voids, the nature of the governance system, the presence of regulations (Delbard, 2008) and employment and labour conditions (Crossland and Hambrick, 2007), among others. For instance, firms operating in non-Anglo-Saxon-tradition countries, such as Japan, and in non-Anglo-Saxon-tradition Europe, view CSR as an implicit element and focus on internal CSR initiatives (i.e., employee-centric CSR) (Jackson and Apostolakou, 2010). Such firms may not formally describe their activities as CSR policies and may view them instead as part of normative compliance (Carroll, 1979). In contrast, firms operating in Anglo-Saxon-tradition countries, such as the US and Australia, emphasise external CSR initiatives (Bennett, 1998; Maignan and Ralston, 2002). Therefore, CSR practices must be analysed in terms of their context.

CSR holds strategic importance for New Zealand's "clean and green" image (Collins et al., 2007). Therefore, the majority of firms in New Zealand voluntarily engage in CSR practices. Despite the voluntary nature of CSR in New Zealand, firms operating in New Zealand must comply with respect to some legal standards. For instance, compliance with the Resource Management Act (RMA) 1991 promotes sustainable resource management and makes firms accountable for their environmental practices (Robertson, 1993). Similarly, the Fair Trading Act 1986 and the Employment Relationship Act 2000 ensure customer protection and employee rights, respectively, in New Zealand. These legislative structures are evident in that the New Zealand government encourages responsible business practices. Since New Zealand closely follows Australia when it comes to financial reporting, after the ASX revised its guidelines in 2014 to enforce sustainability reporting for ASX listed firms, the NZX also initiated[3] CSR disclosure requirements for NZX-listed firms.

In New Zealand, the New Zealand Business Council for Sustainable Development (NZBCSD) and Sustainable Business Network (SBN) are responsible for promoting sustainability (both the concept and practices) among businesses. SBN describes "sustainability" as the integration of social equity, economic growth and environmental management across New Zealand firms. Most of the businesses that promote CSR initiatives are members of these two organisations, with SBN having a significant share (i.e., 470 members in 2018[4]).

Despite these two organisations' efforts, the overall commitment of New Zealand firms to engaging in CSR is still lacking (Kloeten, 2014; KPMG, 2013b). For instance, a Lawrence et al. (2010) survey found only 15 per cent of New Zealand firms report their sustainability/CSR initiatives. Wells et al. (2014) also found limited reporting practices among sampled firms.

More recently, examining the motivation for CSR initiatives in New Zealand, Dobbs and Van Staden (2016) found that the lack of a formalised system was reflected in varied CSR initiatives across NZX-listed firms. Their results suggest that New Zealand firms are not currently fully committed to CSR. In most cases, CSR is used only to create the impression of being concerned about society and stakeholders. This not only raises significant questions about firms' management commitment to CSR adoption but also requires the development of more comprehensive and universal CSR programmes.

We assessed the CSR initiatives of the NZX-listed firms using the AHP and grey-AHP, an MCDM, to address which facets of CSR have received more attention and recognition among NZX-listed firms at large. CSR research among NZX-listed firms at best remains low and requires development, especially after the NZX CG 2017 principles were revised, which require listed companies to report material problems related to CSR. In this regard, there is an inevitable need to address the CSR issues that have triggered both local and global attention.

RESEARCH METHODOLOGY

Despite the surge in CSR publications, best practices and standards for CSR, there is still no agreement on what firms should be responsible for and how. A large number of CSR standards (such as UN Global Compact, ILO standard, ISO, GRI), codes and guidelines (i.e., Organisation for Economic Co-operation and Development and European Union guidelines for CSR) have been created in response to the need to appraise the business impact on society and the environment (Pisani et al., 2017). The majority of them are under criticism because they inhibit innovation and enhance conformity (De Colle et al., 2014).

In practice, CSR might be used in an opaque manner. Some companies claim to be socially responsible while also engaging in CSiR activities. For instance, Enron and BP are labelled as "CSR champions" engaged in CSiR. Based on the growing number of CSiR incidences, consumers have become inherently sceptical when evaluating CSR information (Chen et al., 2016; Connors et al., 2017).

In addition, CSR concepts in accounting and finance overlap with business goal setting, and hence the majority of CSR research in this domain is largely concentrated on linking firms' CSR engagement with their financial performance (Boesso et al., 2013; Chen et al., 2016; Jain and Jamali, 2016) using the neoclassical corporate finance standard (Doś, 2017). These studies differ in terms of variable selection, proxies for CSR and firm performance and selection of time horizon, resulting in inconsistent findings (Malik, 2015; Wang et al., 2016). This, however, is inevitable, since these studies fail to accommodate the intended time frame for CSR projects, types of CSR activities and heterogeneity of CSR projects due to differentiation in the reaction of a complex business environment (Bénabou and Tirole, 2010; Godfrey et al., 2010) – making it impossible to establish an incontestable business case for CSR. Although CSR does not always link with firm value, an increase in CSR activities can be value-enhancing (Malik, 2015). However, this increase should be based on accurate planning, keeping the right balance between ethical commitment to diverse stakeholders and accurate recognition of shareholder preferences (Doś, 2017; Godfrey et al., 2010; Malik, 2015) – hence involving managerial decision-making.

Notably, since there is no standard for firms' goal setting, it is solely up to firms' management on how to determine the criteria for decision-making, including CSR. Management's failure to undertake an accurate instrument in decision-making might result in undesirable consequences (i.e., a high proportion of non-financial to financial outcomes and increased agency costs). Therefore, there is a greater need for studies to improve managerial decision-making to foster transparency and accountability of CSR initiatives. Considering this, we adopted the mixed method based on MCDM to fulfil our study's objectives.

MCDM is a methodological design for evaluating a set of competing options using multiple and often conflicting criteria (Ho et al., 2010; Karaman and Akman, 2018). There is a large body of MCDM techniques, including AHP, grey-AHP and fuzzy-AHP. This is primarily due to there being many different decision-making situations, as well as time and data availability, analytical expertise and administrative requirements.

Our study is centred on the thoughts and perceptions of senior executives on the pre-defined criteria (i.e., questions about CSR), which might be conflicting. In such cases, AHP is a proven method for reconciling expert decisions and providing reliable results (Karaman and Akman, 2018). AHP is one of the most practical and accepted methods in MCDM (Mardani et al., 2015). We adopted AHP along with grey theory to decrypt the hierarchical importance of CSR initiatives – obtained as a result of interviewing the senior managers of NZX-listed "CSR champion" firms. AHP enables a researcher to establish group consensus by weighting the CSR initiatives to select the best suitable criteria (Akman and Dageviren, 2018). Apart from these advantages, the number of respondents to our survey is 41. Therefore, we consider AHP to be an ideal method for this study. A recent literature review confirming the popularity of MCDM, especially after 2010, has highlighted the growth of AHP in many different fields; i.e., economics, education and the supply chain (Doś, 2017; Mardani et al., 2015).

Methodological Framework

We have adopted the mixed-method approach comprised of two phases. In Phase I, CSR initiatives have been identified through qualitative interviews with senior managers of NZX-listed "CSR champion" firms. In Phase II, the relative weights of the CSR programmes were assessed through AHP by implementing the survey questionnaires with the senior executives of all NZX-listed firms. The schematic diagram of the research process is given in Figure 12.1.

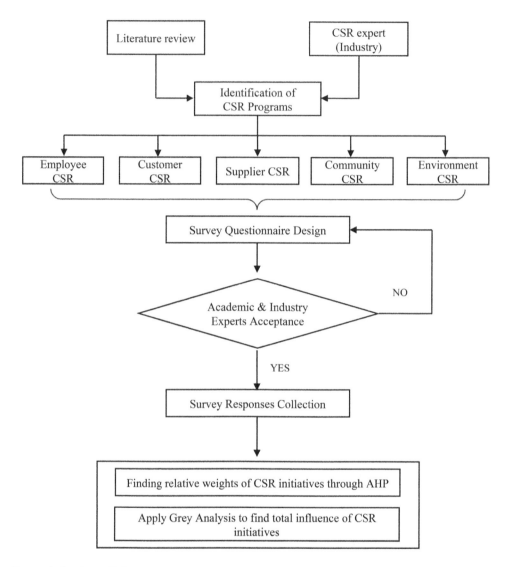

Source: Authors' compilation

Figure 12.1   Research design

Phase I: interviews with senior executives
A critical step in an MCDM setting is to determine the pertinent criteria. Several studies using MCDM have relied on a literature review to develop the criteria (Karaman and Akman, 2018; Mardani et al., 2015). Considering CSR dependency across institutional voids and the scarcity of the literature in an NZX context limits us to depending solely on the literature review for CSR initiatives selection. Therefore, we used face-to-face interviews, targeting senior managers in an actual company setting in the first phase. To do this, we used purposive sampling[5]

for sample selection (Farooq, 2018; Jason and Glenwick, 2016) by employing one criterion,[6] namely that firms had to be listed in the Global Reporting Initiative (GRI) database (see http://database.globalreporting.org/search/). This process resulted in 18 companies meeting the pre-determined sampling criteria. Of the 18 companies, six declined the interview invitation on the grounds of internal re-structuring, management re-shuffling and overall busyness. Finally, we were able to interview 12 company managers.

Although there are studies encouraging scholars to adopt technology (telephonic and video) while conducting interviews (De Villiers et al., 2021; Farooq and De Villiers, 2017), we preferred face-to-face because of two advantages: to build and maintain rapport with interviewees and its ability to visually assess the participant's work environment (De Villiers et al., 2021). All the interviews[7] were conducted at the respondents' company offices, located in three New Zealand cities – Auckland, Wellington and Christchurch – between February and August 2017. The interviewees were well informed and the majority of them were in executive management positions: chief financial officer, company secretary, executive general manager, head of government relations and CSR, and general manager sustainability (see Table 12.1).

Table 12.1   Summary of interviewees and description of interview characteristics

SN	Code	Locations	Designation	Company tenure (years)	Interview duration (h:mm:ss)	Transcription (words)
1	SM1	Auckland	Head of Government Relations & Corporate Responsibility	7	0:54:57	5877
2	SM2	Auckland	Sustainability Manager	10	0:42:01	4603
3	SM3	Wellington	Head of Sustainability	3	0:41:20	4003
4	SM4	Auckland	Executive General Manager	5	0:50:15	7127
5	SM5	Christchurch	Chief Operating Officer & CFO	7	0:45:03	4199
6	SM6	Auckland	Governance & Sustainability Manager	3	0:40:50	4629
7	SM7	Wellington	Chief Financial Officer	8	0:44:31	5334
8	SM8	Wellington	Sustainability Manager	3	0:41:05	5101
9	SM9	Auckland	General Manager Sustainability	2	0:50:22	7874
10	SM10	Auckland	Company Secretary	6	0:38:52	3894
11	SM11	Auckland	Group Chief Financial Officer	3	1:02:11	7706
12	SM12	Wellington	Sustainability Manager	5	0:52:42	7073

Source: Authors' compilation

Next, we thematically analysed the transcripts (Gibbs, 2002) to identify the patterns of meaning (Braun and Clarke, 2006; Farooq, 2018). The data (i.e., sentences and paragraphs) were coded by allocating names/labels, which process was facilitated by the analysis software NVivo 11 (Bazeley and Jackson, 2013). NVivo aids code creation by recording transcripts, creating and editing code names, maintaining a code database, retrieving codes from the database, tracking codes to transcripts, collapsing multiple codes into desired codes, and finally grouping the codes into categories and sub-categories (Bazeley and Jackson, 2013). We started with open coding; i.e., line-by-line reading of the transcript and creating the code names for the issue discussed. The process was repeated, and issues related to sub-categories and related themes were also developed based on the interview guide. The final categories and sub-categories that emerged from the interviews are presented in Table 12.2.

Next, we developed survey questions based on these criteria and sub-criteria with the use of the five-point Likert scale. Notably, we pre-tested (pilot study) the survey questions using two groups of respondents: CSR practitioners and academic experts. For CSR practitioners, the study used all 12 interviewees that participated in the first phase of the research project for two reasons: (i) they are experts in the CSR domain as they already use GRI-based CSR practices, and (ii) they have a prior familiarity with the current research project. In addition to the CSR practitioners, two academic experts were asked to review the questionnaires to ensure the readability and transparency of the questions and criteria. Both groups suggested changes to some of the wording and the sequencing of the questions. These were incorporated into the final survey with the aim of bringing theory and practice together by adopting such procedures.

Table 12.2   *Thematic analysis results of interviewees*

Categories	Sub-categories	Example of interviewee's perception
Employee CSR	Employee Wellbeing Policies (EMP1)	"We offer meaningful employment [...] and wellness type programmes because we want them to be the best that they can be [...] we run bus services to pick them up from locations and bring them to our processing operations." [SM9]
		"I think, we've probably led the sector in terms of how we treat employees. We spend a lot of effort on values and employee engagement, which introduces career retailer wage." [SM11]
	Employee Health and Safety (EMP2)	"We measure health & safety incidents from employee injury ranks, lost time injury ranks, all those sort of things." [SM5]
		"Our target area for CSR include shareholder value maximization, customer satisfaction, health and safety and employee engagement." [SM6]
		"We [provide] employee with effective work place environment." [SM10]
		"[W]e have award schemes. It's about increasing the level of engagement within the business in mainstreaming sustainability and I have that [in] mine also and aspects like health & safety are in there as well so that's an important one." [SM9]
		"[W]e are really focusing on [what] is called HSSSE so it's got an extra 'S' in it and the extra 'S' is for security, health, safety, security and environment." [SM12]
	Equal Employment Opportunities (EMP3)	"[M]aking sure that [...] our employees are treated fairly." [SM05]
		"We [...] are committed to provide timely, accurate and equal information to the stakeholders." [SM3]
		"We are committed to provide equal employment opportunities, without caring for gender, race, religion or nationality." [SM1]
Customer CSR	Product Quality Policies and Procedures (CUS1)	"We adopt customer-friendly practices by delivery price included in sensitive products." [SM11]
		"We have the customer service team [...] We have a research team [that] does market research with our customers." [SM3]
		"We have a customer centre [...] but I didn't mention them at all. [The] main thing with our customers is helping them do the right thing." [SM8]
		"[W]e also have a customer call centre and customer care sort of place." [SM10]

Categories	Sub-categories	Example of interviewee's perception
Customer CSR (continued)	CSR Best Practices Products (CUS2)	"Our focus is on the product quality; we ensure that we are not using low-quality material that harm[s] our customer, both pocket and health [...] we have also loyalty programmes for customers." [SM12]
		"From the customer, then make a turn into point of engagement with customers around that issue to say, well, "Actually we think it's important to you guys, it's important to us [...] that is, what we are doing about it? [We] are sharing it with you, rather than sort of just say, 'It interests us'." [SM11]
		"But we like to put customers first, in a way we design products, in a way we think about things we put them in first." [SM1]
		"We show customers that we focus strongly on CSR practices, have better returns and are more secure at lower risk in the long run as a business." [SM8]
		"We [...] are doing a lot of research and R&D into fabrics where they don't need as much dyeing process, so less water usage in the process of dyeing, less harmful chemicals being used, so we are looking to invest." [SM5]
	Disclosure of CSR-Related Product Features (CUS3)	"We trying to educate customers which Kiwi saver would suits their requirement and that has a direct impact on the customer as they invested their money in a smart way, it's increasing for next step for them." [SM1]
Supplier CSR	Encourage Suppliers for CSR (SUP1)	"You know, we do a lot of work around ethical sourcing and selecting our suppliers that don't exploit child labour, and they don't work at 70-hour shifts, and all that sort of stuff." [SM11]
	Dealing with Responsible Supplier (SUP2)	"[W]hen we talk about supplier practices, [...] then the benefits for that are people who are making their product treated fairly really. So it's benefit for them rather than necessary for us." [SM5]
		"Our main focus of [...] It's like ten priorities we listed out but top five are [...] focused on our supplier, so basically making sure that our suppliers [...] are treated fairly [...] so the people [Supplier] making our products are treated fairly, and so that it stands to do audits at factories that we have top suppliers." [SM5]
	Provide Assistance to Supplier for CSR Improvement (SUP3)	"You know, that has to be safe, healthy, what the customers want, we work with their supply chains to optimise value for them as well for ourselves so there's a whole heap of reasons." [SM9]
Community CSR	CSR Programmes for Local Communities (COM1)	"We do a lot of community-based giving and events around the community, probably those differentiate us a little bit from other organisations." [SM11]
	Engagement with Charity Organisations (COM2)	"We have sponsorships with Red Cross, the Australian Himalayan Foundation, DOC, they sponsor some campgrounds in Marlborough. And we do [...] so we do [...] we donate money." [SM5]
		"We donate money and we [...] Outward Bound is another one, so we donate product to Outward Bound for people to use when they're on the course." [SM6]

Categories	Sub-categories	Example of interviewee's perception
Community CSR (continued)	Relationship with Indigenous Communities (COM3)	"We do stakeholders engagement, peace community and Iwi community engagement, that's really done through corporate affairs but we have regular meetings, bimonthly meetings with local Iwi on the development side of things, we have regular sessions with local board members." [SM2] "We are getting rid of a large amount of bicycles, epoxy bikes, and rather than in the past, they used to cut them up and put them in the scrap metal, but now, giving them to community groups so that they can repaint them and use them for other purposes." [SM8] "We have community funds within our local communities. We try to keep good relationship with local governments in our communities by the right person contact and consultation." [SM7] "We have a lot of staff engagement with our community investment because we are not focused on just giving away cash and hoping that we can get someone else's glory because I've done something good. We are a bit more engaged in that process." [SM4]
	Monitoring Firms' Activities Impact on Communities (COM4)	"We also have internal developed produces to monitor the compliance with regard to communities." [SM3] "[I]t's almost now become more about corporate reputation and kind of license to operate." [SM2] "We have got environmental and communities benchmarks in which we operate, it's about license to operate and it's about being good corporate citizens in those areas where you operate." [SM4]
Environment CSR	Waste Reduction (ENV1)	"We create recycling and waste management kind of thing and then we think about it in terms of sustainability and that bring sustainability in New Zealand." [SM10]
	Effective Resources Management (ENV2)	"We also have a focus on our energy management and waste reduction in our buildings." [SM8] "[T]he environment is more like your environmental compliance as opposed to the environmental initiatives [....] so the environment is the Resource Management Act (RMA) type compliance stuff." [SM12] "Our core business in terms of the renewable electricity generation but also going through the process in terms of monitoring resource use." [SM6]
	Obsolesce Avoidance (ENV3)	"All our product comes [from] factories, packaged in poly bags and cupboard boxes, so [we] try and make sure we recycle everything [...] and we encourage to return damaged or need repairs or whatever, we try and recycle those as well so those are where our main focus is really." [SM5]
	Renewable Energy Usage (ENV4)	"We are being vocal in the conversation around transport electrification given that [...] obviously agriculture is the largest proportion of emissions for New Zealand but within the energy sector, over 40 per cent ... well over 40 per cent, the bulk of the emissions are from the energy sector comes from transport." [SM6] "[W]e make a lot of investment around renewable energy and improvements in energy efficiency, you know, supporting the whole electric vehicles." [SM11]
	Emission Monitoring (ENV5)	"[L]ook at our previously corporate responsibility reports, there is a lot of focus on reducing environmental which is mainly around emissions." [SM1] "We have sort of environment as an area that we think about and focus on, so if you look at our reports, there's various part of it but, for instance, we focus on reduction of greenhouse emissions, we have sort of companies specifically focus[ing] on things like recycling." [SM10]

Source: Authors' compilation

Phase II: survey questionnaires

In this phase, we collected the survey data from all managers of NZX-listed firms. To do this, we developed a database of NZX-listed firms' management, containing publicly available information about executive leaders, including name, designation, LinkedIn profile and email address or phone number. Specifically, each respondent's email address was matched with their LinkedIn profile using the LinkedIn Professional Suite (LPS). LinkedIn matching enabled the researcher to find informed participants by looking at individuals' professional experiences. This process yielded 104 respondents for data collection. Notably, in New Zealand, around 150–160 companies are listed on the NZX. This number excluded participants from the qualitative phase and companies with the same management teams.[8] Considering the NZX market dynamics (i.e., small, open economy), the number of targeted participants, 104, was considered reasonable for the current research. We then adopted a hybrid approach, using both paper-based and online surveys (Qualtrics) to collect the data from senior management of NZX-listed firms. Data cleaning and removing missing responses yielded a total of 41 responses (or a response rate of 39.42 per cent) (see Table 12.3 for respondents' profiles). This allowed the researcher to proceed with the analysis, as it was higher than the 25 per cent documented by Dobbs and Van Staden (2016), who used a sample of NZX-listed companies.

Table 12.3   Sample description of survey questionnaires

	Frequency	Percentage
Respondent tenure (Years)		
0–5	22	53.66
6–10	9	21.95
11–15	2	4.88
16–20	3	7.32
> 21	5	12.20
Respondent designations		
Chief Financial Officer (CFO)	24	58.54
Chief Operating Officer (COO)	2	4.88
Sustainability Manager	4	9.76
Finance Manager	2	4.88
Country Manager	2	4.88
Head of Strategy	1	2.44
Senior Communication Manager	1	2.44
Executive Service Manager	1	2.44
Managing Director	1	2.44
Annual Report Program Manager	1	2.44
Senior Portfolio Manager	1	2.44
Management Accountant	1	2.44
Firm size (number of employees)		
0–99	12	29.27
100–199	0	0.00
> 200	29	70.73
Firm industry		
Agriculture, forestry and fishing	4	9.76
Electricity, gas, water and wastage	5	12.20
Finance and insurance	7	17.07
Health care and social assistance	5	12.20

	Frequency	Percentage
Information, media and telecommunication	5	12.20
Manufacturing	2	4.88
Mining	1	2.44
Rental, hiring and real estate services	3	7.32
Retail	4	9.76
Transport, postal and warehousing	5	12.20

Source: Authors' compilation

AHP AND GREY-AHP METHOD AND ANALYSIS

CSR evaluation is subjective and based on the opinions of senior executives of the proposed criteria, which may be naturally conflicting. In such cases, AHP is a proven method for reconciling expert decisions and providing reliable results (Karaman and Akman, 2018). AHP enables us to establish group consensus by weighting the criteria and sub-criteria (in our case, CSR initiatives) (Akman and Dageviren, 2018). AHP was originally developed by Saaty (1980). AHP attempts to derive criteria scores and weights based on pairwise comparisons between criteria and multiple outputs. Decision-makers are required to make comparisons between each criterion relative to the others using a nine-point semantic scale (Saaty, 1980). To apply AHP, a hierarchy or network structure that illustrates the problem is essential, as well as pairwise relative comparisons (Saaty, 1980; Saaty, 1987) in a systematic manner. This process is elaborated in subsequent sections.

AHP Method and Application

Hierarchy for the decision

The first step in AHP analysis is to build a hierarchy for the decision. This is often known as decision modelling. It simply consists of building a hierarchy to analyse the decision. More specifically, AHP structures a situation into goals, decision criteria and alternatives; it assumes that all of them are independent. It synthesises group consensus, evaluating the criteria and sub-criteria in order to select the leading suitable alternative. For example, Figure 12.2 shows the structural decision station, in which the top level shows the goal, while levels two and three reflect the criteria and sub-criteria that need to be compared in order to achieve the goal. The structuring of the problem into a hierarchy provides an advantage in understanding the decision when set against alternatives (Saaty, 1987).

The next step in AHP involves pairwise comparison. For pairwise comparison, we carry out the pairwise comparison for each criterion and sub-criteria of Figure 12.2. In pairwise comparison, the respondents have to indicate their preference for two elements using the nine-point AHP scale as shown in Table 12.4.

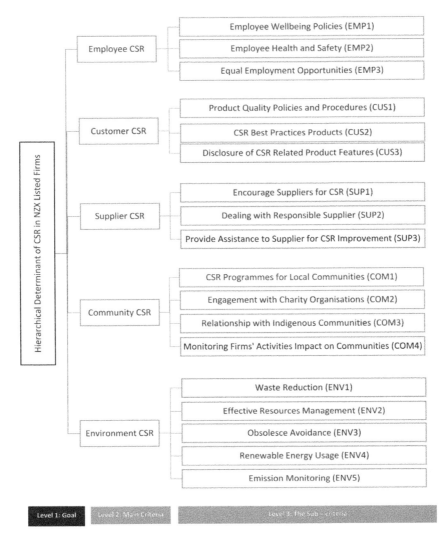

Source: Authors' compilation

Figure 12.2   Hierarchy for organisational CSR practices

Table 12.4   AHP pairwise comparisons

				CA_1									CA_n			
9	8	7	6	5	4	3	2	1	2	3	4	5	6	7	8	9
				SCA_1									SCA_n			
9	8	7	6	5	4	3	2	1	2	3	4	5	6	7	8	9

The pairwise contrasting of n criteria are summarised as an $n \times n$ pairwise assessment matrix. Let us define $C = C_j / j = 122n$ as the set of criteria of CSR programmes. The $n \times n$ evaluation matrix, A, includes a comparison of criteria from the set C. The matrix A is given in Equation (12.1):

$$Matrix\ A = \begin{bmatrix} a_{11} & a_{12} & \cdots & a_{1n} \\ a_{21} & a_{22} & & a_{2n} \\ \vdots & & \ddots & \vdots \\ a_{n1} & a_{n2} & \cdots & a_{nn} \end{bmatrix} \tag{12.1}$$

In this context, based on the AHP hierarchy, given in Figure 12.2, a_{ij} represents the numerical assessment of pairwise comparison between criteria i and j. For instance, if criteria i has absolute importance over criteria j, then $a_{ij} = 9$; conversely $a_{ji} = 1/9$. The entries of matrix A follow the reciprocal property rule as shown in Equation (12.2):

$$a_{ij} \neq 0, a_{ii} = 1, a_{ji} = \frac{1}{a_{ij}} \tag{12.2}$$

A key disadvantage of AHP pairwise comparison is that it requires a large amount of information, as for each hierarchy $N*(N-1)/2$ individual comparisons are required (Hossain et al., 2014; Kallas, 2011; Saaty, 1987). It thus becomes a lengthy task for participants to fill in the information (Kallas, 2011). Due to the amount of time needed to complete this task, respondents usually ignore their past assigned values during the process of new information sharing and thus create inconsistencies (Kallas, 2011). To avoid these inconsistencies, scholars have adopted a Likert scale for data collection and developed a process to transform the Likert scale data into pairwise comparisons (Hossain et al., 2014; Kallas, 2011; Schühly and Tenzer, 2017). In line with previous literature (Kallas, 2011; Hossain et al., 2014; and Schühly and Tenzer, 2017), we also transformed the individual absolute Likert scale answers into pairwise comparisons. Initially following Schühly and Tenzer (2017), the Likert scale answers were transformed using a Saaty nine-point scale as shown in Table 12.5.

Table 12.5   Likert scale and Saaty scale equivalence

Linguistic	Saaty	Likert scale
Extremely Important	9	5
Very Strong (More Important)	7	4
Strong (More Important)	5	3
Moderately More Important	3	2
Equally Important	1	1
2, 4, 6, 8 can be used to express intermediate values for Saaty scale		

Following Kallas (2011), Hossain et al. (2014) and Schühly and Tenzer (2017), we used Equation (12.3) to complete the transformation process and fill in the so-called Saaty matrix.

$$\hat{a}_{ij} = \left| SC_{ik} - SC_{jk} \right| + 1, \tag{12.3}$$

where $\hat{a}_{ij}$ is the estimated pairwise comparative score on the Saaty scale, SC_{ik} is the Likert scale valuation score for individual criteria i – obtained using the five-point Likert scale (1: non-important/strongly disagree to 5: very important/strongly agree) – and C_{jk} is the Likert scale valuation score for other criteria j. For instance, in our case (Figure 12.2), if the SC_{ik} of the criteria I (i.e., employee CSR) for individual k is 5 on the Likert scale and the SC_{jk} for criteria j (i.e., customer CSR) for individual k is 4, then the transformation approach of the paired comparison between i and j is $\hat{a}_{ij} = |4{-}5| + 1 = 2$. This study uses the same approach to fill in the Saaty matrix (Saaty, 2003; Saaty, 1980) for each criteria and sub-criteria item.

Normalisation and weights calculations
The next step after completing the Saaty matrix in AHP is to normalise and obtain the respective weights of each matrix 'A' by dividing the column entries by the corresponding column geometric sum.[9] The principal eigenvector 'w' concurrent to the largest eigenvector λ_{max} of matrix A determines the precedence of the element as shown in Equation (12.4):

$$Aw = \lambda_{max} w \tag{12.4}$$

Consistency of preferences
The final step in AHP involves the calculation of the consistency ratio, as the eminence of AHP results is highly dependent on the congruity of pairwise comparison judgements. For instance, in our case (Figure 12.2), if a respondent rates employee CSR as twice preferred to customer CSR and subsequently rate customer CSR as twice preferred to supplier CSR, then the respondent should rate employee CSR as four times preferred to supplier CSR. When developing AHP, Saaty acknowledged the human decision maker's limitations in terms of absolute consistency and allowed for a certain degree of flexibility during the elicitation of preferences as measured by the consistency ratio (CR). We accomplished CR using a two-step process. Initially, the consistency index (CI) was calculated using Equation (12.5):

$$CI = \frac{\lambda_{max} - n}{n - 1} \tag{12.5}$$

where n is the size of the original comparison matrix. The final CR is obtained from Equation (12.6):

$$CR = \frac{CI}{RI} \qquad (12.6)$$

The random indices (RIs) for a very large number (e.g., 500,000) of randomly generated pairwise comparison matrices, as purposed by Saaty, are shown in Table 12.6.

Table 12.6   AHP random indices for assessing the consistency of pairwise comparison

N	1	2	3	4	5	6	7	8	9	10
Random index	0	0	0.52	0.89	1.11	1.25	1.35	1.40	1.45	1.49

CR usage is imperative in AHP, as it indicates the consistency of the pairwise assessments. In prior literature, 0.1 is accepted as the upper bound (Saaty and Vargas, 2012). Analysis exceeding the upper limit needs to be repeated to improve the ratio (Karaman and Akman, 2018; Saaty and Vargas, 2012). In the current research, CR ratios are well below 0.1, suggesting the consistency of responses (results available upon request). The results for the AHP analysis are presented in the next section.

Grey Relational Analysis

To measure the influence of identified CSR initiators and overall CSR performance of NZX-listed firms, we performed a grey relational analysis using the grey system theory. The grey system theory evolved to overcome the issue of ambiguous and incomplete information (Zhou and Xu, 2006). The grey system theory is a systematic analysis method that utilises the maximum potential of known information (Mathivathanan et al., 2017), reflecting the essence of a present grey system (Zhou and Xu, 2006). Grey systems are generally described by using the grey number, grey equation and grey matrices. " $\otimes$ " represents the grey number – a basic unit that depicts intervals between unknown exact value and known scope (Liu et al., 2011). In grey-AHP, a whitening function is generally used to obtain the close degree of proximity in the interval. The grey approach combined with AHP methods not only helps to overcome the lack of more responses but also helps obtain the essence of total information given in the current scenario to measure the influence of identified CSR initiators and overall CSR performance.

We follow scholars such as Mathivathanan et al. (2017) to integrate the grey approach in AHP. The grey-AHP combines the initial collected response to find the most influential CSR initiatives using the priority weights obtained through the AHP process – getting the final overall grade of responses obtained. The sections below systematically describe the grey-AHP application process.

Establishing a comment set for evaluation indicator
In grey-AHP, we first assign the values on a scale of 4, 3 and 1 against three grades: "highly influencing" [4], "moderately influencing" [3] and "poorly influencing" [1] for framing the comment set of the evaluation index $[V = (4, 3, 1)^T]$.

Development of the evaluation sample matrix

The evaluation indicator system's weight, according to evaluation indicator B_j, is determined as follows:

$$\textbf{\textit{Matrix D}} = \left[d_{ijk} \right], \tag{12.7}$$

where i = number of criteria, j = number of sub-criteria and k = the number of respondents.

Determination of the evaluation grey cluster

We first divide the grey cluster into three grades: "highly influencing", "moderately influencing" and "poorly influencing" (e = 1, 2, 3). The corresponding grey cluster is as follows: (i) $\otimes_1 \in [0,4,\infty]$ and whitenization function $f_1(x)$ is classification for "highly influencing"; (ii) $\otimes_2 \in [0,3,5]$ and whitenization function $f_2(x)$ is classification for "moderately influencing"; (iii) and $\otimes_3 \in [0,1,3]$ and whitenization function $f_3(x)$ is classification for "poorly influencing". The whitenization function can be explicitly written as:

$$f_{1(x)} = \begin{cases} x\big/4 & 0<x<4 \\ 1 & x>4 \\ 0 & else \end{cases} \tag{12.8}$$

$$f_{2(x)} = \begin{cases} 5-x & 0<x\leq3 \\ 1 & 5<x\leq3 \\ 0 & else \end{cases} \tag{12.9}$$

$$f_{3(x)} = \begin{cases} 1 & 0<x\leq1 \\ 3-x/2 & 3<x\leq1 \\ 0 & else \end{cases} \tag{12.10}$$

Calculation of the grey evaluation weight

The evaluation of the indicator B candidate belonging to the evaluation grid cluster has the grey assessment coefficient of:

$$X_{ije} = \Sigma f_e \left(d_{ijk} \right) \tag{12.11}$$

K = 1 to s (total number of respondents)

The evaluation indicator B candidate belongs to the grey cluster. The total grey evaluation quantity is given as:

$$X_{ij} = \Sigma X_{ije} \qquad (12.12)$$

where e = 1, 2, 3

The grey evaluation weight of the *eth* evaluation grey cluster is:

$$r_{ije} = {}^{X_{ije}} \Big/ {}_{X_{ij}} \qquad (12.13)$$

The indicator B that belongs to the grey evaluation weight is:

$$r_{ije} = \left\{ r_{ij1}, r_{ij2}, r_{ij3} \right\} \qquad (12.14)$$

Therefore, the grey evaluated weight matrix is written as:

$$Matrix\ R_i = \left\{ \begin{matrix} r_{i1} \\ r_{i2} \\ r_{i3} \\ \cdots \\ r_{ij} \end{matrix} \right\} = \left\{ \begin{matrix} r_{i11} & r_{i12} & r_{i13} \\ r_{i21} & r_{i22} & r_{i23} \\ r_{i31} & r_{i32} & r_{i33} \\ \cdots & \cdots & \cdots \\ r_{ij1} & r_{ij2} & r_{ij3} \end{matrix} \right\} \qquad (12.15)$$

Calculation of total assessment value

The grey assessment vector of every grey classification B_i is:

$$B_i = W_i * R_i \qquad (12.16)$$

Next, the grey assessment weight vector B is obtained by integrating each assessment of the grey classification as:

$$B = W * R \qquad (12.17)$$

According to the maximum principle, the grey grade of effectiveness can be determined from expression 16. Sometimes judgement will be distorted due to the loss of too much information. To avoid this, B can be considered as a single effectiveness value E_v.

$$E_v = B \cdot V^T \qquad (12.18)$$

Based on the E_v value, a conclusion can be drawn regarding the effectiveness of CSR initiators.

Grey-AHP Application

As discussed earlier, we integrated the grey system theory in AHP to measure the influence of CSR initiatives. After we obtained the weights through AHP, we applied grey clustering. We first established the three grades corresponding to e = 1, 2 and 3 to accommodate the three clusters. For example, consider our respondent score for CSR initiatives under employee CSR, as shown in Table 12.7.

Table 12.7 Responses for CSR initiators under "Employee CSR" criterion

CSR initiators	Number of responses (firms)															
	Code		1	2	3	4	5	6	7	8	.	.	.	38	39	40	41
Employee	EMP1	X11	5	5	3	5	4	3	4	4	.	.	.	4	5	5	5
Employee	EMP2	X12	5	5	4	5	5	3	5	4	.	.	.	5	5	5	5
Employee	EMP3	X13	5	5	5	5	4	3	5	4	.	.	.	4	5	4	5

We first calculated the explicit weight functions for every element. For instance, for criterion C_{i1}, according to Equation (12.11):

$$\text{For e} = 1, \ X_{111} = f_1(5) + f_1(5) + f_1(3) + f_1(5) \cdots \cdots + f_1(5) = 17.75$$

$$\text{For e} = 2, \ X_{112} = f_2(5) + f_2(5) + f_2(3) + f_2(5) \cdots \cdots + f_2(5) = 3.0$$

$$\text{For e} = 3, \ X_{113} = f_2(5) + f_3(5) + f_3(3) + f_3(5) \cdots \cdots + f_3(5) = 1.0$$

Total grey evaluation, $X_{11} = 17.75 + 3.0 + 1 = 21.75$ (from Equation (12.12))

$$r_{111} = r_{111} \Big/ r_{11} = \frac{17.75}{21.75} = 0.816$$

$$r_{112} = r_{112} \Big/ r_{11} = \frac{3}{21.75} = 0.138$$

$$r_{113} = r_{113} \Big/ r_{11} = \frac{1}{21.75} = 0.046$$

Concurrently, the grey evaluation weights for all the CSR initiatives are calculated. The grey evaluated weights matrix, R_i, for the employee CSR category is obtained as follows:

$$R_i = \begin{Bmatrix} 0.816 & 0.138 & 0.046 \\ 0.934 & 0.066 & 0.000 \\ 0.927 & 0.073 & 0.000 \end{Bmatrix}$$

The total grey assessment vector for employee CSR criteria is:

$$B_i = W_i * R_i = (0.909004 \quad 0.081801 \quad 0.009195)$$

$$E_v = B \cdot V^T = (3.89061)$$

Similarly, to employee CSR, we have calculated each CSR initiative and summarised them in Table 12.8. The total grey grade value for CSR initiatives under the employee CSR category is 3.891, which falls in the second cluster (i.e., moderately influencing). This suggests that the overall influence of employee CSR initiatives on firm CSR performance is "moderate". Similar to employee CSR initiatives, we have calculated the grey grade for all five categories using the grey-AHP and the results documented in Table 12.8 fall in the second category cluster, which suggests that the overall effect of CSR initiatives is moderate on each CSR performance criterion.

Table 12.8   Summary of grey-AHP results

CSR initiators		Grey evaluated weighted matrix			Total grey assessment Vector			Grey grade
CSR	Code	R_{ij1}	R_{ij2}	R_{ij3}				
Employee	EMP1	0.816	0.138	0.046	0.909	0.082	0.009	3.891
	EMP2	0.934	0.066	0.000				
	EMP3	0.927	0.073	0.000				
Customer	CUS1	0.639	0.331	0.030	0.567	0.410	0.022	3.522
	CUS2	0.471	0.529	0.000				
	CUS3	0.448	0.530	0.022				
Supplier	SUP1	0.419	0.538	0.043	0.379	0.568	0.053	3.073
	SUP2	0.362	0.599	0.039				
	SUP3	0.356	0.566	0.078				
Community	COM1	0.686	0.314	0.000	0.621	0.372	0.007	3.606
	COM2	0.652	0.348	0.000				
	COM3	0.615	0.385	0.000				
	COM4	0.529	0.441	0.029				
Environment	ENV1	0.652	0.348	0.000	0.665	0.331	0.004	3.656
	ENV2	0.712	0.288	0.000				
	ENV3	0.665	0.335	0.000				
	ENV4	0.681	0.319	0.000				
	ENV5	0.613	0.366	0.022				

FINDINGS AND DISCUSSION

Table 12.9 shows the AHP results obtained for the main criteria. The results suggest that four of these programmes (i.e., employee CSR, customer CSR, community CSR and environment CSR) received higher but equal weightings (i.e., 23.08 per cent) than supplier CSR (7.69 per cent). This illustrates the inefficient supplier CSR understanding among New Zealand firms. Considering the strategic importance of supply chain management, CSR practices among supply chains are inevitable. Firms might possess exemplary records in other CSR dimensions (e.g., employee, community, environment, investors and customers); however, ignorance of supplier-related CSR practices has a greater potential to affect a company's corporate citizen image (Lee and Kim, 2009). For instance, we have witnessed public boycotts of a specific product (e.g., Nike and Shell) for failing to maintain responsible supply chain practices (Locke and Romis, 2007). Considering the importance of supplier-related CSR practices, and a growing number of legislative restrictions and international standards that relate to the environment, labour standards and human rights, it is imperative for NZX-listed firms to accentuate supplier-related CSR issues.

The findings are interesting, as generally it is considered that firms operating in Anglo-Saxon-tradition countries, such as the US, Australia and New Zealand, emphasise external CSR mechanisms (i.e., focusing on external stakeholders) (Dobbs and Van Staden, 2016; Maignan and Ralston, 2002; Matten and Moon, 2008) rather than internal CSR (i.e., focusing on internal stakeholders). While firms operating in non-Anglo-Saxon-tradition countries, such as Japan and in Europe, follow internal CSR or employee CSR (Jackson and Apostolakou, 2010), these results suggest that even though firms in New Zealand focus on explicit CSR, they still view implicit CSR (i.e., employee CSR) as part of normative compliance (Carroll, 1991).

Table 12.9   AHP weights and rank of the main criteria for CSR programmes

	Non-normalised			Normalised		
Criteria	Saaty scale	Weights	Rank	Saaty scale	Weights	Rank
Employee CSR	7	0.2308	1	7	0.2308	1
Customer CSR	7	0.2308	1	7	0.2308	1
Community CSR	7	0.2308	1	7	0.2308	1
Environment CSR	7	0.2308	1	7	0.2308	1
Supplier CSR	5	0.0769	2	5	0.0769	2
Column sum		1.00			1.00	

Table 12.10 reveals the sub-criteria rankings based on AHP local weights and global weights. The results for local weights in Table 12.10 show that "employee health and safety (EMP2)" are considered the most influential (60 per cent) CSR practices, followed by "employee wellbeing policies (EMP1)" and "equal employment opportunities (EMP3)," with each having equal weight (20 per cent) among respondent firms. This finding indicates that measures by the New Zealand government to promote employee health and safety (H&S) in 2015 are effective and that firms consider H&S issues as the number one priority among their employee-related CSR practices. In addition, the regulatory nature of employee H&S often motivates firms to accord priority to this CSR factor. Ignorance of H&S regulations often sparks regulatory intervention (Montero et al., 2009). Thus, management prioritisation of employee H&S promotion can be justified and is in line with prior literature (Cowper-Smith and De Grosbois, 2011). However, considering the significance associated with employee wellbeing (e.g., it is associated with lower levels of employee turnover and high firm performance), it is beneficial for firms to prioritise and subsequently frame "employee wellbeing policies".

In terms of the customer CSR sub-criteria, "product quality policies and procedures (CUS1)" have received the greater attention (60 per cent), compared with "CSR best practices products (CUS2)" and "disclosure of CSR-related product features (CUS3)" with 20 per cent each. This finding indicates that firms are fully aware that product quality has tangible benefits – as product quality is associated with customer satisfaction (Hill and Alexander, 2017) and firm profitability (Malshe and Agarwal, 2015). However, a lower preference for "disclosure of CSR-related product features (CUS3)", such as environmentally friendly labels, shows that firms are not fully recognising the added benefits associated with these practices. This is not surprising, as the CSR concept is still new but growing among New Zealand firms, and demands from the customer for CSR-related products will push firms to provide additional information.

Supplier CSR received a lower but equal preference (33 per cent) among all three indicators; i.e., "encourage suppliers for CSR (SUP1)", "dealing with responsible suppliers (SUP2)" and "provide assistance to the supplier for CSR improvement (SUP3)". Given the importance of supplier-related CSR, these findings are somewhat surprising. The majority of supplier-related scandals for labour abuses across the world for reputable companies (e.g., Nike and Adidas) have fuelled negative public sentiments (Ganesan et al., 2009; Locke and Romis, 2007). This has resulted in an undesirable impact on these companies' reputations, leading to declining sales. A significant number of New Zealand brands are manufactured overseas,[10] in places like China, Bangladesh, Vietnam and India, where the CSR concept is not widely recognised (Chapple and Moon, 2005). Therefore, it is recommended that New Zealand companies promote supplier-related CSR practices across their global supply chain.

Table 12.10   AHP weights and ranking of sub-criteria for CSR practices

| Criteria | Sub-criteria | Normalised pairwise matrix | | | |
		Local weights	Local rank	Global weights	Global rank
Employee CSR	EMP1	0.200	2	0.046	2
	EMP2	0.600	1	0.138	1
	EMP3	0.200	2	0.046	2
Customer CSR	CUS1	0.600	1	0.138	1
	CUS2	0.200	2	0.046	2
	CUS3	0.200	2	0.046	2
Supplier CSR	SUP1	0.333	1	0.026	4
	SUP2	0.333	1	0.026	4
	SUP3	0.333	1	0.026	4
Community CSR	COM1	0.250	1	0.058	3
	COM2	0.250	1	0.058	3
	COM3	0.250	1	0.058	3
	COM4	0.250	1	0.058	3
Environment CSR	ENV1	0.200	1	0.046	2
	ENV2	0.200	1	0.046	2
	ENV3	0.200	1	0.046	2
	ENV4	0.200	1	0.046	2
	ENV5	0.200	1	0.046	2

Note: In this table, Employee Wellbeing Policies (EMP1), Employee Health and Safety (EMP2) and Equal Employment Opportunities (EMP3) are sub-criteria of Employee CSR, whereas Product Quality Policies and Procedures (CUS1), CSR Best Practices Products (CUS2) and Disclosure of CSR-Related Product Features (CUS3) represent sub-criteria of Customer CSR. Supplier CSR sub-criteria include Encourage Suppliers for CSR (SUP1), Dealing with Responsible Supplier (SUP2) and Provide Assistance to Supplier for CSR Improvement (SUP3), while CSR Programmes for Local Communities (COM1), Engagement with Charity Organisations (COM2), Relationship with Indigenous Communities (COM3) and Monitoring Firm Activities Impact on Communities (COM4) reflect sub-criteria for Community CSR. Finally, Waste Reduction (ENV1), Effective Resources Management (ENV2), Obsolesce Avoidance (ENV3), Renewable Energy Usage (ENV4) and Emission Monitoring (ENV5) are sub-criteria of Environment CSR.

Community CSR and environment CSR both received equal but greater attention across all sub-criteria. Under community CSR, CSR programmes for local communities (COM1), engagement with charity organisations (COM2), relationship with indigenous communities (COM3) and monitoring the impact of firms' activities on communities (COM4) all received a score of 25 per cent. These results could be interpreted under the legislative structure of New Zealand (e.g., the Treaty of Waitangi), which encourages New Zealand businesses to maintain a good working relationship with indigenous communities. Under environmental CSR, the study found that waste reduction (ENV1), effective resources management (ENV2), obsolesce avoidance (ENV3), renewable energy usage (ENV4) and emissions monitoring (ENV5) received greater but equal (20 per cent) emphasis from firms' management. These major sub-criteria of environmental CSR are in line with Cowper-Smith and De Grosbois (2011) and Kuo et al. (2016), which found the same sub-criteria among deciding factors in shaping CSR adoption from an environmental standpoint. These results for community CSR and environmental CSR sub-criteria are consistent with Loosemore et al. (2018) and Dobbs and Van Staden (2016), who notes the significance of community and environmental CSR practices across New Zealand firms.

Global weights were obtained by multiplying the local weights of the sub-criteria (the third level in the hierarchy) with the weights of the main criteria (the second level in the hierarchy). They show that employee and customer CSR are the most preferred by NZX-listed companies – followed by community and environmental CSR, which were both equally weighted. Supplier CSR results are consistent with this research's earlier findings, which show supplier CSR to be the least preferred among NZX-listed firms.

In brief, the result of the study proposes that NZX managers need to define CSR strategies focusing on both implicit (employee) and explicit CSR (customer, supplier, community and environment) criteria, respectively. The supplier elements of CSR should be highlighted in setting firm strategies along with improvements of products and services.

Managerial Implications and Limitations and Policy Implications

The study is timely (especially after the NZX push for CSR) and novel in addressing CSR issues by adopting MCDM methods in the NZX context, where firms are struggling to have a formal CSR programme. The interview-based analysis reveals that in New Zealand companies use an inclusive approach and undertake different types of CSR practices, targeting a range of stakeholders (i.e., employees, customers, society, supplier and environment). These results debunk the myth surrounding CSR that generally companies focus on targeted stakeholders (internal CSR vs external CSR). The outcome of this research helps to identify and prioritise specific practices in CSR performance so that a firm can concentrate on developing those CSR practices pertaining to their own requirement. For example, the identified CSR initiatives as a result of the interviews with the NZX-listed "CSR champion" firms' senior leadership can be used as a benchmark for companies that are in the initial stages of CSR adoption or planning to incorporate CSR for compliance purposes. Further, the findings specifically illustrating the organisational preferences of the specific practices in CSR provide insight to the policymakers to develop policies accordingly. For instance, we found NZX-listed companies give little consideration to the supplier aspect of CSR. Such a lack of interest in supplier-related aspects raises significant concerns on companies' overall CSR claims, especially if they involve production and importing from countries that have a poor track record of CSR, particularly related to worker exploitation. We believe our findings are useful for stakeholders, especially those in charge of governance; i.e., directors, policymakers and stock exchanges, interested in promoting responsible business practices.

In addition to policy and practice, this research also contributes to CSR measurement literature. The majority of CSR studies have adopted a third-party rating to assess CSR performance, but this measurement approach suffers from validity and consistency issues (Visser et al., 2010; Zaman et al., 2022) and has received much academic criticism (Chatterji et al., 2015; Giannetti et al., 2015; Rahdari and Rostamy, 2015). This research adopted lived managerial perspective to evaluate CSR, contributing to CSR assessment calls (Pisani et al., 2017; Zaman et al., 2022; Zaman et al., 2021).

CONCLUSION

This study suggests a comprehensive and applicable MCDM model to help disentangle the issue of selection decisions of CSR schemes in the New Zealand context. The study focuses on interview data and executive surveys with NZX-listed firms' management. Initially, the senior executives of "CSR champion" firms were interviewed to explore the CSR initiatives that persist among "CSR champion" listed firms. The thematic analysis of interviewee results, using the stakeholder theory lens, identified the five dominant CSR criteria (i.e., employee CSR, customer CSR, supplier CSR, community CSR and environment CSR) and 18 CSR initiatives. Next, to determine the overall significance of the CSR criteria, we combined AHP weights with grey theory to apply a grey-AHP. The grey-AHP results indicated the current NZX-listed firms are performing moderate practices with respect to each CSR criterion (see Table 12.8). The current regulatory push (NZX CG 2017) is a timely effort to uplift the CSR practices of NZX-listed firms to conform with their counterparts.

Through this research, we have identified the CSR initiatives with an aim of developing a more robust, practical and flexible model for NZX-listed firms. In addition, we have prioritised the identified CSR programmes and practices through AHP application. The use of AHP helps to quantify the qualitative judgement and to eliminate unbalanced judgements and imprecision in the pairwise comparisons.

Our research demonstrates that NZX firms allocate higher weightings to employee CSR, customer CSR, community CSR and environmental CSR compared with supplier CSR. These findings provide additional and novel insights into the literature that only views environmental- and community-related CSR aspects dominant among New Zealand firms (Dobbs and Van Staden, 2016). To extend these findings, by using grey-AHP, we find that overall NZX-listed firms are performing moderate CSR initiatives on individual criteria. The grey-AHP results also confirm inefficient supplier CSR understanding among NZX-listed firms. Considering the strategic importance of supply chain management, CSR practices in the supply chain are crucial for increasing competitiveness and strengthening the chain itself. Discounting supplier-related CSR is dangerous and risks degrading firms' good corporate citizen image (Lee and Kim, 2009), destroying shareholder value and leading to customer boycotts (Lee and Kim, 2009). Therefore, it is recommended that management should integrate supplier-related CSR perspectives into corporate CSR management and strategies.

What is equally important, though, is that companies develop strategies to meet individual and societal needs, underpinned not by a "boiler-plate" approach that grudgingly acknowledges the principles of CSR, but based on a solid foundation of trust and belief in the mantra "We are all in this together."

NOTES

1. For more about the CSR guidelines on the ASX, BSE, NZX and SGX, please see ASX Corporate Governance Council (2014), Bombay Stock Exchange (2013), New Zealand Stock Exchange (2017) and Singapore Exchange Limited (2016).
2. For details, see: www.chapmantripp.com/publications/nzx-to-revise-corporate-governance -requirements.
3. For details, see: www.chapmantripp.com/publications/nzx-to-revise-corporate-governance -requirements.
4. To see SBN members, please visit: https://sustainable.org.nz/members/.
5. In purposive sampling, the participants and key informants are selected either by key characteristics, such as knowledge, skills and demographic (Jason and Glenwick, 2016) or other attributes, that are best suited to the study research questions for better understanding of the research phenomena (Parker and Northcott, 2016). We adopted purposive sampling as only a limited number of NZX-listed firms have a formal CSR programme (Dobbs and Van Staden, 2016).
6. The core assumption with this criterion was that appearing on the GRI database reflects a firm's commitment to CSR. The management in firms fulfilling this criterion is assumed to be more knowledgeable, skilful and well informed about practical aspects of CSR, and we designated those firms as CSR champions.
7. We designed an interview protocol to help the interviewers and to encourage participants to relax and talk freely. The interview protocol contained a welcome note, the interview purpose, the interview format and a set of interview questions, supported by additional questions to enable interviewers to delve deeper and explore sub-themes. We pre-tested the interview protocol with five respondents outside of our sample to ensure the sample's validity and reliability.
8. During the process, it was found that some NXZ listed companies have similar management structures, especially those in the financial industry. For instance, the NZ Bond Fund (NS) and NZ Top 10 Fund (NS) follow the same management structure (see www.nzx.com/markets/nzsx).
9. Saaty (2008) argues that the arithmetic mean is not appropriate, whereas various researchers, such as Aczél and Alsina (1987) and Saaty and Vargas (2012), have proven that geometric means satisfy this condition.
10. See the *NZ Herald* (2018), "Revealed: Where your favorite NZ brands are really made", www .nzherald.co.nz/business/news/article.cfm?c_id=3&objectid=12047848.

REFERENCES

Aczél, J., and Alsina, C. (1987). Synthesizing judgements: A functional equations approach. *Mathematical Modelling*, 9(3–5), 311–20. https://doi.org/10.1016/0270–0255(87)90487–8.

Adams, C., and Zutshi, A. (2004). Corporate social responsibility: Why business should act responsibly and be accountable. *Australian Accounting Review*, 14(34), 31–9. https://doi.org/10.1111/j .1835–2561.2004.tb00238.x.

Akman, E., and Dageviren, M. (2018). Discovering what makes a SME website good for international trade. *Technological and Economic Development of Economy*, 24(3), 1063–79. https://doi.org/10 .3846/20294913.2016.1266709.

ASX Corporate Governance Council (2014). *Corporate Governance Principles and Recommendations*. www.asx.com.au/documents/asx-compliance/cgc-principles-and-recommendations-3rd-edn.pdf.

Baumann-Pauly, D., Wickert, C., Spence, L.J., and Scherer, A.G. (2013). Organizing corporate social responsibility in small and large firms: Size matters. *Journal of Business Ethics*, 115(4), 693–705. https://doi.org/10.1007/s10551–013–1827–7.

Bazeley, P., and Jackson, K. (2013). *Qualitative Data Analysis with NVivo*. SAGE. https://au.sagepub
.com/en-gb/oce/qualitative-data-analysis-with-nvivo/book261349#description.

Bénabou, R., and Tirole, J. (2010). Individual and corporate social responsibility. *Economica*, *77*(305),
1–19.

Bennett, R. (1998). Corporate philanthropy in France, Germany and the UK: International comparisons
of commercial orientation towards company giving in European nations. *International Marketing
Review*, *15*(6), 458–75. https://doi.org/10.1108/02651339810244778.

Bhimani, A., and Soonawalla, K. (2005). From conformance to performance: The corporate responsibilities continuum. *Journal of Accounting and Public Policy*, *24*(3), 165–74. https://doi.org/10.1016/
j.jaccpubpol.2005.03.001.

Boesso, G., Kumar, K., and Michelon, G. (2013). Descriptive, instrumental and strategic approaches to
corporate social responsibility: Do they drive the financial performance of companies differently?
Accounting, Auditing & Accountability Journal, *26*(3), 399–422.

Bombay Stock Exchange (2013). *Regulatory Requirements*. www.bseindia.com/static/about/regulatory
_requirements.aspx?expandable=4.

Brammer, S., Millington, A., and Rayton, B. (2007). The contribution of corporate social responsibility
to organizational commitment. *International Journal of Human Resource Management*, *18*(10),
1701–19. https://doi.org/10.1080/09585190701570866.

Braun, V., and Clarke, V. (2006). Using thematic analysis in psychology. *Qualitative Research in
Psychology*, *3*(2), 77–101. https://doi.org/10.1191/1478088706qp063oa.

Carroll, A.B. (1979). A three-dimensional conceptual model of corporate performance. *Academy of
Management Review*, *4*(4), 497–505. https://doi.org/10.5465/amr.1979.4498296.

Carroll, A.B. (1991). The pyramid of corporate social responsibility: Toward the moral management of organizational stakeholders. *Business Horizons*, *34*(4), 39–48. https://doi.org/10.1016/
0007-6813(91)90005-G.

Chapple, W., and Moon, J. (2005). Corporate social responsibility (CSR) in Asia: A seven-country
study of CSR web site reporting. *Business & Society*, *44*(4), 415–41. https://doi.org/10.1177/
0007650305281658.

Chatterji, A.K., Durand, R., Levine, D.I., and Touboul, S. (2015). Do ratings of firms converge?
Implications for managers, investors and strategy researchers. *Strategic Management Journal*, *37*(8),
1597–1614.

Chen, C.-J., Guo, R.-S.A., Hsiao, Y.-C., and Chen, K.-L. (2016). Business strategies, corporate social (ir)
responsibility and firm performance. *Academy of Management Proceedings*. https://doi.org/10.5465/
AMBPP.2016.10423abstract.

Collins, E., Lawrence, S., Pavlovich, K., and Ryan, C. (2007). Business networks and the uptake of sustainability practices: The case of New Zealand. *Journal of Cleaner Production*, *15*(8), 729–40. https://
doi.org/10.1016/j.jclepro.2006.06.020.

Conner, K.R., and Prahalad, C.K. (1996). A resource-based theory of the firm: Knowledge versus opportunism. *Organization Science*, *7*(5), 477–501. https://doi.org/10.1287/orsc.7.5.477.

Connors, S., Anderson-MacDonald, S., and Thomson, M. (2017). Overcoming the "Window Dressing"
effect: Mitigating the negative effects of inherent skepticism towards corporate social responsibility.
Journal of Business Ethics, *145*(3), 599–621.

Cornelius, N., Todres, M., Janjuha-Jivraj, S., Woods, A., and Wallace, J. (2008). Corporate social
responsibility and the social enterprise. *Journal of Business Ethics*, *81*(2), 355–70. https://doi.org/10
.1007/s10551-007-9500-7.

Cowper-Smith, A., and De Grosbois, D. (2011). The adoption of corporate social responsibility practices in the airline industry. *Journal of Sustainable Tourism*, *19*(1), 59–77. https://doi.org/10.1080/
09669582.2010.498918.

Crossland, C., and Hambrick, D.C. (2007). How national systems differ in their constraints on corporate
executives: A study of CEO effects in three countries. *Strategic Management Journal*, *28*(8), 767–89.
https://doi.org/10.1002/smj.610.

Dattani, P., Still, A., and Pota, V. (2015). *Business Backs Education: Creating a Baseline for Corporate
CSR Spend on Global Education*. UNESCO. www.unesco.org/education/BBE-EPG-Report2015.pdf.

De Colle, S., Henriques, A., and Sarasvathy, S. (2014). The paradox of corporate social responsibility
standards. *Journal of Business Ethics*, *125*(2), 177–91.

Delbard, O. (2008). CSR legislation in France and the European regulatory paradox: An analysis of EU CSR policy and sustainability reporting practice. *Corporate Governance: The International Journal of Business in Society*, 8(4), 397–405. https://doi.org/10.1108/14720700810899149.

De Villiers, C., Farooq, M.B., and Molinari, M. (2021). Qualitative research interviews using online video technology–challenges and opportunities. *Meditari Accountancy Research*, ahead of print. https://doi.org/10.1108/MEDAR-03-2021-1252.

Dobbs, S., and Van Staden, C. (2016). Motivations for corporate social and environmental reporting: New Zealand evidence. *Sustainability Accounting, Management and Policy Journal*, 7(3), 449–72. https://doi.org/10.1108/SAMPJ-08-2015-0070.

Doś, A. (2017). Multi-criteria decision methods for CSR management: Literature review. *Managerial Economics*, 18(1), 63.

Farooq, M.B. (2018). A review of Gadamerian and Ricoeurian hermeneutics and its application to interpretive accounting research. *Qualitative Research in Organizations and Management*, 13(3), 261–83.

Farooq, M.B., and De Villiers, C. (2017). Telephonic qualitative research interviews: When to consider them and how to do them. *Meditari Accountancy Research*, 25(2), 291–316.

Farooq, M.B., and De Villiers, C. (2019). Understanding how managers institutionalise sustainability reporting: Evidence from Australia and New Zealand. *Accounting, Auditing & Accountability Journal*, 32(5), 1240–69.

Farooq, M., Zaman, R., and Nadeem, M. (2021a). AccountAbility's AA1000AP standard: A framework for integrating sustainability into organisations. *Sustainability Accounting, Management and Policy Journal*, 12(5), 1108–39. https://doi.org/10.1108/SAMPJ-05-2020-0166.

Farooq, M., Zaman, R., Sarraj, D., and Khalid, F. (2021b). Examining the extent of and drivers for materiality assessment disclosures in sustainability reports. *Sustainability Accounting, Management and Policy Journal*, 12(5), 965–1002.

Ganesan, S., George, M., Jap, S., Palmatier, R.W., and Weitz, B. (2009). Supply chain management and retailer performance: Emerging trends, issues, and implications for research and practice. *Journal of Retailing*, 85(1), 84–94. https://doi.org/10.1108/CG-08-2015-0109.

Garriga, E., and Melé, D. (2004). Corporate social responsibility theories: Mapping the territory. *Journal of Business Ethics*, 53(1), 51–71. https://doi.org/10.1023/B:BUSI.0000039399.90587.34.

Giannetti, B.F., Agostinho, F., Almeida, C.M.V.B., and Huisingh, D. (2015). A review of limitations of GDP and alternative indices to monitor human wellbeing and to manage eco-system functionality [Review]. *Journal of Cleaner Production*, 87(1), 11–25. https://doi.org/10.1016/j.jclepro.2014.10.051.

Gibbs, G. (2002). *Qualitative Data Analysis: Explorations with NVivo (Understanding Social Research)*. Open University Press.

Godfrey, P.C., Hatch, N.W., and Hansen, J.M. (2010). Toward a general theory of CSRs: The roles of beneficence, profitability, insurance, and industry heterogeneity. *Business & Society*, 49(2), 316–44.

Gupta, A., Briscoe, F., and Hambrick, D.C. (2017). Red, blue, and purple firms: Organizational political ideology and corporate social responsibility. *Strategic Management Journal*, 38(5), 1018–40.

Hawn, O., and Ioannou, I. (2016). Mind the gap: The interplay between external and internal actions in the case of corporate social responsibility. *Strategic Management Journal*, 37(13), 2569–88. https://doi.org/10.1002/smj.2464.

Hill, N., and Alexander, J. (2017). *The Handbook of Customer Satisfaction and Loyalty Measurement*. Routledge. https://doi.org/10.4324/9781315239279.

Ho, W., Xu, X., and Dey, P.K. (2010). Multi-criteria decision-making approaches for supplier evaluation and selection: A literature review. *European Journal of Operational Research*, 202(1), 16–24. https://doi.org/10.1016/j.ejor.2009.05.009.

Hossain, M.F., Adnan, Z.H., and Hasin, M. (2014). Improvement in weighting assignment process in analytic hierarchy process by introducing suggestion matrix and Likert scale. *International Journal of Supply Chain Management*, 3(4). http://citeseerx.ist.psu.edu/viewdoc/download?doi=10.1.1.666.252&rep=rep1&type=pdf.

Hou, J., and Reber, B.H. (2011). Dimensions of disclosures: Corporate social responsibility (CSR) reporting by media companies. *Public Relations Review*, 37(2), 166–8. http://dx.doi.org/10.1016/j.pubrev.2011.01.005.

Jackson, G., and Apostolakou, A. (2010). Corporate social responsibility in Western Europe: An institutional mirror or substitute? *Journal of Business Ethics*, *94*(3), 371–94. https://doi.org/10.1007/s10551-009-0269-8.

Jain, T., and Jamali, D. (2016). Looking inside the black box: The effect of corporate governance on corporate social responsibility. *Corporate Governance: An International Review*, *24*(3), 253–73. https://doi.org/10.1111/corg.12154.

Jain, T., and Zaman, R. (2020). When boards matter: The case of corporate social irresponsibility. *British Journal of Management*, *31*(2), 365–86.

Jason, L., and Glenwick, D.S. (2016). *Handbook of Methodological Approaches to Community-Based Research: Qualitative, Quantitative, and Mixed Methods*. Oxford University Press.

Kallas, Z. (2011). Butchers' preferences for rabbit meat: AHP pairwise comparisons versus a LIKERT Scale valuation. *Proceedings of the International Symposium on the Analytic Hierarchy Process for Multicriteria Decision-making*.

Karaman, A.S., and Akman, E. (2018). Taking-off corporate social responsibility programmes: An AHP application in airline industry. *Journal of Air Transport Management*, *68*, 187–97. https://doi.org/10.1016/j.jairtraman.2017.06.012.

Kloeten, N. (2014). Kiwis lag on corporate social responsibility. *Stuff*. www.stuff.co.nz/business/better-business/10513699/Kiwis-lag-on-corporate-social-responsibility.

KPMG (2013a). *The KPMG Survey of Corporate Responsibility Reporting 2013*. www.kpmg.com/Global/en/IssuesAndInsights/ArticlesPublications/corporateresponsibility/Documents/corporate-responsibility-reporting-survey-2013-execsummary.pdf.

KPMG (2013b). *Survey of Corporate Responsibility Reporting: New Zealand Supplement*. www.kpmg.com/NZ/en/IssuesAndInsights/ArticlesPublications/Documents/KPMG-Corporate-Responsibility-Survey-2013.pdf.

Kuo, T.C., Kremer, G.E.O., Phuong, N.T., and Hsu, C.-W. (2016). Motivations and barriers for corporate social responsibility reporting: Evidence from the airline industry. *Journal of Air Transport Management*, *57*, 184–95. https://doi.org/10.1016/j.jairtraman.2016.08.003.

Lawrence, S., Collins, E., Roper, J., and Haar, J. (2010). *Trends in NZ CSR Practices*. Waikato Management School.

Lee, K.-H., and Kim, J.-W. (2009). Current status of CSR in the realm of supply management: The case of the Korean electronics industry. *Supply Chain Management: An International Journal*, *14*(2), 138–48. https://doi.org/10.1108/13598540910942000.

Lindgreen, A., Swaen, V., and Maon, F. (2009). Introduction: Corporate social responsibility implementation. *Journal of Business Ethics*, *85*(2), 251–6. https://doi.org/10.1007/s10551-008-9732-1.

Liu, H.-C., Liu, L., Bian, Q.-H., Lin, Q.-L., Dong, N., and Xu, P.-C. (2011). Failure mode and effects analysis using fuzzy evidential reasoning approach and grey theory. *Expert Systems with Applications*, *38*(4), 4403–15.

Locke, R.M., and Romis, M. (2007). Improving work conditions in a global supply chain. *MIT Sloan Management Review*, *48*(2), 54. https://sloanreview.mit.edu/article/improving-work-conditions-in-a-global-supply-chain/.

Loosemore, M., Lim, B.T.H., Ling, F.Y.Y., and Zeng, H.Y. (2018). A comparison of corporate social responsibility practices in the Singapore, Australia and New Zealand construction industries. *Journal of Cleaner Production*, *190*, 149–59. https://doi.org/10.1016/j.jclepro.2018.04.157.

Luo, X., and Bhattacharya, C.B. (2006). Corporate social responsibility, customer satisfaction, and market value. *Journal of Marketing*, *70*(4), 1–18.

Lyon, T.P., and Montgomery, A.W. (2015). The means and end of greenwash. *Organization & Environment*, *28*(2), 223–49. https://doi.org/10.1177/1086026615575332.

Maignan, I., and Ralston, D.A. (2002). Corporate social responsibility in Europe and the US: Insights from businesses' self-presentations. *Journal of International Business Studies*, *33*(3), 497–514. https://doi.org/10.1057/palgrave.jibs.8491028.

Malik, M. (2015). Value-enhancing capabilities of CSR: A brief review of contemporary literature. *Journal of Business Ethics*, *127*(2), 419–38.

Malshe, A., and Agarwal, M.K. (2015). From finance to marketing: The impact of financial leverage on customer satisfaction. *Journal of Marketing*, *79*(5), 21–38. https://doi.org/10.1509/jm.13.0312.

Mardani, A., Jusoh, A., Md Nor, K., Khalifah, Z., Zakwan, N., and Valipour, A. (2015). Multiple criteria decision-making techniques and their applications: A review of the literature from 2000 to 2014. *Economic Research-Ekonomska Istraživanja*, *28*(1), 516–71.

Martínez-Ferrero, J., Gallego-Álvarez, I., and García-Sánchez, I.M. (2015). A bidirectional analysis between earnings management and corporate social responsibility: The moderating effect of stakeholder and investor protection. *Australian Accounting Review*, *25*(4), 359–71. https://doi.org/doi:10.1111/auar.12075.

Mathivathanan, D., Govindan, K., and Haq, A.N. (2017). Exploring the impact of dynamic capabilities on sustainable supply chain firm's performance using grey-analytical hierarchy process. *Journal of Cleaner Production*, *147*, 637–53.

Matten, D., and Moon, J. (2008). "Implicit" and "explicit" CSR: A conceptual framework for a comparative understanding of corporate social responsibility. *Academy of Management Review*, *33*(2), 404–24. https://doi.org/10.5465/amr.2008.31193458.

Montero, M.J., Araque, R.A., and Rey, J.M. (2009). Occupational health and safety in the framework of corporate social responsibility. *Safety Science*, *47*(10), 1440–1445. https://doi.org/10.1016/j.ssci.2009.03.002.

New Zealand Stock Exchange (NZX) (2017). *NZX Corporate Governance Code*. www.nzx.com/files/attachments/257864.pdf.

Parker, L.D., and Northcott, D. (2016). Qualitative generalising in accounting research: Concepts and strategies. *Accounting, Auditing & Accountability Journal*, *29*(6), 1100–1131. https://doi.org/10.1108/AAAJ-04-2015-2026.

Pisani, N., Kourula, A., Kolk, A., and Meijer, R. (2017). How global is international CSR research? Insights and recommendations from a systematic review. *Journal of World Business*, *52*(5), 591–614. https://doi.org/10.1016/j.jwb.2017.05.003.

Porter, M.E., and Kramer, M.R. (2002). The competitive advantage of corporate philanthropy. *Harvard Business Review*, *80*(12), 56–68.

Rahdari, A.H., and Rostamy, A.A.A. (2015). Designing a general set of sustainability indicators at the corporate level. *Journal of Cleaner Production*, *108*, 757–71. https://doi.org/10.1016/j.jclepro.2015.05.108.

Robertson, W. (1993). New Zealand's new legislation for sustainable resource management: The Resource Management Act 1991. *Land Use Policy*, *10*(4), 303–11. https://doi.org/10.1016/0264-8377(93)90040-H.

Saaty, R.W. (1987). The analytic hierarchy process: What it is and how it is used. *Mathematical Modelling*, *9*, 161–76. https://doi.org/10.1016/0270-0255(87)90473-8.

Saaty, T.L. (1980). *The Analytical Hierarchy Process: Planning, Priority Setting, Resource Allocation*. McGraw-Hill.

Saaty, T.L. (2003). Decision-making with the AHP: Why is the principal eigenvector necessary. *European Journal of Operational Research*, *145*(1), 85–91. https://doi.org/10.1016/S0377-2217(02)00227-8.

Saaty, T.L. (2008). Decision-making with the analytic hierarchy process. *International Journal of Services Sciences*, *1*(1), 83–98. https://doi.org/10.1504/IJSSCI.2008.017590.

Saaty, T.L., and Vargas, L.G. (2012). *Models, Methods, Concepts & Applications of the Analytic Hierarchy Process* (Vol. 175). Springer Science & Business Media. https://doi.org/10.1007/978-1-4614-3597-6.

Schembera, S. (2018). Implementing corporate social responsibility: Empirical insights on the impact of the UN Global Compact on its business participants. *Business & Society*, *57*(5), 783–825. https://doi.org/10.1177/0007650316635579.

Schühly, A., and Tenzer, H. (2017). A multidimensional approach to international market selection and nation branding in sub-Saharan Africa. *Africa Journal of Management*, *3*(3–4), 236–79. https://doi.org/10.1080/23322373.2017.1375812.

Shen, J., and Jiuhua Zhu, C. (2011). Effects of socially responsible human resource management on employee organizational commitment. *International Journal of Human Resource Management*, *22*(15), 3020–3035. https://doi.org/10.1080/09585192.2011.599951.

Singapore Exchange Limited (2016). *SGX-ST Listing Rules, Practice Note 7.6*. http://rulebook.sgx.com/net_file_store/new_rulebooks/s/g/SGX_Mainboard_Practice_Note_7.6_July_20_2016.pdf.

Turker, D. (2009). Measuring corporate social responsibility: A scale development study. *Journal of Business Ethics*, *85*(4), 411–27. https://doi.org/10.1007/s10551–008–9780–6.

Visser, W., Matten, D., Pohl, M., and Tolhurst, N. (2010). *The A to Z of Corporate Social Responsibility*. John Wiley & Sons.

Voegtlin, C., and Pless, N.M. (2014). Global governance: CSR and the role of the UN Global Compact. *Journal of Business Ethics*, *122*(2), 179–91. https://doi.org/10.1007/s10551–014–2214–8.

Wang, Q., Dou, J., and Jia, S. (2016). A meta-analytic review of corporate social responsibility and corporate financial performance: The moderating effect of contextual factors. *Business & Society*, *55*(8), 1083–121.

Wells, P., Ingley, C., and Mueller, J. (2014). New Zealand corporate sustainability/CSR and the influence of the independent director: "100% Pure" New Zealand. 10th European Conference on Management, Leadership & Governance, Zagreb, Croatia, 12–14 November.

Wickert, C., and De Bakker, F.G. (2015). Managerial struggles during practice implementation: The case of corporate social responsibility. *Academy of Management Proceedings*, *1*. https://doi.org/10.5465/ambpp.2015.62.

Yuan, W., Bao, Y., and Verbeke, A. (2011). Integrating CSR initiatives in business: An organizing framework. *Journal of Business Ethics*, *101*(1), 75–92. https://doi.org/10.1007/s10551–010–0710-z.

Zaman, R., Farooq, M., Khalid, F., and Mahmood, Z. (2021). Examining the extent of and determinants for sustainability assurance quality: The role of audit committees. *Business Strategy and the Environment*, *30*(7), 2887–906.

Zaman, R., Jain, T., Samara, G., and Jamali, D. (2022). Corporate governance meets corporate social responsibility: Mapping the interface. *Business & Society*, *61*(3), 690–752.

Zhou, L., and Xu, S. (2006). Application of grey clustering method in eutrophication assessment of wetland. *Journal of American Science*, *2*(4), 52–7.

13. Do corporate governance codes matter in Africa?

Geofry Areneke, Wafa Khlif, Danson Kimani and Teerooven Soobaroyen

1. INTRODUCTION

'No matter how long a log stays in water, it cannot become a crocodile' (African proverb)

The study of corporate governance (CG) practices continues to attract interest globally, and in the context of emerging and developing countries. In particular, the past two decades have witnessed a notable number of African countries introducing CG codes, ostensibly with a view to enhance the efficiency of their corporate (and state-owned enterprise) sectors, improve private inward investment attractiveness, systematise board processes and decision-making, and eventually help support effective socio-economic development (ACCA, 2017; Nakpodia et al., 2018). South Africa, which is widely viewed as a forerunner of CG reforms in Africa with its emphasis on stakeholder models, also introduced the King Reports (for the first time in 2002) to replace the previous King I Report of 1994. Global policy makers and international institutions (e.g., the World Bank, or WB; International Monetary Fund, or IMF; European Union, or EU; Financial Stability Board), aided by pan-African institutions (African Union, or AU; Pan-African Federation of Accountants; Good Governance Institute; African Development Bank, or AfDB) had anticipated that the implementation of 'international' best practices would help the continent to overcome its traditional lacklustre image from the perspective of foreign investors and multinationals, while fostering change and improved decision-making processes at the board level and underpinning relationships between boards and ultimate owners. Very recent initiatives at the AU[1] suggest a realisation that an African set of principles and guidelines would be more appropriate. At the same time, sustainability and other transparency initiatives (e.g., corporate social responsibility, Sustainable Development Goals, integrated thinking/reporting, climate change disclosure, ethics of the supply chain) have become weaved in with CG code reforms, leading to renewed expectations and pressures on boards and directors (Ntim and Soobaroyen, 2013; Sorour et al., 2020; Wang et al., 2020).

From a functionalist perspective, CG codes are intended to, inter alia, strengthen good/best practices/processes within the board of directors, promote corporate accountability and transparency, safeguard shareholders' rights and mitigate corporate failures. Since the enactment of these codes, a number of academic studies have been published in the African context to examine the role and/or effectiveness of CG codes. However, amidst changing economic environments, and social and political upheavals, there seems to be limited as well as mixed evidence in support of CG codes (e.g., Samaha et al., 2012; Tshipa et al., 2018). CG and board practices, borne out of these codes, remain often weak or inefficient (Nakpodia et al., 2018) and do not appear to deliver the expected benefits outlined earlier. There have also been a number of costly corporate failures attributed to poor governance, including in contexts where a CG code had been implemented and/or enforced (Kimani et al., 2020; Nweke et al., 2020).

Deeper insights into the reasons for such failures or weaknesses, typically from an interpretive perspective, point to a lack of a 'fit' between the provisions of CG codes and the contextual reality of some of the African countries (Wanyama et al., 2013), reflected for instance in terms of how boards and directors reach decisions. The continent encompasses different, and somewhat idiosyncratic, regional, cultural and/or political settings; e.g., North Africa, sub-Saharan Africa, colonial heritage, ownership structures, different stages of economic and stock market development, languages, post-colonial influence (e.g., Britain, France, Belgium and Portugal) and other religious/cultural affiliations (e.g., Islamic traditions; Farah et al., 2021). Some scholars (e.g., Wanyama et al., 2009) suggest that African countries may have hastily adopted CG codes as a means to obtain financial aid from international donors or attract foreign investors to fill severe capital shortages locally, without a genuine intention (including by companies) to live up to the spirit of the CG codes. This view chimes with international cross-country studies of CG code adoption (e.g., Aguilera and Cuervo-Cazurra, 2004, 2009) which suggest that country-level adoption is not only motivated by an effectiveness motive but also by a legitimation motive. Yet very few (if any) African countries were included in prior cross-country studies of CG codes since their level of adoption at the time was quite low (Haxhi and Van Ees, 2010). A more recent review (Cuomo et al., 2016) highlights a marked increase in adoption by developing/emerging economies, albeit that it does not focus on the specific case of African countries.

Other observers, mainly from a critical standpoint, argue that it is unreasonable to expect CG codes to have an impact on CG practices in contextual environments that can otherwise be characterised by weak legal enforcement and regulatory systems (Uddin et al., 2017; Ahmed and Uddin, 2018). Relatedly, some provisions of CG codes borrowed from Western countries seem unable to address various CG challenges, such as the abuse of minority investors' rights (Okpara, 2011), board and executive malpractices (Adegbite et al., 2012) and firm–stakeholders conflicts (Wanyama et al., 2013). Furthermore, actual corporate board practices and decision-making processes, which may for example reflect local ties bound by family, politics, ethnicity/nationalities or colonial heritage, tend to diverge from those stipulated in mainstream CG codes. For example, notions of 'board accountability', 'board oversight', 'independent non-executive directors', 'independent chair' and 'balanced board' often collide with established leadership styles; historical decision-making habits; informality of processes; and personal relationships between shareholders, business partners, political elites and/or family members (Areneke and Kimani, 2019). Transparency and disclosure requirements (a key facet of CG codes) may be shunned due to the impact such information could have on existing ties (Samaha et al., 2012) or are selectively implemented to provide a modicum of legitimacy (Aguilera and Cuervo-Cazurra, 2004) to international market-led audiences (e.g., improving CG indicators; scorecard assessments). At the same time, CG codes themselves become the subject of a process of local change, 'capture' and/or adaptation. Even an appreciation of which African countries have adopted (and on what basis) a CG code is unclear, save for a report by the Association of Chartered Certified Accountants (ACCA, 2017).[2]

After nearly two decades of multiple experiences with the CG codes, in particular for some of the major African economies and a number of academic studies, we therefore raise the following questions: to what extent have these codes made a difference in Africa? If so, how? And if not so, why is this the case and which alternatives may need to be considered, alongside any need for further research – including for board decision-making and processes? Consequently, this chapter seeks to contribute to the debate on the relevance of mainstream CG codes in the African context by:

(a) Identifying the different CG codes adopted in Africa (up to and including 2020) and analysing their evolution (or lack thereof) in relation to different country-level characteristics aspects (origin, content, scope, political systems and stock market development).
(b) Reviewing the academic literature to assess to what extent (if at all) CG codes in African settings have had an influence on corporate outcomes (e.g., performance, disclosure, market liquidity, shareholder rights, sustainability performance, board processes/decision-making), with due consideration of the theoretical underpinnings, empirical approaches and key findings.
(c) Documenting how local CG codes have developed in selected African countries (e.g., Kenya, Nigeria, South Africa and Tunisia), with a view to highlight some of the specific factors/forces behind adoption/implementation.

In addressing the above questions and objectives, the authors draw upon a desk-based research of applicable CG codes and academic/professional articles, supported by their own empirical forays in selected African countries. The next section reviews the state of CG codes in Africa, followed by a review of prior studies and an assessment of the factors underpinning the adoption of CG codes in four selected countries. We conclude with a discussion of these existing insights, the relevance of CG codes in Africa and implications for further research in the field.

2. CORPORATE GOVERNANCE CODES IN AFRICA: EVOLUTION AND CURRENT STATUS

We carry out a documentary review to assess which African countries have issued one or more CG codes in relation to private sector companies (including banks). Since the European Corporate Governance Institute (ECGI) website is often highlighted in the literature as providing a detailed record of applicable codes worldwide (Enrione et al., 2006; Haxhi and Van Ees, 2010; Nordberg, 2020), this was our starting point to survey codes pertaining to African jurisdictions. However, it became apparent that existing codes for some of the African countries were not available on the ECGI website. We therefore extended our search to a range of other authoritative sources (e.g., the WB's *World Development Indicators*, Reports on Observance of Standards and Codes (ROSC), African Development Bank publications), a recent report by the Association of Chartered Certified Accountants (ACCA, 2017) and the worldwide survey by Cuomo et al. (2016). Finally, we reviewed the academic literature (including Francophone articles) to identify any reference to codes of CG in the African context, typically as part of country studies.

This combined search and review process enabled us to identify that 24 African countries (out of 55 recognised states) have one or more existing CG codes (refer to the Appendix). A further two countries, São Tomé and Principe and Lesotho, appear to have respectively a code issued for banks (which could not be sourced) and a soon-to-be-issued code for companies/public interest entities. Furthermore, most of the Francophone African countries incorporate CG code-related clauses in company, banking and/or commercial laws. In particular, l'Organisation pour l'Harmonisation en Afrique du Droit des Affaires[3] (OHADA), through an

Acte Uniforme Révisé relatif au Droit des Sociétés Commerciales et du Groupement d'Intérêt Economique,[4] has sought to establish a common set of legal provisions relative to companies. In its most recent version (2014), the Acte Uniforme refers to some rules on board composition and structure (e.g., board size, audit committee) for listed companies but it does not prescribe detailed provisions one would usually find in mainstream CG codes. Finally, the West African Economic and Monetary Union,[5] consisting of eight (mainly French-speaking) West African countries, has issued a stand-alone CG code applicable to banks and financial institutions (2017) operating in these countries.

What is first noted from the list is that early adopters on the continent (i.e., up to and including 2005) – namely Egypt, Ghana, Kenya, Malawi, Mauritius, Nigeria, Uganda, Tanzania, Zambia, alongside pioneering South Africa – are either the continent's largest or more active economies. These countries may be viewed as part of the diffusion stage associated with the rapid institutionalisation of codes of governance worldwide (Aguilera and Cuervo-Cazurra, 2004, 2009; Enrione et al., 2006; Wanyama et al., 2009). In an empirical study of the cultural factors underpinning the adoption of CG codes in 67 countries, Haxhi and Van Ees (2010) found that a (national) individualist culture was associated with the adoption of a CG code. Furthermore, for countries indicative of a high receptivity to power differences (i.e., high power distance), government, directors' or professional associations tend to be spearheading the adoption of a code while the stock exchange authority and/or other investor-led groups are at the forefront in the case of lower-distance countries. Given the very few African countries included in previous empirical studies (Kenya, South Africa and Nigeria), and arguably the limitation of relying on narrow conceptions of national culture, it is rather difficult to extend these insights to the African continent. From the above-mentioned 10 African countries, a stock exchange or capital market authority developed the code in six instances. One country constituted a joint government–private sector committee to formulate the code, while three countries relied on their local institute of directors. Hence, it would be fair to conclude that the 'hand of the state' is more than often involved (directly or indirectly) in such initiatives. More pertinently the role of transnational institutions (Aguilera and Cuervo-Cazurra, 2009), such as the WB, IMF and Organisation for Economic Cooperation and Development (OECD), has been central in bringing about reforms in many developing countries (e.g., Wanyama et al., 2009; Samaha et al., 2012; Hopper et al., 2017). These efforts were partly a response to the 1997 Asian Financial Crisis, whose consequences affected many developing countries and led to calls for 'global financial stability' (Financial Stability Forum, thereafter Financial Stability Board[6]), leading to the 1999 OECD principles of CG being heavily promoted (Aguilera and Cuervo-Cazurra, 2009) worldwide. The ROSC scheme, jointly managed by the WB and IMF's Financial Sector Assessment Programme (FSAP),[7] was the equivalent of a detailed audit of a country's financial system. It set the scene for multiple recommendations and reforms in the corporate, stock market and financial sectors (e.g., accounting, auditing, company law and CG) of developing countries, ostensibly with a view to 'modernise' the oversight and enforcement regimes. The institutionalisation of the mainstream CG principles can be evidenced by the adoption of the 'comply or explain' regime[8] in seven of the 10 countries, albeit that the 'half-way house' discourse it reflected led to mixed messages with boards, directors and companies in both civil and common law countries (e.g., Soobaroyen and Mahadeo, 2008; Asplund, 2021; Farah et al., 2021). In particular, it is argued that the 'comply' term may have led to minimal implementation of CG regulations and narrow-minded 'box-ticking' behaviour among companies, while the statements to 'explain' were either poor-quality or non-existent explanations. In contrast, Ghana, Egypt and Nigeria articulated a rather more 'voluntary' approach for their codes.

Secondly, signs of the accelerated diffusion of CG codes in Africa are visible within the next decade (2006 to 2015) with 13 countries issuing a code, albeit with some notable commonalities and variations. Firstly, there appears to be a mimetic behaviour at play within the North African countries since Algeria, Libya, Morocco and Tunisia all implemented a code by 2010. At the same time, variations emerge, with Libya only mandating (on a 'comply' basis) a code for banks (2007 and revised 2010), Algeria[9] and Tunisia issuing one on a voluntary basis for companies, and Morocco a 'comply or explain' version. Secondly, a group of countries, associated with the SADC (South African Development Community) region (Botswana, Mozambique, Namibia and Zimbabwe) introduced a CG code that is closely aligned to the South African code (including an 'apply or explain'[10] regime).[11] Thirdly, further variations exist across other regions, with Rwanda implementing a voluntary code for all companies while South Sudan and Liberia (for banks) mandate full compliance. Distinctively, Senegal is the only Francophone West African country that has an 'apply or explain' code in addition to the legal implications set out in the OHADA law. The 'comply or explain' regime is noted only in the case of Ethiopia, and reflective of the shifting opinions away from this approach. Fourthly, from these 13 cases, there is more pluralism in terms of the issuing or 'championing' authorities, classified in terms of stock exchange/capital market authorities (two), central banks (two), government ministry (one), institute of directors (three), and national 'purpose-built' institutions or committees (five). The preponderance of the latter suggests a different strategy of seeking consensus and building on normative/mimetic circuits to design and implement a CG code. Lastly, beyond 2015, there is little evidence of a continued trend in first-time adoption on the continent. Sierra Leone adopted a 'comply or explain' code in 2018 which was issued by a corporate regulator. Lesotho's Institute of Directors appears to be completing the development of its code, following financial support from the AfDB, but it has yet to be made public.[12]

Thirdly, 11 African countries have also gone through the process of revising their codes. In particular, Egypt and South Africa have made multiple revisions. The application regime has also shifted for some countries, towards a 'comply or explain' approach (Egypt, Rwanda), while the 'apply or explain' regime became slightly more widespread (Kenya, Mauritius and Nigeria). Conversely, some of the original adopters have not considered any change over the best part of 15 to 20 years (Tanzania, Zambia). Furthermore, while Ghana and Tunisia did revise their code, the application regime has remained the same (voluntary) and somewhat at odds with the approaches adopted by their neighbouring countries.

Fourthly, given the small number of observations, it is somewhat challenging to consider elaborate statistical analyses such as those performed by studies examining the spread of codes on a worldwide basis (e.g., Aguilera and Cuervo-Cazurra, 2004; Haxhi and Van Ees, 2010), and its relationship to national variables. Notwithstanding, it is noted that the average Democracy Index (compiled by the Economist Intelligence Unit) for the 24 adopting countries is 5.11 over 10, with 14 countries classified as either a hybrid regime, flawed or full democracy. Contrastingly, the average index for non-adopting countries (data available for 25 countries) was 3.5, with most countries (20) classified as authoritarian regimes (Economist Intelligence Unit, 2020). Hence, there seems to be a concurrence between democracy-based indicators and the decision to adopt a CG code. Furthermore, as already highlighted in the literature (Zattoni and Cuomo, 2008), common law countries tend to be more able to adopt and incorporate subtler notions of guidelines and codes (soft law) relative to civil law countries. However, exceptions have been noted in our sample; i.e., Senegal, Rwanda and Tunisia. One can also observe that countries with a sizable stock market (market capitalisation as a percentage of GDP) have adopted a code. Lastly, when it comes to ownership, it is well established that the majority of African businesses tend to have a concentrated ownership structure involving either large private (e.g., family, block ownership) or state shareholders, with key implications for minority shareholders, board composition, decision-making and processes, and stakeholders. Hence, the intentions of a mainstream code may not easily be transposed to such settings.

In conclusion, while we note the diffusion of CG codes has reached just under half of African countries (43 per cent) over a 20-year period, there are notable variations in terms of the application regime, issuing entity, extent of revision/reform and scope of the codes. These findings extend the reports by the ACCA (2017) and Cuomo et al. (2016) in identifying more code-adopting African countries. A further point to consider is the extent to which there is actual 'activity' and 'engagement' in the field (e.g., review of board composition, setting up board committees, adoption of director training, evaluation and assessments by boards) and consequences of their application for companies and stakeholders more widely. One wonders whether the adoption of the code is primarily an end in itself or whether it is a means by which change (e.g., at board decision-making level) can happen, bringing us to a review of the evidence on the consequences/implications of the code.

3.   REVIEW OF (EMPIRICAL) STUDIES ON THE CG CODE IN AFRICA

We have extracted 40 articles from 2000 to 2020 on the EBSCO and SCOPUS databases by relying on these three keywords: 'codes', 'corporate governance', 'Africa'. We have also accessed five edited book chapters related to these keywords. Finally, we sought French-language articles from the CAIRN and HAL databases.

Firstly, a descriptive observation relates to the adopted perspectives on CG codes and the extent to which these perspectives have been explored in scholarly work. The articles reflect three main perspectives underpinning a discussion of the CG code: (1) the links between business and society (12 articles in four journals), (2) the legal perspective (three articles in three journals) and (3) the consequences of the codes in general, albeit mainly from an accounting and finance perspective (25 articles in 18 journals). There are two main periods of publication during 2011–2012 (six articles) and 2019–2020 (seven articles). Otherwise, articles are scattered over the entire studied period with one or two articles per year. In general, articles either adopt a normative approach or seek to validate agency or institutional theory-led theories. South Africa, Nigeria and Kenya are the three most researched contexts. Finally, virtually all the articles are published in English. We briefly review the three key above-mentioned themes.

3.1   Links Between Business and Society (12 Articles in Four Journals)

Most of the articles in this theme approach the national codes of CG in terms of their relationship with ethics in general and business ethics in particular (e.g., Rossouw, 2005, 2019). The potential for codes to act as a mechanism of 'sensitisation' or awareness to signal (and address) concerns about the role and (often deleterious) impact of business on society has been at the core of such discussions. This is notable in the case of South Africa, where about half of the articles focus on the case of the King Report, in terms of studying its evolution over the years; e.g., the gradual integration of ethical requirements and of 'stakeholder inclusivity' in board deliberations (Rossouw, 2019; Van der Merwe, 2020). Some of the findings show how initiatives (e.g., code of ethics) become more meaningful if they can be related to the corporation's corporate social responsibility (CSR) initiatives (Painter-Morland, 2006), reporting practices or shareholders' activism (Amao and Amaeshi, 2008). Other authors look at the fit of the codes in comparison with the 'inspiring' Western models. For example, on one hand, Andreasson (2011) considered the emergence of an 'African' model of CG, and the role of international and domestic factors in shaping South Africa's ongoing reform process. On the other hand, Nakpodia et al. (2018) suggest the need for an integrated system that combines elements of both rule- and principle-based regulation, supported by a multi-stakeholder co-regulation strategy.

Finally, only one article looks at the level of corporate engagement with the code's requirements, including CSR initiatives. Mahadeo and Soobaroyen (2016) found that in Mauritius, the level of engagement is high in the first year of enactment and starts to level off over the years. The authors contend that companies 'appear to have appreciated and rationalized the extent to which implementation would be sufficiently "acceptable" to their constituents' (p. 767). The articles in this section tend to draw on institutional theory as a theoretical perspective to recognise the various pressures that are at play.

3.2 Legal Perspective (Three Articles in Three Journals)

The literature from the legal perspective tends to adopt a normative perspective and argues that to improve CG practices within sub-Saharan African firms, efforts need to be targeted at the board of directors as the foremost CG actors within firms (Kiggundu and Havenga, 2004). Scholars who study CG codes from the legal perspective are mainly engaged in deliberations as to whether a 'hard' law regime presents a more appropriate foundation for the implementation of national CG codes, compared with a 'soft' law approach or even a mixture of both approaches. This is also highlighted by Farah et al. (2021) in a review of CG studies in the Middle East and North Africa (MENA). Those who argue in favour of a hard law regime posit that it is almost impossible for firms located in countries with weak legal environments to adopt appropriate CG practices without the ability of government and regulators to sanction and/or prosecute wrongdoing by non-complying boards and/or firm executives. For instance, Croucher and Miles (2010) propose the enactment of an active enforcement of CG standards as an ideal way to improve CG practices in South African firms, arguing that other approaches, such as the use of a soft law, are unlikely to improve the situation. The authors, however, focus only on the provisions relating to a board's responsibility towards employees in their analysis. This makes it difficult to appreciate whether the directors' mandate to shareholders and lenders should be governed through hard law or soft law, or a combination of both. In a similar vein, Nakpodia et al. (2018) reviewed evidence from Nigeria and argued in favour of a CG regime that is gradual in nature, progressing from a rules-based approach that integrates aspects of soft regulation and hard law. These observations illustrate the mixed views about how national CG codes could be operationalised and enforced. We also argue that the enforceability of CG codes implemented in many African countries relies on several factors, such as safeguarding shareholders' rights, board conduct/process and quality of board decision-making; aspects that have been far less researched on the continent.

3.3   Accounting and Finance Perspective (25 Articles in 18 Journals)

The majority of the reviewed studies on CG codes in Africa have been published in accounting and finance outlets. This research tends to assume two broad dimensions. Firstly, some authors examine the impact of adopting national codes of CG practices on various firm performance metrics. Such metrics include return on corporate investments, share price movements, cost of capital and ability to secure affordable capital/leverage (e.g., see Waweru, 2014). Scholars who focus on the performance-related metrics have assumed a predominantly shareholder-centric viewpoint, with many such studies utilising agency theory as the tool of analysis as well as being grounded in the quantitative tradition (e.g., Munisi and Randøy, 2013; Ntim, 2013; Waweru, 2014).

Secondly, the other significant strand of literature within the accounting and finance domain focuses on the influence of national CG codes on various governance outcomes, including board and director accountability, firm transparency and disclosure (Okike, 2007; Mahadeo and Soobaroyen, 2016). Researchers set out to analyse how embedding CG provisions can enable firms to identify and recruit appropriate board talent, and navigate through crises and/or complex business environments, as well as building mutually beneficial relations with important stakeholder constituencies, including shareholders and other resource providers (see, for instance, Adegbite and Nakajima, 2012; Adegbite, 2015; Kimani et al., 2020). Noticeably, this strand of research moves beyond agency theory to draw on diverse theoretical frameworks, such as institutional theory, legitimacy theory, and other 'social' theories (Wanyama et al., 2009; Soobaroyen and Ntim, 2013; Kimani, 2016; Uche et al., 2016). Efforts by these mainly qualitatively driven studies have been instrumental in understanding issues that impede the efficacy of CG codes adopted in various African countries. For example, Mahadeo and Soobaroyen (2016) highlight how companies in Mauritius respond to the requirements of the CG code, adopting aspects that appear to be beneficial to the small and local business elite, that are fairly uncontroversial (e.g., independent directors) and that signal good societal intentions/ contributions. However, aspects that are more contentious – e.g., disclosure of executive compensation, nomination and appointment policies, related party disclosures – are ignored for fear of upsetting local perceptions. Nakpodia and Adegbite (2018) also report that the boards of many Nigerian firms, despite consisting of a majority of non-executive directors, fail to enact effective boardroom practices. One key reason is that the majority of outside directors hail from social elites (e.g., politicians and military officials) who are themselves known to be involved in unethical/corrupt practices and/or tend to disregard capital market regulations with impunity. Furthermore, Kimani et al. (2020) find that the adoption of a CG code in Kenya has hardly improved board processes, since the work of non-executive directors and accounting and auditing professionals is constrained by a powerful neo-patrimonial culture involving patronage and informal relations. In such cases, accountability towards shareholders and other firm stakeholders is superseded by loyalty towards relatives and/or friends. These examples illustrate cases of companies showing 'apparent' and symbolic compliance with CG codes, such as appointing independent directors or employing qualified accounting/auditing professionals. However, the actions of these CG actors remain constrained by local factors, thus leading to CG outcomes that are either limited in scope/impact or diverging from the intended objectives of developing/adopting national codes of CG practices. A deeper appreciation of these local factors can be developed by considering some country case studies.

4. CASE STUDIES: KENYA, SOUTH AFRICA, NIGERIA, AND TUNISIA

Mindful of the rather limited work on the role of CG codes in Africa and the influence of various political, cultural and social factors, we draw on the following case studies to deepen our understanding of the circumstances leading to the development (and reforms, where relevant) of the code in Kenya, South Africa, Nigeria and Tunisia.

4.1 Kenya: The Long (Neo-Liberal) March Towards a Code

The development of a CG code in Kenya can be seen as part of the initial ground-breaking efforts to implement neo-liberal development policies imposed by international institutions, which was subsequently promoted as part of the UK Commonwealth initiatives and rationalised on the basis of local corporate failures. The events, which culminated in the development of an official CG code, began in the mid-1980s, when Kenya approached the IMF and the WB for financial assistance to address the fiscal challenges the country was experiencing. The financial assistance provided to Kenya was linked to a raft of reforms that were intended to 'correct' Kenya's previous economic policies, thought to have contributed to the fiscal difficulties (Were et al., 2006). These reforms included privatisation of several non-strategic state-owned companies, which were identified as significant sources of government fiscal haemorrhaging (Mwega, 2006; Mwaura, 2007). Other than addressing the issue of inefficient state-owned enterprises (SOEs) draining public resources (Were et al., 2006) and advancing the case for neoliberalism (Levi-Faur, 2005), the privatisation process was also aimed at raising capital for the Kenyan government (Rono, 2002).

The next step involved the creation of a stock exchange market where shares for the privatised state-owned companies are traded, as well as a corporate sector regulatory framework to promote effective management of the listed firms and safeguard shareholders' rights. This second phase of the economic reforms saw the involvement of several other international institutions, including the International Finance Corporation (IFC) and United States Agency for International Development (USAID). The agencies' financial and technical assistance supported the establishment of capital market institutions in Kenya, including the Capital Markets Authority of Kenya and the Nairobi Securities Exchange (Office of Economic and Institutional Reform, 1994). The Capital Markets Authority of Kenya and the Nairobi Securities Exchange would later play a leading role in the drafting of the Kenyan CG code.

Table 13.1 provides a chronological illustration of the major events, which culminated in the process of developing Kenya's CG code.

In addition to the privatisation endeavours, other undesirable occurrences led to further thoughts on developing a national code of CG. The Kenyan banking sector had experienced several crises and failures, attributed to widespread insider lending (i.e., large loans to insiders without collateral), excessive government ownership and interference from politicians (Brownbridge, 1998; Were et al., 2006). Such events, alongside an urgent need for foreign aid and investment, prompted support for a local code of CG; thereby reflective of a strategy of

Table 13.1　　Chronology of events leading to the current CG code in Kenya (CMA 2002 code)

Timeline	Event
Early 1980s: 1980–1984	First phase of (economic) reforms introduced by the IMF and WB – the beginning of privatisation process
1984	Joint study by the IFC and the Central Bank of Kenya recommending creation of a regulatory body for the capital markets
1985–1991	Second phase of (economic) reforms spearheaded by the WB and IMF – the establishment of Capital Markets Authority and formalisation of the Nairobi Securities Exchange
June 1986	Funding agreement signed between the Government of Kenya (GoK) and donors (USAID) to establish a capital market development authority
November 1989	Kenyan parliament passes a bill to set up the Capital Markets Authority of Kenya (CMA) through an act of parliament (Cap 485A, Laws of Kenya)
January 1990	CMA constituted
March 1990	CMA inaugurated
1991	Nairobi Securities Exchange formalised as a private company limited by shares
1991–1996	Third generation of economic reforms spearheaded by the WB and IMF
1997	Commonwealth secretariat held three-day workshop in Kampala, Uganda, on improving performance of companies
November 1998	First CG workshop in Kenya organised by the Nairobi Securities Exchange, CMA, Institute of Certified Public Accountants of Kenya and ACCA
March–August 1999	Private Sector Corporate Governance Trust (PSCGT) reviewed various international codes of CG and drafted a sample Kenyan code
October 1999	PSCGT organised a CG workshop/seminar sponsored by the Ford Foundation, British Department for International Development and Friedrich Ebert Foundation
November 1999	PSCGT sample code published and distributed in Kenya
January 2002	Kenya Shareholders' Association established
April 2002	Formal adoption of Kenya's CG code

Source: Adapted from Kimani (2016) and Kimani et al. (2020).

unlocking capital rather than directly being concerned about improving local accountability and CG practice (ActionAid International Kenya, 2009). At the same time, the development of the code was a protracted one because of strained relations between the key donors. Interestingly, it was through the Commonwealth Secretariat that satisfactory progress ensued due to a more deliberative process (involving the market regulator, stock exchange, professional bodies and corporate owners/managers), thereby preventing dissenting voices from taking prominence. The donor community also provided financial and technical assistance, involving, for instance, the funding of various CG workshops/seminars and funding international speakers, to sensitise local stakeholders on the importance of good CG practices (Gatamah, 2002).

These local events became instrumental to the drafting of a code by the PSCGT (Gatamah, 2002). Within six months, the PSCGT completed a draft CG code for Kenya and 'distributed it to over four hundred corporate organisations, development agencies, embassies and government departments' (Private Sector Corporate Governance Trust, 1999, p. iii), albeit that this was a private initiative with no legal backing or enforceability. As a result, the CG development process was viewed with suspicion. As Gatamah notes:

> [there was] fear that good CG practices [were] an imposition by the donor community to facilitate enhanced dominance of the market by the foreign community [and] to facilitate rent seeking by foreigners in the process of liberalisation and privatisation. (2002, pp. 50–51)

The above statement highlighted a key concern of reforms during the privatisation of state-owned companies; i.e., that foreigners stood to benefit at the expense of local people, such that the flow of foreign capital within developing countries 'is often perceived as a neo-colonialist threat' (Smith and Trebilcock, 2001, p. 238). It was therefore unsurprising to find that local public suspicion ensued when the PSCGT code was issued. Thereafter, the CMA took a keen interest and formed a technical committee to draft an official CG code for Kenya, ostensibly in a bid to address concerns about the misappropriation of resources by their controlling shareholders. The choice of an Anglo-American governance model may have been informed by several considerations, including perceived suitability with Kenya's common law orientation (La Porta et al., 2000), and closeness to the neo-liberal economic order advocated by the Bretton Woods institutions (Reed, 2002). It is also likely that Kenya may have been trying to mimic the then prevailing dominant global economic order, in order to enhance the credibility of her financial markets (Zattoni and Cuomo, 2008).

Despite similarities in the two CG codes – the PSCGT code issued in 1999 and the CMA code issued in 2002 – the privately issued PSCGT code was unable to curb the poor CG practices confronting Kenya's corporate sector. The PSCGT code lacked any legal backing, compared to the (enforceable) CMA code issued by the capital market regulator. The CMA thus ensured the code would be obligatory for firms to minimise non-compliance. More recently, a new code entitled the Code of Corporate Governance Practices for Issuers of Securities to the Public was issued in 2015. Overall, the Kenyans' experience reveals the gradual and pervasive use of neo-liberal ideals (privatisation, ensuring efficient/transparent management) promoting the need for a code. The code did not initially progress due to local concerns that such reforms may embolden foreign ownership and a (dominant) control of local companies. Gradually, however, the code was accepted through a process of dissemination and acculturation within local professional bodies and institutions. Whether the different incarnations of the code have led to significant changes and consequences, including at board level, remains less clear.

4.2 South Africa: Pioneering a Stakeholder-Led Model

Historically, due to the oppressive political environment and notably the apartheid policies, international trade sanctions were imposed against South Africa, thereby stifling the country's economic development (Vaughn and Ryan, 2006). The forced isolation also shielded South African firms from outside competition as sanctions kept international companies out of the country's domestic market, and national firms out of the global capital market (Vaughn and Ryan, 2006; Ntim, 2013; Ntim et al., 2015). Gradually, corporate practices, regulations and domestic laws fell far behind global standards, and, by the late 1980s many of the country's firms were described as 'fuzzy' entities led by self-righteous and entrenched executives (Vaughn and Ryan, 2006; Ntim, 2013). However, the repeal of apartheid and the release of Nelson Mandela from prison allowed the country to be welcomed back to the international economy (Vaughn and Ryan, 2006; Areneke, 2018). Faced with the challenges of returning to the international market and attracting investors, South African firms were compelled to implement CG reforms. Indeed, the South African government and firms equally acknowledged that an improvement in CG rules and policies could enhance the country's ability to achieve increased productivity growth and economic stability; crucial factors for long-term national development (Vaughn and Ryan, 2006; Andreasson, 2011; Areneke, 2018).

In this light, the King Committee on Corporate Governance was formed in 1992 with the task of developing CG codes. Its first report was published in 1994 (King I) and substantially inspired by the UK 1992 Cadbury Committee Report (Vaughn and Ryan, 2006; Andreasson, 2011; Ntim, 2013; Ntim et al., 2015; Areneke, 2018; Machokoto et al., 2020). The first South African CG regime (King I Report) was oriented towards a traditional Anglo-American model with a shareholder-wealth-maximisation approach. In particular, King I reaffirmed a general commitment to market-driven economic courses of action, with little explicit consideration of the legacy of apartheid. However, in 2002 King II moved away from the Anglo-American model to a somewhat 'hybrid' model incorporating both the shareholder- and stakeholder-oriented CG practices. In this respect, 'triple-bottom-line' reporting (Vaughn and Ryan, 2006; Andreasson, 2011; Ntim, 2013) was introduced, requiring firms to report on environmental sustainability and social aspects in addition to traditional reporting on the economic and financial 'bottom line' (Vaughn and Ryan, 2006; Andreasson, 2011; Ntim, 2013; Ntim et al., 2015). Both the 'triple-bottom-line' reporting standard and the implementation of a Socially Responsible Investment Index by the JSE (Johannesburg Stock Exchange) in 2004 are praised as the first of their kind in the world (Vaughn and Ryan, 2006; Andreasson, 2011; Areneke and Kimani, 2019).

In 2009, a third report (King III) was developed with the aim of the continuous promotion of the principles-based approach of King I and King II (Andreasson, 2011) with some of the principles of the King Report legislated in law. In contrast to King I and II, King III applied to all entities, be they private and non-profit or public. More so, its orientation was towards a hybrid CG system that encompasses elements of both 'comply and explain' and 'comply or else'. Indeed, King III at the time of release covered a number of global emerging trends in governance, including alternative dispute resolution, shareholder approval of directors' remuneration, evaluation of directors' and board performance and risk-based internal auditing, IT governance and business rescue (Esser, 2009; Gstraunthaler, 2010; Posthumus et al., 2010; Ioannou and Serafeim, 2014; Areneke, 2018).

In November 2016, the King Committee released the King IV report. This report moved from an 'apply or explain' orientation in King III to 'apply and explain'. In addition, King IV reduced the 75 requirements in King III to 17 with one that applied to institutional investors only. The other 16 principles were oriented towards providing detailed and substantiated evidence that good governance was being practised rather than merely signalling compliance. There was also an emphasis on the roles and responsibilities of stakeholders in holding organisations accountable. Furthermore, King IV's preference for an 'explanation' of practical CG structures reflected a priority for outcomes-based targets instead of a compliance- and rules-based approach from previous King Reports. Specifically, the report encourages organisations to view CG not as an act of 'ticking the box', but as practices that will yield positive outcomes if approached mindfully – while taking into account organisational circumstances.

In summary, the principal objective of the King Report was to encourage the highest CG standards in South Africa by promoting an assimilated approach to CG in the interest of a wide range of stakeholders. Some of these recommendations included encouraging shareholder activism, revising the Companies Act, implementing accounting standards into company law and calling on stakeholders to improve the enforcement of existing rules and regulations (Esser, 2009; Gstraunthaler, 2010; Posthumus et al., 2010; Ioannou and Serafeim, 2014). Indeed, the South African CG code became a pioneering example of how emerging markets in Africa can develop their own solutions and yet align, if not contribute significantly, to 'international best practices' in CG. At the same time, the code sought to address national needs by dovetailing its application with other accountability and social reforms, relating, for instance, to CSR, integrated reporting (recently value reporting) and black economic empowerment as a means for a broader-based and more inclusive development in the country. Notwithstanding the gradual 'maturation' of the code and a number of studies highlighting satisfactory levels of adoption, there remains a long path to greater stakeholder involvement in South African corporate activities.

4.3   Corporate Governance in Nigeria: A Story of Multiple CG Codes and Reforms

Similar to other African countries adopting post-colonial reforms in the 1960s, the country pursued an interventionist development strategy, which entailed restrictions on foreign ownership of firms and an active role of the state in strategic sectors of the economy, particularly oil, and gas and infrastructure (Ahunwan, 2002). Operating with this type of strategic initiative in a context characterised by weak market-based institutions and the absence of a healthy political democracy did not result in the practice of 'good' CG (Areneke and Kimani, 2019; Ahunwan, 2002).

The Nigerian Stock Exchange (NSE) went operational with under 10 stocks in 1961 (Sanda et al., 2005), and as of 2016 it had about 188 listed firms (Areneke and Kimani, 2019) with a total market capitalisation of about N12.88 trillion ($80.8 billion). Although this is remarkable growth, this number is arguably lower than those from other emerging markets such as Malaysia and South Korean exchanges (Sanda et al., 2005). Furthermore, the stock exchange began operations without any regulatory body until 1979, when the Securities and Exchange Commission (SEC) was established (Sanda et al., 2005; Sanda et al., 2010). It took a further 20 years for the Securities and Investment Act (1999) to be adopted.

International economic pressures prompted the country to take on a program of deregulation and economic liberalisation (Ahunwan, 2002). Supporters of these changes point to the potential not only for accelerating economic growth, but also for enhancing responsible CG (Ahunwan, 2002; Akinkoye and Olasanmi, 2014). As a result, in June 2000 the Nigerian SEC established a Committee on Corporate Governance of Public Companies in Nigeria (Okike, 2007). This committee was charged with reviewing CG practices in Nigeria and thereafter providing recommendations for a code of best practice to be implemented by public firms listed in the NSE. The code provided recommendations for directing the firm, the supervision of management actions, transparency and accountability in the firm's governance within the regulatory framework and NSE rules (Okike, 2007).

In 2003, the SEC inaugurated a code of best practices in CG. This code was issued due to the banking crises of the 1990s, which led to the failure of 75 out of the 105 banks operating in Nigeria and a new wave of fraud in the sector that resulted in the failure of an additional 33 banks. In 2006, the Central Bank of Nigeria (CBN) implemented another code of CG for Nigerian banks post-consolidation (Adekoya, 2011; Akinkoye and Olasanmi, 2014). These codes were aimed at supplementing the provisions of the Company and Allied Matters Act of 1990 enacted during the military administration era to regulate all corporate entities in Nigeria (Adekoya, 2011; Akinkoye and Olasanmi, 2014). The Nigeria 2003 code emphasised responsibilities and the structure of the board of directors (Okike, 2007; Adekoya, 2011; Areneke, 2018; Areneke and Kimani, 2019; Areneke and Tunyi, 2020). The 2003 code was derived largely from the UK Cadbury Report and the King I Report of South Africa, and thus reflective of Anglo-American CG regimes. It stipulated the responsibilities of boards for efficient, effective and lawful oversight to ensure that firms are constantly enhancing their value creation for shareholders (Okike, 2007; Adekoya, 2011; Areneke and Tunyi, 2020).

A revised code was introduced in 2011 with a similar emphasis on the responsibilities and the structure of the board of directors (Okike, 2007; Adekoya, 2011; Akinkoye and Olasanmi, 2014; Areneke and Tunyi, 2020). The board was also tasked with ensuring that the value created by the firms is shared among the shareholders and employees while meeting the interests of the other stakeholders of the firm (Okike, 2007; Adekoya, 2011; Akinkoye and Olasanmi, 2014). In addition, the 2011 code included global trends in CG practices, such as appraisal of management's strategic planning, selection, performance, executive compensation and succession planning, among other aspects of the board's activities (Okike, 2007; Adekoya, 2011; Akinkoye and Olasanmi, 2014).

Nigeria's public limited companies are required to have a unitary board system. Although the code specifies a minimum number of five directors on the board, it does not specify an upper limit. The code suggests that the constitution of a corporate board should reflect the scale and complexity of a firm, ensuring diversity of experience without undermining integrity, availability, independence and compatibility with the firm's needs (Okike, 2007). The code also recommended a mix of non-executive and executive directors under the leadership of the chairperson, who should be a non-executive director (Okike, 2007; Areneke and Tunyi, 2020; Areneke, 2018). Furthermore, the 2011 code required triple-bottom-line reporting, including sustainability issues, which are similar to South Africa's King II and III Reports. Shifting from the shareholder-centric perspective of the 2003 code, the 2011 code included stakeholder CG provisions and global CG trends, including alternative dispute resolution; shareholder approval of remuneration of directors; evaluation of directors' and board performance; risk-based internal auditing; social, ethical and cultural diversity; anti-corruption; strategies for HIV/AIDS and other diseases; and environmental reporting (Areneke, 2018; Areneke and Tunyi, 2020). At the time of the 2011 CG code, companies were expected to comply or explain their reasons for non-compliance, in line with the UK 'comply or explain' and the South African King I and II CG orientation. A seventh CG code in Nigeria was issued in 2016, as an attempt by the government to harmonise existing CG codes. Intervention arose because of the concerns raised by some stakeholders, who argued that the proliferation of codes did not appear to promote good CG practices in Nigeria.

On 5 January 2019, a revised code was introduced by the Federal Government of Nigeria. In contrast to the 2011 code, which was applicable only to listed firms, the 2018 code is applicable to all public and private firms, with no clear firm size threshold. However, the code continued with the 'comply or explain' principles of the 2011 code. Furthermore, the 2018 code included principles to limit institutional influence by politicians and elites. Specifically, the code required a transaction between related parties to be disclosed prior to its execution, especially when it is likely to result in a conflict of interest. Moreover, it prohibited firms from appointing individuals at director or top management level if they are involved with regulatory institutions; particularly when the company is under the supervision of the relevant regulatory body. Furthermore, the code includes more emphasis on environmental, social and governance (ESG) responsibilities of firms beyond those set out in the 2011 code.

Table 13.2 summarises the evolution of CG codes in Nigeria (Nweke et al., 2020).

While the 2018 code is applicable to firms irrespective of industry, there are other industry/ sectoral specific codes enacted by various regulatory bodies. This includes the Code of

Table 13.2   *CG codes issued in Nigeria from 2003–2018*

Name of code	Year of issuance/revision	Issuing agency	Sector	Trigger
Code of Corporate Governance for Banks and Other Financial Institutions in Nigeria	2003	Bankers' Committee	Financial services	Banking crisis due to corporate fraud
Code of Corporate Governance for Public Companies in Nigeria	2003 (revised 2008, 2011)	SEC	All sectors	External influence/ fraud
Code of Corporate Governance for Banks in Nigeria-Post-Consolidation	2006 (replaced 2003 Bankers Committee code; revised 2014)	CBN	Financial services	Corporate fraud
Code of Corporate Governance for Licensed Insurance Companies in Nigeria	2008	National Pension Commission (PENCOM)	Financial services	Corporate fraud
Code of Corporate Governance for the Insurance Industry in Nigeria	2009	National Insurance Commission (NAICOM)	Financial services	Corporate fraud
Financial Reporting Council of Nigeria (FRCN) Corporate Governance Code	2016 (suspended 2017)	FRCN	All sectors	Harmonisation of existing codes
Code of Corporate Governance for the Telecommunication Industry	2014 (revised 2016)	Nigerian Communications Commission	Telecommunication	Corporate fraud
Nigerian Code of Corporate Governance (NCCG)	2018	FRCN	All sectors	Institutionalisation of CG norms/ checkmate fraud

Corporate Governance for the Telecommunication Industry 2016 issued by the Nigerian Communications Commission to replace the 2014 Code. In 2014, the CBN issued the Code of Corporate Governance for Banks and Discount Houses in Nigeria to replace its 2006 code. Similarly, it released a CG code in 2008 known as the 'Code of Corporate Governance for Licensed Pension Fund Operators' to regulate pension entities. The National Insurance Commission (NAICOM) followed suit in 2009, issuing its own CG code known as 'Code of Good Corporate Governance for Insurance Industry in Nigeria' to regulate the CG practices of insurance companies. This multiplicity of codes without a clear uniform CG standard across firms and sectors led to organisations facing more than one CG regime that are not necessarily consistent with each other (Adegbite and Nakajima, 2012; Adegbite et al., 2013; Adegbite, 2015; Nakpodia et al., 2018). It appears that the different codes, rather than being a means to improving CG and accountability, have themselves become a 'political football' between different parties – stakeholders, regulators and the state.

4.4   Corporate Governance in Tunisia: A 'Symbolic' Guide Rather than a Code

After its independence from France in 1956, Tunisia suffered two waves of authoritarian regimes until 2011. Under the first regime and pressure from the WB and IMF, Tunisia undertook a vast program of structural reforms (the Structural Adjustment Program, or SAP) to restore overall macroeconomic equilibrium, improve the efficiency and competitiveness of the national economy, and ease inflationary pressures. The second authoritarian regime, which took power in 1987, decided to fully 'liberate' the economy to embrace economic development reforms dictated by the international financial institutions. However, in the Arab political context, domination is an implicit pact built by the regimes with their society with the latter agreeing to leave the public sphere, in return for social development and integration into modern modes of consumption and production (Ben-Hammouda, 2012). For this purpose, the regime uses repression not necessarily in a physically violent way, but rather the practice is to exclude dissidents from economic benefits and rents (Hibou, 2011). Hence, economic institutions remain largely controlled by authoritarian leaders who negotiate socio-economic advantages with economic actors to maintain their dominant situation internally and to project an image of stability externally.

After a few public cases of corruption and mismanagement, and especially the well-known case of Batam in 2002,[13] the government issued a 2005 law on the security of financial transactions. Several laws and legal texts[14] were promulgated in order to guarantee greater transparency in financial transactions. In the mid-2000s, the authoritative Tunisian government integrated in its discourse the concept of CG to enhance future development strategies, promoting the country's image and easing international pressures on the country's development. Tunisia began to follow the international movement and, among others (NEPAD[15]), the AfDB Corporate Governance Strategy (2005),[16] whose main objective was 'the respect of three key principles by companies: transparency, responsibility and accountability'. In 2008, the IACE[17] (Arab Institute of Business Leaders) and the American Centre for International Private Enterprise (CIPE) proposed a *Guide to Good Corporate Governance Practices for Tunisian Companies*. The document summarises several proposals made within different workshops where CEOs, scholars and civil servants discussed the global topic of good governance. In 2009, the Tunisian Centre for Corporate Governance was created with the heavy support of CIPE. Its motto was clear: 'Beyond good intentions, we need to move on to implementation'.

Following the above, Law 2009–16 of 16 March 2009, amending and supplementing the Commercial Companies Code, revised certain provisions relating to public limited companies. This law made the 'avoidance of conflicts of interest' a main topic around which the provisions of Article 200 (new) are structured. Likewise, the scope of application has been extended to certain transactions made even with third parties outside the company. This debate on the conflicts of interest is mostly an 'imported' one as the Tunisian economic sector largely consists of small and medium-sized enterprises (SMEs) and the financial market is quite embryonic. In fact, the Tunisian Stock Exchange was created in 1969 but remained inactive until 1999 with only 16 listed banks and state-owned companies, representing only 1 per cent of the country's GDP. Ten years later, 56 companies were listed on the market, even though more than half of them were financial institutions, with an overall contribution of 16 per cent of GDP. In 2020, the number of listed companies increased to 80, representing different sectors. In the main, three largely concentrated ownership structures exist on the Tunisian market: state-owned companies, family groups and foreign investors.[18]

In 2011, the rules of good governance in financial institutions were reinforced. However, this law was considered more political than economic in terms of reflecting the precarious and dubious context in which Tunisian banks operated during the rule by the former authoritative president and his relatives (non-disclosed mortgages, oligarchical behaviours). This law was the first step towards establishing legal provisions for governance mechanisms, primarily focusing on the board of directors and its prerogatives. In 2012, the *Guide to Good Corporate Governance Practices for Tunisian Companies* was updated with provisions for not only listed companies but also SMEs. The OECD and the IFC (WB) joined as 'supportive partners'. The code, formally labelled as a 'guide', aimed to 'make the Tunisian corporate governance system more transparent and understandable. Its objective is to promote national and international investors, customers, employees and the public's trust in the management and control of Tunisian companies'.

The main provisions of CG outlined in the *Guide* are shareholder rights (highlighting the minorities), board structure and responsibilities, internal audit, external audit, managerial privileges and stakeholder relations. A Tunisian idiosyncrasy is the inclusion of elements of good governance within family businesses and the development of the role of managers, ethics in the conduct of business and the governance of partnerships. However, it remains a 'guide' for companies to adopt on a voluntary basis, while companies adopting such a 'guide' are expected to adhere to the 'adopt or explain' principle.

To illustrate the political rather than the economic perspective of the *Guide*, the Tunisair case is a very appropriate one. Tunisair is the state-owned airline company, listed on the Tunisian Stock Exchange, which provides for a delay of up to two years for the publication of the financial statements. Although the company has adopted the code since inception, it is rather difficult to conceive of a Western representation of good governance when such a prominent company did not publish its financial statements on time and continued to be traded on the stock market, with little explanation from its board. Arguably, the Tunisian code appears to be more of a 'signal' of 'change' in relation to economic and political systems, and in the way the country seeks to renew its portrayal; and thus the code has little or nothing to do with the adoption of practices at the organisational level.

5. DISCUSSION AND REFLECTIONS ON CODES IN AFRICA: THE OXEN BEFORE THE CART?

Based on the case insights and review of the literature provided in the preceding sections, we provide a discussion and reflections on the role and implications of CG codes in Africa.

5.1 What Can One Surmise from Existing Studies and Cases?

In conceptualising how and why codes have been established in Africa, the literature often refers to the 'emerging governance' models, which either display a combination of market-centric or relationship-based features (sometimes within the same country) or only one of the two features. Some of the characteristics and features of the 'emerging governance' model (Bhasa, 2004, p. 14; Mahadeo and Soobaroyen, 2016) are: existence of active capital markets, transition from state-held to widely held firms, emergence of a managerial labour class, formal and functional legal systems, existence of family-held and widely held firms, a nascent market for corporate control and more able regulatory agencies. Our country studies, as well the evidence from the reviewed literature, highlight that many of these structural aspects have remained dominant in Africa and have not significantly changed or been reformed, except for a handful of contexts. This begs the question as to the potential for CG code/reforms to challenge the status quo. There is also little understanding in terms of how board practices and processes occur in the emerging governance model, and how some of these practices/processes are more beneficial in improving governance practices.

Furthermore, and while a notable degree of resistance in the Kenyan context was noted and the South African example remains a rather idiosyncratic case of internal 'regime change', the pressures from the WB and IMF (aided by other international agencies) are at the centre of the implementation of African CG codes with (or without) some modifications. Since CG reforms have become part of development goals, the IMF and WB have significantly enhanced their monitoring of CG in emerging economies, emphasising not only adoption, but also more recently the use of scorecard assessments to motivate reforms (International Finance Corporation, 2014). Early instances of pressures to implement codes have been linked to conditionalities in country-level funding and debt agreements (Siddiqui, 2010; Adegbite et al., 2013; Windsor, 2014; Hopper et al., 2017). However, the emphasis seems to have shifted to a gradual and more subtle embedding of practices via a route of 'normative' pressures and the concomitant popularity of governance indicators, indices and ratings (e.g., as part of ESG metrics). This is made possible by the efforts of a range of professional or other 'intermediary' bodies (e.g., professional accountancy organisations, 'Big Four' firms, institutes of directors, corporate secretaries, universities, CG institutes, suppliers of governance data) pursuing 'well-intentioned' initiatives to promote governance, ethics, accountability and transparency. Yet these aspirations towards better standards of (corporate) behaviour often collide with the 'realities' on the ground, and in practice they become narrowed down to 'what can be (pragmatically) done' (e.g., voluntary codes, non-binding guidance, no willingness to enforce) as opposed to 'what ought to be done'. These pronouncements can become implemented as 'best practice' until a jolt to the system (e.g., a corporate collapse) leads to further questions of relevance and efficacy. Despite the multiplicity of these codes to regulate economic and managerial behaviours in different economic sectors, the African business environment also continues to witness several high-profile corporate scandals, which have resulted in the failure of many companies.

As a recent illustration of this issue, the 2015 collapse of the BAI (British American Insurance) Group in Mauritius[19] revealed long-standing governance, audit and regulatory weaknesses, although the country regularly tops African governance rankings. One important factor is the closely-knit personal or familial relationships between the different business, professional, state or political spheres in Mauritius, which can lead to 'grand coalitions' (Soobaroyen and Mahadeo, 2016) aimed at the sharing of economic wealth, maintaining social welfare and promoting peaceful inter-ethnic/religious relations. Equally, however, such closeness provides spaces for collusion and secrecy to enable fraud, disables independent board oversight, breeds an unwillingness to challenge due to 'reputational risks' and potential negative consequences for the stability of elite networks, and weakens or compromises external regulatory checks and balances. In the latter circumstances, a CG code visibly brings distinctive 'labels' to various actors, players and institutions (e.g., independent director/chairperson, audit committee, external auditors, institutional shareholders, regulator) that in fact mask the underlying (and sometimes nepotistic) interrelationships between parties and substantive, rather than rational, motivations of dominant economic, political and social elites. To a similar extent, Kimani et al. (2020) highlight the role of ethnic considerations in the appointment of directors on corporate boards and the limited efficacy of board oversight.

Most of the reviewed literature highlighted two main reasons for the inefficacy of Western-inspired CG codes in African and other emerging countries. Firstly, some scholars attribute it to a cultural mismatch and one's inability to reflect the institutional peculiarities of emerging economies (Kimani et al., 2015; Nakpodia et al., 2018; Areneke et al., 2019). For example, will an independent non-executive director be able to adequately challenge the chief executive officer, without a consideration of the consequences of operating within a well-connected business and political elite? As Kimani et al. (2020) suggest, patronage-led appointments, the dominance of social/political networks and cultural norms (e.g., respect for the elders) often trump the board-level formalities and processes associated with codes. Codes can also be re-interpreted or selectively applied to meet local imperatives. In view of the latitude offered by comply/apply and/or explain regimes, and while companies can legitimately not comply and then explain the reasons for non-compliance, such an approach does foster a perception that none of the code's provisions are crucial or 'serious' enough to matter if these can be 'explained away'.

Secondly, a lack of enforcement has been attributed to so-called institutional voids (Okike and Adegbite, 2012; Kimani et al., 2015; Okike et al., 2015), mainly in terms of a lack of capacity (including legal powers to investigate and sanction) by the state and oversight institutions. Although many African countries have also been encouraged to establish or reform appropriate oversight bodies (e.g., Financial Reporting Council-type and other sectoral commissions/agencies), the evidence as to the potency of these institutions (inclusive of the purpose-built national committees on CG; e.g., refer to Section 2) is unclear to say the least. Paradoxically, the case of Nigeria has demonstrated a mushrooming of overlapping regulatory agencies, each vying to issue its own code but with little evidence of coordination and effectiveness in addressing governance concerns and failures. Contrastingly, there appears to be little evidence from the African Francophone settings in terms of the implications of the OHADA regime of CG, and there is even less in the case of African SOEs. Although SOEs can be prominent economic actors on the continent and are sometimes expected to adopt a CG code (e.g., Kenya), there is little appreciation of how directors, managers and state actors (officials, politicians) engage with the requirements and expectations.

Furthermore, research evidence on the implications and consequences of a code has led to questions about the relevance of agency theory, and the need to consider theories that incorporate other actors and a consideration of institutionalised practices and habits. As we have noted from the case studies, CG developments in emerging economies are not merely the result of a perceived principal–agent problem, and even so such a 'problem' occurs in a context where the overarching social contract is largely different from the one in Western societies. A related point is the emphasis on quantitative studies and the use of proxies/variables that originate from the mainstream (Western) literature that are often uncritically applied to the African context. In so doing, there appears to be very few variables that emerge from the field to reflect the specificities of African countries, whether from North African, sub-Saharan African, Anglophone, Francophone or Lusophone settings. For example, do African institutional investors (e.g., pension funds) operate in the same way as their European or US counterparts? Also, ownership blocks (family, state, foreign) are typically conceptualised as having 'single-mindedness', while they might more realistically reflect a combination of (varying) local factors and considerations. Furthermore, what is the relevance of a split of roles between the chair of the board and the chief executive officer (duality) if this merely offers the opportunity for local cultural, social and political norms to fuel tensions between these two (nominally) powerful positions? What does it take to be an independent director in Africa, and do we know if such a profile/function is important in terms of bringing change? What distinctive board decision-making processes exist in African contexts where there has not been any mainstream code adopted? Are independent directors really able to represent broader stakeholder concerns and bring them to the boardroom? What does (gender) diversity refer to in an African context and board? Therefore, notwithstanding that such directors have become part of African boards, what is the extent of their influence, if any? These are some of the questions, we argue, that have yet to be unearthed in the African context and need to be explored from a multiplicity of theoretical perspectives.

5.2   What Should We Also Think (Differently) About?

Building on the above, it is argued that many facets of the current African CG environment could be seen as mere ritualistic practice with a view to maintain the status quo. Most research-ers and policymakers do seem to be detached from the articulation of some key questions: why do reforms, such as the ones set out in CG codes, fail to deliver? Are such 'lessons', which have been known to be repeatedly problematic even in the Western world, useful in 'educating' African business elites? One critical path underlying those questions leads us to the neo-colonial perspective, given the already well-established work on the role of accounting in the pursuance of imperialism and colonialism, and how such influences have been 'main-tained' in ex-colonies (e.g., Anisette and Neu, 2004; Lassou and Hopper, 2016; Hopper et al., 2017). As a result, many Arab (Kamla, 2007) and African (Agyemang et al., 2020) countries have continued to be influenced by Western systems and experiences. From this perspective, the importing of 'best practice' codes of CG reinforces the asymmetrical power relationships between Africa and the Western world. The pseudo-benevolence of Western aid (e.g., Bakre and Lauwo, 2016) becomes embodied in knowledge-exchange activities (Hopper et al., 2017), technical cooperation/advice and aid work by development agencies (Lassou et al., 2019; Goddard, 2020), and results in the propagation of a single view/model of 'good governance'. Hence, African directors and boards may unwittingly become part of the continuation of the neo-colonial project.

In this light, we note the work of Mudimbe (1988) in our reflections. While the colonial period of 'occupation' represents, time-wise, an insignificant moment in African history, its repercussions have been nothing short of a grand project to 'organise and transform non-European areas into fundamentally European constructs' (Mudimbe, 1988, p. 1). The seminal work of Mudimbe thus presents three complementary hypotheses: (1) the domination of physical space, (2) the reformation of the natives' mind and (3) the integration of local eco-nomic histories into the Western perspective (Mudimbe, 1988). From a research perspective, these hypotheses can be added to the dual constraint of a reliance on dominant theories (prior-itising an interaction with Western-oriented literature) and gatekeeping by academic journals that define what are the relevant issues and terrain for debate. One should also add the scarcity of funding, which leads many researchers to work as entrepreneurs (at the mercy of philan-thropic 'desires') favouring quantitative production rather than qualitative or critical analysis (Mbembe, 2018). We argue that such research prioritisations have resulted in a somewhat atrophic intellectual debate towards envisioning and establishing different ways of modernity, inclusive of governance practices, for Africa.

Admittedly, for a long time indigenous African thinking has been marginalised (Emmanuel, 1969) and disintegrated (Turnbull, 1962; Mair, 1975) and this has led to an 'incoherent establishment of new social arrangements and institutions' (Mudimbe, 1988, p. 6). Indeed, the first economic modern contact with Africa 'had fallen into the hands of the most unscrupulous financiers and captains of industry' (Césaire, [1950] 1972, p. 23). Since colonial conquest has been built on profit increase without any moral limitations, such thinking has been instilled into African institutions, and arguably board processes, as a direct heritage of that behaviour. Hence, this economic dependence assumes underdevelopment (Mazurui, 1974) and a tendency to see capitalism and corporate board decision-making merely as a search for higher profits regardless of broader consequences. Mudimbe proposed three points explaining this state:

> (1) the capitalist world system is such that parts of the system always develop at the expense of other parts, either by trade or by the transfer of surpluses; (2) the under-development of dependencies is not only an absence of development, but also an organisational structure created under colonialism by bringing non-Western territory into the capitalist world, and (3) despite their economic potential, dependencies lack the structural capacity for autonomy and sustained growth, since their economic fate is largely determined by the developed countries. (1988, p. 3)

Under the colonial era, explorers sought to confirm African inferiority by providing 'proofs' feeding the 'epistemological ethnocentrism' that stops the 'other' from becoming someone equal and different. Moreover, Western 'influence' places African actors under a form of 'symbolic violence' (Bourdieu, 1998), implying that the dominated – here African board members – are keen to acquire aspects of the dominant thinking that justify and normalise the exerted domination. Weak or insufficient independent and indigenous African thinking on CG and board practices thus allows for the intensification of Western influence, which is reflected in a continuous reliance on 'international' institutions (e.g., OECD, International Federation of Accountants, EU) and multinationals to frame revisions to local accounting, board, governance and reporting practices. The use of the imperialistic languages (mainly French and English, see Ngũgĩ wa Thiong'o, 1986) for many of the economic activities (accounting, reporting, contracts, certification of professional accountants and governance experts) also serves to embody a form of subjugation that helps to perpetuate colonialism (Kimani et al., 2020). Currently, the balance of power remains tilted towards Western countries as originators of prescriptions for 'good governance' agendas (see Chang, 2007; Lassou et al., 2019; Kimani et al., 2020), while more recent forays into Africa by other powerful countries (e.g., China) are barely underpinned by such discourses. The propagation of universalised reforms (Anglo-American model of governance) assumes that all countries have similar needs and behaviours. The challenge for the so-called 'developing' countries is to put in place the appropriate institutions, often inspired by the Western liberal state/market model as a shortcut to economic progress (Yousfi, 2017). One therefore asks: is there an alternative to this mainstream governance thinking?

According to Mary Douglas (1986), a cultural analysis (of risk) in finding an alignment or at least a congruence between social codes and CG codes is possible. A culturalist hypothesis puts the norms and the theory that claims to be 'standard' under tension and enriches the possible translations of economic realities. The codes can thus reflect an emergent embedded movement by reconsidering a new indigenous version of capitalism reconnecting with traditional thinking and economic behaviours. The core of this capitalism may rather be determined by the 'traditional' goal of subsistence rather than the drive for growth, whereby demands for labour and capital would be reduced when the subsistence needs of the family and community are assured. What Hyden (1980, 1983) called an 'economy of affection', broadly defined by networks of socio-economic relationships of reciprocity (Sugimora, 2007) and the multiplicity of lifestyles, makes African societies a unique case for a possible redefinition and recasting of capitalism – particularly in view of the contemporary implications of sustainability and climate change. Recent AU efforts to develop an African set of guidelines and principles seem to be a step in the right direction. In the short term, this may also imply lesser importance to local equity capital markets across Africa. A code could also apply to non-listed companies or other corporate entities.

In the longer term, the colonial past can be used as a communication platform for converging interests and calling for localities and practices to become Africanised – as a way to subjugate this common scar and transform it. This is reminiscent of the collective work initiated by Bernard Stiegler (2020), which he refers to as a process of 'internation'. *Internation* designates the entity that would link various localities, through scientific and political exchanges and based on re-functionalised and reticulated technologies; these would allow the circulation of different knowledge with the potential to challenge Western hegemony imposed as a result of past colonial regimes and at the expense of Africa's rich cultural identity and knowledge. In short, *internation* constitutes a process of international trans-individuation based on the opening of localities to each other and their reticulation. To some extent, therefore, could the pioneering achievements of the South African example serve as a beginning of a 'liberation'? In this way, Africa could initiate a transition to scale, by constituting an effective public power and a collective decision-making capacity at the continental level, capable of facing up to the multiplicity of political legal diversity, by making a transition that is at once ecological, economic, technological and social. It can also take example from the richness of the globalisation-from-below (Falk, 2003) movement, which emerges from the network of people undergoing development evident in their everyday lives and practices; far from international institutional pressure. Within this movement, individuals recognise their diversity but also their common interests. In this way, a redefinition of capitalism and governance around the needs of the individual and communities becomes possible.

6.   CONCLUSION

'When kings lose direction, they become servants' (African proverb)

This chapter sought to examine the spread and relevance/efficacy of CG codes in the African context. While we find evidence of the spread of codes in 24 African countries, empirical evidence on the design, implications and consequences of these codes remains very limited, in terms of outcomes, board processes/decision-making and of the different African regional contexts. Empirical work has in the main considered larger economies; i.e., South Africa, Nigeria and Egypt. Furthermore, although there is an emerging evidence base from other code-adopting and/or code-revising countries (e.g., Kenya, Uganda, Ghana, Mauritius), one valuable aspect would be to document practices in other non-adopting countries and in non-private sector contexts (e.g., SOEs) to understand the nature of CG arrangements, board decision-making challenges and benefits. Internationally as well, there is a certain 'taken-for-granted'-ness associated with notions of 'good governance' and the adoption of so-called best practices in developing countries, with few critical reflections on its continued relevance (in its current form). Illustratively, the case studies from Nigeria, Tunisia and Kenya not only reveal the circuits through which codes have been disseminated and the underlying neo-liberal motivations, but also the symbolic/political nature of their adoption, thereby resulting in very little substantive change to corporate arrangements on ownership and board processes/decision-making.

At the same time, we do acknowledge the pioneering features of South Africa's experience, whose reforms have been (and are still) happening alongside a raft of what we refer to as 'economic democratisation' policies and laws fostering corporate accountability, integrated thinking and responsibility. Yet, without a similar consideration of the structural arrangements that are often borne out of history, colonial legacy and financial or political crises, CG codes and pronouncements in other parts of the continent appear to serve very limited and technical purposes. More fundamentally, however, we contend that contemporary academic and policy-making concerns about a technical compliance or application of international codes may also be distracting attention away from examining the indigenous facets and foundations of an African form of CG, and from tackling more explicitly the constraints/logics of neo-colonial and neo-liberal thinking in board processes and decision-making.

In a similar vein, an area that has so far been largely trivialised within CG scholarship in African settings concerns board behaviour and decisions making processes. Driven by a research agenda set in the context of developed economies, studies have generally concentrated on the impact of CG mechanisms on firm performance, from an input–output perspective – thereby consciously or unconsciously conceiving of board decision-making, behavioural processes and directors as similar to the corporate boardrooms in developed economies. Thus, the reality of how African corporate boards function and their decision-making process remains unclear. We believe that attempts towards making sense of the impact of CG practices on firm performance should not be limited to the mere factoring of more CG proxies in the pursuit of 'value creation'; instead one has to explicitly acknowledge and understand how board members lead and make decisions in a given social, regulatory and political environment. For codes of CG to have any meaningful influence on firm-level CG practices, it is therefore crucial to delve into the behaviour of, and dynamics within, boardrooms. Only then can codes be reviewed and adapted to reflect the peculiarities of African leadership, management, ownership and board processes. We therefore invite more 'alternative' research, debate and reflections on these points.

NOTES

1. In May 2019, the AU commenced efforts to develop a CG framework for member countries that was to be hinged on African realities and values, hence the proposed title of 'African (corporate governance) principles'. More information and background about this development is available via this link: https://au.int/sites/default/files/newsevents/workingdocuments/38223-wd-framework_cg_au_guidance_note_oct_19_1.pdf.
2. The ACCA report reports on the case of 15 African countries. As reported later in the chapter, we have identified more cases.
3. Translated as 'The Organisation for the Harmonisation of Business Laws in Africa'.
4. Translated as 'Revised Uniform Act Relative to Commercial Companies and Economic Entities'.
5. Union Économique et Monétaire Ouest Africaine (UEMOA).
6. Refer to www.fsb.org/about/history-of-the-fsb/.

7. As an illustration, out of the 77 CG and 195 accounting and auditing assessments carried out so far, 18 and 50 respectively have focused on African countries (source: World Bank).
8. The 'comply or explain' regime refers to a flexible approach to CG implementation, where a board of directors is allowed flexibility to follow CG regulations that are applicable to the circumstances of their company, whilst simultaneously deferring regulations that might be too cumbersome for the nature of their business and/or costly in relation to the size of their company.
9. There are very few listed companies in Algeria (three) and the intention of the code is to target smaller enterprises, although it is not clear to what extent such entities will find it worthwhile to engage.
10. The 'comply or explain' regime required the explicit adoption of a given CG practice as set out in the CG code, or an explanation as to why this practice was not adopted. The 'apply or explain' regime is deemed to be a more flexible approach to CG implementation, in that the company is expected to adhere to principles (rather than specific requirements) set out in a code, or justify why these principles have not been applied.
11. The exception being Mozambique, whose local institute of directors issued a voluntary code.
12. Refer to: www.maserumetro.com/news/news/corporate-governance-code-complete-but/.
13. A group that took advantage of privileged relations with some banks and the political regime to expand too quickly thanks to multiple acquisitions – clearly contrasting with the financial imbalances that the group was carrying. With unpaid debts, unpaid suppliers, poor internal management and a cyclical stagnation of the market from 2000 onwards, Batam sank into indebtedness and attempted to cover it up by resorting to new bond loans, in particular to feed the working capital of its main ailing subsidiaries. The government tried to 'save' the group with a court-ordered reorganisation, without much success.
14. These include the provisions of Article 262 of the Commercial Companies Code, the decree of the Ministers of National Economy and Finance approving the scale of fees for chartered accountants and auditors of Tunisian companies, as amended by the decree of the Ministers of Finance and National Economy of 23 January 1995.
15. New Partnership for Africa's Development, in French.
16. Stratégie en matiégie de gouvernance d'entreprise du Groupe de la BAD. See www.afdb.org/fr/news-and-events/african-development-bank-afdb-group-corporate-governance-strategy-2656.
17. Institut Arabe des Chefs d'Entreprises.
18. See www.bvmt.com.tn/fr/content/pr%C3%A9sentationhttp://www.bvmt.com.tn/sites/default/files/rapports_activites/2020.pdf.
19. For example, refer to www.mondaq.com/shareholders/575140/the-collapse-of-a-giant.

REFERENCES

ACCA (2017). Balancing rules and flexibility for growth: A study of corporate governance requirements across global markets – Phase 2 Africa. Available at www.accaglobal.com/africa/en/technical-activities/technical-resources-search/2017/june/Balancing-rules-and-flexibility-for-growth.html.
ActionAid International Kenya (2009). *IMF Policies and Their Impact on Education, Health and Women's Rights in Kenya: The Fallacies and Pitfalls of the IMF Policies*. Nairobi: ActionAid International Kenya.
Adegbite, E. (2015). Good corporate governance in Nigeria: Antecedents, propositions and peculiarities. *International Business Review, 24*, 319–30.
Adegbite, E., Amaeshi, K., and Amao, O. (2012). The politics of shareholder activism in Nigeria. *Journal Of Business Ethics, 105*, 389–402.
Adegbite, E., Amaeshi, K., and Nakajima, C. (2013). Multiple influences on corporate governance practice in Nigeria: Agents, strategies and implications. *International Business Review, 22*, 524–38.
Adegbite, E., and Nakajima, C. (2012). Institutions and institutional maintenance: Implications for understanding and theorizing corporate governance in developing countries. *International Studies of Management and Organization, 42*, 69–88.

Adekoya, A.A. (2011). Corporate governance reforms in Nigeria: Challenges and suggested solutions. *Journal of Business Systems, Governance & Ethics*, 6(1). https://doi.org/10.15209/jbsge.v6i1.198.

Aguilera, R.V., and Cuervo-Cazurra, A. (2004). Codes of good governance worldwide: What is the trigger? *Organization Studies*, 25(3), 415–43.

Aguilera, R.V., and Cuervo-Cazurra, A. (2009). Codes of good governance. *Corporate Governance: An International Review*, 17(3), 376–87.

Agyemang, J., Jayasinghe, K., Adhikari, P., Carmel, S., and Abongeh, T. (2020). Calculative measures of organising and decision-making in developing countries: The case of a quasi-formal organisation in Ghana. *Accounting Auditing and Accountability Journal*, 34(2), 421–50.

Ahmed, S., and Uddin, S. (2018). Toward a political economy of corporate governance change and stability in family business groups: A morphogenetic approach. *Accounting, Auditing and Accountability Journal*, 31(8), 2192–217.

Ahunwan, B. (2002) Corporate governance in Nigeria. *Journal Of Business Ethics*, 37, 269–87.

Akinkoye, E.Y., and Olasanmi, O.O. (2014). Corporate governance practice and level of compliance among firms in Nigeria: Industry analysis. *Journal of Business & Retail Management Research*, 9(1), 13–25.

Amao, O., and Amaeshi, K. (2008). Galvanising shareholder activism: A prerequisite for effective corporate governance and accountability in Nigeria. *Journal of Business Ethics*, 82(1), 119–30.

Andreasson, S. (2011). Understanding corporate governance reform in South Africa: Anglo-American divergence, the King Reports, and hybridization. *Business & Society*, 50, 647–73.

Annisette, M., and Neu, D. (2004). Accounting and empire: An introduction. *Critical Perspectives on Accounting*, 15, 1–4.

Areneke, G., and Kimani, D. (2019). Value relevance of multinational directorship and cross-listing on MNEs national governance disclosure practices in sub-Saharan Africa: Evidence from Nigeria. *Journal of World Business*, 54(4), 285–306.

Areneke, G., and Tunyi, A.A. (2020). Chairperson and CEO foreignness and CG quality of emerging markets MNCs: Moderating role of international board interlocks. *International Journal of Finance & Economics*. https://doi.org/10.1002/ijfe.2313.

Areneke, G.N.A. (2018). *Comparative Study of the Impact of Compliance with Corporate Governance Regulations & Internal Governance Mechanisms on Financial Performance of Listed Firms in Africa*. Maidenhead: Open University.

Asplund, A. (2021). From watchdogs towards boards with robust and long-term business sense. *International and Comparative Corporate Law Journal*, 14(2020) 2, University of Oslo Faculty of Law Research Paper No. 2021–04. Available at SSRN: https://ssrn.com/abstract=3770637.

Bakre, O.M., and Lauwo, S. (2016). Privatisation and accountability in a 'crony capitalist' Nigerian state. *Critical Perspectives on Accounting*, 39, 45–58.

Ben-Hammouda, H. (2012). Néo-Patrimonialisme et autoritarisme au cœur des régimes politiques Arabes. In Ben Hammouda, H. (Ed.), *Tunisie: Économie politique d'une révolution*. Louvaine-la-Neuve: De Boeck Supérieur.

Bhasa, P.M. (2004). Understanding the corporate governance quadrilateral. *Corporate Governance*, 4(4), 7–15.

Bourdieu, P. (1998). *La domination masculine*. Paris: Seuil.

Brownbridge, M. (1998). *The Causes of Financial Distress in Local Banks in Africa and Implications for Prudential Policy*. Geneva: United Nations Conference on Trade and Development.

Capital Markets Authority of Kenya (2021). Our history. www.cma.or.ke/index.php?option=com_content&view=article&id=10&Itemid=167.

Césaire, A. (1950). *Discours sur le colonialisme*. Paris: Présence Africaine (*Discourse on Colonialism*. New York: Monthly Review Press, 1972).

Chang, H.-J. (2007). *Bad Samaritans: The Guilty Secrets of Rich Nations and the Threat to Global Prosperity*. London: Random House Business Books.

Croucher, R., and Miles, L. (2010). Corporate governance and employees in South Africa. *Journal of Corporate Law Studies*, 10(2), 367–89.

Cuomo, F., Mallin, C., and Zattoni, A. (2016). Corporate governance codes: A review and research agenda. *Corporate Governance: An International Review*, 24(3), 222–41.

Douglas, M. (1986). *How Institutions Think*. New York: Syracuse University Press.

Economist Intelligence Unit (2020). Democracy Index 2020: In sickness and in health? [Online]. www .eiu.com/n/campaigns/democracy-index-2020/.

Emmanuel, A. (1969). *L'Echange inégal*. Paris: Maspero.

Enrione, A., Mazza, C., and Zerboni, F. (2006). Institutionalizing codes of governance. *American Behavioral Scientist*, *49*(7), 961–73.

Esser, I.M. (2009). The protection of stakeholder interests in terms of the South African King III Report on Corporate Governance: An improvement on King II. *South African Mercantile Law Journal*, *21*(2), 188–201.

Falk, R. (2003). Globalization-from-below: An innovative politics of difference. In Sandbrook, R. (Ed.) *Civilizing Globalization: A Survival Guide*. Albany: SUNY Press.

Farah, B., Elias, R., Aguilera, R., and Abi Saad, E. (2021). Corporate governance in the Middle East and North Africa: A systematic review of current trends and opportunities for future research. *Corporate Governance: An International Review*. Ahead of print.

Gatamah, K. (2002). Strengthening corporate governance: The Kenyan experience. In Organisation for Economic Co-Operation and Development (Ed.) *Official Development Assistance and Private Finance: Attracting Finance and Investment to Developing Countries*. Paris: Organisation for Economic Co-Operation and Development.

Goddard, A. (2020). Accountability and accounting in the NGO field comprising the UK and Africa: A Bordieusian analysis. *Critical Perspectives on Accounting*. Ahead of print.

Gstraunthaler, T. (2010). Corporate governance in South Africa: The introduction of King III and reporting practices at the JSE Alt-X. *Corporate Ownership and Control*, *7*(3), 149–57.

Haxhi, I., and Van Ees, H. (2010). Explaining diversity in the worldwide diffusion of codes of good governance. *Journal of International Business Studies*, *41*(4), 710–26.

Hibou, B. (2011). *Anatomie politique de la domination*. Paris: La Découverte.

Hopper, T., Lassou, P., and Soobaroyen, T. (2017). Globalisation, accounting and developing countries. *Critical Perspectives on Accounting*, *43*, 125–48.

Hyden, G. (1980). *Beyond Ujamaa in Tanzania: Underdevelopment and Uncaptured Peasantry*. London: Heinemann.

Hyden, G. (1983). *No Shortcuts to Progress: African Development Management in Perspective*. London: Heinemann.

International Finance Corporation (2014). *Corporate Governance Scorecards: Assessing and Promoting the Implementation of Codes of Corporate Governance*. Washington, DC: World Bank. Available at: https://openknowledge.worldbank.org/handle/10986/20676.

Ioannou, I., and Serafeim, G. (2014). *The Consequences of Mandatory Corporate Sustainability Reporting: Evidence from Four Countries*. Harvard Business School Research Working Paper.

Kamla, R. (2007). Critically appreciating social accounting and reporting in the Arab Middle East: A postcolonial perspective. *Advances in International Accounting*, *20*(8), 105–79.

Kiggundu, J., and Havenga, M. (2004). The regulation of directors' self-serving conduct: Perspectives from Botswana and South Africa. *Comparative & International Law Journal of Southern Africa*, *37*(3), 272–93.

Kimani, D. (2016). *Investigating Factors Which Influence the Practice of Corporate Governance within the Kenyan Corporate Sector*. Maidenhead: Open University. Available at: http://oro.open.ac.uk/51777/.

Kimani, D., Ullah, S., Kodwani, D., and Akhtar, P. (2020). Analysing corporate governance and accountability practices from an African neo-patrimonialism perspective: Insights from Kenya. *Critical Perspectives on Accounting*. Forthcoming.

Kimani, D., Viney, H., and Kodwani, D. (2015). Corporate governance in less developed countries. *Academy of Management Proceedings*.

La Porta, R., Lopez-De-Silanes, F., Shleifer, A., and Vishny, R. (2000). Investor protection and corporate governance. *Journal of Financial Economics*, *58*, 3–27.

Lassou, P.J.C., and Hopper, T. (2016). Government accounting reform in an ex-French African colony: The political economy of neocolonialism. *Critical Perspectives on Accounting*, *36*, 39–57.

Lassou, P.J.C., Hopper, T., Tsamenyi, M., and Murinde, V. (2019). Varieties of neo-colonialism: Government accounting reforms in Anglophone and Francophone Africa – Benin and Ghana compared. *Critical Perspectives on Accounting*. Forthcoming.

Levi-Faur, D. (2005). The global diffusion of regulatory capitalism. *Annals of the American Academy of Political and Social Science, 598*, 12–32.

Machokoto, M., Areneke, G., and Ibrahim, B.M. (2020). Rising corporate debt and value relevance of supply-side factors in South Africa. *Journal of Business Research, 109*, 26–37.

Mahadeo, J.D., and Soobaroyen, T. (2016). A longitudinal study of the implementation of the corporate governance code in a developing country: The case of Mauritius. *Business & Society, 55*(5), 738–77.

Mair, L. (1975). *Primitive Government.* Gloucester, MA: Peter Smith.

Mazrui, A.A. (1974). *World Culture and the Black Experience.* Seattle: University of Washington Press.

Mbembe, A. (2018). L'Afrique en théorie. *Multitudes, 4*(78), 143–52 (trans. François Ronan Dubois).

Mudimbe, V.Y. (1988). *The Invention of Africa.* London: Indiana University Press.

Munisi, G., and Randøy, T. (2013). Corporate governance and company performance across sub-Saharan African Countries. *Journal of Economics and Business, 70*, 92–110.

Mwaura, K. (2007). Failure of corporate governance in state owned enterprises and the need for restructured governance in fully and partially privatized enterprises: The case of Kenya. *Fordham International Law Journal, 31*(1), 34–75.

Mwega, F.M. (2006). Financial sector reforms in Eastern and Southern Africa. In Mkandawire, T., and Soludo, C.C. (eds) *African Voices on Structural Adjustment.* Nairobi: Africa World Press.

Nairobi Securities Exchange (2021). History of NSE. www.nse.co.ke/nse/history-of-nse.html.

Nakpodia, F., and Adegbite, E. (2018). Corporate governance and elites. *Accounting Forum, 42*(1), 17–31.

Nakpodia, F., Adegbite, E., Amaeshi, K., and Owolabi, A. (2018). Neither principles nor rules: Making corporate governance work in Sub-Saharan Africa. *Journal of Business Ethics, 151*(2), 391–408.

Ngũgĩ wa Thiong'o (1986). *Decolonising the Mind: The Politics of Language in African Literature.* Nairobi: East African Educational Publishers.

Nordberg, D. (2020). Codes and their contexts. In *The Cadbury Code and Recurrent Crisis.* Cham: Palgrave Macmillan.

Ntim, C.G. (2013). An integrated corporate governance framework and financial performance in South African-listed corporations. *South African Journal of Economics, 81*(3), 373–92. https://doi.org/10.1111/j.1813–6982.2011.01316.x.

Ntim, C.G., Opong, K.K., and Danbolt, J. (2015). Board size, corporate regulations and firm valuation in an emerging market: A simultaneous equation approach. *International Review of Applied Economics, 29*(2), 194–220.

Ntim, C.G., and Soobaroyen, T. (2013). Corporate governance and performance in socially responsible corporations: New empirical insights from a neo-institutional framework. *Corporate Governance: An International Review, 21*, 468–94.

Nweke, I.M., Khlif, W., and El Omari, S. (2020). Multiplicity of corporate governance code in Nigeria, the past explains the present. *Journées d'études internationales: Interroger l'histoire du management : ce que le Sud nous apprend,* 9–10 December. DRM-Université PSL-Paris dauphine.

Office of Economic and Institutional Reform (1994). *Kenya: Evaluation of Capital Markets Authority.* Washington, DC: U.S. Agency for International Development.

Okike, E., Adegbite, E., Nakpodia, F., and Adegbite, S. (2015). A review of internal and external influences on corporate governance and financial accountability in Nigeria. *International Journal of Business Governance and Ethics, 10*(2), 165–85.

Okike, E.N. (2007). Corporate governance in Nigeria: The status quo. *Corporate Governance: An International Review, 15*, 173–93.

Okike, E.N.M., and Adegbite, E. (2012). The code of corporate governance in Nigeria: Efficiency gains or social legitimation. *Corporate Ownership and Control, 9*(3–2), 262–75.

Okpara, J.O. (2011). Corporate governance in a developing economy: Barriers, issues, and implications for firms. *Corporate Governance, 11*(2), 184–99.

Painter-Morland, M. (2006). Triple bottom-line reporting as social grammar: Integrating corporate social responsibility and corporate codes of conduct. *Business Ethics: A European Review, 15*(4), 352–64.

Posthumus, S., Von Solms, R., and King, M. (2010). The board and IT governance: The what, who and how. *South African Journal of Business Management, 41*(3), 23–32.

Private Sector Corporate Governance Trust (1999). *Principles for Corporate Governance in Kenya and a Sample Code of Best Practice for Corporate Governance.* Nairobi: Private Sector Initiative for Corporate Governance.

Reed, D. (2002). Corporate governance reforms in developing countries. *Journal of Business Ethics, 37*, 223–47.

Rono, J.K. (2002). The impact of the structural adjustment programmes on Kenyan society. *Journal of Social Development in Africa, 17*(1), 81–98.

Rossouw, G.J. (2005). Business ethics and corporate governance in Africa. *Business and Society, 44*(1), 94–106.

Rossouw, G.J. (2019). The ethics of governance and governance of ethics in the King Reports. *Journal of Global Responsibility, 11*(2), 187–96.

Samaha, K., Dahawy, K., Hussainey, K., and Stapleton, P. (2012). The extent of corporate governance disclosure and its determinants in a developing market: The case of Egypt. *Advances in Accounting, 28*(1), 168–78.

Sanda, A., Mikailu, A.S., and Garba, T. (2005). *Corporate Governance Mechanisms and Firm Financial Performance in Nigeria* (Vol. 149). Nairobi: African Economic Research Consortium.

Sanda, A.U., Mikailu, A.S., and Garba, T. (2010). Corporate governance mechanisms and firms' financial performance in Nigeria. *Afro-Asian Journal of Finance and Accounting, 2*(1), 22–39.

Siddiqui, J. (2010). Development of corporate governance regulations: The case of an emerging economy. *Journal of Business Ethics, 91*, 253–74.

Smith, D.A.C., and Trebilcock, M.J. (2001). State-owned enterprises in less developed countries: Privatization and alternative reform strategies. *European Journal of Law and Economics, 12*, 217–52.

Soobaroyen, T., and Mahadeo, J.D. (2008). Selective compliance with the corporate governance code in Mauritius: Is legitimacy theory at work? *Research in Accounting in Emerging Economies, 8*, 239–72.

Soobaroyen, T., and Mahadeo, J.D. (2016). Community disclosures in a developing country: Insights from a neo-pluralist perspective. *Accounting, Auditing & Accountability Journal, 29*(3), 452–82.

Soobaroyen, T., and Ntim, C.G. (2013). Social and environmental accounting as symbolic and substantive means of legitimation: The case of HIV/AIDS reporting in South Africa. *Accounting Forum, 37*(2), 92–109.

Sorour, K., Boadu, M., and Soobaroyen, T. (2020). The role of corporate social responsibility in organisational identity communication, co-creation and orientation. *Journal of Business Ethics.* Forthcoming.

Stiegler, B. (ed.) (2020). *Bifurquer: Il n'y a pas d'alternative.* Paris: Les liens qui libèrent.

Sugimora, K. (2007). Les paysans africains et l'économie morale. *Revue du Mauss, 2*(30), 185–97.

Tshipa, J., Brummer, L., Wolmarans, H., and Du Toit, E. (2018). The impact of flexible corporate governance disclosures on value relevance: Empirical evidence from South Africa. *Corporate Governance: The International Journal of Business in Society, 18*(3), 369–85.

Turnbull, C.M. (1962). *The Lonely African.* New York: Simon and Schuster.

Uche, C.O., Adegbite, E., and Jones, M. (2016). Institutional shareholder activism in Nigeria: An accountability perspective. *Accounting Forum, 40*(2), 78–88.

Uddin, S., Jayasinghe, K., and Ahmed, S. (2017). Scandals from an island: Testing Anglo-American corporate governance frameworks. *Critical Perspectives on International Business, 13*(4), 349–70.

Van der Merwe, A. (2020). The evolution of the stakeholder-inclusive approach in the King Reports. *Journal of Global Responsibility, 11*(2), 139–46.

Vaughn, M., and Ryan, L.V. (2006). Corporate governance in South Africa: A bellwether for the continent? *Corporate Governance: An International Review, 14*, 504–12.

Wang, R., Zhou, S., and Wang, T. (2020). Corporate governance, integrated reporting and the use of credibility-enhancing mechanisms on integrated reports. *European Accounting Review, 29*(4), 631–63.

Wanyama, S., Burton, B., and Helliar, C. (2009). Frameworks underpinning corporate governance: Evidence on Ugandan perceptions. *Corporate Governance: An International Review, 17*(2), 159–75.

Wanyama, S., Burton, B., and Helliar, C. (2013). Stakeholders, accountability and the theory-practice gap in developing nations' corporate governance systems: Evidence from Uganda. *Corporate Governance: The International Journal of Business in Society, 13*(1), 18–38.

Waweru, N.M. (2014). Determinants of quality corporate governance in sub-Saharan Africa: Evidence from Kenya and South Africa. *Managerial Auditing Journal, 29*(5), 455–85.

Were, M., Ngugi, R., and Makau, P. (2006). Understanding the reform process in Kenya. In Mensah, J. (Ed.) *Understanding Economic Reforms in Africa: A Tale of Seven Nations*. New York: Palgrave Macmillan.

Windsor, D. (2014). Corporate governance as an antidote to corruption in emerging markets. In Boubaker, S., and Nguyen, D. (Eds) *Corporate Governance in Emerging Markets*. Berlin: Springer. https://doi.org/10.1007/978-3-642-44955-0_17.

Yousfi, H. (2017). *Redessiner les relations État/collectivités locales en Tunisie: enjeux socio-culturels et institutionnels du projet de décentralisation*. Paris: Agence française de développement.

Zattoni, A., and Cuomo, F. (2008). Why adopt codes of good governance? A comparison of institutional and efficiency perspectives. *Corporate Governance: An International Review, 16*, 1–15.

APPENDIX

Table 13.A1   List of African corporate governance codes

Country	Year (first introduced)	Subsequent revision(s)	Title of (most recent) CG code	Produced by/issuing entity	Language(s)	Application regime	Application regime (for any new version)
Algeria	2008		2008: Le Code Algérien de Gouvernance d'Entreprise	Algerian Corporate Governance Task Force	French/ Arabic	Voluntary	
Botswana	2013		2013: Botswana Code of Corporate Governance 2016: Botswana Accountancy Oversight Authority (BAOA), in 2016 directed public companies in Botswana to adopt King III Report	Directors Institute of Botswana	English	Apply or explain	
Egypt	2005	2011 and 2016	2016: Egyptian Code of Corporate Governance	Egyptian Institute of Directors	Arabic/ English	Should seek to abide	Comply or explain
Ethiopia	2011		Ethiopian Code for Corporate Governance	Corporate Governance Institute	English	Comply or explain	Comply or explain
Ghana	2002	2010	2010: CG Guidelines on Best Practices 2018: The Banking Business – CG Directive	Securities & Exchange Commission Ghana Bank of Ghana	English	Voluntary Mandatory	
Kenya	2002	2015	Code of CG Practices for Issuers of Securities to the Public	Capital Markets Authority	English	Comply or explain	Apply or explain
Liberia	2012		Corporate Governance Regulation for Financial Institutions	Central Bank of Liberia	English	Mandatory	
Libyan Arab Jamahiriya	2007 2010		2007: Corporate governance regulation. 2010: Corporate governance code for the banking sector	Libyan Stock Market. Central Bank of Libya	Arabic	Comply (2010)	
Malawi	2001	2010	The Malawi Code II (Code of Best Practice for Corporate Governance in Malawi)	Institute of Directors	English	Comply or explain*	Comply or explain
Mauritius	2003	2004, 2016	The National Code of Corporate Governance for Mauritius	National Committee on Corporate Governance	English	Comply or explain	Apply and explain

Country	Year (first introduced)	Subsequent revision(s)	Title of (most recent) CG code	Produced by/issuing entity	Language(s)	Application regime	Application regime (for any new version)
Morocco	2008		2008: Moroccan Code of Good Corporate Governance Practices. 2008: Code for SMEs. 2012: Code for state-owned enterprises	The National Corporate Governance Commission	French	Comply or explain	
Mozambique	2011		Mozambique Corporate Governance Code	Directors Institute of Mozambique (Instituto de Directores de Moçambique)	Portuguese	Voluntary	
Namibia	2014	2016	Corporate governance Code for Namibia (NamCode)	Namibian Stock Exchange and the Institute of Directors in Southern Africa (IoDSA).	English	Apply or explain	
Nigeria	2003	2016	Nigerian Code of Corporate Governance *(suspended and published updated version in 2018)*	Financial Reporting Council of Nigeria	English	Apply or explain	
Rwanda	2009	2012	Guiding Code of Corporate Governance (2009) The Capital Market Corporate Governance Code (2012)	Private Sector Foundation (PSF) Capital Market Authority	English English, French/ Kinyarwanda	Voluntary	Comply or explain
Senegal	2011		Code de Gouvernance des Entreprises	Institut Sénégalais des Administrateurs	French	Apply or explain	
Sierra Leone	2018		National Corporate Governance Code for Sierra Leone	Corporate Affairs Commission	English	Comply or explain	
South Africa	1994	2002, 2009 and 2016	King Report on Corporate Governance	IoDSA	English	Apply or Explain	
South Sudan	2012		The Code of Good Corporate Governance *(appended to the Company Laws, 2012)*	Ministry of Justice	English	Mandatory	
Tunisia	2008	2012	2008: Guide de Bonnes Pratiques de Gouvernance des Entreprises Tunisiennes *(new version in 2012)*	Centre Tunisien de Gouvernance d'Entreprises	French	Voluntary	Voluntary (and explain if applying partially)

Country	Year (first introduced)	Subsequent revision(s)	Title of (most recent) CG code	Produced by/issuing entity	Language(s)	Application regime	Application regime (for any new version)
Uganda	2003		Capital Markets Corporate Governance Guidelines *(Note: CG Guidelines of the private Institute of Corporate Governance first introduced in 2002 and revised in 2008.)*	Capital Market Authority	English	Comply or Explain	
United Republic of Tanzania	2002		Guidelines of Corporate Governance Practices by Public Listed Companies	Capital Markets and Securities Authority	English	Comply or explain	
Zambia	2005		The Lusaka Stock Exchange Corporate Governance Code	Lusaka Stock Exchange	English	Comply or explain	
Zimbabwe	2014		The National Code on Corporate Governance (ZimCode)	ZIMCODE Trust	English	Apply or explain	

Notes: * According to the WB's Report on Observance of Standards and Codes (2007), this requirement was not compatible with the stock market's listing requirements. ** Out of the 55 African countries, 24 including one OHADA country (Senegal) have issued at least one corporate governance code. 16 OHADA countries have incorporated basic CG requirements in their company law. 1 country has seemingly adopted (São Tomé and Principe) but no evidence was found. Another country (Lesotho) is in the process of issuing a code. For the 13 final countries, there is no indication of a code having been adopted.

PART IV

BOARD DECISION-MAKING IN EXTREME SITUATIONS

14. Nonexecutive director influence on informational asymmetries in offshore financial centres

Bruce Hearn, Alexander Mohr, Muhammad Khawar and Jaskaran Kaur

1.   INTRODUCTION

Over the last two decades, there has been a phenomenal increase in the worldwide use of offshore financial centres, or tax havens, in international financial transactions. This is estimated to amount to US$1–1.6 trillion per year in illicit cross-border financial flows, which dwarfs the approximately US$135 billion in annual global foreign aid receipts (Tax Justice Network, 2019). Much of this flows through the Caribbean, which alone acts as a conduit in 40 per cent of all foreign direct investment worldwide (Damgaard et al., 2019). Surprisingly, there is no prior research on the corporate governance of firms' boards of directors within such opaque contexts where this provides an opportunity to uncover the institutional determinants of offshore secrecy. This is of concern given the importance of the monitoring and disciplining function of nonexecutive directors within good governance (Donnelly and Mulcahy, 2008; Zattoni and Cuomo, 2010) as is embedded in most corporate governance legislation and recommendations worldwide (Nowak and McCabe, 2003; Aguilera, 2005). In this chapter, we theoretically and empirically explore how nonexecutive directors' personal ownership impacts firm-level informational asymmetries and how the strength of this effect is influenced by the macro-institutional environment of offshore tax havens.

Theoretically, we develop a novel institution-theoretic approach that facilitates a more accommodating and flexible framework than that of agency theory's restrictive and unrealistic assumption that institutions are merely a thin veil for transactions. We suggest a deeper consideration of institutions (e.g., Aguilera, 2005) that embodies historically contingent interactions between constituencies within Caribbean economies that interact to form the unique offshore jurisdictional architecture. The influence of constituencies such as powerful families prevalent on Caribbean islands transcends firms (Miller et al., 2013) and shapes cultural norms, which emphasize extended social relational interconnectedness and legitimacy through isomorphic conformity (DiMaggio and Powell, 1983) in governance structures. As such, our adoption of an institutional perspective better enables our exploration of rival factors influencing nonexecutive directors. We argue that a trade-off exists between nonexecutive directors' ability to impartially and effectively monitor and appraise the decisions made by their executive counterparts (Fama, 1980; Fama and Jensen, 1983) and their capacity to utilize their social status and interconnectedness (Roberts et al., 2005) in enhancing the legitimacy of their firms, which facilitates access to resources and social capital (Nahapiet and Ghoshal, 1998). We focus on how nonexecutive directors' personal ownership influences this trade-off, which itself is contingent on the wider institutional context. We argue that while firms and their directors are subject to North's (1991) "rules of the game", their behaviour is also subject to a dynamic interplay between firms and the social fabric in the form of external constituencies, within which nonexecutive directors are embedded.

Our first contribution is our focus on a largely ignored yet critical aspect of nonexecutive compensation, namely their personal ownership, and linking this to the informational asymmetry between a firm and its minority principals. Our institutional approach adopts a socialized view that marks a substantial departure from agency theory's (e.g., Jensen and Meckling, 1976) singular emphasis on nonexecutive impartiality in monitoring and disciplining often powerful insiders. Following Roberts et al. (2005), we argue that agency theory fails to consider the essential socialized, collaborative side to nonexecutive directors' roles, which, for instance, includes their close interaction with executives through activities such as mentoring, leadership counselling, experience-based advice, and involvement in and evaluation of strategic decisions. This is a particularly prominent issue in offshore tax havens, which are characterized by extremely dense social networks from which social capital is derived (Nahapiet and Ghoshal, 1998). Therefore, nonexecutive directors' social capital constitutes a critical resource for their firms through their mutual interconnectedness with external constituencies (Nahapiet and Ghoshal, 1998), which are predominantly families.

Our next contribution is our exploration of how various dimensions of the institutional environment in offshore tax havens influence the association between nonexecutive director ownership and informational asymmetry. We consider how well formal institutional frameworks protect the property rights of outside minority principals in the context of external contracting. To do this, we utilize formal institutional quality, which is a national aggregate of the six Worldwide Governance Indicator (WGI) measures (Kaufman et al., 2009) that form the underlying dimensions of institutional quality. We then undertake a more fine-grained analysis of formal institutions by considering, first, whether their offshore jurisdictions have retained European colonial status and, second, whether a fixed currency regime, such as the US dollar, is maintained with their major trading partners. These two institutional contingencies result in considerable differences in national institutional frameworks and are fundamental to the design of offshore institutional frameworks while they also provide deeper insights into the impact of nonexecutive directors on firms' informational asymmetries.

2.   THEORY AND HYPOTHESES

A common theme in the agency-based corporate governance literature is the inherently under-socialized view of discipline within contemporary corporate governance. Individual listed firms are viewed as being subject to a combination of internal and external disciplinary measures (Jensen and Meckling, 1976). Although largely complementary, external disciplinary measures are generally associated with the market for corporate control (Aguilera and Jackson, 2010), whereas internal disciplinary measures are associated with boards of directors who are tasked with monitoring, evaluation and structuring executive compensation packages (Jensen and Meckling, 1976; Fama and Jensen, 1983). Both emphasize motivational alignment between outside principal owners and their inside managerial agents. Nonexecutive directors are charged with representing the interests of outside principals, or owners, as well as with the monitoring and evaluation of executive decision-making. This has led to a number of studies emphasizing a more passive role for nonexecutive directors in the formulation of firm strategy where they rely on CEOs' charismatic drive in this respect (Baysinger and Hoskisson, 1990; Golden and Zajac, 2001). Moreover, it underscores a more prescriptive view of nonexecutive directors based on normative tenets of agency theory in which the focus is on their ability to monitor and appraise the decision-making of their executive counterparts. Rival views have been developed that focus on the association of firm performance with nonexecutive directors' independence from vested corporate ownership or controlling interests (Aguilera, 2005; Roberts et al., 2005), their "busyness" in terms of shared directorships with other firms (Falato et al., 2014) and their contribution to the gender balance of boards of directors (Adams and Ferreira, 2009).

Seminal work by Roberts et al. (2005) sought to address the limitation of this under-socialized view of nonexecutive directors through an interview-based qualitative study. A critical failure of more remote views of generic "monitoring" is their lack of addressing the role of accountability. This is achieved through executives working collaboratively with nonexecutives, who are seen as equal peers and from whom advice, mentoring and counsel are sought to assist executives in leading and formulating strategy (Roberts et al., 2005; Shen, 2005). The lack of consideration of social interconnectedness in the prior literature is a serious shortcoming and limits the applicability of more prescriptive agency-based research. Moreover, a more fine-grained socialized view of nonexecutives underscores the professional boundaries associated with their roles and the dilemmas they face when challenging executive excesses. In particular, nonexecutives of a firm may have been recruited by their executive counterparts or the CEO, which leads to a degree of subordination and hence conflict of interest in exercising their impartial monitoring and evaluative role. Notably, Shen (2005) argued that nonexecutives face considerable social sanctions or ostracizing by incumbent executives and senior management teams within the firms they are involved in if they initiate the disciplinary aspect of their monitoring roles. Such disciplining measures range from influencing CEO succession and insisting on the independence of committees nominating CEOs to imposing restrictions on executive bonuses, benefits and pay awards as well as questioning the validity of contract formation, which is a particularly difficult issue in extended family firms and business groups due to nepotism and cronyism. Nonexecutive directors are likely held "hostage" by the potential for detrimental social actions against them by executives.

Collectively, these arguments emphasize the complementarity between social collaboration and the monitoring aspects of nonexecutive directors' roles. This is especially true across different structures of boards of directors, with the most prevalent structures worldwide being those of unitary and dual tiers. The former structure envisages a single-tier board comprised of equal and opposite executive and nonexecutive counterparts, where both have legal fiduciary status; this structure is deemed optimal in affording protections for minorities within the dispersed ownership model of Berle and Means (1932). Conversely, the latter structure involves two tiers, with the higher of the two being a supervisory board composed solely of nonexecutive directors, many of whom represent the interests of block owners, and a subordinate level consisting of a management board staffed by senior management. This latter dual-tier model is better at accommodating the controlling interests of large block owners, such as extended families, within a firm. However, while in the former unitary structure the nonexecutive role is equal parts collaboration and monitoring, in the latter structure there is a much greater emphasis on collaboration. In that type of structure, an emphasis on collaboration is essential to nonexecutives' role in negotiating between rival block-holder interests and acting as an interface between block-owner interests and senior management on subordinate management boards. This highlights an even more socialized role than that envisaged by Roberts et al. (2005) in arguing that nonexecutives' collaborative function has been overlooked.

Building on the notion that the structure of boards of directors facilitates the accommodation of rival block-owner controlling interests, a significant feature across small, isolated, predominantly island economies such as those of the Caribbean is a proliferation of family interests. These interests overwhelmingly dominate Caribbean societies with often disproportionate influence over all realms of society. They are also based on deeply ingrained conservatism and opacity, which form the bedrock of informal culture. This in turn emphasizes dense social interconnectedness and the profound importance of social capital (Nahapiet and Ghoshal, 1998) in relational contracts. In such circumstances, nonexecutive directors and their executive counterparts are predominantly drawn from an extremely small director talent pool where all of the potential candidates are embedded within the overarching family governance system. This has two implications. The first is that the genuine independence of nonexecutives from their executive counterparts is questionable. The second is that there is a great emphasis on very dense and overlapping social relationships. Both of these implications underscore the overwhelmingly socialized and collaborative nature of the relationships, including those of nonexecutive directors with their executive counterparts. Given these considerable informational asymmetries, minority outside investors face potentially huge downside risks (Jensen and Meckling, 1976).

Furthermore, a particular feature of small, isolated economies is the density of overlapping social connections, which constitute a critical resource for firms in the form of social capital (Nahapiet and Ghoshal, 1998). These connections are based on cognitively embedded cultural constructs that form the basis of extensive relational contracting systems (see West, 2014; Berger et al., 2015) predominantly based on indigenous families. Business is undertaken through extended, highly socialized interactions involving benevolence towards members of one's own ethnic, clan and familial networks (Berger et al., 2015), while adverse selection and moral hazard are mitigated by the reputation-based credibility of oneself and one's affiliated group (Coleman, 1988). This underscores the superficial nature of nonexecutive independence and a much deeper and more socialized aspect of their roles, where they are closely associated with executive directors (Roberts et al., 2005). Given this heightened emphasis on social collaboration, we argue that greater nonexecutive director ownership is associated with their increasing inability to impartially and effectively monitor insiders on behalf of outside minorities. We argue that this leads to increased informational asymmetry, which leads us to formulate the following hypothesis:

Hypothesis 1: Nonexecutive director ownership is positively associated with informational asymmetry.

Institutional Contingency Effects

While we expect that the level of nonexecutive director ownership will *generally* affect the extent of information asymmetry in our research context, we also anticipate that this will be moderated by the variation in national institutional settings. This supports our further exploration of these environmental contingency factors through three additional interactive terms. These terms are the formal regulatory institutional quality in a specific offshore jurisdiction and two closely related subcomponents, namely whether the offshore jurisdiction has retained its European colonial status and whether it has adopted a fixed peg exchange rate regime. These last two distinct characteristics of national institutional environments facilitate the investigation of external investors' evaluations of informational asymmetry risk, as captured by our dependent variable, in relation to the *effectiveness* of nonexecutive directors in monitoring.

We argue that formal regulatory institutional quality captures the quality of the external contracting protections afforded to otherwise vulnerable outside minority owners or principals. Furthermore, it is a direct reflection of the demographic structure of the underlying national polity, as envisioned by North (1991, 1994). In particular, lower levels of formal institutional quality are associated with weaker protections of minority property rights. More specifically, the legal and judicial systems in such environments are relatively under-developed, often with incomplete bodies of prior case history in common law systems or dysfunctional bureaucracy in civil code systems. North (e.g., 1991, 1994) argued that demographically narrow national polities under the hegemonic control of empowered elites effectively stymie equitable social and economic reforms to protect their vested interests at the national level. The consequences of this under-development of formal institutional architecture are twofold. First, there is a much greater emphasis on dense socialized interactions and relational contracting, which form the basis for mitigating adverse selection and moral hazard. These attributes emphasize the much more collaborative, socialized role for nonexecutive directors acting in conjunction with their executive counterparts. Second, owing to the deficiencies or voids in formal regulatory frameworks (Khanna and Palepu, 2000), there is a lack of recognition of the role of nonexecutive directors in terms of monitoring and evaluation. Consequently, there is greater emphasis on the role of block owners, such as the handfuls of extended families that comprise the majority of block owners in firms, and their associated nonexecutives, in socialized interconnectedness. This affords minimal protections against infringements of minority property rights, which leads to elevated informational asymmetry.

In contrast, as formal institutional quality improves, regulatory frameworks become more equitable and national polities become more demographically inclusive (North, 1991, 1994). There is greater independence of legal and judicial systems from national executives, and elevated protections for external contracting facilitate the national adoption of international best practices in governance. These practices are typically based on optimal minority shareholder welfare protection, which affords much greater recognition of the impartial monitoring role of nonexecutive directors. Higher-quality formal institutional architecture also implies that nonexecutive directors have improved access and recourse to legal redress, inhibiting insider expropriation. This argument for high formal institutional quality is very similar to the theorization from studies undertaken in developed economies such as the US (Dalton and Dalton, 2005) and UK (Mura, 2007). Doidge et al. (2007) argued that the technologies used for expropriation are rendered more costly for insiders than simply reinvesting cash flows back into their firms to achieve a lower cost of capital and hence narrowing bid–ask spreads from reduced adverse selection. These arguments lead us to test the following:

Hypothesis 2: The positive association between nonexecutive director ownership and informational asymmetry is negatively moderated by formal institutional quality.

Thus far, we have only considered the quality of the aggregate external contracting environment or formal institutional framework. However, there is notable variation in formal institutional frameworks across the Caribbean region. A defining characteristic is the relative smallness and isolation of the territories. Our narrow regional focus on the Caribbean increases our ability to theorize about the dichotomy between developed and developing/emerging frameworks in the typology of national jurisdictions in the international business literature (Meyer and Sinani, 2009; Cantwell et al., 2010; Wang et al., 2012). The developed country frameworks are characterized by reliability and impartiality in the application of the rule of law supporting external contracting, while the developing country frameworks contain institutional voids, or deficiencies in the protection of minority property rights. Our institutional theorization addresses Allred et al.'s (2017) call for a third category of formal frameworks, which account for offshore tax havens. Next, we address the theoretical concern that in the context of small open economies and offshore financial centres, formal institutional quality that is aggregated in its construction fails to adequately capture the distinctive attributes associated with formal institutional architecture. This is particularly true in the case of smaller territories that have retained their European colonial status, foregoing independence, and those that are independent but have adopted a highly restrictive, macroeconomic fixed peg exchange rate regime.

The smallness and isolation of Caribbean territories has led to fundamental questions regarding the viability of their economies due to the prohibitive costs of providing public goods and services. Such economic concerns have led the overwhelming majority of island and archipelago states to either retain their European colonial status or to gain independence while initiating a restrictive fixed peg exchange rate arrangement with a major trading partner, predominantly the US. Territories that elect to retain European colonial status are inherently very small and isolated, which underscores their relative autonomy and discretion in decision-making within an otherwise restrictive colonial relationship with the European colonial metropole. Consequently, these smaller territories have disproportionate control over the design of their own national formal institutional frameworks in terms of the exact elements that are adopted and assimilated into the island's context.

This historical process of assimilation is inextricably intertwined with the dynasties of, at most, a handful of elite families that are central to the broader national institutional heritage. An outcome of this collusion is that essentially family-dominated island authorities can also work closely with the European colonial metropole to secure diplomatic "protection", which bestows huge benefits in terms of negotiating international tax treaties and avoiding the "blacklisting" of the territories due to nefarious tax evasion activities and accusations of money laundering. In this way, smaller territories that retain their colonial status acquire substantial competitive advantages in comparison to their sovereign peers, which is a major benefit arising from their bifurcated jurisdictional frameworks. Consequently, smaller colonial territories have strategic advantages in attracting the lucrative registration of international and multinational enterprises (Dyreng et al., 2013; Allred et al., 2017) seeking to exploit the territories' secrecy as a means of aggressive tax management. These firms benefit from the protections afforded by some of the highest-quality formal institutional architectures in terms of property right protections while also benefitting from the considerable secrecy afforded by the bifurcation.

Such secrecy is an outcome of the underlying culturally imbued conservatism associated with overwhelmingly dominant local family institutions, which are also associated with extensive social relational contracting, personal networks and social trust (Granovetter, 1973). These characteristics supersede the largely superfluous notion of impartiality within external contracting. This implies that there is heightened collaboration, rather than impartial monitoring and evaluation, in the relationship between nonexecutive directors and their executive counterparts. Such socialized collaboration is exceptionally strong given the powerful family-based cultural foundations linking these two types of directors; i.e., where members of both categories are drawn from the same family-based cultural framework. As a consequence of these institutional arguments, we argue that the European colonial status of a territory further accentuates, or positively moderates, the main association between nonexecutive director ownership and informational asymmetry.

Hypothesis 3: The positive association between nonexecutive director ownership and informational asymmetry is positively moderated by a territory's preservation of its European colonial status.

As an alternative to retaining a colonial relationship, many small territories have opted for political independence while simultaneously adopting a fixed peg exchange rate with a dominant trading partner, such as the US dollar. The benefits of such a restrictive currency arrangement are that while effectively surrendering control of macroeconomic policy and interest rates to those determined by the dominant foreign partner, it facilitates the attraction of supplementary foreign investment through the conveyance of stability and credibility in the indigenous regulatory environment (Kingsley and Graham, 2017). A critical and often overlooked element in the adoption of a fixed exchange rate is the typically extremely large amount of formal institutional architecture that must be adopted and assimilated which is essential for institutionally supporting the arrangement. This ranges from essential legal and judicial architecture to government apparatus where we extend the arguments of Ellis et al. (2017) in terms of the portability of institutional frameworks from a dominant country to its satellite.

Consequently, we argue that in Caribbean territories that have adopted fixed peg exchange rate regimes there is considerable adoption of the formal institutional architecture established in the developed world that is essential to support the arrangement. This constitutes an effective tie between the smaller satellite economy and its dominant partner both in terms of macroeconomic arrangements but also in formal institutional architecture (Kingsley and Graham, 2017). Therefore, the smaller territory adopts modernized formal institutional architecture yet at the same time in being independent is wholly reliant on the indigenous national polity to enact the political processes which are directly responsible for the assimilation of institutional architecture and the reform of existing institutional frameworks. The wholesale reliance on an indigenous polity for institutional reform is very different from colonial relationships where collusive local families effectively have near total autonomy underneath the overarching political protection of a dominant metropole acting as benefactor (Hines, 2010; Cobb, 2001). Given the fundamental importance of the underlying national polity in assimilating and reforming institutional architecture in fixed exchange rate regimes, this is reflective of an equal emphasis on institutional support for external, arm's-length contracting. Consequently, despite potential inadequacies the frameworks within fixed-currency-regime satellite countries provide institutionalized support for the role of nonexecutive directors in terms of impartiality and effective monitors in protecting minority investor welfare. Increasing nonexecutive director ownership will therefore act as a motivational alignment mechanism, thereby reducing informational asymmetries between minority investors and insiders.

Conversely, in Caribbean territories that have more flexible exchange rates, where these are a myriad of less restrictive exchange rate arrangements bestowing greater sovereign discretion over macroeconomic affairs, there is a lack of impetus towards the smaller economy adopting another dominant country's formal institutional architecture. Consequently, there is a total reliance on the independent national polity to determine the evolution of national institutional frameworks through indigenous political process (North, 1991, 1994). This is subject to the demographic narrowness and lack of inclusivity of national polities which stymie political processes, thereby impeding more equitable institutional reform (North, 1991, 1994), where this ultimately leads to voids or deficiencies in external contracting (Khanna and Palepu, 2000). In essence, larger territories with sovereignty in terms of political independence and macroeconomic arrangements are more prone to weaknesses arising from the limitations of national polities dominated by social elites and resulting cronyism (Moon and Schoenherr, 2021). More importantly, they lack the impetus in adopting, assimilating and reforming their institutional frameworks to match the quality of a dominant partner economy as would be the case in fixed currency arrangements. Given the voids in external contracting, there is a greater emphasis on relational contracting and social collusion to engender socialized trust (Granovetter, 1973) in firms' resource acquisition. These arguments collectively emphasize much weaker support for nonexecutive directors' roles in terms of impartiality and monitoring, and an emphasis on social collusion where informational asymmetries between insiders and minority investors are exacerbated.

In summary, these arguments imply that a fixed currency regime in a territory will reduce, or negatively moderate, the association between nonexecutive ownership and informational asymmetry.

Hypothesis 4: The positive association between nonexecutive director ownership and informational asymmetry is negatively moderated by a fixed peg exchange rate currency regime.

3.   DATA

Our Caribbean sample comprises formal securities markets that attract domestic and foreign listed firms. Consequently, we omit the informal Saint Vincent and the Grenadines Securities Exchange, which lacks recognition by national regulators; the Haitian Stock Exchange in francophone République d'Haïti; and the Bolsa de Valores de la República Dominicana in Hispanic (Spanish-speaking) República Dominicana. The latter two markets have attracted no equity listings since their inception. Our final omission is the Dutch Caribbean Securities Exchange in Curaçao, Netherlands Antilles, which is designated an offshore market focusing solely on the attraction of international listings.[1] This leads to a final sample comprising eight established equity markets: those of Bermuda, the Bahamas, Barbados, the Cayman Islands, Jamaica, the regional Eastern Caribbean Securities Exchange, Trinidad & Tobago, and Guyana.

The dataset is unique and is constructed in three stages. The first stage involves the compilation of a comprehensive list of firms with listed ordinary shares. These are single-class voting rights, namely one share equals one vote. Thus, entities with primary listings of dual- or multiple-class shares, preference shares and convertible instruments are removed from consideration. A list of listed firms is compiled for each Caribbean stock exchange from 2000 or its year of inception, whichever date is earliest. These lists also consider new listings, suspensions and de-listings that occurred during the period 2000–2017 inclusive to account for potential survivorship bias in the final dataset. Such listing data are obtained from the national stock exchanges (see Appendix, Table 14.A1). This results in 179 listed firms.

The second stage in the construction of the dataset involves the procurement of the individual listed firms' annual reports from across the Caribbean region. Some firms' annual reports are obtained directly from the national stock exchange websites of the Bahamas, Bermuda, Jamaica and Trinidad & Tobago. Other firms' annual reports are obtained directly from the national exchanges of Barbados and the Eastern Caribbean Securities Exchange, and additional direct procurement is undertaken from the national regulator (GASCI) in the case of Guyana. Individual listed firms' websites are used for procurement in the case of the Cayman Islands, which is relatively efficient given the handful of listings. Additional recourse to individual listed firms is undertaken across the Caribbean region to supplement the original data collection and augment any missing values (annual reports). This leads to an unbalanced panel sample of 171 listed firms' annual reports. However, there is some variation in the consistency of the availability of the annual reports and there are various omissions prior to 2004. All of the firm-specific balance sheet and governance variables are sourced directly from the collected annual reports.

The third and final step in constructing the dataset is in the procurement of secondary market financial trading data. This entails the systematic collection of daily bids, asks, closing prices, traded volumes, and numbers of shares issued and outstanding. These data are sourced exclusively from Bloomberg for Jamaica and Trinidad & Tobago. However, they are collected directly from the respective exchanges for Guyana, the Bahamas, Barbados, the Cayman Islands, Bermuda and Eastern Caribbean. All data are converted to US$ end-of-period equivalent values to facilitate comparison in a multi-country sample. This leads to a final sample of 146 listed firms with secondary trading data across 14 years.

4.   METHODS

4.1   Dependent Variable

We measure the costs associated with a single buy or sell order submission into a trading system compared to the full spread, which is representative of a "round trip" consisting of both the buy and sell legs when buying into and then liquidating a trading position (see Stoll, 2000). This is calculated by averaging the current month's average bid–ask spread and the preceding month's average bid–ask spread. The average monthly bid–ask spread is estimated by subtracting the monthly average end-of-day closing bid (buying) prices from their ask (selling) price equivalents and then dividing this number by the midpoint of those monthly average bid–ask prices.[2]Our use of averages minimizes outliers and averages out the highs and lows in quotes that result from monthly sampling.

Central to our theorization is the notion that informational asymmetry between insiders and outsiders can be represented as a form of measurable cost. We adopt the bid–ask spread as our cost construct, which provides a measure of the costs involved in equilibrating price differences attached to buy and sell orders, as reflected in bid and ask prices, respectively, to consummate trades and clear the market for a given asset (Box and Griffith, 2016). These trading costs, captured in the price differences, are informational in nature and relate to the probability of an uninformed market participant trading with an informed counterpart (Glosten and Harris, 1988). In larger markets, this model is extended to capture the costs for designated market-maker brokers, who are contractually obliged to maintain markets in less actively traded, smaller assets, in terms of their risks from trading assets between uninformed and informed traders (Madhaven, 1992; Bollen et al., 2004).

However, in extremely small markets where there are at most a handful of brokers, we argue that the information and market design circumstances are slightly different. First, the minimal order flow underscores the lack of viability for market-maker brokers who would otherwise receive compensation through holding a monopoly position in certain assets – a position derived from their market-making obligation. Here, the bid–ask spread additionally includes the brokers' order-processing costs, their compensation for their services in the form of monopoly rents and asymmetric information costs (Collin-Dufresne and Fos, 2015). Second, there is a considerable emphasis on the stock exchanges, as well as the associated clearing facilities, and all the stock brokers to jointly "maintain" the markets so that the markets do not succumb to "failure" owing to exacerbated informational asymmetries. We argue that the implications of this are twofold. On the one hand, there is a need to maintain legitimacy through the application of globally recognized regulatory norms embodied in notions of "best practices". This is exemplified through often voluminous regulatory measures designed to counter insider information trading, which occurs in predominantly large, developed markets such as London and New York. This need to maintain legitimacy implies that brokers quote bid and ask prices to their external minority investor clients that at least best estimate the true level of the underlying informational asymmetry within the market for a given firm or asset. However, on the other hand, great importance is attached to the signals of quality and credible contracting that are associated with listed firms, such as retained ownership by nonexecutive directors; such signals are deemed to reliably convey the otherwise concealed true value of listed firms.

We argue that in smaller stock markets with a high barrier to entry and a handful of licenced brokers, powerful interdependencies exist within the brokerage community, curbing excessively high gains on trades and overly high monopoly rents. This constitutes a form of market discipline in these dense communities, which is essential given that the sole means of economic viability for brokers is to levy bid–ask spreads within the trading price discovery mechanism. This is similar to the fledgling local foreign exchange brokerage markets in the Caribbean, where the market power of individual brokers influences their monopoly rent extraction and ultimately influences the exchange rate (Khemraj and Pasha, 2014). Finally, a critical issue in these smaller stock markets is that informational asymmetry becomes so significant that it precipitates a prohibitive widening of bid–ask spreads to protect uninformed investors from being outpriced by investors with superior information (Vayanos and Wang, 2007).

In summary, these arguments emphasize that bid–ask spreads are attributable to a combination of brokers' order processing costs, monopoly rent compensation for their price discovery services and adverse selection. The order-processing costs and monopoly rents are largely a function of adverse selection. Consequently, bid–ask spreads are useful as an evaluative measure of informational asymmetry.

4.2   Explanatory Variable

Our study uses one explanatory variable, namely the percentage of ownership by all nonexecutive directors. Individual nonexecutive directors are identified from the director biography sections of the annual reports. Their individual personal ownership holdings are sourced from the shareholder sections, which are usually in the appendices or notes of annual reports. It should be noted that we identify personal nonexecutive director holdings as those holdings that are attributed to their individual selves, whereas holdings that are attributed to nonexecutive directors who are part of a family or business group entity fail to count for the individual director but instead count towards the family or business group. Thus, nonexecutive ownership is the ownership that is attributable to independent nonexecutives, which is the focus of our first hypothesis. We follow previous studies (e.g., Filatotchev and Bishop, 2002; Dalton et al., 2003) and use the percentage ratio of the total number of ordinary shares nonexecutives own to the total number of firm shares issued and outstanding.

4.3   Moderating Variables

Our three moderators are measured as follows. The first moderating variable, namely formal institutional quality, is measured using the WGI index. The variable is formed from the equally weighted average of the six WGI metrics[3] (Kaufman et al., 2009). The six dimensions are (1) voice and accountability, (2) political stability and the absence of violence/terrorism, (3) government effectiveness, (4) regulatory quality, (5) the rule of law and (6) the control of corruption. Detailed definitions of the six metrics and their sources are provided in Table 14.A1. These six dimensions range in value from -2.5 to +2.5 but are rebased here to a 0–10 scale prior to aggregation. To mitigate collinearity concerns, formal institutional quality is centred and normalized.

Our second moderator is the European colony variable, which takes the value of 1 if the listing jurisdiction is a European colony and zero otherwise. Our measure for the third moderator takes the value of 1 if the listing jurisdiction has a fixed peg exchange rate regime with a dominant country trading partner and zero otherwise. It should be noted that due to the fixed currency regime and formal institutional quality variables being almost perfectly collinear, we include the three moderating variables in separate models. Therefore, the European colony retention variable is included with the formal institutional quality and fixed currency regime variables, but the latter two variables are not included together in any model. The inclusion of all interactive terms is accompanied by rigorous checks on the variance inflation factors (VIFs), which are consistently under the value of 4 in all of the models.

4.4   Control Variables

Our choice of controls is very specific in order to align our study with the market microstructure literature. This is of critical importance given that our dependent variable is the quoted bid–ask spread, which we use as a proxy for informational asymmetry. We adopt three sets of controls.

The first control is a single *ownership control*, which aggregates all of the block ownerships in the listed firms other than the ownership that forms the basis of the main effect, namely that of the founder or non-founder directors. This control is included to mitigate potential omitted variable bias and is reported in annual percentage terms. The values are extracted from ownership holdings statements or the notes/appendices sections within the annual reports.

The second control is an *institutional control* represented by the aggregate stock market capitalization to gross domestic product (GDP) ratio, expressed as an annual percentage and obtained from the World Bank database. This control captures the degree of the importance of stock market intermediation in the wider economy.

The third control is a set of specific *microstructural controls* prescribed by the market microstructural finance literature (see Stoll, 1978, 2000); these microstructural controls capture four dimensions of market microstructures, each of which is converted to its natural logarithm. *Price* is measured as the monthly average daily closing price for each stock and is calculated over the preceding trading month. This controls for the discreteness of the effects of quoted trade price clustering at fractional levels, such as 1/8,[4] and the resultant impact on the spreads (Harris, 1994). *Volatility* is measured as the daily standard deviation of stock price returns, which is determined from the differences between the daily closing stock prices, as expressed in local currency terms. This controls for potential changes in the value of the inventory holdings of market makers, where such additional risks are included in the spreads (Bollen et al., 2004). *Traded volume* is measured as the total number of shares traded daily for each listed stock, averaged over each month. The above three variables are averaged across the preceding year. Transactional volumes are related to order-processing risks in that lower volumes incur higher order-processing costs, which are in turn reflected in the spreads (Stoll, 1978). *Size* is the final variable, and following Schnatterly et al. (2008) we drop market capitalization as the measure and adopt total assets, which mitigates concerns over collinearity with stock prices while being relatively constant over the course of the preceding year. Large firms have more transparent informational environments owing to the higher analyst coverage that results from their inclusion in blue chip indices as well as the media and press coverage that results from the size and complexity of their operations. While the opposite is true for smaller firms, these firms are less compliant with the dispersed ownership model and more likely to be governed by dominant block owners, such as families. This exacerbates informational asymmetries, leading to higher spreads. Closing stock prices and traded volumes are obtained on a daily basis directly from each national stock exchange. The total number of shares issued and outstanding and the total assets for each firm are obtained directly from the respective annual report.

4.5   Empirical Model

We construct pooled OLS regression models based on unbalanced panels with firm-years as the units of observation. In line with Schnatterly et al. (2008), our pooled estimators draw on both cross-sectional (firms) and time series dimensions, which addresses a shortcoming in the prior literature in which only individual cross-sections were considered (e.g., Stoll, 2000). However, this design presents two modelling concerns. The first concern is the presence of stochastic martingales within the price time series data-generating processes, which is an issue in finance-based studies. This is mitigated by our use of low-frequency annual data and a sample group comprising highly illiquid and price-static markets. The second concern relates to potential autocorrelation and heteroscedastic issues regarding the time series component in the errors. To circumvent these issues, we adopt industry[5] and time (year) binary effects. These binary effects also facilitate controlling for latent or unobservable differences between firms, such as differences in industries, levels, regulation, or governance and ownership, in line with Schnatterly et al. (2008). Next, we apply White's cross-sectional standard error and covariance estimator, which take into account potential period (time series) clustering while clustering by country in the standard errors.

Three sets of regressions are estimated. The first corresponds to the main effect, namely the nonexecutive director category of block ownership. This allows for testing the main effect suggested in Hypothesis 1. The second and third sets correspond to moderation by the WGI institutional quality index as suggested in Hypothesis 2 and by the European colony and a fixed peg exchange rate regime as suggested in hypotheses 3 and 4, respectively.

5.   EMPIRICAL RESULTS

5.1   Descriptive Statistics

The evidence in Table 14.1 reveals a number of distinct trends in the listed firms across the Caribbean region as a whole. Formal institutional quality is notably the highest in the European colonial territories of Bermuda (77.85 per cent) and the Cayman Islands (76.44 per cent) and progressively decreases in other notable offshore financial centres such as the Bahamas (76.14 per cent), with the weakest formal institutional quality appearing in the much larger, developing economies of Trinidad & Tobago (56.97 per cent), Jamaica (55.23 per cent) and Guyana (45.76 per cent). One prominent exception in this trend is Barbados, with a value of 80.21 per cent. Generally, this trend is reversed for the average firm bid–ask spreads, where Bermuda has the highest values (21.68 per cent) and Trinidad & Tobago the lowest values (2.85 per cent). There are some notable exceptions, however, such as the severely under-developed securities market in Guyana (18.22 per cent).

Despite the dominance of English common law across the sample countries, with the exception of Saint Lucia's French civil code (White, 1961) and Guyana's mixed Roman-Dutch system (Lee, 1914; Cooray, 1974), only 56.90 per cent of the firms in the sample have single-tier, unitary boards of directors, which are ubiquitous to Anglophone governance systems. This is largely explained by the prevalence of extended family business groups across the region, which often have overlapping control over certain firms, as the dual-tier structure is preferable in accommodating those overlapping interests. The board sizes are large, comprising between eight and 10 directors on average, while over 70 per cent of these directors are nonexecutive directors. Typically, between 15 per cent and 25 per cent of them are independent nonexecutive directors, underscoring the lack of genuine independence across the island jurisdictions, where family institutions overwhelmingly dominate. Finally, nonexecutive director ownership is less than 2 per cent across the sample, subject to significant variation between countries. This relatively low level of nonexecutive ownership is reflective of findings of similarly low nonexecutive ownership by others, such as Dalton et al. (2003) in a sample of US firms, Mura (2007) in a sample of UK listed firms and Filatotchev (2005) in a sample of UK IPO (initial public offering) firms.

Further evidence of the variation across the Caribbean region is shown in Table 14.2. The bid–ask spreads are both high and variable, while nonexecutive director ownership is 1.3 per cent on average, with a standard deviation of 4.6 per cent and a range of zero to 50 per cent. Formal institutional quality also exhibits substantial variation across the sample, although it should be noted that this variable is statistically normalized. Furthermore, 11.2 per cent of the sample firms are located in the European colonial territories of Bermuda and the Caymans, while 41.7 per cent of the sample firms are located in fixed peg exchange rate, or currency, regimes.

Table 14.1   Descriptive statistics

Market	N	State-level	Firm-level	Board-level					
		Institutional quality	Bid–ask spread	Board type: Unitary	Dual-tier	Board size	Ratio of nonexecutive directors	Ratio of independent nonexecutive directors	Nonexecutive director ownership
	#	% [SD]	% [SD]	%	%	# [SD]	% [SD]	% [SD]	% [SD]
Atlantic									
Bermuda	14	77.85 [2.90]	21.68 [24.32]	24.40	75.60	9.46 [3.47]	71.61 [13.00]	16.88 [12.39]	1.33 [3.40]
Northwest									
Cayman Islands	3	76.44 [4.21]	…	12.00	88.00	9.00 [0.00]	73.09 [7.69]	11.69 [10.78]	0.38 [1.04]
The Bahamas	18	76.14 [4.75]	9.95 [17.57]	45.50	54.50	8.49 [2.01]	69.29 [26.52]	23.89 [18.98]	4.11 [11.18]
Jamaica	72	55.23 [1.73]	12.97 [17.79]	57.40	42.60	8.80 [2.38]	77.98 [17.24]	25.27 [16.73]	0.69 [1.86]
Eastern									
Barbados	17	80.21 [2.66]	11.29 [11.12]	45.10	54.90	8.69 [2.23]	75.61 [16.17]	16.31 [13.28]	0.50 [1.00]
ESCE	13	68.72 [5.67]	12.11 [13.90]	42.00	58.00	9.19 [1.72]	91.54 [16.89]	22.91 [16.42]	0.23 [0.69]
Leeward Islands									
St. Kitts & Nevis	5	69.99 [6.00]	11.65 [12.50]	40.00	60.00	8.38 [1.87]	88.58 [20.14]	21.78 [11.21]	0.46 [0.94]
Windward Islands									
Dominica	1	69.49 [2.54]	10.19 [6.85]	32.50	66.20	8.85 [2.10]	78.24 [13.88]	26.34 [18.74]	1.69 [8.84]
Saint Lucia	3	72.03 [4.45]	19.71 [21.59]	0.00	100.00	10.00 [0.00]	100.00 [15.27]	23.20 [9.88]	0.02 [0.02]
Grenada	3	62.92 [1.68]	7.09 [6.07]	62.90	37.10	10.28 [1.50]	99.04 [2.69]	34.12 [25.46]	0.00 [0.00]
St. Vincent & the Grenadines	1	69.71 [3.39]	…	0.00	100.00	9.25 [1.03]	76.56 [9.05]	6.25 [5.17]	0.00 [0.00]
Southern									
Guyana	12	45.76 [1.87]	18.22 [25.73]	100.00	0.00	7.37 [2.41]	62.49 [21.68]	7.82 [8.91]	1.81 [4.71]
Trinidad & Tobago	30	56.97 [1.58]	2.85 [2.23]	100.00	0.00	9.42 [2.28]	75.74 [16.94]	14.52 [15.22]	2.33 [5.88]
Sample average	171	64.79 [11.88]	12.17 [17.83]	56.90	43.10	8.83 [2.42]	75.64 [19.74]	20.18 [16.49]	1.45 [5.29]

Notes: Table 14.1 reports the number of firms, *N*, per country and includes all firms currently listed alongside all firms that were listed and then subsequently delisted or that suspended their listings during the sample timeframe of 2000 to 2017. This mitigates survivorship bias. The firm-level bid–ask spread is the quoted bid–ask spread. State-level institutional quality is the equally weighted average of the six WGI metrics, as defined by Kaufman et al. (2009) and sourced from http://info.worldbank .org/governance/wgi/index.aspx#faq. Board size is the total number of directors serving on the board of directors. The ratio of nonexecutive directors is the percentage of board members that are nonexecutive directors. The ratio of independent nonexecutive directors is the ratio of independent nonexecutive directors to the total board size. Nonexecutive ownership is the percentage level of ownership held by nonexecutive directors. SD is the standard deviation across the listed firms and years within a particular country.

There is also considerable variation in the importance of stock market finance in relation to national GDP across the region, with an average of 65 per cent, a standard deviation of 30.0 per cent and a range of zero to 164.5 per cent.

5.2   Bivariate Analysis

The evidence from the bivariate correlation analysis (Table 14.2) reveals minimal correlations among the variables, while the majority are statistically significant ($p \leq 0.05$). There is one notable exception: the correlation between the formal institutional quality and fixed currency regime variables (0.929, $p \leq 0.01$). This supports our decision not to include both of these variables in any one of our models. This omission from joint inclusion is further justified by the VIF analysis, where following the removal of one of the two variables, all of the VIFs are less than 4 in absolute value. It is also worth noting that due to our small sample size and the acute sensitivity of financial time series variables to potential collinearity in the time series dimension of pooled estimators, we extensively use VIFs as a means to determine which model best minimizes the issues and potential risks associated with collinearity as well as heteroscedasticity and autocorrelation in errors.

5.3   Multivariate Results

The results of the empirical tests performed on our first two hypotheses are shown in Table 14.3. Notably, in model 1, there is a large positive association (+0.485, p ≤ 0.005) in the main effect between nonexecutive director ownership and bid–ask spreads. This evidence statistically supports Hypothesis 1. It is in line with Heflin and Shaw's (2000) thesis that increased block ownership exacerbates informational asymmetries, leading to increased adverse selection risk for minorities as reflected in wider bid–ask spreads. In practical terms, this implies that a one-standard-deviation increase in nonexecutive director ownership leads to a 48.5 per cent increase in bid–ask spreads.

Next, we moderate the ownership variable by the normalized formal institutional quality index. Our results are reported in model 2, Table 14.3. These results reveal a large, positive and statistically significant main effect association between nonexecutive ownership and bid–ask spreads (+0.733, $p \leq 0.005$), which is moderated by formal institutional quality (-0.569, $p \leq 0.005$). This supports Hypothesis 2. In practical terms, the moderation partially cancels out the main effect, implying that a one-standard-deviation increase in nonexecutive director ownership is accompanied by a 16.4 per cent net increase in bid–ask spreads in higher-quality formal institutional jurisdictions compared to their lower-quality counterparts. This reduction in bid–ask spreads in the context of high institutional quality is akin to the findings of single-country studies of the impact of nonexecutive ownership on various measures of firm performance, such as by Dalton et al. (2003), which exclusively focus on large developed markets such as the US and Europe.

Next, we introduce the moderating European colonial status retention and fixed exchange rate regime variables. In model 3, Table 14.3, we moderate by retaining the European colonial status of the listing jurisdiction. The main association between nonexecutive ownership and bid–ask spreads (+0.428, $p \leq 0.01$) is further positively moderated by the binary effect of European colonial status retention (+0.717, $p \leq 0.01$). This provides statistical support

Table 14.2a   Descriptive statistics and correlations

		Mean	Std. Dev.	Max	Min	1	2	3
1	Quoted bid–ask spread	0.121	0.170	2.000	0.000	1.000		
2	Nonexecutive ownership	0.013	0.046	0.500	0.000	0.049*	1.000	
3	European colony	0.112	0.315	1.000	0.000	0.200**	0.012	1.000
4	Fixed currency regime	0.417	0.493	1.000	0.000	0.086**	-0.005	0.419**
5	Formal institutional quality	0.457	0.527	1.312	-0.527	0.055*	-0.009	0.441**
6	Market cap/GDP ratio	0.650	0.309	1.654	0.000	-0.007	-0.164**	-0.195**
7	Block own excl. nonexecutive	0.477	0.565	4.697	0.021	-0.007	0.005	0.452**
8	Log (Price, US$)	-0.587	2.353	4.024	-7.699	-0.048*	0.102**	0.390**
9	Log (Volatility)	11.432	3.009	19.660	1.609	-0.169**	-0.079**	-0.257**
10	Log (Volume)	-4.263	1.139	1.401	-9.957	0.291**	-0.042†	0.185**
11	Log (Total Assets)	18.319	2.179	23.201	9.348	-0.271**	-0.029	0.028

Notes: The table outlines the Pearson correlations between all of the variables as well as the individual variable means and standard deviations. The state-level institutional quality index has been normalized. † p<0.10; *p<0.05; **p<0.01.

Table 14.2b Descriptive statistics and correlations (continued)

		4	5	6	7	8	9	10	11
1	Quoted bid-ask spread								
2	Nonexecutive ownership								
3	European colony								
4	Fixed currency regime	1.000							
5	Formal institutional quality	0.929**	1.000						
6	Market cap/GDP ratio	-0.320**	-0.270**	1.000					
7	Block own excl. nonexecutive	0.210**	0.294**	-0.114	1.000				
8	Log (Price, US$)	0.649***	0.613**	-0.354	0.275***	1.000			
9	Log (Volatility)	-0.625**	-0.501**	0.272	-0.115**	-0.689***	1.000		
10	Log (Volume)	-0.031	-0.023	0.123	-0.051*	-0.357***	0.241**	1.000	
11	Log (Total Assets)	0.159**	0.154**	-0.211	0.062*	0.429**	0.013	-0.195**	1.000

Notes: † p<0.10; *p<0.05; **p<0.01

for Hypothesis 3. In practical terms, this implies that a one-standard-deviation increase in nonexecutive director ownership is accompanied by a 114.5 per cent increase in bid–ask spreads in jurisdictions maintaining European colonial status compared to jurisdictions that are independent.

In model 4, Table 14.3, we moderate by assigning the listing jurisdiction a fixed peg exchange regime. The main association between nonexecutive ownership and bid–ask spreads $(+0.712, p \leq 0.005)$ is negatively moderated by the binary effect of the fixed peg currency regime $(-0.597, p \leq 0.005)$. This provides statistical support for Hypothesis 4. In practical terms, the moderation cancels out some of the main association, with a one-standard-deviation increase in nonexecutive director ownership accompanied by a 52.58 per cent increase in bid–ask spreads in jurisdictions maintaining a fixed peg currency exchange rate regime compared to those that have independently managed floating-rate arrangements.

More generally, across the controls, there is a consistently negative and statistically significant association between all block owners (other than nonexecutive directors) and bid–ask spreads. This implies that a one-standard-deviation decrease in other block ownership leads to a decrease of between 3.4 per cent and 3.5 per cent in bid–ask spreads. There is also a consistently negative association between the ratio of market capitalization to GDP and bid–ask spreads, where a 1 per cent increase in this ratio leads to between a 1.7 per cent and 1.8 per cent reduction in bid–ask spreads. Finally, market microstructural controls and stock prices lack statistical significance, stock price volatility is positively associated with bid–ask spreads, and both traded volume and total assets are negatively associated with bid–ask spreads. These associations are in line with those found by both Stoll (2000) and Schnatterly et al. (2008). As a final note on our diagnostic statistics, the adjusted R^2s from all of the models are in line with those in the literature.

Using model parameter estimates, we input a range of values for nonexecutive ownership, first, in conjunction with the continuous normalized formal institutional quality index measure and, second, in conjunction with the binary metrics accounting for the listing jurisdictions retaining European colonial status and maintaining a fixed exchange rate regime. These moderation plots are shown in figures 14.1 to 14.3.

The evidence from Figure 14.1 reveals that at low levels of nonexecutive director ownership, there is little impact on informational asymmetry across the entire range of formal institutional quality in terms of variation in bid–ask spreads. Conversely, at increasing levels of nonexecutive director ownership, there is substantial variation in relation to formal institutional quality. Notably, at low levels of formal institutional quality, higher nonexecutive director ownership is associated with extremely high informational asymmetry, as reflected in the bid–ask spreads. As formal institutional quality improves this informational asymmetry, the bid–ask spreads rapidly decrease to negligible levels.

The evidence from the binary interactive plots in figures 14.2 and 14.3 supports the above finding in that in Figure 14.1, informational asymmetry in terms of bid–ask spreads rises much more steeply in the context of increasing nonexecutive director ownership within jurisdictions with European colonial status as opposed to sovereign territories. Conversely, in Figure 14.2, informational asymmetry, in the form of bid–ask spreads, is negligibly higher in the context of nonexecutive director ownership in fixed exchange rate regimes compared to comparable floating currency regimes.

Table 14.3   Nonexecutive director ownership and bid–ask spread OLS regression resultsa, b, c

	Dependent variable: Quoted bid–ask spread			
	Main effect	Moderated effect	Moderated effect	Moderated effect
	Model 1	Model 2	Model 3	Model 4
Intercept	0.853 [0.10]***	0.834 [0.10]***	0.867 [0.09]***	0.837 [0.10]***
Explanatory variables				
H1: Nonexecutive own	+0.485 [0.17]***	+0.733 [0.17]***	+0.428 [0.17]**	+0.712 [0.15]***
H2: x Institutional quality	–	-0.569 [0.21]***	–	–
H3: x European colony	–	–	+0.717 [0.43]*	–
H4: x Fixed currency regime	–	–	–	-0.597 [0.22]***
Institutional quality	–	-0.001 [0.01]	–	–
European colony	+0.069 [0.01]***	+0.072 [0.01]***	+0.062 [0.01]***	+0.072 [0.01]***
Fixed currency regime	-0.007 [0.01]	–	-0.009 [0.01]	-0.001 [0.01]
Ownership control				
All other block holders own	-0.033 [0.02]*	-0.035 [0.02]*	-0.035 [0.01]**	-0.034 [0.02]*
Institutional control				
Market cap/GDP	-0.017 [0.00]***	-0.017 [0.00]***	-0.018 [0.00]***	-0.017 [0.00]***
Microstructural controls				
Log (Price, US$)	-0.001 [0.01]	-0.001 [0.01]	-0.001 [0.01]	-0.002 [0.01]
Log (Volatility)	0.039 [0.01]***	-0.012 [0.00]***	-0.013 [0.00]***	-0.012 [0.00]***
Log (Volume)	-0.013 [0.00]***	0.038 [0.01]***	0.038 [0.01]***	0.038 [0.01]***
Log (Total Assets)	-0.021 [0.00]***	-0.021 [0.00]***	-0.021 [0.00]***	-0.021 [0.00]***
N (Obs)	1,343	1,343	1,343	1,343
F-statistic (prob.)	12.022 [0.00]	12.027 [0.00]	11.824 [0.00]	11.943 [0.00]
Log-likelihood	691.61	696.32	693.13	695.00
Adjusted R2	0.2519	0.2566	0.2530	0.2551

Notes: The table reports the OLS regression results from the unbalanced panels of the dependent variable (bid–ask spread) against the explanatory and control variables on a sample of 146 firms with up to 14 year-long time periods, leading to 1,343 firm-year observations. a White's cross-section standard errors and covariances (d.f. corrected) are in parentheses. b The robust standard errors and c industry and time fixed effects are included. † $p<0.10$; *$p<0.05$; **$p<0.01$; ***$p<0.005$.

5.4   Supplementary Analysis

As a final exercise, we moderate our main association between nonexecutive director ownership and the dependent variable by each of the six disaggregated WGI formal institutional quality dimensions. It is notable when moderating with one dimension that we aggregate the remaining five and include this value as a control to mitigate omitted variable bias. The results are presented in Table 14.4, where models 6 and 9 have visibly higher adjusted R2s and log-likelihood ratios than all of the other models, corresponding to moderation by corruption control and rule of law, respectively. This evidence emphasizes that corruption control and the rule of law are the two principal dimensions influencing bid–ask spreads across Caribbean offshore financial centres.

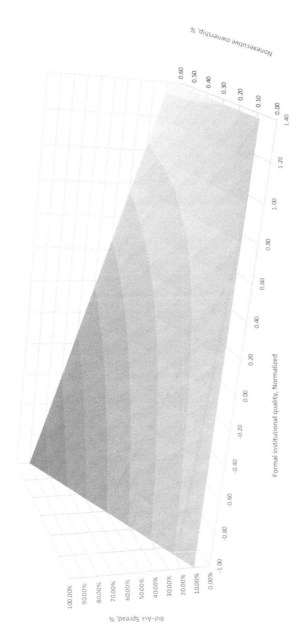

Figure 14.1   NED ownership and informational asymmetry (institutional quality)

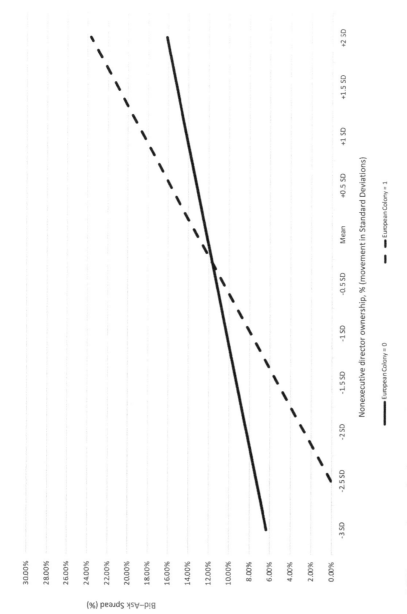

Figure 14.2   NED ownership and informational asymmetry (jurisdictions)

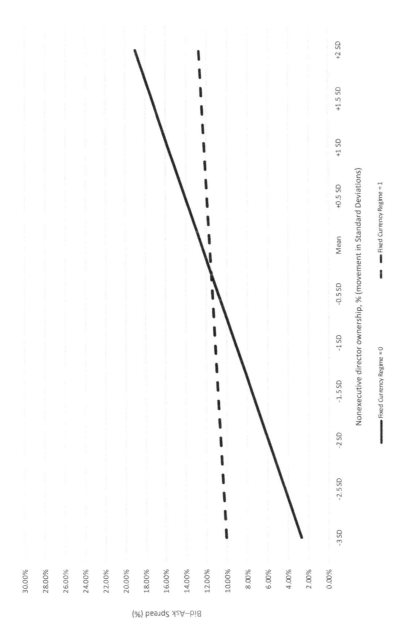

Figure 14.3   NED ownership and informational asymmetry (currency regime)

Table 14.4   Moderation by various dimensions of institutional quality regression resultsa, b, c

	Controls	CC	PS	GE	RL	RQ	VA
	Model 5	Model 6	Model 7	Model 8	Model 9	Model 10	Model 11
Intercept	0.855 [0.10]***	0.832 [0.10]***	0.836 [0.10]***	0.839 [0.10]***	0.835 [0.10]***	0.819 [0.10]***	0.819 [0.10]***
Nonexecutive own*CC	–	-0.408 [0.14]***	–	–	–	–	–
Nonexecutive own*PS	–	–	-0.681 [0.27]**	–	–	–	–
Nonexecutive own*GE	–	–	–	-0.567 [0.23]**	–	–	–
Nonexecutive own*RL	–	–	–	–	-0.492 [0.16]***	–	–
Nonexecutive own*RQ	–	–	–	–	–	-0.497 [0.24]**	–
Nonexecutive own*VA	–	–	–	–	–	–	-0.871 [0.40]*
Main effects							
Nonexecutive own	0.485 [0.17]***	0.626 [0.13]***	0.667 [0.15]***	0.764 [0.18]***	0.611 [0.12]***	0.722 [0.17]***	1.066 [0.31]***
Corruption Control (CC)	–	0.038 [0.01]***	–	–	–	–	–
Political Stability (PS)	–	–	-0.023 [0.02]	–	–	–	–
Government Effectiveness (GE)	–	–	–	0.032 [0.03]	–	–	–
Rule of Law (RL)	–	–	–	–	-0.029 [0.01]**	–	–
Regulatory Quality (RQ)	–	–	–	–	–	-0.023 [0.02]	–
Voice & Accountability (VA)	–	–	–	–	–	–	0.033 [0.03]
All other institutions	-0.002 [0.00]	-0.013 [0.01]**	0.005 [0.00]	-0.007 [0.01]	0.007 [0.00]**	0.002 [0.00] †	-0.004 [0.00]
Institutional controls							
European colony	0.070 [0.01]***	0.077 [0.01]***	0.065 [0.01]***	0.074 [0.01]***	0.069 [0.01]***	0.086 [0.02]***	0.075 [0.01]***

	Controls	CC	PS	GE	RL	RQ	VA
	Model 5	Model 6	Model 7	Model 8	Model 9	Model 10	Model 11
Market cap./GDP	-0.017 [0.00]***	-0.017 [0.00]***	-0.016 [0.00]***	-0.019 [0.00]***	-0.019 [0.00]***	-0.018 [0.00]***	-0.017 [0.00]***
Ownership control							
All other block holders own	-0.033 [0.02]*	-0.031 [0.01]**	-0.035 [0.02]**	-0.036 [0.02]**	-0.036 [0.02]**	-0.031 [0.01]**	-0.034 [0.01]**
Microstructural controls							
Log (Price, US$)	-0.001 [0.01]	-0.001 [0.01]	-0.001 [0.01]	-0.001 [0.01]	-0.001 [0.01]	-0.001 [0.01]	-0.001 [0.01]
Log (Volume)	-0.013 [0.00]***	-0.011 [0.00]***	-0.012 [0.00]***	-0.013 [0.00]***	-0.013 [0.00]***	-0.011 [0.00]***	-0.012 [0.00]***
Log (Volatility)	0.039 [0.01]***	0.037 [0.01]***	0.038 [0.01]***	0.038 [0.01]***	0.038 [0.01]***	0.037 [0.01]***	0.037 [0.01]***
Log (Total Assets)	-0.021 [0.00]***	-0.021 [0.00]***	-0.021 [0.00]***	-0.021 [0.00]***	-0.021 [0.00]***	-0.021 [0.00]***	-0.021 [0.00]***
F-statistic (prob.)	12.037 [0.00]	11.818 [0.00]	11.729 [0.00]	11.725 [0.00]	11.799 [0.00]	11.734 [0.00]	11.673 [0.00]
Log-likelihood	691.84	697.59	696.17	696.10	697.29	696.25	695.27
Adjusted R2	0.2522	0.2574	0.2558	0.2558	0.2571	0.2559	0.2548

Notes: The table reports the OLS regression coefficients for the annual quoted half-spreads on each of the six disaggregated WGI institutional dimensions and firm liquidity characteristics for 146 firms across eight jurisdictions. The six dimensions are CC (for corruption control), PS (political stability), GE (government effectiveness), RL (the rule of law), RQ (regulatory quality) and VA (voice and accountability), which are defined by Kaufman et al. (2009) and sourced from http://info.worldbank.org/governance/wgi/index.aspx#faq. The firm liquidity characteristics are price, volume, daily return volatility and total assets. All are natural log scaled. There are 1,341 observations derived from 146 listed firms over 14 years. a Industry and time (year) binary fixed effects are included in all cases. b White's cross-section standard errors and covariances (d.f. corrected) are in parentheses. † p<0.10; *p<0.05; **p<0.01; *** p<0.005.

6.   DISCUSSION

Our study is the first to undertake an exploration of the impact of nonexecutive director ownership on informational asymmetry as captured by firms' traded stocks' bid–ask spreads within an offshore jurisdictional context. In accordance with our expectations, we find that higher levels of nonexecutive director ownership are associated with substantially elevated informational asymmetry. Our use of bid–ask spreads quoted by stockbrokers within markets is a unique measure of informational asymmetry and is based on the brokers' estimates of the levels of informational asymmetry in a given listed firm's stock in relation to the anticipated trading cost incurred by outside minority investors. Conceptually, our findings are intuitive given the smallness of predominantly offshore island economies, which are almost entirely controlled by handfuls of families that have a hegemonic influence over the national institutional frameworks. Such extensive familial influence underscores the extensive socialization of these nascent island economies and the density of social interconnectedness upon which they are founded. In such contexts, nonexecutive directors are inherently socially interconnected both to firm owners, who are predominantly families, and to the extended families that hegemonically control the island economies. This leads to notions of nonexecutive directors being impartial monitors and their independence and avoidance of conflicts of interest being at best superfluous. We argue that nonexecutive directors need such dense social interconnectedness to facilitate access to resources. However, from the perspective of outside minority investors or stakeholders, these traits constitute significant risks to their property rights given the reduced emphasis on monitoring, which is reflected in increased informational asymmetry and quoted bid–ask spreads.

Empirically, we extend this underlying relationship between nonexecutive director ownership and informational asymmetry in the form of quoted bid–ask spreads through moderation by three institutional metrics. Our first moderator is formal institutional quality, and our findings indicate that nonexecutive director ownership is associated with heightened informational asymmetry and related bid–ask spreads only at lower levels of formal institutional quality. Conversely, nonexecutive director ownership has a nearly negligible impact on informational asymmetry at either lower levels of ownership or progressively higher formal institutional quality. Intuitively, lower institutional quality environments provide fewer protections for external contracting, with a resulting emphasis on relational contracting through social interconnectedness. Nonexecutive directors within such contexts are valued in terms of their social connections that facilitate access to resources and convey the legitimacy of their firms. However, such interconnectedness in conjunction with the reduced effectiveness of impartial monitoring implies higher informational asymmetry and thus elevated bid–ask spreads. We argue that the opposite is true in contexts of higher formal institutional quality, where external contracting is more prevalent and better supported.

Finally, we extend our analysis by moderating by two additional institutional characteristics, namely whether the jurisdictions are European colonies and whether the jurisdictions have a fixed exchange rate regime. Our findings reveal that nonexecutive director ownership is associated with considerably higher informational asymmetry, in terms of bid–ask spreads, in jurisdictions that are European colonies compared to those that are sovereign. This is seemingly counterintuitive in that it goes against various assertions of the "law and finance" research that link institutional quality with "better" governance at the firm level (La Porta et al., 1998; La Porta et al., 1999). Next, our evidence reveals that in the context of jurisdictions that are sovereign and have a fixed exchange rate regime, the association between nonexecutive director ownership and informational asymmetry, or bid–ask spreads, is reduced. This is contrary to the findings regarding the moderating impact of European colonial status and provides support for Allred et al.'s (2017) argument that offshore tax havens constitute a "third" institutional category outside the current dichotomy between "developed" and "developing/ emerging" country frameworks. Our study is the first to explore the impact of the institutional environment on the governance attributes of boards of directors and particularly nonexecutive directors.

Our study has a number of limitations. The first limitation is that it is constrained to only listed firms in the mostly English-speaking Caribbean region. It excludes unlisted firms and vehicles that are more typically used in aggressive tax engineering strategies by controlling owners. The second limitation is that it would be useful to widen the study to encompass the non-anglophone Caribbean region, where similar offshore centres are notably present: the Netherlands Antilles of Aruba, Curaçao, and Sint Maarten. Finally, the third limitation is that, ideally, the sample coverage should include all offshore jurisdictions worldwide to facilitate comparability. However, a major constraint in all three limitations are the severe impediments in obtaining data, which are a function of the secrecy and asset protections we study.

7. CONCLUSIONS

Our study explores the association between nonexecutive director ownership and informational asymmetry in the form of bid–ask spreads quoted by stockbrokers to minority outside investors. It also provides a multi-level analysis of the formal institutional embeddedness of this association. Practitioners are able to gain better insights into the effectiveness of nonexecutive directors in terms of their ownership mitigating informational asymmetry, which is particularly important in the opaque context of firms' burgeoning use of offshore financial centres and tax havens. Practitioners can also gain insights into the extent of the influence of nonexecutive director ownership under certain predetermined, contextually embedded conditions.

REFERENCES

Adams, R.B., and Ferreira, D. (2009). Women in the boardroom and their impact on governance and performance. *Journal of Financial Economics*, 94(2), 291–309.

Aguilera, R.V. (2005). Corporate governance and director accountability: an institutional comparative perspective. *British Journal of Management*, 16, 39–53.

Aguilera, R.V., and Jackson, G. (2010). Comparative and international corporate governance. *Academy of Management Annals*, 4(1), 485–556.

Allred, B.B., Findley, M.G., Nielson, D., and Sharman, J.C. (2017). Anonymous shell companies: a global audit study and field experiment in 176 countries. *Journal of International Business Studies*, 48, 596–619.

Baysinger, B., and Hoskisson, R.E. (1990). The composition of boards of directors and strategic control: effects on corporate strategy. *Academy of Management Review*, 15(1), 72–87.

Berger, R., Silbiger, A., Herstein, R., and Branes, B.R. (2015). Analyzing business-to-business relationships in an Arab context. *Journal of World Business*, 50, 454–64.

Berle, A. and Means, G. (1932). *The Modern Corporation and Private Property*. New York, Macmillan.

Bollen, N.P.B., Smith, T., and Whaley, R.E. (2004). Modelling the bid/ask spread: measuring the inventory-holding premium. *Journal of Financial Economics*, 72, 97–141.

Box, T., and Griffith, T. (2016). Price clustering asymmetries in limit order flows. *Financial Management*, 45(4), 1041–66.

Cantwell, J., Dunning, J.H., and Lundan, S.M. (2010). An evolutionary approach to understanding international business activity: the co-evolution of MNEs and the institutional environment. *Journal of International Business Studies*, 41, 567–86.

Christie, W.G., and Schultz, P.H. (1994). Why do NASDAQ market makers avoid odd-eighth quotes? *Journal of Finance*, 49(5), 1813–40.

Cobb, S.C. (2001). Globalization in a small island context: creating and marketing competitive advantage for offshore financial services. *Geografiska Annaler*, 83B(4), 161–74.

Coleman, J.S. (1988). Social capital in the creation of human capital. *American Journal of Sociology*, 94, S95–S120.

Collin-Dufresne, P., and Fos, V. (2015). Do prices reveal the presence of informed trading? *Journal of Finance*, 70(4), 1555–82.

Cooray, L.J.M. (1974). The reception of Roman-Dutch law in Sri Lanka. *Comparative & International Law of South Africa*, 7(3), 295–320.

Dalton, D., Daily, C., Certo, S.T., and Roengpitya, R. (2003). Meta-analysis of financial performance and equity: fusion or confusion? *Academy of Management Journal*, 46, 13–26.

Dalton, C.M., and Dalton, D.R. (2005). Boards of directors: utilizing empirical evidence in developing practical prescriptions. *British Journal of Management*, 16, S91–S97.

Damgaard, J., Elkjaer, T., and Johannesen, N. (2019). The rise of phantom investments: empty corporate shells in tax havens undermine tax collection in advanced, emerging market, and developing economies. *Finance & Development*, 56(3), 11–13.

DiMaggio, P., and Powell, W. (1983). The iron cage revisited: institutional isomorphism and collective rationality in organizational fields. *American Sociological Review*, 48, 147–60.

Doidge, C., Karolyi, A., and Stulz, R. (2007). Why do countries matter so much for corporate governance? *Journal of Financial Economics*, 86, 1–39.

Donnelly, R., and Mulcahy, M. (2008). Board structure, ownership, and voluntary disclosure in Ireland. *Corporate Governance: An International Review*, 16(5), 416–29.

Dyreng, S.D., Lindsay, B.P., and Thornock, J.R. (2013). Exploring the role Delaware plays as a domestic tax haven. *Journal of Financial Economics*, 108, 751–72.

Ellis, J.A., Moeller, S.B., Schlingemann, F.P., and Stulz, R.M. (2017). Portable country governance and cross-border acquisitions. *Journal of International Business Studies*, 48(2), 148–73.

Falato, A., Kadyrzhanova, D., and Lel, U. (2014). Distracted directors: does board busyness hurt shareholder value? *Journal of Financial Economics*, 113(3), 404–26.

Fama, E.F. (1980). Agency problems and the Theory of the Firm. *Journal of Political Economy*, 88(2), 288–307.

Fama, E.F., and Jensen, M.C. (1983). Separation of ownership and control. *Journal of Law & Economics*, 26(2), 301–25.

Filatotchev, I. (2005). Effects of executive characteristics and venture capital involvement on board composition and share ownership in IPO firms. *British Journal of Management*, 17, 75–92.

Filatotchev, I., and Bishop, K. (2002). Board composition, share ownership, and "underpricing" of UK IPO firms. *Strategic Management Journal*, 23, 941–55.

Glosten, L.R., and Harris, L.E. (1988). Estimating the components of the bid/ask spread. *Journal of Financial Economics*, 21, 123–42.

Golden, B.R., and Zajac, E.J. (2001). When will boards influence strategy? Inclination x Power = Strategic Change. *Strategic Management Journal*, 22, 1087–111.

Granovetter, M.S. (1973). The strength of weak ties. *American Journal of Sociology*, 78(6), 1360–80.

Harris, L. (1994). Minimum price variations, discrete bid-ask spreads, and quotation sizes. *Review of Financial Studies*, 7, 149–78.

Heflin, F., and Shaw, K.W. (2000). Blockholder ownership and market liquidity. *Journal of Financial and Quantitative Analysis*, 35(4), 621–33.

Hines, J.R., Jr. (2010). Treasure islands. *Journal of Economic Perspectives*, 24(4), 103–25.

Jensen, M.C., and Meckling, W. (1976). Theory of the firm: managerial behavior, agency costs, and ownership structure. *Journal of Financial Economics*, 3, 305–60.

Kaufman, D., Kraay, A., and Mastruzzi, M. (2009). *Governance Matters VIII: Governance Indicators for 1996–2008*. Washington, DC: World Bank Policy Research Unit.

Khanna, T., and Palepu, K. (2000). Is group affiliation profitable in emerging markets? An analysis of diversified Indian business groups. *Journal of Finance*, 55(2), 867–91.

Khemraj, T., and Pasha, S. (2014). The determinants of bid-ask spread in the Guyanese FX market. *Journal of Developing Areas*, 48(2), 39–62.

Kingsley, A.F., and Graham, B.A.T. (2017). The effects of information voids on capital flows in emerging markets. *Journal of International Business Studies*, 48(3), 324–43.

La Porta, R., Lopez-de-Silanes, F., and Shleifer, A. (1999). Corporate ownership around the world. *Journal of Finance*, 54, 471–518.

La Porta, R., Lopez-de-Silanes, F., Schliefer, A., and Vishny, R. (1998). Law and finance. *Journal of Political Economy*, 106(6), 1113–55.

Lee, R.W. (1914). Roman-Dutch Law in British Guiana. *Journal of the Society of Comparative Legislation*, 14(1), 11–23.

Lesmond, D.A. (2005). Liquidity of emerging markets. *Journal of Financial Economics*, 77, 411–52.

Madhaven A. (1992). Trading mechanisms in securities markets. *Journal of Finance*, 47(2), 607–41.

Meyer, K.E., and Sinani, E. (2009). When and where does foreign direct investment generate positive spillovers? A meta-analysis. *Journal of International Business Studies*, 40(7), 1075–94.

Miller, D., Le Breton-Miller, I., and Lester, R.H. (2013). Family firm governance, strategic conformity, and performance: institutional vs. strategic perspectives. *Organization Science*, 24(1), 189–209.

Moon, T., and Schoenherr, D. (2021). The rise of a network: spillover of political patronage and cronyism to the private sector. *Journal of Financial Economics*, forthcoming. https://doi.org/10.1016/j.jfineco.2021.09.014.

Mura, R. (2007). Firm performance: do non-executive directors have minds of their own? Evidence from UK panel data. *Financial Management*, Autumn, 81–112.

Nahapiet, J., and Ghoshal, S. (1998). Social capital, intellectual capital, and the organizational advantage. *Academy of Management Review*, 23(2), 242–66.

North, D.C. (1991). Institutions. *Journal of Economic Perspectives*, 5, 97–112.

North, D.C. (1994). The historical evolution of polities. *International Review of Law and Economics*, 14, 381–91.

Nowak, M.J., and McCabe, M. (2003). Information costs and the role of the independent corporate director. *Corporate Governance: An International Review*, 11(4), 300–307.

Roberts, J., McNulty, T., and Stiles, P. (2005). Beyond agency conceptions of the work of the non-executive director: creating accountability in the boardroom. *British Journal of Management*, 16, 5–26.

Schnatterly, K., Shaw, K.W., and Jennings, W.W. (2008). Information advantages of large institutional owners. *Strategic Management Journal*, 29, 219–27.

Shen, W. (2005). Improve board effectiveness: the need for incentives. *British Journal of Management*, 16, S81–S89.

Stoll, H.R. (1978). The supply of dealer services in securities markets. *Journal of Finance*, 33, 1133–51.

Stoll, H.R. (2000). Friction. *Journal of Finance*, 55(4), 1479–514.

Tax Justice Network (2019). Financial Secrecy Index. www.financialsecrecyindex.com/en/ (accessed 29 January 2020).

Vayanos, D., and Wang, T. (2007). Search and endogenous concentration of liquidity in asset markets. *Journal of Economic Theory*, 136, 66–104.

Wang, C., Hong, J., Kafouros, M., and Wright, M. (2012). Exploring the role of government involvement in outward FDI from emerging economies. *Journal of International Business Studies*, 43(7), 655–76.

West, A. (2014). Ubuntu and business ethics: problems, perspectives and prospects. *Journal of Business Ethics*, 121(1), 47–61.

White, D. (1961). Some problems of a hybrid legal system: a case study of St Lucia. *International and Comparative Law Quarterly*, 30, 862–81.
Zattoni, A. and Cuomo, F. (2010). How independent, competent and incentivized should non-executive directors be? An empirical investigation of good governance codes. *British Journal of Management*, 21(1), 63–79.

APPENDIX

The table documents a non-exhaustive representation of data and information sources from the Caribbean region.

Table 14A.1   Data sources

Market	Information source
Caribbean	Databases: Bloomberg LLP; Thomson Perfect Information Portal & Datastream
Bermuda	Bermuda Stock Exchange library, Hamilton, Bermuda and website: www.bsx.com/
	Hamilton-based interviews (11/2016 and 05/2019):
	Bermuda Stock Exchange: James S. McKirdy (Chief Compliance Officer)
	Bermuda Monetary Authority (BMA): Tessa Ingham (Analyst)
	Bermuda Chamber of Commerce: Kendaree Burgess (Executive Director)
	Bermuda Government: Victoria Taylor, Executive Officer
	Listed firm: Ozics Holdings Ltd (Auvo Kaikkonen, CEO); Cohort Ltd (Tracey Packwood); Bermuda Commercial Bank Ltd (Charlene Gilbert)
Barbados	Barbados Stock Exchange, Bridgetown, Barbados and website: www.bse.com.bb/
	Bridgetown-based interviews (07/2011 and 11/2016):
	Barbados exchange: Marlon E. Yarde (GM); Barry Blenham (Operations); Donna Hope (Operations Manager)
	Central Bank of Barbados: Financial Division
The Bahamas	Bahamas Stock Exchange, Nassau, The Bahamas and website: http://bisxbahamas.com/
	Nassau-based interviews (05/2019):
	Bahamas International Securities Exchange [BISX]: Keith Davies (CEO); Holland Grant (COO)
	Chamber of Commerce: Jeffrey N. Beckles (CEO)
	Securities Exchange Commission of The Bahamas (Senior Analysts)
	Bahamas Venture Capital Fund c/o Baker Tilly Managers: Joan Octaviano (Head of Audit)
	Bahamas Development Bank: Director (Mme Pelicanos)
	University of The Bahamas graduate school of business: Remelda Moxley (Dean)
	Listed firm: Bank of Bahamas (Leashawn McPhee); Emera (Dina Bartolacci Seely); Commonwealth Bank (Gina Greene); ICBL (Jenifer Clarke); Doctors Hospital (Joanne Lowe)
Cayman Islands	CISX, Cayman Islands Exchange, Georgetown, Grand Cayman and website: www.csx.ky
	Georgetown, Grand Cayman-based interviews (05/2019):
	Cayman Islands Exchange: Sandy McFarlane (Operations Manageress)
	Cayman Islands Development Bank: Tracy Ebanks (General Manager/CEO)
	Cayman National Securities: Erol Babayigit (Vice President)
Jamaica	JSE, Jamaican Stock Exchange, Kingston, Jamaica and website: www.jamstockex.com/
	Kingston-based interviews (07/2016):
	Jamaican Stock Exchange: Marlene J. Street Forrest (General Manager); Sandra Shirley (Principal e-campus); Charlette Eddie-Nugent (Listings Manager); Neville R. Ellis (Operations Manager)
	JSE electronic media marketing event (07/2016): Spanish Court Hotel Annex, Kingston, Jamaica
	Bank of Jamaica: Financial services division interviews
Eastern Caribbean	ECSE, Basseterre, St Kitts & Nevis and website: www.ecseonline.com/
	Basseterre-based interviews (11/2011):
	Eastern Caribbean Stock Exchange: Trevor E. Blake (GM); Sherizan Mills (Operations Officer)
	Eastern Caribbean Central Bank visit (11/2011)
	Telephone-based interviews (06/2016–08/2016):
	Eastern Caribbean Stock Exchange: Trevor E. Blake (GM); Sherizan Mills (Operations Officer)
	Nevis, Charlestown-based interviews (11/2011): Financial district in Charlestown, Nevis;
	St Lucia-based interviews (11/2011): Financial district, Castries, St Lucia

Market	Information source
Guyana	GASCI, Guyana Securities Council, Georgetown and website: www.gasci.com/
	Telephone-based interviews (08/2015 to 01/2017): Cheryl Ibbott (CEO, Guyana Securities Council c/o Bank of Guyana); Vick (Compliance Officer, Guyana Securities Council)
Trinidad & Tobago	TTSE, Trinidad & Tobago Stock Exchange, Port of Spain and website: http://ttsec.org.tt/
	Trinidad, Port of Spain-based procurement (06/2016 to 07/2016):
	Trinidad, Ministry of Finance: Melissa Mattoo and Christine Frank (Communications Officers)
	Trinidad, Central Bank of Trinidad & Tobago: Candice Dilbar (Research Economist)
	Trinidad, listed firm: National Enterprises Ltd (Keisha Armstrong, Head of Secretariat)
	Tobago: Scarborough and Canaan-based interviews in financial district (06/2016 to 07/2016)

15. The impact of the audit committee and internal audit function on board decision-making during an extreme financial crisis

Khairul Ayuni Mohd Kharuddin and Ilias G. Basioudis

1.   INTRODUCTION

The 2007–2008 global financial crisis (GFC) received a great deal of attention from investors, the media, governments and others, who in turn focused on and scrutinised various aspects of accounting, auditing and financial reporting within the generic corporate governance function in the financial markets. The effectiveness of the corporate governance function and the regulatory framework themselves had also become a global concern in the most severe financial crisis for many decades. Therefore, a comprehensive empirical study on corporate governance, audit quality and earnings quality, and the impact on firm decision-making during the period is warranted.

It is a well-accepted fact that the quality of company reported earnings affects investors' confidence and allocation of resources in the financial market. Company reported earnings are, however, prone to legitimate management manipulations, but the established functions of corporate governance and external auditing serve as direct monitoring mechanisms of the company's financial reporting process. As these two functions also have a potentially direct impact on the degree of earnings management[1] exercised by the companies' management, the importance of their role and effectiveness cannot be over-emphasised. Empirical research provides support for the notion that characteristics of effective company corporate governance, such as the board of directors and the audit committee function, as well as the internal audit function, lead to fewer earnings management activities[2] and in a broader sense to a higher quality of financial reporting (earnings) and audit quality.

As is well documented, the 2007–2008 GFC resulted in the collapse or privatisation of many high-profile companies (for example, Northern Rock, Royal Bank of Scotland, Lloyds and Alliance & Leicester in the UK; Fannie Mae, Freddie Mac, Lehman Brothers and Merrill Lynch in the US; ABN Amro in the Netherlands; and many others around the world), with many critics blaming the external auditors and corporate governance for their failure to prevent such a crisis from happening in the first place. We contend that the GFC provides a relevant setting to study the impact of overall corporate governance effectiveness in constraining earnings management. The opportunistic pressures for both auditors and managers are more prevalent during an extreme financial distress period as compared to a booming economic situation. In such crisis periods, managers are normally struggling to meet or beat the company financial performance – a condition described by sales reductions, more bad debts and greater obsolete inventory, thus increasing managers' propensity to manipulate earnings (Dechow and Schrand, 2004; Charoenwong and Jiraporn, 2009; Lang et al., 2011; Habib et al., 2013). More specifically, auditors lost clients during the GFC due to firms' insolvency (Pál, 2010); hence auditors might have relied on clients' economic importance in the past, thus possibly compromising their independence (Sharma et al., 2011), and auditors consistently failed to warn the firms on their going concern status before the GFC, where most failed companies received an unqualified audit report just a few months prior to the firms' filing of bankruptcy, thus raising questions on auditors' capability to spot financial irregularities (Sikka, 2009).

Furthermore, following the financial crisis, the UK regulator, the Financial Reporting Council (FRC), introduced for the first time in 2010 (with many updates since then) the Corporate Governance Code, the UK Stewardship Code and the Audit Firm Governance Code with the aim of improving the quality of governance and financial reporting in the public listed companies in the UK, after taking into account lessons learned from the 2008 financial crisis (FRC, 2010).

Hence, corporate governance research during and following the GFC period is important, considering the changing financial reporting landscape and regulatory environment which has impacted the role played by corporate governance and external auditors. Moreover, there has been no published study jointly examining the relationship between various aspects of corporate governance, external audit and earnings management in the UK in the period during and subsequent to the financial crisis. Therefore, the financial crisis setting makes it interesting to analyse the effect of corporate governance on audit quality and earnings quality to see whether the findings would turn out differently as compared to other studies carried out during non-crisis periods. The corporate governance features examined in this study are the internal audit function, and audit committee characteristics relating to its size, independence, expertise and activity.

This study supports the argument that a company's corporate governance function and the auditor's quality characteristics cannot be isolated from one another when analysing their effect on earnings and audit quality, as the auditor's monitoring role and reporting decision vary depending on the strength of the company's corporate governance structure (Larcker and Richardson, 2004). Furthermore, findings from prior auditor choice studies suggest that the auditor's differentiation strategy (such as the auditor's industry specialisation) is valued by the board of directors, audit committee and shareholders as signalling a higher-quality audit, as they are more likely to choose industry-specialist auditors instead of relying just on a blanket brand name (Abbott and Parker, 2000; Beasley and Petron, 2001; Velury et al., 2003; Kane and Velury, 2004; Chen et al., 2005). This study employs a rigorous approach in measuring earnings quality using proxies such as discretionary accruals and the likelihood of issuing a modified audit opinion or going concern report.

The study contributes to the extant literature by examining the effectiveness of two aspects of corporate governance function, namely the audit committee and the presence of an internal audit unit, in conjunction with the impact of the GFC, on company decision-making and auditor reporting decisions. Similarly to prior literature, we capture four characteristics of the audit committee (size, independence, expertise and activity). We also intercept the above relationships by applying the joint industry–expert auditor framework that is used in prior studies (Francis et al., 2005, in the US; Basioudis and Francis, 2007, in the UK), and hence we provide support in this specific area of research with scant prior evidence.

What do we find? Only one of the two aspects of corporate governance function is shown to have made a meaningful impact on the quality of reported earnings and audit quality in the UK in the period of extreme crisis. We obtain consistent evidence of a significant constraining of earnings management and a higher likelihood of an auditor issuing a modified or going concern report in the presence of an active internal audit department. We can conclude that the internal audit function achieved an important improvement to the quality of financial reporting and audit quality during the GFC in the UK. Further, the overall picture from the study's results leads us to assume that none of the audit committee characteristics successfully deterred earnings management, or influenced auditor reporting decisions in the GFC period, although there are some instances of an audit committee parameter that encouraged conservatism effectively or increased audit quality in some sub-samples in that period. We can determine that there was little evidence of an audit committee's involvement in company financial decisions or auditor decision-making in the crisis period of 2008–2010. Finally, after applying the joint industry–specialist auditor framework in our study, we document that those auditors who were jointly national and city-specific industry leaders helped restrain clients' earnings management and were inclined to issue more modified or going concern reports to their clients during the crisis in the period 2008–2010.

On reflection, our empirical findings demonstrate that both the internal and external audit functions were an important aspect of companies' overall governance mission and improved the quality of the reported earnings as well as audit quality. Thereby, we argue that both functions supported organisation (listed company, audit firm) decision-making and board performance management during an extreme financial crisis.

The remainder of the chapter is structured as follows. The following section reviews the relevant literature and presents the hypothesis development. Section 3 describes the research design of the study, and the penultimate section discusses the empirical findings. The last section summarises and concludes the study.

2.   LITERATURE REVIEW AND HYPOTHESES DEVELOPMENT

Earnings Quality and Audit Quality during Crises

Earnings management and the impact on earnings quality as well as auditors' decision-making and its impact on audit quality could be magnified during extreme crises. For instance, during the GFC companies experienced a fall in their profitability, drops in consumer demand, employee layoffs, spending being slashed and expansion plans being halted, and they tried to find new ways to survive until the financial crisis subsided. Therefore, in such harsh economic environment conditions for companies, managers could manage earnings upward to avoid presenting unanticipated results and potentially report an acceptable level of losses (DeFond and Jiambalvo, 1994; Charitou et al., 2007; Arthur et al., 2015; Lisboa and Kacharava, 2018). In doing so, their objective could be to restore investor and stakeholder confidence in the company and the market and signal that the position of the company was not far worse than its competitors in the industry (Beidleman, 1973; Khanchel, 2011; Cimini, 2015). On the other hand, crises can favour big bath practices, where managers decide to manage earnings downward and ultimately report even worse earnings in order to able to enhance future earnings (Asquith et al., 1994; DeAngelo et al., 1994; Filip and Raffournier, 2014).

Similarly, the GFC negatively impacted audit quality and led regulators and others (including investors, financial media, etc.) to question whether auditors duly discharged their auditing duties (Woods et al., 2009; Geiger et al., 2014). For example, auditors were heavily criticised for failing to apply properly the auditing standards in connection with specific financial reporting areas that were significantly affected by the economic crisis (Humphrey et al., 2009). Conversely, audit firms claimed that there was a significant increase in the auditors' effort and in the propensity to issue going concern opinions, and research studies show an increase in audit quality during the GFC (Xu et al., 2011; Xu et al., 2013; Geiger et al., 2014), albeit many have argued that going concern opinions should have been issued in the years before the onset of the GFC.

The Monitoring Role of the Audit Committees and Internal Audit

According to the first UK Corporate Governance Code (2010), the board of directors' responsibilities include "setting the company's strategic aims, providing the leadership to put them into effect, supervising the management of the business and reporting to shareholders on their stewardship". This suggests that the board of directors plays a very strategic and tactical role in determining business success. Thus, it follows that in order to be able to discharge their respective duties and responsibilities effectively, it is very important that the directors possess the appropriate balance of skills, experience, independence and knowledge of the company. The UK Companies Act (2006) also outlines the company board's duties in ensuring transparency and fairness in a firm's financial reporting, and further it stipulates that all accounts of public listed companies that have been prepared and approved by the directors have to be independently audited by an external auditor to verify their credibility, objectivity and reliability.

In order to carry out its responsibility effectively, the board may, however, delegate its authority to sub-committees, such as the audit committee, nomination committee and remunerations committee. In spite of this, such delegation of authority does not make the board less accountable for the sub-committees' actions. The audit committee is of particular interest in this study. This is because this committee has a direct link with the financial reporting process of a firm and represents the firm's liaison with the external auditor. The formation of the audit committee aims to enhance the integrity of the reported numbers, thus maintaining investors' confidence in the financial market. The successful implementation of the committee's tasks also helps to reduce management's opportunistic behaviour, improve staff accountability, increase internal control effectiveness, enhance audit quality and strengthen the function of the board of directors while helping them to meet their legal responsibilities (Wolnizer, 1995).

Many researchers, particularly in Anglo-American settings, have examined the relationship between corporate governance and accounting or auditing outcomes. Among the earlier studies are those by Turley and Zaman (2004), Gramling et al. (2004), DeFond and Francis (2005), Cohen et al. (2007), Schneider (2009), García-Meca and Sánchez-Ballesta (2009), Bédard and Gendron (2010), and Lin and Hwang (2010). Consistently, most of these meta-analysis studies have generally found evidence which supports the notion that an effective board and audit committee are associated with "good" accounting and auditing outcomes, and more effective internal controls within the business environment (Carcello et al., 2011).

The most popular characteristics of the board and audit committee that have been examined are mainly their independence and expertise (Beasley, 1996; Dechow et al., 1996; Abbott et al., 2004), whereas accounting outcomes are normally measured in terms of lower earnings management (e.g., Klein 2002), lower restatements (e.g., Abbott et al., 2004) or fraudulent financial reporting (e.g., Beasley, 1996; Beasley et al., 2000). Auditing outcomes that have been examined include auditors' reporting decisions (e.g., Carcello and Neal 2000, 2003), auditor type (e.g., Beasley and Petron, 2001) and auditor fees (e.g., Carcello et al., 2002; Abbott et al., 2003). Overall, research has demonstrated that the two roles of the board and audit committee are integral in the company financial reporting process in order to protect shareholders' interests and maintain investors' confidence in the financial markets.

Moreover, the internal audit function plays an important role in facilitating the audit committee in its financial reporting oversight role (Goodwin and Yeo, 2001; Goodwin, 2003). Abbott et al. (2012) and Pizzini et al. (2015) report evidence that external auditors' reliance on the client's internal audit function helps increase audit efficiency, resulting in reduced audit delay and better audit quality. Zain et al. (2015) show that the reliance of external auditors on the internal auditor's work is contingent on the quality of the client's internal audit function.

Therefore, the corporate governance characteristics examined in this study are audit committees and the internal audit function. As in previous research, we examine four audit committee characteristics, namely size, independence, expertise and activity in relation to audit quality and earnings quality. The presence of a client's strong control environment safeguarded by the audit committee and the internal audit function leads to enhanced client financial reporting and reliance by the external auditor. This in turn affects earnings quality (e.g., Chan et al., 2008; Gleason et al., 2017) and audit quality (Hay et al., 2008; Bame-Aldred et al., 2013), but also company and audit firm board decision-making (e.g., Cheng et al., 2013; Feng et al., 2015; D'Mello et al., 2017).

Audit committee size, audit quality and earnings quality

Audit committee size is an important attribute of good corporate governance as it contributes to the effectiveness of the committee's function, which in turn affects the company's overall financial reporting quality. The first UK Corporate Governance Code (2010)[3] required company boards to establish an audit committee comprised of at least three members. The suggestion of a minimum number of members on the audit committee, without an upper limit, expresses the regulatory bodies' view in the UK that they place great emphasis on ensuring the audit committees are sufficiently staffed.

A larger audit committee represents greater resources, talents, skills and knowledge invested by the company to be certain of overseeing more carefully the financial reporting process (Vafeas, 2000; Bédard et al., 2004; Norman et al., 2007; Lin and Hwang, 2010), and thus it is argued a more effective monitoring is accomplished. Larger audit committees are more likely to withstand pressures of management collusion (Dezoort and Salterio, 2001) and are able to pay more attention to the overall financial accounting process (Anderson et al., 2004).

Results of studies on the effect of audit committee size on audit quality, financial reporting outcomes and earnings quality are inconclusive. Prior studies (such as Abbott et al., 2003; Vafeas and Waegelein, 2007; Hoitash and Hoitash, 2009; Zaman et al., 2011) have found a positive association between the audit committee size and audit fees. Few other studies report negative associations between audit committee size and auditor independence (Hoitash and Hoitash, 2009), auditor switches (Archambeault and DeZoort, 2001), adverse rulings by the FRRP[4] (Song and Windram, 2004), financial restatements (Lin et al., 2006) and lower accrual estimation error (Kent et al., 2010).

On the contrary, Abbott et al. (2004) and Bédard et al. (2004) report no significant relationship between audit committee size and earnings management capturing earnings quality. There are also studies which show no significant association between audit committee size and audit and financial reporting measures such as audit fees (O'Sullivan, 1999), restatements

(Abbott et al., 2004) and accruals (Baxter and Cotter, 2009). Given the mixed results from previous studies, this study makes no directional prediction, and the hypothesis is stated below in the null form, as follows:

H1: There is no significant relationship between the size of audit committees and earnings and audit quality.

Audit committee independence, audit quality and earnings quality

The independence of the audit committee is another key characteristic for effective monitoring of the financial reporting process. It is assumed that independent directors within the audit committee are better at monitoring than their insider counterparts (DeFond and Francis, 2005) and are more likely to report questionable managerial financial reporting practices to appropriate authorities (Baxter and Cotter, 2009). The independence of the audit committee is also a subject of increasing regulatory interest. The first UK Corporate Governance Code (2010) recommended that all listed companies establish and maintain a fully independent audit committee.

Based on prior literature, an audit committee that is independent preserves the objectivity of the internal and external auditors (Vicknair et al., 1993; Deli and Gillan, 2000; Abbott et al., 2003), is more questionable of management actions (Baysinger and Butler, 1985), is more conservative and supportive of the proposed audit adjustment and auditor's effort (Dezoort et al., 2003; Abbott et al., 2003), and reduces management threats to replace or dismiss the existing auditor when a modified opinion is being issued (Knapp, 1985; Carcello and Neal, 2000, 2003; Abbott et al., 2003; Hoitash and Hoitash, 2009).

Other studies by Carcello et al. (2002), Abbott et al. (2003), and Mitra et al. (2007) report a positive association between audit committee independence and audit fees. On the contrary, Zaman et al. (2011) have reported a negative association between audit committee independence and audit fees. Koh et al. (2007) and Kent et al. (2010) have suggested that higher audit committee independence is associated with higher accruals quality. Nevertheless, Osma and Noguer (2007) and Baxter and Cotter (2009) have failed to find any significant association between audit committee independence and accruals. In light of the above discussion, the following null hypothesis is proposed:

H2: There is no significant relationship between audit committee independence and earnings and audit quality.

Audit committee financial expertise, audit quality and earnings quality

Audit committee financial expertise is regarded as a very important aspect of corporate governance, given the complex nature of financial reporting. In the UK, the first Corporate Governance Code (2010) recommended that "at least one member of the audit committee should have significant, recent and relevant financial experience".

Given the paucity of regulations in prescribing precisely a definition of financial expert, previous studies have measured audit committee financial expertise in several ways, such as accounting financial experts (for example, directors with an accounting qualification such as the CPA [Certified Public Accountant] or CA [Chartered Accountant]), non-accounting financial experts (for example, directors with experience as chairperson, chief executive officer or chief financial officer), and non-financial experts (for example, directors who are neither accounting nor non-accounting financial experts) (DeFond et al., 2005; Krishnan and Visvanathan, 2007, among others). Other studies have measured audit committee financial expertise using the US Securities Exchange Commission's (SEC's) various definitions of a financial expert, such as audit partner experience (Naiker and Sharma, 2009), industry expertise (Cohen et al., 2010) and auditing expertise (Barua et al., 2010).

Farber (2005) has reported that fraudulent firms have fewer financial experts on their audit committees. Similarly, Abbott et al. (2003), Xie et al. (2003), Bédard et al. (2004), Abbott et al. (2004) and Lo et al. (2010) note that the presence of financial expertise on the audit committee has a significant positive association with financial reporting/earnings quality measures. In contrast, Carcello and Neal (2003) and Zaman et al. (2011) do not report any benefit of such expertise on earnings quality. Examining accounting expertise particularly, prior research shows empirical evidence of a strong positive association between accounting financial expertise and earnings quality (Krishnan, 2005; Krishnan and Visvanathan, 2007; Baxter and Cotter, 2009; Dhaliwal et al., 2010).

From the above discussion, the following hypothesis is proposed (in the null form):

H3: There is no significant relationship between audit committee financial expertise and earnings and audit quality.

Audit committee activity, audit quality and earnings quality

Audit committee activity is another important corporate governance characteristic which contributes to effective financial reporting. In the research literature, the effectiveness of the audit committee in discharging properly its roles and responsibilities is measured based on the committee's meeting activities (Song and Windram, 2004), as the frequency of audit committee meetings indicates its level of diligence and activity (Peasnell et al., 2005; Yang and Krishnan, 2005).

It is deemed that active audit committees that frequently meet are more attentive and have better understanding of their roles and responsibilities (Abbott et al., 2003). During the meetings, audit committee members have the opportunity to put an emphasis on financial statement accuracy, control effectiveness and audit quality discussions, financial report wording, and questioning management and auditors on their actions/decisions (Gendron et al., 2004).

McMullen (1996) has found that the incidences of accounting errors, irregularities and illegal acts are lower in companies with active audit committees. Abbott et al. (2000) and Beasley et al. (2000) document that there is lower likelihood for companies to be sanctioned for fraud and aggressive accounting when the audit committee frequently meets. Abbott et al. (2004) have reported that financial restatements are unlikely to happen to companies that meet at least four times a year. Other studies (for example, Vafeas, 2005; Goodwin-Stewart and Kent, 2006; Krishnan and Visvanathan, 2007; Stewart and Munro, 2007; Hoitash et al., 2009; Hoitash and Hoitash, 2009; Engel et al., 2010; Kent et al., 2010; and Zaman et al., 2011) have found support for higher audit committee meetings frequency in relation to audit fee, non-audit fee ratio and earnings quality. However, some other empirical studies, such as Abbott et al. (2003), Bédard et al. (2004), and Baxter and Cotter (2009), have found an insignificant association between earnings quality and audit committee meeting frequency. The results of a meta-analysis study by Lin and Hwang (2010) document an overall significant negative relationship between the number of audit committee meetings and earnings management. Given the mixed findings in prior literature, the hypothesis below is stated in the null form as follows:

H4: There is no significant relationship between audit committee activity and earnings and audit quality.

Internal audit function, audit quality and earnings quality

The International Auditing Standard (ISA) 610 "Using the Work of Internal Auditors" explicitly recognises the potential relevance of internal auditing to the financial reporting process, which makes the internal audit an important function in promoting the quality of financial reporting. Further, ISA 610 provides guidance on how the external auditor's reliance on the work of internal auditors could affect the nature, timing and extent of audit procedures performed by the external auditor.

Additionally, and according to the Institute of Internal Auditors, the internal audit's role encompasses both assurance activity as well as consulting activity, playing a key role in corporate governance and risk management, instead of narrowly focusing on evaluating and strengthening internal controls per se. Given the increased capability and scope of internal audits today, the presence of the internal audit function within a company facilitates the external audit process (Schneider, 2009) by reducing the risk of material misstatements (Lin et al., 2011; Prawitt et al., 2011) as well as improving internal governance processes (Munro and Stewart, 2010), particularly when agency costs are high (Adams, 1994).

Based on the prior literature, the role and scope of the internal audit in the last twenty years or so does not solely focus on evaluating and improving the firm's internal control, but also includes corporate governance and risk management (IIA, 1999; Cohen et al., 2004; Gramling et al., 2004; Basioudis, 2014). This emerging role of the internal audit would surely have an effect on the external auditors' reliance decisions (Munro and Stewart, 2010; Schneider, 2009). According to Goodwin-Stewart and Kent (2006), companies are more likely to use an internal audit when agency costs are high (Adams, 1994). The internal audit function plays an important role in facilitating the audit committee in its financial reporting oversight role (Goodwin and Yeo, 2001; Goodwin, 2003). Abbott et al. (2012) and Pizzini et al. (2015) report evidence that external auditors' reliance on the internal audit function of the client helps increase the external audit efficiency, resulting in reduced external audit delay. Zain et al. (2015) show that the reliance of external auditors on the internal auditor's work is contingent on the quality of the client's internal audit function.

Further research in the audit fee studies by Anderson et al. (1993), Felix et al. (2001), Prawitt et al. (2011), Abbott et al. (2012), Mohamed et al. (2012) and Zain et al. (2015) provides evidence of a negative association between internal audit and audit fees, while other studies by Walker and Casterella (2000), Goodwin-Stewart and Kent (2006) and Hay et al. (2008) have found a positive relationship between the presence of internal audit function and external audit fees.

Other research in this area by Abbott et al. (2012) and Pizzini et al. (2015) has reported that internal audit function quality and its coordination with external auditors increases the external audit efficiency by reducing external audit delay, whereas Lin et al. (2011) find the coordination between the external auditor and the internal audit function improves audit quality as it increases material weakness disclosures. Prawitt et al. (2011) document that internal audit function quality increases earnings quality. A meta-analysis study by Bame-Aldred et al. (2013) reports that reliance on internal audit function can also influence other factors, such as litigation risk and external audit efficiency, as well as the overall quality of the financial statements.

In light of the above discussion, we propose the following hypothesis (in the null form):

H5: There is no significant relationship between the internal audit function and earnings and audit quality.

3.   RESEARCH DESIGN

Data and Sample Selection

The study examines the impact of the various audit committee characteristics and the internal audit function on board decision-making in the UK during the GFC. The initial sample of companies listed on the London Stock Exchange (LSE) between year 2008 to 2010 comprises approximately 7,427 observations. This sample is then reduced to exclude small listed companies that were not followed by the FAME database[5] (4,315), listed companies from the financial services sector (350), governmental institutions (1,253), incomplete data (248), listed companies on the LSE that were audited by non-UK audit firms (25), as well as companies with missing data for the audit quality and earnings quality analyses (202). Following the UK study of Basioudis and Francis (2007), samples with fewer than two observations per city–industry combination are also eliminated (213), as to allow for the application of the national–city framework for the auditor industry-specialisation analysis. The final usable sample in this study consists of 1,001 listed companies on the LSE for the accruals and going concern models. The sample selection procedure and data attrition are shown in Table 15.1.

Table 15.1   Sample selection procedures

Description	2008	2009	2010	Pooled
All LSE listed firms	2,724	2,414	2,289	7,427
Less: Firms not followed by FAME database	(1,706)	(1,380)	(1,229)	(4,315)
Less: Financial firms	(112)	(117)	(121)	(350)
Less: Public administration and defence, health and education, other services firms	(401)	(415)	(437)	(1,253)
Less: Firms with incomplete financial data	(27)	(7)	(10)	(44)
Less: Firms audited by other than UK audit offices	(10)	(7)	(8)	(25)
Less: Firms with unavailable annual reports	(53)	(66)	(35)	(154)
Less: Firms with missing corporate governance data	(15)	(22)	(13)	(50)
Less: Sample with less than two observations per city-industry combination	(67)	(71)	(75)	(213)
Less: Firms with incomplete data to calculate *DISC_ACC*	(5)	(8)	(9)	(22)
Final sample for *DISC_ACC* and *A_OPINION*	328	321	352	1,001

In determining auditor specialisation, we calculated various market shares to be able to determine the top leader at the joint level, national industry level and city-specific industry level. In order to make sure that industries included as many companies as possible, we used all companies in our sample with available audit fees data ($N = 1,747$), even if some companies had to be eliminated later due to missing data or unavailability of data for some other variables in our models. The industry classification used in this study is based on the FAME categorisation of major industry sectors, where the numerous LSE industry codes (SIC codes) of similar industry nature are being categorised into thirteen major industry sectors.

Model Specification

The study used two well-established audit/earnings quality models to examine the impact of the audit committee and internal audit function on board decision-making during an extreme financial crisis. The two audit/earnings quality proxies that are examined in this study are: (1) the discretionary accruals measure (*DISC_ACC*) which controls for firm's performance based on Kothari et al. (2005), and (2) the likelihood of a company receiving a modified or going concern audit opinion (*A_OPINION*), adopted from Francis and Yu (2009). The earnings quality model for discretionary accruals is as follows:

$$DISC\_ACC = \alpha + \beta_1 LTA + \beta_2 PYTAC + \beta_3 LEV + \beta_4 MB + \beta_5 CFO + \beta_6 LOSS + \beta_7 ALTMAN + \beta_8 ACSZIE + \beta_9 ACINDP + \beta_{10} ACEXP + \beta_{11} ACMEET + \beta_{12} SECOND + \beta_{13} JOINT + \beta_{14} CITYONLY + \beta_{15} NATONLY + Year\ fixed\text{-}effects + Industry\ fixed\text{-}effects + \varepsilon \qquad (15.1)$$

Following Kothari et al. (2005), we calculate the *DISC_ACC* model in Equation (15.1) above in several steps. Firstly, we calculate the non-discretionary accrual (NONDISC_ACC), where the following equation is estimated by year and industry: $NONDISC\_ACC = a_1 (1/LTA) + a_2 (DREV - DREC/LTA) + a_3 (PPE/LTA) + a_4 (LROA)$, where: *LTA* = total assets in year *t*-1; *DREV* = change in revenues; *DREC* = change in receivables; *PPE* = gross property, plant, and equipment in year *t*; and *LROA* = return on assets in year *t*-1. Industry is based on the FAME categorisation of major industry sectors, as noted earlier. Before *NONDISC_ACC* is calculated, the coefficients parameters a_1, a_2, and a_3 are estimated using an OLS regression for all firms with available data within the same industry and year. For this purpose, we adopt the methodology used in a UK study by Athanasakou et al. (2009), which sets a minimum of six firms in each industry per year. Therefore, we use the following equation: $ACCRUALS = a_1 (1/LTA) + a_2 (DREV - DREC/LTA) + a_3 (PPE/LTA) + a_4 (LROA) + e$, where: *ACCRUALS* = net income from continuing operations minus operating cash flow in year *t* scaled by total assets at year *t*-1; all other variables are as defined above. Finally, the discretionary accruals are calculated using the equation: $DISC\_ACC = ACCRUALS - NONDISC\_ACC$, where: *DISC_ACC* = discretionary accruals and all other variables are as defined earlier.

The control variables included in Equation (15.1) above are found in prior studies to be significantly related to company's level of discretionary accruals (Choi et al., 2010; Reichelt and Wang, 2010; Francis et al., 2013; Kharuddin et al., 2021). For the control variables, as in Ashbaugh et al. (2003), lagged total accruals (*PYTACC*) are used to control for reversal of accruals overtime. Consistent with Reichelt and Wang (2010), lower discretionary accruals are expected for companies that are larger in size (*SIZE*), and have higher leverage (*LEV*) and bankruptcy risk (*ALTMAN*),[6] as well as for those clients of the second-tier audit firms (*SECOND*). Whereas higher discretionary accruals are expected for companies with higher prior year and current year total accruals (*PYTACC* and *TACC*), as well as companies with bottom-line losses (*LOSS*). Following Kothari et al. (2005) and Choi et al. (2010), cash flow from operation is included in the model to control for the potential correlation between accruals and cash flows (*CFO*), and a negative sign is expected. Following Kharuddin et al. (2021), an industry-specialist auditor who is a joint national and city industry leader (*JOINT*) is more likely to constrain earnings management and issue modified or going concern audit opinions to their clients, relative to national specialist (*NATONLY*) or city industry specialist alone (*CITYONLY*).

The basic *DISC_ACC* model is augmented, as shown in Equation (15.1), by including audit committee characteristics, following Klein (2002) and Bédard et al. (2004). Finally, the *DISC_ACC* model is estimated as the industry and year fixed-effects model to control for systematic differences in fees across the thirteen industries and three-year period examined in the sample.

The audit quality model for the likelihood of a company receiving a modified audit opinion/ going concern report is as follows:

$$A\_OPINION = \alpha + \beta_1 LTA + \beta_2 TACC + \beta_3 LEV + \beta_4 MB + \beta_5 CFO + \beta_6 LOSS + \beta_7 ALTMAN + \beta_8 ACSZIE + \beta_9 ACINDP + \beta_{10} ACEXP + \beta_{11} ACMEET + \beta_{12} SECOND + \beta_{13} JOINT + \beta_{14} CITYONLY + \beta_{15} NATONLY + Year\ fixed\text{-}effects + Industry\ fixed\text{-}effects + \varepsilon \qquad (15.2)$$

For the *A_OPINION* model, we adopt Francis and Yu (2009)'s method where they have used the full sample for their going concern analysis and then rerun the same analysis on a restricted sample of financially distressed companies. We utilise the full sample ($N = 1,001$) for our main *A_OPINION* analysis and re-perform the same test using a restricted sample of financially distressed firms ($N = 794$) as a sensitivity check. We expect the sign on the coefficient for *SIZE* to be negative (Reynolds and Francis, 2000). As per Reichelt and Wang (2010), we expect that clients with higher accruals (*TACC*) are more likely to receive modified audit opinion. Further, consistent with Prawitt et al. (2009), Reichelt and Wang (2010), and Francis et al. (2013), firms with high growth opportunities (*MB*) are associated with higher discretionary accruals.

4.   RESULTS AND DISCUSSION

Descriptive Statistics

In Table 15.2, we provide descriptive statistics for the variables used in our earnings and audit quality models. We present the results based on the sample size of 1,001 observations. The mean value for *DISC_ACC* is 0.095, similar to a UK study by Kharuddin et al. (2021). Based on the mean *A_OPINION*, it seems that on average 10 per cent of the companies in the sample received a modified or going concern audit opinion during the sample period examined. This is slightly lower than Kharuddin et al. (2021), who reported a 16 per cent average for the period 2008–2011. Audit committees on the UK boards have, on average, three members (*ACSIZE*), and 93.6 per cent of the audit committee members are comprised of independent non-executive directors (*ACINDP*). These audit committee findings are comparable to Kharuddin et al. (2021) and suggest a vast improvement in the audit committee independence level, given the earlier reported frequency of 53 per cent in 2001–2005 (Zaman et al., 2011). Further, on average, 30.6 per cent of the audit committee composition is represented by directors having accounting or financial expertise (*ACEXP*). Audit committees in this study meet on average three times during the year (*ACMEET*), which is comparable to Kharuddin et al. (2021) and Zaman et al. (2011), but slightly lower as compared to Adelopo et al. (2012), who documented average meeting frequency of four times a year.

Table 15.2   Descriptive statistics (N = 1,001)

Variable	Mean	Std. Dev.	Min	Max
DISC_ACC	0.095	0.129	0.000	0.830
A_OPINION	0.093	0.290	0.000	1.000
SIZE	8.123	1.061	5.880	10.640
PYTACC	0.310	0.503	0.000	2.420
TACC	0.085	0.065	0.012	0.221
LEV	0.120	0.150	0.000	0.600
MB	1.731	1.390	0.160	4.520
CFO	0.028	0.237	-1.150	0.470
LOSS	0.311	0.463	0.000	1.000
ALTMAN	0.975	0.796	-0.020	4.090
ACSIZE	2.984	0.914	2.000	6.000
ACINDP	0.936	0.177	0.000	1.000
ACMEET	2.999	1.452	1.000	15.000
ACEXP	0.294	0.259	0.000	1.000
INTAUD	0.509	0.500	0.000	1.000
SECOND	0.199	0.399	0.000	1.000
JOINT	0.197	0.398	0.000	1.000
CITYONLY	0.096	0.295	0.000	1.000
NATONLY	0.033	0.179	0.000	1.000

Correlation

We tabulate the Pearson correlation analysis in Table 15.3 including all variables shown in both of our regression models. Again, this table is based on the sample size of 1,001 observations. In general, the correlation matrix shows that our earnings and audit quality measures and independent variables are moderately co-correlated and none of the variables are highly correlated above 0.7. The Variance Inflation Factor (VIF) is also below 10 according to the cut-off point by Hair et al. (2010) in all of the regression models, suggesting that multicollinearity does not pose any serious problem to our dataset.

Table 15.3   Correlation matrix (N = 1,001)

		A	B	C	D	E	F	G	H	I	J
A	DISC_ACC	1.000									
C	A_OPINION	0.258*	1.000								
B	SIZE	-0.278*	-0.250*	1.000							
D	PYTACC	0.160*	0.138*	-0.117*	1.000						
E	TACC	0.519*	0.202*	-0.244*	0.081*	1.000					
F	LEV	-0.201*	-0.135*	0.491*	-0.079*	-0.097*	1.000				
G	MB	0.013	-0.079*	0.172*	0.015	0.007	-0.022	1.000			
H	CFO	-0.356*	-0.345*	0.464*	-0.091*	-0.158*	0.198*	0.117*	1.000		
I	LOSS	0.234*	0.238*	-0.418*	0.055*	0.273*	-0.192*	-0.128*	-0.434*	1.000	
J	ALTMAN	-0.147*	-0.232*	0.077*	-0.094*	-0.104*	-0.108*	0.129*	0.258*	-0.287*	1.000
		K	L	M	N	O	P	Q	R	S	
K	ACSIZE	1.000									
L	ACINDP	0.004	1.000								
M	ACMEET	0.396*	0.117*	1.000							

		A	B	C	D	E	F	G	H	I	J
N	ACEXP	0.054*	0.084*	0.181*	1.000						
O	INTAUD	0.409*	0.175*	0.472*	0.175*	1.000					
P	SECOND	-0.210*	-0.039	-0.210*	-0.112*	-0.307*	1.000				
Q	JOINT	0.214*	0.095*	0.144*	0.110*	0.279*	-0.246*	1.000			
R	CITYONLY	0.028	-0.003	0.040	0.028	0.041	-0.162*	-0.161*	1.000		
S	NATONLY	-0.009	-0.039	-0.035	0.013	-0.020	-0.092*	-0.091*	-0.060*	1.000	

Notes: * is significant at p<0.05. All p-values are two-tailed.

Regression Results

Earnings quality – discretionary accruals (DISC_ACC)

Panel A in Table 15.4 reports the results on the effect of audit committee characteristics and internal audit on company earnings quality as captured by discretionary accruals (*DISC_ACC*). Discretionary accruals represent the amount of a company's abnormal or unexpected accruals and are the amount of earnings that have been potentially distorted through managerial discretion (i.e., earnings management) (Reichelt and Wang, 2010). The *DISC_ACC* model examines the effects of audit committee characteristics and internal audit from the demand side of the audit market.

Interestingly, none of the audit committee characteristics (*ACSIZE, ACINDP, ACEXP* and *ACMEET*), as captured in this study (and prior literature), are found to be significantly related to discretionary accruals (*DISC_ACC*). Given that the variation between these characteristics among the companies does not seem to contribute to improved quality of financial reporting through constraining earnings management, the insignificant results for the audit committee variables in this study imply that the role of audit committees and by extension of the corporate governance in the public listed firms may have only been ceremonial in nature during the GFC in the UK.

This assumption is possibly consistent with the pressures created by the GFC and felt by the directors of listed companies, whom were assumed to be seen to conform to their environmental pressures (for example, meet the requirement of the corporate governance best practices, such as the FRC, 2008, and the UK Corporate Governance Code, 2010). These results are also consistent with the proposition under the institutional theory, where companies follow the legal requirements of laws and regulations in order to simply maintain their legitimacy, instead of intending to achieve an effective governance and monitoring role, particularly in the financial reporting process and during a crisis.

These non-significant findings on overall audit committee effectiveness are consistent with Xie et al. (2003), Choi et al. (2004) and Lin et al. (2006). But they contradict earlier non-UK findings (for example, Abbott et al., 2000; Klein, 2002; Abbott et al., 2004; Davidson et al., 2005) which documented the occurrence of earnings management decreases with independence of the audit committee. Further, the finding of insignificant effects for audit committee size in this study is consistent with Xie et al. (2003) and Bédard et al. (2004), but is in contrast to Yang and Krishnan (2005), who report that audit committee size is negatively associated with abnormal accruals. With regard to audit committee diligence, the finding of this study is consistent with Bédard et al. (2004) and Yang and Krishnan (2005), who also fail to find such an association, as opposed to other studies which reported negative associations between earnings management and the number of audit committee meetings (Xie et al., 2003; Vafeas,

2005; Lin et al., 2006; Koh et al., 2007; Kent et al., 2010). In general, empirical results in this area of research are less consistent and conclusive.

The other variable of interest in this study, the internal audit (*INTAUD*), is found to be negatively and significantly related to discretionary accruals (*DISC_ACC*), at 5 per cent level (one-tail). This finding is consistent with Prawitt et al. (2011), who report that an internal audit represents a detection and deterrent mechanism that moderates earnings management, but contrary to Davidson et al. (2005), who reported an insignificant relationship between the two.

Exploring the impact of auditor specialisation, the coefficient for *JOINT* is negative and weakly significant (significant at 10 per cent level, one-tailed test), while the coefficients for *CITYONLY* and *NATONLY* are not significant at any conventional level. This indicates that the Big 4 audit firms which are joint national and city-specific industry leaders reduce the magnitude of discretionary accruals, but not when they are city-industry leaders or national industry leaders alone. In other words, an audit firm's joint (industry, city) industry leadership was an important condition to constrain accrual-based earnings management during the GFC in the UK. This finding is consistent with a recent study by Kharuddin et al. (2021) in the UK and Reichelt and Wang (2010) in the US. However, this finding is in contrast to Choi et al. (2010), who have documented in the US for the period 2000 to 2005 that the effect of office-level industry expertise dominates the effect of national-level industry expertise in deterring management's opportunistic earnings manipulation.

All control variables are significant at 5 per cent level in the predicted directions in most of the model estimations, except for *SIZE*, *LOSS* and *ALTMAN*, which are not significant at any conventional levels. Consistent with Reichelt and Wang (2010), Francis et al. (2013) and Minutti-Meza (2013), *DISC_ACC* is larger for firms with higher prior year total accruals (*PYTACC*), lower leverage (*DE*), lower operating cash flow (*CFO*) and higher growth opportunities (*MB*). Also, consistent with Reichelt and Wang (2010) and Minutti-Meza (2013), discretionary accruals are lower for clients audited by the second-tier audit firms (*SECOND*).

Table 15.4　*Regression results for earnings and audit quality (N = 1,001)*

Dependent variables	Panel A: DISC_ACC			Panel B: A_OPINION		
	Coefficient	t-statistic	p-value	Coefficient	t-statistic	p-value
SIZE	-0.004	-0.580	0.559	-0.011	-0.640	0.521
PYTACC	0.024	2.290	0.022			
TACC				0.458	2.660	0.008
LEV	-0.054	-2.040	0.042	-0.058	-0.990	0.323
MB	0.007	2.200	0.028	-0.003	-0.510	0.609
CFO	-0.123	-3.180	0.002	-0.261	-3.900	0.000
LOSS	0.006	0.440	0.658	0.012	0.420	0.676
ALTMAN	-0.007	-1.260	0.209	-0.043	-4.120	0.000
SECOND	-0.017	-1.630	0.104	-0.026	-1.010	0.314
ACSIZE	0.001	0.150	0.879	-0.012	-1.040	0.298
ACINDP	-0.013	-0.520	0.604	-0.014	-0.250	0.802
ACEXP	-0.004	-1.250	0.210	0.012	1.270	0.205
ACMEET	0.018	0.900	0.368	0.018	0.360	0.720
INTAUD	-0.018	-1.780	0.075	-0.052	-2.350	0.019
JOINT	-0.010	-1.380	0.169	0.038	1.940	0.053
CITYONLY	-0.002	-0.140	0.891	-0.025	-0.840	0.400

Dependent variables	Panel A: DISC_ACC			Panel B: A_OPINION		
	Coefficient	t-statistic	p-value	Coefficient	t-statistic	p-value
NATONLY	0.021	0.600	0.548	0.014	0.310	0.755
Intercept	0.134	2.440	0.015	0.227	2.000	0.045
R-squared		0.249			0.235	
Year Fixed-Effects		Yes			Yes	
Industry Fixed-Effects		Yes			Yes	

Note: Industry fixed effects and year fixed effects are not reported for brevity, and t-statistics and significance levels are calculated using the White (1980) robust standard errors to correct for heteroscedasticity.

Audit quality – audit opinion (A_OPINION)

Panel B in Table 15.4 reports the results on the effect of audit committee characteristics and internal audit function on audit quality as measured by the likelihood of a listed company receiving a modified audit opinion or going concern audit report (*A_OPINION*). The *A_OPINION* model examines the effects of audit committee characteristics and internal audit from the supply side of the audit market.

Similar to the earnings quality analysis above, the audit quality results show that none of the audit committee variables examined in this study and the prior literature (*ACSIZE*, *ACINDP*, *ACEXP* and *ACMEET*) are found to be significantly related to the auditor's propensity to issue modified or going concern audit opinions. These insignificant results for the audit committee variables imply that auditors did not perceive that the audit committee played a significant or differential role in improving financial reporting quality during the GFC in the UK. This outcome is consistent with our earlier findings in Panel A of Table 15.4.

However, as before, the other variable of interest, the internal audit function (*INTAUD*), is found to be negatively and significantly related to *A_OPINION* (significant at 5 per cent level, two-tail). This indicates that during and after the GFC in the UK, the presence of a client's strong control environment safeguarded by the internal audit function led to high reliance by the external auditor, and contributed to a lower assessment of client audit risk and higher level of trust by the external auditor regarding the client's internal control system. This in turn caused the auditor to assess that there was less need to issue a modified or going concern opinion in the period 2008–2010 when an internal audit function was present in the client business.

Furthermore, the coefficient for *JOINT* is significantly positive (significant at 10 per cent level, two-tail), while the coefficients for *CITYONLY* and *NATONLY* are not significant at any conventional level. Consistent with Kharuddin et al. (2021) in the UK and Reichelt and Wang (2010) in the US, this finding indicates that only the Big 4 audit firms that are jointly national and city-specific industry leaders are more likely to issue a modified or going concern audit opinion to their clients, but not when they are either national or city industry leaders alone. This finding suggests that only the joint specialists were able to use adequately the in-depth knowledge of their client's industry and, as a result, they were better equipped in assessing their clients' business risk, detecting significant irregularities/errors and expressing their opinion more conservatively during the crisis. In doing so, they successfully protected their reputation and minimised litigation risk during the turbulent period of 2008–2010[7] (Reichelt and Wang, 2010; Chi and Chin, 2011).

All control variables in the audit quality model are significant at p<0.10 in the predicted directions in most of the model estimations, except for *SIZE*, *LEV*, *MB*, *LOSS* and *SECOND*, which are not significant at any conventional levels. In sum, the insignificant findings in respect of the audit committee effectiveness in improving earnings quality during the sample period 2008 to 2010 could be argued to be partly motivated by the economic and financial conditions during the GFC when companies were facing a difficult time trying to maintain and improve their performance in the public equity market. Given the nearly universal harm inflicted by the crisis, the inability of audit committees to improve company earnings quality in the period 2008–2010, as shown in this chapter, may imply a lack of knowledge and expertise on behalf of audit committee members to be able to receive and interpret information and evaluate how managers chose accounting policies and how they measured economic profits and losses during that difficult period. Furthermore, by looking at the big picture, it can be argued that company boards of directors and audit committee members failed to prevent the crisis in the first place (together of course with various other stakeholders in the capital markets, such as securities analysts, ratings agencies, auditors, news media, investors, politicians and regulators), which may suggest a lack of understanding on how complex global economies and financial systems work at all levels.

Similarly, the presence of audit committees within companies' governance function seems to have little influence on auditors' decision-making. Audit quality as shown in the chapter is neither diminished nor improved during and after the GFC by the involvement of audit committees in providing oversight of the client financial reporting process.

On the other hand, the internal audit function in companies is shown to have improved both earnings quality and audit quality during the GFC. Further, when the auditor is a specialist at both the national and city-specific level, then earnings quality and audit quality are also shown to be improved in the crisis. It seems that joint specialists providing the external audit service helped clients to increase the quality and reliability of the reported financial statements as well as enhancing the audit process and outcome in the GFC. Taken together, it seems that the ineffective monitoring role of an audit committee in constraining accruals manipulation was moderated by the presence of an effective internal audit function and industry-specialist auditors during and after the GFC in the UK.

Sensitivity Analyses

To confirm whether the earlier documented results in Table 15.4 are robust across different sample characteristics, we re-ran the same analyses on various sub-samples based on client size and risk categorisation.

Different company markets
To examine the effectiveness of the audit committee and internal audit function in constraining discretionary accruals in different clients markets, we split the full sample ($N = 1,001$) into two sub-samples based on FTSE 350 ($N = 329$) and non-FTSE 350 ($N = 672$) categorisation. The results of the analyses are presented in Table 15.5. The *INTAUD* variable is negative and significant for both markets of FTSE 350 and non-FTSE 350 companies, indicating that the presence of an internal audit function helped to constrain earnings management and enhanced company earnings quality in both markets during and after the GFC. This result is consistent with our main results in Table 15.4. For FTSE 350 companies, we find for the first time some significance in two audit committee variables. The coefficient for *ACSIZE* is positive and weakly significant (at 10 per cent level, one-tail), implying that when the size of the audit

committee is large, it contributes to higher discretionary accruals. On the contrary, the coefficient for *ACEXP* (significant at 10 per cent level, one-tail) is negative and weakly significant, suggesting that audit committees with more financially expert members enhanced earnings quality in the FTSE 350 market only during the crisis.

Table 15.5   *Regression results on DISC_ACC for FTSE 350 and non-FTSE 350 sub-samples*

	FTSE 350 (N = 329)			Non-FTSE 350 (N = 672)		
Dependent variables	Coefficient	t-statistic	p-value	Coefficient	t-statistic	p-value
SIZE	-0.015	-1.680	0.095	0.005	0.390	0.696
PYTACC	0.006	0.470	0.642	0.029	2.380	0.018
LEV	-0.071	-2.160	0.031	-0.045	-1.220	0.224
MB	0.002	0.450	0.655	0.006	1.260	0.208
CFO	-0.023	-0.210	0.833	-0.145	-3.510	0.000
LOSS	0.026	0.890	0.373	-0.007	-0.500	0.617
ALTMAN	-0.007	-0.790	0.430	-0.006	-0.820	0.414
SECOND	0.007	0.230	0.817	-0.024	-2.060	0.040
ACSIZE	0.007	1.570	0.118	-0.005	-0.560	0.575
ACINDP	0.024	0.550	0.583	-0.021	-0.760	0.445
ACEXP	-0.004	-1.470	0.143	-0.002	-0.270	0.786
ACMEET	0.004	0.210	0.830	0.015	0.550	0.586
INTAUD	-0.034	-1.410	0.159	-0.020	-1.840	0.066
JOINT	0.001	0.170	0.861	-0.022	-1.800	0.072
CITYONLY	0.006	0.500	0.615	-0.013	-0.620	0.533
NATONLY	0.097	0.910	0.364	-0.004	-0.140	0.891
Intercept	0.174	2.530	0.012	0.098	1.080	0.281
R-squared		0.225			0.257	
Year fixed effects		Yes		Yes	Yes	Yes
Industry fixed effects		Yes		Yes	Yes	Yes

Note: Industry fixed effects and year fixed effects are not reported for brevity, and t-statistics and significance levels are calculated using the White (1980) robust standard errors to correct for heteroscedasticity.

On the other hand, for the non-FTSE 350 sample, the audit committee findings are more aligned to the results reported in the main analysis in Table 15.4, where no audit committee variable is shown to be significant and *INTAUD* and *JOINT* are significantly and negatively related to *DIS_ACC* at 5 per cent level (one-tail). These results confirm our earlier conclusion in Table 15.4 that the presence of *INTAUD* and *JOINT* helped increase the quality of earnings.

In Table 15.6, we examine the effect of the audit committee and internal audit function on *A_OPINION* for the FTSE 350 and non-FTSE 350 listed companies. The *INTAUD* variable is negative and significant for both markets of FTSE 350 and non-FTSE 350 companies. This result is consistent with our main results in Table 15.4 and suggests that the presence of an internal audit function led to high reliance by the external auditor on the client's internal control systems, which in turn contributed to auditors assessing lower audit risk and sequentially less need to issue a modified or going concern opinion. Interestingly, in the FTSE 350 market only, we find *CITYONLY* to be negative and weakly significant (at 10 per cent level, one-tail), suggesting that industry-specialised auditors who were city-specific industry leaders only were likely to compromise their audit quality by showing less likelihood to issue a modified or going concern audit opinion to their FTSE 350 clients during and after the crisis. This result should be interpreted with caution given the extreme nature of the crisis.

On the other hand, and consistent with our main results in Table 15.4, the coefficient for *JOINT* is positive and significant (at 5 per cent level, one-tail) in the non-FTSE 350 market only. For the non-FTSE 350 sample, we also find that *ACEXP* is positive and weakly significant (at 10 per cent level, one-tail). This suggests that a higher proportion of audit committees with accounting or financial knowledge and experience led auditors to issue more modified or going concern audit opinions in this market and in the specific period of study. This further implies that the auditor's reporting decision was affected in a negative way in the presence of experienced audit committee directors.

Table 15.6   *Regression results on A_OPINION for FTSE 350 and non-FTSE 350 sub-samples*

Dependent variables	FTSE 350 (N = 329)			Non-FTSE 350 (N = 672)		
	Coefficient	t-statistic	p-value	Coefficient	t-statistic	p-value
SIZE	-0.009	-0.720	0.472	-0.010	-0.380	0.705
TACC	0.732	4.790	0.000	0.449	2.150	0.032
LEV	-0.077	-1.700	0.090	-0.090	-0.970	0.331
MB	0.002	0.310	0.753	-0.002	-0.180	0.855
CFO	-0.470	-7.490	0.000	-0.207	-2.710	0.007
LOSS	-0.006	-0.230	0.818	0.023	0.650	0.519
ALTMAN	-0.020	-1.540	0.124	-0.056	-3.790	0.000
SECOND	-0.101	-2.330	0.020	-0.006	-0.210	0.835
ACSIZE	-0.005	-0.560	0.574	-0.016	-0.850	0.396
ACINDP	-0.087	-1.250	0.214	-0.002	-0.030	0.973
ACEXP	0.011	0.960	0.335	0.020	1.360	0.173
ACMEET	-0.001	-0.030	0.973	0.047	0.610	0.544
INTAUD	-0.171	-2.750	0.006	-0.040	-1.580	0.114
JOINT	0.008	0.720	0.475	0.057	1.690	0.092
CITYONLY	-0.030	-1.490	0.136	-0.012	-0.280	0.778
NATONLY	-0.014	-0.460	0.649	0.045	0.780	0.433
Intercept	0.354	2.830	0.005	0.202	1.080	0.279
R-squared	0.581			0.208		
Year fixed effects	Yes			Yes	Yes	Yes
Industry fixed effects	Yes			Yes	Yes	Yes

Note: Industry fixed effects and year fixed effects are not reported for brevity, and t-statistics and significance levels are calculated using the White (1980) robust standard errors to correct for heteroscedasticity.

High- and low-risk companies
Next, we examine whether there is differentiated earnings quality and audit quality between high- and low-risk listed companies, and we follow prior research on auditor independence (Geiger and Raghunandan, 2001; Geiger and Rama, 2003; Basioudis et al., 2008) by defining risk as the probability of a company being financially distressed. We determine a financial distress company using the probability-of-bankruptcy model introduced by Hopwood, McKeown, and Mutchler (1994) and modified by Geiger and Raghunandan (2001). The sample is equally divided into two sub-samples of 501 and 500 companies each, the former representing high-risk companies and the latter corresponding to auditors' low-risk clients. The two sub-samples were split based on the median value of the probability-of-bankruptcy score. Tables 15.7 and 15.8 provide the results for the *DISC_ACC* and *A_OPINION* models respectively.

For the high-risk sample in Table 15.7, results are not consistent with our main results in Table 15.4. None of the test variables in Table 15.4 is significant in this high-risk sample. Additionally, we find that audit committees with higher proportions of members who are financially experts, represented by the *ACEXP* variable, constrain earnings management (significant at 5 per cent level, one-tail), whereas city industry-specialist auditors, *CITYONLY*, allow greater earnings manipulation (significant at 10 per cent level, one-tail). These additional results appear for the first time in determining *DISC_ACC* and earnings quality, and given the challenges presented by the crisis, they should be cautiously construed. On the other hand, the results for the low-risk sample are consistent with Table 15.4's main results. Both coefficients of *INTAUD* and *JOINT* are found to be negatively and significantly related to *DISC_ACC*.

Table 15.7   *Regression results on DISC_ACC for high- and low-risk sub-samples*

	High-risk (N = 501)			Low-risk (N = 500)		
Dependent variables	Coefficient	t-statistic	p-value	Coefficient	t-statistic	p-value
SIZE	-0.004	-0.470	0.638	0.005	0.410	0.682
PYTACC	0.040	1.860	0.064	0.018	1.490	0.136
LEV	-0.042	-1.330	0.184	-0.048	-1.130	0.260
MB	0.008	2.620	0.009	0.003	0.430	0.670
CFO	-0.002	-0.030	0.972	-0.187	-3.840	0.000
LOSS	0.037	1.660	0.098	-0.018	-1.010	0.313
ALTMAN	-0.004	-0.600	0.551	-0.022	-0.710	0.478
SECOND	0.001	0.040	0.970	-0.034	-2.040	0.042
ACSIZE	-0.002	-0.500	0.616	0.008	0.850	0.395
ACINDP	-0.014	-0.590	0.554	-0.010	-0.230	0.819
ACEXP	-0.007	-2.060	0.040	-0.001	-0.140	0.889
ACMEET	0.032	1.140	0.256	-0.004	-0.140	0.893
INTAUD	-0.010	-0.880	0.379	-0.035	-2.110	0.036
JOINT	0.004	0.440	0.659	-0.038	-2.760	0.006
CITYONLY	0.017	1.300	0.193	-0.035	-1.170	0.241
NATONLY	0.024	0.560	0.574	0.017	0.310	0.755
Intercept	0.101	1.850	0.065	0.078	0.840	0.400
R-squared		0.205			0.287	
Year fixed effects		Yes		Yes	Yes	Yes
Industry fixed effects		Yes		Yes	Yes	Yes

Note: Industry fixed effects and year fixed effects are not reported for brevity, and t-statistics and significance levels are calculated using the White (1980) robust standard errors to correct for heteroscedasticity.

When we examine the impact of the audit committee and internal audit on *A_OPINION* for the high-risk audit clients in Table 15.8, similar to *DISC_ACC* results and opposite to our main findings in Table 15.4, we find that none of the main test variables are significant. Alternatively, we show that *ACEXP* is positive and weakly significant (at 10 per cent, one-tail), indicating the positive impact of directors with financial expertise on audit quality. On the contrary, national specialists and city industry specialists, *NATONLY* and *CITYONLY*, seemed to show less likelihood to issue a modified or going concern opinion in the high-risk clients during and after the GFC. When we examine the market with low-risk companies, the results are consistent with those in Table 15.4. In other words, the *INTAUD* has a negative impact and the *JOINT* shows a positive impact on audit quality.

Table 15.8   Regression results on AUDIT_OPINION for high- and low-risk sub-samples

Dependent variables	High-risk (N = 501)			Low-risk (N = 500)		
	Coefficient	t-statistic	p-value	Coefficient	t-statistic	p-value
SIZE	-0.033	-2.690	0.007	-0.024	-0.830	0.408
TACC	0.449	2.550	0.011	0.474	1.670	0.097
LEV	-0.010	-0.230	0.816	-0.092	-0.840	0.403
MB	0.002	0.390	0.698	-0.003	-0.260	0.799
CFO	-0.273	-2.580	0.010	-0.201	-2.180	0.030
LOSS	-0.032	-1.320	0.188	0.026	0.570	0.570
ALTMAN	-0.015	-1.490	0.137	-0.142	-2.030	0.043
SECOND	-0.007	-0.280	0.779	-0.024	-0.520	0.603
ACSIZE	0.004	0.430	0.670	-0.015	-0.630	0.526
ACINDP	-0.007	-0.150	0.880	-0.005	-0.050	0.959
ACEXP	0.015	1.320	0.188	0.015	1.080	0.283
ACMEET	0.009	0.230	0.815	0.027	0.310	0.760
INTAUD	-0.001	-0.070	0.946	-0.058	-1.370	0.172
JOINT	-0.006	-0.530	0.596	0.127	2.800	0.005
CITYONLY	-0.024	-1.480	0.139	0.003	0.050	0.960
NATONLY	-0.034	-1.560	0.118	0.109	1.150	0.249
Intercept	0.262	2.900	0.004	0.356	1.760	0.079
R-squared		0.255			0.245	
Year fixed effects		Yes		Yes	Yes	Yes
Industry fixed effects		Yes		Yes	Yes	Yes

Note: Industry fixed effects and year fixed effects are not reported for brevity, and t-statistics and significance levels are calculated using the White (1980) robust standard errors to correct for heteroscedasticity.

Income-increasing/decreasing discretionary accruals

Finally, we examine the effect of audit committee characteristics and the internal audit function on income-increasing and income-decreasing discretionary accruals. As the value of discretionary accruals could be in both directions – that is, income-increasing and income-decreasing – the impact of the effect of the crisis on income-increasing earnings management (i.e., companies with positive discretionary accruals) and income-decreasing earnings management (i.e., companies with negative discretionary accruals) is examined separately. The sample is divided into two sub-samples based on the sign of the company's discretionary accruals. The results are presented in Table 15.9.

In Panel A of Table 15.9, the empirical results for the income-increasing accruals support partially the main findings in Table 15.4. The *INTAUD* reduced the earnings management and therefore increased earnings quality in 2008–2010. While the main results reveal no effect of audit committee characteristics on *DISC_ACC*, the *ACSIZE* is negative and significant (at 5 per cent level, one-tail) in the income-increasing accruals sub-sample. This means that companies with larger audit committees (*ACSIZE*) had lower income-increasing discretionary accruals and hence higher earnings quality in the period 2008–2010. On the other hand, in Panel B of Table 15.9, we find that only the *JOINT* is negative and significant (at 5 per cent level, one-tail), which means that only industry specialists who are joint national and city-specific industry leaders constrained income-decreasing earnings management during and after the GFC. This result is consistent with our overall results in Table 15.4, and with the non-FTSE 350 sub-sample and in the low-risk market.

Table 15.9   *Regression results on income-increasing and income-decreasing DISC_ACC for high- and low-risk sub-samples*

Dependent variables	Panel A: Income-increasing DISC_ACC (N = 403)			Panel B: Income-decreasing DISC_ACC (N = 598)		
	Coefficient	t-statistic	p-value	Coefficient	t-statistic	p-value
SIZE	0.000	0.000	0.996	-0.009	-0.810	0.419
TACC	0.032	2.470	0.014	0.014	0.980	0.325
LEV	-0.028	-0.680	0.499	-0.072	-2.030	0.042
MB	0.004	1.010	0.314	0.010	2.210	0.028
CFO	-0.170	-3.560	0.000	-0.105	-1.550	0.123
LOSS	-0.012	-0.470	0.641	0.014	0.800	0.426
ALTMAN	0.000	0.030	0.980	-0.011	-1.370	0.173
SECOND	-0.005	-0.400	0.691	-0.026	-1.570	0.116
ACSIZE	-0.011	-1.830	0.068	0.006	0.820	0.413
ACINDP	0.001	0.020	0.982	-0.025	-0.760	0.448
ACEXP	-0.004	-1.200	0.230	-0.003	-0.600	0.548
ACMEET	0.038	1.280	0.202	0.002	0.080	0.938
INTAUD	-0.018	-1.340	0.180	-0.015	-1.040	0.300
JOINT	0.005	0.450	0.653	-0.021	-1.910	0.056
CITYONLY	-0.013	-0.600	0.549	0.001	0.070	0.944
NATONLY	0.040	0.490	0.621	0.008	0.240	0.811
Intercept	0.083	1.290	0.197	0.193	2.280	0.023
R-squared		0.361			0.230	
Year fixed effects		Yes		Yes	Yes	Yes
Industry fixed effects		Yes		Yes	Yes	Yes

Note: Industry fixed effects and year fixed effects are not reported for brevity, and t-statistics and significance levels are calculated using the White (1980) robust standard errors to correct for heteroscedasticity.

5.   SUMMARY AND CONCLUSION

Our study investigates the effects of audit committee and internal audit function on board decision-making during the period of an extreme financial crisis. The sample of the study comprised all companies listed in the LSE between 2008 and 2010 financial periods; i.e., during and immediately after the GFC.

Based on the results of our full sample, the role of the audit committee is viewed as passive and more ceremonial in nature during the sample period investigated, given that the variation between these characteristics among the companies does not contribute to improved quality of audit and financial reporting through constraining earnings management in the UK public listed companies during the financial crisis period. This interesting insignificant finding[8] in respect of audit committee (and, by extension, corporate governance) effectiveness could be argued to be partly motivated by the economic and financial conditions during the financial crisis when companies were facing a difficult time trying to maintain and improve their performance in the public equity market.

However, there are some mixed results on the audit committee effects when we perform sub-sample analyses. We find evidence that audit committee size contributed to higher accruals manipulation in FTSE 350 companies, while audit committees with higher proportions of financial expertise helped to moderate this negative effect. We also find that higher proportions of financial expertise reduced accruals manipulation in the sample of companies with higher risk of bankruptcy. Nevertheless, the evidence suggests that larger audit committees constrained income-increasing discretionary accruals. Our overall results are somehow mixed with regard to audit committee effectiveness in the GFC, but they are consistent with the inconclusive prior research. However, we tend to argue based on the overall empirical results of this study that perhaps audit committees did not provide a high-level oversight function, and earnings quality was not really modified by audit committees during the GFC.

In a similar vein, auditor reporting decision and audit quality do not seem to be influenced by the presence of audit committees in the GFC period. However, in the smaller non-FTSE 350 sample and in markets with companies showing higher risk of bankruptcy, a higher proportion of financial experts in the audit committee actually contributed to a higher likelihood of that company receiving modified or going concern audit opinions. Similarly to the argument made regarding the earnings quality in the preceding paragraph, overall results seem to indicate that audit committee characteristics were not valued by auditors in determining the likelihood of issuing modified or going concern audit opinions to their clients and, hence, audit quality was hardly affected by audit committees in the GFC period under investigation.

The results indicate that our second variable of interest, the presence of an internal audit function in a listed company, helps to constrain the magnitude of discretionary accruals and, therefore, improves earnings quality. This finding about the importance of the internal audit function is also consistent across various sub-samples, including the FTSE 350 sample and non-FTSE 350 sample, and in companies with low risk of bankruptcy and income-decreasing accruals. We can safely conclude that the internal audit function provided support in improving the quality of financial reporting in the GFC period.

Likewise, auditors value the presence of an internal audit function in arriving at their audit opinion, if it is either a modified or a going concern report. Although the percentage of companies that had an internal audit was still low at 50 per cent in the 2008–2010 period, the presence of this function in those companies had a significant effect on improving the audit firms' quality of external audit service. We also find the positive effect of the internal audit function on audit opinion in the FTSE 350 and non-FTSE 350 samples and in companies with low risk of bankruptcy.

Another interesting finding deriving from this study is that joint national and city-specific industry audit leaders effectively reduced companies' level of earnings manipulation through discretionary accruals. Joint auditor specialists appear to be better able to mitigate opportunities for client management to engage in opportunistic behaviour that can affect earnings quality in the GFC period. This finding is consistent across various sub-samples, including the non-FTSE 350 sample, and in companies with low risk of bankruptcy and income-decreasing discretionary accruals. Additionally, our results reveal that the joint national and city-specific industry specialist auditors were most conservative and careful in issuing their audit opinion, meaning they were more likely to issue modified or going concern audit opinions to their clients in the 2008–2010 period. It can be said that beyond enriching audit quality, joint specialists also helped improve the quality of the client internal information environment that supports decision-making and performance management. This finding is also consistent across two sub-samples, including the non-FTSE 350 sample and the sample with companies in low risk of bankruptcy.

Taken altogether, it seems that the ineffective monitoring role of audit committees in promoting company earnings quality and audit quality during and after the financial crisis in the UK capital market was moderated by the presence of an effective internal audit function and auditors who were joint national and city-specific industry specialists. Based on our results, we can conclude that the presence of the internal audit function supported companies in the discharging of their responsibilities and contributed to the quality of financial decision-making. The alignment of external auditor (mainly the joint industry specialist) with the client's internal audit function seemed to affect upwards the quality of the respective internal information environments and, ultimately, helped support improved client decision-making and performance management. Therefore, it can be argued that the complementary functions of internal and external audit created additional value by improving the processes and information to support client management decisions but also auditor reporting decisions.

These findings are of potential interest to policy makers, practitioners and investors as the issues relating to audit quality, earnings quality and the two functions of corporate governance (audit committee and internal audit) are pertinent for investor protection in the financial market. More specifically, we argue it is critical that policy makers adopt a balanced and evidence-based perspective that recognises the importance of academic research as, in turn, effective and proportionate remediating of any shortcomings in the markets can be applied. Internal and external audit are complementary functions within the assurance framework and our study shows that both are essential for the effective governance of an organisation. Perhaps internal and external audit practitioners should find more ways to ensure their work is coordinated and there is an efficient use of resources. It is also important that regulators and policy makers take into account the complementarity of internal and external audits when developing new policies related to audit and corporate governance. It is clear from our study that audit committees need to enhance their personal development and step up their engagement with (internal and external) auditors and the company board, as well as the management and preparers of financial information. Finally, given the inefficiencies and dysfunction of mainly the audit committee function in the GFC period, as reported in this study, investors should perhaps not rely on audit committees to monitor and evaluate company performance, but instead they need to be more active in receiving useful information from companies and assessing firm value.

NOTES

1. Earnings management represents an inverse measure of earnings quality.
2. Earnings management is estimated in the prior literature using various proxies such as discretionary accruals (Peasnell et al., 2000, 2005; Klein, 2002; Koh, 2003; Xie et al., 2003; Bédard et al., 2004; Larcker and Richardson, 2004; Yang and Krishnan, 2005), earnings restatements (Ferguson et al., 2004), income smoothing (Chung et al., 2002) and accounting conservatism (Ahmed and Duellman, 2007; Krishnan and Visvanathan, 2007), among others.
3. The FRC has updated the UK Corporate Governance many times since 2010; the latest version of it was published on 1 July 2018.
4. In the UK, action against companies by the Financial Reporting Review Panel (FRRP) for defective financial statements has been used as an equivalent signal to SEC Enforcement Actions in the US.
5. FAME is an acronym for Financial Analysis Made Easy, a comprehensive database for UK private and publicly listed companies maintained by Bureau Van Dijk.

6.   The Altman score measures the likelihood of company survival. Lower (higher) scores measure greater (lesser) bankruptcy risk.
7.   We should note here that the UK auditors did not raise any concerns with regard to their banking clients, nor issued any going concern opinions, prior to the events unfolding at the start of the GFC. Our study does not include the financial companies in the sample.
8.   This finding is statistically insignificant, but as the editor has pointed out, one could argue that this insight is not insignificant at all when someone tries to understand and explain the main reasons of the GFC.

REFERENCES

Abbott, L., Parker, S., and Peters, G. (2012). Audit Fee Reductions from internal Audit-Provided Assistance: The Incremental Impact of Internal Audit Characteristics. *Contemporary Accounting Research*, 29 (1): 94–118.

Abbott, L.J., Park, Y., and Parker, S. (2000). The Effects of Audit Committee Activity and Independence on Corporate Fraud. *Managerial Finance*, 26 (11): 55–67.

Abbott, L.J., and Parker, S. (2000). Auditor Selection and Audit Committee Characteristics. *Auditing: A Journal of Practice & Theory*, 19 (2): 47–66.

Abbott, L.J., Parker, S., and Peters, G.F. (2004). Audit Committee Characteristics and Restatements. *Auditing: A Journal of Practice & Theory*, 23: 69–87.

Abbott, L.J., Parker, S., Peters, G.F., and Raghunandan, K. (2003). The Association between Audit Committee Characteristics and Audit Fees. *Auditing: A Journal of Practice & Theory*, 22 (2): 17–32.

Adams, M.B. (1994) Agency Theory and the Internal Audit. *Managerial Auditing Journal*, 9 (8): 8–12.

Adelopo, I., Jallow, K., and Scott, P. (2012). Multiple Large Ownership Structure, Audit Committee Activity and Audit Fees: Evidence from the UK. *Journal of Applied Accounting Research*, 13 (2): 100–121.

Altman, E.I. (1983). *Corporate Financial Distress*. Wiley Interscience, New York.

Anderson, D., Francis, J.R., and Stokes, D.J. (1993). Auditing, Directorships, and the Demand for Monitoring. *Journal of Accounting and Public Policy*, 12 (4): 353–75.

Anderson, R.C., Mansi, S.A., and Reeb, D.M. (2004). Board Characteristics, Accounting Report Integrity, and the Cost of Debt. *Journal of Accounting and Economics*, 37: 315–42.

Ahmed A.S, and Duellman, S. (2007). Accounting conservatism and board of director characteristics. *Journal of Accounting and Economics*, 43 (2–3): 411–37.

Archambeault, D.S., and DeZoort, T. (2001). Auditor Opinion Shopping and the Audit Committee: An Analysis of Suspicious Auditor Switches. *International Journal of Auditing*, 5: 33–52.

Arthur, N., Tang, Q., and Lin, Z. (2015). Corporate Accruals Quality during the 2008–2010 Global Financial Crisis. *Journal of International Accounting, Auditing and Taxation*, 25: 1–15.

Ashbaugh, H., LaFond, R., and Mayhew, B.W. (2003) Do Non-Audit Services Compromise Auditor Independence? Further Evidence. *Accounting Review*, 78 (3): 611–39.

Asquith, P., Gertner, R., and Scharfstein, D. (1994). Anatomy of Financial Distress: An Examination of Junk-Bond Issuers. *Quarterly Journal of Economics*, 109: 625–58.

Athanasakou, V.E., Strong, N.C., and Walker, M. (2009). Earnings Management or Forecast Guidance to Meet Analyst Expectations? *Accounting and Business Research*, 39 (1): 3–35.

Bame-Aldred, C.W., Brandon, D.M., Messier, W.F. Jr., Rittenberg, L.E., and Stefaniak, C.M. (2013). A Summary of Research on External Auditor Reliance on the Internal Audit Function. *Auditing: A Journal of Practice & Theory*, 32 (1): 251–86.

Barua, A., Rama, D., and Sharma, V.D. (2010). Audit Committee Characteristics and Investment in Internal Auditing. *Journal of Accounting and Public Policy*, 29 (5): 503–13.

Basioudis, I.G. (2014). "Aligning the internal audit function with strategic objectives", in *QFinance: The Ultimate Resource*, 5th Revised Edition. Bloomsbury Publishing, London.

Basioudis, I.G., and Francis, J.R. (2007). Big 4 Audit Fee Premiums for National and Office-Level Industry Leadership in the United Kingdom. *Auditing: A Journal of Practice & Theory*, 26 (2): 143–66.

Basioudis, I.G., Papakonstantinou, E., and Geiger, M.A. (2008). Audit Fees, Non-Audit Fees and Auditor Going-Concern Reporting Decisions in the United Kingdom. *Abacus*, 44 (3): 284–309.

Baxter, P., and Cotter, J. (2009). Audit Committees and Earnings Quality. *Accounting and Finance*, 49: 267–90.

Baysinger, B., and Butler, H. (1985). Corporate Governance and the Board of Directors: Performance Effects of Changes in Board Composition. *Journal of Law, Economics and Organization*, 1: 101–24.

Beasley, M.S. (1996). An Empirical Analysis of the Relation between the Board of Director Composition and Financial Statement Fraud. *Accounting Review*, 71 (4): 443–65.

Beasley, M.S., Carcello, J.V., Hermanson, D.R., and Lapides, P.D. (2000). Fraudulent Financial Reporting: Consideration of Industry Traits and Corporate Governance Mechanisms. *Accounting Horizons*, 14 (4): 441–54.

Beasley, M.S., and Petron, K.R. (2001). Board Independence and Audit Firm Type. *Auditing: A Journal of Practice & Theory*, 20 (1): 97–114.

Bédard, J., and Gendron, Y. (2010). Strengthening the Financial Reporting System: Can Audit Committees Deliver? *International Journal of Auditing*, 14 (2): 174–210.

Bédard, J., Chtourou, S.M., and Courteau, L. (2004). The Effect of Audit Committee Expertise, Independence and Activity on Aggressive Earnings Management. *Auditing: A Journal of Practice & Theory*, 23: 55–79.

Beidleman, C.R. (1973). Income Smoothing: The Role of Management. *Accounting Review*, 48 (4): 653–67.

Carcello, J.V., Hermanson, D.R., Neal, T.L., and Riley, R.A. (2002). Board Characteristics and Audit Fees. *Contemporary Accounting Research*, 19 (3): 365–84.

Carcello, J.V., Hermanson, D.R., and Ye, Z. (2011). Corporate Governance Research in Accounting and Auditing: Insights, Practice Implications, and Future Research Directions. *Auditing: A Journal of Practice & Theory*, 30 (3): 1–31.

Carcello, J.V., and Neal, T.L. (2000). Audit Committee Composition and Auditor Reporting. *Accounting Review*, 75 (4): 453–67.

Carcello, J.V., and Neal, T.L. (2003). Audit Committee Characteristics and Auditor Dismissals following "New" Going-Concern Reports. *Accounting Review*, 78 (1): 95–117.

Chan, K.C., Farrell, B., and Lee, P. (2008). Earnings Management of Firms Reporting Material Internal Control Weaknesses under Section 404 of the Sarbanes–Oxley Act. *Auditing: A Journal of Practice & Theory*, 27(2), 161–79.

Charitou, A., Lambertides, N., and Trigeorgis, L. (2007). Earnings Behaviour of Financially Distressed Firms: The Role of Institutional Ownership. *Abacus*, 43: 271–96.

Charoenwong, C., and Jiraporn, P. (2009). Earnings Management to Exceed Thresholds: Evidence from Singapore and Thailand. *Journal of Multinational Financial Management*, 19 (3): 221–36.

Chen, Y.M., Moroney, R., and Houghton, K. (2005). Audit Committee Composition and the Use of an Industry Specialist Audit Firm. *Accounting and Finance*, 45 (2): 217–39.

Cheng, M., Dhaliwal, D., and Zhang, Y. (2013). Does Investment Efficiency Improve after the Disclosure of Material Weaknesses in Internal Control over Financial Reporting? *Journal of Accounting and Economics*, 56: 1–18.

Chi, H.Y., and Chin, C.L. (2011). Firm versus Partner Measures of Auditor Industry Expertise and Effects on Auditor Quality. *Auditing: A Journal of Practice & Theory*, 30 (2): 201–29.

Choi, J.H., Jeon, K.A., and Park, M.L. (2004). The Role of Audit Committees in Decreasing Earnings Management: Korean Evidence. *International Journal of Accounting, Auditing and Performance Evaluation*, 1 (1): 37–60.

Choi, J., Kim, C., Kim, J., and Zang, Y. (2010). Audit Office Size, Audit Quality, and Audit Pricing. *Auditing: A Journal of Practice & Theory*, 29 (1): 73–97.

Chung, R., Firth, M., and Kim J.-B. (2002). Institutional Monitoring and Opportunistic Earnings Management. *Journal of Corporate Finance*, 8 (1):29–48.

Cimini, R. (2015). How Has the Financial Crisis Affected Earnings Management? A European Study. *Applied Economics*, 47 (3): 302–17.

Cohen, J., Krishnamoorthy, G., and Wright, A. (2004). The Corporate Governance Mosaic and Financial Reporting Quality. *Journal of Accounting Literature*, 23: 87–152.

Cohen, J., Krishnamoorthy, G., and Wright, A. (2010). Corporate Governance in the Post Sarbanes–Oxley Era: Auditors' Experiences. *Contemporary Accounting Research*, 27 (3): 751–86.

Cohen, J.R., Krishnamoorthy, G., and Wright, A.M. (2007). The Impact of Roles of the Board on Auditors' Risk Assessments and Program Planning Decisions. *Auditing: A Journal of Practice & Theory*, 26 (1): 91–112.

Davidson, R., Goodwin-Stewart, J., and Kent, P. (2005). Internal Governance Structures and Earnings Management. *Accounting and Finance*, 45 (2): 241–67.

DeAngelo, H., DeAngelo, L., and Skinner, D. (1994). Accounting Choice in Troubled Companies. *Journal of Accounting and Economics*, 17 (1–2), 113–43.

Dechow, P., and Schrand, C. (2004). *Earnings Quality*. CFA Institute Research Foundation, Charlottesville.

Dechow, P., Sloan, R., and Sweeney, A. (1996). Causes and Consequences of Earnings Manipulation: An Analysis of Firms Subject to Enforcement Actions by the SEC. *Contemporary Accounting Research*, 13: 1–36.

DeFond, M., and Jiambalvo, J. (1994). Debt Covenant Violation and Manipulation of Accruals: Accounting Choice in Troubled Companies. *Journal of Accounting and Economics*, 17 (1–2): 145–76.

DeFond, M.L., and Francis, J.R. (2005). Audit Research after Sarbanes–Oxley. *Auditing: A Journal of Practice & Theory*, 24: 5–30.

DeFond, M.L., Hann, R.N., and Hu, X. (2005). Does the Market Value Financial Expertise on Audit Committees of Boards of Directors? *Journal of Accounting Research*, 43 (2): 153–93.

Deli, D.N., and Gillan, S.L. (2000). On the Demand for Independent and Active Audit Committees. *Journal of Corporate Finance*, 6: 427–45.

DeZoort, F.T., Hermanson, D.R., and Houston, R.W. (2003). Audit Committee Member Support for Proposed Audit Adjustments: A Source Credibility Perspective. *Auditing: A Journal of Practice & Theory*, 22: 189–205.

DeZoort, F.T., and Salterio, S. (2001). The Effects of Corporate Governance Experience and Financial Reporting and Audit Knowledge of Audit Committee Members' Judgments. *Auditing: A Journal of Practice & Theory*, 20 (2): 31–48.

Dhaliwal, D.S., Naiker, V., and Navissi, F. (2010). The Association between Accruals Quality and the Characteristics of Accounting Experts and Mix of Expertise on Audit Committees. *Contemporary Accounting Research*, 27 (3): 787–827.

D'Mello, R., Gao, A., and Jia, Y. (2017). Internal Control and Internal Capital Allocation: Evidence from Internal Capital Markets of Multi-Segment Firms. *Review of Accounting Studies*, 22: 251–87.

Engel, E., Hayes, R., and Wang, X. (2010). Audit Committee Compensation and the Demand for Monitoring of the Financial Reporting Process. *Journal of Accounting and Economics*, 49: 136–54.

Farber, D.B. (2005). Restoring Trust After Fraud: Does Corporate Governance Matter? *Accounting Review*, 80: 539–61.

Felix, W.L., Gramling, A.A., and Maletta, M.J. (2001). The Contribution of Internal Audit as a Determinant of External Audit Fees and Factors Influencing This Contribution. *Journal of Accounting Research*, 39 (3): 513–34.

Feng, M., Li, C., McVay, S.E., and Skaife, H. (2015). Does Ineffective Internal Control over Financial Reporting Affect a Firm's Operations? Evidence from Firms' Inventory Management. *Accounting Review*, 90 (2): 529–57.

Ferguson, M.J., Seow, G.S., and Young, D. (2004). Non-Audit Services and Earnings Management: UK Evidence. *Contemporary Accounting Research*, 21 (4): 813–41.

Filip, A., and Raffournier, B. (2014). Financial Crisis and Earnings Management: The European Evidence. *International Journal of Accounting*, 49 (4): 455–78.

Francis, J.R., Michas, P.N., and Seavey, S.E. (2013). Does Audit Market Concentration Harm the Quality of Audited Earnings? Evidence from Audit Markets in 42 Countries. *Contemporary Accounting Research*, 30 (1): 325–55.

Francis, J.R., Reichelt, K., and Wang, D. (2005). The Pricing of National and City-Specific Reputations for Industry Expertise in the US Audit Market. *Accounting Review*, 80 (1): 113–36.

Francis, J.R., and Yu, M.D. (2009). Big 4 Office Size and Audit Quality. *Accounting Review*, 84 (5): 1521–52.

FRC (2010). *The UK Approach to Corporate Governance*. Financial Reporting Council, London.

García-Meca, E., and Sánchez-Ballesta, J.P. (2009). Corporate Governance and Earnings Management: A Meta-Analysis. *Corporate Governance: An International Review*, 17 (5): 594–610.

Geiger, M.A., and Raghunandan, K. (2001). Bankruptcies, Audit Reports, and the Reform Act. *Auditing: A Journal of Practice & Theory*, 20 (1): 187–95.

Geiger, M.A., Raghunandan, K., and Riccardi, W. (2014). The Global Financial Crisis: U.S. Bankruptcies and Going-Concern Audit Opinions. *Accounting Horizons*, 28: 59–75.

Geiger, M.A., and Rama, D.V. (2003). Audit Fees, Non-Audit Fees, and Auditor Reporting on Stressed Companies. *Auditing: A Journal of Practice & Theory*, 22 (2): 53–69.

Gendron, Y., Bédard, J., and Gosselin, M. (2004). Getting Inside the Black-Box: A Filed Study of Practices in "Effective" Audit Committees. *Auditing: A Journal of Practice & Theory*, 23 (1): 153–71.

Gleason, C.A., Pincus, M., and Olhoft Rego, S. (2017). Material Weaknesses in Tax-Related Internal Controls and Last Chance Earnings Management. *Journal of the American Taxation Association*, 39 (1): 25–44.

Goodwin, J. (2003). The Relationship between the Audit Committee and the Internal Audit Function: Evidence from Australia and New Zealand. *International Journal of Auditing*, 7: 263–78.

Goodwin, J., and Yeo, T.Y. (2001). Two Factors Affecting Internal Audit Independence and Objectivity: Evidence from Singapore. *International Journal of Auditing*, 5: 107–25.

Goodwin-Stewart, J., and Kent, P. (2006). Relation between External Audit Fees, Audit Committee Characteristics and Internal Audit. *Accounting and Finance*, 46: 387–404.

Gramling, A.A., Maletta, M.J., Schneider, A., and Church, B.K. (2004). The Role of the Internal Audit Function in Corporate Governance: A Synthesis of the Extant Internal Auditing Literature and Directions for Future Research. *Journal of Accounting Literature*, 23: 194–244.

Habib, A., Bhuiyan, B.U., and Islam, A. (2013). Financial Distress, Earnings Management and Market Pricing of Accruals during the Global Financial Crisis. *Managerial Finance*, 39 (2): 155–80.

Hair, J.F., Black, W.C., Babin, B.J., and Anderson, R.E. (2010). *Multivariate Data Analysis: A Global Perspective*, 7th ed. Pearson Prentice Hall, Upper Saddle River.

Hay, D., Knechel, W.R., and Ling, H. (2008). Evidence on the Impact of Internal Control and Corporate Governance on Audit Fees. *International Journal of Auditing*, 12 (1): 9–24.

Hoitash, R., and Hoitash, U. (2009). The Role of Audit Committees in Managing Relationships with External Auditors after SOX: Evidence from the US. *Managerial Auditing Journal*, 24 (4): 368–97.

Hoitash, U., Hoitash, R., and Bédard, J.C. (2009). Corporate Governance and Internal Control Over Financial Reporting: A Comparison of Regulatory Regimes. *Accounting Review*, 84 (3): 839–67.

Hopwood, W., McKeown, J.C., and Mutchler, J. F. (1994), A Re-Examination of Auditor versus Model Accuracy within the Context of the Going-Concern Opinion Decision. *Contemporary Accounting Research*, 10 (2): 409–31.

Humphrey, C., Loft, A., and Woods, M. (2009). The Global Audit Profession and the International Financial Architecture: Understanding Regulatory Relationships at a Time of Financial Crisis. *Accounting Organisations & Society*, 34: 810–25.

IIA (Institute of Internal Auditors) (1999). *A Vision for the Future: Professional Practices Framework for Internal Auditing*. Institute of Internal Auditors, Altamonte Springs.

ISA 610 (2010). Using the Work of Internal Auditors: The International Auditing Standard. Available at: www.ifac.org/download/a034–2010-iaasb-handbook-isa-610.pdf (accessed 22 November 2010).

Kane, G.D., and Velury, U. (2004). The Role of Institutional Ownership in the Market for Auditing Services: An Empirical Investigation. *Journal of Business Research*, 57: 976–83.

Kent, P., Routledge, J., and Stewart, J. (2010). Innate and Discretionary Accruals Quality and Corporate Governance. *Accounting and Finance*, 50: 171–95.

Khanchel, I. (2011). An Examination of the Naïve-Investor Hypothesis in Accruals Mispricing in Tunisian Firms. *Journal of International Financial Management & Accounting*, 22 (2): 131–64.

Kharuddin, K.A.M., Basioudis, I.G., and Farooque, O.A. (2021). Effects of the Big 4 National and City-Level Industry Expertise on Audit Quality in the United Kingdom. *Journal of International Accounting, Auditing and Taxation*. In press.

Klein, A. (2002). Audit Committee, Board of Director Characteristics, and Earnings Management. *Journal of Accounting and Economics*, 33 (3): 375–401.

Knapp, M.C. (1985). Audit Conflict: An Empirical Study of the Perceived Ability of Auditors to Resist Management Pressure. *Accounting Review*, 60 (2): 202–11.

Koh, P.S. (2003). On the Association Between Institutional Ownership and Aggressive Corporate Earnings Management in Australia. *British Accounting Review*, 35: 105–28.

Koh, P.S., LaPlante, S.K., and Tong, Y.H. (2007). Accountability and Value Enhancement Roles of Corporate Governance. *Accounting and Finance*, 47: 305–33.

Kothari, S.P., Leone, A.J., and Wasley, C.E. (2005). Performance Matched Discretionary Accruals. *Journal of Accounting and Economics*, 39: 163–97.

Krishnan, G.V., and Visvanathan, G. (2007). Reporting Internal Control Deficiencies in the Post-Sarbanes–Oxley Era: The Role of Auditors and Corporate Governance. *International Journal of Auditing*, 11: 73–90.

Krishnan, J. (2005). Audit Committee Quality and Internal Control: An Empirical Analysis. *Accounting Review*, 80: 649–75.

Lang, M., Lins, K.V., and Maffett, M. (2011). Transparency, Liquidity and Valuation: International Evidence on When Transparency Matters Most. *Journal of Accounting Research*, 50: 729–74.

Larcker, D.F., and Richardson, S.A. (2004). Fees Paid to Audit Firms, Accrual Choices and Corporate Governance. *Journal of Accounting Research*, 42 (3): 625–58.

Lin, J., Li, J., and Yang, J. (2006). The Effect of Audit Committee Performance on Earnings Quality. *Managerial Auditing Journal*, 21 (9): 921–33.

Lin, J.W., and Hwang, M.I. (2010). Audit Quality, Corporate Governance and Earnings Management: A Meta-Analysis. *International Journal of Auditing*, 14: 57–77.

Lin, S., Pizzini, M., Vargus, M., and Bardhan, I.R. (2011). The Role of the Internal Audit Function in the Disclosure of Material Weaknesses. *Accounting Review*, 86 (1): 287–323.

Lisboa, I., and Kacharava, A. (2018). Does Financial Crisis Impact Earnings Management? Evidence from Portuguese and UK. *European Journal of Applied Business and Management*, 4 (1): 80–100.

Lo, A.W.Y., Wong, R.M.K., and Firth, M. (2010). Can Corporate Governance Deter Management from Manipulating Earnings? Evidence from Related-Party Sales Transactions in China. *Journal of Corporate Finance*, 16: 225–35.

McMullen, D.A. (1996). Audit Committee Performance: An Investigation of the Consequences Associated with Audit Committees. *Auditing: A Journal of Practice & Theory*, 15 (1): 87–103.

Minutti-Meza, M. (2013). Does Auditor Industry Specialization Improve Audit Quality? *Journal of Accounting Research*, 51 (4): 779–817.

Mitra, S., Hossain, M., and Deis, D.R. (2007). The Empirical Relationship between Ownership Characteristics and Audit Fees. *Review of Quantitative Financial Accounting*, 28: 257–85.

Mohamed, Z., Mat Zain, M., Subramaniam, N., and Wan Yusoff, W.F. (2012). Internal Audit Attributes and External Auditors' Reliance on Internal Audit: Implications for Audit Fees. *International Journal of Auditing*, 16 (3): 268–85.

Munro, L., and Stewart, J. (2010). External Auditors' Reliance on Internal Audit: The Impact of Sourcing Arrangements and Consulting Activities. *Accounting and Finance*, 50 (2): 371–87.

Naiker, V., and Sharma, D. (2009). Former Audit Partners on the Audit Committee and Internal Control Deficiencies. *Accounting Review*, 84 (2): 559–87.

Norman, M.S., Takiah, M.I., and Mohd, M.R. (2007). Audit Committee Characteristics and Earnings Management: Evidence from Malaysia. *Asian Review of Accounting*, 15 (2): 147–63.

O'Sullivan, N. (1999). Board Characteristics and Audit Pricing Post-Cadbury: A Research Note. *European Accounting Review*, 8 (2): 253–63.

Osma, B.G., and Noguer, B.G. (2007). The Effect of the Board Composition and Its Monitoring Committees on Earnings Management: Evidence from Spain. *Corporate Governance: An International Review*, 15 (6): 1413–28.

Pál, T. (2010). The Impact of the Economic Crisis on Auditing. *European Integration Studies*, 8 (1): 131–42.

Peasnell, K.V., Pope, P.F., and Young, S. (2000). Detecting Earnings Management Using Cross-Section Abnormal Accruals Models. *Accounting and Business Research*, 30: 313–26.

Peasnell, K.V., Pope, P.F., and Young, S. (2005). Board Monitoring and Earnings Management: Do Outside Directors Influence Abnormal Accruals? *Journal of Business Finance and Accounting*, 32: 1131–46.

Pizzini, M., Lin, S., and Ziegenfuss, D.E. (2015). The Impact of Internal Audit Function Quality and Contribution on Audit Delay. *Auditing: A Journal of Practice & Theory*, 34 (1): 25–58.

Prawitt, D.F., Sharp, N.Y., and Wood, D.A. (2011). Reconciling Archival and Experimental Research: Does IA Contribution Affect the External Audit Fees? *Behavioral Research in Accounting*, 23 (2): 187–206.

Prawitt, D.F., Smith, J.L., and Wood, D.A. (2009). Internal Audit Quality and Earnings Management. *Accounting Review*, 84 (4): 1255–80.

Reichelt, K.J., and Wang, D. (2010). National and Office-Specific Measures of Auditor Industry Expertise and Effects on Audit Quality. *Journal of Accounting Research*, 48 (3): 647–86.

Reynolds, J.K., and Francis, J. (2000). Does Size Matter? The Influence of Large Clients on Office-Level Auditor Reporting Decisions. *Journal of Accounting and Economics*, 30: 375–400.

Schneider, A. (2009). The Nature, Impact and Facilitation of External Auditor Reliance on Internal Auditing. *Academy of Accounting and Financial Studies Journal*, 13 (4): 41–53.

Sharma, V.D., Sharma, D.S., and Ananthanarayanan, U. (2011). Client Importance and Earnings Management: The Moderating Role of Audit Committees. *Auditing: A Journal of Practice & Theory*, 30 (3): 125–56.

Sikka, P. (2009). Financial Crisis and the Silence of the Auditors. *Accounting, Organizations and Society*, 34 (6–7): 868–73.

Song, J., and Windram, B. (2004). Benchmarking Audit Committee Effectiveness in Financial Reporting. *International Journal of Auditing*, 8 (3): 195–207.

Stewart, J., and Munro, L. (2007). The Impact of Audit Committee Existence and Audit Committee Meeting Frequency on the External Audit: Perceptions of Australian Auditors. *International Journal of Auditing*, 11: 51–69.

Turley, S., and Zaman, M. (2004). The Corporate Governance Effects of Audit Committees. *Journal of Management and Governance*, 8 (3): 305–32.

Vafeas, N. (2000). Board Structure and the Informativeness of Earnings. *Journal of Accounting and Public Policy*, 19: 139–60.

Vafeas, N. (2005). Audit Committees, Boards, and the Quality of Reported Earnings. *Contemporary Accounting Research*, 22 (4): 1093–1122.

Vafeas, N., and Waegelein, J. (2007). The Association between Audit Committees, Compensation Incentives and Corporate Audit Fees. *Review of Quantitative Finance and Accounting*, 28: 241–55.

Velury, U., Reisch, J.T., and O'Reilly, D.M. (2003). Institutional Ownership and the Selection of Industry Specialist Auditors. *Review of Quantitative Finance and Accounting*, 21 (1): 35–48.

Vicknair, D., Hickman, K., and Carnes, K.C. (1993). A Note on Audit Committee Independence: Evidence from the NYSE on Grey Area Directors. *Accounting Horizons*, 7 (1): 53–57.

Walker, P.L., and Casterella, J.R. (2000). The Role of Auditee Profitability in Pricing New Audit Engagements. *Auditing: A Journal of Practice & Theory*, 19 (1): 157–67.

White, H. (1980). A Heteroskedasticity-Consistent Covariance Matrix Estimator and a Direct Test for Heteroskedasticity. *Econometrica*, 48: 817–38.

Wolnizer, P.W. (1995). Are audit committees red herrings? *Abacus*, 31 (1): 45–66.

Woods, M., Humphrey, C., Dowd, K., Liu, Y.L., 2009. Crunch Time for Bank Audits? Questions of Practice and the Scope for Dialogue. *Managerial Auditing Journal*, 24: 114–34.

Xie, B., Davidson, W., and DaDalt, P. (2003). Earnings Management and Corporate Governance: The Roles of the Board and the Audit Committee. *Journal of Corporate Finance*, 9 (3): 295–317.

Xu, Y., Carson, E., Fargher, N., Jiang, L. (2013). Responses by Australian Auditors to the Global Financial Crisis. *Accounting and Finance*, 53: 301–38.

Xu, Y., Jiang, A.L., Fargher, N., and Carson, E. (2011). Audit Reports in Australia during the Global Financial Crisis. *Australian Accounting Review*, 21: 22–31.

Yang, J., and Krishnan, J. (2005). Audit Committees and Quarterly Earnings Management. *International Journal of Auditing*, 9: 201–19.

Zain, M.M., Zaman, M., and Mohamed, Z. (2015). The Effect of Internal Audit Function Quality and Internal Audit Contribution to External Audit on Audit Fees. *International Journal of Auditing*, 19 (3): 134–47.

Zaman, M., Hudaib, M., and Haniffa, R. (2011). Corporate Governance Quality, Audit Fees and Non-Audit Fees. *Journal of Business Finance & Accounting*, 38 (1&2): 165–97.

APPENDIX

This appendix describes the variables that are used in this study.

DISC_ACC   = magnitude and direction of discretionary accruals based on the model by Kothari et al. (2005), which controls for firm's performance

A_OPINION   = indicator variable, 1 = received modified audit opinion or going concern audit report, 0 = otherwise

LTA   = natural log of total assets in GBP'000

LEV   = ratio of long-term debt to total assets

PYTACC   = net income from continuing operations minus operating cash flow in year t-1 scaled by total assets at year t-2

MB   = the market value of equity divided by book value of equity

CFO   = operating cash flow in year t scaled by total assets at year t-1

LOSS   = indicator variable, 1 = loss in any past three years, 0 = otherwise

ALTMAN   = Altman's (1983) score

TACC   = net income from continuing operations minus operating cash flow in year t scaled by total assets at year t-1

ACSIZE   = number of directors on audit committee

ACINDP   = proportion of non-executive directors on audit committee

ACEXP   = proportion of directors with accounting or financial expertise on audit committee

ACMEET   = number of audit committee meetings

INTAUD   = indicator variable, 1 = presence of internet audit function; 0 = otherwise

SECOND   = indicator variable, 1 = client of second-tier audit firms, 0 = otherwise

JOINT   = indicator variable, = 1 if the audit firm is the top-ranked by market share nationally and the audit office is the top-ranked by city industry market share, 0 = otherwise

CITYONLY   = indicator variable, = 1 if the audit firm is not the top-ranked by market share nationally and the audit office is the top-ranked by city industry market share, 0 = otherwise

NATONLY   = indicator variable, = 1 if the audit firm is the top-ranked by market share nationally and the audit office is not the top-ranked by city industry market share, 0 = otherwise.

16. Cycles of corporate fraud: a behavioural economics approach

Richard Fairchild and Oliver Marnet

INTRODUCTION

In recent years, the corporate sector has again been rocked by managerial fraud and scandals. The standard economics (*Homo economicus*) economics view, à la Becker (1974), is that criminal (and fraudulent) behaviour is driven by fully rational agents, who perform a very calculative and mathematical cost–benefit analysis (CBA) of crime/fraud commission: weighing up, in a very rational unemotional manner, the economic/monetary benefits of the crime/fraud commission, and the expected costs (the probability of being caught multiplied by the economic penalties if caught). This approach emphasises that rigorous monitoring (by watchdogs such as auditors, independent directors and regulators), coupled with strong punishment threats towards miscreants, can be effective in deterring corporate crime and fraud.

In contrast, the more recent paradigm of behavioural economics combines standard economics, psychology and sociology to recognise that real-world humans are not always fully rational, unemotional, non-psychological all-calculating maximisers of expected utility (Simon, 1957; Janis, 1972; Tversky and Kahneman, 1974; Kahneman and Tversky, 1979; Thaler, 1980, 2015; Loewenstein, 1996; Rabin, 2002). The behavioural economics (*Homo sapiens*) approach examines the effects of including bounded rationality, psychology, and emotions into the economics models, and into the agents' preferences. Particularly in relation to corporate crime and fraud, behavioural economists have cast doubt on Becker's fully rational, unemotional, non-psychological CBA approach. Real-world criminals may be myopic (the immediate benefits of the crime are salient; the long-term expected costs are too far in the future to be considered). In this chapter, motivated by Dan Ariely's research into crime, we add to the behavioural economics approach to consider a deeper, psychoanalytical, Freudian approach to crime and fraud commission. Indeed, Ariely (2008) argues that emotions often play a key role in the decision to commit crime: criminals often gain emotional excitement at 'getting away' with the perfect crime.

The purpose of this chapter is four-fold. First, we consider the theoretical and empirical research from the behavioural economics perspective of crime, with a focus on corporate fraud. Second, we analyse, in detail, some of the (behavioural and psychoanalytical) game-theoretic approaches to corporate fraud; this is interesting in terms of both the modelling approaches and what they reveal to us about real-world factors affecting corporate fraud. Third, we apply the behavioural economics/psychoanalytical framework to real-world cases. Fourth, we consider real-world policy implications arising from the behavioural economics approach. Finally, we discuss the most recent research into corporate fraud, and conclude.

1.   BEHAVIOURAL ECONOMICS AND THE SLIPPERY SLOPE TO FRAUD

Behavioural and psychoanalytical game-theoretic approaches emphasise that two particular phenomena may lead to managerial fraud in the corporate sector: (a) the tendency for fraud to start on a small scale, perceived by perpetrators as insignificant and inconsequential, but which may 'mount up' over time to large cumulative fraud; and (b) formerly ethical managers becoming 'infected' by the behaviour of unethical managers within an organisation.

In this chapter, we consider a simple framework in which a manager commits a series of small frauds over time (initially perceived as insignificant). At some critical point the frauds accumulate to a magnitude where they 'activate' the manager's super-ego. At that point, guilt looms large, which may be sufficient to motivate the manager to cease her fraudulent behaviour, and to admit to previous indiscretions. However, if regret dominates, the manager may be 'entrapped' into continuing to further hide fraud. In a second version of the model, we consider an organisation consisting of two managers: one ethical/non-fraudulent and one unethical/fraudulent. We consider how the unethical manager's behaviour may 'infect' the ethical manager, so that the latter is induced to commit fraud, due to the unethical culture of the organisation. We employ our theoretical analysis to help to understand a real-world fraud case (Enron) in which fraud began at small individualistic levels, but quickly escalated and became institutionalised throughout the organisation, destroying the company. We conclude with policy and ethical implications, and suggestions for future research.

Setting the Scene

There is no shortage of recent episodes of destructive managerial fraudulent behaviour and egregious activity. Prominent cases at the firm level (for example, Enron, Parmalat, Xerox, Tyco, American International Group (AIG), Lehman Brothers and Satyam, amongst many others), and at the individual level ('rogue traders' such as Nick Leeson at Barings Bank, Jérôme Kerviel at Societe Generale, Kweku Adoboli at UBS, and John Rusnak at AIB), repeatedly brought the issue of corporate fraud to public attention.

Given the prominence of such high-profile fraud cases, there have been increasing demands for tougher corporate regulation, stronger governance and monitoring (e.g., by corporate boards), and more stringent reporting and accounting standards (e.g., SOX, 2002, in the USA; the European Union's Audit Directive, 2014; and numerous updates to the UK's governance and auditing framework – FRC, 2016). A common feature of such tougher financial regulations is that they aim to deter fraud and other undesired managerial behaviour through yet more stringent monitoring and harsher economic penalties. However, it must be questioned just how effective tougher regulations and punishments are in deterring fraud given that corporate fraud continued seemingly unabated after the introduction of similar measures in the past.

The debate over the efficacy of addressing corporate fraud through tough governance, regulation and punishment threats is important from both an academic and practitioner perspective. Insights into this debate are provided by considering the traditional rational economics framework (the rational choice model, in which agents are fully rational, unemotional, unbiased, perfect all-calculating maximisers of expected utility: the *Homo economicus* approach), compared with the behavioural economics framework (which incorporates psychology, bounded rationality and emotions into the decision-making model: the real-world *Homo sapiens* approach).

We consider the behavioural economics/psychoanalytical approach to corporate fraud. This approach enables us to consider the economic and behavioural factors affecting managerial corporate fraud. The approach provides important insights into the following questions. Why are managers (as human beings) susceptible to fraudulent activity? Why do some managers engage in such behaviour, while others are able to resist it? Is it easy for managers to face up to their misdoings, and 'come clean'? Or is there a form of 'fraud entrapment' with a 'slippery slope', particularly when the manager has committed a series of small frauds over time, which may result in a large cumulative amount of fraud? Are some humans naturally more prone to fraud than others, or are fraudulent managers products of the culture and environment within their organisations (the classic 'nature versus nurture' debate)?

A further question for scholars to consider is whether managerial fraud is primarily the result of an economic, CBA-type decision, or are there also behavioural/psychological/emotional factors at play? This final question is particularly important, and relevant to the debate over whether tough regulations and punishment threats are likely to be effective in deterring managerial corporate fraud.

Corporate Fraud: Economic Versus Behavioural Factors

How effective can tough financial regulation and strong punishment threats be at deterring corporate fraud? In this chapter, we consider a behavioural game-theoretic framework of managerial fraud, incorporating both a dynamic aspect (current managerial fraud activity may be affected by past, accumulated, misdemeanours over time; thus, managers at the individual level may become entrapped into fraudulent activity), and an organisational/cultural/environmental aspect (such that ethical managers may be dominated and induced into fraud by the existence of unethical managers and an organisational culture which nurtures unethical behaviour; consider, for example, the culture of fraud at Enron, and its remuneration and promotion system which encouraged fraud).

The seminal work on the economics of crime was developed by Becker (1974). He considers criminal activity occurring as a result of a fully rational CBA. That is, he considered criminals who weigh up the benefits of the crime (for example, how much money will they be able to steal?) against the costs of the crime (the cost of effort of committing it, the probability of being caught, the extent of the punishment if they are caught, and so forth). Hence, according to Becker, criminals are fully rational, all-calculating, unemotional, self-interested maximisers of expected utility. Becker's approach implies that tough financial regulation and strong punishment threats can be effective at deterring corporate fraud.

We have been motivated by two main departures from Becker's (1974) economic calculus of criminal (fraudulent/unethical) activity. Discussing the psychological/psychoanalytical underpinnings of fraud at the individual level, Ariely (2008, p. 203) suggests:

> Sigmund Freud explained it this way. As we grow up in society, we internalise the social virtues. This internalisation leads to the development of the superego. In general, the superego is pleased when we comply with society's ethics, and unhappy when we don't.

Ariely notes that, according to this Freudian framework, the super-ego provides us with the warm glow that comes from charitable, other-regarding and ethical acts, such as returning a lost wallet to its owner. However, given the existence of a super-ego, and our resulting desire to be honest, why are criminal activity and fraud so widespread? According to Ariely, the super-ego is only active (helping, monitoring and managing our honesty) when we are engaged in large transgressions. For small crimes or frauds, Ariely argues that the super-ego stays asleep, and we do not consider how these small crimes reflect on our honesty. The crimes are simply too small to activate the super-ego. There may come a point in the process where, after committing a series of small frauds, the manager suddenly realises the cumulative extent of those frauds, and the super-ego awakes. At this point in time, the manager may then own up to past misdemeanours, or become entrapped in fraud, due to regret.[1]

Slippery Slope to Fraud: Competing Forces Model of Crime

Our framework is close in spirit to the analysis of Van Winden and Ash (2012). These authors analyse the behavioural economics of crime, and develop a 'Competing Forces' model of criminal/fraudulent behaviour. As they point out, current crime-deterrence policies (from governments, law-makers, regulators and other organisations) suffer from being based on Becker's (1974) standard economics approach, in which criminals conduct a fully rational CBA of crime commission. Becker's approach emphasises strong punishment threats as an effective deterrence; the behavioural economics approach calls this finding into question.

We build on the behavioural economics model of Van Winden and Ash (2012). Their 'Competing Forces' model incorporates rationality, cognitive biases and emotions. They analyse people as being 'boundedly rational, being motivated by emotions as well as cognition. Analytically, this approach conceptualises criminal behaviour (B) as the product of a dual process of cognition (C) and emotion (E)' (p. 6).

Interestingly, Van Winden and Ash consider a linear 'action space' of criminality, ranging from zero (minimum criminality) to 1 (maximum criminality level). Then, 'We conceptualise the criminal's cognitive and emotional decision systems as generators of force-fields in the action space ... (the model) can be used to show the action tendencies or forces on behaviour at a given level of x' (2012).

Their model provides a useful means of considering when cognitive and emotional forces act in the same direction, or opposite directions, to push the criminal to more or less crime. We will demonstrate parallels in our behavioural/psychoanalytical model: we, too, consider an action space for fraud (the manager can commit fraud each period in an interval from zero to a maximum amount). Further, we consider cases where there are competing cognitive and emotional forces 'pushing' the manager in one direction or the other (towards maximum or minimum fraud).

Motivated by the model of Van Winden and Ash (2012), we note the following departures in our approach:

(a) We focus on conscious and unconscious emotions in a psychoanalytical framework (considering a human's super-ego, which may be asleep for small frauds, or awake for larger frauds), and the interaction between these emotions and a rational CBA.

(b) We incorporate the emotions of regret, guilt, pride. Our approach implies a dual-selves model.

(c) We introduce the effect of managerial fraud-hiding efforts, and we consider the possibility of managerial entrapment into fraud (neither of which are included in the model of Van Winden and Ash, 2012).

Our analysis of managerial entrapment into fraud has parallels with the work in behavioural corporate finance of Statman and Caldwell (1987), who incorporate regret theory, and regret aversion, into a prospect theory framework to understand managerial entrapment into a failing corporate project, thus refusing to abandon it. The losing project induces the manager to be risk-seeking (prospect theory: people are risk-seeking when facing losses), and regret aversion further cements this entrapment, as the manager postpones the pain of revealing (to the market and to herself) that he made a mistake in investing in a bad project. In our model, we can think of the manager being entrapped into fraud, and continuing to hide it to postpone the painful regret of revealing her fraud.

The second point of departure for our analysis has been motivated by the work of Kulik et al. (2008), who analyse the effect of organisational group culture on the spread of unethical practice throughout the organisation. Particularly, they consider how a culture that rewards unethical behaviour may result in the spread of unethical behaviour from unethical to ethical managers. After developing their conceptual framework, Kulik et al. (2008) apply it to the case of Enron, with its stacking system for managerial promotion/firing which effectively rewarded and motivated unethical behaviour.[2]

Our analysis considers how the Freudian psychoanalytical framework, with the existence of a super-ego, can explain how managers may fall onto the 'slippery slope' to fraud, and may become entrapped in fraud, due to emotions such as regret. In a similar vein, Schrand and Zechman (2011) consider how the behavioural factor of managerial *overconfidence* may result in this slippery slope to fraud. These authors empirically analyse how overconfident executives with an optimism bias initially and unintentionally overstate earnings. In subsequent periods, when the executives become aware of their financial misreporting, they may then become entrapped into intentional mis-statement to cover it up. Our formal analysis could explain Schrand and Zechman's conceptual framework, and their results: in the initial period, the super-ego is asleep. At a critical point the super-ego awakens, and the manager may then be entrapped in deliberate mis-statement.

Fleming and Zyglidopoulos (2008) present a *process* model that analyses the escalation of deception in organisations. Similar to our analysis, they consider how once-ethical organisations ('Enron, WorldCom, Arthur Andersen and Lucent, did not start out deceitful') can become involved in a process of fraud escalation and entrapment ('If undetected, an initial lie can begin a process whereby the ease, severity and pervasiveness of deception increases overtime so that it eventually becomes an organizational level phenomenon.'), noting that their paper contributes to 'a growing body of research that looks beyond "bad" individuals for the causes of corporate illegality' (p. 837). This emphasises the importance of the 'nature versus nurture' debate, and sets the scene for our analysis, inspired by Kulik et al. (2008), that ethical managers may be 'infected' by an unethical culture.[3]

The seemingly frequent recurrence of scandals may point to potentially inadequate or inappropriate legislative responses, which gives rise to the question of whether more fundamental issues are being overlooked. In a review of a series of frauds, and legislative responses, that occurred throughout the twentieth century, Rockness and Rockness (2005) for example, focus on purely economic reasons for managerial fraudulent behaviour. Following Becker's (1974) analysis, these authors argue that 'The incentives for management to engage in unethical practices were driven by personal gain, ego and greed illustrated by opportunistic and exploitative executive behavior to achieve personal objectives … The use of incentive-based compensation schemes provided the incentives … for fraudulent financial reporting' (p. 32).

In contrast, findings from cognitive psychology and behavioural studies suggest that decision-making is not exclusively based on logical reasoning, but is also subject to numerous heuristics and cognitive biases (Tversky and Kahneman, 1974; Kahneman and Tversky, 1979; Fischhoff, 2002), affect (Slovic et al., 2002, 2004), visceral factors (Schelling, 1984; Loewenstein, 1996; Loewenstein and Lerner, 2003), and pressures towards conformity with the group or authority (Asch, 1951; Janis, 1972). Divergence from utility maximisation over time adds a temporal dimension to this literature (Strotz, 1955; Thaler, 1981; Laibson, 1997). Cohan (2002) considers corporate governance failings at Enron in terms of information blockage and information myopia. He analyses how these effects may have been driven by a combination of factors: economic (e.g., deliberate concealment of information by officers: 'only telling the boss what one perceives the boss wants to hear'; p. 281), behavioural (e.g., bounded rationality, cognitive dissonance, confirmatory bias, groupthink, false-consensus effect) and unconscious emotions.

2.   GAME THEORY, CORPORATE GOVERNANCE AND ETHICS

Our approach employs a game-theoretic analysis to consider the economic and behavioural factors affecting managerial fraud in organisations such as Enron. Other game-theoretic approaches exist that analyse various aspects of corporate governance and ethics. For example, in a series of papers, Sacconi (1999, 2006, 2007) develops a conceptual, philosophical and game-theoretic analysis of a social contract approach (which considers all stakeholders) to understanding ethical behaviour in an organisation. Cast in the new institutional theory of the firm framework, Sacconi's contractarian approach focuses on unethical behaviour regarding the abuse of authority, and the effects of contracts necessarily being incomplete, due to *ex post* uncertainty and unforeseen circumstances that cannot be fully understood or described in the *ex ante* initial contract. In Sacconi's papers, this *ex post* uncertainty can be mitigated in the initial contract by appealing to 'fuzzy logic' and 'fuzzy set' theory. In practical terms, this approach argues for loose, principles-based contracts, rather than strict rules-based contracts. Furthermore, Sacconi argues that the social contract can be considered, in practical terms, as a firm's code of ethics.

In addition to arguing for a principles-based 'fuzzy' social contract, Sacconi's series of papers gradually develop the 'story' along the following lines. First, he considers the optimum framework for the initial social contract. Sacconi (2006) argues that the contract should be *ex ante* acceptable to all parties, and hence *implementable*. The way that Sacconi deals with this is as follows. The social contract is based on economic bargaining models, particularly Nash bargaining[4] over the expected economic surplus generated from the organisational relationship. This bargaining is structured in such a way to ensure fairness and impartiality; hence all parties are happy to sign it, and it is indeed implementable.

In Sacconi (2007), he argues that *ex ante* implementability is one thing; however, *ex post* compliance is quite another. Why should parties adhere to the initial agreement as the situation unfolds? This speaks directly to the *ex post* abuse of authority. Sacconi (2007) argues that such *ex post* opportunism can be mitigated by long-run and dynamic reputation effects, and he considers a repeated Prisoner's Dilemma game[5] in which reputation drives compliance and mutual cooperation.

Sacconi's work is based on a *Homo economicus* approach, in which the players are self-interested, fully rational, unemotional, non-psychological, unbiased maximisers of expected utility. Hence, compliance has to be individually rational, and is enforced by fear of damaged future reputation if agents defect from the agreement (the 'shadow of the future' in repeated Prisoner's Dilemma terminology).[6] Furthermore, it is assumed that agents, being fully rational, can calculate, and can fully comprehend, the extent of the effects of their defection.

In our model, we consider *Homo sapiens*, not *Homo economicus*. The manager in our analysis is capable of feeling emotions and may be psychologically biased; in particular, we consider a psychoanalytical approach, in which a manager's ethicality is governed by her super-ego, not by external economic factors, such as reputation. In our dynamic model, the manager may not be able to 'look ahead' rationally (unlike in Sacconi's approach), since her super-ego may be asleep for small frauds. Sacconi's rational economics approach may be considered in terms of standard economics and standard game theory; our approach, on the other hand, may be considered as falling into the realm of behavioural economics and behavioural game theory. Comparing our approach with Sacconi's is useful for considering real-world fraud cases, such as Enron. The Enron case demonstrates that the fully rational *Homo economicus* approach may not be appropriate of sufficient in real-world fraud cases: fraud and abuse of authority can arise and spread in an organisation through psychological, behavioural and emotional channels.

Another game-theoretic approach has been developed by Cosimano (2004). He employs a repeated Prisoner's Dilemma framework, with punishment threat, to analyse why Tier 1 financial institutions failed to carry out their fiduciary duties in auditing, monitoring and controlling Enron. Cosimano's approach is heavily based on the economic approach in which fully rational self-interested utility-maximising agents act opportunistically unless constrained by future punishment threats. Hence, Cosimano argues for strong contracts, legal codes and punishment. We argue, supported by our behavioural game-theoretic analysis, that policy makers need to understand both the economic and the behavioural/psychological factors affecting fraud commission and fraud entrapment.

The Model

We consider corporate fraud both at the individual and corporate network level. In our first analysis, we focus on the economic, behavioural and psychological factors affecting individual managerial fraudulent behaviour, and the role of the super-ego in fraud entrapment, abstracting from any environmental and organisational effects. In our second analysis in our chapter, we incorporate environmental, contextual and organisational effects by considering 'fraud infection' across the dyad.

Model 1: Single manager
We begin by considering a behavioural model that analyses managerial fraudulent behaviour at an individual level. We consider a manager who has the opportunity to commit fraud in each period of her firm's existence. Particularly, we focus on a manager who initially considers fraud on a period-by-period (myopic) basis, and considers fraud as small and inconsequential.

Each period, there is a probability that the fraud is discovered (by, for example, external stakeholders, such as auditors, regulators, investors, the general public). Since the manager views this fraud as small and inconsequential, she underestimates her utility loss in terms of lost reputation and financial punishment. During this period of the game, the manager focuses on an *economic* CBA of fraud commission. However, at a critical period, the manager is 'hit' with the realisation that each period's small fraud has 'mounted up' to a large cumulative fraud. This activates her 'super-ego', which is capable of considering behavioural feelings of guilt and regret. Hence, the manager now conducts a *behavioural* CBA of fraud commission.

We model this game formally as follows. During the first time period from period 1 to a critical period n_c, the manager's super-ego remains asleep. At the critical period n_c, the manager's super-ego awakes. In each period, the unethical manager makes two decisions: (a) how much fraud to commit, and then (b) how much effort to exert in hiding the fraud. We solve each period's optimal decision-making 'backwards': that is, in each period, we solve for the manager's optimal fraud-hiding efforts, given the fraud level, and then move back to determine her optimal fraud level in that period. We denote fraud in period n as f_n, and we assume that there is a maximum level of fraud $\bar{f}$ that she can commit each period. We denote her fraud-hiding effort as e. Effort is costly for the manager: her cost-of-effort function is βe^2. This exhibits increasing marginal cost of effort.

Each period, there is an exogenously-given probability $q \in [0,1]$ that the manager's fraudulent activity will be discovered (by external stakeholders, such as the company's auditor, the regulator, the investors, the general public). We assume that if any level of fraud is discovered, the organisation collapses (as in the Enron case), and the manager suffers a huge economic (lost job, lost reputation, lost future employment elsewhere) and behavioural/emotional/psychological (guilt, regret) utility loss. She may also suffer legal punishment/imprisonment (which has huge economic and behavioural/emotional/psychological costs).

In order to solve the game, we need to specify a payoff function for the period in which the super-ego is asleep, and for the period when the super-ego awakes. When the super-ego is asleep, the manager's expected payoff in each period $n \in [1, n_C]$ is:

$$\pi_n = (1-q)f_n + q\left[f_n\left(1-(1-\gamma e)\hat{r}\right)\right] - \beta e^2 \tag{16.1}$$

The first term represents the manager's expected payoff in the case that fraud is not discovered. f_n represents the level of fraud that the manager commits in period n (one of the manager's two decisions each period). The first term captures the idea that the unethical manager gains positive utility from committing fraud. If the fraud is not discovered (which happens with probability $1-q$), this utility is undiminished. The second term represents the manager's payoff in the case that fraud is discovered (which occurs with probability q). In that case, the manager's payoff from committing fraud is diminished by her *perception of* lost reputation $\bar{r}$ from being discovered as fraudulent. γ represents her fraud-hiding ability: recall that e is her fraud-hiding effort. Thus, the higher is the product of her ability and effort γe, the more fraud she is able to hide in the case that fraud is discovered. For example, if $\gamma e = 0$, she does not hide any fraud: if fraud is discovered, she suffers 'full-utility loss': $f_n\left(1-\hat{r}\right)$. As γe increases, her

utility loss due to perceived loss of reputation reduces. At the maximum level of $\gamma e=1$, the

manager suffers no utility loss when fraud is discovered: $f_n\left(1-(1-\gamma e)\hat{r}\right)$ becomes f_n. The

final term in Equation (16.1) is the manager's cost of fraud-hiding effort.

In Equation (16.1), we are modelling the idea that, when the super-ego is asleep, the manager only considers fraud in the current period: she ignores/writes-off previous fraud, does not consider cumulative fraud and focuses on current-period fraud. This reflects the idea that she considers fraud as 'small and inconsequential'.

Furthermore, in the period when the super-ego is asleep, she focuses on an *economic* CBA; thus, she considers the economic cost of lost reputation. Furthermore, she considers her *perception* of lost reputation. We assume that she underestimates this factor: the true lost reputation is $R>\hat{r}$. Note that the true lost reputation will appear in payoff (16.2) below, when the manager's super-ego awakes.

We solve for the manager's optimal (that is, payoff-maximising) fraud level and fraud-hiding efforts in the period of the dormant super-ego 'backwards': that is, we first take as given the manager's choice of fraud level in period n, and find her optimal effort level by solving $\dfrac{\partial \pi_n}{\partial e}=0$ in Equation (16.1). We then substitute that optimal effort level into Equation (16.1), and solve $\dfrac{\partial \pi_n}{\partial f_n}$. Under certain parameter assumptions, we obtain the following.

Lemma 1: In the period when the super-ego is asleep: $n\in[1.n_C)$, *The unethical manager only considers fraud in each period (ignoring previous cumulative fraud); therefore, she views fraud as small and inconsequential, and she commits maximum fraud per period:* $f_n=\overline{f}$.
The unethical manager exerts fraud-hiding effort

Therefore, M's fraud-hiding effort is positively related to the probability of fraud discovery, the level of (maximum) fraud in period n, her ability to hide fraud and her perceived lost reputation from being discovered. Note that she underestimates the true lost reputation from fraud discovery, so she undersupplies fraud-hiding effort (that is, if she understood the true level of lost reputation, she would work harder to hide fraud). Her fraud-hiding effort is negatively related to her effort-cost of hiding fraud.

Before considering the period where the super-ego awakes, it is worth considering one of our assumptions in more detail. We have assumed that, if fraud is discovered, the organisation collapses, the manager loses her job and the game ends. However, above we have modelled the business-as-usual case, where the game continues for the full term of the dormant super-ego, with the manager committing the same maximum fraud and fraud-hiding efforts as in result 1, identically for each of the periods $n\in[1,n_C)$. Of course, as the game continues through this time interval, the probability of fraud discovery by outsiders, such as the auditor, increases. In our model, the probability of *avoiding* fraud discovery by the time we arrive at period n is $(1-q)^n$.

Our modelling approach is based on the firm continuing. One way is to consider a very low probability of fraud discovery. As an example, if we assumed that the probability of fraud discovery is $q=0.1$ (10 per cent chance of being discovered/90 per cent chance of getting away with it each period!) then the probability of avoiding fraud discovery by the time we arrive at period 5 is $0.9^5 = 0.59$. Even surviving fraud investigations to period 10 has quite a high probability: $0.9^{10} = 0.35$. Our model then focuses on the case where the firm avoids fraud discovery for a sufficiently long period to make our model meaningful.

We now turn to considering the critical time period n_C where the super-ego awakes. We consider that the super-ego awakes when the 'small and inconsequential' period frauds mount up to a large level of cumulative fraud that triggers the super-ego. Thus, we define a critical level of cumulative fraud F_C, where, if $F \in [0.F_C)$, the manager's super-ego is dormant. If we reach period F_C without fraud being discovered (see discussion above), the super-ego awakes.

In result 1 above, we demonstrated that, when the super-ego was asleep, the manager exerted the same level of fraud each period, being the maximum physical amount per period $\overline{f}$. Therefore, the critical level of fraud F_C, at which the super-ego is awakened, can be translated into a critical time period $N_C = \dfrac{F_C}{\overline{f}}$. To clarify analysis, we assume that $\overline{f}$ divides into F_C exactly, so that, at N_C, cumulative fraud has reached the exact level of critical fraud (this is not an essential assumption, but it makes the analysis neater and clearer).

Thus, when we reach period N_C, cumulative fraud is such that the super-ego awakens. We specify the unethical manager's payoff, when the super-ego awakens, as follows:

$$\pi = (1-q)\big(F_C[1-G]\big) + qF_C\big(1-\gamma eG - (1-\gamma e)(R+r)\big) - \beta e^2 \tag{16.2}$$

We designed this payoff to capture the various conflicting economic and behavioural/psychological/emotional factors in the fraudulent manager's mind when the super-ego awakens, and she realises the extent and level of her cumulative fraud. The reader is invited to compare payoff (16.2) with earlier payoff (16.1) when the super-ego was asleep: we observe parallels in these two payoffs.

When the super-ego was asleep, the manager only considers period fraud (thus f_n in payoff (16.1)). Now that the super-ego is awake, she considers cumulative fraud F_C in equation (16.2). As in equation (16.1), the unethical manager gains some positive utility from fraud commission (Ariely discusses how criminals and fraudsters may gain some pleasure and excitement from 'committing the perfect crime', cheating the system and getting away with it![7]); but now, in Equation (16.2), the positive utility comes from cumulative, not period, fraud.

As in Equation (16.1), the payoff in Equation (16.2) captures both the case where fraud is not discovered (with exogenous probability $1-q$), and the case where fraud is discovered (with exogenous probability q). The first term of Equation (16.2) demonstrates that when the super-ego awakes, then, if fraud is not discovered, the manager enjoys the excitement of committing cumulative fraud F_C. However, compared to Equation (16.1) when the super-ego was asleep, the manager now feels a level of guilt, acting as a psychological 'cost' on utility: $(1-G)$. Note that G is a fraction between zero and 1, and represents the proportion of the utility from F_C 'lost' due to painful feelings of guilt.

The second term in Equation (16.2) represents the case where the fraud is discovered. In our model, the manager's fraud-hiding effort e reduces the amount of fraud to be discovered: effectively, the harder that she works at hiding fraud, the more fraud that she can put out of sight of external bodies, such as the auditor. For example, in the Enron case, much managerial effort was exerted in creating complex accounting methods and financial instruments, such as special-purpose entities (SPEs), to hide large levels of fraud from the external auditor.

In the second term of payoff 2, R represents her true lost reputation when her fraud is discovered. We focus on the case where $R > \hat{r}$ (that is, the manager underestimated her lost reputation when considering small frauds in equation (16.1), but now realises the true extent R of her lost reputation if the cumulative fraud is now discovered). Furthermore, in the second term, r represents managerial regret from committing fraud after it is discovered. As noted earlier in the paper, this follows the behavioural research into regret theory (Bell, 1982; Loomes and Sugden, 1982) which suggests that people only feel regret when the loss becomes 'real'. Also, as noted previously, the manager only feels guilt G if fraud is not discovered.

In our model, the manager has no control over the probability q of fraud discovery (for example, the manager cannot 'make' the auditor discover fraud: if the auditor lacks independence, and wishes to 'turn a blind eye', or exerts low effort into finding fraud).[8] Thus, when considering her *expected* payoff, she faces two possible guilt situations: in the first case, she feels guilt when fraud is not discovered (the first term of Equation (16.2)); in the second, she feels guilt when fraud is discovered, but she has hidden some away (e.g., in SPEs) – this is captured in the second term of Equation (16.2).

The second term in payoff 2 captures an interesting trade-off for the unethical manager when the super-ego is awake. The manager feels guilt G for the amount of fraud hidden (being discovered and 'coming clean' is 'good for the soul'). On the other hand, the manager suffers from both lost reputation and regret due to the amount of fraud discovered. The manager thus faces an interesting trade-off and economic/psychological conflict in her mind when deciding on her fraud-hiding efforts: as she increases these efforts, she gains in terms of reducing the negative effects of lost reputation and regret. However, she increases the utility loss associated with guilt. These two opposing effects are interesting. Lost reputation and regret drive the manager to work harder to hide fraud, while guilt drives her to work *less* hard to hide fraud: her optimal fraud-hiding effort depends on which of these two effects dominate. Result 2 captures this trade-off in the manager's fraud decision.

We solve for the manager's optimal fraud level and fraud-hiding efforts exactly as described when deriving result 1. We obtain proposition 1 (which incorporates lemma 1 to give the complete picture). Note that proposition (1b), that the manager reduces period fraud to zero, depends on certain parameter assumptions.

Proposition 1:

When $N \in [0, N_C]$, *the super-ego lies dormant. The manager only considers period fraud.* *She commits the maximum 'small' fraud each period:* $f_n = \overline{f}$, *and exerts fraud-hiding efforts*

$$e^* = \frac{q \overline{f} \gamma \hat{r}}{2\beta}.$$

When $N > N_C$, *the super-ego is activated, and the manager experiences feelings of guilt and regret. Furthermore, she now turns her attention to cumulative fraud. The manager reduces her period fraud to zero. Although she commits no more fraud, she exerts fraud-hiding efforts*

$$e^* = \max\left(\frac{q F_C \gamma [R + r - G]}{2\beta}, 0 \right) \text{ (in order to hide the existing cumulative fraud). When her guilt is}$$

low compared to lost reputation and regret: $G < R + r$, *the manager exerts some fraud-hiding efforts. When her guilt is high compared to lost reputation and regret:* $G > R + r$, *she reduces her fraud-hiding efforts to zero.*

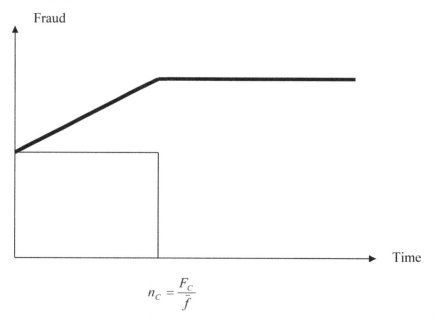

$$n_C = \frac{F_C}{\overline{f}}$$

Figure 16.1   *Manager's fraud commission as a function of time: super-ego asleep versus super-ego awake (diagram reflects Proposition 1)*

We summarise these results in Figures 16.1 and 16.2.

In Figure 16.1, the thinner lines represent per-period fraud. The thick black lines represent cumulative fraud. In summary, the manager uses a cost–benefit calculation (as in Ariely's discussion). Up to time $N_C = \frac{F_C}{\overline{f}}$, she views the frauds as small, her guilt is low, and therefore

Fraud-hiding
Efforts

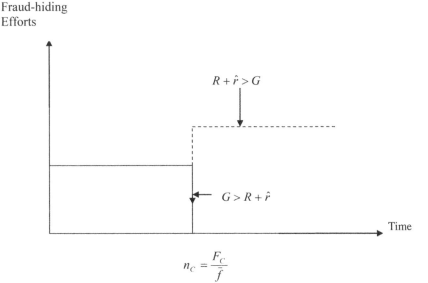

$$n_C = \frac{F_C}{\hat{f}}$$

Figure 16.2   Manager's fraud commission as a function of time: super-ego asleep versus
super-ego awake (diagram reflects Proposition 1)

she commits fraud. After time $N_C = \dfrac{F_C}{\hat{f}}$, fraud becomes large enough that her super-ego kicks

in, activating guilt, such that she stops fraud.

Figure 16.2 captures an interesting effect: although the manager stops committing fraud, her fraud-hiding efforts are determined by her relative feelings of guilt and regret, together with her lost reputation. If guilt dominates, then she reduces her fraud-hiding efforts to zero. If lost reputation/regret dominates, she *increases* her fraud-hiding efforts (as she now considers cumulative, rather than period, fraud). This can be considered as a kind of fraud entrapment. In the early periods, she perceived the fraud as minor, and so committed it without guilt, and exerted low fraud-hiding efforts. In the latter periods, she views the cumulative fraud as large, and is now entrapped into hiding it.

A Dyadic Model of Fraud Infection

Thus far, we have considered an individual manager, acting in isolation. We now extend the model to consider the possibility that unethical practice (such as fraud) may spread throughout an organisation, as unethical actors 'infect' ethical actors. In this work, we have been inspired by Kulik et al.'s (2008) conceptual model of the spread of unethical behaviour. Following the second part of Kulik et al.'s model, we focus on a dyadic relationship between two types of manager: an ethical (non-fraudulent) and unethical (fraudulent) manager. We note a difference between the two managerial types that has important policy and ethical considerations. The unethical manager acts exactly as in model 1, as described in results 1 and 2. That is, he performs a CBA, with the super-ego asleep for the first n_c periods (purely economic CBA), after which the super-ego awakes (economic and behavioural CBA). In performing these calculations, the unethical manager considers the probability of fraud discovery. In contrast, the ethical manager does not perform such a CBA, and does not consider the probability of being caught. In our model, the ethical manager acts according to his character (is it in his character to commit fraud?), but may also be affected by the organisational culture.

We model this as follows. The unethical manager still faces the payoff as in (16.1), and acts as in the first model, as described in results 1 and 2. The ethical manager, on the other hand, is a different 'beast' and has the following payoff:

$$\pi_E = U - gf_n + \psi \tag{16.3}$$

where U represents the ethical manager's 'base utility' from working in the organisation, and gf_n represents his guilt (parameter g) from committing period fraud f_n. Due to the multiplicative nature of this element of his payoff, g can be thought of as 'guilt per unit of fraud'. Thus, the higher is g, and/or the higher is f_n, the higher the total guilt felt by the ethical manager. We assume that g is strictly positive for the ethical manager; thus, in the absence of the final parameter ψ of equation (16.3), payoff π_E is strictly decreasing in guilt. That is, an ethical manager would optimally choose zero fraud to maximise his payoff.

It is the final parameter of equation (16.3), ψ, that brings the interest to our dyadic model. We term ψ the unethical infection parameter, and it provides the link from the unethical manager's to the ethical manager's behaviour, as follows.

We model unethical infection as:

$$\psi = \theta\Delta(n-1) \text{ if } f_n(E) = f_n(U)$$

$$\psi = 0 \text{ if } f_n(E) < f_n(U) \tag{16.4}$$

The first part of Equation (16.4) states that the ethical manager only gains utility ψ if he 'matches' the unethical manager's level of fraud: $f_n(E) = f_n(U)$. If he commits any level of fraud lower than the unethical manager, $f_n(E) < f_n(U)$, then the ethical manager gains zero utility from unethical infection: $\psi = 0$.

θ is the unethical infection rate: that is, the extent to which unethicality spreads across an organisation from unethical to ethical members. Δ is the 'organisational reward' for being unethical. Thus, for example, in Enron, we would expect both parameters to be large: much research demonstrates that Enron was organised such that both the infection rate and the rewards for being unethical were large in Enron. Breaking down the total level of unethical infection to these two factors (infection rate, and organisational rewards for unethical behaviour) may be interesting for empirical analysis of fraud across organisations, as we suggest that both elements play a role in the spread of fraud. The factor $(n-1)$ is in the equation to represent the growing pressure on the ethical manager to commit fraud as time goes on.

In our dyadic model, the actions of the unethical manager remain as in model 1 (that is, he is isolated from the behaviour of the ethical manager). Thus, the unethical manager continues to commit maximum fraud in the period when the super-ego remains asleep: $N \in [1, N_C]$

Thus, given that the unethical manager commits maximum fraud per period, then (16.4) demonstrates that the ethical manager only achieves $\psi = \theta \Delta(n-1)$ if he mimics the unethical manager by committing maximum fraud in the period. If he commits any amount of fraud lower than the maximum per-period level, he will commit less fraud than the unethical manager, and his unethical reward, from (16.4), will be $\psi = 0$. Formally, incorporating (16.4) into (16.3), the ethical manager's payoff, when he commits less-than-maximum per-period fraud (given that the unethical manager is committing maximum fraud in each period) is:

$$\pi_E = U - gf_n. \tag{16.5}$$

On the other hand, if the ethical manager mimics the unethical manager by committing maximum per-period fraud, the ethical manager's payoff is:

$$\pi_E = U - gf_n + \theta \Delta(n-1). \tag{16.6}$$

Considering (16.5) and (16.6), the ethical manager's payoff is decreasing in fraud in (16.5) (that is, for any level of fraud up to, but just less than, the maximum level). If the ethical manager commits maximum fraud, then his payoff jumps up by the final term in (16.6).

Therefore, from (16.5) and (16.6), the ethical manager either commits zero fraud, or maximum fraud. Thus, (16.5), with zero fraud, becomes:

$$\pi_E = U \tag{16.5a}$$

In order to decide on his optimal level of fraud (zero or maximum), he simply compares (16.5a) and (16.6), to observe which is larger. This reduces to the following result. The ethical manager commits maximum fraud in a period if $\theta \Delta(n-1) > gf_n$; otherwise, he commits zero fraud. We note the following. In the first period $(n=1)$, the ethical manager faces zero unethical infection: $\psi = \theta \Delta(n-1) = 0$. Thus, (16.5a) > (16.6), and he commits zero fraud. Now, throughout the period when the super-ego is asleep, such that the unethical manager commits maximum per-period fraud, the ethical manager's unethical infection pressure is growing with the passing periods, due to the inclusion of $n-1$ in the infection equation. The ethical manager switches from zero fraud to maximum fraud in the period where Equation (16.6) switches from being less than, to becoming greater than (16.5a). Note that (16.5a) = (16.6) when $\theta \Delta(n-1) = gf_n =>$

$$(n-1)' = \frac{gf_n}{\theta \Delta} \tag{16.7}$$

Thus, $(n-1)'$ represents the critical period whereby, for $n-1 < (n-1)'$, the ethical manager commits zero fraud. When $n-1 > (n-1)'$, the ethical manager switches dramatically from zero to maximum fraud. Payoff (16.6) captures the following dilemma for the ethical manager: the second term demonstrates that he feels guilt at committing fraud (this is what defines him as an ethical manager, in contrast to the unethical manager, with dormant super-ego). However, he faces organisational pressure, from the infection rate and from the organisational rewards from mimicking the unethical manager. This ethical dilemma is captured further in (16.7): the more ethical he is (higher numerator in (16.7)), the later the critical period at which he switches from zero to maximum fraud to mimic the unethical manager. On the other hand, the higher the organisational unethical infection pressure (the denominator in (16.7), the *earlier* the period at which he switches from zero to maximum per-period fraud.

We note that, given the parameter values in (16.7), and given the exogenous period N_C at which the unethical manager's super-ego awakes, it is possible that the ethical manager is able to resist the unethical infection parameter for the entire period that the unethical manager's super-ego is dormant (this is the case where $n' > N_C$). On the other hand, if $n' \in [0, N_C]$ the ethical manager will be able to resist, and commit zero fraud for the period $n \in [0, n']$, but will switch to maximum per-period fraud when $n \in [n', N_C]$ In order to clarify this analysis, we work with the following numerical parameter values: $U=1,000; g=5; f_n=500$; and the infection parameters are $\theta=0.5; \Delta=1000$. For the unethical manager, we consider the case where his super-ego awakes at the cumulative fraud level: $\overline{F}=5,000$. Since the maximum per-period fraud is $f_n=500$, this implies that the critical period at which the unethical manager's super-ego awakens is: $n_C = \dfrac{\overline{F}}{f_n} = 10$. Consider the ethical manager. Given the parameter values above, we compare (16.5a) (zero fraud) and (16.6) (maximum fraud) to examine the ethical manager's behaviour in each round.

Ethical Manager's Fraud Decision as a Function of Time

Figure 16.3 summarises the ethical manager's fraud decision period-by-period.

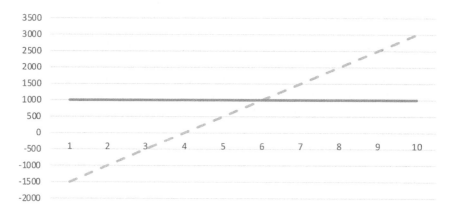

Figure 16.3   *Ethical manager's payoff (zero fraud versus maximum fraud) by period*

The horizontal line is his payoff from committing zero fraud (16.5a). The upward sloping line is his payoff from committing maximum fraud (payoff 16.6). The figure demonstrates that he switches from zero to maximum fraud at period 6. We can easily check that this is consistent with the critical period in (16.7):

$$(n-1)' = \frac{gf_n}{\theta\Delta} = \frac{5*500}{0.5*1000} = 5 => n' = 6. \tag{16.7}$$

The unethical manager's super-ego awakes

We assume the following. If the ethical manager is able to resist committing fraud for the entire period where the unethical manager's super-ego is dormant (that is, $n' > N_C$,) then, when the unethical manager's super-ego awakes, and he behaves as in result 1, the ethical manager remains ethical (i.e., remains uninfected), and continues to ignore the behaviour of the unethical manager, continuing to commit zero fraud. On the other hand, if $n' < N_C$, the ethical manager switches to maximum fraud during the period where the unethical manager's super-ego is dormant. In this case, we assume that, once the unethical manager's super-ego awakes, the ethical manager has become so infected by the unethical manager that he, in effect, becomes an unethical manager, and acts as in result 1. Both managers (ethical and unethical) stop committing fraud, but may or may not exert fraud-hiding efforts for the cumulative fraud, depending on whether $G < R+r$ or $G > R+r$.

This has interesting organisational implications. In the former case, where $n' > N_C$, there is only one level of cumulative fraud, committed by the unethical manager. In the latter case, $n' < N_C$, the ethical manager becomes infected (doubling the level of organisational fraud in the periods when he becomes infected), and equally as entrapped as the unethical manager when the super-ego awakes. In the case that $G < R+r$, they both exert cumulative fraud-hiding efforts once the super-ego awakes.

In Figure 16.4, we consider the case where $N_C = 10$. Given our parameter values above, we obtained $n' = 6$. Thus, in Figure 16.4, we are considering the case where $n' < N_C$, such that the unethical manager commits maximum per-period fraud of $f_n = 500$ each period, and the ethical manager commits zero fraud up to $n = n' = 6$, but becomes infected at that period, and jumps to maximum fraud for the remaining four periods $n \in [n' = 7, N_C = 10]$. When the super-ego awakes at $N_C = 10$, both managers (ethical and unethical) stop committing fraud. Thus, in periods 1–6, the per-period fraud is 500 (committed only by the unethical manager). In periods 7–10, the per-period fraud is 1000 (committed by both managers). Thus, when the unethical manager's super-ego awakes, the cumulative fraud level is $6*500 + 4*1000 = 7,000$. At this point, they both stop committing fraud. However, if $G < R+r$, both managers become entrapped into exerting fraud-hiding efforts.

The unethical manager's super-ego is asleep for the first 10 periods, and so the unethical manager commits the maximum amount of fraud per period ($f_n = 500$). The ethical manager commits zero fraud per-period until period $n' = 6$. At this point, the infection parameter dominates, and the ethical manager switches from zero to maximum period fraud of 500, mimicking the unethical manager. Hence, the period fraud doubles from 500 to 1000 (unethicality has 'swept across the dyad'); hence, the kink in the figure at period 6. At period 10, the super-ego

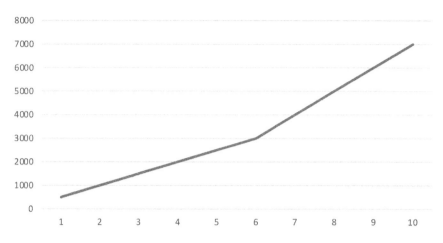

Figure 16.4   Cumulative fraud in the dyad

awakes, and both managers stop committing fraud at the cumulative level of 7000 (although, depending on the economic and behavioural parameters in their payoffs, they may continue to hide it; recall result 2). Although we have only considered a dyad, we could develop this work to consider a network of managers across the organisation. What our dyadic analysis has demonstrated is that unethicality may gradually spread across managers over time, and that total fraud may then 'snowball', increasing at an ever-greater rate.

3.   REAL-WORLD UNETHICAL INFECTION: THE ENRON CASE

In this section, we follow up our theoretical analysis by considering the case of Enron. Enron provides an example where fraud and unsustainable business practices appear to have become endemic with a promotion system in place which effectively encouraged unethical behaviour. As noted by Kulik et al. (2008), Enron nurtured an organisational culture in which unethical managers were rewarded for performance even if this involved committing a fraud, and where ethical managers were incentivised to copy this behaviour.

Although the extent and scale of the *ex post* investigation of the collapse of Enron was unprecedented, the most accessible studies are still those emanating from the internal enquiry set up by Enron shortly after the commencement of the US Securities and Exchange Commission (SEC) investigation (the Powers report: Powers et al., 2002) and the monumental enquiries of the bankruptcy examiners (Batson, 2002, 2003a, 2003b, 2003c; Goldin, 2003).[9] The Powers report focuses primarily on the scale of Enron's off-balance-sheet activities, transactions between Enron and its unconsolidated SPEs, the use of transactions with these SPEs to seek to protect Enron's reported profitability in the two years immediately ahead of its collapse, and the opportunity for improper personal benefit afforded to certain of Enron's senior executives from such transactions.

The bankruptcy examiners' reports give a wider perspective on the extent and manner of the manipulation of Enron's financial reporting in terms of income, cash flows and the balance sheet picture. The great majority of these manipulations were, individually, designed to comply with US GAAP (generally accepted accounting principles) and the details of the trans-actions giving rise to the manipulations were known to the auditors. However, the bankruptcy examiner's (Batson's) view was that, in a great many cases, the compliance with US GAAP was illusory and that overall the combined effect was a massive distortion of the financial statements. Details of this distortion which, in the opinion of the bankruptcy examiner, led to overstatement of profit by 96 per cent, of operating cash flows by 105 per cent and an under-statement of liabilities by 116 per cent in the final set of fully audited financial statements, those for the year end 31 December 2000 (Batson, 2003a).

On the face of it, Enron's corporate governance structure was a model of good practice. Enron's Audit and Compliance Committee, chaired by Robert Jaedicke, Emeritus Professor of Accounting and former Dean of the Graduate School of Business at Stanford, and including Wendy Gramm, a former chair of the US Commodity Futures Trading Commission, and Lord Wakeham, both a qualified accountant and a previous UK energy minister, was a dis-tinguished one. The external audit was carried out by Arthur Andersen, one of the then Big Five auditors. There was an active risk and compliance function internal to the firm. Enron had produced a Code of Ethics, a document of 64 pages signed by Kenneth Lay (Enron CEO and Chairman), outlining the company's firm commitment to conducting business affairs in accordance with all applicable law and in the highest moral and honest manner, with the last known edition produced in July 2000 (now an exhibit in the Smithsonian's National Museum of American History). The only potential reservation would be that the internal audit function was outsourced to Andersen, the external auditors, a practice which has been prohibited in the US since implementation of the Sarbanes Oxley Act of 2002, and in the European Union since implementation of the 2014 Regulation regarding statutory audit of public-interest entities.[10]

It is arguable whether anything could have prevented the collapse of Enron subsequent to the initial revelations of financial irregularities. Nonetheless, a more effective corporate governance structure, effective internal control, an effective risk management system and a committed risk committee might have been able to check management excesses in terms of remuneration and might have both reduced the scale of the loss and the spread of the fraudu-lent behaviours and significantly affected where the losses fell by ensuring more appropriate financial reporting practices and the prevention of schemes whereby net cash outflows were incurred for the purpose of financial reporting manipulation.

In addition to the documented unquestionably poor financial reporting, the sub-standard auditing provided by Arthur Andersen, and the failures of effectively all of the standard corpo-rate governance mechanisms right up to the company's demise, we question how an organisa-tion's behaviour – and with this we make reference to what one must assume to be a majority of key personnel, including the members of the board who are the basis for the 'tone at the top' – came to wholeheartedly embrace a myriad of inopportune, in many instances unethi-cal, and regularly unlawful, business practices, which on the whole and in their final impact would seem to have resulted in its unexpectedly sudden and inglorious demise. Here, the case contributes to an understanding of the antecedents to and the spread of unethical behaviour, its spread across the organisation and its development into the de facto norm.

Kulik et al. (2008) note the corrosive effects on ethical behaviour of forced competi-tion systems in organisations. Enron's stacking system implemented a strict system of intra-organisational competition amongst employees, and refers to a forced-ranking system which forced out low performers every six months. Alas, forced-ranking systems may not only be ineffective and inefficient (Pfeffer and Sutton, 2006), but may foster the spread of unethical behaviour between individuals after the behaviour has emerged but before unethical behaviour had become normalised. Kulik et al. (2008) argue that such systems may result in organisation-wide corruption as an unintended consequence, an interpretation that had earlier been suggested by Pfeffer and Sutton (2006), quoting McKinsey consultants Michaels et al. (2001):

> A couple of years ago, one of us gave a speech at a renowned (but declining) high-technology firm that used a forced-ranking system. They called it a stacking system. Managers were required to rank 20 per cent of employees as A players, 70 per cent as Bs, and 10 per cent as Cs. Just as The War for Talent advises, they gave the lion's share of rewards to As, modest rewards to Bs, and fired the Cs. But in an anonymous poll, the firm's top 100 or so executives were asked which company practices made it difficult to turn knowledge into action. The stacking system was voted as the worst culprit. This is not just one company's experience. A survey of more than 200 human resource professionals … found that … more than half of the companies [surveyed] used forced ranking. (p. 107)

Losers in a stacking system are under pressure to adopt the behaviours of the winners at the dyadic (person to person) level in order to thrive and survive in organisations. This can then lead to the spread of unethical behaviour if the winners at least sometimes succeed by making unethical decisions and the losers adapt to the behaviour of the winners (Kulik et al., 2008). With regard to the effects on behaviour, established behaviour patterns (including what may originally be seen as corrupt, fraudulent, unethical or unacceptable behaviour) may subsequently be interpreted as the acceptable norm, without necessarily being interpreted as 'improper'.

Enron's stacking system likely induced behaviour which in hindsight is clearly inappropriate, unethical, even fraudulent, but at the time may largely have been viewed as acceptable behaviour necessary to survive and succeed in a highly competitive environment. Hence, competitive, aggressive, unethical behaviour may become acceptable, indeed highly valued and rewarded, leading to highly selective perceptions of acceptable behaviour, regardless of and in contrast to Enron's professed core values, summarised in Enron's four values of respect, integrity, communication, excellence ('R.I.C.E.') and its Code of Ethics, values which in reality were routinely violated and undermined. A stacking system, and the rewards from perceived dominant behaviours and outcomes this enabled and encouraged, may well reinforce biases in judgement and decision-making processes noted elsewhere, such as a susceptibility of individuals to drift from accepted or prescribed behavioural norms (Maccoby, 2000), the tendency to acquiesce to or uncritically accept assertions (Prentice, 2000a, 2000b; Coffee, 2001; Langevoort, 2001); and socio-psychological effects on the quality of judgements and decision-making of groups (Janis, 1989).

Committing small transgressions to start with, and 'blanking' them in the mind as 'too small to worry about', 'acceptable' or 'a necessary means to survival', or deviating from acceptable behaviour only by an amount seen as noise, immaterial or within a range of acceptable variances, the individual effectively sets a new anchor for acceptable behaviour, potentially placing himself or herself on a slippery slope towards outright fraud.[11] Where this is rewarded in a forced-ranking system which measures success by crude shot-term numeric/financial performance indicators which underestimate risk and make no allowance for the likelihood of success of the proposed venture (note how systematically Enron offloaded business ventures into SPEs which not only took liabilities off the consolidated financial statements, but also allowed imaginary 'profits' to be booked), this can become self-reinforcing. Hence, an unintended consequence of Enron's stacking system may have been that the behaviour of the winner(s) of one round of the competition is quickly adopted by the loser(s), who either develop the characteristics and skills necessary to win in the next round or face removal from the organisation.

Recent research into biological mechanisms underlying the development of fraudulent behaviour supports this interpretation on how small transgressions may gradually lead to larger ones, and how small deviations from a moral code (or standard, rule, law, regulation) may, over time, escalate into material deviations with potentially devastating consequences (Garrett et al., 2016). Effectively, the brain may become 'immune' to the effects of deception, akin to an anchor creeping ever further away from the ideal spot, with the individual over time committing ever bigger frauds, a phenomenon possibly supported by, and potentially pre-disposed towards, over-optimism (Schrand and Zechman, 2011), a character trait typically favoured within organisations.

Hence, in the absence of a realisation within the organisation of the need for a strong and fixed moral guide (an anchor which stays firmly affixed), or moderating factors which pull the individual and group back towards the moral beacon if their anchors have 'slipped', competitive internal interactions can lead to the spread of unethical behaviour from bad apples to good apples and can eventually become so ingrained that the remaining good apples have either been completely side-lined (while observing the bad apples' success and promotions) or have left the organisation. As the remaining good apples may not be seen as successful by the forced-ranking system, they may forcibly be weeded out until only those willing to play the game within the organisation remain; i.e., they accept the prevailing norm, an outcome not unlike Akerlof's 'Market for "Lemons"' (1970), where bad products drive out the good, and only the lemons (unethical individuals in our example) remain.[12] A race to the bottom may thus result in organisations with potentially disastrous results.

Whereas governance at board level should have picked up on the detrimental effects of its internal tournament system, and should have introduced moderating factors and circuit-breakers, to induce a counterculture with high ethical standards or ethical leadership (or both; see Trevino et al., 2000), to overcome the corrosive side-effects of the stacking system, or avoid it in the first place, the tone at Enron's top was hardly focused on providing such moderation, and instead focused on (perceived) success at all cost, creating an environment where unethical behaviour became the celebrated norm. To some extent, Enron's stacking system not only de-emphasised ethical controls but strongly conditioned employees towards unethical behaviour. In this respect, the described pressures on performance echo Milgram's 1963 experiment on obedience to authority where honest, ethical and good-intentioned individuals were prepared to perform acts conflicting with their (original) personal conscience, even if this meant causing serious injury and distress (in Milgram's experiment), or in our case to expose the company to unsustainable liabilities and risks.[13]

Just as groups may escalate commitment to a lost cause where groupthink takes hold (Janis, 1972; Staw, 1976; Weick, 1983), individuals can be subject to gradual escalation of self-serving dishonesty (Weick, 1964; Garrett et al., 2016). This can potentially have devastating outcomes when a forced-ranking system with great rewards for the winners not only leads to the frequent emergence of unethical behaviour, but results in widespread diffusion of such patterns permeating the organisation (Kulik et al., 2008). Committed ethical leadership would likely have been able to put an end to such a diffusion of unethical practice. Enron, alas, was one example where some corrupt (or possibly ignorant) people at the top reinforced unethical grassroots behaviour, with many remaining elements of the governance paradigm busy playing the three wise monkeys.

4.   POLICY IMPLICATIONS OF OUR ANALYSIS FOR AUDITING AND ORGANISATIONAL SYSTEMS

Anastasopoulos and Anastasopoulos (2012) present a dynamic game-theoretic analysis of auditing for fraud and misreporting. They model a two-player game between an auditor (who chooses between two strategies: basic audit or a more costly extended audit, which provides a greater probability of discovering fraud if it has been committed) and an auditee (who decides between committing fraud and not committing fraud). These authors' paper can be considered in the fully rational, non-psychological and non-emotional traditional economics framework. Their main findings surround audit quality and audit tenure: they recommend a more comprehensive audit to deter rational fraud commission.

In contrast, we have employed a behavioural economics approach, incorporating psychology and emotions, to consider managerial fraud in an organisation. Our main implications for auditing systems and organisational design are as follows:

(a) In designing monitoring and auditing systems to check for managerial misbehaviour and fraud, it is important to note that managers may not be aware of their fraudulent behaviour, especially in the early days of fraud, and when this fraud is 'small'. This is the period when the manager's super-ego may be asleep.

(b) When the manager's super-ego is asleep, traditional deterrence threats, such as in-depth auditing, monitoring and punishments (such as fines, firing from the job, and potential prison sentences) may be wholly ineffective, as managers will not be aware that they are committing any offence. Van Winden and Ash (2012) emphasise the importance of educating managers in ethical behaviour.

(c) When the super-ego awakes, the manager may then be weighing up the economic and behavioural/psychological/emotional benefits of owning up to fraud versus hiding it (similar to Van Winden and Ash's (2012) competing forces model). Excess threat may be counterproductive, and lead to more fraud-hiding!

(d) Finally, design of the organisational systems and structures, and the method of motivating, rewarding and compensating employees may have a crucial effect on the spread of unethical and fraudulent behaviour across the organisation. For example, a culture that obsessively rewards 'performance' at all costs, and is tough on mistakes, may lead to unethical behaviour spreading across the organisation, infecting once-ethical employees. The organisational culture at Enron, together with its 'stacking system', is a prime example of a structure to be avoided.

The Fraud Triangle

Our analysis has parallels with the work that considers the Fraud Triangle (Cressey, 1951; Cressey, 1953; Sutherland and Cressey, 1978; Albrecht, 2014), which suggests three conditions that need to be present for fraud to take place: motive/pressure, opportunity and rationalisation. The Fraud Triangle is most useful in studying why and how individuals commit fraud, and in the prevention, deterrence, detection and investigation of fraud. Following Cressey (1953), Albrecht et al. (1984) compiled a list of variables (red flags) associated with the perpetration of fraud, and reached the conclusion that it was a combination of three forces that underlie the incidence of fraud (thus creating the seminal Fraud Triangle). In concluding their study into fraud and fraud prevention, Albrecht et al. (1984) suggested that the three factors interact to determine whether an individual commits fraud or not, without making the claim to be able to explain every case of fraud. Albrecht et al. (1984) add that anything that contributes to the capability of perpetrating or concealing fraud increases the opportunity for fraud. Albrecht (1991) further notes that all three elements must be present for fraud to occur (although mere perception of pressure or opportunity suffices), later adding further triangles relevant to understanding fraud (Albrecht et. al., 1995). Of direct importance to our study is the triangle presenting ways to fight fraud, with these elements: prevention, detection and investigation (Albrecht et al., 1995).

Our model aims to further add to the understanding of fraud, by investigating the rationalisation of fraud (the third leg/element of the Fraud Triangle, originally from Cressey, 1953, and eventually adopted by Albrecht in formulating the model) in the presence of a regulator. We build on Davis and Pesch (2013), who develop an agent-based modelling (ABM) approach to examine the emergent dynamics of the spread of fraud across organisations. In their ABM, they also draw from Cressey's (1953) and Albrecht et al.'s (1984) Fraud Triangle, in order to consider heterogeneous agents working within an organisation, characterised by differing levels of motive, opportunity and attitude towards fraud: these varying characteristics contribute to an agent being honest or, conversely, fraudulent.

Like Davis and Pesch (2013), our model considers the Fraud Triangle factors of motive, opportunity and attitude. Furthermore, we consider a 'moral hazard' (hidden action) element, not considered in Davis and Pesch (2013). That is, we consider a manager who chooses how much fraud to commit each period, and how much costly effort to exert in hiding it from the regulator, who, in turn, is exerting effort into trying to find it.

Comparison of Our Framework with Existing Conceptual Research

We have considered both economic and behavioural factors affecting the manager's fraud decisions. Our work is close in spirit to Van Winden and Ash (2012). We are also motivated by the conceptual behavioural economics analyses of fraud conducted by Di Micela da Silveira (2013) and Rafeld et al. (2017).

Kulik et al. (2008) conceptualise how fraud and unethical behaviour was endemic and spread rapidly across and throughout Enron. They note that this spread of fraud was driven both from the top down but was also driven from the 'bottom up', and horizontally across layers within the organisation. Kulik et al. (2008) further argue that the organisational culture at Enron (the 'tone at the top' at board level, the employee stacking system – a compensation system which effectively rewarded fraudulent, dishonest behaviour) allowed this spread of unethical fraudulent behaviour to thrive.

Kulik et al. (2008) begin their conceptual analysis of the spread of fraud within Enron by considering two inter-related frameworks: the theory of reasoned action (TRA) (Ajzen 1985), and the theory of planned behaviour (TPB) (Ajzen and Fishbein 1980; Fishbein and Ajzen, 1975). As they state, 'the theory of reasoned action assumes that individuals are rational, that they make use of all available information, and that they evaluate the possible implications of their action before they decide to engage or not engage in a particular decision' (p. 708). Although this work appears in the 'management' literature, we draw parallels to our work by noting that this is the *Homo economicus* approach in the standard economics literature.

The TPB has parallels with our behavioural economics approach to fraud, by extending the TRA framework to include heterogenous individual attitudes, subjective norms and perceived behavioural control. This approach emphasises the gap between (unethical/fraudulent) intentions and behaviour (the intention/behaviour gap is a key element considered in behavioural economics, and particularly in nudge theory). Kulik et al. (2008) note that, in the TPB, the attitude towards the behaviour refers to the individual's positive or negative assessment of engaging in that behaviour. 'An individual's attitude is a multiplicative component consisting of the individual's strength of belief associated with the behaviour and the individual's subjective evaluation or weighted importance of the belief's attribute' (p. 709). In our behavioural economics framework, this would feature in the manager's utility function (his economic and behavioural CBA) in the parameters relating to his (perceived) gains from fraud commission, his (perceived) lost reputation from fraud discovery, and behavioural factors such as guilt and regret.

The further factor in TPB is 'perceived behavioural control'. This refers to the individual's perceptions of the ease or difficulty of performing the behaviour. We note that this may relate to the Fraud Triangle in terms of opportunity to commit fraud. In our model, this opportunity to commit fraud relates to the maximum amount of fraud that can be physically committed per period.

From Kulik et al.'s 2008 discussion, we note the TPB has parallels with both our behavioural economics model and the Fraud Triangle. The Fraud Triangle emphasises three factors: (a) pressure (or incentives) to commit fraud, (b) the opportunity to commit fraud and (c) rationalisation (the individual's attempts to justify his fraud commission, which would include subjective norms). What the TPB and the Fraud Triangle emphasise is that not every manager who could commit fraud will commit fraud. The 'subjective norm-rationalisation' factor emphasises that the fraud decision is heterogenous across managers who face the same fraud opportunities. In our model, we focus on widespread corruption in an organisation consisting of fraudulent managers.

Di Micela da Silveira (2013) provides a conceptual analysis of a behavioural economics approach to corporate fraud. He argues that the problem with the current approach, and the policy recommendations that arise, is that it is heavily based upon the standard fully rational *Homo economicus* approach. He argues that it is vitally important that a new behavioural economics approach is developed that considers three main building blocks: (a) a systematic focus on mitigating managerial cognitive biases in making their fraud decisions; (b) continuous encouragement of employee-executive awareness of unselfish, long-term cooperative behaviours; and (c) the development of new corporate strategies designed to greatly reduce the likelihood of fraud through a deeper understanding of psychological motives. Indeed, the author emphasises that management engages in both an economic and a behavioural CBA towards fraud commission. Di Micela da Silveira (2013) notes several psychological factors that seem to be relevant in people's fraud-commission decisions. This includes the ability to rationalise dishonest acts. This ties in with the TPB, discussed by Kulik et al. (2008), and with the Fraud Triangle. In our model, the manager rationalises his behaviour through his economic (when the super-ego is asleep) and his behavioural CBA (when the superego is awake).

Rafeld et al. (2017) consider behavioural patterns in fraud commission and rogue trading at the lone/individual level. Rafeld et al. (2017) base their analysis heavily on Tittle's (1995, 2004) control balance theory (CBT). CBT identifies an individual's desire for autonomy (trying to escape from control, and to exercise more control over others). In CBT, individuals become psychologically distressed by perceived control deficits (excess control from others) or control surpluses (excess control over others). According to the theory, individuals act to minimise these control imbalances. A key aspect emphasised by Tittle's CBT is that the desire to commit fraud is heterogeneous. Control imbalances are subjective, environment-driven, and depend on opportunity and motivation. As in the TPB, not all managers who can commit fraud will do so. This work demonstrates the parallels between a behavioural economics approach to corporate fraud and the Fraud Triangle: both approaches emphasise motive, opportunity and rationalisation/attitude.

The Role of the Regulator

Regulators' real-world incentives: two cases

Our model demonstrated that we do not only need to consider corporate management's economic and behavioural incentives to engage, or not, in fraud. We should also understand that regulators are self-interested entities too, with their own self-interested set of economic (agency) and behavioural issues and incentives. As Benabou and Tirole (2010) argue, regulators are not necessarily the benevolent social planners of standard economics: they have their own self-interested agendas. If the regulator is not correctly motivated to regulate, then there is an incentive for her to not exert costly effort in searching for fraud, with a small probability of finding it. In our model, we considered how the regulator might be motivated to the job through gaining utility from positive economic factors (reputation) and behavioural/emotional factors (excitement, pride in a job well done). Conversely, we considered the possibility of negative economic/behavioural punishments (job loss, lost reputation) from not doing a good job.

Two real-world examples where these factors came into play relate to (a) the 2019 Kingman enquiry into the effectiveness of the Financial Reporting Council (FRC), and (b) the resignation of Martin Wheatley from the Financial Conduct Authority (FCA) in 2015. In 2019, Sir John Kingman was asked by the British Government's Secretary of State, the Rt Hon Greg Clark MP, to conduct a 'root and branch' review into the FRC. As a result of this review, Kingman referred to the FRC as a 'ramshackled house, cobbled together, with all sorts of extensions over time … it is time to build a new house' (quoted in Bunney 2018) and recommended that the FRC should be replaced with an independent statutory regulator, called the Audit, Reporting and Governance Authority. In the context of our model, we can say that the members of the FRC have suffered huge economic, behavioural and reputational utility losses from this report, and from losing their jobs. If they had anticipated this threat, this may have driven them to do their job more thoroughly, albeit still being hindered by institutional shackles.

In our second example, we consider Martin Wheatley, who resigned from his position as CEO of the FCA in 2015. The *Financial Times* (FT) reported, in its online Financial News page (19 March 2018) that Wheatley was effectively ousted from his position by the then Chancellor George Osborne, who moved to install a 'different leadership' at the FCA. The case demonstrates how fragile and tenuous a regulator's position may be. Ironically, Wheatley is described by the FT as a 'tough-talking regulator, who ... would "shoot first and ask questions later".' Perhaps he was considered to be too tough: he 'had riled the banking community during his tenure with a string of record fines'. In the interview with the FT, Wheatley claims that he had been replaced at the FCA due to a political mood change at the Conservative government. However, the FT also notes that his position was made very difficult following a botched FCA media briefing that resulted in billions of pounds being wiped off the values of life insurers. This was 'the writing on the wall' for Martin Wheatley, who was placed on 'gardening leave'.

5. BEHAVIOURAL ECONOMICS AND CORPORATE FRAUD: RECENT POLICY RESEARCH

The FCA, in its 2016 policy publication 'Behaviour and Compliance in Organisations', provides an in-depth consideration of the behavioural economics factors affecting corporate fraud. The document has striking parallels with our theoretical analysis in this chapter. That is, it considers the economic factors (managerial economic incentives) and behavioural factors affecting corporate compliance decisions. Furthermore, the FCA then proceeds to consider social factors and social context. In a parallel to our discussion of super-ego, the FCA furthermore considers morality in its analysis. In its policy report, it begins by posing the question:

> What determines compliance? Standard economic models suggest that a fully rational decision maker would compare the expected benefits of rule breaking with the expected costs, the latter determined by a combination of the probability of detection and the size of punishment in the event of detection. (p. 5)

The FCA report emphasises that this economic CBA approach has limitations, and suggests that behavioural economics demonstrates that real-word humans do not always respond to incentives in a strictly rational way. For instance, widespread corporate fraud persists in spite of increasingly heavy penalties.

This is the focus of the FCA's 2016 report, the behavioural economics approach to corporate fraud and compliance. It examines how individual managerial biases (such as overconfidence, salience, vividness, preference biases), group pressure and groupthink at the collective managerial level, together with individuals' inherent conscience and morality, may affect the propensity to commit corporate fraud. A key emphasis of the FCA report is that it is not just individual psychological biases that affect fraud commission. Social context and group behaviour can play a key role. It refers to the strong evidence that corporate fraud and the likelihood of rule-breaking may be affected by organisational culture and social norms. Interestingly, the FCA refers to experimental evidence (reported in the FCA Occasional Paper 24, *Behaviour and Compliance in Organisations*, December 2016[14]) that rule-breaking is contagious. The evidence demonstrates that it becomes more widespread when we observe people form our own group cheating and breaking rules, while observing 'outsiders' cheating can actually cause us to reduce our egregious behaviour. Furthermore, organisational ideologies which provide a social justification for rule-breaking can be ruinous.

The FCA considers the example of collusion amongst NASDAQ market makers to reduce competition, thus violating competition law and increasing the colluders' profit margins. This collusion was sustained as a social norm through an ideology that justified collusion in terms of ethics and professionalism, with failure to follow the convention being regarded as 'unethical' and 'unprofessional'. The case of LIBOR manipulation[15] provides another example of social norms and cultural ideologies sustaining rule-breaking. Thus, in addition to the fully rational CBA comparison of economic cost and benefits of compliance versus fraud, the FCA report advocates that regulators consider the behavioural biases that can affect the corporate players' CBA analysis (as in our model earlier in this chapter) by noting that 'Behavioural biases can affect the way people compare the costs and benefits of non-compliance, leading to increased wrongdoing' (p. 7).

In addition to a consideration of the behavioural biases affecting corporate fraud commission, the FCA places strong emphasis on morality (in our model, we consider this through the role of the super-ego). It argues that regulators can increase compliance by enhancing moral considerations. The FCA presents evidence that firms can enhance compliance, and reduce fraud, by having managers and employees commit to abide by moral codes, and to use constant reminders to reinforce ethical behaviour. Interestingly, the report further notes that increased compliance, and fraud reduction, can be achieved by informing staff of the consequences of their non-compliance for consumers (thus emphasising that people are not completely self-interested: humans are capable of 'other-regarding' behaviour), and by engaging employees' moral reasoning.

The individual biases that the FCA report considers include present bias, which can lead to time-inconsistent preferences, thereby increasing the perceived benefits of rule-breaking, and endowment effects, which can result in excessive attachment to existing poor governance processes. Overconfidence can result in people having excessive faith in their ability to avoid detection and unwarranted confidence in their firm's internal controls. Salience and vividness effects can result in people paying selective attention to information in their decision-making. Groupthink can lead firms to make poor decisions, leading to poor governance processes.

The FCA report also refers to the practicalities of the newly introduced Senior Managers and Certification Regime in the UK:[16]

> Regulators also have a key role in reinforcing the importance of individual morality and responsibility in decision-making. The Senior Manager Regime introduced in the UK is an example of the increased focus on individual responsibility for actions that is consistent with the principles in this paper. Regulators need to consider whether compliance decisions by firms and employees are taken in a context that promotes moral reasoning rather than as part of, for example, "tick box compliance", which risks reducing the salience of ethics in firms' decision-making. (p. 3)

Thus, the FCA report focuses on the behavioural economics of *corporate* fraud.

There has been parallel policy research investigating the behavioural economics of individual *non*-corporate fraud. For example, the Swiss RE Institute[17] examines fraud at an individual, non-corporate level in its economic insights document, *Behavioural Economics: Shaping Optimal Decision-Making, Including Fraud Prevention, in Insurance Buying*.[18] The Institute notes that insurers are currently focusing on the rational economics approach in deterring fraud (à la Becker), placing great emphasis on detection, with heavy investment in advanced analytics. It argues that behavioural economics allows a better understanding of consumer biases that may lead to sub-optimal decision-making. Insurers can use this information to influence consumer behaviours including to reduce fraud:

> In our view, understanding why people commit fraud in the first place is equally important, and here BE can help. Different behavioural biases can lead consumers to commit opportunistic claims fraud, especially soft fraud or *claims padding* (inflating claims amounts to more than actual values), the most common type of insurance fraud. (p. 1; emphasis in original)

In the Institute's view, three key biases drive insurance fraud: social norms, the endowment effect and mental accounting. The social norm bias is where people tend to follow what others do. If a majority of consumers in a social sub-group are perceived to pad their claims as a matter of course, others in that same group are likely to follow suit.

The endowment effect is when people think their possessions are worth more than they are and inflate associated insurance claims in the case of a loss event. Another factor at play is mental accounting, when people mentally separate their money into specific accounts. If they perceive a deductible to be high and/or unfair, mental accounting may lead them to effectively compensate for this higher price by padding claims.

The Swiss RE Institute finally suggests that such frauds around insurance claims have been a long-standing drain on insurer profits. Using behavioural economics to understand the underlying behavioural economics biases behind these frauds, insurers can design ways and means of reducing fraud. For example, the way choices are presented can persuade consumers towards increased disclosure. Reframing the act of fraud whereby the broader policyholder population is presented as victim also helps. Shaping consumer behaviours can also help insurers improve claims process efficiency.

Another organisation that has focused on the behavioural economics of non-corporate fraud is the Behavioural Insights Team (BIT) in the UK.[19] The Team was set up in the UK in 2010 by the then Prime Minister David Cameron, who was keen to use insights from behavioural economics and nudge theory to affect public and corporate economic behaviour, such as fraud and compliance. In its report (2012), BIT analyses the behavioural economics of personal (non-corporate) fraud, and the potential effect of the use of nudges to reduce it. It notes that:

> Fraud, error and debt cost the UK economy billions of pounds each year – £21 billion is lost to fraud in the public sector, a further £96 billion is lost to errors, while £7–8 billion is lost in uncollected debt. These significant sums of money are ultimately borne by UK taxpayers, so any measures that reduce fraud, error and debt in a cost-effective way are to be welcomed. (p. 3)

The BIT report considers the behavioural economics factors contributing to non-corporate fraud (with many parallels to those considered in the FCA report on corporate fraud and compliance). The BIT (colloquially known as the 'Nudge Unit') discusses experimental interventions (nudges) that it attempted to reduce fraud. It is interesting to note that these behavioural nudge experiments were not artificial, in the lab … they were experiments involving actual people, and actual cases of fraud, that were draining money from the system.

As the BIT report notes:

> These trials are now up and running and preliminary results are very positive. For example, Trial 1 advanced £160 million of tax debts to the Exchequer over the six-week period of the trial, the two behavioural letters in Trial 2 brought in over £1 million from doctors in additional yield to HM Revenue and Customs, while Trial 6 saved Manchester City Council up to £240,000 in council tax discounts. (p. 3)

The report goes on to note that 'Overall, these trials showed effect sizes of up to 30 percentage points, underlining the key role that behavioural insights can play in tackling fraud, error and debt' (p. 3).

Importantly, the BIT experiments show that even relatively minor changes to processes, forms and language can have a significant, positive impact on behaviour, and can often save the public time and money too. 'Indeed, if trialled on a national scale, we expect that these interventions will save hundreds of millions of pounds' (p. 3).

The UK BIT and the Swiss RE Institute reports have useful parallels with the FCA report discussed at the beginning of this section, emphasising the importance of looking beyond the rational CBA approach, to consider the lessons from behavioural economics, examining the effects of behavioural and psychological biases and emotions on fraud. This enables policy makers, corporations and institutions (such as auditors and regulators) to think beyond purely economic monitoring and punishment approaches, and to consider behavioural interventions and nudges to reduce corporate and non-corporate fraud.

Corporate Fraud during the Covid Crisis

Some analysts have noted that corporate fraud has become particularly prevalent and insidious during the current Covid crisis, which began at the start of 2020. For example, EY (2020) analyse the increase in corporate fraud during the Covid pandemic, employing Cressey's (1953) Fraud Triangle framework, and investigate how Covid-19 has affected (a) incentive or pressure, (b) opportunity and (c) rationalisation in relation to fraud commission.[20] EY note that during the Covid pandemic 'The risk of internal fraud has heightened due to an abrupt change in working practices, as well as increasing pressure on organisations and employees.'

The main points of the EY analysis suggest that:

(a) Enterprise-wide controls to prevent and detect fraud and network breaches may not be designed to operate in near-100 per cent virtual environments.
(b) Anti-fraud, compliance and cybersecurity concerns may also have been de-prioritised in favour of maintaining business-as-usual (BAU) services.
(c) The reliance on staff to comply with policies and operate those controls is also under strain: as many people are working remotely, they may become disengaged and their actions may be subject to less scrutiny and oversight; similarly, financial and other concerns caused by Covid-19 may cause those in important oversight roles to be less vigilant.
(d) There may be pressure on organisations and staff to report positive results – i.e., demonstrating organisations are operating as usual without a negative impact on earnings and profitability, or staff compensation and incentive plans.

As EY note: 'The new challenges posed by the COVID-19 pandemic present heightened risks across all elements of The Cressey fraud triangle (1953).' Particularly in terms of rationalisation (which has parallels with the behavioural economics approach), the report suggests that:

> Employees may find it easier to rationalise defrauding their company if they think they won't be getting a raise or bonus this year. This is more likely where incentive compensation is a large proportion of total compensation, or the method of incentive compensation is narrowly focused on short-term performance or affected by earn-out provisions at acquired operations. Employees may be more inclined to commit fraud if long periods of remote working make them feel disengaged or undervalued.

6.   CONCLUSION

In this chapter, we have analysed the combined effects of economic, behavioural, psycholog-ical, emotional and psychoanalytical factors on managerial propensity to commit corporate fraud. We began by reviewing relevant existing literature on the (behavioural) economics of crime and fraud in order to set the scene. We noted that much of the existing academic research and policy approach has been based upon the standard economics rational CBA set forth by Becker (1974). According to this approach, miscreants perform a rational CBA of committing crime or fraud: that is, they ask themselves, 'What are the financial benefits of committing the fraud, and what are the expected costs (the financial loss, such as economic fines and sanc-tions, loss of job and status, imprisonment, multiplied by the probability of being caught)?' The Becker approach thus advocates tougher financial regulation, stronger punishment threats, and setting up systems that improve the chances of catching the criminals and fraudsters.

Clearly the Becker approach has failed to reduce the incidence of corporate fraud. In the chapter, we then proceeded to consider the existing research that employs a behavioural eco-nomics approach to analysing corporate fraud. We noted that this approach removes the focus from economic CBA factors, and focuses instead upon behavioural, psychological, emotional and psychoanalytical factors. We were particularly interested in Dan Ariely's psychoanalytical analysis, where he considered a Freudian framework, incorporating a super-ego, which mon-itors our behaviour and acts as our moral compass. When committing small and seemingly inconsequential frauds, our super-ego remains asleep. When cumulative fraud hits a critical level, our super-ego awakes, and we suddenly are struck by the enormity of our wrongdoing, and act accordingly.

Motivated by the behavioural economics and psychoanalytical research into corporate fraud, we then proceeded to develop a behavioural game-theoretical framework that analysed managerial fraud commission in the early periods of small fraud, where the super-ego remains asleep, and in the subsequent periods, after the critical point where the super-ego awakes.

Furthermore, we developed a second, related model, whereby we analysed the spread of fraud across an organisation from unethical to ethical managers. We termed this 'fraud infec-tion/fraud contagion', and related our model to the real-world case of Enron.

After an in-depth analysis of the behavioural economics of the Enron fraud case, we con-sidered the relationship of our analysis to the Fraud Triangle, and then briefly outlined how behavioural economic factors could crucially affect the efficacy of a key watchdog (the finan-cial regulator) in deterring corporate fraud. The chapter concluded with an in-depth discussion of how real-world policy makers (such as the FCA and BIT in the UK) are beginning to under-stand, and employ, the behavioural economics approach in developing policies to address corporate fraud. We concluded with a very topical discussion of the behavioural economics factors driving the relationship between the current Covid crisis and corporate fraud. In doing so, we drew from the research policy webpage provided by EY.

We suggest that our behavioural economics framework provides a basis for future academic and practitioner/policy maker research. It would be useful to further develop the model to consider the effect of other psychological and behavioural biases and emotions, such as overconfidence, anger, fear and shame. In our fraud contagion model, we have focused on the managerial dyad. The model would be further strengthened by considering a complete and complex organisational network. Furthermore, we could include an auditor or regulator as an additional player in the game. At the empirical level, we could extend our analysis beyond the Enron case to consider how our framework applies to other corporate frauds and scandals. Furthermore, we could employ experimental and neuro-economic techniques to test for the economic and psychological determinants of managerial fraud in a lab setting. Nevertheless, it is hoped that our current analysis in this chapter contributes to a better understanding, and ultimately reduction, of corporate fraud.

NOTES

1. The pioneers of regret theory were Loomes and Sugden (1982), and Bell (1982). These authors developed economic models incorporating the emotion of regret and, in particular, the potential for humans to exhibit *regret aversion*. In our fraud model, we are appealing to their idea, based on psychological evidence, that individuals are able to anticipate the regret that they will feel from a bad decision, or bad outcome. Furthermore, according to regret theory, individuals are able to delay feeling regret by postponing the actualisation of the bad outcome. In our model, when the superego awakes, the manager realises the regret that he will feel due to the cumulative fraud that he has committed, but is able to postpone that by continuing to hide it. He anticipates that, once the fraud is discovered, his regret will 'flood his consciousness'.

2. Trinkaus and Giacalone (2005) present an interesting analysis of the spread of unethical behaviour across a broader set of stakeholders (beyond internal management) in Enron: specifically, they consider why the external watchdogs (such as institutional investors, and external auditors) were not 'barking'; i.e., were acquiescing in the widespread fraud.

3. Indeed, Sims and Brinkmann (2003) argue that Enron's collapse was driven by its culture, and the authors argue that 'Culture matters more than codes'.

4. The Nash bargaining model was developed by Nobel Prize-winning game theorist/economist John Nash. Nash bargaining is based on concepts of cooperation and fairness. The solution of the game is that the bargainers share the economic surplus equally; hence its importance as a consideration in the social contract.

5. A Prisoner's Dilemma game arises in economic game theory, and considers the case where two competing actors would both benefit from mutual cooperation, but who have each have individual incentives to defect from an agreement. They both defect and both end up worse off. In a repeated Prisoner's Dilemma game, individual defection in one round of play can be punished by the other player; this punishment threat may be enough to maintain mutual cooperation throughout all rounds of play.

6. We do not focus on the reputation-damaging/economic punishment threat mechanism for enforcing ethical compliance/non-abuse of authority in our chapter. Instead, we focus on the latter issue: control of unethical behaviour by the super-ego, and the 'bounded rationality' of managers when committing small frauds, such that the super-ego remains asleep. In a future paper, we will work on developing Sacconi's work to consider whether players may comply with the social contract due to social preferences (fairness, trust, empathy) in a one-shot game, rather than the punishment threat in a repeated game.

7. See, for example, Ariely's (2010) Blog: 'How to Commit the Perfect Crime' at http://danariely.com/2010/06/05/how-to-commit-the-perfect-crime/.

8. We emphasise that, in our current analysis, we do not consider the auditor as a player in the game. The probability of fraud discovery q is exogenously given, but may implicitly capture our discussion on the reasons why the probability of fraud discovery is beyond the manager's control, such as the psychological motivations of the auditor herself. Many papers exist, considering a game-theoretic approach in which a manager and an auditor are both players in the game. See Anastasopoulos and Anastasopoulos (2012) for a good example of such a game-theoretic approach, plus a good review of related literature.

9. There is also an extensive academic literature reviewing and interpreting aspects of the Enron saga – examples of which include Benston et al. (2003) and Benston (2006).

10. The ability to purchase both external and internal audit from the same firm has been a source of controversy for some time and the SEC had brought into force rules (probably unworkable) limiting

the extent to which clients could purchase internal audit from their external auditor. Post Sarbanes–Oxley there is now a complete prohibition of joint purchase. The 2014 EU Regulation (Regulation (EU) No 537/2014) prohibits a number of non-audit services that can be provided by the external auditor; see: http://eur-lex.europa.eu/legal-content/EN/TXT/?uri=uriserv%3AOJ.L_.2014.158.01 .0077.01.ENG.

11. Anchoring and adjustment is a psychological heuristic made popular by the seminal work of Tversky and Kahneman (1974) that influences the way people intuitively use an initial piece of information to make subsequent judgments. According to this heuristic, people start with an implicitly suggested reference point (the 'anchor') and make subsequent adjustments to it to reach their judgement. Where an unethical manager's behaviour is seen as the norm, this may form an anchor or reference point against which someone's own behaviour may be judged. Further deviations from the anchor might be seen as insignificant, and thus acceptable, setting off a process which may lead to significant deviations from the originally accepted norm.

12. In 'The Market for "Lemons": Quality Uncertainty and the Market Mechanism', Akerlof (1970) describes the demise of markets as a result of asymmetric information. Where an organization embraces a forced-ranking system, this can lead to situations where ethical behaviour is driven out by unethical behaviour patterns, as it does not pay to be ethical, and as ethical individuals are forced out since they simply may not be competitive in an unethical environment.

13. Presumably, Enron's star employees at least originally had some of these characteristics if the ethics education at the top MBA programmes from which Enron typically recruited is worth the fees charged.

14. www.fca.org.uk/publication/occasional-papers/op16–24.pdf.

15. See this link for a discussion of the LIBOR manipulation scandal: https://www.investopedia.com/ terms/l/libor-scandal.asp.

16. www.fca.org.uk/firms/senior-managers-certification-regime.

17. www.swissre.com/institute/.

18. www.swissre.com/institute/research/sigma-research/economic-insights-behavioural-economics .html.

19. www.bi.team/.

20. www.ey.com/en_uk/disrupting-financial-crime/financial-crime/covid-19-implications-internal -fraud.

REFERENCES

Akerlof, G.A. (1970). The Market for 'Lemons': Quality Uncertainty and the Market Mechanism. *Quarterly Journal of Economics*, 84(3): 488–500.

Albrecht, W.S. (1991). Fraud in Government Entities: The Perpetrators and the Types of Fraud. *Government Finance Review*, December: 27–30.

Albrecht, W.S. (2014). Iconic Fraud Triangle Endures: Metaphor Diagram Helps Everybody Understand Fraud. *Fraud Magazine*, July/August. Available at: www.dkcpas.com/content/client/7fa6b31cca001 f1ab32e5d2a03a5b153/uploads/iconic-fraud-triangl.pdf.

Albrecht, W.S., Howe, K.R., and Romney, M.M. (1984). *Deterring Fraud: The Internal Auditor's Perspective*. Altamonte Springs, Institute of Internal Auditors' Reseach Foundation.

Albrecht, W.S., Williams, T.L., and Wernz, G.W. (1995). *Fraud: Bringing Light to the Dark Side of Business*. Burr Ridge, Irwin.

Anastasopoulos, N.P., and Anastasopoulos, M.P. (2012). The Evolutionary Dynamics of Audit. *European Journal of Operational Research*, 1 216: 469–76.

Ariely, D. (2008). *Predictably Irrational*. New York, Harper Publishers.

Asch, S.E. (1951). Effects of Group Pressure Upon the Modification and Distortion of Judgement, in Guetzkow, H. (Ed.), *Groups, Leadership and Men*. Pittsburgh, Carnegy Press.

Ajzen, I. (1985). From intention to actions: A theory of planned behavior. In J. Kuhl, & J. Beckman (Eds.), *Action control: From cognition to behavior* (pp. 11–39). New York: Springer-Verlag.

Ajzen, I., and Fishbein, M. (1980). *Understanding attitudes and predicting social behavior*. Englewood Cliffs, NJ: Prentice-Hall.

Batson, N. (2002). *First Interim Report of Neal Batson Court Appointed Examiner*. Available at: www .enron.com/corp/por/pdfs/InterimReport1ofExaminer.pdf.

Batson, N. (2003a). *Second Interim Report of Neal Batson Court Appointed Examiner*. Available at: www.enron.com/corp/por/pdfs/examiner2/InterimReport2ofExaminer.pdf.

Batson, N. (2003b). *Third Interim Report of Neal Batson Court Appointed Examiner*. Available at: www .enron.com/corp/por/pdfs/examiner3/ExaminersReport3.pdf.

Batson, N. (2003c). *Final Report of The Court Appointed Bankruptcy Examiner*. Available at: www .enron.com/corp/por/examinerfinal.html.

Becker, G. (1974). Crime and Punishment: An Economic Approach. In Becker, G., and Landes, W. (Eds), *Essays in the Economics of Crime and Punishment*. New York, NBER Publishers: 1–54.

Behavioural Insights Team (2012). *Applying Behavioural Insights to Reduce Fraud, Error and Debt*. London, UK Cabinet Office.

Bell, D.E. (1982). Regret in Decision-Making Under Uncertainty. *Operations Research*, 30(3): 961–81.

Benabou, R., and Tirole, J. 2010. Individual and Corporate Social Responsibility. *Economica*, 77: 1–19.

Benston, G. (2006). Fair-Value Accounting: A Cautionary Tale from Enron. *Journal of Accounting and Public Policy*, 25(4): 465–84.

Benston, G., Bromwich, M., Litan, R.E., and Wagenhofer, A. (2003). *Following the Money: The Enron Failure and the State of Corporate Disclosure*. Washington, DC, AEI-Brookings Joint Center for Regulatory Studies.

Bunney, J. (2018). Kingman Review Calls for Abolition of FRC as Audit Regulator. *Accountancy Daily*, December 18. Available at: https://www.accountancydaily.co/kingman-review-calls-abolition -frc-audit-regulator.

Coffee, J.C. (2001). *The Acquiescent Gatekeeper: Reputational Intermediaries, Auditor Independence and the Governance of Accounting*. Columbia Law School, Center for Law and Economics Studies Working Paper, No. 191. Available at SSRN: http://ssrn.com/abstract=270944.

Cohan, J.A. (2002). 'I Didn't Know' and 'I Was Only Doing My Job': Has Corporate Governance Careened out of Control? A Case Study of Enron's Information Myopia. *Journal of Business Ethics*, 40(3): 275–99.

Cosimano, T.F. (2004). Financial Institutions and Trustworthy Behavior in Business Transactions. *Journal of Business Ethics*, 52(2): 179–88.

Cressey, D.R. (1951). Why do trusted persons commit fraud?: A social-psychological study of defalcators. *Journal of Accountancy*, 92 (577).

Cressey, D.R. (1953). *Other People's Money: A Study in the Social Psychology of Embezzlement*. Glencoe, Free Press.

Davis, J.S., and Pesch, H.L. (2013). Fraud dynamics and controls in organizations. *Accounting, Organizations and Society*, 38(6–7), 469–83. https://doi.org/10.1016/j.aos. 2012.07.005

Di Miceli Da Silveira, A. (2013). *Corporate Scandals of the 21st Century: Limitations of Mainstream Corporate Governance Literature and the Need for a New Behavioral Approach*. SSRN Working Paper.

European Union (2014). Directive 2014/56/EU of the European Parliament and of the Council. Available at: https://eur-lex.europa.eu/legal-content/EN/TXT/?uri=celex%3A32014L0056.

EY (2020). Covid-19 Implications: Internal Fraud. Available at: www.ey.com/en_uk/disrupting-financial -crime/financial-crime/covid-19-implications-internal-fraud.

Financial Conduct Authority (2016). *Behaviour and Compliance in Organisations*. Occasional Paper No. 24.

Financial Reporting Council (FRC) (2016). Press Release: Revised UK Corporate Governance Code, Guidance on Audit Committees, and Auditing and Ethical Standards. Available at: https://www.frc .org.uk/news/april-2016/revised-uk-corporate-governance-code,-guidance-on.

Fischhoff, B. (2002). Heuristics and Biases in Application. In Gilovich, T., Griffin, D., and Kahneman, D. (Eds), *Heuristics and Biases*. Cambridge, Cambridge University Press: 730–48.

Fishbein, M., and Ajzen, I. (1975). *Belief, attitude, intention and behavior: An introduction to theory and research*. Reading, MA: Addison-Wesley.

Fleming, P., and Zyglidopoulos, S.C. (2008). The Escalation of Deception in Organizations. *Journal of Business Ethics*, 81: 837–50.

Garrett, N., Lazzaro, L.C., Ariely, D., and Sharot, T. (2016). The Brain Adapts to Dishonesty. *Nature Neuroscience*, 19: 1727–32.

Goldin, H. (2003). *Report of Harrison J. Goldin, The Court-Appointed Examiner in the Enron North America Corp. Bankruptcy Proceeding, Respecting His Investigations of the Role of Certain Entities in Transactions Pertaining to Special Purpose Entities.* Available at: www.enron.com/corp/por/pdfs/ SPEReport11142003.pdf.

Janis, I.L. (1972). *Victims of Groupthink: A Psychological Study of Foreign-Policy Decisions and Fiascos.* Boston: Houghton Mifflin.

Janis, I.L. (1989). *Crucial Decisions: Leadership in Policymaking and Crisis Management.* New York, Free Press.

Kahneman, D., and Tversky, A. (1979). Prospect Theory: An Analysis of Decision under Risk. *Econometrica*, 47(2): 263–91.

Kulik, B.W., O'Fallon, M.J., and Salimath, M.S. (2008). Do Competitive Environments Lead to the Rise and Spread of Unethical Behavior? Parallels from Enron. *Journal of Business Ethics*, 83: 603–723.

Laibson, D. (1997). Golden Eggs and Hyperbolic Discounting. *Quarterly Journal of Economics*, 112(2): 443–77.

Langevoort D.C. (2001). *Monitoring: The Behavior Economics of Inducing Agents' Compliance with Legal Rules.* University of Southern California Law School, Center for Law, Economics and Organization, Research Paper No. C01–7. Available at SSRN: http://ssrn.com/abstract=276121a.

Loewenstein, G. (1996). Out of Control: Visceral Influences on Behaviour. *Organizational Behavior and Human Decision Processes*, 65(3): 272–92.

Loewenstein, G., and Lerner, J.S. (2003). The Role of Affect in Decision-making. In Davidson, R.J., Goldsmith, H.H., and Scherer, K.R. (Eds), *Handbook of Affective Science.* New York: Oxford University Press: 619–42.

Loomes, G., and Sugden, R. (1982). Regret Theory: An Alternative Theory of Rational Choice Under Uncertainty. *Economic Journal*, 92(368), 805–24.

Maccoby, M. (2000). Narcissistic Leaders. *Harvard Business Review*, 78(1): 69–77.

Michaels, E., Hanfield-Jones, H., and Axelrod, B. (2001). *The War for Talent.* Boston: Harvard Business School Press.

Milgram, S. (1963). Behavioral Study of Obedience. *Journal of Abnormal and Social Psychology*, 67(4): 371–78.

Pfeffer, J., and Sutton, R.I. (2006). *Hard Facts, Dangerous Half-Truths, and Total Nonsense: Profiting from Evidence-Based Management.* Boston: Harvard Business School Press.

Powers, W., Troubh, R., and Winokur, H. (2002). Report of Investigation by the Special Investigative Committee of the Board of Directors of Enron Corp. Available at: http://energycommerce.house.gov/ 107/hearings/02052002Hearing481/hearing.htm.

Prentice, R.A. (2000a). The SEC and MDP: Implications of the Self-Serving Bias for Independent Auditing. *Ohio State Law Journal*, 61(5): 1597–670.

Prentice R.A. (2000b). The Case of the Irrational Auditor: A Behavioral Insight into Securities Fraud Litigation. *Northwestern University Law Review*, 95(1): 133–219.

Rabin, M. (2002). *A Perspective on Psychology and Economics.* Economics Department, University of California (Berkeley) Working Paper E02–313. Available at: http://repositories.cdlib.org/iber/econ/ E02–313.

Rafeld, H., Fritz-Morgenthal, S., and Posch, P. (2017). Behavioural Patterns in Rogue Trading: Analysing the Cases of Nick Leeson, Jérôme Kerviel and Kweku Adoboli. *Journal of Financial Compliance*, 1(2): 156–71.

Rockness, H., and Rockness, J. (2005). Legislated Ethics: From Enron to Sarbanes–Oxley, the Impact on Corporate America. *Journal of Business Ethics*, 57(1): 31–54.

Sacconi, L. (1999). Codes of Ethics as Contractarian Constraints on the Abuse of Authority within Hierarchies: A Perspective from the Theory of the Firm. *Journal of Business Ethics*, 21(2–3): 189–202.

Sacconi, L. (2006). A Social Contract Account for CSR as an Extended Model of Corporate Governance (I): Rational Bargaining and Justification. *Journal of Business Ethics*, 68(3): 259–81.

Sacconi, L. (2007). A Social Contract Account for CSR as an Extended Model of Corporate Governance (II): Compliance, Reputation, and Reciprocity. *Journal of Business Ethics*, 75(1): 77–96.

Schelling, T.C. (1984). *Choice and Consequence: Perspectives of an Errant Economist*. Cambridge: Harvard University Press.

Schrand, C.M., and Zechman, S.L.C. (2012). Executive Overconfidence and the Slippery Slope to Financial Misreporting. *Journal of Accounting and Economics*, 53(1): 311–29.

Simon, H.A. (1957). *Models of Man: Social and Rational – Mathematical Essays on Rational Human Behavior in a Social Setting*. New York, John Wiley.

Sims, R.R, and Brinkmann, J. (2003). Enron Ethics (Or: Culture Matters More than Codes). *Journal of Business Ethics*, 45: 243–56.

Slovic, P., Finucane, M.L., Peters, E., and MacGregor, D.G. (2002). The Affect Heuristic. In Gilovich, T., Griffin, D., and Kahneman, D. (Eds), *Heuristics and Biases*. Cambridge, Cambridge University Press: 397–420.

Slovic, P., Finucane, M.L., Peters, E., and MacGregor, D.G. (2004). Risk as Analysis and Risk as Feelings: Some Thoughts about Affect, Reason, Risk, and Rationality. *Risk Analysis*, 24(2): 311–22.

Statman, M., and Caldwell, D. (1987). Applying Behavioral Finance to Capital Budgeting: Project Terminations. *Financial Management*, 16(4): 7–15.

Staw, B.M. (1976). Knee-Deep in the Big Muddy: A Study of Escalating Commitment to a Chosen Course of Action. *Organizational Behavior and Human Performance*, 16(1): 27–44.

Strotz, R.H. (1955). Myopia and Inconsistency in Dynamic Utility Maximization. *Review of Economic Studies*, 23(3): 165–80.

Sutherland, E. H., and Cressey, D. R. (1978). *Criminology* (10th ed.). Philadelphia: Lippincott.

Swiss RE Institute (2019). *Behavioural Economics: Shaping Optimal Decision-Making, including Fraud Prevention, in Insurance Buying*. Available at: www.swissre.com/dam/jcr:590b3918-f583–4f42–885d -4a1ad92f24ed/EI_16_2019_Behavioural_Economics.pdf.

Thaler, R.H. (1980). Toward a Positive Theory of Consumer Choice. *Journal of Economic Behavior & Organization*, 1(1): 39–60.

Thaler, R.H. (1981). Some Empirical Evidence on Dynamic Inconsistency. *Economics Letters*, 8(3): 201–7.

Thaler, R.H. (2015). *Misbehaving: The Making of Behavioral Economics*. New York, W.W. Norton & Company.

Tittle, C.R. (1995). *Control balance: Toward a general theory of deviance*. Boulder: CO: Westview.

Tittle, C.R. (2004). Refining control balance . *Theoretical Criminology* 8 395–428. (2004). http://dx.doi .org/10.1177/1362480604046657.

Trevino, L.K., Hartman, L.P., and Brown, M. (2000). Moral Person and Moral Manager. *California Management Review*, 42(4): 128–42.

Trinkaus, J., and Giacalone, J. (2005). The Silence of the Stakeholders: Zero Decibel Level at Enron. *Journal of Business Ethics*, 58(1/3): 237–48.

Tversky, A., and Kahneman, D. (1974). Judgment under Uncertainty: Heuristics and Biases. *Science*, 185(4157): 1124–31.

US House of Representatives (2002). H.R. 3763 – 107th Congress: Sarbanes–Oxley Act of 2002. Available at: www.govtrack.us/congress/bills/107/hr3763.

Van Winden, F., and Ash, E. (2012). On the Behavioural Economics of Crime. *Review of Law and Economics*, 8(1): 181–213.

Weick, K.E. (1964). Reduction of Cognitive Dissonance through Task Enhancement and Effort Expenditure. *Journal of Abnormal and Social Psychology*, 68: 533–39.

Weick, K.E. (1983). Stress in Accounting Systems. *Accounting Review*, 58(2): 350–69.

Index

Printed and bound by CPI Group (UK) Ltd, Croydon, CR0 4YY

16/04/2025

14658396-0005